1 & 2 SAMUEL

THE NIV
APPLICATION
COMMENTARY

From biblical text . . . to contemporary life

1 & 2 SAMUEL

THE NIV APPLICATION COMMENTARY

From biblical text . . . to contemporary life

BILL T. ARNOLD

ZONDERVAN™

GRAND RAPIDS, MICHIGAN 49530 USA

ZONDERVAN™

The NIV Application Commentary: 1 and 2 Samuel
Copyright © 2003 by Bill T. Arnold

Requests for information should be addressed to:
Zondervan, *Grand Rapids, Michigan 49530*

Library of Congress Cataloging-in-Publication Data

Arnold, Bill T., 1955-
    1 and 2 Samuel : the NIV application commentary from biblical text — to contemporary life / Bill T. Arnold.
       p. cm. — (The NIV application commentary)
    Includes bibliographical references and index.
    ISBN 0-310-21086-0
    1. Bible. O.T. Samuel — Commentaries.   I. Title: First and Second Samuel.   II. Title.
III. Series.
    BS1325.53 .A76 2003
    222'.4077 — dc21
                                                     2002010350
                                                        CIP

All Scripture quotations, unless otherwise indicated, are taken from the *Holy Bible: New International Version*®. NIV®. Copyright © 1973, 1978, 1984 by International Bible Society. Used by permission of Zondervan. All rights reserved.

Printed in the United States of America

05 06 07 08 /❖ DC/ 10 9 8 7 6 5 4

DEDICATION
FOR MY HEROES OF 1939 – 1945

MY FATHER
SERGEANT WALTER L. ARNOLD
83rd Division, 329th Infantry Regiment
Bronze Star, Combat Infantry Badge
European-African-Middle East Theater Medal (5 battle stars)
American Theater Medal, Good Conduct Medal, World War II Victory Medal

MY UNCLE
CORPORAL JAMES H. ARNOLD
1346th Army Air Force Base Unit, Air Transport Command
Carbine Marksman
Asiatic-Pacific Theater Medal (2 battle stars)
American Theater Medal, Good Conduct Medal, World War II Victory Medal

MY UNCLE
PRIVATE FIRST CLASS ANDREW R. ARNOLD
95th Division, 377th Infantry Regiment
European-African-Middle East Theater Medal (3 battle stars), Purple Heart,
American Theater Medal, Good Conduct Medal, World War II Victory Medal
1925 – 1998

MY UNCLE
CORPORAL CECIL B. ARNOLD
504th Military Police Battalion
Army of Occupation Medal, World War II Victory Medal

MY UNCLE

STAFF SERGEANT HOBART SPIRES

100th Bomb Group, 349th Squadron

European-African-Middle East Theater Medal (1 battle star), Purple Heart,

Presidential Unit Citation (Oakleaf Cluster), Air Medal (5 Oakleaf Clusters),

Good Conduct Medal, American Defense Ribbon

Killed in action over Berlin (March 6, 1944)

1920–1944

MY MENTOR AND FRIEND

LIEUTENANT COLONEL CLARENCE A. OLSEN

66th Division, G-2 (Counter-Intelligence Corps - Special Agent)

Liaison Agent (French Underground)

Croix de Guerre (avec palme)

Décoration Militaire (avec palme)

Interpreter at Post-Potsdam Conferences

Translator for General Lucius Clay, US Military Governor (Berlin, Germany)

Security Office (US Embassy, Paris & US Army Seine Area Command)

Foreign Liaison Officer (Pentagon & Foreign Military Attachés in Washington, DC)

West Point Military Academy (Chief of French Department)

Presidential Citation for Meritorious Service at West Point

MY TEACHER AND FRIEND

PROFESSOR WERNER WEINBERG, PH.D.

Survivor of Bergen-Belsen

1915–1997

Contents

The NIV Application Commentary Series

When complete, the NIV Application Commentary
will include the following volumes:

To see which titles are available,
visit our web site at www.zondervan.com

NIV Application Commentary
Series Introduction

THE NIV APPLICATION COMMENTARY SERIES is unique. Most commentaries help us make the journey from our world back to the world of the Bible. They enable us to cross the barriers of time, culture, language, and geography that separate us from the biblical world. Yet they only offer a one-way ticket to the past and assume that we can somehow make the return journey on our own. Once they have explained the *original meaning* of a book or passage, these commentaries give us little or no help in exploring its *contemporary significance*. The information they offer is valuable, but the job is only half done.

Recently, a few commentaries have included some contemporary application as *one* of their goals. Yet that application is often sketchy or moralistic, and some volumes sound more like printed sermons than commentaries.

The primary goal of the NIV Application Commentary Series is to help you with the difficult but vital task of bringing an ancient message into a modern context. The series not only focuses on application as a finished product but also helps you think through the *process* of moving from the original meaning of a passage to its contemporary significance. These are commentaries, not popular expositions. They are works of reference, not devotional literature.

The format of the series is designed to achieve the goals of the series. Each passage is treated in three sections: *Original Meaning, Bridging Contexts,* and *Contemporary Significance.*

THIS SECTION HELPS YOU UNDERSTAND the meaning of the biblical text in its original context. All of the elements of traditional exegesis—in concise form—are discussed here. These include the historical, literary, and cultural context of the passage. The authors discuss matters related to grammar and syntax and the meaning of biblical words.¹ They also seek to explore the main ideas of the passage and how the biblical author develops those ideas.

After reading this section, you will understand the problems, questions, and concerns of the *original audience* and how the biblical author addressed those issues. This understanding is foundational to any legitimate application of the text today.

THIS SECTION BUILDS A BRIDGE between the world of the Bible and the world of today, between the original context and the contemporary context, by focusing on both the timely and timeless aspects of the text.

God's Word is *timely*. The authors of Scripture spoke to specific situations, problems, and questions. The author of Joshua encouraged the faith of his original readers by narrating the destruction of Jericho, a seemingly impregnable city, at the hands of an angry warrior God (Josh. 6). Paul warned the Galatians about the consequences of circumcision and the dangers of trying to be justified by law (Gal. 5:25). The author of Hebrews tried to convince his readers that Christ is superior to Moses, the Aaronic priests, and the Old Testament sacrifices. John urged his readers to "test the spirits" of those who taught a form of incipient Gnosticism (1 John 4:1–6). In each of these cases, the timely nature of Scripture enables us to hear God's Word in situations that were *concrete* rather than abstract.

Yet the timely nature of Scripture also creates problems. Our situations, difficulties, and questions are not always directly related to those faced by the people in the Bible. Therefore, God's word to them does not always seem relevant to us. For example, when was the last time someone urged you to be circumcised, claiming that it was a necessary part of justification? How many people today care whether Christ is superior to the Aaronic priests? And how can a "test" designed to expose incipient Gnosticism be of any value in a modern culture?

Fortunately, Scripture is not only timely but *timeless*. Just as God spoke to the original audience, so he still speaks to us through the

---

1. Please note that in general, when the authors discuss words in the original biblical languages, the series uses a general rather than a scholarly method of transliteration.

pages of Scripture. Because we share a common humanity with the people of the Bible, we discover a *universal dimension* in the problems they faced and the solutions God gave them. The timeless nature of Scripture enables it to speak with power in every time and in every culture.

Those who fail to recognize that Scripture is both timely and timeless run into a host of problems. For example, those who are intimidated by timely books such as Hebrews, Galatians, or Deuteronomy might avoid reading them because they seem meaningless today. At the other extreme, those who are convinced of the timeless nature of Scripture, but who fail to discern its timely element, may "wax eloquent" about the Melchizedekian priesthood to a sleeping congregation, or worse still, try to apply the holy wars of the Old Testament in a physical way to God's enemies today.

The purpose of this section, therefore, is to help you discern what is timeless in the timely pages of the Bible—and what is not. For example, how do the holy wars of the Old Testament relate to the spiritual warfare of the New? If Paul's primary concern is not circumcision (as he tells us in Gal. 5:6), what *is* he concerned about? If discussions about the Aaronic priesthood or Melchizedek seem irrelevant today, what is of abiding value in these passages? If people try to "test the spirits" today with a test designed for a specific first-century heresy, what other biblical test might be more appropriate?

Yet this section does not merely uncover that which is timeless in a passage but also helps you to see *how* it is uncovered. The authors of the commentaries seek to take what is implicit in the text and make it explicit, to take a process that normally is intuitive and explain it in a logical, orderly fashion. How do we know that circumcision is not Paul's primary concern? What clues in the text or its context help us realize that Paul's real concern is at a deeper level?

Of course, those passages in which the historical distance between us and the original readers is greatest require a longer treatment. Conversely, those passages in which the historical distance is smaller or seemingly nonexistent require less attention.

One final clarification. Because this section prepares the way for discussing the contemporary significance of the passage, there is not always a sharp distinction or a clear break between this section and the one that follows. Yet when both sections are read together, you should have a strong sense of moving from the world of the Bible to the world of today.

THIS SECTION ALLOWS the biblical message to speak with as much power today as it did when it was first written. How can you apply what you learned about Jerusalem, Ephesus, or Corinth to our present-day needs in Chicago, Los Angeles, or London? How can you take a message originally spoken in Greek, Hebrew, and Aramaic and communicate it clearly in our own language? How can you take the eternal truths originally spoken in a different time and culture and apply them to the similar-yet-different needs of our culture?

In order to achieve these goals, this section gives you help in several key areas.

(1) It helps you identify contemporary situations, problems, or questions that are truly comparable to those faced by the original audience. Because contemporary situations are seldom identical to those faced by the original audience, you must seek situations that are analogous if your applications are to be relevant.

(2) This section explores a variety of contexts in which the passage might be applied today. You will look at personal applications, but you will also be encouraged to think beyond private concerns to the society and culture at large.

(3) This section will alert you to any problems or difficulties you might encounter in seeking to apply the passage. And if there are several legitimate ways to apply a passage (areas in which Christians disagree), the author will bring these to your attention and help you think through the issues involved.

In seeking to achieve these goals, the contributors to this series attempt to avoid two extremes. They avoid making such specific applications that the commentary might quickly become dated. They also avoid discussing the significance of the passage in such a general way that it fails to engage contemporary life and culture.

Above all, contributors to this series have made a diligent effort not to sound moralistic or preachy. The NIV Application Commentary Series does not seek to provide ready-made sermon materials but rather tools, ideas, and insights that will help you communicate God's Word with power. If we help you to achieve that goal, then we have fulfilled the purpose for this series.

The Editors

General Editor's Preface

IF PLAYWRIGHT ARTHUR MILLER is correct in defining a great play as one in which you discover facets of your own character, then the two books of Samuel can be read as great plays. From Hannah's reaction to her infertility in 1 Samuel to David's desperate act of worship to stop the plague in 2 Samuel 24, these two books seem like nonstop character studies.

If you like to read biographies, the two Samuels are for you. If you are in need of a sure-fire Sunday school series to teach, the life of King David will keep them coming Sunday after Sunday. And, as Bill Arnold so expertly shows in the pages of this commentary, the application of biblical truth to everyday living is immediate and direct. God speaks through these pages.

Why do we hear God's voice so clearly through the lives of Hannah, Samuel, Eli and his sons, Saul, David, and David's family? What is it about the stories of these people that make us think we have met them? How do they remind us of people we know in everyday life?

A couple of "isn'ts." It isn't because we are reminded of our own specific life problems and successes through these characters. Samuel was a priest, David was a king. They lived three thousand years ago under circumstances so foreign to our way of life we can hardly imagine it. And it isn't necessarily that we identify with the sins these characters committed. David coveted his neighbor's wife and ordered her husband's murder so he could have her. Such deeds most of us only have nightmares about.

Rather, the reason we find the applications so immediate has deep theological roots. No matter what role we play, what deeds we do, or what culture gives form to our humanity, we are all created in God's image. We all have the same "father." We are made the same way. If you dig deep enough, underneath every role, deed, and culture you find a person made to seek God. It is the deepest, most basic urge we have. That is why we can read biographies of kings and arch-criminals and see ourselves in them.

There is a second reason why we find these applications so immediate. It is because we are all sinners saved by grace. We recognize not only our parentage, we recognize our common condition. When the prophet Nathan accuses David of murder and adultery in 2 Samuel 12, he points a long, bony finger at David and says, "You are the man," and all of us flinch. We have not all committed adultery, yet in the deepest recesses of our hearts we all have sins we are desperately trying to hide.

Similarly, when David sings his beautiful song of praise to God in 2 Samuel 22, thanking his Creator for delivering him from all his enemies, both external and internal, we immediately feel the warmth surrounding our hearts. We remember all the times in our lives when God's grace was sufficient to overcome the worst we could manage.

The two books of Samuel, therefore, have something to say about similarity and difference. One of the most important lessons of the twentieth century is the importance of difference. Through psychology we have learned the value of recognizing individual differences, of seeing each of us as unique as a snowflake. The study of anthropology has made us see the value of recognizing cultural differences, that the cultures in which we live dramatically shape the way we look at the world—so much so that people from different cultures can witness the same event and see radically different things. Such lessons are making enormous contributions to the ways we do evangelism and mission.

The books of Samuel, however, remind us of the importance of similarity. The lessons of difference must always be balanced by the lesson of similarity. We are so different from Samuel and David. But the same God made us, the same God saved us, and the same God keeps us safe. We call to that God who is worthy of praise, and we are saved from our enemies.

Terry C. Muck

Author's Preface

AT THE COMPLETION OF THIS PROJECT, I have more people than usual to acknowledge for their support. I begin by expressing my gratitude to the trustees and administration of Asbury Theological Seminary for a sabbatical in the fall of 2000, which made it possible to complete the first draft of the commentary.

I have also benefited greatly from my colleagues in the Old Testament department at Asbury, who make it such a delightful place to work. Mary Fisher, Sandra L. Richter, Brian D. Russell, Lawson G. Stone, and David L. Thompson have enriched my thinking and fine-tuned my methodology on a number of points. In addition, Brent A. Strawn's office was directly across the hall from mine the entire time I worked on this commentary. We shared countless conversations about the books of Samuel, leonine imagery in the ancient Near East, and too many other topics to mention (forgive me, Holly). Unfortunately, just as we were both finishing our respective books, Brent was called to another place of ministry, leaving us all the poorer.

The nature of this series as an "application commentary" especially offered me an opportunity to swim beyond the waters in which I normally move most comfortably, that of Old Testament and ancient Near Eastern studies. The Contemporary Significance sections often opened areas that raised more questions for me than I was prepared to answer. I have therefore especially enjoyed the help of colleagues who are critics of contemporary culture, and I have been more dependent than usual upon them for help with interpreting their various disciplines, as well as more mundane guidance such as bibliography.

Such cooperative bonhomie has been rewarding and has created in me a desire for more consistent dependence on each other in our research. It has also made me more thankful than ever for the privilege of ministering in a Christian academic context, and especially for my colleagues at Asbury. On more than one occasion, I consulted with the following colleagues about a variety of topics: Scott R. Burson, Kenneth J. Collins, Joel B. Green, George G. Hunter III, Christine Pohl, James R. Thobaben, Jerry L. Walls, and Ben Witherington III. I am also grateful to my student assistant, Paul Cook, for his help with the indexes.

The team at Zondervan has been helpful, as always. But I owe much especially to Robert Hubbard for his amazing editorial leadership. His many detailed and insightful comments have improved the manuscript at numerous points, and I am sure the book could have been improved even further had I accepted more of his suggestions. His sacrificial leadership as editor remains exemplary for us all. I am also indebted to Terry Muck and Verlyn Verbrugge for their careful efficiency and professionalism.

Finally, I dedicate this book to family and friends who sacrificed so much during World War II. In particular, I offer this work in appreciation of my father, my uncles, and two friends who mentored me at different stages of my life. The events of that war interrupted their happy youths and altered their lives forever.[1] Though it happened a long time ago, I have only recently come to realize how much they suffered in order to make it possible for me to work and live in freedom today. These loved ones have surrounded me and nurtured me at different stages of my life. I am sure I will never fully comprehend the degree of their sacrifice and the degree to which they are my true heroes.

---

1. In the case of Professor Weinberg, the details have been preserved in his own gripping narrative: Werner Weinberg, *Self-Portrait of a Holocaust Survivor* (Jefferson, N.C.: McFarland, 1985).

Abbreviations

AB	Anchor Bible
ABD	*Anchor Bible Dictionary*
ABRL	Anchor Bible Reference Library
AHw	*Akkadisches Handwörterbuch*
AnBib	Analecta biblica
AnOr	Analecta orientalia
ATJ	*Ashland Theological Journal*
BA	*Biblical Archaeologist*
BAR	*Biblical Archaeology Review*
BASOR	*Bulletin of the American Schools of Oriental Research*
BBR	*Bulletin for Biblical Research*
BDB	Brown, Driver, Briggs, *Hebrew and English Lexicon of the Old Testament*
BHS	*Biblia Hebraica Stuttgartensia*
Bib	*Biblica*
BibSac	*Bibliotheca sacra*
BWANT	Beiträge zur Wissenschaft vom Alten und Neuen Testament
BZAW	Beihefte zur Zeitschrift für die alttestamentliche Wissenschaft
CANE	*Civilizations of the Ancient Near East*
CBC	Cambridge Bible Commentary
CBQ	*Catholic Biblical Quarterly*
CBQMS	Catholic Biblical Quarterly Monograph Series
ConBOT	Coniectanea biblica, Old Testament Series
COS	*The Context of Scripture*
CTU	*The Cuneiform Alphabetic Texts from Ugarit, Ras Ibn Hani, and Other Places*
DBI	*Dictionary of Biblical Imagery*
DCH	*Dictionary of Classical Hebrew*
DDD²	*Dictionary of Deities and Demons in the Bible* (2d ed.)
EBC	*The Expositor's Bible Commentary*
EDBT	*Evangelical Dictionary of Biblical Theology*

EHAT	Exegetisches Handbuch zum Alten Testament
ErIsr	*Eretz-Israel*
HALOT	*Hebrew and Aramaic Lexicon of the Old Testament*
HBT	*Horizons in Biblical Theology*
HSM	Harvard Semitic Monographs
HTS	Harvard Theological Studies
HUCA	*Hebrew Union College Annual*
ICC	International Critical Commentary
IDBS	*The Interpreter's Dictionary of the Bible*, Supplementary Volume
IEJ	*Israel Exploration Journal*
Int	*Interpretation*
ITC	International Theological Commentary
JANESCU	*Journal of Ancient Near Eastern Society of Columbia University*
JAOS	*Journal of the American Oriental Society*
JBL	*Journal of Biblical Literature*
JETS	*Journal of the Evangelical Theological Society*
JNES	*Journal of Near Eastern Studies*
JNSL	*Journal of Northwest Semitic Languages*
JSNTSup	Journal for the Study of the New Testament Supplement Series
JSOTSup	Journal for the Study of the Old Testament Supplement Series
JSS	*Journal of Semitic Studies*
LXX	Septuagint (Greek translation of the Old Testament)
MT	Masoretic Text
NAC	New American Commentary
NASB	New American Standard Bible
NCB	New Century Bible
NDBT	*New Dictionary of Biblical Theology*
NEB	New English Bible
NIBCOT	New International Biblical Commentary on the Old Testament
NICNT	New International Commentary on the New Testament
NICOT	New International Commentary on the Old Testament
NIDOTTE	*New International Dictionary of Old Testament Theology and Exegesis*
NIV	New International Version

NIVAC	NIV Application Commentary
NJB	New Jerusalem Bible
NJPS	New Jewish Publication Society (version of the Tanak)
NLT	New Living Translation
NRSV	New Revised Standard Version
OBO	Orbis biblicus et orientalis
OEANE	*The Oxford Encyclopedia of Archaeology in the Near East*
OTG	Old Testament Guides
OTL	Old Testament Library
RSV	Revised Standard Version
SBLDS	Society of Biblical Literature Dissertation Series
SBLMS	Society of Biblical Literature Monograph Series
SHANE	Studies in the History and Culture of the Ancient Near East
SJLA	Studies in Judaism in Late Antiquity
SOTBT	Studies in Old Testament Biblical Theology
SWBA	Social World of Biblical Antiquity
TA	*Tel Aviv*
TDOT	*Theological Dictionary of the Old Testament*
TOTC	Tyndale Old Testament Commentaries
TrinJ	*Trinity Journal*
TynBul	*Tyndale Bulletin*
TZ	*Theologische Zeitschrift*
VT	*Vetus Testamentum*
VTSup	Supplements to Vetus Testamentum
WBC	Word Biblical Commentary
ZAW	*Zeitschrift für die alttestamentliche Wissenschaft*

Introduction

The books of 1 and 2 Samuel contain some of the most beloved narratives of the Bible: the boy-prophet Samuel asleep in the tabernacle at Shiloh, the blasphemous Philistine giant Goliath, the beautiful but forbidden Bathsheba, and Absalom's senseless rebellion. Perhaps less well-known to many readers are the contributions of these books to Israel's concept of "messiah" and the emphasis on the Davidic covenant. All these and many more are combined with an occasional poetic section to relate the acts of God in Israel's early monarchy. Together they create an extended narrative or historical book.

As historical books, 1–2 Samuel introduce the reader to scores of people and places over nearly a century of history. This commentary will make no attempt to discuss every geographical, historical, or grammatical detail of the text because of the nature of the volume as an "application commentary" and because of the constraints of space. For greater detail on these issues, the reader is encouraged to consult the critical commentaries, the best of which are noted often in the footnotes and listed in the bibliography.

Reading Israel's History Books

TODAY'S READERS SOMETIMES FORGET that the Bible's "historical books" were not meant to present a history of Israel and that we as Christians are not nurtured primarily by a study of history in and of itself. One of my former teachers warned that commentators working on the historical books are sometimes so fascinated by historical questions that they often neglect "their main business," which is "the elucidation of what the books mean to convey."[1] Though the literary genre of these books is historical narrative, we should remember their real nature as sermonic tracts. They invite us to follow the historical acts of God in early Israel, but they do much more besides. The narrative

---

1. Matitiahu Tsevat, "Israelite History and the Historical Books of the Old Testament," in *The Meaning of the Book of Job and Other Biblical Studies: Essays on the Literature and Religion of the Hebrew Bible* (New York: Ktav, 1980), 177.

in 1–2 Samuel invites us to enter into the story, to become part of the continuing saga of God's work in the world. Although this commentary will necessarily deal with certain pertinent historical features of these two biblical books, we will focus primarily on these books as "witnessing tradition." In order to hear God's invitation to become part of that tradition, we need to keep four guidelines before us as we proceed through 1–2 Samuel.[2]

(1) The Bible's historical narratives illustrate indirectly or subtly truths explained more directly elsewhere in Scripture. When relating historical events, individual narrators fall on a scale ranging between "showing" and "telling." Some merely present the story ("showing") without interrupting to explain the significance. These narrators rely on the sheer power of the story, leaving implications to the reader. Others insert authoritative explanations to evaluate motives or qualities of characters ("telling").[3] In general, 1–2 Samuel favor "showing" to "telling." On rare occasions, the historian has inserted explicit comments, but in most cases the bare power of the story carries the reader forward. On the one hand, this "showing" technique presents us with some of the most compelling episodes of the Bible. On the other hand, the theological significance of individual episodes may be expounded elsewhere in Scripture, or not at all, leaving us to make our own application.

(2) Narratives of the Old Testament historical books may have three levels of interpretation: the *universal*, the *national*, and the *individual*.[4] (a) The *universal* level refers to narratives that contribute to the universal work of God in creation. This level of interpretation has creation itself at its beginning and the culmination of Christ's work in the end times as its conclusion. (b) The national level has to do with the macrostory of God's redemptive work in Israel. This level of contribution has the call of Abraham and the ancestral narratives as its beginning point and the restoration of Judah in the postexilic period as its conclusion. (c) The individual level of interpretation consists of the thousands of

---

2. See John Goldingay, *Models for Interpretation of Scripture* (Grand Rapids: Eerdmans, 1995), 1–86.

3. M. H. Abrams, *A Glossary of Literary Terms* (5th ed.; New York: Hold, Rinehart and Winston, 1988), 23. See also Goldingay's use of the four Gospels to illustrate the varieties among the Bible's historical books (*Models*, 73–76).

4. For some of what follows, see the popular-level book on hermeneutics by Fee and Stuart, where they discuss these as top, middle, and bottom levels (Gordon D. Fee and Douglas Stuart, *How to Read the Bible for All Its Worth* [Grand Rapids: Zondervan, 1982], 73–78).

episodes that comprise the other two. In Old Testament narratives, every individual narrative contributes to the national level of interpretation, which makes its own contribution to the universal level.[5] In 1–2 Samuel in particular, we will be dealing with some of the most important narratives in the Bible on the national level. But there are many texts in which we will work with multiple levels at once; that is, the individual narrative will have both a national and universal application.

(3) The events narrated in 1–2 Samuel serve as the backbone for God's revelation, but they are not themselves his revelation for our times. Instead, the events are encapsulated in sacred writings as God's revelation. If in reading historical books our purpose is to reconstruct the events as they happened, we miss the truth and power of the narrative. The historian assumes the reality of certain key occurrences as actual historical events, and it would be impossible to read the books rightly without considering that history. But these narratives are "more than history, not less than history"; that is, they place before us an interpretation of God's mighty acts and their implications for our lives.[6] That interpretation is as important as the events themselves.

This point has important implications for our reading of 1–2 Samuel, because today's Christian readers are sometimes distressed by apparent contradictions in biblical narrative. But the very presence of history writing in the Old Testament creates an interesting paradox. On the one hand, history is an important instrument of revelation, the means of theologizing favored by Israelite authors, and in most cases they assumed the events they were describing actually occurred. On the other hand, the historians were not concerned with writing an exact history, that is, history in a modern sense.[7] Ancient Israelite historiography is not the same as modern history writing. Historiography by definition involves

---

5. As Fee and Stuart explain, when Jesus spoke of the Old Testament as bearing witness to him (John 5:37–39), he referred to the universal level of interpretation. He represents the central act of that macrostory of redemption, and the subjection of creation to him represents the climax of its plot. He was thus not referring to every individual narrative of the Old Testament (*How to Read the Bible*, 75).

6. Goldingay, *Models*, 32.

7. As was once popular in biblical studies, to write history *wie es eigentlich geschehen ist* ("as it actually happened"). The quote is most often associated with Leopold von Ranke, the nineteenth-century rationalist historian, who believed the past could be reconstructed with great confidence based on original sources and objective strategies. See Gerald T. Sheppard, "Biblical Interpretation in the 18th and 19th Centuries," in *Historical Handbook of Major Biblical Interpreters*, ed. D. K. McKim (Downers Grove, Ill.: InterVarsity Press, 1998), 257–80, esp. 269–72.

various levels of interpretation: selection, organization, and the drive to establish patterns of causation.[8] Biblical historiography, in contradistinction to modern history writing since the Enlightenment, locates the causes of human events in the passions and purposes of Yahweh, the God of Israel.[9]

So, for example, an earnest and careful reader trying to reconstruct the events of Saul's life or David's reign may become confused at a number of critical junctures, because chronology was not particularly important to our historians. The sequence of events was at times moved around in order to make the theological point of the text. For example, the details of the Philistine-Israelite war in the Jezreel Valley recorded in 1 Samuel 28–31 are arranged thematically in order to contrast Saul and David, so that the chronological sequence of the events was altered (see comments on 1 Sam. 29–30). Likewise, there are features of the reign of David reported out of chronological sequence in order to portray David under the blessing and David under the curse.[10]

All of this warns us not to look to the Bible for a positivistic reconstruction of Israelite history. We must be satisfied with less than a complete picture of "what really happened" and strive to read Scripture for the right purposes. We must come to see history as a primary, though not the exclusive datum for theology.[11] Instead, we must learn to read these books as "kerygmatic history," or "preached history."[12] In reviewing Israel's early monarchy, this extended sermon seeks to apply

---

8. Richard D. Nelson, *The Historical Books* (Interpreting Biblical Texts; Nashville: Abingdon, 1998), 21–24.

9. In a similar vein, ancient Near Eastern historiography in general rooted the causal line also in the divine realm, as did Israel. The difference between Israel and Mesopotamia is, among other things, their different views of divinity, which resulted further in different forms and types of historiography. See Bill T. Arnold, "The Weidner Chronicle and the Idea of History in Israel and Mesopotamia," in *Faith, Tradition, and History: Old Testament Historiography in Its Near Eastern Context*, ed. A. R. Millard, J. K. Hoffmeier, and D. W. Baker (Winona Lake, Ind.: Eisenbrauns, 1994), 129–48.

10. Eugene H. Merrill, "The 'Accession Year' and Davidic Chronology," *JANESCU* 19 (1989): 101–12; see the commentary on 2 Sam. below, passim.

11. Elmer A. Martens, "The Oscillating Fortunes of 'History' within Old Testament Theology," in *Faith, Tradition, and History: Old Testament Historiography in Its Near Eastern Context*, ed. A. R. Millard, J. K. Hoffmeier, and D. W. Baker (Winona Lake, Ind.: Eisenbrauns, 1994), 313–40, esp. 335–40.

12. Hans Walter Wolff, "The Kerygma of the Deuteronomic Historical Work," in *The Vitality of Old Testament Traditions*, ed. W. Brueggemann and H. W. Wolff (Atlanta: John Knox, 1975), 83–100; Nelson, *Historical Books*, 29.

the lessons of that past, in order for the reader to repent and submit to God's leading.

(4) Christian readers should also be sensitive to the supracultural nature of biblical truth. The task of interpretation is only complete when we have learned to apply the truth of the text to our own culture, and also—to borrow a term from missiologists—to contextualize biblical truth for cultures other than our own.[13] Before we even speak about cultures "other than our own," we need to stress that North American culture itself is moving further beyond modernism. As it does, contextualization of biblical truth will become increasingly more important for all Christians living here. The Old Testament historical books can fill an important desideratum in this case. Our generation has a profound need to hear more preaching from the narratives of the Old Testament, because postmoderns perceive life as a drama or narrative. The means of truth communication in 1–2 Samuel, in short, are especially needed in our times.[14]

The Israelite Historians

WHO WROTE 1 AND 2 SAMUEL? Technically, the authors are anonymous.[15] The Talmud preserves the rabbinic tradition that these books were written by prophets who lived contemporaneously with the events described.[16] As we will see, much of what we have in 1–2 Samuel has been narrated from a decidedly prophetic point of view, and there is nothing within the books themselves to preclude the notion that several prophets contributed to these narratives. But the

---

13. For more on this, see Grant R. Osborne, *The Hermeneutical Spiral: A Comprehensive Introduction to Biblical Interpretation* (Downers Grove, Ill.: InterVarsity Press, 1991), 318–38.

14. Thomas Elton Artmann, "Doctrinal Preaching in an Emerging Postmodern Age" (D. Min. diss.; Lexington, Ky.: Asbury Theological Seminary, 1998), 41.

15. In fact, it is strictly speaking impossible to refer to an "author" for these books, because there were many hands involved in the writing, compiling, arranging, and editing process, all anonymously. This commentary deals with the received text of Jewish and Christian tradition, concerning itself only with the "final form" of 1–2 Samuel. Thus, we make no attempt to comment on the meaning of various stages of the traditions (e.g., about Saul or David) at different points in Israel's history.

16. So Samuel wrote 1 Samuel 1–24, and the rest was written by Nathan and Gad (*b. B. Bat.* 14b and 15a). The tradition is likely based on 1 Chron. 29:29: "As for the events of King David's reign, from beginning to end, they are written in the records of Samuel the seer, the records of Nathan the prophet and the records of Gad the seer."

fact remains, the books of Samuel are anonymous, like many other Old Testament books.

Over the past six decades, biblical scholars have devised a theory to explain the origins and composition of 1–2 Samuel, and it is fair to say we have reached something of a consensus. The books of Samuel appear to have been a portion of a longer work tracing Israel's history from Moses to the destruction of Jerusalem by the Babylonians in 586 B.C. This longer history was comprised of Deuteronomy (at least in part), plus Joshua, Judges, 1–2 Samuel, and 1–2 Kings.[17] These books present a theological history of Israel, evaluating Israel's past in light of the covenant relationship established in Deuteronomy and relying on the so-called "retribution theology" established there. Based on the curses and blessings of Deuteronomy 28, the doctrine of retribution assumes the idea of reward for obedience to the covenant and punishment for disobedience. Such a guiding principle evaluated national and individual successes and failures in terms of the consequence of faithfulness or disobedience to Mosaic, or Deuteronomic, law. As a result, this extended history is commonly referred to as the Deuteronomistic History.[18]

Of the books contained in the Deuteronomistic History, 1–2 Samuel have the least amount of editorial and compositional detail that may be considered distinctively "Deuteronomistic." Most assume this is because the historian took large portions of previously existing materials (or "sources") and folded them into his extended treatment.

---

17. That is, the "Former Prophets" of the Hebrew canon, which excludes Ruth, 1–2 Chronicles, Ezra, Nehemiah, and Esther from the historical books per se. In contrast to our Protestant canon, these later historical books are included in the "Writings," or the third and final portion of the Hebrew canon.

18. The theory was first proposed by Martin Noth in 1943 and has been the subject of intense study for decades (Martin Noth, *The Deuteronomistic History* [JSOTSup 15; 2d ed.; Sheffield: Sheffield Academic Press, 1991]). Though the idea of a Deuteronomistic History has gone through significant modification, it stands today as the best explanation of origins of these historical books. For more information, see A. Graeme Auld, "The Former Prophets: Joshua, Judges, 1–2 Samuel, 1–2 Kings," in *The Hebrew Bible Today: An Introduction to Critical Issues*, ed. S. L. McKenzie and M. P. Graham (Louisville, Ky.: Westminster John Knox, 1998), 53–68; Steven L. McKenzie, "Deuteronomistic History," *ABD*, 2:160–68; Steven L. McKenzie and M. Patrick Graham, eds., *The History of Israel's Traditions: The Heritage of Martin Noth* (JSOTSup 182; Sheffield: Sheffield Academic Press, 1994); Mark A. O'Brien, *The Deuteronomistic History Hypothesis: A Reassessment* (OBO 92; Freiburg/Göttingen: Universitätsverlag/Vandenhoeck & Ruprecht, 1989).

It seems likely that the historian had available three narrative units, which presumably had an independent history before being used to produce the books of Samuel. These were: (1) the ark narrative (1 Sam. 4:1b–7:1, and perhaps also 2 Sam. 6);[19] (2) the history of David's rise (1 Sam. 16:14–2 Sam. 5);[20] and (3) the court history (otherwise known as the succession narrative, 2 Sam. 9–20; 1 Kings 1–2).[21]

These portions provided the skeletal features used by the final author of the books of Samuel. At places they appear to have been supplemented with other materials, serial lists, and appendices to comprise the whole package. The parameters for some of these sources—and indeed the independent existence of some of them—has been called into question by recent literary investigations of the received text of the books of Samuel.[22] Regardless of the origins of individual pieces, it would be a mistake to underestimate the degree of intentionality behind the present arrangement of the books of Samuel and one would miss the grander scale in view in the narrative of Saul, David, and Solomon.

For years scholars have argued that these three main narrative units noted above were some of the world's earliest and finest works of history (this was said especially of the court history). Likewise, it is often

---

19. The parameters for each of the sources listed here are often debated by scholars. On the source problems of Samuel, see Baruch Halpern, *The Constitution of the Monarchy in Israel* (HSM 25; Chico, Calif.: Scholars Press, 1981), 149–74. On the ark narrative in particular, see Patrick D. Miller Jr. and J. J. M. Roberts, *The Hand of the Lord: A Reassessment of the "Ark Narrative" of 1 Samuel* (Baltimore: John Hopkins Univ. Press, 1977), and P. Kyle McCarter Jr., *I Samuel* (AB 8; New York: Doubleday, 1980), 23–26.

20. Mettinger believes the original source was more extensive, comprising 1 Sam. 15– 2 Sam. 7. Tryggve N. D. Mettinger, *King and Messiah: The Civil and Sacral Legitimation of the Israelite Kings* (ConBOT 8; Lund: C.W.K. Gleerup, 1976), 33–47.

21. Leonhard Rost, *The Succession to the Throne of David*, trans. M. D. Rutter and D. M. Gunn (Sheffield: Almond, 1982); trans. of *Die Überlieferung von der Thronnachfolge Davids* (BWANT 3.6; Stuttgart: Kohlhammer, 1926); P. Kyle McCarter Jr., "Plots, True or False: The Succession Narrative as Court Apologetic," *Int* 35 (1981): 355–67; T. Ishida, "'Solomon Who Is Greater Than David': Solomon's Succession in 1 Kings I–II in the Light of the Inscription of Kilamuwa, King of YᵓDY-Samᵓal," in *Congress Volume: Salamanca, 1983*, ed. J. A. Emerton (VTSup 36; Leiden: Brill, 1985), 145–53. See also Robert P. Gordon, "In Search of David: The David Tradition in Recent Study," in *Faith, Tradition, and History: Old Testament Historiography in Its Near Eastern Context*, ed. A. R. Millard, J. K. Hoffmeier, and D. W. Baker (Winona Lake, Ind.: Eisenbrauns, 1994), 285–98.

22. For summary, see Robert Alter, *The David Story: A Translation with Commentary of 1 and 2 Samuel* (New York: W. W. North, 1999), x–xii.

asserted that these pieces were composed soon after the events themselves and were therefore relatively accurate historically. In the last few decades, scholars have routinely argued instead that these books are products of the late preexilic age, the exilic, or in some cases, even the postexilic period, and that they contain little if anything of historical value (see below). As a result, the earlier consensus about these sources has collapsed. The arguments for the exilic and postexilic date for these narrative units of Samuel are not convincing, however, and this commentary will assume their earlier provenance.[23]

Israel's Early United Monarchy

THE FIELD OF OLD TESTAMENT studies has gone through significant upheaval in recent decades.[24] Through much of the twentieth century until the mid–1970s, there were two competing approaches to the history of Israel, which together dominated the field. On the one hand, scholars who emphasized archaeology were generally more optimistic about the degree to which we could reconstruct the events of ancient Israel's history, including the judges period, the Exodus, and for some, the ancestral age (today we call such scholars "maximalists"). These scholars were often associated with William F. Albright, and those working within this framework are sometimes categorized as the American archaeological school. On the other hand, scholars working with the traditio-historical approach were less optimistic, especially about the ancestral age, the Exodus, and the judges period ("minimalists"). Scholars such as Albrecht Alt and Martin Noth best exemplify this approach, which flourished especially in Germany.

Despite the wide differences between these approaches, they were remarkably united on one thing: the United Monarchy of ancient Israel. With the kingdoms of David and Solomon, it was assumed we could have confidence about the events of this period. However, in the closing decades of the twentieth century, this consensus crumbled.[25]

---

23. See Gary N. Knoppers, "The Historical Study of the Monarchy: Developments and Detours," in *The Face of Old Testament Studies: A Survey of Contemporary Approaches*, ed. D. W. Baker and B. T. Arnold (Grand Rapids: Baker, 1999), 212–15.

24. For overview of these developments, see David W. Baker and Bill T. Arnold, eds., *The Face of Old Testament Studies: A Survey of Contemporary Approaches* (Grand Rapids: Baker, 1999).

25. Gary N. Knoppers, "The Vanishing Solomon: The Disappearance of the United Monarchy from Recent Histories of Ancient Israel," *JBL* 116 (1997): 19–44; idem, "Historical

Histories of Israel written during the 1980s often evinced caution about anything prior to David. During the 1990s, this caution gave way to radical skepticism, or as one scholar has called it, "nihilism."[26] It is not unusual for scholars today to deny the possibility of knowing anything at all about the history of early Israel, including the United Monarchy of the tenth century B.C., and some have even called into question the existence of David and Solomon. Instead, these kings are often seen as fictitious characters created in the Persian or Hellenistic periods.

The United Monarchy (minus Solomon) is, however, the period we are dealing with in this commentary (ca. 1025–965 B.C.).[27] The books of Samuel comprise the primary texts narrating the rise of Israel's monarchy, the failure of King Saul, and the towering figure of King David. Were we to accept the arguments of many scholars today, we would be forced to conclude that David may not have existed and that in any case we can know practically nothing about him. Are we to accept the results of minimalistic scholarship on Israel's United Monarchy? Is it possible that these individuals never existed?

The assumption adopted for this commentary is that such skepticism is unwarranted. It is beyond our purposes here to survey the problems involved, but it may be simply stated that the scholarship has been unduly affected by issues other than the evidence available.[28] We should remember that these ancient Hebrew texts had a long history of transmission. The form in which we have received the Bible reflects the later periods to be sure, but this does not preclude a growth of tradition coming from earlier times. In addition, the variability and

---

Study of the Monarchy: Developments, 215–21; see the fascinating volume edited by Lowell K. Handy, *The Age of Solomon: Scholarship at the Turn of the Millennium* (SHANE 11; Leiden: Brill, 1997).

26. Knoppers, "The Vanishing Solomon," 19–20.

27. For the dates and archaeological survey of the period, see Amihai Mazar, *Archaeology of the Land of the Bible, 10,000–586 B.C.E.* (ABRL; New York: Doubleday, 1990), 368–402. On the impossibility of fixed dates for this early period, see Hayim Tadmor, "The Chronology of the First Temple Period: A Presentation and Evaluation of the Sources," in J. Alberto Soggin, *An Introduction to the History of Israel and Judah* (rev. ed.; Valley Forge, Pa.: Trinity International, 1993), 394–417, esp. 408–9; and Mordecai Cogan, "Chronology: Hebrew Bible," *ABD*, 1:1002–11, esp. 1009.

28. See V. Philips Long, *The Art of Biblical History* (Foundations of Contemporary Interpretation 5; Grand Rapids: Zondervan, 1994), 120–68; Bill T. Arnold, "The Quest for the Historical Israel Continued," *ATJ* 24 (1992): 92–103.

adaptability within the Hebrew language itself suggests a long period of development and a diverse cultural milieu.[29] We actually have impressive evidence for the United Monarchy, including material remains discovered by archaeologists, epigraphic (i.e., textual) evidence from extrabiblical sources, and the literary evidence from the Bible itself. Based on this evidence, we can have confidence that Samuel, Saul, and David were historical individuals and that Saul and David did in fact rule a unified state of Israel.[30]

Contents of 1 and 2 Samuel

"YAHWEH IS KING." This is an important message in Israelite theology, which is taught explicitly in many texts and is used as a praise theme in several psalms. The ramifications of such a doctrine in the context of the ancient Near East are profound. Since Israel eventually extended the idea to include Yahweh's sovereignty over the whole world, it came to have an impact on Israel's relationship to the other nations.[31]

The idea that Yahweh is king has its origins in the very self-identity of the nation of Israel. At the heart of her understanding of her relationship with God is the concept of covenant. Scholars have often debated whether there exists a theological center (German *Mitte*) in the Old Testament, that is, whether there is a single unifying theme or motif that holds the various parts together.[32] I would argue that there is no actual center, that instead the various materials collected in the

---

29. Ian Young, *Diversity in Pre-Exilic Hebrew* (Tübingen: Mohr, 1993), passim.

30. See the conclusions of Knoppers, "The Vanishing Solomon," 33–43. One archaeologist stated recently that the sudden transformation of Hazor, Megiddo, and Gezer from burnt-out ruin heaps into "roughly comparable complex fortified governmental centers" would have forced him to invent David and Solomon had the Bible not already supplied their names. The archaeological evidence demands a conqueror and an administrator to have effected such a transformation. John S. Holladay Jr., "The Kingdoms of Israel and Judah: Political and Economic Centralization in the Iron IIA-B (ca. 1000–750 B.C.E.)," in *The Archaeology of Society in the Holy Land*, ed. Thomas E. Levy (London: Leicester Univ. Press, 1995), 368–98 (quote is from 371).

31. On the kingship of God, see Philip J. Nel, "מלך," *NIDOTTE*, 2:956–65, esp. 960–63.

32. John H. Hayes and Frederick Prussner, *Old Testament Theology: Its History and Development* (Atlanta: John Knox, 1985), 257–60; Gerhard F. Hasel, *Old Testament Theology: Basic Issues in the Current Debate* (rev. ed.; Grand Rapids: Eerdmans, 1975), 77–103.

Old Testament adhere as they do simply because of their common origins in the people of ancient Israel.[33] But one of the themes that has received the most attention over the years, and one that is clearly *a* central theme of the Old Testament, is that of *covenant*.

Since the 1950s and the pioneering work of George Mendenhall, most scholars have admitted a close relationship between ancient Near Eastern political treaties and certain crucial passages of the Old Testament.[34] In particular, the Hittite suzerainty treaties of the fourteenth and thirteenth centuries B.C. give us a glimpse of the way a superior king of one dominant nation might relate to a vassal, or weaker king, of a neighboring nation. The parallels between these ancient political treaties and certain covenant passages of the Old Testament are undeniable, since they share the same structure and, in some cases, even the same detailed outline. In particular Exodus 20–24, Joshua 24, and especially the book of Deuteronomy seem to be organized deliberately according to the structure of these ancient treaties.[35]

It is beyond my purposes here to review the importance of these observations.[36] But it is necessary for our reading of 1–2 Samuel to remember that the concept of covenant became Israel's most important and pervasive relational metaphor in the Old Testament. This became the best way to describe Israel's relationship with God, who is thereby portrayed as the Great King and Israel as the weaker vassal. Therefore, from Israel's earliest recollections of national origins (the Mosaic covenant) and in its greatest theological explanations of its relationship with Yahweh (Ex. 20–24 and Deuteronomy), God most often assumed the position of King of Israel. The concept of God's kingship over Israel appears in numerous other passages of the Old Testament, and certain royal psalms celebrate his kingship (Ps. 47; 93; 96; 98; 99; 100).

---

33. The concept of the person and presence of God may serve as an organizing tenet for the whole, though it is so broad as to be of little value theologically. See Samuel L. Terrien, *The Elusive Presence* (New York: Harper, 1978).

34. See George E. Mendenhall, *Law and Covenant in Israel and the Ancient Near East* (Pittsburgh: Biblical Colloquium, 1955), 32–34.

35. Dennis J. McCarthy, *Treaty and Covenant: A Study in Form in the Ancient Oriental Documents and in the Old Testament* (rev. ed.; Rome: Biblical Institute, 1981).

36. For discussion and introduction to the extensive bibliography on this topic, see John H. Walton, *Ancient Israelite Literature in Its Cultural Context* (Grand Rapids: Zondervan, 1989), 95–109.

It should not surprise us, then, that the transition from theocracy to monarchy, which is narrated mostly in 1 Samuel, was an agonizing process in the life of ancient Israel.[37] Contemporary scholarship has offered several attempts to explain the transition, the most helpful new approaches applying anthropological or macrosociological theory to the traditional archaeological and textual data.[38] So James Flanagan, for example, identifies the rule of Saul and David as "chiefdoms," a type of society that often precedes in social development a monarchy with centralized power.[39] But regardless of the historical and sociological specifics, the books of Samuel are primarily devoted to narrating the beginnings of the new Israelite institution of kingship. Thus 1 Samuel 1–7 may be said to describe the prelude to the monarchy, chapters 8–15 its advent, and chapters 16–31 its establishment. Likewise, 2 Samuel 1–20 narrate the consolidation of the monarchy under David, while chapters 21–24 function as an epilogue to the books generally.[40]

As 1–2 Samuel narrate the rise and establishment of Israel's new monarchy, they offer answers to two questions. What is the acceptable nature of the Israelite monarchy? And, who can serve suitably as king in this new institution? The first question is addressed primarily in 1 Samuel 1–15 and the second in 1 Samuel 16–2 Samuel 24, though several features of the second question are addressed much earlier in 1 Samuel 1–15 as well.

In addressing the first question, 1 Samuel 1–15 illustrate the deficiencies of the older model of the tribal confederation centered on priesthood and tabernacle at Shiloh and preserved from invasions by military judges. Both the religious and political superstructure failed. By the time the reader reaches 1 Samuel 12, it becomes obvious to

---

37. Israel's request in 1 Sam. 8:7 amounted to a rejection of Yahweh as king. See G. E. Gerbrandt, *Kingship According to the Deuteronomistic History* (Atlanta: Scholars Press, 1986), 148.

38. For helpful review, see Charles E. Carter, "Opening Windows onto Biblical Worlds: Applying the Social Sciences to Hebrew Scripture," in *The Face of Old Testament Studies*, 421–33.

39. James W. Flanagan, *David's Social Drama: A Hologram of Israel's Early Iron Age* (JSOTSup 73 and SWBA 7; Sheffield: Almond, 1988), 304–18; Robert Donald Miller II, "A Social History of Highland Israel in the 12th and 11th Centuries B.C.E." (Ph.D. diss., Ann Arbor: The University of Michigan, 1998).

40. Ronald F. Youngblood, "1, 2 Samuel," *EBC* (Grand Rapids: Zondervan, 1992), 3:1050–51.

Samuel, the most ardent adversary of the monarchy, that kingship is necessary and, if rightly constituted, even desirable. Much of Samuel's energy in chapters 8–12 is then devoted to constituting the new institution.[41] Ideally there was always to be a close relationship between Israel's human kingdom and God's kingdom.

But Yahweh was king in earliest Israel (Ex. 15:18; Num. 23:21; Deut. 33:5), and this was not a concept that could be relinquished in the new monarchy. So from the earliest conceptions of Israelite monarchy, this was the hard question: How was the human king related to the divine king? Ultimately, as 1 Samuel shows, Israel settled the question in a way similar to the way this was handled in Assyria and Babylonia. The real king was the deity, while the human king was just a representative or viceroy. The human king was chosen by the deity to fulfill his wishes in the human kingdom.[42] The kingship of Saul was thus limited as a conditional appointment or covenant. As long as he served under the inspiration of the spirit of God and as long as he avoided violation of the ancient tribal legal traditions, he would serve as Yahweh's vicegerent.[43]

So to this first question on the nature of Israelite monarchy, 1 Samuel 1–15 is clear that Yahweh must continue to rule Israel, even after a human leader comes to power. There are, of course, many historical and sociological issues involved, and in certain ways, Israel was not unlike her neighbors in regards to her transition to monarchy. But 1 Samuel 1–15 is less concerned with these than with the theological significance of the shift. Christoph Barth has summarized the issue well:

---

41. When I refer to early Israel's monarchy as an "institution," I do not intend to conjure up the debate over the definition of "state," in which Max Weber's use of "institution" (*Anstalt*) was so important. See Christa Schäfer-Lichtenberger, "Sociological and Biblical Views of the Early State," in *The Origins of the Ancient Israelite States*, ed. V. Fritz and P. R. Davies (JSOTSup 228; Sheffield: Sheffield Academic Press, 1996), 85–88.

42. For references, see J. J. M. Roberts, "Zion in the Theology of the Davidic-Solomonic Empire," in *Studies in the Period of David and Solomon and Other Essays*, ed. Tomoo Ishida (Winona Lake, Ind.: Eisenbrauns, 1982), 99. One of the central functions of all Mesopotamian kings was to serve as the primary human link with the gods. All rulers from Hammurabi to Nabonidus claimed they were called by a great god, who had chosen them for the office and who maintained an intimate link with the human king (cf. Ps. 2:7). See H. W. F. Saggs, *Babylonians* (Peoples of the Past 1; Norman, Okla.: Univ. of Oklahoma Press, 1995), 135–37.

43. See comments on 1 Sam. 9:1–10:8; also Frank Moore Cross, *Canaanite Myth and Hebrew Epic: Essays in the History of the Religion of Israel* (Cambridge, Mass.: Harvard Univ. Press, 1973), 220–21.

> For Israel ... monarchy as a political and social system also had a theological dimension, for the Israelites were in relation to the eternal kingdom in which God rules in love and justice. The interest of Israel lay not so much in the institution of kingship as such but in God's use of the institution as Ruler over his people and humanity. The Lord, the God of Israel, wants just government. It is to this end that he acts, raising up kings here and overthrowing them there.[44]

We will see that the second question (Who may serve suitably as king?) begins to be addressed in the institution of prophetic anointing. But the story begins even earlier with the assertion that Yahweh himself has been Israel's king thus far and that in reality he must always remain king. He governed in the past through certain religious and political institutions (i.e., priesthood and tabernacle, with its ark at Shiloh and the network of judges). Paradoxically, these must all be transformed in the new monarchy, yet they must also remain the same. The priesthood will be resuscitated, the tabernacle relocated and rebuilt as a permanent structure to house the ark, and the judges system reconfigured and absorbed by the monarchy. But as symbols of Yahweh's kingship, they will remain.

Israel's new monarchy will be structured as a vice-regency—the Lord will remain Israel's king but will rule through human designees. As to who can serve suitably as king, the human viceroy is to be anointed with oil by one of Yahweh's prophets and guided by Yahweh's spirit. He will also be received by the people by public acclamation. The rest of 1–2 Samuel is devoted to illustrating—first by negative example (Saul) and then by positive example (David)—who may serve suitably as Yahweh's viceroy.

Biblical historiography seeks to explore the past in order to influence both the present (that of the author) and the future. Like the ancient Egyptian and Mesopotamian practice of monumental inscriptions placed in walls or foundations of public buildings or erected on stone pillars, biblical historiographers consciously intended their history writing to become part of a continued witnessing tradition.[45] In

---

44. Christoph Barth, *God with Us: A Theological Introduction to the Old Testament* (Grand Rapids: Eerdmans, 1991), 188–89.

45. Nelson, *Historical Books*, 25–27.

the case of 1–2 Samuel, the biblical historian was consciously attempting to recount the past as a means of lending support and legitimacy to the Israelite monarchy as constituted in the Davidic dynasty. Thus, the two central questions cited above are also programmatic for Israel's future. I could rephrase my questions: What *should* the monarchy be like, and Who *should* the king of Israel be like? The answers: Israel's monarchy should always be as Samuel intended, and the king should always be like David.

As part of ancient Hebrew Scriptures, 1–2 Samuel define the nature and significance of kingship for Israel's future. As part of our Christian canon, they speak with power to our understanding of the work of Christ in the world generally. Today's Christian readers now stand in the great stream of the biblical historian's posterity. The books of Samuel were intended to be programmatic for Israel's monarchy, and so they argue that Israel's kingdom should have certain defining characteristics and that Israel's king must meet a given set of criteria. In light of our understanding of the revelation given through Jesus Christ, today's Christian readers accept the idea that the ancient Israelite historian wrote better than he understood. The Israelite stream of messianism, by which ancient believers perceived God's work in their nation Israel and through their king, now takes on a broader application.

The future perspective of the historian is thus transformed from a programmatic treatise on what the nature of Israelite kingship ought to be into a theological treatise on the actual character of the Messiah. So the books of Samuel, which have their own innate authority as inspired texts from God, assume also for the Christian reader special appeal as texts that shape and inform our understanding of the life and mission of Jesus Christ.

Theological Themes of 1 and 2 Samuel

BESIDES THE IMPORTANT concept of divine kingship, 1–2 Samuel develop other concepts linked with it in ancient Israelite thought. Primary among these are Israel's emerging concept of a "messiah" or "anointed one," the condemnation of abuses of power, and the books' prophetic emphasis on confession and repentance.

(1) Israel's belief in an ideal anointed leadership does not appear on the scene suddenly or fully developed but emerges gradually and subtly

in 1–2 Samuel. So, for example, as 1 Samuel begins, the role of the holy place (ark of the covenant and tabernacle) and the priesthood are important themes. But these institutions are not fulfilling their proper roles and are not serving Yahweh or Israel as intended, primarily because of the leadership at the time. Eventually the difficulties find partial resolution in David's capture of Jebus/Jerusalem in 2 Samuel 5–6. Thus, the *three* institutions—Israel's new monarchy, the central worship site, and the priesthood—are then explicitly tied together in David, Jerusalem, and Zadok. In essence, all the themes relevant to Israel's burgeoning messianism are developed, some to nearly complete form.[46] Later in Old Testament thought and in the intertestamental period, messianism grew out of this Davidic ideal through the prophets.

The concept of an ideal anointed one arises gradually and is sustained in the narrative. But at the same time the severe shortcomings of David call the whole venture into question. Earlier, Israel's need for a king is first justified and then met by the anointing and reign of King Saul. But his rejected rulership only serves to highlight the need for a righteous and just king. When this is met by the ideal king David, God gives promises that a son of David will rule forever (2 Sam. 7). But the disappointing flaws in David create a tension in the narrative: the ideal and hope of David versus his failures. This contrast between the ideal and the actual in the narratives of 1–2 Samuel creates a "deliberately emphasized antinomy," creating a tension that ultimately drives the reader past the pages of 1–2 Samuel themselves for the answers.[47]

Subsequent Old Testament prophetic texts carry the tension further, sustaining the ideal figure of David's son with the realization that few, if any, of his descendants live up to that ideal.[48] In 1–2 Samuel these

---

46. P. R. Ackroyd, *The Second Book of Samuel* (CBC; Cambridge: Cambridge Univ. Press, 1977), 8; and J. J. M. Roberts, "The Old Testament's Contribution to Messianic Expectations," in *The Messiah: Developments in Earliest Judaism and Christianity*, ed. James H. Charlesworth (Minneapolis: Fortress, 1992), 39–51, esp. 42–43.

47. The words are those of Philip E. Satterthwaite ("David in the Books of Samuel: A Messianic Hope?" in *The Lord's Anointed: Interpretation of Old Testament Messianic Texts*, ed. P. E. Satterthwaite, R. S. Hess, and G. J. Wenham [Carlisle: Paternoster, 1995], 64–65). See also Rolf P. Knierim, "The Messianic Concept in the First Book of Samuel," in *Jesus and the Historian: Written in Honor of Ernest Cadman Colwell*, ed. F. T. Trotter (Philadelphia: Westminster, 1968), 20–51, esp. 42.

48. For representative examples, see Isa. 11:1–2; Jer. 23:5; Amos 9:11–15.

ideas are presented only in germinal form. Satterthwaite has grasped the role and position of the books of Samuel in the rise of biblical messianism:

> Expectation and present reality have not as yet fully diverged. Yet the books of Samuel have gone at least partly along the way towards the position represented by the prophetic texts. David's own shortcomings raise questions concerning the kingdom he inaugurates, yet at his best he represents an ideal. If the books of Samuel do not resolve this tension, they do at any rate clearly mark out its contours.[49]

(2) In addressing the two central questions outlined above, the extended narrative of 1–2 Samuel contains another important theme lying just beneath the surface, that is, the use and abuse of power. Who has power or authority in Israel, and how will it be exercised? In many respects, Israel's king would be like other kings of the world. But the distinctive feature of Israelite kingship was not only that the king was the chosen and anointed one but that the king must accept Yahweh's authority and lead the people in submission to Yahweh's sovereignty. At stake, of course, is the manner in which the human king would use or abuse his God-given power. Will the Israelite king, like other kings both ancient and modern, manipulate and conspire in the process of ruling? Or will he submit to Yahweh's rulership and acknowledge certain divinely established limits to his power?

The first anointed one failed in this regard (Saul). Though the second one also abused power, he quickly and earnestly repented, and he genuinely accepted divinely ordained limits to his power (David). Thus, 1–2 Samuel contain a powerful message, which is the logical corollary to the definition of Israel's monarchy as a circumscribed and limited office. The abuse of the power that comes to us by virtue of office or position is an indication that we are not worthy of that office or position. To wield institutional power rightly, one must be willing to submit to God's righteous and sovereign direction. Just as in Israel, the Lord's anointed one must be willing to serve as a vice-regent; he must acknowledge that he, too, serves at the wishes of an even greater authority, God himself.

---

49. Satterthwaite, "David in the Books of Samuel," 65.

(3) These two themes (messianism and the right use of power) are concerns of other Old Testament authors as well. But a third theme transcends these and binds them together in the books of Samuel, namely, the definition and nature of repentance. A wholistic reading of the final form of 1–2 Samuel reveals a pattern in which the three protagonists of our story (Samuel, Saul, and David) serve to highlight and emphasize the definition and nature of confession and repentance. These three present us with three "portraits of repentance." The macrostructure in 1–2 Samuel supports the idea that the trajectories of the three main figures work together to define and illustrate the author's fundamental message.

The concept of turning to Yahweh (*šwb*) is, of course, central to many of the canonical prophets, particularly Hosea, Joel, and Jeremiah.[50] Thus, as I have said, important theological concepts taught explicitly elsewhere in Scripture are often illustrated in the historical books. The books of Samuel therefore contribute graphic illustration to the Bible's teaching on the precise nature of confession and repentance through the three portraits of Samuel, Saul, and David.

(a) At a critical juncture in Israel's history, the prophet Samuel seized a moment of tragedy in order to call the nation to repentance. The opening six chapters of 1 Samuel condemn a wicked Elide priesthood at Shiloh and a nation plagued with sin and failure. At this critical moment in Israel's history, Samuel used terminology characteristic of later prophetic preaching to call for a "return" (*šwb*) to Yahweh (see comments on 1 Sam. 7:2–4 for linguistic details). Such genuine repentance is required to restore a right relationship with Yahweh, and it involves at once both a turning away from the sins that have caused the separation and a returning unto God. This return must be "whole-hearted," implying there can be no divided loyalties or opinions when one returns to Yahweh. In the case of Samuel's appeal in 1 Samuel 7, repentance involved a repudiation of Israel's allegiance to Canaanite gods of fertility and a renewed commitment to serve Yahweh exclusively. Samuel's message synopsizes the Old Testament prophetic concern for repentance and stands like a watchtower over the rest of the books of Samuel.

---

50. For particular references, see Jer. 18:1–12; Hos. 14:1–2; Joel 2:12–13. This theme may be another indication of the role of the prophets in the compilation of 1–2 Samuel.

This first portrait includes not only the sermon Samuel preached (1 Sam. 7:3) but also its effects. With his help, the Israelites came to understand the nature of wholehearted turning to God as both a repudiation of past sins and exclusive devotion to Yahweh. Samuel gathered them at Mizpah for prayer and fasting, and Israel's corporate confession was succinct and genuine (7:6): "We have sinned against the LORD." This brings us to the first of three illustrations of confession, all using the verb "sinned" (ḥṭʾ). Samuel's instruction was effective; the Israelites confessed and repented. The Lord responded at once with victory and peace, where before there had been only failure and defeat.[51] This first portrait of repentance is paradigmatic for the rest of 1–2 Samuel by defining and illustrating the nature of true confession and repentance.

(b) The second portrait of confession, Saul, teaches by way of contrast. As the first example (Samuel at Mizpah) was genuine and effective, the second was insincere and futile. The portrait of Saul in 1 Samuel 15 is *not* the way to repent! His words and actions were self-serving and self-vindicating. His confession is coerced by the prophet bit by bit, and even then it is disingenuous. He *acknowledges* wrongdoing instead of *repudiating* it; Saul regrets his actions because they leave him vulnerable, not because they were self-destructive and offensive to God.

Saul's words of confession are the same as Israel's at Mizpah: "I have sinned" (1 Sam. 15:24; repeated in 15:30), but the words alone are not enough. He fails to exemplify the same wholehearted repentance Israel illustrates. Instead, his words are followed by more words of defensive argumentation, deflection, and rationalization. His "I have sinned" is followed by an unfortunate "because." He sinned, *because* he "was afraid of the people" (almost implying "it was all *their* fault").[52] Our reading of Saul will reveal that he was more concerned with placating Samuel and the people of Israel than he was with seeking forgiveness and restoration from Yahweh.

---

51. Note esp. the summarizing evaluations of the narrator: "The Philistines were subdued" (1 Sam. 7:13), and "there was peace between Israel and the Amorites" (7:14).

52. The causal connector (*ki*) is obscured in the NIV. Compare NRSV and esp. NJPS, where the logical connector becomes disjunctive: "I did wrong ... *but* I was afraid of the troops and I yielded to them."

If Samuel's message of repentance is a watchtower over the rest of 1–2 Samuel and Israel's confession at Mizpah is a positive example of its effects, then conversely, Saul stands as a benchmark of failure. His confession illustrates precisely the results of resisting Samuel's instruction and the self-destructive consequences of an unrepentant heart. He said the right words, but his heart and his actions belied his recalcitrant spirit.

(c) The third portrait of repentance is David. The prophet who brought the message is different, but the message itself is the same. Nathan has replaced the revered Samuel, but his firm "You are the man!" confronts David with the same powerful lessons (2 Sam. 12:7). Like the Israelites at Mizpah, David has learned well the prophetic lesson of confession and repentance. The terminology we have now come to expect is sincere and genuine to the core. David's "I have sinned" (12:13) is not followed by recrimination or self-vindication. His words stand alone, exposed, naked, and vulnerable. David is a broken man. The king who boldly took what was not rightfully his acknowledges his guilt. He serves as an illustration for the sermon Samuel preached so many years before.

Outline of the Books of Samuel

I. Israel's Need for a King (1 Sam. 1–7)
  A. Shiloh Narratives (1 Sam. 1–3)
    1. The Birth of Samuel (1 Sam. 1:1–28)
    2. Hannah's Song and Eli's Failure (1 Sam. 2:1–36)
    3. The Call of Samuel(1 Sam. 3:1–4:1a)
  B. Ark Narratives (1 Sam. 4–7)
    1. The Philistines Capture the Ark of the Covenant (1 Sam. 4:1b–11)
    2. Eli's Death and Ichabod's Birth (1 Sam. 4:12–22)
    3. The Ark's Sojourn in Philistia and Return to Israel (1 Sam. 5:1–7:1)
    4. Samuel's Call to Repentance (1 Sam. 7:2–4)
    5. Israel's Confession at Mizpah (1 Sam. 7:5–17)
II. The Rise and Fall of Saul, Israel's First King (1 Sam. 8–15)
  A. Saul Becomes King (1 Sam. 8–12)
    1. Israel Demands a King (1 Sam. 8:1–22)
    2. Saul Becomes Israel's First King (1 Sam. 9:1–10:27)
    3. Saul Delivers the City of Jabesh Gilead (1 Sam. 11:1–15)
    4. Samuel's Final Exhortations (1 Sam. 12:1–25)
  B. God Rejects Saul (1 Sam. 13–15)
    1. Saul Offers Sacrifice At Gilgal (1 Sam. 13:1–22)
    2. Leadership Crisis During Philistine Wars (1 Sam. 13:23–14:52)
    3. Saul Rejects the Word of the Lord (1 Sam. 15:1–35)
III. The Rise of David, Israel's Promised King (1 Sam. 16–2 Sam. 4)
  A. David in Saul's Court (1 Sam. 16–20)
    1. Samuel Anoints David (1 Sam. 16:1–13)
    2. David Enters Saul's Service (1 Sam. 16:14–23)
    3. David and Goliath (1 Sam. 17:1–58)
    4. Conflict Between Saul and David (1 Sam. 18:1–30)

Bibliography

Commentaries on 1 and 2 Samuel

Ackroyd, P. R. *The First Book of Samuel*. CBC. Cambridge: Cambridge Univ. Press, 1971.

_____. *The Second Book of Samuel*. CBC. Cambridge: Cambridge Univ. Press, 1977.

Alter, Robert. *The David Story: A Translation with Commentary of 1 and 2 Samuel*. New York: W. W. North, 1999.

Anderson, A. A. *2 Samuel*. WBC 11. Dallas, Tex.: Word, 1989.

Baldwin, Joyce. *1 and 2 Samuel: An Introduction and Commentary*. TOTC 8. Downers Grove, Ill.: InterVarsity Press, 1988.

Bergen, Robert D. *1, 2 Samuel*. NAC 7. Nashville, Tenn.: Broadman & Holman, 1996.

Brueggemann, Walter. *First and Second Samuel*. Interpretation. Louisville, Ky.: John Knox, 1990.

Evans, Mary J. *1 and 2 Samuel*. NIBCOT 6. Peabody, Mass.: Hendrickson, 2000.

Gordon, Robert P. *I and II Samuel: A Commentary*. Grand Rapids: Zondervan, 1986.

_____. *1 and 2 Samuel*. OTG. Sheffield: Sheffield Academic Press, 1984.

Hertzberg, Hans Wilhelm. *I and II Samuel*. OTL. Philadelphia: Westminster, 1964.

Jobling, David. *1 Samuel*. Berit Olam. Collegeville, Minn.: Liturgical, 1998.

Keil, C. F., and Franz Delitzsch. *Biblical Commentary on the Books of Samuel*. Trans. J. Martin. Grand Rapids: Eerdmans, 1956.

Klein, Ralph W. *1 Samuel*. WBC 10. Waco, Tex.: Word, 1983.

Mauchline. J. *1 and 2 Samuel*. NCB. London: Marshall, Morgan and Scott, 1971.

McCarter, P. Kyle, Jr. *1 and 2 Samuel*. 2 vols. AB 8, 9. New York: Doubleday, 1980 and 1984.

McKane, William. *I and II Samuel*. Torch Bible Commentaries. London: SCM, 1963.

Newsome, James D. *I Samuel, II Samuel*. Knox Preaching Guides. Philadelphia: Westminster John Knox, 1982.

Payne, David F. *I and II Samuel*. Westminster Daily Study Bible. Philadelphia: Westminster John Knox, 1982.

Smith, H. P. *A Critical and Exegetical Commentary on the Books of Samuel.* ICC. Edinburgh: T. & T. Clark, 1898.

Spina, Frank Anthony. "1 and 2 Samuel." Pages 358–87 in *Asbury Bible Commentary.* Edited by Eugene E. Carpenter and Wayne McCown. Grand Rapids: Zondervan, 1992.

Youngblood, Ronald F. "1, 2 Samuel." Pages 551–1104 in *EBC*, vol. 3. Edited by Frank E. Gaebelein. 12 vols. Grand Rapids: Zondervan, 1992.

Other Significant Works Related to 1 and 2 Samuel

Ahlström, Gösta W. "Administration of the State in Canaan and Ancient Israel." Pages 587–603 in vol. 1 of *Civilizations of the Ancient Near East.* Edited by Jack M. Sasson. 4 vols. New York: Simon & Schuster, 1995.

Arnold, W. R. *Ephod and Ark.* HTS 3. Cambridge, Mass.: Harvard Univ. Press, 1917.

Ash, Paul S. *David, Solomon and Egypt: A Reassessment.* JSOTSup 297. Sheffield: Sheffield Academic Press, 1999.

Auld, A. Graeme. *Kings Without Privilege: David and Moses in the Story of the Bible's Kings* Edinburgh: T. & T. Clark, 1994.

_____. "Re-Reading Samuel (Historically): 'Etwas mehr Nichtwissen.'" Pages 160–69 in *The Origins of the Ancient Israelite States.* Edited by Volkmar Fritz and Philip R. Davies. Sheffield: Sheffield Academic Press, 1996.

Bailey, Randall C. *David in Love and War: The Pursuit of Power in 2 Samuel 10–12.* JSOTSup 75. Sheffield: JSOT, 1990.

Birch, Bruce C. *The Rise of the Israelite Monarchy: The Growth and Development of I Samuel 7–15.* Missoula, Mont.: Scholars Press, 1976.

Brettler, Marc Z. "Biblical Literature as Politics: The Case of Samuel." Pages 71–92 in *Religion and Politics in the Ancient Near East.* Edited by Adele Berlin. Bethesda, Md.: Univ. Press of Maryland, 1996.

_____. *The Creation of History in Ancient Israel.* London: Routledge, 1995.

_____. *God Is King: Understanding an Israelite Metaphor.* Sheffield: JSOT, 1989.

Campbell, Antony F. *The Ark Narrative (1 Sam 4–6; 2 Sam 6): A Form-Critical and Traditio-Historical Study.* Missoula, Mont.: Scholars Press, 1975.

_____. *Of Prophets and Kings: A Late Ninth-Century Document (1 Samuel 1–2 Kings 10.* CBQMS 17. Washington, D.C.: Catholic Biblical Association, 1986.

Carlson, R. A. *David, the Chosen King.* Stockholm: Almqvist & Wiksell, 1964.

Conroy, Charles. *Absalom Absalom! Narrative and Language in 2 Sam 13–20.* AnBib 81. Rome: Pontifical Biblical Institute, 1978.

Day, John, ed. *King and Messiah in Israel and the Ancient Near East: Proceedings of the Oxford Old Testament Seminar.* JSOTSup 270. Sheffield: Sheffield Academic Press, 1998.

Edelman, Diana. *King Saul in the Historiography of Judah*. JSOTSup 121. Sheffield: JSOT Press, 1991.

_____. "Saul ben Kish in History and Tradition." Pages 142–59 in *The Origins of the Ancient Israelite States*. Edited by Volkmar Fritz and Philip R. Davies. Sheffield: Sheffield Academic Press, 1996.

Eslinger, Lyle M. *House of God or House of David: The Rhetoric of 2 Samuel 7*. JSOTSup 164. Sheffield: JSOT, 1994.

_____. *Kingship of God in Crisis: A Close Reading of 1 Samuel 1–12*. Sheffield: Almond, 1985.

Exum, J. Cheryl, ed. *The Historical Books: A Sheffield Reader*. The Biblical Seminar 40. Sheffield: Sheffield Academic Press, 1997.

Flanagan, James. *David's Social Drama: A Hologram of Israel's Early Iron Age*. JSOTSup 73 and SWBA 7. Sheffield: Almond, 1988.

Fokkelmann, Jan P. *Narrative Art and Poetry in the Books of Samuel: A Full Interpretation Based on Stylistic and Structural Analyses*. 4 vols. Assen, The Netherlands: Van Gorcum, 1981, 1986, 1990, 1993.

Foresti, Fabrizio. *The Rejection of Saul in the Perspective of the Deuteronomistic School: A Study of 1 Sam 15 and Related Texts*. Rome: Edizione del Teresianum, 1984.

Fritz, Volkmar, and Philip R. Davies, eds. *The Origins of the Ancient Israelite States*. JSOTSup 228. Sheffield: Sheffield Academic Press, 1996.

Garsiel, Moshe. "Word Play and Puns as a Rhetorical Device in the Book of Samuel." Pages 181–204 in *Puns and Pundits: Word Play in the Hebrew Bible and Ancient Near Eastern Literature*. Edited by Scott B. Noegel. Bethesda, Md.: CDL Press, 2000.

Gerbrandt, Gerald E. *Kingship According to the Deuteronomistic History*. Atlanta: Scholars Press, 1986.

Gordon, Robert P. "David's Rise and Saul's Demise: Narrative Analogy in 1 Samuel 24–26." *TynBul* 31 (1980): 37–64.

_____. "In Search of David: The David Tradition in Recent Study." Pages 285–98 in *Faith, Tradition, and History: Old Testament Historiography in Its Near Eastern Context*. Edited by A. R. Millard, J. K. Hoffmeier, and D. W. Baker. Winona Lake, Ind.: Eisenbrauns, 1994.

_____. "Who Made the Kingmaker? Reflections on Samuel and the Institution of the Monarchy." Pages 255–69 in *Faith, Tradition, and History: Old Testament Historiography in Its Near Eastern Context*. Edited by A. R. Millard, J. K. Hoffmeier, and D. W. Baker. Winona Lake, Ind.: Eisenbrauns, 1994.

Gunn, David M. *The Fate of King Saul: An Interpretation of a Biblical Story*. JSOTSup 14. Sheffield: JSOT, 1980.

_____. *The Story of King David: Genre and Interpretation*. JSOTSup 6. Sheffield: JSOT, 1978.

Halpern, Baruch. *The Constitution of the Monarchy in Israel*. HSM 24. Chico, Calif.: Scholars Press, 1981.

_____. "The Construction of the Davidic State: An Exercise in Historiography." Pages 44–75 in *The Origins of the Ancient Israelite States*. Edited by Volkmar Fritz and Philip R. Davies. Sheffield: Sheffield Academic Press, 1996.

Howard, David M., Jr. "The Case for Kingship in the Old Testament Narrative Books and the Psalms." *TrinJ* 9 (1988): 19–35.

Ishida, Tomoo. *The Royal Dynasties in Ancient Israel*. BZAW 142. Berlin: W. de Gruyter, 1977.

_____, ed. *Studies in the Period of David and Solomon and Other Essays*. Winona Lake, Ind.: Eisenbrauns, 1982.

Knierim, R. "The Messianic Concept in the First Book of Samuel." Pages 20–51 in *Jesus and the Historian: Written in Honor of E. C. Colwell*. Edited by F. T. Trotter. Philadelphia: Westminster, 1968.

Knoppers, Gary N. "Ancient Near Eastern Royal Grants and the Davidic Covenant: A Parallel?" *JAOS* 116 (1996): 670–97.

_____. "The Historical Study of the Monarchy: Developments and Detours." Pages 207–35 in *The Face of Old Testament Studies*. Edited by D. W. Baker and B. T. Arnold. Grand Rapids: Baker, 1999.

_____. "The Vanishing Solomon: The Disappearance of the United Monarchy from Recent Histories of Ancient Israel." *JBL* 116 (1997): 19–44.

Levenson, Jon D. "1 Samuel 25 as Literature and History." *CBQ* 40 (1978): 11–28.

_____, and Baruch Halpern. "The Political Import of David's Marriages." *JBL* 99 (1980): 507–18.

Long, V. Philips. *The Art of Biblical History*. Grand Rapids: Zondervan, 1994.

_____. "Historiography of the Old Testament." Pages 145–75 in *The Face of Old Testament Studies*. Edited by D. W. Baker and B. T. Arnold. Grand Rapids: Baker, 1999.

_____. *The Reign and Rejection of King Saul: A Case for Literary and Theological Coherence*. SBLDS 118. Atlanta: Scholars Press, 1989.

Malamat, Abraham. "A Political Look at the Kingdom of David and Solomon and Its Relations with Egypt." Pages 189–204 in *Studies in the Period of David and Solomon and Other Essays*. Edited by Tomoo Ishida. Winona Lake, Ind.: Eisenbrauns, 1982.

Martin, J. "Studies in 1 and 2 Samuel, Part 1: The Structure of 1 and 2 Samuel." *BibSac* 141 (1984): 28–42.

_____. "Studies in 1 and 2 Samuel, Part 2: The Literary Quality of 1 and 2 Samuel." *BibSac* 141 (1984): 131–45.

_____. "Studies in 1 and 2 Samuel, Part 3: The Text of Samuel." *BibSac* 141(1984): 209–22.

McCarter, P. Kyle, Jr. "The Apology of David." *JBL* 99 (1980): 489–504.

McConville, J. Gordon. *Grace in the End: A Study in Deuteronomic Theology.* Grand Rapids: Zondervan, 1993.

Mendenhall, George E. "The Monarchy." *Int* 29 (1975): 155–70.

Merrill, Eugene H. "The 'Accession Year' and Davidic Chronology," *JANESCU* 19 (1989): 101–12

Mettinger, Tryggve N. D. *King and Messiah: The Civil and Sacral Legitimation of the Israelite Kings.* ConBOT 8. Lund: C. W. K. Gleerup, 1976.

Meyers, Carol, "David as Temple Builder." Pages 357–76 in *Ancient Israelite Religion: Essays in Honor of Frank Moore Cross.* Edited by Patrick D. Miller Jr., P. D. Hanson, and S. D. McBride. Philadelphia: Fortress, 1987.

Miller, Patrick D., and J. J. M. Roberts. *The Hand of the Lord: A Reassessment of the "Ark Narrative" of 1 Samuel.* Baltimore: Johns Hopkins Univ. Press, 1977.

Miscall, Peter D. *1 Samuel: A Literary Reading.* Bloomington, Ind.: Indiana Univ. Press, 1986.

Moberly, R. W. L. "Theology of the Old Testament." Pages 452–78 in *The Face of Old Testament Studies.* Edited by D. W. Baker and B. T. Arnold. Grand Rapids: Baker, 1999.

Momigliano, A. "Biblical Studies and Classical Studies: Simple Reflections About Historical Method." *BA* 45 (1982): 224–28.

Nassaman, Nadav. "Sources and Composition in the History of David." Pages 170–86 in *The Origins of the Ancient Israelite States.* Edited by Volkmar Fritz and Philip R. Davies. Sheffield: Sheffield Academic Press, 1996.

Polak, F. H. "David's Kingship—A Precarious Equilibrium." Pages 119–47 in *Politics and Theopolitics in the Bible and Postbiblical Literature.* Edited by H. G. Reventlow, Y. Hoffman, and B. Uffenheimer. JSOTSup 171. Sheffield: Sheffield Academic Press, 1994.

Polzin, Robert. *David and the Deuteronomist: 2 Samuel.* Indiana Studies in Biblical Literature. Bloomington, Ind.: Univ. of Indiana Press, 1993.

_____. *Samuel and the Deuteronomist: A Literary Study of the Deuteronomic History.* 2 vols. San Francisco: Harper & Row, 1989.

Roberts, J. J. M. "The Davidic Origin of the Zion Tradition." *JBL* 92 (1973): 329–44.

_____. "In Defense of the Monarchy: The Contribution of Israelite Kingship to Biblical Theology." Pages 377–96 in *Ancient Israelite Religion: Essays in Honor of Frank Moore Cross.* Edited by Patrick D. Miller, Jr., P. D. Hanson, and S. D. McBride. Philadelphia: Fortress, 1987.

_____. "The Old Testament's Contribution to Messianic Expectations." Pages 39–51 in *The Messiah.* Edited by J. H. Charlesworth. Minneapolis: Fortress, 1992.

_____. "Zion in the Theology of the Davidic-Solomonic Empire." Pages 93–108 in *Studies in the Period of David and Solomon and Other Essays*. Edited by Tomoo Ishida. Winona Lake, Ind.: Eisenbrauns, 1982.

Sacon, Kiyoshi K. "A Study of the Literary Structure of 'The Succession Narrative'." Pages 27–54 in *Studies in the Period of David and Solomon and Other Essays*. Edited by Tomoo Ishida. Winona Lake, Ind.: Eisenbrauns, 1982.

Satterthwaite, P. E. "David in the Books of Samuel: A Messianic Expectation?" Pages 41–65 in *The Lord's Anointed: Interpretation of Old Testament Messianic Texts*. Edited by P. E. Satterthwaite, R. S. Hess, and G. J. Wenham. Carlisle: Paternoster, 1995.

Schäfer-Lichtenberger, Christa. "Sociological and Biblical Views of the Early State." Pages 78–105 in *The Origins of the Ancient Israelite States*. Edited by Volkmar Fritz and Philip R. Davies. Sheffield: Sheffield Academic Press, 1996.

Schniedewind, William M. *Society and the Promise to David: The Reception History of 2 Samuel 7:1–17*. Oxford: Oxford Univ. Press, 1999.

Seow, C. L. *Myth, Drama, and the Politics of David's Dance*. HSM 44. Atlanta: Scholars Press, 1989.

Stirrup, A. "'Why Has Yahweh Defeated Us Today Before The Philistines?' The Question of The Ark Narrative." *TynBul* 51 (2000): 81–100.

Tsevat, Matitiahu. "The Biblical Account of the Foundation of the Monarchy in Israel." Pages 77–99 in *The Meaning of the Book of Job and Other Biblical Studies: Essays on the Literature and Religion of the Hebrew Bible*. New York, Ktav, 1980.

_____. "Israelite History and the Historical Books of the Old Testament." Pages 177–87 in *The Meaning of the Book of Job and Other Biblical Studies: Essays on the Literature and Religion of the Hebrew Bible*. New York, Ktav, 1980.

_____. "Samuel, I & II." Pages 777–81 in *IDBS*. Edited by K. Crim. Nashville: Abingdon, 1976.

_____. "Studies in the Book of Samuel: I, Interpretation of I Sam. 2:27–36, The Narrative of *Kareth*." *HUCA* 32 (1961): 191–216.

Vannoy, J. Robert. *Covenant Renewal at Gilgal: A Study of I Samuel 11:14–12:25*. Cherry Hill, N.J.: Mack, 1978.

de Vaux, Roland. "The King of Israel, Vassal of Yahweh." Pages 152–66 in *The Bible and the Ancient Near East*. Trans. D. McHugh. Garden City, N.Y.: Doubleday, 1971.

Willis, J. T. "The Function of Comprehensive Anticipatory Redactional Joints in I Samuel 16–18." *ZAW* 85 (1973): 294–314.

_____. "The 'Repentance' of God in the Books of Samuel, Jeremiah, and Jonah." *HBT* 16 (1994): 156–75.

1 Samuel 1

THERE WAS A certain man from Ramathaim, a Zuphite from the hill country of Ephraim, whose name was Elkanah son of Jeroham, the son of Elihu, the son of Tohu, the son of Zuph, an Ephraimite. ²He had two wives; one was called Hannah and the other Peninnah. Peninnah had children, but Hannah had none.

³Year after year this man went up from his town to worship and sacrifice to the LORD Almighty at Shiloh, where Hophni and Phinehas, the two sons of Eli, were priests of the LORD. ⁴Whenever the day came for Elkanah to sacrifice, he would give portions of the meat to his wife Peninnah and to all her sons and daughters. ⁵But to Hannah he gave a double portion because he loved her, and the LORD had closed her womb. ⁶And because the LORD had closed her womb, her rival kept provoking her in order to irritate her. ⁷This went on year after year. Whenever Hannah went up to the house of the LORD, her rival provoked her till she wept and would not eat. ⁸Elkanah her husband would say to her, "Hannah, why are you weeping? Why don't you eat? Why are you downhearted? Don't I mean more to you than ten sons?"

⁹Once when they had finished eating and drinking in Shiloh, Hannah stood up. Now Eli the priest was sitting on a chair by the doorpost of the LORD's temple. ¹⁰In bitterness of soul Hannah wept much and prayed to the LORD. ¹¹And she made a vow, saying, "O LORD Almighty, if you will only look upon your servant's misery and remember me, and not forget your servant but give her a son, then I will give him to the LORD for all the days of his life, and no razor will ever be used on his head."

¹²As she kept on praying to the LORD, Eli observed her mouth. ¹³Hannah was praying in her heart, and her lips were moving but her voice was not heard. Eli thought she was drunk ¹⁴and said to her, "How long will you keep on getting drunk? Get rid of your wine."

¹⁵"Not so, my lord," Hannah replied, "I am a woman who is deeply troubled. I have not been drinking wine or beer; I was pouring out my soul to the LORD. ¹⁶Do not take your servant

for a wicked woman; I have been praying here out of my great anguish and grief."

[17]Eli answered, "Go in peace, and may the God of Israel grant you what you have asked of him."

[18]She said, "May your servant find favor in your eyes." Then she went her way and ate something, and her face was no longer downcast.

[19]Early the next morning they arose and worshiped before the LORD and then went back to their home at Ramah. Elkanah lay with Hannah his wife, and the LORD remembered her. [20]So in the course of time Hannah conceived and gave birth to a son. She named him Samuel, saying, "Because I asked the LORD for him."

[21]When the man Elkanah went up with all his family to offer the annual sacrifice to the LORD and to fulfill his vow, [22]Hannah did not go. She said to her husband, "After the boy is weaned, I will take him and present him before the LORD, and he will live there always."

[23]"Do what seems best to you," Elkanah her husband told her. "Stay here until you have weaned him; only may the LORD make good his word." So the woman stayed at home and nursed her son until she had weaned him.

[24]After he was weaned, she took the boy with her, young as he was, along with a three-year-old bull, an ephah of flour and a skin of wine, and brought him to the house of the LORD at Shiloh. [25]When they had slaughtered the bull, they brought the boy to Eli, [26]and she said to him, "As surely as you live, my lord, I am the woman who stood here beside you praying to the LORD. [27]I prayed for this child, and the LORD has granted me what I asked of him. [28]So now I give him to the LORD. For his whole life he will be given over to the LORD." And he worshiped the LORD there.

FIRST SAMUEL 1–7 narrates the ministry of Samuel during one of the most critical moments of Israel's history. The first section (chs. 1–3) legitimizes Samuel by describing the holy events surrounding his birth and his sensitivity to God's call during his childhood. The emphasis on the righteousness of Samuel and his family is heightened by contrasts with Eli and his wicked sons, the priests of the tabernacle at Shiloh. The second section (chs. 4–7, the so-called "ark narratives") describes the early wars between Israel and the Philistines and again shows the importance of Samuel's ministry.[1]

Modern scholarship has speculated about a variety of sources for 1 Samuel 1–7. It is possible that the historian has combined three traditions: (1) Shiloh traditions highlighting Samuel (1 Sam. 1–3); (2) an ark narrative (1 Sam. 4–6, more precisely 4:1b–7:1); (3) a chapter on the leadership of Samuel as judge in Israel (1 Sam. 7, or 7:2–17).

But it is also obvious that the author of the book intends us to read these chapters together. They contain a clear structural coherence that is intentional from the start.[2] (1) In chapters 1–3, Samuel arrives during a time in which Israel was experiencing peace. This unit reveals the sins of the house of Eli and the righteous character of Samuel and his family, and it mentions the "ark of God" for the first time in these books (1 Sam. 3:3). Its overarching concern is doubtless to provide the background for Samuel, the one who will deliver Israel in the coming crisis. (2) The second unit (4:1b–7:1) describes the Philistine crisis itself, in which the Philistines commanded a decisive military advantage over the Israelites. Without a single reference to Samuel, the ark narrative tells of the punishment of the house of Eli and the loss of the ark to the Philistines. (3) In the final section (7:2–17), Samuel is reintroduced into the narrative as the one who leads Israel to repentance and deliverance. Regardless of the sources used by the historian, the literary structure of the canonical form of the text is the focus of our interpretation.

Samuel is one of those great Bible figures who seems larger than life. In terms of Old Testament history, he was an important transitional figure at one of the most important turning points in the life of the nation, namely, the rise of Israelite kingship. Ever since Moses had led the nation out of Egypt, the Israelites had been a loosely organized confederation of tribes governed as a theocracy. God was their king, and he ruled through designated human leaders. During the centuries prior to Samuel, the tribes were independent, joining only temporarily for purposes of joint military forays organized and led by divinely appointed judges. Now in 1 Samuel 1–3, Samuel is introduced as an important step from theocracy to monarchy. He is a judge like others

---

1. Robert P. Gordon has found impressive evidence for the authenticity of these early Samuel narratives ("Who Made the Kingmaker? Reflections on Samuel and the Institution of the Monarchy," in *Faith, Tradition, and History: Old Testament Historiography in Its Near Eastern Context*, ed. A. R. Millard et al. [Winona Lake, Ind.: Eisenbrauns, 1994], 255–69, esp. 262).

2. John T. Willis, "An Anti-Elide Narrative Tradition from a Prophetic Circle at the Ramah Sanctuary," *JBL* 90 (1971): 288–308; idem, "Cultic Elements in the Story of Samuel's Birth and Dedication," *Studies in Theology* 26 (1972): 33–61; idem, "Samuel Versus Eli: I Sam. 1–7," *TZ* 35 (1979): 201–12.

in the book of Judges. But he is also a prophet, like those great prophets who would later play an important role in Israel's history. Samuel was forging new territory for Israel.

As we know from the concluding unit of the Judges (Judg. 17–21), the period in which Samuel was born was one of great moral apostasy. During this time everyone did what was right in his or her own opinion (Judg. 17:6; 21:25). The nation seemed to be adrift without a moral conscience, nor did it have any external moral compass to give definition to righteousness. The leadership was perverse, and the people were wicked. It was obvious to the author of Judges that the nation was headed for total disaster unless God provided a righteous king to lead the people.

Thus, 1 Samuel 1 introduces Samuel by relating the unique circumstances of his birth. The narrative emphasizes the devotion and ethical character of Samuel's parents, which provides a stark contrast to the apostate and degenerate nation of Israel at this time. Clearly, God has special plans for Samuel. His birth is a momentous event in salvation history, separating the period of the judges from that of the kings.

Background of Hannah and Her Problems (1:1–8)

THE OPENING UNIT of this chapter introduces Samuel's family. The details of geography and family heritage (1:1–2) are clues that Samuel was born to propitious circumstances, and these details anticipate the significance of his birth. The fact that Elkanah's long line is preserved in the sacred traditions indicates that Samuel is from aristocracy. In fact, the Chronicler gives the added detail that Samuel's line is from the Kohathite family of Levitical priests (1 Chron. 6:26–27, 33–34), who were originally responsible for caring for the ark of the covenant (Num. 3:31). Nor is Elkanah's polygamy a problem (1 Sam. 1:2), since such practices were not uncommon in the Old Testament.[3] Indeed, Hannah's inability to conceive children may well have given rise to the need for a second wife.[4]

This opening paragraph contains several features that illustrate the righteousness of Samuel's parents. Elkanah is depicted as an upstanding Israelite who cares deeply for his family and carefully attends to his religious com-

---

3. In fact, the presence of more than one wife may be further indication of Elkanah's exalted financial status. Polygamy was never God's ideal plan for marriage. The Bible clearly sanctions marriage as the union of one man and one woman (Gen. 2:18, 24). At the same time, Elkanah and Peninnah may be compared to Abraham and Hagar, whose relationship was culturally arranged because of Sarah's barrenness (and Hannah's), and such a relationship may not strictly be considered polygamy (Gen. 16:4–16).

4. As with Sarah, Rachel, and Leah before her (Gen. 16:2; 30:3, 9).

mitments. (1) He gives himself faithfully to the proper worship of Yahweh at great personal cost and sacrifice ("year after year this man went up," 1:3). The law of Moses mandated regular trips to the tabernacle to worship (Deut. 16:16), and Elkanah is a faithful Israelite, concerned to fulfill his vows to Yahweh. The yearly festival in view here is likely the Feast of Tabernacles, celebrated at the end of each summer (Lev. 23:33–43), though it may also have been a private, personal pilgrimage distinct from the regularly pre-scribed requirements.[5] (2) Elkanah carefully and generously distributes meat to his family, likely a common practice during the festivals in which certain sacrifices were offered (1:4). (3) Finally, Elkanah loves Hannah deeply, despite her unenviable position as a barren wife (1:5, 8).

The concluding statement of verse 2 sets up the painful situation for Hannah: "Peninnah had children, but Hannah had none." In the ancient social setting, the most important role for a wife was to bear children. Men of financial means needed to have a male heir to continue the line, and barren wives suffered the embarrassment and shame of seeing another wife provided for their husbands, as Hagar did for Sarah and Bilhah for Rachel. Elkanah's impressive past (1:1) will find a future in Peninnah's children rather than through his favorite wife, Hannah. Hannah's intense pain is exacerbated by the insufferable cruelty inflicted on her by her counterpart, Peninnah: "Her rival kept provoking her in order to irritate her" (1:6). This is a perpetual burden for Hannah, since it recurs each year at the time for the festival in Shiloh (1:7).

The passing reference to the ruling priestly family is a subtle reminder that the nation has strayed far from God (1:3): "Hophni and Phinehas, the two sons of Eli, were priests of the LORD." The next few chapters reveal just how apostate the priestly leadership has become. But even as this becomes clear in the narrative, it is equally clear that Samuel has been prepared from birth to lead the nation back to God.

Hannah's Prayer (1:9–18)

WHILE AT THE Lord's temple for the festival at Shiloh, Hannah weeps and prays earnestly, making a vow to Yahweh.[6] In despair, she turns to Yahweh for help. Her years of barrenness have convinced her that any children born

---

5. Ralph Klein, *1 Samuel* (WBC 10; Waco, Tex.: Word, 1983), 6.

6. Prior to David's capture and expansion of Jerusalem, Shiloh was the site of the tabernacle of Yahweh, which housed the ark of the covenant. First Samuel 1–3 assumes a more permanent building that served as the sanctuary of the Lord during part of the judges period, as is implied by terms such as "temple" (*hekal*, 1:9), "doorpost" (*mᵉzuzah*, 1:9), and "doors" (*delet*, 3:15). Some have suggested that a permanent structure was erected to replace the tabernacle at Shiloh (Joyce Baldwin, *1 and 2 Samuel: An Introduction and Commentary* [TOTC;

to her will be nothing short of a miraculous gift from God. Therefore, she vows to return such a precious gift to God forever, if he will only answer her cry. Her vow also promises that "no razor will ever be used on his head" (1:11), which implies the so-called "Nazirite" vow.

The term *nazir* ("Nazirite") is defined in Numbers 6, where a man or woman can make a special vow of separation to Yahweh. The vow involves a period of time in which the Nazirite abstains from wine and other products of the vine, uses no razor on his or her head, and avoids contact with dead bodies. Numbers 6 probably regulated and standardized an already ancient Semitic institution. After the period of separation was over, Numbers 6 prescribed a ritual for terminating the vow. Interestingly, in the case of Samson (Judg. 13) and Samuel, the vow does not appear to be temporary but permanent. Thus, Hannah is offering her unborn child as a permanent Nazirite, whose life will be wholly and exclusively God's.[7]

The encounter between Eli and Hannah contains an ironic twist. Eli represents the corrupt and apostate leadership of the priesthood and Hannah the simple faith that issues from suffering and pain. Yet Eli mistakes her earnestness for drunkenness. The spiritual leader of the nation is unable to discern the spiritual significance of this woman's struggle. In the end, he recognizes in her the faith he was supposed to represent (1:17). After she has poured out her soul to Yahweh (1:15), she finds a new peace with herself and her circumstances. She is able to eat and is no longer disconsolate (1:18).

The Birth of Samuel (1:19–20)

THESE VERSES REVEAL a quick answer to Hannah's prayer. After their return trip home, Elkanah "lay with Hannah his wife," which in Hebrew is simply he "knew" her. The original language is graphic at this point. Elkanah knows her and Yahweh remembers her, as he remembered Rachel when he opened her womb (Gen. 30:22). God's remembering someone in the Old Testament (*zkr*) does not mean that he has forgotten them, only that his memory is consistent with his promises and that he will take action (Ex. 2:23–25).[8] Such language emphasizes his faithfulness when confronted with the earnest need and prayer of his people.

Downers Grove, Ill.: InterVarsity Press, 1988], 65–68), but the use of "Tent of Meeting" in 2:22 is difficult to explain (see also 2 Sam. 7:6). Perhaps a semipermanent porch with doors and doorposts had been built at the entrance to the tabernacle in Shiloh (C. F. Keil and Franz Delitzsch, *Biblical Commentary on the Books of Samuel*, trans. J. Martin [Grand Rapids: Eerdmans, 1956], 23, 50–51).

7. Jackie A. Naudé, "נזר," *NIDOTTE*, 3:73–74.

8. To "remember" in the Old Testament is so closely associated with action that it is sometimes synonymous for action (Leslie C. Allen, "זכר," *NIDOTTE*, 1:1102–3).

Birth narratives play an important role in biblical literature. They generally have specific features, all of which are present in Samuel's birth narrative. (1) The birth of the child marks a turning point, or at least some significant episode in Israel's history. (2) The narratives usually reveal something of the baby's character or future role in Israel's history. (3) Individuals whose births are announced in such a way are the solution to a dire problem. (4) Finally, such birth narratives always emphasize the providential significance of the new character's name.

As an example of such birth announcements, the arrival of Isaac was the answer to Abraham's and Sarah's barrenness, and as the child of the ancestral promises, Isaac's birth was a linchpin of ancestral faith (Gen. 21:1–4). The birth of Moses was the eventual salvation of the Israelites from Egypt (Ex. 2:1–10). The birth of Samson announced a new period of Israelite dominance of the Philistines (Judg. 13:2–5, 24–25). Isaiah could even predict the future birth of Immanuel, who would inaugurate a new messianic age (Isa. 7:14–17). Clearly the birth of Samuel into such circumstances marked for the narrator the dawning of a new day in Israel. The birth narratives of Jesus, of course, stand in this biblical tradition as the ultimate turning point in salvation history (Matt. 1:20–25; Luke 1:31–33).

Samuel's name is difficult, but it probably means "His name is El [God]," suggesting that Samuel's God is the true God.[9] Hannah's explanation for the name is controversial, since the verb "ask" is not related etymologically to "Samuel": She named him Samuel, saying, "because I asked [šʾl] the Lord for him" (1:20). The root šʾl ("ask") is used frequently throughout this narrative, leading many commentators to argue that the author has expropriated traditions about the birth of Saul, whose name is a perfect match for Hannah's explanation (šaʾul, "requested one"). In this theory, the original traditions legitimized and valued Saul's kingship. This argument suggests that the historian had a negative view of Saul and therefore uses these naming traditions to legitimize the prophet Samuel instead. If this is indeed how the traditions developed, the author is saying that "the real deliverer is not the first king, but the last judge."[10]

However, birth narratives in the Old Testament commonly use paronomasia, or wordplays, in announcing the name of a child. Thus here, Hannah's explanation plays on the similarity of sound between "Samuel" (šᵉmuʾel) and "I asked for him" (šᵉʾiltiw). As a result, while it may be *possible* that our author has used materials originally written about Saul to describe Samuel's birth, it is not *likely* for a wide variety of reasons.[11] Etymological precision was not the

---

9. On this and the discussion to follow, see McCarter, *I Samuel*, 62–63.
10. Hans Wilhelm Hertzberg, *I and II Samuel* (OTL; Philadelphia: Westminster, 1964), 26.
11. Gordon, "Who Made the Kingmaker?" 263–69.

norm in such Old Testament passages, but rather association by assonance (similarity of sounds). The Hebrew words for "ask" and "request" are enough like "Samuel" to make Hannah's name-giving typical of other Old Testament examples. Her play on Samuel's name is not attempting a precise etymological connection. It is a rather typical "naming" wordplay, and it emphasizes her confidence in God's faithfulness to answer prayer.

Hannah Fulfills Her Vow (1:21–28)

ALMOST A YEAR has passed since the family's last visit to Shiloh ("in the course of time Hannah conceived and gave birth to a son," 1:20). Contrary to their previous custom, Hannah decides not to accompany Elkanah and the rest of the family during the annual festival. But when the boy is old enough to live in Shiloh permanently (two or three years old), Hannah feels able to fulfill her vow (1:21–23). She takes him to Shiloh and worships Yahweh in gratitude for his gracious gift (1:24). She reminds Eli that she was the woman who prayed so earnestly, and she publicly confesses that Yahweh has answered her prayer.

In a striking wordplay that continues the play on Samuel's name, Hannah states that Yahweh has granted her petition (*š°elati*), which she had requested (*ša°alti*, 1:27). In language that illustrates how appropriate her response is, she dedicates him (*biš°iltihu*, from the same verbal root) to Yahweh; all his life Samuel will be dedicated (*ša°ul*) to Yahweh. In remarkable faithfulness to her vow and in one of the most sobering scenes of devotion in the books of Samuel, Hannah finds it possible to return to God what he has so graciously given to her. Having come to God with nothing, she now returns to Shiloh to give back that which means everything.

HANNAH'S PROBLEM AND ITS SOLUTION. The internal literary structure of 1 Samuel 1 shows the timeless message of Samuel's birth narrative. The chapter opens with a problem. Hannah's pain is more than she can bear. A barren wife was seen as an embarrassment in the ancient world. Children were gifts of God, but they were also important economically in the ancient social structure. They contributed to the family wealth through their work, they cared for their parents in old age, and they ensured the future of the family by inheriting the family wealth. Hannah's inability to fulfill what was seen as her raison d'être was devastating. When Elkanah follows social custom by having a second wife so that children can be brought into the home, that second wife proves to be a constant source of pain and agony to Hannah. Peninnah hurts her deeply, to the point of emotional depression (she weeps and cannot eat, 1:7).

Hannah's earnest prayer in the Shiloh sanctuary is the pivotal point in the narrative. After Eli blesses her, she is able to eat, and "her face was no longer downcast" (cf. vv. 7–8, 18). There is a telling contrast between the Hannah who is too despondent to eat and the Hannah who emerges from God's presence full of hope and confidence. Though her circumstances have not yet changed, she has found a peace with God, a peace that leaves her buoyant and capable of returning with her family. The way in which the narrative immediately turns to the birth of Samuel (1:19–20) brings quick resolution to Hannah's problem. In response to her changed circumstances, she piously fulfills her vow by giving the boy over to the Lord.

This problem-solution literary structure enables us to focus on the timeless features of this text, which we should use in building a bridge to our contemporary context. This passage is not advocating polygamy for our times, though it does not condemn Elkanah's polygamy. The practice of multiple wives was always and forever less than God's ideal for Israel (Gen. 2:18, 24), and if we read this text in light of others in the Old Testament, it is clear that, wherever practiced, polygamy resulted in problems (e.g., Gen. 16:4; 30:1). While Elkanah is following cultural custom, especially in light of Hannah's barrenness, this is certainly not the timeless truth we would apply to today's context. Rather, the problem-solution structure we have observed above, pivoting as it does around Hannah's prayer in the Shiloh sanctuary, emphasizes Hannah's personal piety and highlights the importance of Samuel's birth.

A new era in salvation history. Hannah's spiritual sensitivity and devotion are the anvil God uses to hammer out his will for her and her family. Moreover, Hannah's piety results in the introduction of Samuel into the biblical story, whose significance goes far beyond Elkanah's and Hannah's circumstances. His arrival in salvation history is notable on two levels. (1) This chapter (taken together with chs. 2–3) begins a new stage in God's overarching plan of salvation as it unfolds in the pages of the Old Testament. (2) The account of Samuel's birth reveals the way God uses holy individuals and the circumstances of their lives to accomplish his purposes. Let us look at these separately.

(1) This chapter introduces Samuel as the miraculous and gracious gift of God to Hannah and to the nation Israel. The recurring wordplay in his birth narrative using the name Samuel and the forms of the root "ask, request" portrays Samuel as the one desperately needed, not only for Hannah but especially for the whole nation.

This broader, national significance of the passage is apparent from its location at the beginning of 1 Samuel. The book of Judges had concluded with accounts of brutal intertribal warfare and cruel acts of cultic and moral disobedience. The birth of Samuel is cast against this shocking backdrop. Israel is barren like Hannah; each has a desperate need that only God can satisfy. The chapter opens with the account of God's intervening on behalf of both Hannah and Israel. He delivers Hannah from her barrenness and intervenes in the history of Israel. The deliverance is the same for Hannah and Israel, that is, the birth of a weak and innocent child. The birth of Samuel signals the end of Hannah's painful sterility and Israel's anchorless apostasy.

This scenario reminds us of other times in biblical history when the birth of a child was the answer to hopelessness and desperate need. Isaac's birth marked the fulfillment of the great ancestral promises and the beginning of God's salvation from sin. Moses' birth initiated the beginning of salvation for the nation of Israel, so long in bondage to Egypt. And the birth of the Messiah will initiate an era of salvation (Isa. 9:6–7). God seems to find particular delight in using the ultimate in weakness and vulnerability—a newborn baby—as the means of accomplishing his great purposes. In human weakness, God's strength can be seen with greater clarity. When the apostle Paul pleaded for the Lord to take away his thorn in the flesh, God told him, "My grace is sufficient for you, for my power is made perfect in weakness." Thus Paul could say, "I will boast all the more gladly about my weaknesses, so that Christ's power may rest on me" (2 Cor. 12:9).

(2) The significance of Samuel's birth narrative centers not on Samuel himself but on his mother, Hannah. Much of the Old Testament historical books are devoted to narrating events surrounding Israelite leadership: kings and prophets. Indeed, the majority of 1–2 Samuel will center around Samuel himself and the two kings he anoints, Saul and David. But here, as elsewhere in a few other instances, the narrative considers events related to an average Israelite family. Elkanah was apparently from aristocracy, but he was no king or leading priest. He was only an individual who worked, ate, and took his family to Shiloh regularly for religious observances. His wife Hannah became the center of the narrative because of her pain and the saintly way in which she and Elkanah handled themselves.

All of this illustrates the way God continually works out his purposes through the everyday affairs of righteous people. He is looking for people whom he can afford to bless, and in Hannah, God finds a woman who can be trusted. Building on her devotion, God provides Israel's future deliverer through her, illustrating again that God takes the weakness and barrenness of his people to demonstrate his might. The chapter is a witness to God's transforming power, which creates a new historical possibility where none has existed.[12] Hannah waits—and worships—in her barrenness, and so does Israel. The answer for both is a surprising gift of grace.

 CHRISTIANITY AND POSTMODERNISM. Samuel was born in a period of great moral and spiritual crisis. Israelite society had become ethically pluralistic, and everyone was doing whatever seemed right in his or her own opinion (Judg. 17:6; 21:25). Without righteous leadership, the nation was perilously close to ruin. Internal moral decay was leading to social unrest and conflict. This portrait of ancient Israel offers alarming parallels with modern culture, which at the beginning of the twenty-first century has been described as *postmodern*.

It is impossible to define with precision what current philosophers mean by postmodernism. Indeed, few generations have been able to analyze and critique their own philosophical climate. But most agree that postmodern America is committed to at least three principles.[13] (1) Postmodernism is postrationalistic. It rejects the idea that truth is absolute and purely rational. By dethroning the human intellect, postmoderns accept other paths to truth besides reason, such as the emotions and intuition.

(2) Postmodernism is postindividualistic. Rejecting modernism's paradigm of the self-determining, autonomous individual, who stands outside any community, postmoderns prefer to think of the individual within community.

(3) Postmodernism is postnoeticentric, which means it desires more than knowledge for knowledge's sake. Our world today is full of data and information. But postmoderns want more than purely intellectual apprehension. They want to know how to live well. Knowledge is of no value unless it works, unless it helps the postmoderns get along in life. In this sense, the fiercely pragmatic postmodern will consider something "true" if it works. If it does not work, then it is not true regardless of how much empirical data seems to support it.

Of course, much of this philosophy is not bad. American culture has needed more emphasis on the community and social responsibility. But one of the consequences of this combination of ideas is the assumption that there is no absolute truth governing the universe. Since truth has to be defined for each context, it is up to each community to determine truth in the sense of

---

12. Walter Brueggemann, *First and Second Samuel* (Interpretation; Louisville, Ky.: John Knox, 1990), 12.

13. Stanley J. Grenz, *A Primer on Postmodernism* (Grand Rapids: Eerdmans, 1995).

finding what works for it and its individuals. Truth, then, is communally defined. The community accepts as truth the laws and ideals agreed upon by the majority. Truth is determined by a sort of collective knowledge (or ignorance, as the case may be).

The many cultural differences between twenty-first-century America and ancient Israel at the time of Samuel's birth are obvious. Such profound historical and sociological differences over three millennia are hard to imagine. Nevertheless, human nature is limited in its inherent, psychological composition. As finite beings, humans are not very creative or imaginative in expressing their desire to be independent of God's covenants and loving direction. Israel's tendency to fall into rebellion over and over again, as narrated in Judges, is not unlike America's propensity to strive for a secular, nonreligiously driven society. The libertarian impulses in America during the last half of the twentieth century provide parallels to ancient Israel's rebuff of Yahweh's covenant in the period just prior to Samuel's birth. More apropos theologically and more alarmingly, the church has displayed similar propensities toward abandoning biblical principles and redefining the nature of life with God.

God's answer today is the same as then, and Samuel's birth presents us with two aspects of that answer. When a nation is in such despair, the only hope is the appearance of righteous individuals, both in national leadership and in the common citizenry. First Samuel 1 announces both. Samuel is the coming new leadership, and he is given to the nation through a righteous family. Let us consider the significance of this passage in terms of leadership and individual responsibility.

(1) Israel's problems were deeply rooted in the national psyche, but they were compounded by her failed religious leadership. Eli and his sons were so perverse that they provided no hope of renewal. Without godly leadership, any nation faces eventual ruin. The birth of Samuel provided hope for the future for Israel. So too for modern states, the role of leadership should not be overlooked. The twentieth century has left behind examples of tyrannical despots who manipulated the nations in their charge and inflicted untold pain and suffering on the masses (Adolf Hitler, Romania's Ceausescu, Cambodia's Pol Pot, and Iraq's Saddam Hussein, to name the most notorious). But other national leaders too have allowed the spiritual infrastructure of their nations to deteriorate through less dramatic and less obviously evil policies.

Now, the beginning of the twenty-first century has produced Osama bin Laden, in perhaps a chilling forewarning of the kind of despotism we can expect in the future. As illustrated by 1 Samuel 1, God desires to use godly leaders to reform nations. In the Old Testament, kingship was a source of great potential good for the nation Israel. It became the means through which God himself would eventually redeem his people (i.e., through the Messiah). But kingship was also a potential for great evil. These principles are no less true of the Christian church generally, which also suffers from a lack of godly leadership.

(2) The second necessary element in the spiritual rebirth of a nation is probably more important, though it receives less attention in the Bible and in the modern world: the importance of a godly citizenry. A devout ruler alone cannot reform a rebellious and sinful populace. Interestingly, the good news of this passage begins with the righteous, everyday affairs of a faithful family. Through her suffering and trials, Hannah was used as an instrument of God to initiate spiritual rebirth in Israel. Like Elizabeth and Mary after her, she was honored by God with miraculous conception in order to show God's mercy and grace and to continue his salvation story. But without a host of other, nameless Israelites who also prayed and lived their lives in quiet devotion, such reform would not be possible. These individuals become the salt and light of their society (Matt. 5:13–16).

I believe the Bible illustrates that social change and reformation takes place *primarily* in this way. As the waves of the sea slowly and gradually alter the landscape of the seashore, we need billow after billow of godly people, swelling up to contribute their influence on our culture and slowly to chip away at the evil in our society. To use another metaphor, as the slow but incessant drip, drip of water on a granite boulder will eventually change its surface, so Christians must be faithful to God's Word, living devout and godly lifestyles over the long duration in order to reform the church and the nation.

(3) Finally, we should also note the connection between Hannah's suffering and her effective prayer. She had every reason to be bitter (1:10). She was incapable of bearing children, Peninnah ridiculed her, Elkanah was unable to comfort her, and Eli mistook her motives. Yet rather than capitulate to her emotions, she let her circumstances drive her to prayer. Hannah's profound pain prodded her to an abiding faith, which issued forth in earnest prayer. Her prayer and vow exemplify the persistent and tenacious kind of faith that is borne out of pain and suffering. She is an example of the believing soul lost in desire before a heavenly Father. Bonhoeffer summarizes Jesus' teaching on prayer in this way:

> We are privileged to know that he knows our needs before we ask him. This is what gives Christian prayer its boundless confidence and its joyous certainty. It matters little what form of prayer we adopt or how many words we use, what matters is the faith which lays hold on God and touches the heart of the Father who knew us long before we

came to him. Genuine prayer is never "good works," an exercise or a pious attitude, but it is always the prayer of a child to a Father. Hence it is never given to self-display, whether before God, ourselves, or other people. If God were ignorant of our needs, we should have to think out beforehand *how* we should tell him about them, *what* we should tell him, and *whether* we should tell him or not. Thus faith, which is the mainspring of Christian prayer, excludes all reflection and premeditation.[14]

The introduction of Samuel into the biblical story line begins with the heartfelt and effective prayer of his mother: "The prayer of the righteous is powerful and effective" (James 5:16b, NRSV).

---

14. Dietrich Bonhoeffer, *The Cost of Discipleship*, rev. ed. (New York: Macmillan, 1959), 181.

1 Samuel 2

THEN HANNAH PRAYED and said:

"My heart rejoices in the LORD;
  in the LORD my horn is lifted high.
My mouth boasts over my enemies,
  for I delight in your deliverance.

2 "There is no one holy like the LORD;
  there is no one besides you;
  there is no Rock like our God.

3 "Do not keep talking so proudly
  or let your mouth speak such arrogance,
for the LORD is a God who knows,
  and by him deeds are weighed.

4 "The bows of the warriors are broken,
  but those who stumbled are armed with strength.
5 Those who were full hire themselves out for food,
  but those who were hungry hunger no more.
She who was barren has borne seven children,
  but she who has had many sons pines away.

6 "The LORD brings death and makes alive;
  he brings down to the grave and raises up.
7 The LORD sends poverty and wealth;
  he humbles and he exalts.
8 He raises the poor from the dust
  and lifts the needy from the ash heap;
he seats them with princes
  and has them inherit a throne of honor.

"For the foundations of the earth are the LORD's;
  upon them he has set the world.
9 He will guard the feet of his saints,
  but the wicked will be silenced in darkness.

"It is not by strength that one prevails;
10   those who oppose the LORD will be shattered.

He will thunder against them from heaven;
  the LORD will judge the ends of the earth.

"He will give strength to his king
  and exalt the horn of his anointed."

¹¹Then Elkanah went home to Ramah, but the boy ministered before the LORD under Eli the priest.

¹²Eli's sons were wicked men; they had no regard for the LORD. ¹³Now it was the practice of the priests with the people that whenever anyone offered a sacrifice and while the meat was being boiled, the servant of the priest would come with a three-pronged fork in his hand. ¹⁴He would plunge it into the pan or kettle or caldron or pot, and the priest would take for himself whatever the fork brought up. This is how they treated all the Israelites who came to Shiloh. ¹⁵But even before the fat was burned, the servant of the priest would come and say to the man who was sacrificing, "Give the priest some meat to roast; he won't accept boiled meat from you, but only raw."

¹⁶If the man said to him, "Let the fat be burned up first, and then take whatever you want," the servant would then answer, "No, hand it over now; if you don't, I'll take it by force."

¹⁷This sin of the young men was very great in the LORD's sight, for they were treating the LORD's offering with contempt.

¹⁸But Samuel was ministering before the LORD—a boy wearing a linen ephod. ¹⁹Each year his mother made him a little robe and took it to him when she went up with her husband to offer the annual sacrifice. ²⁰Eli would bless Elkanah and his wife, saying, "May the LORD give you children by this woman to take the place of the one she prayed for and gave to the LORD." Then they would go home. ²¹And the LORD was gracious to Hannah; she conceived and gave birth to three sons and two daughters. Meanwhile, the boy Samuel grew up in the presence of the LORD.

²²Now Eli, who was very old, heard about everything his sons were doing to all Israel and how they slept with the women who served at the entrance to the Tent of Meeting. ²³So he said to them, "Why do you do such things? I hear from all the people about these wicked deeds of yours. ²⁴No, my sons; it is not a good report that I hear spreading among

the LORD's people. ²⁵If a man sins against another man, God may mediate for him; but if a man sins against the LORD, who will intercede for him?" His sons, however, did not listen to their father's rebuke, for it was the LORD's will to put them to death.

²⁶And the boy Samuel continued to grow in stature and in favor with the LORD and with men.

²⁷Now a man of God came to Eli and said to him, "This is what the LORD says: 'Did I not clearly reveal myself to your father's house when they were in Egypt under Pharaoh? ²⁸I chose your father out of all the tribes of Israel to be my priest, to go up to my altar, to burn incense, and to wear an ephod in my presence. I also gave your father's house all the offerings made with fire by the Israelites. ²⁹Why do you scorn my sacrifice and offering that I prescribed for my dwelling? Why do you honor your sons more than me by fattening yourselves on the choice parts of every offering made by my people Israel?'

³⁰"Therefore the LORD, the God of Israel, declares: 'I promised that your house and your father's house would minister before me forever.' But now the LORD declares: 'Far be it from me! Those who honor me I will honor, but those who despise me will be disdained. ³¹The time is coming when I will cut short your strength and the strength of your father's house, so that there will not be an old man in your family line ³²and you will see distress in my dwelling. Although good will be done to Israel, in your family line there will never be an old man. ³³Every one of you that I do not cut off from my altar will be spared only to blind your eyes with tears and to grieve your heart, and all your descendants will die in the prime of life.

³⁴"'And what happens to your two sons, Hophni and Phinehas, will be a sign to you—they will both die on the same day. ³⁵I will raise up for myself a faithful priest, who will do according to what is in my heart and mind. I will firmly establish his house, and he will minister before my anointed one always. ³⁶Then everyone left in your family line will come and bow down before him for a piece of silver and a crust of bread and plead, "Appoint me to some priestly office so I can have food to eat."'"

HANNAH'S PRAYER HAS been answered. The Lord has given this wonderful woman a son, and she has dedicated him to God's service in the tabernacle at Shiloh (ch. 1). Thus far we have only been given a hint of the problems in Shiloh itself. Eli the priest and his two sons were introduced in the previous unit (1:3, 9), but their characters have not yet been described. Eli's inability to discern the nature of Hannah's prayer may ironically and subtly tell us something about him (1:12–14). But in chapter 2 we learn that the venerable old priestly family at Shiloh is exceedingly corrupt. In fact, the next two chapters reveal the bleak spiritual condition of the nation Israel itself. Official religious leadership is corrupt beyond hope (2:12–17, 22–25), and the nation has no access to a reforming prophetic message (3:1). It is to such a world that Samuel has been given for service.

This chapter contains three sections. Hannah's prayer of thanksgiving is followed by a section devoted to the contrast between Eli's sons and the young Samuel. It concludes with a dramatic condemnation of Eli's priesthood. Together these sections play a significant role in characterizing Samuel further and preparing us for what follows in the rest of 1 Samuel. While Eli's sons continue to grow in their sin and rebellion, Samuel grows in stature and righteousness. Once again we see that God is carefully preparing ancient Israel's kingmaker.

Hannah's Song (2:1–11)

OLD TESTAMENT HISTORICAL narratives occasionally insert poetry to supplement a particular episode. Such poems are usually a prayer, a song, or a speech of the central character, and they frequently crystallize the important theological themes of the episode.[1] Verse 1 says Hannah prayed this poem, but it is also known as the "Song of Hannah" because of its hymnic qualities. In this instance, the poem in 2:1–11 is an eloquent expression of the theological significance of the birth of Samuel (as such, it brings closure to ch. 1 more than it introduces ch. 2).

This little poem also plays an important structuring role in 1–2 Samuel generally. It corresponds in a kind of point–counterpoint fashion with two poems near the conclusion of the two-volume book. David's song of praise (2 Sam. 22:1–51) and his last words (2 Sam. 23:1–7) are poems serving as theological summaries of King David's reign and are central to the final unit's

---

1. Martin Noth saw such speeches as one of the main instruments used by the historian for expressing theology, along with narrative summaries and prayers (*The Deuteronomistic History* [JSOTSup 15; Sheffield: JSOT, 1981], 4–11).

interpretation of David as charting a course for Israel's future messianic hopes.[2] In other words, Hannah begins 1–2 Samuel by celebrating what Yahweh has done and will do in the future, while David concludes the book by celebrating Yahweh's faithfulness.

As hermeneutical bookends, these poems interpret the narratives of 1–2 Samuel, especially highlighting the significance of Yahweh's anointed one.[3] Hannah's song points to the future and anticipates God's power to answer prayer and to reverse one's fortunes. David's thanksgiving hymn looks backward to celebrate numerous times when the Lord has delivered him (2 Sam. 22:1–51). His last words look both backward and forward by defining his special relationship with God as a "covenant," which must become the paradigm for all future kings of Israel (2 Sam. 23:1–7).[4] Thus, these poems at the beginning and end of 1–2 Samuel speak to each other in antiphonal unity. They interpret the narratives between them and tie those narratives together as authoritative canon for believing readers, ancient and modern.

Hannah's prayer spans the height and depth of Israelite theology and relates it to her circumstances. She begins with an introduction (2:1) that announces the personal joy she has in her relationship with Yahweh: *"my* heart rejoices," *"my* horn is lifted high," *"my* mouth boasts," and *"I* delight." The concept of the exalted horn is a Hebrew idiom that has never been satisfactorily explained (*harim qeren*).[5] It appears to be a metaphor in which the horns and head of an animal are held high as a symbol of triumph and power (Dan. 8:3, 5, 9).[6] When one's horn is elevated, it seems to involve visible distinction or exaltation and sometimes designates perpetual distinction through one's offspring. It is especially meaningful here that Hannah rejoices in Yahweh, who has lifted her horn, implying both her visible vindication before Peninnah and her lasting strength through her offspring. This is a point to which she returns at the center of her song in verse 5b: "She who was barren has borne seven children, but she who has had many sons pines away."

Hannah's joy and triumph are firmly rooted in the singular holiness of Yahweh (2:2). Only he is transcendent in power and moral character, and only he is a Rock: "There is no one besides you." From this certitude flows her confidence, and she bursts forth in a stream of assertions that result from it. The arrogant have no right to continue boasting, for Yahweh knows everything

---

2. See my Original Meaning introduction to 2 Sam. 21–24, below.

3. For the verbal and thematic parallels linking Hannah's and David's poems, see Nelson, *Historical Books*, 115, and Brevard S. Childs, *Introduction to the Old Testament As Scripture* (Philadelphia: Fortress, 1979), 272–75.

4. Philip E. Satterthwaite, "David in the Books of Samuel," 43–44.

5. McCarter, *I Samuel*, 71–72; Michael L. Brown, "קֶרֶן," *NIDOTTE*, 3:990–92.

6. Alternatively, one's horn can be cut off, representing humiliation and defeat (Jer. 48:25).

(2:3). Strength is not found in military might, wealth, or honor but in relation to the sovereign Yahweh, who gives to whom he will and who will thunder from heaven and judge the ends of the earth (2:10a).

In the closing phrases of the poem, we return to the idea of the exalted horn, which forms an inclusio, or literary envelope, for the whole (2:10b): "He will give strength to his king and exalt the horn of his anointed." This is the first time the king of Israel is referred to as "the anointed one." The mention of Yahweh's king raises the question: Did someone from later in Israel's history, during the monarchy, add this conclusion, or did Hannah speak prophetically here? Though it is possible that verse 10b was added at a later time, the entire poem can be identified as a song of triumph, thanking Yahweh for victory over one's enemies. It is possible that the song originated at the Shiloh sanctuary and that Hannah, having learned it in her regular practice of worship, simply adapted the celebratory song for her new wonderful circumstances. Since the final reference to Yahweh's king and anointed forms the inclusio with verse 1, it seems likely that it was an original part of the form and structure of the poem. The need for a king had been established during the judges period (cf. Judg. 21:25), and we therefore have no reason to deny this verse as original to the poem.

More importantly, these concluding phrases of Hannah's song emphasize the Lord's anointed as especially chosen by God and empowered for the task of leading Israel (also a theme of David in 2 Sam. 22:51). This is the kind of king Israel longs for and needs. He uses God's power to bring about surprising reversals and to defeat Israel's enemies. This description of Yahweh's anointed becomes programmatic for the narratives that follow.[7]

After this conclusion to Hannah's song, the narrator leaves us with the simple observation: "Elkanah went home to Ramah, but the boy ministered before the LORD under Eli the priest" (2:11). As if to illustrate that strength is derived only from one's relationship with Yahweh, we are left with this contrast. The boy Samuel stays behind to serve Yahweh and grow in his devotion to God as he grows in stature. By contrast, the hapless Eli seems destined to rely on his own strength, derived from priestly tradition and status. But Hannah's song is the harbinger of things to come.

Contrast Between Eli's Sons and Samuel (2:12–26)

THIS UNIT IS dominated by a literary contrast. It artfully alternates between the sinful practices of Eli's wicked sons and the innocent purity and righteousness of Samuel and his family. First, the rapacious and unholy actions of

---

7. Satterthwaite, "David in the Books of Samuel," 48, and J. J. M. Roberts, "The Old Testament's Contribution to Messianic Expectations," 39–51.

Hophni and Phinehas (2:12–17) are contrasted with the righteous conduct of Samuel's family and the Lord's blessing on them (2:18–21). This is followed by Eli's unheeded rebuke of his sons (2:22–25), contrasted finally with a concluding statement of Samuel's continued maturity, both physically and spiritually (2:26). Such literary interchange heightens both Samuel's good qualities and Eli's sons' bad qualities.

The general statement of verse 12 sets the tone for verses 12–17: "Eli's sons were wicked men; they had no regard for the LORD." The designation "wicked men" (lit., "sons of Belial") in these opening chapters of 1 Samuel refers to cultic abuses, that is, a lack of regard for the proper worship of Yahweh.[8] It is ironic that Eli earlier mistakenly assumed Hannah was a "wicked woman" (1:16; lit., "daughter of Belial"); in reality, it is his own sons who are the scoundrels, showing only contempt for Yahweh's sacrifices. Hannah was a righteous woman, but Eli does not know righteousness when he sees it.

The specific nature of the sins of Hophni and Phinehas has to do with their rights as priests. The Old Testament law provided proper and just ways for priests to share in certain meat portions of animals offered at the tabernacle (Lev. 7:28–36; Deut. 18:3). But Eli's sons at Shiloh have devised their own system, using a fork to pilfer the choicest meat, including the fat usually burned entirely for Yahweh. If the worshiper does not yield to the grasping priests, Eli's sons threaten to take it by force. The narrator summarizes their great sin as "treating the LORD's offering with contempt" (2:17).

The positive evaluation of Samuel and his family likewise begins with a general statement, setting the tone for 2:18–21: "Samuel was ministering before the LORD—a boy wearing a linen ephod." The linen ephod was a garment worn by priests at that time, and the "little robe" supplied by his mother each year (presumably since he outgrew them) may have been an outer cloak worn over the ephod.[9] This ideal scene, so lovingly describing the adorned little priest, is surely a dramatic contrast to the grasping and avaricious sons of Eli. Through the years, Eli comes to appreciate this devout family, blessing them and praying that Yahweh will honor their faithfulness. Hannah, attentively supplying young Samuel with his annual priestly garment, also conceives and gives birth over the years to five more children (2:21). Her barrenness has not resumed after Samuel's birth, nor has Yahweh withdrawn his pleasure from this wonderful family.[10]

---

8. Klein, *1 Samuel*, 9.

9. Keil and Delitzsch, *Samuel*, 36.

10. Eli's blessing (2:20–21a) stands at the center of a chiastic structure for ch. 2, indicating its importance to the narrative. See Michael Fishbane, "I Samuel 3: Historical Narrative and Narrative Poetics," in *Literary Interpretations of Biblical Narratives*, ed. K. R. R. Gros Louis and J. S. Ackerman; 2 vols. (Nashville: Abingdon, 1974, 1982), 2:194–96.

Meanwhile, Eli is either unwilling or unable to control his wayward sons. When he learns of their sexual exploits and their public reputation (2:22–23), he rebukes them and warns them of the inevitable consequences of their actions. But they reject his words, "for it was the LORD's will to put them to death" (2:25). Like the Pharaoh of the Exodus, who first hardened his own heart and then continued to resist God's grace until God himself gave him over to his own obstinate nature, so Hophni and Phinehas are clearly committed to their course of action. In their hearts, there is no turning back. As Wesley said: "They had now sinned away their day of grace. They had long hardened their hearts. And God at length gave them up to a reprobate mind and 'determined to destroy' them (II Chron. 25:16)."[11] But Samuel, by contrast, continues to mature physically as well as spiritually (1 Sam. 2:26).

Samuel's maturation in 1 Samuel 1–3 can be traced through four carefully orchestrated statements of the narrator.

1. "The boy ministered before the LORD under Eli the priest" (2:11; cf. 3:1). The irony here is that young Samuel is nurtured in the faith by Eli, the high priest, whose own sons are so wicked that his priestly line will eventually be deposed.
2. "The boy Samuel grew up in the presence of the LORD" (2:21). This time there is no mention of Eli's influence. Samuel is simply maturing in "the presence of the LORD."
3. "The boy Samuel continued to grow in stature and in favor with the LORD and with [people]" (2:26). As Samuel matures, he learns to live in such a way as to please God and those around him. Hophni and Phinehas have learned neither, having no regard for the sacrifices of Yahweh (2:17) or the rights of other humans (2:22–25).
4. "The LORD was with Samuel as he grew up, and he let none of his words fall to the ground" (3:19).

In each of the last three statements, Samuel is described by the root *gdl* ("grow, mature, become great"). Note in 2:17 how the narrator characterizes the sins of Hophni and Phinehas as "very great [*gᵉdolah*] in the LORD's sight." Thus, both Samuel and the sons of Eli are "great." Samuel is becoming a great man of God, while Hophni and Phinehas are becoming great sinners.[12]

Prophecy Against Eli's Priesthood (2:27–36)

THE SUDDEN AND UNEXPECTED APPEARANCE of "a man of God" (2:27) in Old Testament narrative is seldom good news. Such anonymous prophetic figures

---

11. John Wesley, *Wesley's Notes on the Bible*, ed. G. Roger Schoenhals (Grand Rapids: Zondervan, 1987), 181.

12. Brueggemann, *First and Second Samuel*, 22–23.

often bring messages of impending judgment. This pericope contains the features of prophetic speech often used by such prophets to announce judgment against an individual, a genre of speech well known elsewhere in the Old Testament.[13] Such prophetic speech has a discernible form: introduction, followed by accusation and then by the announcement of judgment. As is typical, the prophetic "Thus says Yahweh" introduces the whole speech (*koh ʾamar ywhw;* NIV "This is what the LORD says," 2:27). It is followed by the accusation, which here takes the form of a question. This particular accusation in fact contains three questions: "Did I not clearly reveal myself to your father's house...?" "Why do you scorn my sacrifice and offering...?" and "Why do you honor your sons more than me ...?" (2:27–29).

The final stage of the prophetic speech is the announcement of judgment, which begins with the "therefore" in 2:30. Typically such announcements contain a singular statement of punishment about to befall the person to whom the speech is directed. Occasionally, as in our case against Eli, the announcement contains a contrast motif in which the offense of the guilty party is contrasted with the fact that he has received many benefits from Yahweh. In this passage, Yahweh reminds Eli that he had committed himself by divine oracle to the Elide house as priests (*nᵊʾum yhwh;* NIV "the LORD declares"), that they would minister before the Lord "forever." But as elsewhere in the Bible, such divine eternal promises are conditioned on continued faithfulness, even where such conditions are not specifically spelled out. Will the Lord abide the sinful and wicked behavior of Eli's sons? The answer is an emphatic "Far be it from me!" (3:30). The condition for continued good favor with God is stated succinctly, requiring only four words in Hebrew: "Those who honor me I will honor, but those who despise me will be disdained."

There is one more important component of the prophetic judgment speech against an individual pertinent to this passage. The greater part of the announcement of such speeches is usually connected to the declaration of a "sign" (*ʾot*), as in the familiar "therefore the LORD himself will give you a sign" (Isa. 7:14). One needs a sign only when the thing announced is expected to appear later, perhaps years later. The sign attests to the validity of the speech in the immediate historical context in which it is delivered. So the sign is announced in 2:34: "What happens to your two sons, Hophni and Phinehas, will be a sign [*ʾot*] to you."

---

13. Claus Westermann, *Basic Forms of Prophetic Speech,* trans. H. C. White (repr. of 1967 ed.; Louisville, Ky.: Westminster John Knox, 1991), 142–63; Bill T. Arnold, "Forms of Prophetic Speech in the Old Testament: A Summary of Claus Westermann's Contributions," *ATJ* 27 (1995): 30–40.

The specifics of God's judgment against Eli are both corporate and personal. The entire house of Eli will suffer the consequences of the present wickedness. Every one of its members will die early, making Eli the last old man in his priestly line (2:22). But the immediate and personal application for Eli relates to his sons, Hophni and Phinehas (2:34–36): They will both die on the same day! Yahweh will raise up in their place a faithful priest, who "will minister before my anointed one always" (2:35).

The fulfillment of this prophecy comes in stages. First, Eli's sons meet an untimely and tragic death, resulting also in the pitiable end of Eli's life (1 Sam. 4). Many years later, eighty-five of Eli's descendants meet a violent death in one of the darkest episodes of Israel's first king, Saul (22:6–23). Eventually, Eli's line of descendants is completely displaced by the Zadokite priests under Solomon (1 Kings 2:26–27). This illustrates the way in which Old Testament prophecy often finds fulfillment—first in a partial and incomplete way in the near future, and then in more complete and final ways in the remote future.

Bridging Contexts

HANNAH'S SONG. The Israelites had the wonderful ability of singing their theology. Hannah's song of thanksgiving contains many indications that it was adapted from the nation's repertoire of hymns. Her references to enemies, warriors, princes, and eventually a king lead to the conclusion this was a public hymn that she learned in her regular habit of worship. The appropriateness of her song is obvious, since her barrenness has been turned to joy by Yahweh's power, just as Israel's bleakness will soon be turned to exultation through the ministry of Samuel, the kingmaker. Thus, Hannah has learned how to praise through regular worship, and it serves her well when she wants to express her gratitude to God. In this way, worship often prepares us for life.

Hannah's song of thanksgiving expresses great confidence in the loving sovereignty of God and expresses gratitude for what he has done. What God has done in the past, he is doing again, now through Hannah. By starting with the holy transcendence of Yahweh, as Hannah does in verse 2, the Israelites are able to see that every blessing in life is from God. Indeed, even those circumstances that we may not consider as "blessings" are from God, since he alone is holy.

God's sovereignty is not mechanical determinism but knowledge that everything is in his hands and that whatever deliverance comes our way is from him. Just as he will some day exalt the horn of his anointed and give strength to his king (2:10), so Hannah can rejoice in her own exalted horn (2:1). God has lifted her head in vindication, because she trusted in him. But the exaltation of the meek also sets the tone for the rest of 1–2 Samuel.[14] After the elevation of Hannah, we will read of the elevation of Samuel, Saul, and eventually David. This rise from humble surroundings to distinction (and power) is indeed the paradigm for what is about to happen for Israel as a nation.

Mary, the mother of Jesus, apparently patterned her own great prayer of praise and gratitude after Hannah's song (the "Magnificat," Luke 1:46–55).[15] The two hymns have similarities in their beginnings, and they share several common themes. The circumstances of the two women were very different, of course, yet both conceived miraculously. Hannah sang her hymn of praise after Samuel's birth, while Mary sang her hymn prior to her son's birth. Unlike Hannah's situation, Mary's was an unexpected (and at first unwanted?) surprise blessing. But she came to accept and rejoice in God's will for her life and was confident in his sovereign rule.

Samuel and Eli's sons. The middle unit of this chapter highlights the differences between Samuel and the sons of Eli (2:12–26). The interchanging contrast between them pits the wicked actions of Eli's sons against the innocent and submissive behavior of Samuel. Eli's sons greedily exploit their position as priests, using power to gratify their own desires.

The narrator portrays a growing urgency about their sin. Their presumptuous actions intensify as the narrative unfolds. At first they steal food not rightfully theirs. Then they sexually abuse the women serving in the tabernacle. Their abhorrent behavior becomes widely known in Israel, and Eli realizes the severity of their sins. Samuel, by contrast, is the boy priest who innocently goes about his work, performing the services of the Lord (2:18). He is lovingly cared for by his mother, who brings him a fresh priestly garment each year and who is herself blessed by God's good favor with more children. And Samuel gradually becomes mature in his faith.

The narrative's way of contrasting the two paths of life—that followed by Samuel and that chosen by Eli's sons—is a chilling lesson in the importance of individual responsibility for life's choices. Hophni, Phinehas, and Samuel are not of totally dissimilar backgrounds and social privileges. Hophni and Phinehas are the sons of the high priest at Shiloh; Samuel is the son of a priestly family from nearby Ramah. They must have had similar religious education and opportunities. But the sons of Eli become great in their sins while Samuel became great in his faith. How does one explain the differences? Sin is deceptive and has a hardening effect on the human heart. When people continuously choose sinful attitudes and actions, they gradually become

---

14. McCarter, *I Samuel*, 76.
15. Compare also Zechariah's song in Luke 1:68–79.

hardhearted and turn away "from the living God." But those who persist in the faith will grow stronger and stand firm to the end in the confidence they had at first (Heb. 3:12–15).

Prophetic condemnation. The final unit of this chapter is the prophetic condemnation of the house of Eli (2:27–36). The formulaic pattern of introduction, accusation, and announcement as noted above prepares us for the fall of Eli (1 Sam. 4) and the concomitant rise of the fortunes of Samuel (1 Sam. 7). Eli and Samuel are headed in opposite directions. Eli was meant to be the nation's spiritual leader during the premonarchic period. But his inability to control his wicked sons clearly removed him from that role. It is appropriate, then, that his replacement as spiritual leader and eventual king-maker for Israel is Samuel.

The statement in which Yahweh retracts his commitment to Eli's family has enduring significance. Verse 30 is notable for its assertion that Yahweh is repealing a promise he had previously stated as eternal. In addition to the promise of Aaronic priesthood (Ex. 29:9; Num. 25:13), this verse indicates a commitment to Eli's house or descendants as priests: "I promised that your house ... would minister before me forever." But the surpassing wickedness of Eli's sons leads God to nullify that promise.

In other words, God's eternal decrees are formally conditional. Eli's family do not meet those conditions (2:30); thus, they will not benefit from the Aaronic promises. As elsewhere in Old Testament thought, the benefits of God's promises are conditioned on people's faithfulness, "a condition which applies to God's promises even when it is not explicitly stated."[16] Thus, we may surmise that while God's promises are eternal, the specific and individual benefits of those promises are contingent on continued faithfulness.

SINGING. SOMETIMES YOU JUST HAVE TO SING! Hannah had to sing! God had turned her barrenness into joy. By using one of Israel's national hymns, she was bidding the nation to sing along with her. And her song reveals that she understood full well the significance of God's sovereign, gift-giving love.

Attendance in public worship is important for numerous reasons. One of those is how it instills in us the ability to relate our circumstances to God's love and his work in our lives. Our hymns and songs of worship are second only to the reading and exposition of the biblical text. Whether it is the

---

16. Baldwin, *1 and 2 Samuel*, 62; Brueggemann, *First and Second Samuel*, 23.

Scripture choruses many of us use in our modern churches or the great classic hymns of the Christian faith, such singing of theology helps shape our thinking and prepares us for the day when we just cannot help ourselves, and we too have to sing.

Sin among church leaders. The contrast between Samuel and Eli's sons in this chapter is a lesson for all religious professionals, as well as for individuals deeply involved in the life of their local congregation. Martin Luther King Jr. once admitted to being frustrated by ministers of the gospel who often "aren't concerned about anything but themselves."[17]

As the son of a pastor, I grew up watching parishioners and other pastors in our denominational connection. I will never fully understand the number of people intimately plugged into the business of the church—both local and general—who seem to persist in sin because of a hardness of heart. Some of the most hateful behavior I have ever witnessed has come from denominational leaders and local church officials. There is something about throwing oneself into the everyday affairs of the church, into the routine business of doing "church work," that is deceptive. It soothes our conscience and makes us feel we are in the right state of mind spiritually. But proximity to God's work is no substitute for submission to the grace of God.

As Hophni and Phinehas warn us, it is possible to handle the things of God regularly (they officiated Israel's worship services!) and fail to have a heart that is sensitive to God's will. In fact, it may be that those of us who daily handle the things of Christ are the ones most prone to forget their significance and fall into a laissez-faire approach to the gospel of God. In my current position as a seminary professor, the words edited by the fourteenth-century priest Thomas Hemerken of Kempen (better known as Thomas à Kempis) are apropos:

> What good does it do to speak learnedly about the Trinity if, lacking humility, you displease the Trinity? Indeed it is not learning that makes a [person] holy and just, but a virtuous life makes him pleasing to God. I would rather feel contrition than know how to define it. For what would it profit us to know the whole Bible by heart and the principles of all the philosophers if we live without grace and the love of God? Vanity of vanities and all is vanity, except to love God and serve Him alone.[18]

---

17. A passing comment in Dr. King's last sermon, delivered in Memphis on the eve of his assassination, April 3, 1968. See "I See the Promised Land," in *A Testament of Hope: The Essential Writings of Martin Luther King, Jr.*, ed. James Melvin Washington (San Francisco: Harper & Row, 1986), 279–86 (quote is from 282).

18. Thomas à Kempis, *The Imitation of Christ* (Milwaukee: Bruce Publishing, 1962), 1–2.

So what profit was there in being priests for Hophni and Phinehas? And what profit is there in being the chairperson of your local church's board of trustees or the administrative superintendent of your denomination? Indeed, these types of service are all commendable. But without the sensitive heart of the young Samuel, our service is useless.

Conditionality of benefits. The last section of chapter 2 contains prophetic condemnation of Eli's house. This pericope has several issues germane to our contemporary context, but I mention just one here. The conditionality of Eli's benefits and privileges under the Aaronic priesthood has many parallels to the contemporary church. Most Christians today attach themselves to institutions that they feel are squarely within God's will and therefore are worthy of his continued blessings. These institutions can be whole denominations, individual local churches, Christian colleges or seminaries, an evangelistic association, or even a particular evangelist or minister. People often feel that because a certain institution has been faithful and effective in ministry in the past, it is worthy of continued financial support. But some Christians go further and lend such credibility to that institution (or individual) that they may not hear when God announces, "Far be it from me!" (2:30).

My own denomination has been wonderfully used of God in the history of the United States. I know many ministers who feel they could never leave our church because of an emotional attachment to the church as institution. We should always be aware that there are many valid Christian ministries, and no one organization or denominational group is above reproach. Like Eli's priesthood, God does not bless forever any institutionalized form of Christianity as is. Institutions that fail to remain faithful to their calling and to uphold biblical principles of discipleship will eventually lose God's favor. As painful as it often is, today's Christian needs to realize that Eli's priesthood did not last forever. There came a time for God to let it go and to look to new leadership to carry forward his work.

1 Samuel 3:1–4:1a

❦

THE BOY SAMUEL ministered before the LORD under Eli. In those days the word of the LORD was rare; there were not many visions.

²One night Eli, whose eyes were becoming so weak that he could barely see, was lying down in his usual place. ³The lamp of God had not yet gone out, and Samuel was lying down in the temple of the LORD, where the ark of God was. ⁴Then the LORD called Samuel.

Samuel answered, "Here I am." ⁵And he ran to Eli and said, "Here I am; you called me."

But Eli said, "I did not call; go back and lie down." So he went and lay down.

⁶Again the LORD called, "Samuel!" And Samuel got up and went to Eli and said, "Here I am; you called me."

"My son," Eli said, "I did not call; go back and lie down."

⁷Now Samuel did not yet know the LORD: The word of the LORD had not yet been revealed to him.

⁸The LORD called Samuel a third time, and Samuel got up and went to Eli and said, "Here I am; you called me."

Then Eli realized that the LORD was calling the boy. ⁹So Eli told Samuel, "Go and lie down, and if he calls you, say, 'Speak, LORD, for your servant is listening.'" So Samuel went and lay down in his place.

¹⁰The LORD came and stood there, calling as at the other times, "Samuel! Samuel!"

Then Samuel said, "Speak, for your servant is listening."

¹¹And the LORD said to Samuel: "See, I am about to do something in Israel that will make the ears of everyone who hears of it tingle. ¹²At that time I will carry out against Eli everything I spoke against his family—from beginning to end. ¹³For I told him that I would judge his family forever because of the sin he knew about; his sons made themselves contemptible, and he failed to restrain them. ¹⁴Therefore, I swore to the house of Eli, 'The guilt of Eli's house will never be atoned for by sacrifice or offering.'"

¹⁵Samuel lay down until morning and then opened the doors of the house of the LORD. He was afraid to tell Eli the vision, ¹⁶but Eli called him and said, "Samuel, my son."

Samuel answered, "Here I am."

¹⁷"What was it he said to you?" Eli asked. "Do not hide it from me. May God deal with you, be it ever so severely, if you hide from me anything he told you." ¹⁸So Samuel told him everything, hiding nothing from him. Then Eli said, "He is the LORD; let him do what is good in his eyes."

¹⁹The LORD was with Samuel as he grew up, and he let none of his words fall to the ground. ²⁰And all Israel from Dan to Beersheba recognized that Samuel was attested as a prophet of the LORD. ²¹The LORD continued to appear at Shiloh, and there he revealed himself to Samuel through his word.

⁴:¹And Samuel's word came to all Israel.

THIS SECTION CONTAINS one of our most endearing pictures of the great prophet. As a young boy serving in the Lord's house, Samuel is stirred in the night by the voice of God. For everyone who has received the call of God and struggled with the authenticity of that calling, this passage has personal significance.

The Word of the Lord Was Rare (3:1)

EASILY LOST IN our familiarity with this narrative is the way the historian has framed the account with an emphasis on "the word" of Yahweh. The opening verse reminds us that Samuel is serving Yahweh under Eli's tutelage. But there is no widespread prophetic ministry of "the word of the LORD" in those days.

To be more specific, the narrator informs us "there were not many visions" (3:1). The rarity of the prophetic word is of particular interest to our author, and this entire episode of Samuel's call should be read in this light. Samuel receives a message related to Eli's priesthood (3:11–14), but his calling has wider significance because it also initiates a new era in which God's word is received and proclaimed. Under Moses and Joshua, God had spoken, and his word had led the nation, both in its great victories and through its miserable failures. But during the judges period, "all the people did what was right in their own eyes" (Judges 17:6; 21:25 NRSV). Now under Eli's priesthood, the nation is languishing without an adequate prophetic ministry.

Our author—who may have been a prophet (see introduction)—has a special appreciation for the importance of living under the authority of Yahweh's word. Without such direction, the nation (or any individual) will wander aimlessly and eventually fall into self-destructive behavior. The word of Yahweh is necessary if Israel is to survive this dangerous time. The author returns to this at the end of chapter 3 when he tells us that Samuel has matured into a "trustworthy" prophet (NIV "attested as a prophet"), whose words do not fall to the ground (i.e., they come true, 3:19–20). Furthermore, Yahweh continues to appear ("reveal himself") to Samuel at Shiloh "through his word" (3:21). In this context, this episode is not simply about the end of Eli's priesthood but about the beginning of Samuel's prophetic leadership ("Samuel's word came to all Israel," 4:1a) and renewed communication between God and Israel.

The Word of the Lord Came to Samuel (3:2–14)

THE OPENING CHAPTERS of 1 Samuel appear to presuppose a semipermanent structure built around the ancient tabernacle.[1] If it were similar to the later temple complex in Jerusalem, it would have included rooms or apartments as part of its outer court for the priests' quarters. The reference to Samuel's sleeping in the temple near the ark of the covenant does not mean he is actually sleeping in the Most Holy Place, only that he has a room with the priests, presumably adjacent or near Eli's quarters.[2] This arrangement is in case the infirm Eli ("he could barely see," 3:2) needs the youth during the night. Thus, when Samuel hears a voice, it is only natural for him to expect that Eli needs something urgently. The fact that the lamp of God has not yet gone out indicates that the call comes in the early morning hours, just before the oil is gone (cf. Ex. 27:21).

Yahweh's call of Samuel is narrated in 3:4–10, and the divine message conveyed to the prophet-in-the-making in 3:11–14. The call itself is the cherished picture of the young Samuel who responds to Yahweh (and Eli) in childlike fashion. But the message of doom delivered as part of the theophany is not childlike or endearing.

Samuel's recurring self-announcement ("Here I am; you called me") is the expression of those who volunteer themselves for service. He is placing himself at the disposal, at the beck and call, of his master. Samuel is willing to serve, but he is confused about the identity of the one calling him. The

---

1. See Youngblood, "1, 2 Samuel," 572. It is unnecessary to posit two separate traditions, one that thought there was a tent-shrine, "house of Yahweh," and the other a permanent temple, "temple of Yahweh," at Shiloh (McCarter, *I Samuel*, 60).

2. Keil and Delitzsch, *Samuel*, 49–51; against H. P. Smith, *A Critical and Exegetical Commentary on the Books of Samuel* (ICC; Edinburgh: T. & T. Clark, 1989), 26, and most other commentators.

single Hebrew word translated "Here I am" (*hinneni*, 3:4) can be a common greeting, but it is often a more subtle indication that a servant hears and obeys. It is especially significant when someone hears and obeys the divine call (Gen. 22:1, 11; Ex. 3:4; Isa. 6:8).

Samuel is still inexperienced in the way of Yahweh (he "did not yet know the LORD," 3:7). He has not yet experienced him in that way that leads to intimate and lasting relationship with God, which relationship will eventually make Samuel a great prophet: "The word of the LORD had not yet been revealed to him" (3:7; cf. 3:19–21). That is about to change. His willingness to serve, together with his holy parentage and his childlike acceptance of religious instruction, prepares Samuel to experience Yahweh in a new way. His lack of knowledge of Yahweh leads to confusion in this moment of call, but eventually Eli, a man who at some point in his past understood and appreciated the ways of Yahweh, discerns that it is God who is calling the youth (3:8). Samuel is about to enter into this new experience with Yahweh, a relationship that Eli's sons never had: "They had no regard [i.e., did not know] the LORD" (2:12).

After calling Samuel three times, Yahweh now "came and stood there" (3:10). Apparently Samuel is now receiving not only a word but also a vision, significant because we have been told that both word and vision were rare in those days (3:1). The call of Samuel thus far has been an idyllic, childlike exchange. But when Yahweh reveals the message to Samuel (3:11–14), it is anything but idyllic or childlike.[3] In the Old Testament, ears "tingle" when people receive news of approaching punishment (2 Kings 21:12; Jer. 19:3). Yahweh informs Samuel that he is about to fulfill his word spoken through the anonymous "man of God" regarding the end of Eli's priesthood (2:27–36). There is no turning back now ("The guilt of Eli's house will never be atoned for by sacrifice or offering," 3:14).

Samuel the Prophet (3:15–4:1a)

WHEN MORNING COMES, Samuel goes about his daily routine, opening the doors of the house of Yahweh. He is afraid to tell Eli the dreadful message. But when Eli presses him, Samuel is the ever-obedient servant: "Here I am" (3:16). Samuel tells the elderly priest the truth, to which Eli responds with gloomy resignation. Surely he understands that the sovereign Yahweh is free to punish sin and is just in doing so. As for Samuel, he must have understood that his role is changing. He was accustomed to priestly service from

---

3. Brueggemann, *First and Second Samuel*, 25. Just as Eli's blessing of Samuel's family was the chiastic center of ch. 2, so here the divine oracle against Eli forms the literary center of ch. 3 (Fishbane, "I Samuel 3," 2:193).

his early childhood. But now he has received a prophetic message by means of dramatic divine revelation, and further, he has served as Yahweh's mouthpiece to deliver that message to its intended audience, Eli.

The emphasis of 3:19–21 is the validity of Samuel's prophetic ministry. The narrator itemizes four facts that confirm Samuel's important role as Israel's new hope for revival and deliverance from her spiritual lethargy.

(1) Yahweh continues to grant his supernatural presence to Samuel as he matures. In the ancestral narratives, the presence of Yahweh was linked to the all-important land promise (Gen. 26:3, 24; 28:15). Joseph had been blessed with the presence of God (Gen. 39:2, 3, 21, 23). For Moses and the children of Israel, Yahweh's presence guided them in a column of cloud by day, a pillar of fire by night, and eventually filled the newly constructed tabernacle in the desert in the form of his Shekinah glory (Ex. 13:21; 14:19; 40:34). Similarly, the presence of Yahweh will later be with King David (1 Sam. 16:18; 18:12). So with Samuel, the abiding presence of Yahweh demonstrates that the circumstances of his life (and career) are not left to human influence alone. Yahweh is at work to raise him up as a prophet, which leads to the next fact emphasized in this paragraph.

(2) The historian informs us that Yahweh "let none of his words fall to the ground" (3:19). This particular expression denotes the success of Samuel's prophetic words. The "falling" of a word is its failure to come to fruition. When God defined the nature of Israelite prophecy, he said he would put his own words in the prophet's mouth (Deut. 18:18), and the Israelites would be able to distinguish true prophets from false prophets by whether or not their prophecies came true (18:21–22). True prophets spoke words that could never "fall" (*npl*), so that Jehu was sure Yahweh would not allow any of Elijah's words to fall (2 Kings 10:10). Elsewhere Yahweh assured Israel that he does not permit his own word to fall (Josh. 21:45; 23:14; 1 Kings 8:56).[4]

(3) The validity of Samuel's ministry is demonstrated in his public acclaim (3:20). The expression "from Dan to Beersheba" designates the northern and southern most extremities of united Israel and occurs elsewhere in the narratives about King David (2 Sam. 3:10; 17:11; 24:2, 15). It is obvious to all Israel: Samuel has become a prophet of Yahweh.

The noun "prophet" (*nabiʾ*) until recently had not been attested outside the Bible.[5] We were aware of an ancient verb used in Mesopotamia for "call by name, call to duty," from which it had been deduced to mean "one

---

4. Allan M. Harman, "נָפַל," *NIDOTTE*, 3:129.

5. Daniel E. Fleming, "*Nabû* and *Munabbiatu*: Two New Syrian Religious Personnel," *JAOS* 113.2 (1993): 175–83; idem, "The Etymological Origins of the Hebrew *nabîʾ*: The One Who Invokes God," *CBQ* 55 (1993): 217–24.

summoned" or "one called for a specific assignment." But now we have evidence that the noun was used in other ancient Semitic cultures related to Israel with a similar meaning. Recognition of Samuel as a prophet of Yahweh places him in the company of others who walk through the pages of Israel's salvation history: Moses, Elijah, and the writing prophets Isaiah, Jeremiah, Ezekiel and the twelve so-called Minor Prophets, to name a few.

(4) The final legitimizing feature of Samuel's new role is the continued manifestations of Yahweh to Samuel at Shiloh, where God reveals himself "through his word" (3:21). The night call is not an exceptional appearance of Yahweh to Samuel, but rather the first of a series: "Yahweh kept on appearing in Shiloh."[6] The author's emphasis on "through his word" brings him full circle to the theme from which he began the chapter. Yahweh's word was rare in those days, but now that has changed. Samuel has grown from boy-priest to approved prophet. As the one who receives and proclaims the word of Yahweh, he is now prepared to assume the roles of prophet, priest, and judge. Eventually, through Yahweh's word, he will also become the kingmaker for ancient Israel.

Samuel's greatness has an interesting paradoxical appearance. On the one hand, his role in the transition from judge to king together with his experience as a priest means he assumes within himself significant features of Israelite leadership. His role as a prophet (*nabi'*) makes him, like Moses before him, a leader par excellence. On the other hand, his greatness is most clearly seen in appointing other leaders: Saul as Israel's first king, and then David as Israel's greatest. It is his greatness as noted here—that is, as Israel's prophet, priest, and judge—that makes it possible for him to serve as her kingmaker. "Thus he pointed, not to himself, but to the Lord's anointed, by whom 'the Lord will judge the ends of the earth' (1 Sam. 2:10)."[7]

Bridging Contexts

TRUTHS ABOUT GOD'S WORD. The passage before us is about God's call on the life of the boy Samuel and the effectual work of God's revealed word. Israel had been without Yahweh's preserving and rejuvenating word for some time ("the word of the LORD was rare," 3:1). But with this episode, God is once again revealing his word through Samuel with good effect (3:21). The work of Yahweh's word occurs on several levels in this chapter, since it has a *transforming* effect in Samuel's young

---

6. Klein's translation (*1 Samuel*, 30).
7. Baldwin, *1 and 2 Samuel*, 65.

life and an *informing* consequence in Eli's. The passage presents at least three timeless truths for us to consider.

(1) God's Word is true and certain, presenting undeniable parameters in which life must be lived and enjoyed. The word for Eli, through the new prophetic role of Samuel, is a message of certain doom (3:11–14). In the message revealed about Eli, the Lord emphasizes that he will certainly carry out his judgment against the hapless priestly family "from beginning to end" (3:12). The prophetic word in the Old Testament is certain and sure, whether for good or ill. The Lord is free to change his course of direction according to the response of the people; genuine repentance leads to certain forgiveness while persistent sin leads to inescapable judgment (Jer. 18:1–10). But God is the one who sets the standard, and his Word announces the verdict. Either way, the Word of the Lord is true and will certainly find fruition in the lives of those for whom it is intended.

The Old Testament is clear that God's Word is eternal, unlike ephemeral things of this life ("the word of our God stands forever," Isa. 40:8). Jesus equates his message with the eternal significance of the Old Testament Word of Yahweh: "Heaven and earth will pass away, but my words will never pass away" (Luke 21:33; cf. Matt. 5:17–18). Without doubt, believers today can rest assured that God's Word is still active as a warning for those who consistently reject his grace and as a comfort for those who hear his call.

(2) God's Word represents a claim on individual lives, calling us to service and submission. This passage is not only about God's condemnation of Eli's house but also about God's call for Samuel to serve in a new prophetic ministry. The author writes in order to legitimate Samuel as the new leadership, while delegitimating the old. In 3:9–10, Eli patiently instructs Samuel on how to respond to God's call, and Samuel is totally dependent on Eli. But in 3:17–18, the roles are reversed. Now Samuel informs Eli of God's message, and Eli is dependent on Samuel to learn that word.[8] Sometimes a new beginning requires the end of an old way.

Samuel has entered into a new relationship with God and has learned a new service. He has been accustomed to his priestly responsibilities, but now he serves also as prophet. The text illustrates the work of God's Word in summoning his people to submission to his will and way. It is about hearing the divine call and answering, "Here I am." Like Samuel, many contemporary Christians must hear the call and enter into a new relationship with God, a relationship committed to proclaiming the Word to the world. The text of 1 Samuel 3 is meant to arouse us out of our lethargy, as

---

8. Michael Fishbane, "I Samuel 3," 2:193–96.

it aroused Samuel from his early-morning sleep. Let our answer be like his: "Here I am!"

(3) God's Word has a renewing and transforming force for all who respond to his call. The powerful spoken word of Yahweh in this passage transforms Samuel. At the beginning, he is a young intern priest who does not know the Lord or the Lord's ways with humankind. He is unaware of God's voice or call and seems naive about Eli's leadership. But at the end of the chapter, he is a bold prophet announcing Yahweh's intentions to the elder priest. He has become the regular means of prophetic revelation and is widely recognized in Israel as God's authorized spokesman. Yahweh is with Samuel as he matures, and he continues to reveal himself to Samuel "through his word" (3:19–21).

Israel recognizes the importance of the transforming and saving work of God's Word. The Old Testament prophets understood their ministry as a proclamation of his redemptive Word to the nation (Isa. 6:5–7; 40:6–9; Jer. 1:9–10; Ezek. 2:8–3:4; Amos 7:14–16). The eighth-century prophet Amos portrays the great day of Yahweh's judgment as one in which the life-giving and transforming Word of Yahweh will be withdrawn. There will be a famine in the land—not a famine of bread or water but of hearing the words of Yahweh. The people will be left to wander from sea to sea, seeking a word of Yahweh, but they will not find it (Amos 8:11–12). Nothing is more terrifying because without Yahweh's transforming Word, there is no hope.[9]

To inform and to form. God speaks to his people of every generation. He does not often speak audibly, as he does here to the young Samuel. But he continues to speak clearly through his written Word to all who will listen.

In God's appearance to Samuel, his Word functions in two ways: God speaks both to inform and to invite. His revelation to Samuel informs the young prophet of his intentions regarding the house of Eli. But God's "Samuel! Samuel!" is also an invitation to enter into a new, deeper relationship with him. While Samuel did not *know* God prior to this point (3:7), henceforth he will.

The Bible pictures God's Word with this twofold character throughout.[10] As ancient kings spoke for two purposes, to enact laws and to link themselves

---

9. Another possible "bridging contexts" issue arising from this text is the specific means of revelation for today's Christian believer compared to the prophetically transmitted "word" of Yahweh in this text. For more on this, however, see the Bridging Contexts section for 1 Sam. 23:1–29.

10. For what follows, see J. I. Packer, *Knowing God* (Downers Grove, Ill.: InterVarsity Press, 1973), 98–105.

to their people, so God's Word in the Bible refers to things around us, but it also relates to us directly. He speaks both to *inform* us and to *form* us, both for *information* and for *formation*. As Creator God, his words come as sovereign fiat ("let there be ..."). But he also speaks royal *Torah*, or righteous instruction, in order to bring us to himself. J. I. Packer has summarized the twofold nature of the Word of God as follows:

> God, our Maker, knows all about us before we say anything (Ps. 139:1–4); but we can know nothing about Him unless He tells us. Here, therefore, is a further reason why God speaks to us: not only to move us to do what He wants, but to enable us to know Him so that we may love Him. Therefore God sends His word to us in the character of both information and invitation. It comes to woo us as well as to instruct us; it not merely puts us in the picture of what God has done and is doing, but also calls us into personal communion with the loving Lord Himself.[11]

The Word that God addresses to contemporary believers is both an instrument of government, whereby he informs us how we ought to live, and also a means of fellowship, whereby he invites us into personal relationship with him.

One of the greatest modern illustrations I have found of this inviting and transforming power of God's Word is the life of the philosopher Emile Cailliet. He was born in a small village in France near the end of the nineteenth century.[12] His early education was committed to naturalism, leaving no room for God or supernatural intervention in human affairs. But his naturalistically inspired studies in philosophy proved of little help during front-line experiences as a lad of twenty in World War I. Confronted with the horrors of war, he asked:

> What use, the ill-kept ancient type of sophistry in the philosophic banter of the seminar, when your own buddy—at the time speaking to you of his mother—dies standing in front of you, a bullet in his chest? Was there a meaning to it all? A [person] can endure anything if only it appears meaningful. But what of the caprices of Fate, what of random killing, of senseless ordeal? Deep in the mud during long winter nights when silent knives became arms of predilection on both sides, I wondered. By then, my thinking had no longer anything to do with philosophy taken for the sake of a qualifying exam. ... I too felt,

---

11. Ibid., 99.

12. For what follows, see his book *Journey into Light* (Grand Rapids: Zondervan, 1968), 12–18.

not with my reason but with my whole being, that I was naked and—
war or no war—destined to perish miserably when the hour came.[13]

The impact of the naturalistic presuppositions Emile had absorbed proved
one of utter pessimism. "The moment came when I was overwhelmed by
the inadequacy of my views. What could be done about it? I did not know.
Who was I, anyway? Nay, *what* was I? These fundamental questions of human
existence remained unanswered."[14]

One night a bullet found Cailliet, too. An American field ambulance crew
saved his life, and after a nine-month hospital stay, he was discharged and
resumed his graduate studies. But he had to admit that the books no longer
seemed like the same books, nor was his motivation the same. Reading at
length in philosophy and literature, he found himself probing in depth for
meaning. He testifies:

> During long night watches in the foxholes I had in a strange way been
> longing—I must say it, however queer it may sound—for a book that
> would understand me. But I knew of no such book. Now I would in
> secret prepare one for my own private use. And so, as I went on read-
> ing for my courses I would file passages that would speak to my con-
> dition, then carefully copy them in a leather-bound pocket book I
> would always carry with me. The quotations, which I numbered in red
> ink for easier reference, would lead me as it were from fear and anguish,
> through a variety of intervening stages, to supreme utterances of
> release and jubilation.[15]

At last, the day came when he put the finishing touches on, as he said it,
"the book that would understand me." He describes a beautiful, sunny day,
in which he sat under a tree and opened his precious anthology. As he read,
however, he was overcome by a growing disappointment. Instead of speaking to his condition as he expected, the passages only reminded him of their
context, of the circumstances of his labor over their selection. Then, Cailliet says, he knew that the whole undertaking would not work, simply because
it was of his own making. It carried no strength of persuasion. In a dejected
mood, he put the little book back into his pocket.

On that same day, Cailliet's wife had come into the possession of a Bible
by extraordinary circumstances. Emile had always been adamant that religion
would be taboo in their home, and at the age of twenty-three he had never

---

13. Ibid., 12–13.
14. Ibid., 14.
15. Ibid., 16.

even seen a Bible. But at the end of that disappointing day, when she apologetically tried to explain how she had providentially (as he would later realize!) picked up a copy of the Bible, he was eager to see it. He describes what happened next:

> I literally grabbed the book and rushed to my study with it. I opened it and "chanced" upon the Beatitudes! I read, and read, and read—now aloud with an indescribable warmth surging within.... I could not find words to express my awe and wonder. And suddenly the realization dawned upon me: This *was* the Book that would understand me! I needed it so much, yet, unaware, I had attempted to write my own—in vain. I continued to read deeply into the night, mostly from the gospels. And lo and behold, as I looked through them, the One of whom they spoke, the One who spoke and acted in them, became alive in me.[16]

Cailliet goes on to explain that the circumstances in which the Bible had found him were undeniable. While it seemed absurd to speak of a book understanding a man, this could be said of the Bible because its pages were animated by the presence of the living God and the power of his mighty acts. To that God, Cailliet prayed that night, and the God who answered was *the same God* of whom it was spoken in the Bible.

When I heard recently a similar incident involving a young couple in Germany, it made me marvel again at the transforming power of God's Word. I have a friend who is the pastor of a church in Bietigheim, Germany, near Stuttgart. He related to me the story of a Chinese man named Xiao-Hu Huang, who together with his German wife, Kirstin, live near Stuttgart. He was Buddhist and she was an unbeliever. She went into a bookshop in search of a book in Chinese as a special birthday gift for him. The only Chinese book available was a Chinese translation of the Bible. Reluctantly, she purchased it for him, hoping it would nonetheless show the special thought she had given to his birthday.

At first, Xiao-Hu was not happy. But as he began to read, he was gradually persuaded of the truth contained in these pages. He began to speak to Kirstin about his new perspective, and this time she became angry. This was, after all, her cultural heritage, and she had chosen to reject it. The differences in opinion led to open conflict in their marriage. So Kirstin began to read the Bible too, not to understand her husband's new faith but in order to refute his new beliefs. In the process, she also became persuaded of the truth of the

16. Ibid., 18.

message in God's Word. They both began to grow in their Christian faith simply by studying the Bible. But they soon realized they needed the support of other believers. In 1996, they were both baptized in the Freie Christen Gemeinde, Bietigheim, where they continue as faithful disciples of Christ.

Such power and authority has led Christian thinkers through the ages to pursue the truths of God's Word with unrestrained vigor. John Wesley longed to learn God's truth with single-minded focus:

> I am a spirit come from God and returning to God; just hovering over the great gulf, till a few moments hence I am no more seen—I drop into an unchangeable eternity! I want to know one thing, the way to heaven—how to land safe on that happy shore. God himself has condescended to teach the way: for this very end he came from heaven. He hath written it down in a book. O give me that book! At any price give me the Book of God! I have it. Here is knowledge enough for me. Let me be *homo unius libri* ["a man of one book"].[17]

The lessons of Samuel and Eli will continue to unfold in the spellbinding narratives of 1 Samuel. As they do, we do well to remember the tragic consequences of God's Word against Eli and the transforming power of that Word in Samuel.

---

17. John Wesley, *The Works of John Wesley*, Vol. 1: *Sermons I, 1–33*, ed. Albert C. Outler (Bicentennial ed.; ed. F. Baker; Nashville: Abingdon, 1984), 104–5.

1 Samuel 4:1b–11

NOW THE ISRAELITES went out to fight against the Philistines. The Israelites camped at Ebenezer, and the Philistines at Aphek. ²The Philistines deployed their forces to meet Israel, and as the battle spread, Israel was defeated by the Philistines, who killed about four thousand of them on the battlefield. ³When the soldiers returned to camp, the elders of Israel asked, "Why did the LORD bring defeat upon us today before the Philistines? Let us bring the ark of the LORD's covenant from Shiloh, so that it may go with us and save us from the hand of our enemies."

⁴So the people sent men to Shiloh, and they brought back the ark of the covenant of the LORD Almighty, who is enthroned between the cherubim. And Eli's two sons, Hophni and Phinehas, were there with the ark of the covenant of God.

⁵When the ark of the LORD's covenant came into the camp, all Israel raised such a great shout that the ground shook. ⁶Hearing the uproar, the Philistines asked, "What's all this shouting in the Hebrew camp?"

When they learned that the ark of the LORD had come into the camp, ⁷the Philistines were afraid. "A god has come into the camp," they said. "We're in trouble! Nothing like this has happened before. ⁸Woe to us! Who will deliver us from the hand of these mighty gods? They are the gods who struck the Egyptians with all kinds of plagues in the desert. ⁹Be strong, Philistines! Be men, or you will be subject to the Hebrews, as they have been to you. Be men, and fight!"

¹⁰So the Philistines fought, and the Israelites were defeated and every man fled to his tent. The slaughter was very great; Israel lost thirty thousand foot soldiers. ¹¹The ark of God was captured, and Eli's two sons, Hophni and Phinehas, died.

Original Meaning

AS NOTED IN THE INTRODUCTION, 1 Samuel 4 begins a unit often termed "the ark narrative" (4:1b–7:1). The focus of the narrative shifts away from Samuel, the one born and raised to lead Israel into the next great period of her history. The ark narrative portends what the needs for that next period of Israelite history are going to be. These chapters trace the fortunes of the ark of the covenant—from its capture at Ebenezer, its sojourn in Philistia, and its eventual arrival at Kiriath Jearim. Their purpose is to celebrate the power of Yahweh's ark, Israel's greatest sacred symbol. At the same time they contain a warning about Israel's deep-rooted problems that led to the lack of respect and care for the ark. Though Samuel returns in chapter 7 to provide leadership for a national revival, Israel's propensity to attempt to manipulate God will continue to present problems for the nation and for the kings who will eventually lead her.

The first unit of the ark narrative reports on renewed hostilities between Israel and the Philistines (4:1b—4). After initial defeat at the hands of their enemies, Israel tries to give the conflict the appearance of a Yahweh war (or a so-called "holy war") by manipulating the ark of the covenant (4:5—9). But because of the nation's sin and lack of righteous leadership, their action only results in more loss and humiliation (4:10—11).

War with the Philistines (4:1b—4)

WE BEGIN WITH a textual difficulty that has an impact on our understanding of the events described here. As the Hebrew text stands now (reflected in the NIV), we are left with no idea who the aggressors are in this conflict, the Philistines or the Israelites. The Israelites simply go to war against the Philistines. But the LXX has an additional sentence at the beginning of our text, which appears to have been unintentionally omitted in the received Hebrew (or Masoretic) text: "In those days the Philistines assembled for war against Israel."[1] This reading removes any ambiguity, making it clear that the Philistines are the aggressors.

This general introduction to the ark narrative, in fact, describes the hostilities between the Philistines and Israelites that dominated Israel's history for nearly two centuries, during the days of the judges and the early monarchy. This persistent conflict, in which neither side achieved a decisive defeat of the other, is the historical backdrop against which we should read part of Judges, all of 1 Samuel, and much of 2 Samuel. The Philistine threat presented Israel with its greatest challenge since entering the Promised Land. During the judges period, Israel had been oppressed by various nomadic peoples uninterested in permanent conquest or empire building. But in the Philistines, the Israelites were confronted with a technologically advanced force that

---

1. In all likelihood, the Greek is the original reading because the shorter Hebrew reading can be explained as an unintentional error based on homoioteleuton (or "similar endings"). For full discussion, see Klein, *1 Samuel*, 37; McCarter, *I Samuel*, 102–3; Hertzberg, *I and II Samuel*, 45.

had hegemony on its mind, a people interested in more land and permanent domination.

The Philistines appeared in southwestern Canaan around the beginning of the Iron I period, approximately 1200 B.C., apparently as part of the migrating "sea peoples" attested in Egyptian sources.[2] They were to play an important role in Old Testament history for the next two centuries. They settled in the southwestern coastal plains, occupying principally five cities as a unified Philistine pentapolis: Gaza, Ashdod, Ashkelon, Gath, and Ekron (Josh. 13:3; Judg. 3:3). Each city was governed by a "lord," sometimes called simply "king."[3] The significance of the five Philistine lords will become clear later in the ark narrative.

Though neither side held the decisive advantage, the Philistines began to dominate during the middle of the eleventh century, when they gained a militarily strategic advantage in the use of iron technology, for reasons that are not entirely clear (1 Sam. 13:19–21). They desired to expand into the fertile central hill region, only recently settled by the new Israelite population. But the Israelites needed further holdings to the west, making this a classic battle over *Lebensraum*. During the judges period, Philistine encroachment into Israelite territory had resulted in the relocation of the tribe of Dan (Judg. 18). Now continued aggression threatened to result in more losses in Israel's heartland.

In 4:2, the Philistines rout the Israelites, killing about four thousand soldiers at Ebenezer. The relationship between this Ebenezer and the place by the same name in 7:12 is uncertain. Several scholars feel the two Ebenezers should be distinguished from each other for geographical reasons.[4] Though that is probably true, we should not miss the literary symmetry created by the use of the same geographical name. The ark narrative begins with a loss to the Philistines at Ebenezer, but it concludes with a victory at a new Ebenezer.[5] What is lost to the Philistines will some day be restored. Though these are separate Ebenezers, Israel comes to understand the full significance of God's help in their time of need (see comments on ch. 7).

The question asked by the elders of Israel in 4:3 about this defeat reflects the Israelite concept of the sovereignty of Yahweh. They have suffered a horrible defeat at the hands of the Philistines, and they can only assume that

---

2. For summary, see David M. Howard Jr., "Philistines," in *Peoples of the Old Testament World*, ed. A. J. Hoerth, G. L. Mattingly, and E. M. Yamauchi (Grand Rapids: Baker, 1994), 231–50; Trude Dothan, "Early Philistines," *OEANE*, 4:310–11.

3. The term (*seren*) appears to be the only truly Philistine word preserved in the Bible.

4. Klein, *1 Samuel*, 41; Youngblood, "1, 2 Samuel," 609.

5. McCarter, *I Samuel*, 149; Jeffries M. Hamilton and John F. Kutsko, "Ebenezer," *ABD*, 2:259–60.

Yahweh has brought this defeat on them. In a sense, they are right. One of the main themes of the ark narrative is that Israel suffers terribly because of the wicked leadership at Shiloh. The sins of Eli and his sons Hophni and Phinehas have national and military consequences.

Yet the course of action chosen by the elders is misguided. They presume they can reverse the horrible events of that day by treating the ark of the covenant as though it were a magical wand. They can simply wave this ancient and sacred object in front of Yahweh and have instant success before their enemies. But the sins of Eli are not being addressed, and God cannot be manipulated. Presumably, these are the same "elders of Israel" who later unwisely request a king when Samuel grew old (8:4–5).

The reference to "the ark of the covenant of the LORD Almighty, who is enthroned between the cherubim" is a tacit condemnation of these actions. The elders and people of Israel assume they have lost the battle because Yahweh was not present with them. By fetching the ark, they want to ensure that Yahweh will indeed go with them into battle, and they think the presence of this religious symbol will ensure victory.

What is the ark of the covenant, and why do the elders of Israel think it will bring them luck? Construction of the ark was commissioned at Mount Sinai along with the other furnishings for the tabernacle (Ex. 25:10–22). The ark was simply a wooden rectangular box, less than four feet long, covered with gold. On top were two winged creatures ("cherubim") facing each other, with their outstretched wings touching at the tips across the top of the box. The ark served a practical function as a depository for certain other sacred objects. Initially it housed only the covenant tablets from Mount Sinai (Ex. 25:16), but eventually it also contained a portion of manna as well as Aaron's rod (Heb. 9:4).

But the powerful imagery of the ark is due to its understanding in ancient Israel as the visible sign of the presence of Yahweh. As the narrator states in 4:4, Yahweh is "enthroned between the cherubim."[6] The ark serves as Yahweh's footstool or podium (1 Chron. 28:2; Ps. 99:5; 132:7). Its top is the divine throne itself, and the cherubim flanking the throne may reflect Canaanite royal thrones in which winged sphinxes were used.[7] For the Israelite people, this box symbolizes the very presence of Yahweh.

---

6. Apparently the full name of the ark was "the ark of the covenant of the LORD Almighty, who is enthroned between the cherubim" (4:4). The title "LORD Almighty" (lit., "Yahweh of hosts") became prominent in the Jerusalem cult (see, e.g., Ps. 24), as did the concept that Yahweh was enthroned on the cherubim (Isa. 37:14–16; cf. also Ps. 99:1–3).

7. That is, the invisible Yahweh is perceived as a seated monarch with sphinxes on either side (Frank Moore Cross, *Canaanite Myth and Hebrew Epic: Essays in the History of the Religion of Israel* [Cambridge, Mass.: Harvard Univ. Press, 1973], 69; McCarter, *I Samuel*, 105–6). Recent

As a symbol of God's presence, the ark also came to have a significant military function. When Moses led the Israelite nation away from Mount Sinai for the first time, the ark led them through the desert as a means of protection and guidance. Whenever the ark marched before the nation on a new venture, Moses would say, "Rise up, O LORD! May your enemies be scattered; may your foes flee before you" (Num. 10:35). On one particularly memorable occasion, the ark served an important military function as part of Israel's holy war against the inhabitants of the Promised Land. Yahweh instructed Joshua to give the ark a prominent role in the capture of Jericho (Josh. 6:4, 6–7). The dramatic success on that day surely must have created vivid images of military triumph, which would have been attached to the ark of the covenant.

The elders and people of Israel long for that success and presumably think they can re-create the circumstances of holy war used so effectively in Joshua's day. They unfortunately view the ark as an infallible talisman or a military palladium that ensures victory.[8] In this way, they hope to guarantee Yahweh's presence in battle and assure success. But what they fail to realize is that "if God willed defeat for his people, a thousand arks would not bring success."[9]

The subtle reference in 4:4b is a reminder that this is not holy war: "And Eli's two sons, Hophni and Phinehas, were there with the ark of the covenant of God." Far from an intrusive or irrelevant historical note, the narrator reminds the reader that along with the ark come the wicked sons of Eli. As long as this situation persists, Yahweh will not bless Israel's wars, and the ark will not serve a military role. The presence of such wicked priests (2:22–25)

---

scholarship has refined our understanding of the religious symbolism of the ark. Early Israel was not simply iconoclastic (rejecting images of God), as certain later biblical passages seem to imply. Rather, Israel appears to have shared a common ancient Near Eastern "aniconism," in which the divine *is* visually represented, albeit without pictorial images, whether human or animal. The use of a standing stone or a stone pillar to represent a god is "material aniconism," whereas "empty-space aniconism" uses a throne or pedestal to indicate the presence of the divinity. Israel's ark of the covenant is a close example of the latter, the cherubim serving as a throne for the invisible Yahweh (Ex. 25:22). Tryggve N. D. Mettinger, *No Graven Image? Israelite Aniconism in Its Ancient Near Eastern Context* (ConBOT 42; Stockholm: Almqvist & Wiksell, 1995), esp. 18–20; Theodore J. Lewis, "Divine Images and Aniconism in Ancient Israel," *JAOS* 118 (1998): 36–53.

8. The ark "was conceived of as the battle station from which Yahweh, the divine warrior, the creator of the divine armies, fought for Israel." The march of the ark before the armies of Israel "occupied a place of importance both in the ritual of holy war and in the conceptualization underlying it." Patrick D. Miller Jr., *The Divine Warrior in Early Israel* (HSM 5; Cambridge, Mass.: Harvard Univ. Press, 1973), 158.

9. Youngblood, "1, 2 Samuel," 595.

with the ark of the covenant is incompatible with the presence of Yahweh. In Hannah, God found a worthy woman he could afford to bless (ch. 1). In contrast, the nation now appears incapable of bearing God's blessing; they have in a sense precluded those blessings because of their sins.

The Ark of the Covenant Arrives (4:5–9)

LIKE THE IMPRESSIVE victory at Jericho, the Israelites hope a mighty war cry combined with the presence of the ark of the covenant will do the trick (Josh. 6:5, 20). Their earth-shattering outcry alarms the Philistines, who have heard of the Israelite deity and what he did to the Egyptians (1 Sam. 4:8). Ironically, the Philistines prove to be more adept at interpreting Israelite history than the Israelites themselves. While Israel draws the wrong conclusion from Joshua's victory at Jericho, the uncircumcised Philistines see the implications of Moses' plagues and the miraculous deliverance from Egypt. They may be limited by pagan polytheism, but the Philistines understand that Israel's God is more powerful than anything they have ever experienced. Note 4:7: "We're in trouble! Nothing like this has happened before." Unfortunately, Israel has become negligent in its worship of this miracle-working God. The sins of Shiloh will not be overcome by mimicking the successes of yesteryear.

Strangely, the fear and alarm caused by the Israelite war cry arouses the Philistines to fight even harder (4:9). Whereas Joshua's war cry caused the walls of Jericho to fall down immediately (Josh. 6:20), the Israelite battle cry here has the effect of strengthening the enemy's resolve. Rather than securing victory, Israel's attempt to re-create ancient holy war ensures their defeat. Furthermore, in genuine holy war, "terror" precedes the Israelite army to soften the enemy and to make victory possible (Deut. 11:25). Here, however, when the Israelites try to terrorize the Philistines in their own strength, their contrived dread has the reverse effect, making it possible for the enemy to muster the necessary strength for battle (1 Sam. 4:9).

The Capture of the Ark (4:10–11)

IN THESE TWO BRIEF VERSES, the extreme consequences of Israel's stratagems become apparent. The Philistines are emboldened for the battle, Israel suffers enormous losses, the ark of the covenant is captured, and Eli's sons die!

The loss of thirty thousand ground infantry is indeed a "very great" slaughter. However, we should be sensitive to the hyperbolic way in which ancient Israelite authors used numbers. The loss of four thousand soldiers in 4:2 may well be a metaphoric statement for an excessively large number of military casualties, something often expressed by 400, 4,000, or 40,000.[10] The appalling number of Israelite losses recorded here may be part of what has recently been described as "a rhetorical device common in ancient Near Eastern literature," specifically, the use of large numbers as figures of speech in theologically based narratives.[11]

What a shock this second defeat must have been! The presence of the ark would allegedly guarantee Yahweh's presence, and the Israelites presumed his presence also guaranteed military victory. Now, however, there is only one possible conclusion. Their defeat at the hands of the Philistines is not a result simply of Yahweh's absence, but rather of their own spiritual crisis. The second loss and the capture of the ark of the covenant mean the defeat can only be understood as the will of Yahweh.[12] The losses of 4:1b–11 are due to a theological crisis in Israelite society that goes far beyond a failed military strategy. Their earlier military defeat did not occur because Yahweh was absent from Israel's midst. On the contrary, he was chastening his people because of their moral and ethical failures at Shiloh. If God is now absent from their midst on the battlefield—despite the presence of the ark of the covenant—it is because they have driven him away by breaking the covenant.

Since the purpose of an original ark narrative was presumably to glorify the ark itself, the original telling of this story may have made no attempt to identify the causes of Israel's defeat at the hands of the Philistines.[13] But as the text now stands in the canon, the arrangement of the materials makes it clear that the causes of the defeat are to be found in the failure of the Elide priesthood, even if not stated unequivocally.[14] The culmination of Samuel's prophecy in chapter 3 and its acceptance by Eli, along with 4:12–22, which relate the death of Eli and the final closure of his priestly line, remove all doubt: Israel lost this war with the Philistines because of the wickedness of Eli and his sons.

Furthermore, the absence of the prophet Samuel in this pericope strikes a deafening silence. His introduction in chapter 3 as the new means of divine

---

10. J. B. Segal, "Numerals in the Old Testament," *JSS* 10 (1965): 12; John W. Wenham, "Large Numbers in the Old Testament," *TynBul* 18 (1967): 19–53, esp. 30–32.

11. David M. Fouts, "A Defense of the Hyperbolic Interpretation of Large Numbers in the Old Testament," *JETS* 40 (1997): 387.

12. Brueggemann, *First and Second Samuel*, 32.

13. As argued long ago by the scholar who first isolated the ark narrative; cf. Leonhard Rost, *The Succession to the Throne of David* (Sheffield: Almond, 1982), 6–34; trans. of *Die Überlieferung von der Thronnachfolge Davids* (Stuttgart: W. Kohlhammer, 1926); see Patrick D. Miller Jr. and J. J. M. Roberts, *The Hand of the Lord: A Reassessment of the "Ark Narrative" of 1 Samuel* (Baltimore: John Hopkins Univ. Press, 1977).

14. Robert P. Gordon, *1 and 2 Samuel* (OTG; Sheffield: Sheffield Academic Press, 1984), 32.

revelation in Israel makes his disappearance here significant, symbolizing Israel's presumption. In a way that anticipates Saul's failures and David's strengths, the Israelites fail to consult and heed the prophetic voice available to them.

Bridging Contexts

INTERPRETING MILITARY VICTORY. In order to build an interpretive bridge to our context, it is necessary to address the way military victory was interpreted in the Old Testament as a sign of God's blessing. In Exodus 17, Yahweh blessed Moses and the Israelites with victory over the Amalekites, dramatically authenticated by the elevation of "the rod of God." As long as Moses held up the rod, with the help of Aaron and Hur, Israel prevailed (17:8–16). Military success was obviously linked to Yahweh's blessing in the time of Joshua (Josh. 6–8), and King David came to be viewed as the ideal king partially because Yahweh blessed him with military success (2 Sam. 7:1). Many more examples could be given. The gloomy question of the elders of Israel here reflects the agonizing theological dilemma presented by the first defeat at the hands of the Philistines. Where have they gone wrong? What can they do to reverse their military fortunes?

Historically, these events come near the conclusion of Israel's judges period. There is no king yet in Israel, though the kingmaker, Samuel, is now in preparation. The nation is still under the tribal confederation known from the book of Judges. In that context, we have come to expect certain patterns of behavior concerning warfare (see Judg. 2:10–23). The formula cited there had four ingredients.[15] (1) Israel sinned against Yahweh: "The Israelites did evil in the eyes of the LORD." (2) Yahweh then gave them over into the power of an enemy nation: "The LORD handed them over to raiders who plundered them." (3) This foreign oppression led the people to repent: "But when the Israelites cried out to the LORD...." (4) Finally, Yahweh sent a judge to deliver them: "The LORD raised up judges, who saved them out of the hands of these raiders." This picture is a straightforward interpretation of Israelite history based on Deuteronomy's retribution theology: Faithfulness to the covenant meant success, but failure to live for God meant defeat.

Thus, early in the book of Judges, the Israelites recognized that military failure was linked to their sin, and they turned to the Lord in repentance. With repentance came military deliverance. But the book of Judges also traces a

---

15. The number of components in this literary framework may be analyzed in different ways. See K. Lawson Younger Jr., *Judges and Ruth* (NIVAC; Grand Rapids; Zondervan, 2002), 35.

slow moral deterioration, which is illustrated by the gradual unraveling of this literary cycle. By the time of the Philistine domination in Judges 13, the reader becomes convinced that the system of the judges is not working and Israel is no longer repentant.[16] In the final unit of the book (Judg. 17–21), when everyone is doing what is right in his own eyes, decisions are based not on principle but on pragmatism.

In this historical and literary context, the narrative of 1 Samuel 4 contributes to the continuing moral decline. Here the elders of Israel appear bewildered and confused by the Philistine victory. But rather than leading the people in national repentance, they make other arrangements. The ill-fated decision to bring the ark of the covenant to the battle line is apparently an attempt to re-create the holy wars of Moses and Joshua. As such, it is a futile exercise in self-dependence. Military victory is viewed as dependent on the Israelite ability to arouse the wrath and power of Yahweh to inflict defeat on his enemies. This is neither the repentance of the early portions of the book of Judges nor the holy war of Joshua. This is a manipulative attempt to determine the outcome of battle for self-preservation.

The expression "holy war" is not used in the Old Testament. It was introduced by modern scholars to designate certain wars of the Israelites that were unique to their specific cultural and historical circumstances. Such wars were endorsed and directed by Yahweh. He initiated the conflict and ensured its success. Such sacral wars, or "Yahweh wars," were often preceded by religious rituals, such as sacrifices or even circumcision. The Israelites marched into these wars with reduced numbers and less-effective weaponry. God called on them to take action and participate in some way (shouting, marching, proceeding behind the ark of the covenant), but he was the important participant, fighting on behalf of the nation. The victory was often celebrated in songs of praise to Yahweh. Furthermore, all spoil of such wars was strictly devoted to Yahweh; nothing could be held by the victorious Israelites, as though they had won the prize. Everything and everyone captured was under the "ban" (*ḥerem*, totally devoted to Yahweh) and had to be destroyed.[17] Continued military successes were contingent on continued obedience. The failure at Jericho to devote all the plunder to Yahweh resulted in the defeat at Ai (Josh. 7).

The events in 1 Samuel 4 are related to Israel's sacred rites of war. This is particularly clear from the reference in verse 5 to the "great shout," a war cry

---

16. Ibid., 34–43.

17. Tremper Longman III and Daniel G. Reid, *God Is a Warrior* (SOTBT; Grand Rapids: Zondervan, 1995), 32–47; Patrick D. Miller Jr., *The Divine Warrior;* Gerhard von Rad, *Holy War in Ancient Israel,* trans. Marva J. Dawn (Grand Rapids: Eerdmans, 1991), 41–51.

typical of holy war in the Old Testament (see Josh. 6:5).[18] The elders of Israel find an answer to their question of verse 3 ("Why did the LORD bring defeat upon us... ?") in the ancient traditions of holy war, especially as practiced under the leadership of Joshua. They see the Philistines as God's enemies and worthy of extermination, just like the people of Jericho. The Israelites see themselves as ensuring victory by imitating what worked in the past.

Unfortunately, the situations are not comparable. Yahweh has not initiated this conflict as in holy wars. While the Israelites are correct in seeking a religious explanation for their defeat, their chosen course of action to secure help from Yahweh is misguided. Instead of remorse and repentance, they attempt to compel Yahweh into providing victory regardless of the unacceptable leadership at Shiloh. This is a shameful attempt at manipulation— an effort to use Yahweh's sacred presence for purposes of self-preservation, despite the irreligious leadership at Shiloh. Little wonder the Philistine wars of 1 Samuel 4 are doomed to failure.

THE CHRISTIAN AND WAR. So what of the Bible's understanding of holy war? The twenty-first century opened tragically with extremists in the Middle East calling for *jihad* or modern holy war.[19] After the attacks on the World Trade Center and the Pentagon on September 11, 2001, some in America spoke of our military response as though it were a holy war, while the country debated whether the United States was waging a "just war" in Afghanistan.[20] Does 1 Samuel 4 inform a balanced Christian response to armed conflict, especially in cases in which war seems unavoidable? How should today's Christians respond to conflict?

It would be easy to use this account of war between the Philistines and the Israelites to discuss Christian reactions to violence in general. But the passage raises questions that are much more specific in application and that involve issues debated for centuries by Christians. The Israelites assumed in verse 3 that God was on their side and they only had to guarantee his presence in the battle to secure victory. Likewise, the Philistines believed the gods were actively involved in both sides of armed conflict. All of this surely stems from the ancient Near Eastern assumption that each nation's deity was

---

18. Von Rad, *Holy War*, 48.

19. Roland Jacquard, "The Guidebook of Jihad," *Time* 158, no. 19 (Oct. 29, 2001): 58; Jeffery L. Sheler, "Alive in the Presence of their Lord," *U.S. News & World Report* 131, no. 13 (Oct. 1, 2001): 38.

20. Ann Scott Tyson, "Weighing War in Afghanistan on a Moral Scale," *Christian Science Monitor* 93, no. 228 (Oct. 19, 2001): 3.

responsible for the outcome of wars. A defeated nation must have had an inferior deity!

How does this relate to modern Christians' attitudes to armed warfare? How should followers of Christ react to armed conflict? What about warfare between nations in today's world? What is a Christian response? Christians succeed in avoiding this topic until forced to deal with international conflicts. Most of us give little thought to the question until confronted with hard choices, in which case we are ill-prepared to give a reasoned response. Through the ages, well-meaning, conscientious Christians have responded to war in one of three ways, each of which is incompatible with the others: war as crusade, pacifism, and justifiable war.[21]

(1) Some believers have considered war as a crusade of good against evil. This was certainly Israel's understanding of nearly all her wars, and it is not surprising in light of the use of holy war early in her history. But as we see in this episode, war is seldom so simply defined as God's people versus God's enemies. Nor is this view of warfare limited to "the Crusades," in which the church conceived of itself as the representative of God on earth and from this premise drew the tragic and misguided conclusion that there was no greater glory than to fight infidels and heretics for God (A.D. 1096–1272).[22] Rather, nearly every war in history has produced soldiers guilty of horrible atrocities against humanity, which are often defended as acceptable behavior due to the wickedness of the enemy.

By definition, crusaders tend to view certain wars as struggles of absolute good against absolute evil, and therefore they seek to pursue absolute and unlimited goals in the struggle. As a result, crusaders seek the unqualified and unrestricted destruction of the wicked enemy. The very "rightness" of their cause leaves no restrictions on the means of the war, and they sometimes advocate slaughter of the enemy as though God has no concern for them.[23]

---

21. For what follows here, see Joseph L. Allen, *War: A Primer for Christians* (Nashville: Abingdon, 1991). For more detail on these issues, see Joseph L. Allen, *Love and Conflict: A Covenantal Model of Christian Ethics* (Nashville: Abingdon, 1984); Roland H. Bainton, *Christian Attitudes toward War and Peace: A Historical Survey and Critical Re-evaluation* (New York: Abingdon, 1960); Paul Ramsey, *The Just War: Force and Political Responsibility* (New York: Scribners, 1968); Michael Walzer, *Just and Unjust Wars: A Moral Argument with Historical Illustrations* (New York: Basic Books, 1977).

22. Not only the Muslims suffered. Thousands of Jews in Europe were slaughtered by Crusaders on their way to the Holy Land. See Chaim Potok, *Wanderings: Chaim Potok's History of the Jews* (New York: Fawcett Crest, 1978), 400–407.

23. Lt. General George S. Patton was noted for making shocking statements in his campaign against the Nazis during World War II. For example, on Christmas Day, 1944, he wrote in his diary as follows: "A clear, cold Christmas, lovely weather for killing Germans, which seems a bit queer, seeing Whose birthday it is" (Gerald Astor, *A Blood-Dimmed Tide: The Battle of the Bulge by the Men Who Fought It* [New York: Bantam Doubleday Dell, 1992], 325).

Such an approach expects holy war will result in the perfect conditions of a world utopia. This position is obviously not acceptable for Christians, though it has been adopted in various settings in church history.

(2) Christian pacifists believe that war is always wrong, under any conditions. In general, there are two types of Christian pacifists: pragmatic pacifists and witnessing pacifists.[24] (a) The pragmatic pacifist argues that nonviolent resistance "works" and, given enough time, will produce better results than war, even on the international level. Pragmatic pacifists often cite as examples of the effectiveness of nonviolent resistance Mahatma Gandhi's nonviolent campaign for Indian independence and Dr. Martin Luther King Jr.'s leadership, particularly in the Montgomery bus boycott of 1955–1956.

But pragmatic pacifism has come under considerable criticism in the Christian community. It fails to recognize the depth of human sin, and its practical outcome is a moral preference for tyranny over war. The pragmatic pacifist argues that tyranny will implode whenever it meets nonviolent or passive resistance but is only increased and polarized by a violent response. But experience teaches that unresisted tyranny in fact grows and spreads, threatening to become global. Others have objected that pragmatic pacifists significantly overestimate the effectiveness of nonviolence. But perhaps most telling of all has been the criticism that the supposed nonresistance commanded in the New Testament is quite different from nonviolent resistance. The principle in Matthew 5:39, "Do not resist one who is evil," appears to be an ethic that seeks no success in power struggles, while the pragmatic pacifist claims to win the power struggle by nonviolent means.[25]

(b) The witnessing pacifist, by contrast, contends that war is always immoral regardless of whether it produces better consequences. War is simply incompatible with Christian discipleship, and a refusal to participate in violence is the only proper Christian witness.[26] Agreeing that nonviolence often produces superior results, nonetheless, the witnessing pacifist acknowledges this may not always be the case. The desired outcome, however, is not power or success but obedience to Christ's law of love.[27]

---

24. Allen, *War*, 20–23.

25. See the criticisms of Reinhold Niebuhr, *Moral Man and Immoral Society* (New York: Scribners, 1932), 231–56, and others of Niebuhr's writings; see summary in Allen, *War*, 25.

26. Allen, *War*, 21–23; for the best presentation of witnessing pacifism, see John H. Yoder, *The Politics of Jesus* (Grand Rapids: Eerdmans, 1972), 115–34, 233–50.

27. Some pacifists appear to use both pragmatic and witnessing arguments. This was apparently Dr. Martin Luther King Jr.'s approach in his campaign for racial justice in the 1950s and 1960s; see his *Stride Toward Freedom: The Montgomery Story* (New York: Harper & Row, 1958), 101–7, 213–24.

All Christians everywhere should appreciate the emphasis of the witnessing pacifists on a radical commitment to Jesus and Christian discipleship. However, Christians are not agreed on the definition of Christian love at this point. If love is primarily defined as covenant faithfulness to our neighbors, many believe there are times when war is the only answer to tyranny. Moreover, it is possible to argue that a refusal to intervene on behalf of those suffering under tyrannical oppression means Christians bear responsibility for the evil inflicted on innocent victims. Though I believe the witnessing pacifist position is inadequate, I think we should always take seriously the arguments and recognize differences in the way various members of the church define love and Christian responsibility.

(3) The third approach to war is the just-war tradition. Since the end of Roman persecution of Christians in the early fourth century A.D., many Christians began to believe that the use of force was justifiable for the state under certain conditions. Ambrose and Augustine in the late fourth and early fifth centuries formulated the first Christian definitions of justifiable war.[28] Much of modern Christian thinking is still dependent on their early formulations. During most of modern history, just-war thinking received less attention until the years leading up to and including the Second World War. With the rise of technological advancements in warfare during the second half of the twentieth century, this question has taken on new importance for Christians, who are responsible to formulate in advance our beliefs on the issue in an effort to have an impact on our society and participate in forming policy.

Just-war doctrine is based on the covenant relationship between God and his creation, which emphasizes the value of all human life.[29] Further, this position admits the prevalence of evil and the persistence of human conflict in the world. Particularly, the abusive and unjust oppression of poorer or weaker neighbors, whether individually inflicted or nationally, calls for responsible Christian reactions. The just-war position teaches that *sometimes* the Christian's respect for human life calls for the use of force to protect and defend victims from their attackers. But motivation is determinative, as Augustine argued. Such action must not arise out of selfish desire but must be the result of desire to help other people. It is not a work of love, just-war thinkers argue, to turn the cheek of another person so they may be struck a second time.

Over the years, Christian just-war thinkers have developed a set of criteria to help determine when armed conflict is justifiable and when it is not. Though there are various lists of criteria, in general they include several

---

28. Allen, *War*, 31.
29. Ibid., 32–33.

of the following principles.[30] Primary among these criteria is the need to establish "just cause," in that an egregious wrong has been committed or is about to be committed. Usually this involves an unjust attack on a group of innocent or helpless victims, rights that have been revoked unjustly, or the annulment of a just political order. Also, it must be clear that armed intervention is the last resort to resolution, after every peaceful alternative has been eliminated. Other criteria include "legitimate authority" ("Who should decide?"), a clear "declaration" of war aims, and "proportionality" (the idea that the evil effects of war should not exceed the evil to be prevented by going to war). Others sometimes mentioned are reasonable chance of success and right intention. Though it is not necessary that every criterion be present before armed conflict is justified, some combination of these will, it is hoped, avoid the use of war in a way that just-war thinkers would deem unchristian.

The Old Testament has often been abused in the debates on pacifism versus just war. We should remember that Israelite holy war was a unique, unrepeatable phenomenon. Modern believers are never presented with situations that compare to Israel's holy wars. It is illegitimate for North American Christians to appeal to the Old Testament for support of any armed conflict. Conversely, it is not legitimate to use Old Testament narrative material to illustrate the unchristian practice of crusading against God's enemies. The Old Testament presents multifaceted perspectives on war, and the assemblage of cultural and historical conditions surrounding most of those wars are in no way related to most modern conflicts.

This episode between Israel and the Philistines in 1 Samuel 4 presents us with a picture of Israelites who refused to repent of sin and acknowledge national responsibility for guilt. In this case, warfare was unavoidable, and it would have been an opportunity for repentance and dependence on God for deliverance. This had been the experience of the Israelites throughout the judges period. Armed conflict had given rise to occasions of tribal (and sometimes even national) sorrow for sin and turning to God. But in this episode, military defeat broke their presumption. They simply assumed they were in the right, and they failed to consult God (note again the absence of Samuel here). They trusted the *means* of their covenant relationship (the ark of the covenant) rather than the *God* of that relationship. They attempted to use holy-war shortcuts in order to manipulate God, which is another symptom of their spiritual decay. What is missing in all of this is genuine repentance (see 7:2—4).

---

30. Ibid., 36.

Similarly in modern America, Christians must beware of the presumption that "God is on our side."[31] Such sentiment implies we are a righteous nation, which regularly recognizes guilt and sin and has repented and turned to God. The Allied forces during the Second World War were, I believe, certainly justified in their armed resistance of the Axis nations. The heroic accolades being heaped on the World War II generation during the closing decades of the twentieth century were, I believe, justified, even overdue. Their heroic efforts were required to defeat Nazism and Fascism.

But America's past in successfully engaging in justified wars is no guarantee that she is right in all her military actions, any more so than Israel could presume that Yahweh was going to provide victory against the Philistines. At the end of the day, it is the responsibility of individual Christians to hold the government responsible for any actions taken on behalf of the nation. In every case, occasions of armed conflict should also be occasions of repentance and turning to God for forgiveness for sin and injustice in our own society. This was ultimately Israel's mistake, and it certainly serves as a warning for believers living in modern America.

Moreover, this passage has a message for more general kinds of conflict involving Christians, not just armed military warfare among nations. Anytime someone confronts us or attacks our character, we should humbly seek to determine whether we have acted presumptuously or failed to seek God's will. The Israelites failed to acknowledge their sin and guilt and acted as though God were obligated to favor them in their war with the Philistines.

Sometimes Christians assume an arrogant posture of righteousness in the face of opposition. But we must remember that Christ seeks followers who humbly acknowledge that we have no righteousness apart from our relationship with him. Living for Jesus does not mean we are always right or that we will always "win." Sometimes we will need correction and the discipline provided by others. Unlike the Israelites in this passage, we must never assume that God owes us something or that we can control the outcome of personal conflict by appealing to our relationship with God. After all, our life with God is all of grace and depends not one bit on our own merit.

---

31. After World War II, my father brought home a belt buckle from a German uniform. It bears the chilling inscription, *Gott mit uns,* "God is with us."

1 Samuel 4:12-22

THAT SAME DAY a Benjamite ran from the battle line and went to Shiloh, his clothes torn and dust on his head. ¹³When he arrived, there was Eli sitting on his chair by the side of the road, watching, because his heart feared for the ark of God. When the man entered the town and told what had happened, the whole town sent up a cry.

¹⁴Eli heard the outcry and asked, "What is the meaning of this uproar?"

The man hurried over to Eli, ¹⁵who was ninety-eight years old and whose eyes were set so that he could not see. ¹⁶He told Eli, "I have just come from the battle line; I fled from it this very day."

Eli asked, "What happened, my son?"

¹⁷The man who brought the news replied, "Israel fled before the Philistines, and the army has suffered heavy losses. Also your two sons, Hophni and Phinehas, are dead, and the ark of God has been captured."

¹⁸When he mentioned the ark of God, Eli fell backward off his chair by the side of the gate. His neck was broken and he died, for he was an old man and heavy. He had led Israel forty years.

¹⁹His daughter-in-law, the wife of Phinehas, was pregnant and near the time of delivery. When she heard the news that the ark of God had been captured and that her father-in-law and her husband were dead, she went into labor and gave birth, but was overcome by her labor pains. ²⁰As she was dying, the women attending her said, "Don't despair; you have given birth to a son." But she did not respond or pay any attention.

²¹She named the boy Ichabod, saying, "The glory has departed from Israel"—because of the capture of the ark of God and the deaths of her father-in-law and her husband. ²²She said, "The glory has departed from Israel, for the ark of God has been captured."

THE ACCOUNT OF THE HEAVY LOSSES at the hands of the Philistines and, more importantly, the capture of the ark of the covenant are followed by two related episodes: the death of Eli (4:12–18) and the birth of Ichabod (4:19–22). The first event is directly related to the military defeat and brings closure to elements of the Shiloh narrative in 1 Samuel 1–3. The second is another birth narrative. But unlike the birth narrative of Samuel in chapter 1, this account does not introduce a new period in Israel's history but rather the end of the previous era.

The accounts of Eli's death and Ichabod's birth together serve an important role in the narrative. The prophetic condemnation of Eli's family line has been firmly established by the words of the anonymous "man of God" in 2:27–36 and Samuel's words in 3:11–14. This passage narrates the dramatic confirmation of those divine pronouncements. The punishment against Hophni and Phinehas (4:11) now affects two additional generations.[1] Their father, the elderly Eli, dies at the news from the battlefield, and Phinehas's son, Ichabod, is deprived of his grandfather, uncle, father, and mother—all in a single day, the day of his birth.

The Death of Eli (4:12–18)

ON THE FATEFUL day in which the Philistines capture the ark, a runner comes to Shiloh with appropriate signs of distress: torn clothes and dust on his head (4:12). The messenger's pitiable report contains four parts building in climactic fashion (4:17). First, the Israelite army has been put to flight before the Philistines. Then he reports the news of heavy casualties. Third, Eli's own sons are both dead. Finally, the ark of God has been captured. We are not told of Eli's reaction to the first three pieces of news. But at the mention of the ark's capture, he falls, and because of his advanced age and great girth, he does not survive the fall. The narrator intends us to understand that Eli is practically unaffected by the news of his sons' deaths, supposing that he has given up on them as hopeless.

The Birth of Ichabod (4:19–22)

THE BIRTH AND naming of Ichabod appears to be patterned by the narrator after the birth of Benjamin to Rachel (Gen. 35:16–19). When read in this way, this pericope is significant not only for Ichabod's name (see below) but also because of the contrast between his birth and Benjamin's. As here, Rachel's midwife tried to comfort the mother by assuring her that she is giving birth

---

1. Robert D. Bergen, *1, 2 Samuel* (NAC 7; Nashville: Broadman & Holman, 1996) 93.

to a son. Also like this passage, Rachel names her son with her dying breath. But in this case, the wife of Phinehas seems to draw no comfort from the fact that she is delivering a son: "She did not respond or pay any attention" (4:20). She is so overcome by the loss of the ark that she can take no comfort in the birth of a son, an event that would otherwise be the highest joy for an Israelite woman. The fact that Yahweh is no longer present with Israel on the battlefield leads to the strange name of Eli's new grandson.

The name "Ichabod" requires explanation. It uses a form of the Hebrew negative so rare that it leaves the precise meaning of the name somewhat in doubt. The negative particle (ʾi-) is prefixed to the ordinary term for "glory" (*kabod*), so that the name presumably means "no glory." Since this negative particle is used more frequently in other Semitic languages (particularly Phoenician), we can be reasonably certain of its meaning, which is supported by the context. However, another possibility is that the prefixed particle introduces a question (paralleled in Ugaritic) and that the name really means, "Where is the glory?"[2]

In any case, Ichabod's mother is acknowledging the central role played by the ark in Israel's history. Yahweh's glory filled the tabernacle as the culminating moment in the desert at Mount Sinai (Ex. 40:34–35). The significance of his "tabernacling" or "dwelling" (Heb. *škn*) in the midst of his people later gave rise to the postbiblical theological term "Shekinah-glory," which designated God's own presence with his people. The ark of the covenant was the visible sign of Yahweh's presence. Its top was the divine throne itself, since he was "enthroned between the cherubim" (4:4, see comments). It was the most visible and powerful symbol of Israel's covenant relationship with Yahweh (cf. Ex. 25:10–22; 37:1–9). The loss of the ark was such a startling and sad event that this young mother can only wonder what glory there is in Israel and what hope there will be for her new son.

The use of repetition in 4:21–22 reveals the narrator's concern. He is afraid we may misunderstand Ichabod's mother and the true source of her distress in this, her moment of death. She sees no glory left to Israel because of the capture of "the ark of God" in addition to the deaths of her father-in-law and husband (4:21b). The focusing restatement of 4:22 removes all doubt: God's glory has departed from Israel because the "ark of God" has been captured. The phrase combining the ark of God and "captured, taken" (passive of *lqḥ*, "take") occurs five times in this chapter (4:11, 17, 19, 21, 22; cf. 5:1) and summarizes the initial content of the unit. With the capture of the sacred ark, "we reach a point in Israelite history lower than any since the captivity in Egypt."[3] The

---

2. McCarter, *I Samuel*, 115–16.
3. Hertzberg, *I and II Samuel*, 50.

loss of the ark is a moment of total despair, because it symbolizes the loss of Israel's unique covenant relationship with Yahweh and leaves her future in doubt. The narrator understands this; so do Eli and Ichabod's mother.

After this episode, Shiloh receives little attention. It is generally assumed that when the Philistines capture the ark, they also destroy the city, though the passage does not say this. For the narrator, the ark of God is more important than the physical remains of a worship center at Shiloh that once housed the ark. The narrative in 1 Samuel 1–3 implies that a semipermanent porch with doors and doorposts had been built at the entrance to the tabernacle in Shiloh.[4] Recent archaeological evidence seems to confirm that the Shiloh sanctuary was destroyed at the hands of the Philistines in the days of Eli, during the eleventh century B.C.[5] Another city that appears to play an important role during this period is Samuel's hometown of Ramah (1:19; 2:11; 7:17). It may have served as a new religious center after the fall of Shiloh. Some have even suggested the narratives of 1 Samuel 1–7 were compiled at Ramah.[6]

The significance of the fall of Shiloh was not lost on subsequent generations. This sanctuary had served as a central worship place for the early Israelites, housing the most sacred of worship articles, the ark of the covenant. But the town stood now as an example for future Israelites that Yahweh's grace and favor are conditioned on continued obedience and submission to his will. Jeremiah particularly interpreted the city of Shiloh as an object lesson for his audiences in Jerusalem. The town of Shiloh, though still inhabited in Jeremiah's day (Jer. 41:5), stood as a testimony against those in Jerusalem who felt that the great city of David was indestructible because it housed the temple. Jeremiah invited his fellow citizens to journey to Shiloh to see for themselves what Yahweh had done to the place where long ago he first made a dwelling for his name and where the ark of the covenant had been housed (7:12, 14; 26:6, 9).

THE NATURE OF **divine judgment.** God's verdict on Eli's sons seemed irrevocable. The narrative of 1 Samuel has presented two prophetic condemnations of the Elide priestly family prior to the military debacle of the Philistine battles in 1 Samuel 4. The anonymous "man

---

4. Keil and Delitzsch, *Samuel*, 23, 50–51.

5. Israel Finkelstein, *The Archaeology of the Israelite Settlement* (Jerusalem: Israel Exploration Society, 1988), 228–32; idem, "Excavations at Shiloh 1981–1984, Preliminary Report," *TA* 12 (1985): 123–80.

6. John T. Willis, "An Anti-Elide Narrative Traditiony," 307.

of God" announced that God repealed his previous commitment to Eli's house because of the sins of Hophni and Phinehas, so that their priestly line would not continue (2:30–33). The young Samuel was the instrument of the second prophetic word, in which God renounced the sons of Eli as well as Eli's own failure to discipline and control them (3:11–14). Now chapter 4 identifies the losses at the hands of the Philistines as the fulfillment of those prophecies. The narrative has marched inexorably forward from prophetic word to historical fulfillment. Eli will be the last old man of his line, and even the birth of his grandson is marred by ignoble loss.

The connection between national humiliation at the hands of the Philistines and the judgment of Eli's house in 1 Samuel 4 has surprisingly broadened the sweep of the judgment. Though the earlier condemnations highlighted the guilt of Eli and his sons, this unit shows that ultimately it is the nation itself that suffers the consequences and, to some degree, bears responsibility. The judgment extends to the entire people of Israel, the people whom Eli was called and consecrated to serve.[7]

Both Eli and Ichabod's mother understand the scale and significance of the judgment. Their reactions to the devastating news show that both see the catastrophic implications of the loss of the ark. Eli's reaction is so immediate and calamitous that it leaves him no time to respond (4:18). The young woman articulates the scope of God's judgment with the name "Ichabod" and the subsequent statement, "The glory has departed from Israel" (4:21–22). This unnamed (and unfortunate) character gives voice to the narrator's concerns: God is gone! He has departed. More precisely, he has been driven away by the sins of his own people, especially the Elide priesthood. And his judgment is not limited to the few individuals condemned in the prophetic pronouncements, as the defeat at the hands of the Philistines demonstrates. Indeed, the people of Israel bear the responsibility for the crimes of Hophni and Phinehas, just as they also permitted (or endorsed) their iniquitous behavior.

The Bible has plenty to say about judgment—from the curses of the Garden of Eden (Gen. 3:14–19), to the ominous warnings against covenant-breaking in Deuteronomy (Deut. 27:15–26; 28:15–68), to the prophetic condemnation of Jeroboam I and Manasseh in the books of Kings (2 Kings 17:21–23; 21:10–12; 23:26; 24:3–4). Nor can this be dismissed as an Old Testament aberration. Matthew concludes his version of the Olivet Discourse with the famous prediction that Christ will one day judge humankind, rewarding those who faithfully follow him but sending others into everlasting perdition (Matt. 25:31–46). Indeed, the judgment of God is central to

---

7. Brueggemann, *First and Second Samuel*, 32–33.

New Testament thought, without even appealing to the frightening apocalyptic sections of Revelation. But ironically, most of modern American culture, including much of twentieth-century evangelicalism, omits this ingredient of biblical revelation in its teaching and preaching.

This unit of 1 Samuel should instruct us about divine judgment. The portrait here is not of a God who is vindictive, who cruelly hammers unrepentant victims with random violence from heaven. Instead, as the nameless woman in 4:21–22 states, God is gone. He has reluctantly accepted the reality of Israel's sin and responded accordingly. Divine judgment, then, is not so much the *vengeful presence* of an angered God but the *imposed absence* of the loving and protecting God. He has been driven away by the sin of his people, and with his departure the nation also loses his grace.

This should come as no surprise to anyone reading the Old Testament closely. The book of Deuteronomy, for example, contains many warnings that in essence establish a principle of exile: If and when Israel drives away the sustaining presence of God, the nation will inevitably lose the land (Deut. 28:63; 29:27–28). Such punishment is the form the love of God takes in response to human sin and rebellion.

In a sense, this episode is the climactic moment of the judges period. As we have noted, during that period, the nation constantly fell into political and military anarchy as a result of sin. As the literary cycle recorded in Judges 2 illustrates, when Israel cried out to the Lord, God saved them from their adversaries. But in this episode, Israel does not cry out to the Lord, and so God is absent. The loss of the ark and the subsequent loss of the priestly line and presumably the religious center at Shiloh are visible consequences of the persistence of sin in national Israel.

GOD'S FAITHFULNESS TO HIS WORD. This unit brings into focus two important issues much needed in our contemporary context: the faithfulness of God to bring his Word to fruition and the judgment of God. The Old Testament historical books often delight in showing direct correspondence between a prophetic pronouncement and its subsequent fulfillment in the events narrated. This prophecy-fulfillment framework may even be considered a structural technique in the historical books. Prophets announce some imminent event, which is then fulfilled in a subsequent narrative.[8]

---

8. See, e.g., 1 Kings 13:2–3 and 2 Kings 23:16–18. For discussion and more examples, see Richard D. Nelson, *Historical Books*, 71–72.

As we have seen, the deaths of Eli and his sons had been announced by the anonymous "man of God" (2:30–33) and by the young Samuel (3:11–14). Chapter 4 then describes the nation's defeat at the hands of the Philistines, which leads us to this section on the death of Eli and his sons. The point of this prophecy-fulfillment pattern is that these events are divinely driven, that God's Word through his prophets is true, and that God's will is being accomplished in and through these events. Prophetic history marches with certainty from word to fulfillment. God's Word is to be trusted and his prophets believed.

God's faithfulness in his judgment. The significance of these timeless truths for today's audience lies not only in the concept of the comforting and assuring "promises of God" for Christians as we live alien lives in this increasingly hostile world. Rather, we should also hear the prophetic warning of divine judgment in this passage. God's prophetic word often warns of his intent to punish unrepentant sin as an expression of his love and holiness. In this particular text, Yahweh's goodness and love are evident not so much in his good gifts to his saints but in his faithfulness to punish and destroy those who oppose him in unrelenting disdain. His presence is gone; those left behind are "Ichabod"!

This feature of biblical revelation is often neglected or suppressed in many of today's Christian contexts. Such disregard for scriptural truth is illustrated best by our society's convictions on the existence of hell and the possibility of eternal perdition in contrast to that of only a few generations ago. Whereas hell was once accepted as a fact of life (or death!) and contributed to the cultural shaping of most nations in the West, it now occupies little serious attention in our culture generally, even among some Christian traditions. The dictum of Bertrand Russell, shocking for its time, has become a reality in today's church, let alone in contemporary society: "Hell is neither so certain nor as hot as it used to be."[9]

This text invites us to trace the trajectory of God's prophetic word of judgment through Scripture and history into today's world. As such the text must serve as a corrective to our disbelief. Despite the reticence of today's theologians and philosophers, scriptural authority and the testimony of the church place the doctrine of hell closer to the heart of traditional Christian belief than most want to admit. Indeed, it has recently been suggested that the doctrine of hell, at least in some form, is essential if Christianity is to avoid trivialization.[10]

---

9. Bertrand Russell, *Why I Am Not a Christian* (New York: Simon & Schuster, 1957), 195, quoted in Jerry L. Walls, *Hell: The Logic of Damnation* (Notre Dame, Ind.: Univ. of Notre Dame Press, 1992), 2.

10. Walls, *Hell*, 7–8.

Positively stated, a full-orbed appreciation of God's perfect goodness can only be defended if we hold it in balance with at least some traditional concept of hell. Furthermore, such an understanding of God's judgment as an element of his perfect goodness needs once again to play a role in the church's "moral pedagogy of our society."[11] For those of us who accept Scripture as the primary authority for our theology, the only alternatives are universalism or annihilationism. But these are unacceptable on both exegetical and philosophical grounds.[12]

This text provides a striking example of God's punishment of those for whom the choice of evil has become fully consistent, as when our historian characterized Eli's sons as "wicked men," who "had no regard for the LORD" (2:12). God responded by announcing through two prophetic messengers that those who despise him will be disdained (2:30) and that the guilt of Eli's house will not be atoned for by sacrifice or offering (3:14). When the choice of evil becomes decisive for an individual, it never "bottoms out," meaning there is little if any prospect for a return to good. This may at least be part of what is involved in the biblical metaphor of hell as a "bottomless pit."[13]

One leading Christian philosopher has argued that humans can come to choose evil so decisively that they deceive themselves into believing evil is good (or at least that it holds sufficient advantage over good), with the result that humans consistently and thoroughly prefer evil to good. Thus, hell comes to be preferred over heaven.[14] God's response to such persistent evil, narrated in this text, may serve as a corrective to contemporary views of sin, salvation, and the mercy of God.

---

11. Ibid., 157.
12. Ibid., 158–59.
13. Ibid., 120.
14. Ibid., 113–38.

1 Samuel 5:1–7:1

FTER THE PHILISTINES had captured the ark of God,
they took it from Ebenezer to Ashdod. ²Then they carried the ark into Dagon's temple and set it beside
Dagon. ³When the people of Ashdod rose early the next day,
there was Dagon, fallen on his face on the ground before the
ark of the LORD! They took Dagon and put him back in his
place. ⁴But the following morning when they rose, there was
Dagon, fallen on his face on the ground before the ark of the
LORD! His head and hands had been broken off and were lying
on the threshold; only his body remained. ⁵That is why to this
day neither the priests of Dagon nor any others who enter
Dagon's temple at Ashdod step on the threshold.

⁶The LORD's hand was heavy upon the people of Ashdod
and its vicinity; he brought devastation upon them and
afflicted them with tumors. ⁷When the men of Ashdod saw
what was happening, they said, "The ark of the god of Israel
must not stay here with us, because his hand is heavy upon us
and upon Dagon our god." ⁸So they called together all the
rulers of the Philistines and asked them, "What shall we do
with the ark of the god of Israel?"

They answered, "Have the ark of the god of Israel moved
to Gath." So they moved the ark of the God of Israel.

⁹But after they had moved it, the LORD's hand was against
that city, throwing it into a great panic. He afflicted the people of the city, both young and old, with an outbreak of
tumors. ¹⁰So they sent the ark of God to Ekron.

As the ark of God was entering Ekron, the people of Ekron
cried out, "They have brought the ark of the god of Israel
around to us to kill us and our people." ¹¹So they called
together all the rulers of the Philistines and said, "Send the ark
of the god of Israel away; let it go back to its own place, or it
will kill us and our people." For death had filled the city with
panic; God's hand was very heavy upon it. ¹²Those who did
not die were afflicted with tumors, and the outcry of the city
went up to heaven.

⁶:¹When the ark of the LORD had been in Philistine territory seven months, ²the Philistines called for the priests and

the diviners and said, "What shall we do with the ark of the LORD? Tell us how we should send it back to its place."

³They answered, "If you return the ark of the god of Israel, do not send it away empty, but by all means send a guilt offering to him. Then you will be healed, and you will know why his hand has not been lifted from you."

⁴The Philistines asked, "What guilt offering should we send to him?"

They replied, "Five gold tumors and five gold rats, according to the number of the Philistine rulers, because the same plague has struck both you and your rulers. ⁵Make models of the tumors and of the rats that are destroying the country, and pay honor to Israel's god. Perhaps he will lift his hand from you and your gods and your land. ⁶Why do you harden your hearts as the Egyptians and Pharaoh did? When he treated them harshly, did they not send the Israelites out so they could go on their way?

⁷"Now then, get a new cart ready, with two cows that have calved and have never been yoked. Hitch the cows to the cart, but take their calves away and pen them up. ⁸Take the ark of the LORD and put it on the cart, and in a chest beside it put the gold objects you are sending back to him as a guilt offering. Send it on its way, ⁹but keep watching it. If it goes up to its own territory, toward Beth Shemesh, then the LORD has brought this great disaster on us. But if it does not, then we will know that it was not his hand that struck us and that it happened to us by chance."

¹⁰So they did this. They took two such cows and hitched them to the cart and penned up their calves. ¹¹They placed the ark of the LORD on the cart and along with it the chest containing the gold rats and the models of the tumors. ¹²Then the cows went straight up toward Beth Shemesh, keeping on the road and lowing all the way; they did not turn to the right or to the left. The rulers of the Philistines followed them as far as the border of Beth Shemesh.

¹³Now the people of Beth Shemesh were harvesting their wheat in the valley, and when they looked up and saw the ark, they rejoiced at the sight. ¹⁴The cart came to the field of Joshua of Beth Shemesh, and there it stopped beside a large rock. The people chopped up the wood of the cart and sacrificed the cows as a burnt offering to the LORD. ¹⁵The Levites

took down the ark of the LORD, together with the chest containing the gold objects, and placed them on the large rock. On that day the people of Beth Shemesh offered burnt offerings and made sacrifices to the LORD. ¹⁶The five rulers of the Philistines saw all this and then returned that same day to Ekron.

¹⁷These are the gold tumors the Philistines sent as a guilt offering to the LORD—one each for Ashdod, Gaza, Ashkelon, Gath and Ekron. ¹⁸And the number of the gold rats was according to the number of Philistine towns belonging to the five rulers—the fortified towns with their country villages. The large rock, on which they set the ark of the LORD, is a witness to this day in the field of Joshua of Beth Shemesh.

¹⁹But God struck down some of the men of Beth Shemesh, putting seventy of them to death because they had looked into the ark of the LORD. The people mourned because of the heavy blow the LORD had dealt them, ²⁰and the men of Beth Shemesh asked, "Who can stand in the presence of the LORD, this holy God? To whom will the ark go up from here?"

²¹Then they sent messengers to the people of Kiriath Jearim, saying, "The Philistines have returned the ark of the LORD. Come down and take it up to your place." ⁷:¹So the men of Kiriath Jearim came and took up the ark of the LORD. They took it to Abinadab's house on the hill and consecrated Eleazar his son to guard the ark of the LORD.

Original Meaning

AFTER THE LOSS OF THE ARK OF THE COVENANT to the Philistines and the end of the priestly family, one can only imagine what might happen next to Israel. They have no theological mechanism for interpreting the disaster of 1 Samuel 4. Yahweh seemed unwilling or unable to deliver, and now the throne of Yahweh, the symbol of his very presence, is in the hands of their most bitter adversary. Should the Philistines mount a serious military offensive at this moment, the Israelites can only assume they will be utterly wiped out.

Both the Israelites and Philistines are about to learn a big lesson about Yahweh. These nations are interpreting the world through the lenses of their own theological systems. Like any ancient Near Eastern people-group, the Philistines would draw certain conclusions after their capture of the ark of the covenant. They had heard of Yahweh's victories against Egypt, and that gave them reason to be alarmed. But now they conclude Yahweh is an inferior deity, unable to protect Israel in their new situation in Canaan and impotent in the face of the Philistine deity, Dagon. But the events narrated next belie that interpretation. Both Israel and the Philistines are about to learn something about the freedom and power of Israel's God.

These two chapters relate the ark's seven-month sojourn in Philistia, its return to Israel, and the subsequent events in Beth Shemesh and Kiriath Jearim.

The Ark of the Covenant in Philistia (5:1–12)

YAHWEH WILL NOT permit the Israelites to use the ark of the covenant as though it were a magical wand. But neither can he permit the Philistines to demean him as a trophy of their victory. This episode illustrates that Yahweh himself is responsible for Israel's defeat and that, contrary to appearances, he is not powerless in the hands of Israel's enemies.

Ashdod was apparently the chief city of the Philistine pentapolis and was located just a few miles from the coast and thirty miles southwest of Ebenezer.[1] Gath and Ekron were further inland. Dagon was the principal deity of the Philistines, though he is widely known elsewhere in ancient Near Eastern religion. His cult is attested from the Early Bronze Age throughout the Iron Age down to Hellenistic times. We know little about his nature or character, including the etymological significance of his name. At Ugarit, he is at times identified as the father of the storm god Baal Haddu.[2]

Scholars believe the Philistines arrived in Palestine near the beginning of the Iron Age, probably around 1200 B.C. They appear to have adapted to Canaanite culture nicely, and the acquisition of Yahweh's ark would have been typical of ancient Near Eastern religious syncretism. They must have thought it odd that Israel did not possess an actual idol of its God. But they, like other groups who encountered Israel, would have accepted the ark of the covenant as a physical surrogate for the Israelite deity. Placing the ark "beside Dagon" (5:2) would confirm that Israel's deity was now supporting their efforts to establish hegemony not only along the coastal plains but also in the highlands, where the Israelites had settled. The Philistines could only have been encouraged by this development.

---

1. Moshe Dothan, "Ashdod," *ABD*, 1:477–82.

2. John F. Healey, "Dagon," *DDD*[2], 216–19; Karel van der Toorn, "Theology, Priests, and Worship in Canaan and Ancient Israel," *CANE*, 3:2047; J. J. M. Roberts, *The Earliest Semitic Pantheon* (Baltimore: Johns Hopkins Univ. Press, 1972), 18–19; Helmer Ringgren, *Religions of the Ancient Near East*, trans. J. Sturdy (Philadelphia: Westminster, 1973), 133, 135.

But on the first morning after placing the ark next to Dagon, the Philistines find Dagon in a position of subservience and worship, prostrate before Yahweh's ark (5:3). On the following morning, Dagon has lost his head and hands (5:4). Decapitation and cutting off hands was not infrequent in ancient warfare (17:51, 54; 31:9). In fact, such practices were intended to produce trophies for the victorious (see 31:8–10; for a means of determining correct body count, see 18:25, 27).[3] In a graphic text from the Ugaritic Baal Cycle, Anat, the goddess of love and war, fought against her enemies, with heads hanging on her back and palms on her belt (*CTU* 1.3 ii 5–16).[4] Thus, the condition of Dagon's torso on the second morning is a sign of military defeat.

The imagery presented here is that of a divine contest in which at first Yahweh merely humiliates the Philistine god. But the second victory (like the second Philistine defeat of the Israelites in ch. 4) is more devastating. By leaving only Dagon's torso, Yahweh proves that the previous night's work is not coincidental. Israel's God is victorious over the Philistines' conquering divine hero, who has supposedly brought military success against Israel. This time, however, Yahweh defeats Dagon *in his own temple!*

The added detail that the executed Dagon's extremities are found "lying on the threshold" is interesting (5:4). The narrator inserts the historical note in verse 5 to explain why "to this day" priests of Dagon step over the threshold of the temple of Dagon in Ashdod. The superstitious custom of jumping over the threshold of a sacred place was known in ancient Palestine, even practiced by idolatrous priests in Jerusalem (Zeph. 1:4, 9).

This insertion in verse 5 is an example of what is frequently called an "etiology," that is, a narrative that gives the past reason for a present reality. Often such etiologies use the expression "to this day" (as we have it in v. 5). Though most scholars assume etiological texts are by definition unhistorical (and usually label them "legends" or "folklore"), this assumption is patently unnecessary. The term "etiology" is purely descriptive.[5] Such etiological narratives are known from around the world, and many can be verified as expressing genuine historical events. The narrator here is simply drawing inferences from the events described for his own day. Dagon's humiliation and defeat before Yahweh cast a long shadow across Philistine history.

---

3. Antony F. Campbell, *The Ark Narrative (1 Sam. 4–6; 2 Sam. 6): A Form-Critical and Traditio-Historical Study* (Missoula, Mont.: Scholars Press, 1975), 86.

4. Dennis Pardee, "The Baʿlu Myth," COS, 1.86:241–74, esp. 250 (ii 5–16); Neal H. Walls, *The Goddess Anat in Ugaritic Myth* (Atlanta: Scholars Press, 1991), 163–66; Miller and Roberts, *The Hand of the Lord*, 46.

5. A. R. Millard, "Story, History, and Theology," in *Faith, Tradition, and History*, 40–41; for a slightly different approach, see Richard S. Hess, *Joshua: An Introduction and Commentary* (TOTC; Downers Grove, Ill.: InterVarsity Press, 1996), 110–11.

There is one final irony in the loss of Dagon's hands, which in Hebrew can connote a loss of power. The mention of this detail in 5:4 introduces a motif in the narrative that is quickly picked up again in 5:6: "The LORD's hand was heavy upon the people of Ashdod." Counting the mention of Yahweh's hand against Egypt in the form of the plagues (4:8), the expression or similar expressions occurs eight times in these chapters (5:6, 7, 9, 11; 6:3, 5, 9).[6] In such expressions in the ancient Near East, plagues were often described as the maleficent effects of the "hand" of a god. Thus in the Philistine mind, there is no doubt that the plague of tumors is due to the hand of Yahweh. This is especially evident by the way in which the plague seems to move with the ark to each city, first Ashdod, then Gath and Ekron.[7] All the while, the handless (i.e., powerless) Dagon can do nothing about it.

In sum, the Philistines have now learned the hard lesson, which the Israelites themselves learned in chapter 4. No one can manipulate or control Yahweh simply by obtaining possession of the ark of the covenant. He is sovereign and free, and though he is enthroned between the cherubim atop the sacred sarcophagus, the sum of his personhood can never be reduced to it alone. He is not chained to his throne. Yahweh is simply bigger than the Israelite or Philistine theological configuration of him. They have both grossly underestimated his power and holiness.

The Philistines Send the Ark of the Covenant Back (6:1–12)

THIS PARAGRAPH IS LOADED WITH QUESTIONS, reflecting the confusion and concern of the Philistines. First, they approach their religious leaders for advice on how to end the plague and its consequences (6:2). When they are advised to send the ark of Yahweh back with an offering, they respond with another question (6:4a): "What guilt offering should we send to him?" The Philistine priests and diviners ask rhetorically why the Philistines should harden their hearts like the Egyptians (6:6). But beyond these frantic questions, the overarching question here is not expressed in so many words: Has Yahweh, the God of Israel, really brought this on them or is it mere chance?

The priests and diviners recommend a test to determine whether the catastrophic events are really of Yahweh. The test is the use of two cows to carry the ark back to Israelite territory (6:7–12). Cows with young calves dependent on them and unaccustomed to pulling a cart would likely turn back and fail to deliver the ark to Israel. But these cows go straight toward Beth Shemesh, without turning right or left. And "the five rulers of the Philistines

---

6. Miller and Roberts, *The Hand of the Lord*, 48.

7. Traditionally identified as bubonic plague, though other explanations are possible. See McCarter, *I Samuel*, 123.

saw all this" (6:16). Thus they learn that they have not conquered Israel's God when they captured his ark.

The presence of the ark of Yahweh in the Philistine territory for "seven months" may be figurative, indicating the fullness or completion of the ark's sojourn (6:1). The Philistines decide they have seen enough; it is time to return the ark to Israel.

The Philistines are Israel's bitter enemies, but they are also a deeply religious people. Indeed, there was no such thing as atheism in the ancient world. All peoples believed in deities and the supernatural influences of the world around them. Through plagues and mysterious statue desecration, the Philistines have learned to respect Yahweh, the national patron God of Israel. Now they want to know how to receive healing and ransom so that Yahweh's hand can be stayed. The NIV of 6:3 has been corrected by the LXX and Qumran variant: "Then you will be healed. Once you have been ransomed, why should his hand not turn away from you?"[8] They are interested in determining whether Israel's god is really responsible for their troubles, and if he is, then by all means they want to placate him and escape his wrath.

The recommended offering for Yahweh ("five gold tumors and five gold rats," 6:4) apparently uses sympathetic magic. The departure of the golden statues is probably intended to effect the removal of the rodents and disease from the region of the Philistine pentapolis. There must have been resistance on the part of the Philistines to make such a costly sacrifice to Israel's god, since the priests and diviners warn them against making the same mistakes the Egyptians had made (6:6). The term "honor" (6:5) and the verb for "to harden one's heart" (6:6) are from the same Hebrew root (*kbd*), creating an interesting wordplay: It is better to honor Israel's God than to harden one's heart as the Egyptians did.[9] Ironically, the Philistine priests and diviners are now urging their people (almost preaching to them!) to give glory and honor to Yahweh, the God of Israel. What a fascinating turn of events!

The proof that Yahweh was the genuine source of the Philistine's afflictions comes in the nature of the ark's return to Israel (6:7–12). The first destination of the ark on its return to Israel was about nine miles southeast of Ekron, Beth Shemesh. Archaeologists have uncovered evidence of Philistine influence at Beth Shemesh during the judges period, and it apparently functioned as a border town between Israel and Philistia, though the

---

8. McCarter, *I Samuel*, 129, 133.

9. Lit., "to give *honor*" (a noun in 6:5, *kabod*) and "why do you *harden* your hearts" (Piel of *kbd* in 6:6).

Philistines clearly view it as Israelite territory in this passage.[10] The cows act against nature (because their new calves are not with them), but under divine compulsion (without turning to the right or to the left), taking the cart straight to Beth Shemesh.[11]

The Ark of the Covenant at Beth Shemesh and Kiriath Jearim (6:13–7:1)

THE ARK OF God must be paid its due respect, whether by the Philistines or the Israelites. The Israelites are at first overjoyed to see the ark of Yahweh returned to their borders (6:13). The people of Beth Shemesh join in worshipful thanksgiving by sacrificing the cows to Yahweh before the ark, attended by the Levites. But it is a short-lived victory. The loss of seventy citizens of that city may have been the result of disease passed from Philistine contacts. But in the minds of the Israelites, it is because they have not properly cared for the sacred symbol of Yahweh's covenant (6:19): "because they had looked into the ark of the LORD." The ark was not to be opened, or even touched, out of respect for Yahweh (2 Sam. 6:6–7). "It was important that the Israelites see the recovery of the ark not as a transfer of control from Philistia back to Israel but as it was—an expression of God's sovereignty over both Philistia and Israel."[12]

The pitiable question of the citizens of Beth Shemesh acknowledges the loss of Shiloh as the proper cult center for the fledgling nation (6:20): "To whom will the ark go up from here?"[13] The driving question is: Where should the ark be housed now that we have lost Shiloh and now that Eli's family is dead? Beth Shemesh fails to care for the ark properly and so is struck by a plague not unlike that suffered by the Philistines. Now its citizens look to pass the responsibility onto others. The people of Kiriath Jearim accept the task, consecrating Eleazar the son of Abinadab to guard (lit., "keep") the ark.

Kiriath Jearim is approximately fifteen miles east-northeast of Beth Shemesh in the Israelite heartland. It has a second name, Baalah, which may indicate it had previously been a Canaanite high place and therefore associated with worship, as Shiloh had been.[14] The geographical progression from Philistia to Beth Shemesh, and then to Kiriath Jearim, is part of a larger

---

10. Stratum III (Iron Age I) produced a significant amount of Philistine pottery, as might be expected, given the city's location near the Philistine plain. William G. Dever, "Beth-shemesh," *OEANE* 1:311–12; Fredric Brandfon, "Beth-shemesh," *ABD*, 1:696–98.

11. Youngblood, "1, 2 Samuel," 604–5.

12. Mary J. Evans, *1 and 2 Samuel* (NIBCOT; Peabody, Mass.: Hendrikson, 2000), 34.

13. As narrated in 4:1–22.

14. Jeffries M. Hamilton, "Kiriath-Jearim," *ABD*, 4:84–85.

story told in the books of Samuel. Twenty years later, the ark is taken from Kiriath Jearim by Yahweh's specially anointed servant David and placed in Yahweh's chosen location, Jerusalem (2 Sam. 6:17). The exile of the ark and its eventual migration to Jerusalem reflects God's choice of Jerusalem, which is ultimately behind David's selection of that city as the new capital of unified Israel.[15] These events form the inspiration for the psalmist's mediations in Psalm 78:60–62, 65–69:

> He abandoned the tabernacle of Shiloh,
>   the tent he had set up among men.
> He sent the ark of his might into captivity,
>   his splendor into the hands of the enemy.
> He gave his people over to the sword;
>   he was very angry with his inheritance. . . .
> Then the Lord awoke as from sleep,
>   as a man wakes from the stupor of wine.
> He beat back his enemies;
>   he put them to everlasting shame.
> Then he rejected the tents of Joseph,
>   he did not choose the tribe of Ephraim;
> but he chose the tribe of Judah,
>   Mount Zion, which he loved.
> He built his sanctuary like the heights,
>   like the earth that he established forever.

YAHWEH AND ANCIENT NEAR EASTERN RELIGION. At the beginning of the ark narrative, Israel attempted to manipulate Yahweh. The result was disastrous. Israel had lost the cult center at Shiloh, the Elide priesthood, and the ark of the covenant. Furthermore, Israel was without theological explanation. How were the Israelites to understand their military defeat and, more importantly, the loss of the ark to the Philistines? And what about the Philistines? How were they to understand their victory and capture of the ark? This unit presents a fascinating portrait of the Philistines and their religious conceptions, by which they try to explain their capture of the ark and the subsequent disaster.

The Philistines were not unlike other nations of the ancient Near East, for whom polytheism was a fundamental assumption that lay at the heart of

---

15. Barth, *God with Us*, 240–41.

their worldview. Though some people only served one god or a few gods officially, they nonetheless recognized the existence of dozens, even hundreds of deities, as many as there were natural and social forces in the world.[16] These deities were coterminous, or by nature immanent, in the world. They were correspondent to, or continuous with, all other things that existed. Socially, the deities were much like humans. As opposed to Genesis theology, in which God created humans in his image, ancient theology accepted gods in human image. They had births, deaths, families, and physical needs.

In addition, the ancients believed the deities were susceptible to the forces of magic. Most nations of the ancient world practiced a wide variety of magical arts, including formulaic recitations and imitative acts, which they thought could manipulate and exploit the powers of the divine and natural realms. Such beliefs were probably behind the statement in 5:5 that Philistines entering the temple of Dagon at Ashdod refused to step on the threshold. Sympathetic or imitative magic is certainly also behind the use of five gold tumors and five gold rats to represent the five Philistine cities.

This explains the power of the symbolic acts described in 1 Samuel 5. Idolatry was central to the ancient worldview, since the idol was an actual extension of the deity's essence. Placing Yahweh's ark beside Dagon's idol was symbolic of Dagon's victory. But the loss of Dagon's hands and head turned the tables. And wherever the ark of Yahweh traveled in Philistia, it worked its power, teaching the ancient Philistines through their own idolatrous worldview that Yahweh was all-powerful, even in their own backyard.

When the Philistines encountered God in such a way, they went to their priests and diviners, the latter being specialists in "reading" the divine realm through various practices.[17] This was their way of trying to placate the deity. They were limited in their understanding of God because their minds were darkened. They "exchanged the glory of the immortal God for images made to look like mortal man and birds and animals and reptiles" (Rom. 1:23). At least we can say the Philistine priests and diviners had come to honor Yahweh, and they learned from the stories they had heard about the hardhearted Egyptians (1 Sam. 6:5–6). Though their use of golden images (idols!) as offerings to Yahweh was not adequate, they appear to have learned that Israel's God, unlike their own deities, could not be so easily manipulated.

The tragic events at Beth Shemesh reveal ironically that Israel had not learned the same lesson. Israel's covenant relationship with Yahweh was so radically different that the nation's worldview was also supposed to be unique.

---

16. For more on what follows, see Bill T. Arnold, *Encountering the Book of Genesis: A Survey of Its Content and Issues* (Grand Rapids: Baker, 1998), 49–51.

17. Malcolm J. A. Horsnell, "קסם," *NIDOTTE*, 3:945–51; McCarter, *I Samuel*, 132.

The Israelites believed that Yahweh is alone in the realm of deity and singularly responsible for all other natural and social forces of the universe. Therefore he is not coterminous or immanent in the world. Rather, he is transcendent and unlike humans, having no beginning or end, no family relationships, and no physical needs. Furthermore, magic and all magical practices were forbidden for Israel (Ex. 22:18; Lev. 19:26, 31; 20:6, 27; Deut. 18:10–11).

But who are the real idolaters here? Israel had been equally guilty of attempting to manipulate Yahweh. The use of the ark of the covenant to guarantee military victory came perilously close to imitative magic, or at least pagan religious warfare. And now the losses at Beth Shemesh reveal a propensity to disregard him, failing to glorify him and give thanks to him (Rom. 1:21). Israel had been given the riches of divine self-disclosure. God had revealed his nature to ancient Israel, and this was to make her unique in the ancient world.

But her actions were not matching his grace! She had not learned to allow the truths of his self-revelation to penetrate her own worldview and transform her character. Israel had failed to learn what the Philistines were discovering without the benefit of unique divine revelation: God cannot be manipulated! His ark cannot be used as an idol! We expect the Philistines to try to control him. But sadly, the Israelites have exerted their energy trying to twist God into their image as well. One need not be a Philistine to act idolatrously.

The irony is that the Philistines understand the significance of Israel's unique theology better than the Israelites. This is apparent in the many allusions to the Exodus narrative observed by the Philistines themselves. They understand that their choices, when confronted with Yahweh's awesome power, are either honoring him or hardening their own hearts, as Pharaoh before them had done (1 Sam. 6:5–6). This reference is the counterpart of 4:7–8 earlier in the ark narrative, when the Philistines first recognize that their situation is not unlike Pharaoh's.

Together these references link the entire ark narrative to the Exodus memory.[18] The gold offerings going with Yahweh from Philistia are reminiscent of Israel's departure from Egypt with gold and silver (Ex. 11:2). The unit's emphasis on the "hand of the LORD" may reflect the Exodus narrative's use of the "arm" and "hand" of God.[19] The Philistines decide to release Yahweh,

---

18. Brueggemann, *First and Second Samuel*, 42, Walter Brueggemann, *Theology of the Old Testament: Testimony, Dispute, Advocacy* (Minneapolis: Fortress, 1997), 177.

19. James Hoffmeier, "The Arm of God Versus the Arm of Pharaoh in the Exodus Narratives," *Bib* 67 (1986): 378–87; Brent A. Strawn, "The Strong Hand and Outstretched Arm of God in the Light of Amarna Iconography" (paper presented at the annual meeting of the Society of Biblical Literature, Orlando, Fla., Nov. 21, 1998).

just as Pharaoh was required to "let my people go." Unlike Pharaoh, however, the Philistines decide to honor Yahweh rather than to harden their hearts.

In a sense, the ox-drawn procession of Yahweh along the road to Beth Shemesh is another Exodus. In the Exodus proper, Yahweh came out of Egypt along with his people. But in this episode, Yahweh departs Philistia alone, without his people Israel. In the first Exodus, Yahweh's people were liberated from their slavery and bondage. Here, Yahweh has liberated himself so that his people may finally be liberated from their inadequate understanding of his great character.

How wonderful that God chooses to snatch victory from the jaws of defeat! After the loss of the ark in chapter 4, these chapters narrate God's own actions to overturn the defeat. This narrative functions in 1 Samuel as a wonderful reason for hope, since God in his grace initiated his own exaltation and return to Israel's people. There is a certain freshness about Yahweh. He does things new and unexpected that catch his people by surprise. Furthermore, he alone initiates such new acts of deliverance. No one else can force his timing. In 1 Samuel 1–3, he has initiated the arrival of a new prophet and judge, who will lead Israel into the future, a future she can hardly begin to anticipate. In the ark narrative, he has turned Israel's pitiable failure into an opportunity for further self-disclosure of his surpassing nature. He has again initiated deliverance in a hopeless situation.

VIEWING GOD AND HIS WORK IN THE WORLD. Like Israel of old, the Christian church has been blessed with a unique view of reality. God's self-disclosure has placed truth in the hands of believers, which makes the church a counterculture in the world. The two worldviews represented in this text, Israelite and Philistine, reflect the basic options still available today. In order to draw out the significance of this text for contemporary society and culture, we will need to consider the way today's readers view God's work in the world.

George Hunter, my colleague at Asbury, told recently of a conversation he had with two executives he met while waiting to board their planes in the Cincinnati airport.[20] His simple question generated rich conversation: "Do you believe in God?" The first businessman appealed to the complexity and intricacy of the cosmos as evidence that God exists. It drove him to conclude: "I believe there is a God behind it all." The second was somewhat less

---

20. For what follows, see George G. Hunter III, "God at a Distance," *The Wall Street Journal* (April 24, 1998), w13.

sanguine, pointing out the sheer size of the universe, which makes humankind look so insignificant.

Our planet is one of nine in our solar system. Our sun is one of a hundred million stars in our galaxy. Our Milky Way galaxy is one of a hundred million galaxies in the known universe. Granting what we know today about the vastness of space, it's a stretch to believe that we could matter to the God behind all this.

Professor Hunter uses the assessment of these two executives to critique the understanding of God that has prevailed for generations in most societies of the Western world, namely, deism. Since the Enlightenment, British deism taught that the universe was a closed system, functioning like a well-timed machine with no need for God. Deism allowed for the existence of One Supreme Being, who started it all but whose function in creation was reduced to that of First Cause only. God is now like a "Cosmic Watchmaker," who after having designed and created it all, has now left it to run on its own.[21] He is distant and uninvolved, transcendent but not immanent. Enlightenment thinkers believed that what the world needed was more education and freedom to liberate people and allow humankind to evolve into the civilized and advanced culture that we could become.

With the collapse of the Enlightenment project and the arrival of a postmodern reaction, people are abandoning the idealistic thought that humans are advanced enough, intelligent enough, or even civilized enough to produce a more desirable world. Modernism has not brought the promises of the Enlightenment to fruition. People today are routinely reconsidering the assumption that the universe is a closed system. On the contrary, many educated people today reach for the great Beyond in a multitude of ways, as those listed by Professor Hunter: karma, curses, ghosts, angels, evil spirits, telepathy, astrological powers, out-of-body experiences, and mystery in many forms.

Recently in my local newspaper, I read of the growing phenomenon of "Sufism," the seventh-century mystical Islamic devotion emphasizing a relationship with God expressed through poetry, whirling movement, and meditation. In March 2001, the eighth Sufism Symposium was being held in California's Bay Area, where approximately three to four thousand Sufis live. Organizers of the symposium claimed Sufism is growing because of "a great longing within people's souls to find more spirituality."[22]

---

21. A classic comparison, which appears to date back to the late fourteenth century. See Michael H. Macdonald, "Deism," *Evangelical Dictionary of Theology*, ed. Walter A. Elwell (Grand Rapids: Baker, 1984), 304.

22. So, the article explains, Sufism is to Islam what Zen is to Buddhism or Kabbalah is to Judaism. Lisa Fernandez, "Mystical Branch of Islam Growing," *Lexington Herald-Leader* (March 24, 2001), C9.

At the very time when many postmoderns are seeking God in these illegitimate ways, God seems evermore distant. Deism still clings, for God seems for many to be as far away as ever. As Hunter observes, for most in the West, it still requires a "stretch" to believe we matter to God. But biblical revelation breaks into this worldview and shatters it. Biblical truth offers an alternate view of reality that makes the others impossible. God, the transcendent Creator of the universe, is also immanent and thus immanently involved in the world.

The Bible's witness is remarkably consistent on this point. God broke into Abram's world and committed himself to Abram as friend and protector. Similarly, God broke into ancient Israel's world and met them on Mount Sinai in order to bind himself to them in covenant love. In this text he crashed into the Philistine world in order to teach them that their various ways of explaining and understanding divine presence are all wrong. And Israel also learns in this text that the immanent God cannot be ignored, manipulated, or mishandled. He cares for them too much to allow them to misunderstand his nature.

As Professor Hunter explains, the rest of biblical revelation is unmistakable at this point. Of everything else the Bible teaches, this much is clear: We matter to God! The rest stands or falls on this remarkable claim—revolutionary for its time as well as for our day. Indeed, God is intimately involved in the clothing of the lilies and concerned with wounded sparrows (Matt. 6:26–30; 10:29; Luke 12:6, 24–28). In fact, God cares about everything in this world: birds, plants, animals, everything—but especially people. He numbers the hairs on our heads, which illustrates the depth and breadth of his knowledge and concern for us (Matt. 10:30; Luke 12:7).[23]

The message of this text is greatly needed in today's world. It illustrates that the Philistine worldview—which is so similar in many ways to today's postmodern New Age perspective—is inadequate. God is not coterminous with the forces of nature, nor is he created in our image. He is not susceptible to the forces of magic or idolatry. He cannot be manipulated or pressed into service whenever we feel threatened or at risk. The God of Israel is in fact immanent and in control; he is victorious over all the forces of our world, just as he was victorious over the Philistine god Dagon.

But the Philistine worldview was not the only one corrected in this text. The Israelites also had to reconsider the way they viewed God. Their

---

23. The point of these metaphors is not deliverance from danger. Rather, the point is "that sparrows can be bought and sold and that humans can suffer persecution, but not apart from God's attentiveness, not outside of God's care, not in a way that circumvents the redemptive plan of God" (Joel B. Green, *The Gospel of Luke* [NICNT; Grand Rapids: Eerdmans, 1997], 483).

monotheism must be complete and thorough. It marked Israel as unique in the world and made Israel's voice a counterculture in the ancient Near East. Even when Israel failed to live up to the grace Yahweh had given, even when Israel seemed no more enlightened than the Philistines and attempted to manipulate and control God, God brought victory from the jaws of defeat.

Thus, this text speaks to both the world and the church today. It offers to the world a glimpse into this alternate reality, a reality in which God *does* care. He cares enough to break into the world and offer himself to the Philistines of our day as a full and beautiful revelation of his nature. He cares enough to become vulnerable, even to be captured by the enemy and to be treated as a trophy. But in the end, God will be victorious.

But this text also offers the church a glimpse into this alternate view of reality, which has theoretically marked believers off as unique in the world. This glimpse reminds us that God has cared enough for us to break into our world too, to become vulnerable to our sinful idolatry, even to allow himself to be exploited by the very ones who call on his name. We must, therefore, become thoroughly monotheistic; we must eschew all forms of idolatry; and we must learn again that because he cares for us, we must celebrate his freedom to move in our lives as he chooses.

1 Samuel 7:2–4

𝖎

IT WAS A long time, twenty years in all, that the ark remained at Kiriath Jearim, and all the people of Israel mourned and sought after the LORD. ³And Samuel said to the whole house of Israel, "If you are returning to the LORD with all your hearts, then rid yourselves of the foreign gods and the Ashtoreths and commit yourselves to the LORD and serve him only, and he will deliver you out of the hand of the Philistines." ⁴So the Israelites put away their Baals and Ashtoreths, and served the LORD only.

THIS IMPORTANT PARAGRAPH introduces the final chapter of the first extended unit of 1 Samuel (chs. 1–7). The so-called Shiloh narratives (chs. 1–3) traced Yahweh's intervention on Israel's behalf. He initiated and orchestrated the downfall of the nation's wicked priestly leadership and replaced it with Samuel, his chosen leader for the next great period of Israel's history. The ark narrative (chs. 4–6) related another deliverance at the hands of Yahweh. He turned military and spiritual defeat into victory for Israel, even if the people failed to understand his nature or the full implications of his salvation.

These two units appear on the surface to have little to do with each other. But woven together into a single narrative tapestry, they prepare us for the anointing of Saul and ultimately for the arrival of Israel's greatest king, David. In various ways, these narratives introduce us to the great kingmaker, Samuel, and to the concept that Israel desperately needs a king.

Permeating the whole is this wonderful and perplexing truth: Israel is still living in relationship with Yahweh. Her religious leadership has been wicked. She has tried to manipulate God and to use him for military advantage over the enemy. In sum, she has been plagued with sin and failure. But through it all, he graciously continues to find a way to save her and draw her closer to himself. After chapter 7 the narrative leads directly to the issue of kingship.[1] In the present passage, the text deals more directly with the relationship

---

1. The precise relationship of ch. 7 to the ark narrative is uncertain (Youngblood, "1, 2 Samuel," 593–94, 607), though the essential unity of chs. 1–7 is widely accepted (see Willis, "An Anti-Elide Narrative Tradition").

between Israel and Yahweh. The ark has been returned to Israel, but the Philistine military threat is as serious as previously. Nothing has really been resolved, only now Samuel stands as a legitimate prophet to lead the people and reexamine their relationship with Yahweh.

For twenty years, the ark rests in Kiriath Jearim, presumably without a proper tabernacle (such as it had in Shiloh). The people during this time apparently have a change of heart. Whereas their mourning in 6:19 was the result of the tragedy at Beth Shemesh ("The people mourned because of the heavy blow the LORD had dealt them"), their remorse in 7:2 is accompanied by a seeking after Yahweh.[2] Functioning in his role as prophet, Samuel seizes the opportunity, seeing that the people are ready for genuine repentance.

Verse 3 contains a number of set phrases characteristic of Israelite prophetic preaching. Some scholars take their combination here as indication that this verse (or indeed, this paragraph) is a later addition by an exilic redactor.[3] It may indeed be true that these so-called "Deuteronomistic" themes have a shared common origin and may even be part of a larger editorial framework. But they probably also reflect genuine Israelite prophecy at its best, even in the earlier periods.

The first of these characteristic phrases is the most important Old Testament expression for repentance: "if you are returning to the LORD." To "return" (*šwb*) to the Lord implies acknowledging, confessing, and forsaking sinful behavior (cf. Jer. 3:22–4:2 for the steps of repentance), making it possible to be reinstated in a right relationship with him. It is both a turning away from one's sins, which have caused the separation, and a turning unto Yahweh, who can forgive and restore.

This returning is intensely personal. It is not a mechanical or physical positioning but a relational and associative allegiance. It occurs throughout Old Testament literature but notably in Deuteronomy (Deut. 4:30; 30:2), prophetic texts interspersed in the historical books (2 Kings 17:13; 2 Chron. 7:14; 30:6), and particularly in the prophets. "Returning" (or simply "turning") is particularly important in Jeremiah's preaching[4] and is the climactic call in Hosea (Hos. 14:1–2). Perhaps the text that illustrates best the use of this word in the prophets is Joel 2:12–13:

---

2. Bergen, *1, 2 Samuel*, 106. But the NIV of 7:2 smoothes over a difficult textual problem, and the word for "mourn" here is nonetheless different (and much more rare) than that of 6:19.

3. McCarter, *I Samuel*, 142–43; Hans Walter Wolff, "The Kerygma," 83–100.

4. William L. Holladay, *The Root Šûbh in the Old Testament, with Particular Reference to Its Usage in Covenantal Contexts* (Leiden: Brill, 1958), 128–39, 152–54, 156–57.

"Even now," declares the LORD,
  "return to me with all your heart,
  with fasting and weeping and mourning."
Rend your heart
  and not your garments.
Return to the LORD your God,
  for he is gracious and compassionate,
slow to anger and abounding in love,
  and he relents from sending calamity.

But such returning to Yahweh must by definition be wholehearted. The combination of "returning" with "the whole heart" has been identified as central to the preaching of Old Testament historical narrative.[5] Samuel, as Joel would do later, calls on Israel to return to Yahweh "with all your hearts" (7:3). Halfhearted returning will not do. Most such references to the "heart" in the Old Testament (*lebab* and *leb*) refer to the seat of one's intellectual commitments rather than singularly to human emotions, as we tend to use it in modern English.[6]

Such repentance, if it is to be genuine, must also be accompanied by three other characteristics, according to Samuel in 7:3. These characteristics are marked in the text by three phrases, each beginning with an imperative verb. (1) "Rid yourselves of the foreign gods and the Ashtoreths." This imperative (*hasiru*, Hiphil of *swr*) connotes a putting away, or laying aside, of something to be picked up no more. The Ashtoreths were local manifestations of one of the important goddesses of Canaan, the goddess of love and fertility.[7] As the Israelites put away their "Baals and Ashtoreths" (7:4), they are rejecting the leading Canaanite deities of fertility, which were associated especially

---

5. Wolff, "The Kerygma," 90–100.

6. Esp. when used in this repentance idiom with *šwb*. The "heart" is the locus of a variety of emotions, as well as of thought (*DCH*, 4:497–509). Additionally, the term often translated "soul" or "living being" (*nepeš*) may serve as the seat of emotions (BDB 660, number 6), and the plural "kidneys" and other words for innards may serve as the seat of emotion and affection (*kelayot*, BDB 480, number 2; *DCH*, 4:424–25). The Old Testament identifies emotions physiologically as follows: anger was located in the head (esp. the nose and mouth), a range of emotions in the heart, and distress in the innards or liver. See Mark S. Smith, "The Heart and Innards in Israelite Emotional Expressions: Notes from Anthropology and Psychobiology," *JBL* 117 (1998): 427–36, esp. 434.

7. The Heb. spelling of her name (Ashtoreth for Astarte) appears to be a deliberate scribal distortion, reflecting the vowels of the word "shame" (*bošet*) (John Day, "Ashtoreth [deity]," *ABD*, 1:491–94). The motivation for the spelling is in dispute, however, since it may have intended to elicit a suggestive parallel to the revocalizing of the name for Israel's God, *yhwh* becoming *ꜣadonay* (see Nicholas Wyatt, "Astarte," *DDD*[2], 109–14, esp. 112–13).

with sexual rituals at local Canaanite shrines. Their identification as "foreign gods" is more than a reference to their non-Israelite origins. They are, in fact, *other* than Yahweh, who requires exclusive devotion ("serve him only," 7:3; see below). The Lord cannot be worshiped along with other gods as though he merely supplements their benefits. To worship Yahweh is to reject all others.

(2) The next phrase of Samuel's call to repentance is "commit yourselves to the LORD." Literally, the Hebrew idiom is to fix or establish (imperative *hakinu*) one's heart on something, which often pictures a fixing or setting permanently one's heart on Yahweh. The idea communicated here is one of tenacious determination to remain faithful and loyal to God; it is the antithesis of being stubborn and rebellious (Ps. 78:8, see also 2 Chron. 30:19; Ezra 7:10). This commitment is a logical, though not necessarily chronological, concomitant of the first imperative. When one fixes one's heart on Yahweh, it involves a repudiation of the fertility gods of Canaan. These are two sides of the same theological commitment, and one automatically entails the other. Loyalty to Yahweh requires rejection of Baal and Ashtoreth.

(3) "Serve him only." This imperative (*ʿibduhu*) is the common word for "serve" and, in the context of serving a deity, connotes "worship."[8] The restrictive modifier "only" gets at one of the most important distinguishing characteristics of Israelite religion: Yahweh requires exclusive devotion. Syncretism, or the worship of Yahweh alongside other deities, is forbidden for the ancient Israelite. The Philistines had followed an idolatrous approach to God; they presumed upon his sovereign freedom, as though he were Baal or Dagon or some other ancient Near Eastern deity. There is something about this God of Israel unlike any other deity of the ancient Near East: You either worship him "only" or not at all.[9] Any repentance that clings to vestiges of hope in other gods is no repentance at all.

Samuel concludes his plea by noting that such genuine, heartfelt repentance will result in deliverance from "the hand of the Philistines." The capture of the ark and subsequent humiliation of Israel had been blamed on the sins of Eli and his family. But Samuel's preaching now makes it clear that there are wider and more disturbing origins of Israel's failure. The nation has succumbed to the cultural pressure to worship local deities in addition to their devotion to Yahweh. They have walked away from exclusive service to Yahweh; they have rejected him. As is typical in biblical narrative, the text

---

8. Eugene Carpenter, "עבד," *NIDOTTE*, 3:304–9.

9. Yehezkel Kaufmann, *The Religion of Israel: From Its Beginnings to the Babylonian Exile* (Chicago: Univ. of Chicago Press, 1960), 13–20; J. Andrew Dearman, *Religion and Culture in Ancient Israel* (Peabody, Mass.: Hendrickson, 1992), 142–44.

---

looks beyond the political and military causes for events to the more important explanation, the theological one. The nation has failed because its leadership is corrupt; what is more, her population has abandoned Yahweh. If there is to be a future for Israel and they are to continue in Yahweh's land, they will have to face their own sin and repent.

Samuel's role as a prophet of God is to explain the nature of repentance and call the people to it without timidity. He calls on them to turn their sorrow and remorse into genuine repentance. Such repentance works from the inside outward. It begins with a heartfelt turning to God, an internal commitment to make one's relationship with God a priority over everything else. It moves from this to actions—either a rejection of wrongful deeds or a renewed commitment to righteous deeds. It is not enough to regret; one must also repent from sin.

The paragraph ends with the terse but encouraging statement, "So the Israelites put away their Baals and Ashtoreths, and served the LORD only" (4:4). Samuel's preaching is effective, and the Israelites are now prepared to be led into their future.

REPENTANCE. THIS PASSAGE is an important one for understanding the nature of biblical repentance. There are two errors in how most modern Christians perceive repentance. (1) We tend to think of it only as remorse or a sorrow for having done something wrong. But this passage and others teach us that repentance is primarily a radical turning to God as truly God, which involves also a turning away from our sin and from other gods. It is possible to be painfully sorry for something we have done, but make no effort to stop the painful action.

(2) We often think of repentance as it relates to a single individual, or more precisely, as it relates to a specific deed committed. But Samuel is calling the people of Israel to repent *as a nation* for their sinful behavior. In fact, biblical repentance is often national in scope, and the nation is generally led to such contrition by a decisive leader who calls them to repentance, instructs them in the nature of repentance, and repents by example.

Repentance was obviously a central theme in the earliest stages of Christianity. John the Baptist came "preaching a baptism of repentance for the forgiveness of sins" (Mark 1:4). The core of Jesus' early ministry may be summarized succinctly: "Repent and believe the good news!" (Mark 1:15). The Greek words for repentance (the noun *metanoia* and the verb *metanoeo*) have "change of mind" at their root meaning, but they clearly connote much more in these contexts.[10] It seems likely that in these early Christian uses, repentance has the full and rich content of the Old Testament in view and denotes the complete reorientation of the sinner (cf. 2 Cor. 7:9−10).

An early example occurs in Genesis 35, where Jacob returns to Bethel, builds an altar to God, and leads his entire household in corporate repentance. Interestingly, the same phrase for laying aside foreign gods is used in 35:2 as we find in 1 Samuel 7:3: "Get rid of the foreign gods you have with you." Centuries later, the Lord appeared to King Solomon after the dedication of the new temple. God promised that in years to come, whenever calamity struck his people, he would forgive and heal the land if they repented (2 Chron. 7:14): "If my people, who are called by my name, will humble themselves and pray and seek my face and turn [šwb] from their wicked ways, then will I hear from heaven and will forgive their sin and will heal their land."

Jeremiah's classic object lesson of the potter working at the wheel, shaping the pot of his own choosing, is another example of prophetic repentance (Jer. 18:1−12). Though the overarching theme of that passage is the sovereign freedom of Yahweh to act as he chooses, the prophet is also making a point about repentance. God may plan to punish any given nation for their sins. But given due prophetic warning, if that nation repents (šwb, v. 8) of its evil, God will change his plans and act toward that nation in a different manner. Likewise, if God plans to bless a nation, which however commits some evil act, God will reverse his plans for blessing the nation (v. 9). The point of the object lesson, of course, is that Israel should repent (v. 11): "Turn [šwb] from your evil ways, each one of you, and reform your ways and your actions."

We also have examples in the Old Testament of national leaders repenting on behalf of the people, even when those leaders did not themselves hold responsibility for the sins committed. Ezra is informed that leaders and officials of the people have intermarried with the foreigners of Canaan, making themselves susceptible to the abominable practices of the Canaanites (Ezra 9:1−2). His reaction is one of personal shame and sorrow (9:3−4). That evening, he leads the people in a prayer of national confession, in which he speaks repeatedly of "our sins" and "our guilt" (9:5−15). Finally, he concludes, "Here we are before you in our guilt, though because of it not one of us can stand in your presence" (9:15). In a moving display of unity, a large crowd of Israelites, "men, women and children," gather around him and join in the prayer of confession and repentance (10:1).

One of the most moving prayers of the Old Testament is that of Daniel on behalf of his people in Daniel 9:4−19. After acknowledging that God is

---

10. J. M. Lunde, "Repentance," *New Dictionary of Biblical Theology*, ed. T. Desmond Alexander and Brian S. Rosner (Leicester, Eng.: Inter-Varsity Press, 2000), 726−27.

a covenant-keeping God, Daniel confesses the sins of his ancestors in strikingly personal terms:

> We have sinned and done wrong. We have been wicked and have rebelled; we have turned away from your commands and laws. We have not listened to your servants the prophets, who spoke in your name to our kings, our princes and our fathers, and to all the people of the land. (Dan. 9:5–6)

It is important to remember that most of the sins Daniel is confessing were committed before his birth. He is leading the people in repentance for national sins committed by their ancestors but which have lasting consequences for the people in Daniel's day.

All too often in the modern church, repentance is tucked away in the personal and private lives of people who want to obtain absolution without thought for the continuing effects of sin. We look for exoneration rather than justification and restoration. We prefer to concentrate on the compartmentalized sins of our lives at this controlled and controllable moment rather than to view the ugliness of our idolatry on the grand stage of life. It is not only the passing adulterous thought or murderous deeds of today or yesterday that the Bible addresses when it speaks of repentance; rather, it refers to the lifelong pattern of idolatry that needs confessing.

It is our human tendency to turn away from God unto the gods of fertility all around us, to neglect our relationship with him in our pathetic attempt to grasp the promise of momentary significance by depending on anything other than God. The Bible calls us to repent of our pattern of sin, to repudiate the worldly life of idolatry, which seeks to find meaning in any other way besides living in harmony with him and him only. It is perhaps time to consider whether the church's emphasis on personal repentance actually hinders the biblical call to repent as a church, as the people of God.

IT IS ALWAYS easier to attend a church service once a week and to listen to a public prayer of confession than to acknowledge and confront personal sin and guilt. Perhaps more than any other twentieth-century author, Dietrich Bonhoeffer stated most forcefully the inconsistency of a gospel without a call to repentance: "Cheap grace means the justification of sin without the justification of the sinner." Cheap grace, taught Bonhoeffer, is that grace we bestow on ourselves and is in truth "the deadly enemy of our Church."

Cheap grace is the preaching of forgiveness without requiring repentance, baptism without church discipline, Communion without confession, absolution without personal confession. Cheap grace is grace without discipleship, grace without the cross, grace without Jesus Christ, living and incarnate.[11]

Bonhoeffer has shown that such grace is counterfeit and ineffective. Similarly, John Wesley spoke of repentance as the "porch of religion," while faith is its door and holiness "religion itself."[12] One cannot avoid the porch of repentance while walking through the door of faith. Moreover, repentance does not cease, Wesley thought, once we enter the door, but rather becomes a way of life.[13] The more we grow in grace and the more we become Christlike, we experience a commensurate awareness of sin and move more readily toward genuine repentance.

A few years ago, I met a man named Jim (not his real name). Through a series of seemingly unrelated encounters, Jim and I became casual acquaintances, which is to say we knew each other's first names and generally began to acknowledge each other's existence. Jim and I had nothing in common. He knew nothing of me as a professor of Old Testament to ministerial students. Our lives crossed periodically so that he saw me routinely in public, dressed as most professors have to dress. He probably saw me as one of those professional types who work in office buildings and go out for "power lunches." I am sure he must of thought of me as one of those "college boys," who was incapable of changing the oil in my car or dry-walling a house. By contrast, Jim was one of those men in the work force who was "between jobs." He had a number of handyman skills, but he always seemed to be "down on his luck." When I met him, he was working at a modest job making minimum wages and barely making ends meet.

With so little in common, it was somewhat surprising that with continued regular encounters over the period of several months, our acquaintance began to develop into a friendship, with genuine interest in each other's lives. One day when we had opportunity to have a lengthier conversation, Jim began to tell me about troubles he was having with his girlfriend. Neither were Christians, and they had been living together for quite some time. But things were

---

11. Bonhoeffer, *The Cost of Discipleship*, 45–60. The quotes are from pages 45–47.

12. *The Works of John Wesley*, 14 vols., ed. Thomas Jackson (London: Wesleyan Conference Office, 1872; repr. Grand Rapids: Baker, 1978), 8:472; Kenneth J. Collins, *The Scripture Way of Salvation: The Heart of John Wesley's Theology* (Nashville: Abingdon, 1997), 55.

13. Thus, Wesley speaks of an "evangelical repentance," which occurs after one has been justified and involves a change of heart related to inbred sin (Collins, *Scripture Way*, 155–56).

ed and worried. We had by now become bet-
inity to tell him about my personal faith and
nity as the answer to his questions.

emely negative. He related experiences from
icult for him to see God and Christianity in a
lings were raised by a single mother in near
membered the day when, as a small boy, he
d sisters were asked to leave a church service
ly dressed for worship. That rejection was Jim's
tianity. He wanted nothing to do with it. But
rtunities to explain that the way that particular
as not really Christian and that God was the

in my office, Jim called me. In one of our con-
my office number, though he had never been to
the seminary or really talked much about what I do for a living. On this day,
he was in real trouble. His girlfriend had moved out of their home, and Jim
sounded almost suicidal. At my invitation, Jim came to my office to talk. He
shared honestly and openly about their problems. They had aired out their
differences in a serious fight, and she had broken off their relationship and
moved out for good. His family lived in another state, and he was lonely and
depressed.

I felt that Jim knew enough about me and what I believed that he must have
sought me out for a specific reason. He knew what I would say. I believed he
was reaching out for guidance, some means of finding peace and forgiveness.
For the first time in our friendship, I had an opportunity to explain systemat-
ically the simple gospel message and invite Jim to become a Christian. He was
ready and willing to listen. That day, I invited Jim to pray and accept Christ
as his personal Savior. He hesitated. He wanted to go home and think more
about what I was saying. We prayed, and Jim left my office.

Happily Jim did not delay long. Within days, he called me again. With
near euphoria he told me of his acceptance of the gospel. He had reread the
verses I shared and in fact had started reading the Bible all during the night.
He related that when he prayed alone, he felt an overwhelming sense of joy
and forgiveness that he had never known before. The honesty with which
Jim shared these developments and the innocence of his understanding of
them was refreshing and sincere. We began meeting weekly for Bible study
and prayer, and over the next month or so, Jim grew as fast as any new Christian I had ever seen.

Then one day Jim came to my office for our weekly meeting with the news
that he and his girlfriend were getting back together. She was moving back

in, and Jim was so happy. He saw it as confirmation that his new relationship with Christ was the answer to his problems. As yet, he saw no contradiction between his new faith and his relationship with his girlfriend. After they began living together again, Jim and I continued our meetings, and I began praying about how to handle the situation. After a few weeks, I decided that the next meeting would be a time for me to explain to Jim the inconsistency between his love for Christ and his continued relationship with his girl-friend, at least under their current arrangement. I prayed about how to explain everything and prepared myself for several options in the conversation.

What happened in our meeting that day was a beautiful testimony to God's grace in our lives. After an opening prayer and before I could begin with my plans to confront Jim, he surprised me with the news that he had asked his girlfriend to leave. He said he could not understand what had changed. He was shocked that he was the one breaking off their relationship. He honestly confessed that something about their relationship "just didn't feel right anymore." When I began to explain delicately what I believed was happening in his life, he was amazed and excited to know more. Jim was no longer comfortable with her because he was a different Jim. His new faith had invited God's grace into this life, and God was in the process of changing Jim from the inside out. I explained that as he grew in grace, God would undoubtedly begin to reveal more things about his life that would need to change.

God's grace and love were sufficient to make all of this happen. Within a year, Jim met a Christian woman at a church he was attending. She became his wife. I have come to believe that Jim is a wonderful illustration of the correlation of devotion to God and repentance from sin. He learned repentance when he first became a Christian, but he also "turned from" his illicit relationship with this girlfriend as he grew in grace. The way he did it willingly, without my nudging, illustrated the genuineness of his faith and the effectiveness of God's grace in his life.

As 1 Samuel 7:2–4 teaches, there is a natural connection between committing ourselves to the Lord exclusively and ridding ourselves of the foreign gods, whatever they may be in our contemporary context. We will put away our Baals and Ashtoreths, not only because we must, but because they no longer function as they once did. They no longer satisfy if the Lord is truly our object of worship. For today's believers, any object of our affection may potentially become a "foreign god," interfering with our relationship with God. Whenever and wherever this happens, the message of the prophet needs to be heard again: Return to the Lord wholeheartedly by ridding yourselves of foreign gods, committing yourselves to the Lord, and serving him only!

As important as these truths are, we must not lose sight of the corporate scope of the present passage. As Samuel led the nation in communal repentance and as Ezra and Daniel led Old Testament believers of their day in corporate repentance, so today's Christians must call the contemporary church, in all its rich diversity, to prayers of repentance for past sins.

Many Christians in North America appear to be unwilling to face the sins of our own ancestry against African Americans and Native Americans. Centuries of racial prejudice and forced slavery are crimes that beg for repentance. Many white Americans today refuse to take personal responsibility for our nation's sins and to repent for the crimes of our heritage. But the biblical principle is clear. Like Samuel, Ezra, and Daniel, we should ourselves repent for the nation's sins and call the nation as a whole to join in that repentance. Once the church orders its own house, we will be in a position to model repentance to the larger society, leading the nation to repentance. But until the church rises up to unite the nation in one voice of national repentance, it is unlikely that God will hear from heaven, forgive our sin, and heal our land (2 Chron. 7:14b).

1 Samuel 7:5–17

THEN SAMUEL SAID, "Assemble all Israel at Mizpah and I will intercede with the LORD for you." ⁶When they had assembled at Mizpah, they drew water and poured it out before the LORD. On that day they fasted and there they confessed, "We have sinned against the LORD." And Samuel was leader of Israel at Mizpah.

⁷When the Philistines heard that Israel had assembled at Mizpah, the rulers of the Philistines came up to attack them. And when the Israelites heard of it, they were afraid because of the Philistines. ⁸They said to Samuel, "Do not stop crying out to the LORD our God for us, that he may rescue us from the hand of the Philistines." ⁹Then Samuel took a suckling lamb and offered it up as a whole burnt offering to the LORD. He cried out to the LORD on Israel's behalf, and the LORD answered him.

¹⁰While Samuel was sacrificing the burnt offering, the Philistines drew near to engage Israel in battle. But that day the LORD thundered with loud thunder against the Philistines and threw them into such a panic that they were routed before the Israelites. ¹¹The men of Israel rushed out of Mizpah and pursued the Philistines, slaughtering them along the way to a point below Beth Car.

¹²Then Samuel took a stone and set it up between Mizpah and Shen. He named it Ebenezer, saying, "Thus far has the LORD helped us." ¹³So the Philistines were subdued and did not invade Israelite territory again.

Throughout Samuel's lifetime, the hand of the LORD was against the Philistines. ¹⁴The towns from Ekron to Gath that the Philistines had captured from Israel were restored to her, and Israel delivered the neighboring territory from the power of the Philistines. And there was peace between Israel and the Amorites.

¹⁵Samuel continued as judge over Israel all the days of his life. ¹⁶From year to year he went on a circuit from Bethel to Gilgal to Mizpah, judging Israel in all those places. ¹⁷But he always went back to Ramah, where his home was, and there he also judged Israel. And he built an altar there to the LORD.

SAMUEL'S CALL TO REPENTANCE in 7:2–4 was stated in general terms. The nature of repentance was broadly defined, and no specifics were given other than the Israelite rejection of foreign gods. In this portrait of Israel's confession before God at Mizpah, however, the narrative presents us with a specific example of national repentance in a formal public ceremony led by Samuel.

Repentance at Mizpah (7:5–6)

MIZPAH WAS LOCATED in the tribe of Benjamin, just eight miles north of Jerusalem. It afforded views to the west across the valleys toward Philistia and hosted other national convocations during the period of the judges and early monarchy (1 Sam. 10:17; cf. Judg. 20:1; 21:8).[1] As an important city in early Israel, it was an appropriate location for national confession. It is possible that the water ceremony (7:6) symbolized the washing away of corporate guilt.

Israel's confession in verse 6 makes a significant contribution to the overall message of 1–2 Samuel: "We have sinned against the LORD." The historian responsible for the books of Samuel seems especially interested in defining and illustrating the nature of genuine confession and repentance. The immediately preceding paragraph defined repentance (7:2–4); this one formalizes the national repentance publicly and illustrates confession. Moreover, the extended narrative beautifully makes the point by presenting three poignant scenes in which individuals make the statement: "I/We have sinned (against the LORD)." The books of Samuel use these scenes as "portraits of repentance."

(1) In this passage the venerable prophet Samuel leads a unified and repentant nation of Israel in effective and persuasive corporate repentance. The narrative uses this example to establish and illustrate the nature of true repentance so that the reader knows full well what should and can happen when anyone genuinely repents of sin.

(2) The second scene is King Saul's self-serving and equivocating repentance in 15:24, 30. Though the same phrase is used ("I have sinned"), we will see below that Saul's repentance is disingenuous. He is defensive and argumentative, and even though he uses the right words, they are completely insincere. Saul stands in stark contrast to this first scene. His portrait is a negative example of confession, and thus the reader learns from the long and sad narrative of Saul's fall what happens when an individual fails to repent.

(3) The final confessing scene is that of King David when confronted by the prophet Nathan in 2 Samuel 12:13. Again the same words are used

---

1. Patrick M. Arnold, "Mizpah," *ABD*, 4:879–81; Jeffrey R. Zorn, "Naṣbeh, Tell en-," *OEANE*, 4:101–3.

("I have sinned against the LORD"). But unlike Saul, David is portrayed as genuinely remorseful and makes no attempt at self-vindication or justification.[2] These "portraits of repentance" in 1–2 Samuel create a point-counterpoint balance and teach the importance of true repentance.

Decisive Victory (7:7–11)

IN 1 SAMUEL 4, the Israelites lost to the Philistines because they attempted to manipulate God by bringing the ark of the covenant into the battle. They had no leadership to warn them against such action, and the military defeat was at the same time a spiritual failure. Now, however, Samuel has replaced the unfortunate Eli and his ignoble sons. The military threat has not changed, but this time the people implore Samuel to continue interceding on their behalf (7:8). Nothing has really changed—and yet everything has changed. The Philistines are still there and still menacing. But the people have now repented from worshiping Canaanite gods and from trying to manipulate Yahweh. Now they seek Yahweh's help, demonstrated in their reliance on Samuel to offer acceptable sacrifices to Yahweh and to pray effectual prayers (7:9).

The result is a rousing military victory in which Yahweh thunders "with loud thunder," apparently referring to a storm that breaks up the Philistine battle lines and allows the Israelites to pursue them down the hill.[3] The location of Beth Car is unknown, though from this text we assume it is near Mizpah in the territory of Benjamin.[4]

"Ebenezer": The Lord Has Helped Us (7:12–14)

THE HEBREW "EBENEZER" is a compound word meaning literally "stone of help";[5] it commemorates the place where Yahweh helped Israel. Early Israelites used stones in a variety of ways. They could mark territorial boundaries or tombs; they could represent the twelve tribes or a male heir (Gen. 31:44–49; 35:19–20; Ex. 24:4; 2 Sam. 18:18, respectively).[6] Frequently, such stones were simply commemorative, and Samuel's Ebenezer may have been like hundreds

---

2. As if to emphasize this point one final time, the narrator returns to this portrait of David, who repeats the important confession formula again at the conclusion of the books of Samuel (2 Sam. 24:10, 17).

3. Some scholars have recognized an early "Yahweh war" tradition behind this account, which may support the historicity of the event. See Peter Weimar, "Die Jahwekriegserzählungen in Exodus 14, Josua 10, Richter 4 und 1 Samuel 7," Bib 57 (1976): 38–73, esp. 63–69.

4. Jeffries M. Hamilton, "Beth-Car," ABD, 1:683.

5. Or perhaps "the stone (called) Help," DCH, 1:113.

6. A growing number of scholars believe early Israel shared with other peoples of Syria-Palestine the practice of "material aniconism" (see comments on 4:4).

of royal victory stelae used throughout the ancient world.[7] In this case, it may have been inscribed with an account of Israel's victory over the Philistines.

As we noted on 4:1, this is probably not the same locale as the Ebenezer mentioned there (see comments). But the two Ebenezers (4:1 and 7:12) tie these chapters together thematically and contrast the humiliating defeat in chapter 4 with the victory in chapter 7.[8] This is a new Ebenezer! Israel lost to the Philistines at the old Ebenezer because they trusted in their external symbols of Yahweh's power. But on this occasion near Mizpah, repentant Israel experiences afresh Yahweh's help in their time of need.

This stone monument is more than a reminder for future generations that Yahweh helped in this battle against the Philistines. It is that, but it is more. It also serves the present generation by driving a benchmark in the ground and acknowledging that this victory is not a result of their own strength or brilliant military strategy. Yahweh had spoken with a loud thunder (lit., "with a great voice," 7:10), and this stone acknowledges his help.

Summary of Samuel's Ministry (7:15–17)

THIS BRIEF CONCLUSION states simply that Samuel uses his hometown, Ramah, as a base. He travels on a yearly circuit to serve as judge for all Israel. The spectacular victory over the Philistines and the concluding reference to "peace" in 7:14 draw deliberate comparisons between Samuel and the charismatic leaders in the book of Judges. But there are differences as well. Samuel is established on a more permanent basis, partly because of the loss of the priesthood and the cult shrine at Shiloh. His jurisdiction is broader than previous judges. He is truly a pivotal figure in the transition from tribal confederation under the temporary leadership of various judges to a centralized monarchic government, as we will see in the next major unit of 1 Samuel.

Bridging Contexts

MONUMENTS OF GOD'S **saving work**. The Israelites frequently erected monuments. The patriarchs in Genesis built local altars for worship, which they did at nearly every important stop along their pilgrimage (Gen. 8:20; 12:7–8; 13:18; 22:9; 26:25; 33:20; 35:1). But the use of a commemorative stone was more than an act of worship. It also acknowledged God's mighty saving acts and drove a benchmark as a turning point for the worshiper. It symbolized a new act on God's part,

---

7. Marguerite Yon, "Stelae," *OEANE*, 5:79–82.

8. Because the "Ebenezer" references serve as a literary envelope for chs. 4–7, some scholars feel the parameters of the ark narrative should include ch. 7 (i.e., 4:1b–7:17).

which meant the worshiper would never be the same again. It was a permanent reminder that in this place at this point in time, God acted in such a way that the future has new prospects.

Jacob set up such a stone at Bethel to acknowledge that God had met him there in a special way and that he understood his life would now be different (Gen. 28:16–22; see also 35:14). In an important covenant ceremony, Moses erected twelve stone pillars to represent the twelve tribes of Israel (Ex. 24:4). Joshua used twelve stones to mark the place where God led the people of Israel across the Jordan River on dry ground (Josh. 4:1–9). The stones were meant to prompt the question among their children, "What do these stones mean?" Thus a permanent reminder could be established that Yahweh "did to the Jordan just what he had done to the Red Sea" (4:23).[9] Joshua used a stone monument later when he reestablished the covenant between Yahweh and Israel at Shechem (24:25–26). Thus, such commemorative markers were used for holy sites where God had appeared in a dream, provided miraculously for the nation, or renewed his covenant relationship with them.

Thus, Samuel is here continuing an old and sacred tradition of marking the time and place where God had touched his people in a significant way. Unlike other commemorative stones, however, Samuel gives this memorial a name, "Ebenezer" ("Stone of Help"), because the Lord had helped Israel here. This victory was more than a well-fought and justly deserved triumph. This victory, this "help," had its origin in the Lord and was a gift of his grace.

Christianity is a historical religion. Its origins in Old Testament faith and its beginnings in Jesus of Nazareth teach us to commemorate what God has done. The Old Testament Passover and Jesus' Last Supper with his disciples are means of marking the momentous events that stand as central saving acts of God. They are monuments of God's saving work.

EBENEZER STONES. We have many stone monuments in America. On a recent trip to Washington, D.C., with my family, we reveled in the magnificent monuments of that impressive city. Most commemorate the contributions of giants in our national history, such as the granite monuments to Washington, Jefferson, and Lincoln (my personal favorite). Others provide permanent reminders of the sacrifices Americans have made through the decades to defend and protect our freedom,

---

9. Robert L. Hubbard Jr., "'What Do These Stones Mean?': Biblical Theology and a Motif in Joshua," *BBR* 11 (2001): 1–26, esp. 3–12.

such as the Vietnam War Memorial, the Vietnam Women's Memorial, and the Tomb of the Unknown Soldier in Arlington National Cemetery. Currently, former U.S. Senator Robert Dole is raising funds for a World War II memorial, which he hopes to build on the mall in Washington. Most smaller communities have monuments honoring war dead from the Civil War or one of the World Wars; usually these list the names of local citizens who made the ultimate sacrifice rather than naming God as our Helper (like the Ebenezer stone).

Perhaps the most meaningful of all our national monuments stands in New York Harbor, the Statue of Liberty. No other national monument holds the significance of the grand lady of liberty, who has welcomed millions to our shores over the past century. My father shares his memory of returning from the battlefields of Europe after World War II. His ship was entering New York Harbor with the Statue of Liberty well in sight when a small tugboat came out to meet them. On the deck of the little boat was a band and a group of choristers singing, "Welcome Home, Boys, Welcome Home." My father says that everyone of those hardened combat veterans was standing on deck looking at Lady Liberty with tears in their eyes as they realized they had survived the war and it was over.

As important and meaningful as these national monuments are, none of them speaks to the needs addressed by Israel's Ebenezer monument. The Ebenezer stood in Samuel's day as a reminder of what *God* had done for the nation of Israel. As a matter of fact, the name itself emphasized that their victory was solely of God. On that day when he thundered from heaven, they were the undeserving beneficiaries of his saving work. It was not a monument to an abstract concept such as "liberty" or "justice," nor was it a memorial to individuals who had contributed much or sacrificed most. This was a reminder that repentance and faith had been effective and that God had been faithful to his word; God had *acted* on their behalf. America could use such a monument. In many ways, our annual Thanksgiving Day serves—or at least should serve—as such a commemorative event.

In 1999, I had the honor of returning to Europe with my father, who had been a sergeant in the European Theater of Operations in 1944–1945. We visited many places he remembered from those horrible months when so many of his buddies were killed or wounded. To our surprise, we discovered that hundreds of cities and villages across France, Luxembourg, and Belgium have monuments, often in their town squares, commemorating the sacrifices of soldiers in the U.S. Army. For example, in Sainteny in northern France, we found a monument with the inscription, "Hommage aux 83° et 4° D.I. U.S." ("Dedicated to the US 83rd and 4th Infantry Divisions"). It is only a small monument in a tiny town square in a village in Normandy. There are no large crowds walking by the monument. But for those who do, it stands as a perpetual reminder of my father's work and the sacrifices of his friends to save Sainteny so many years ago.

It was fascinating to see how many of these monuments mention the specific date and outfit or infantry regiment that first entered their city to liberate it from the Nazis. We were visiting primarily those monuments dedicated to the fighting men of the 329th Infantry Regiment (83rd Division), but we discovered many monuments to soldiers from the United States, the United Kingdom, and Canada. Over half a century after the war ended, the citizens of these towns remember and acknowledge their gratitude. After years of Nazi oppression, the specific moment and place of liberation was worth marking, and the liberators will not be forgotten.

It struck me that we Christians need similar Ebenezer stones to commemorate our liberation from oppression. We should likewise commemorate the specific ways God has led us to freedom from our own failures and sin, and we should, like Samuel of old, always acknowledge: "Thus far has the LORD helped us."

On a more individual level, it is also helpful to realize that most of us should have specific and personal ways of commemorating and acknowledging God's grace in our lives. Perhaps it is even helpful to picture mentally certain Ebenezer stones at critical turning points in our lives, when God has acted and we have responded to his grace. We frequently, and quite naturally, associate those singular moments when he touched us by his grace with certain times and places. These become our metaphorical Ebenezer stones. Over time they can take on powerful symbolic significance for us as we journey our Christian pathway, and we grow to cherish the memories of that touch of grace. Such reminders can also inspire us to raise new Ebenezers and to join with the body of believers everywhere in celebrating the saving work of Jesus, as is stated in this classic Christian hymn:

> Here I raise my Ebenezer;
> Hither by thy help I'm come;
> And I hope, by Thy good pleasure,
> Safely to arrive at home.
> Jesus sought me when a stranger,
> Wand'ring from the fold of God;
> He, to rescue me from danger,
> Interposed his precious blood.[10]

---

10. "Come, Thou Fount of Ev'ry Blessing," *The Methodist Hymnal: Official Hymnal of the Methodist Episcopal Church, South, and the Methodist Episcopal Church* (Nashville: Publishing House of the M. E. Church, South, 1905), 23.

1 Samuel 8:1-22

WHEN SAMUEL GREW old, he appointed his sons as judges for Israel. ²The name of his firstborn was Joel and the name of his second was Abijah, and they served at Beersheba. ³But his sons did not walk in his ways. They turned aside after dishonest gain and accepted bribes and perverted justice.

⁴So all the elders of Israel gathered together and came to Samuel at Ramah. ⁵They said to him, "You are old, and your sons do not walk in your ways; now appoint a king to lead us, such as all the other nations have."

⁶But when they said, "Give us a king to lead us," this displeased Samuel; so he prayed to the LORD. ⁷And the LORD told him: "Listen to all that the people are saying to you; it is not you they have rejected, but they have rejected me as their king. ⁸As they have done from the day I brought them up out of Egypt until this day, forsaking me and serving other gods, so they are doing to you. ⁹Now listen to them; but warn them solemnly and let them know what the king who will reign over them will do."

¹⁰Samuel told all the words of the LORD to the people who were asking him for a king. ¹¹He said, "This is what the king who will reign over you will do: He will take your sons and make them serve with his chariots and horses, and they will run in front of his chariots. ¹²Some he will assign to be commanders of thousands and commanders of fifties, and others to plow his ground and reap his harvest, and still others to make weapons of war and equipment for his chariots. ¹³He will take your daughters to be perfumers and cooks and bakers. ¹⁴He will take the best of your fields and vineyards and olive groves and give them to his attendants. ¹⁵He will take a tenth of your grain and of your vintage and give it to his officials and attendants. ¹⁶Your menservants and maidservants and the best of your cattle and donkeys he will take for his own use. ¹⁷He will take a tenth of your flocks, and you yourselves will become his slaves. ¹⁸When that day comes, you will cry out for relief from the king you have chosen, and the LORD will not answer you in that day."

¹⁹But the people refused to listen to Samuel. "No!" they said. "We want a king over us. ²⁰Then we will be like all the other nations, with a king to lead us and to go out before us and fight our battles."

²¹When Samuel heard all that the people said, he repeated it before the LORD. ²²The LORD answered, "Listen to them and give them a king."

Then Samuel said to the men of Israel, "Everyone go back to his town."

WITH CHAPTER 8, we begin a new unit in 1–2 Samuel, which continues through chapter 12. These chapters narrate the rise of Israelite monarchy. As we stated in the introduction, this unit contains both positive and negative attitudes toward the concept of kingship in ancient Israel. Rather than postulate contradictory original sources for the unit, it is possible to see an interchange between the pro- and antimonarchic materials intended to complement each other: 8:1–22 (negative), 9:1–10:16 (positive), 10:17–27 (negative), 11:1–11 (positive), 11:12–12:25 (negative).[1] This also argues ultimately for the unity of the final form of chapters 8–12.

Literary studies in recent decades have shown that 1 Samuel 9–11 function as a central unit on the accession of Saul, which is framed by ideological speculation about the nature of kingship itself (chs. 8 and 12).[2] This central accession core contains a three-part process of divine designation, victory, and confirmation.

From the beginning, we are struck by the fact that the narrative almost completely ignores sociological and political factors in the transition from tribal confederation to monarchy.[3] These must have involved significant, per-

---

1. Dennis J. McCarthy, "The Inauguration of Monarchy in Israel: A Form-Critical Study of 1 Samuel 8–12," *Int* 27 (1973), 401–12; J. Robert Vannoy, *Covenant Renewal at Gilgal* (Cherry Hill, N.J.: Mack, 1978), 197–239; Childs, *Introduction to the Old Testament*, 277–78.

2. D. Edelman, "Saul's Rescue of Jabesh-Gilead (1 Sam. 11:1–11): Sorting Story from History," *ZAW* 96 (1984): 195–209, esp. 198; see also Baruch Halpern, "The Uneasy Compromise: Israel between League and Monarchy," in *Traditions in Transformation: Turning Points in Biblical Faith*, ed. B. Halpern and J. D. Levenson (Winona Lake, Ind.: Eisenbrauns, 1982), 59–96; V. Philips Long, *The Reign and Rejection of King Saul: A Case for Literary and Theological Coherence* (Atlanta: Scholars Press, 1989), 183–90.

3. See Tsevat's distinction between "generalizing history" (i.e., information on the social, economic, cultural, and religious background) and "individualizing history" (i.e., particular circumstances, special events, and specific individuals). Matitiahu Tsevat, "Israelite History," 177–87, esp. 185–87. In this case, the generalizing history must be reconstructed from

---

haps even excruciating, changes for ancient Israel. But the author is primarily concerned with the theological specifics of this monumental development. In fact, the narrative in these early chapters centers not on the new king at all but rather on Samuel. The prophet, the man of God, is Yahweh's chosen king-maker, and he stands behind, alongside, and even above the new king.[4]

Israel Asks for a King (8:1–9)

THE ELDERS OF Israel are right to be concerned about Samuel's sons suc-ceeding him as the spiritual conscience of the nation. Joel and Abijah, his des-ignated successors, are unrighteous and unjust, being easily bribed in their judgments. Dynastic succession had not been effective among the judges or the priests (Judg. 9:1–57; 1 Sam. 2:12–17). Israel had been down this path before. Why should the next generation of leaders necessarily come from Samuel's family? Perhaps there would be a better way.

So the Israelites are justified in planning for the future, and we certainly cannot fault them for approaching Samuel about what they should do after his death. The problem arises in the nature of their suggestion. This request for a king (really, it is a demand) is the fundamental problem that finds res-olution in chapters 8–12 and actually overshadows the rest of 1 Samuel. As we will see, the Israelite demand for a king in 8:5 is sinful in its motives, self-ish in its timing, and cowardly in its spirit (see Bridging Contexts section).

The motivation for Israel's demand for a king will become clearer as the passage unfolds. But it is clear enough already in the elders' words of verse 5: "Appoint a king to lead us, such as all the other nations have."[5] The use of the word "king" (*melek*) is an uncontested reference to monarchy, which had been portrayed as undesirable, though necessary, in the judges period (cf. Judg. 8:22–28; also Jotham's fable in 9:7–15; see also 17:6; 18:1; 19:1; 21:25). When the elders ask Samuel to appoint a king to "lead" them (lit., "judge" them), they clearly have in mind more than a simple change of leaders. They want a change of institutions; they want a fundamental change of national constitution.[6]

---

other sources. Tsevat maintains that the study of individualizing history is a secondary task of biblical interpretation, but is worthwhile because it contributes to a better understand-ing of the historical books.

4. Hertzberg, *I and II Samuel,* 65.

5. These elders are presumably the same body who decided to use the ark of the covenant as a good-luck charm in the war with the Philistines (1 Sam. 4:3).

6. McCarter, *I Samuel,* 160. The term *judge* now takes on predominantly the concept of leadership in war; "the juridical element is totally absent." Matitiahu Tsevat, "The Biblical Account of the Foundation of the Monarchy in Israel," in *The Meaning of the Book of Job and Other Biblical Studies,* 85.

This is a request for a paradigm shift of political structures, rejecting the older form of charismatically chosen judges who led in peacetime and who occasionally also served as temporary military commanders in such defensive wars as were necessary. Requesting a "king" to "lead" is tantamount to a rejection of Samuel's godly judgeship and ministry of prophecy.

Motivation for such a request is stated succinctly, requiring only two words in Hebrew: "such as all the other nations have" (see also 8:20). This alarming statement reveals a profound dissatisfaction with who they are as a people. They have been constituted as the people of God, established in covenant at Mount Sinai, informed by Torah instruction, and led and protected by divinely ordained religious judges. Now this very identity is in doubt. They seek a status on the level with their new neighbors, the Canaanites. They have lived among them for at least two centuries, and now they want to become like them. They have grown weary of being unique; they seek conformity and security. But as the passage makes clear, they are grasping for something they fail to understand and will lose the very things they hope to ensure by having a king.

At first sight, Yahweh's response to Samuel may seem harsh: "It is not you they have rejected, but they have rejected me as their king" (8:7). Yahweh cites the long-standing pattern of sin and rebellion since the Exodus as evidence that the people of Israel will persist in their demand for a king (8:8). In fact, this speech of Yahweh uses characteristic vocabulary to illustrate that their request is tantamount to other episodes of rebellion from Israel's history: "forsaking me and serving other gods."[7] He is painfully aware that even given the warnings against kingship, Israel will not relent. Furthermore, Gideon had also perceived human kingship as a rejection of Yahweh's rule, reflecting the long-standing Israelite belief in theocracy (i.e., the kingship of God; Judg. 8:23; cf. 1 Sam 12:12). "The meaning of the kingship of God, according to the Bible, is the denial to [humankind] of the concentration and permanence of power."[8] To demand otherwise is to wrest power away from God.

Samuel Warns Against Kingship (8:10–18)

AT YAHWEH'S DIRECTION, Samuel details the consequences of the kingship Israel desires. At this point, the reader may object that kingship had been the plan of Yahweh from before the beginning of Israel as a nation (Gen. 17:6, 16; 49:10; Ex. 19:6; Num. 24:17–19; Deut. 17:14–20). The Lord's warning against kingship may seem duplicitous.

---

7. Klein, *1 Samuel*, 75–76.
8. Tsevat, "Foundation of the Monarchy," 91.

It is true that Yahweh was not opposed to an Israelite monarchy. Rather, he was opposed to the *kind* of monarchy Israel is now demanding! She wants a king *like the nations around her*, a kingship that will bring her power and political influence. The problem of Israel's request is aptly summarized by Ronald Clements:

> The sharpness of the criticism of the kingship expressed here is not in order to reject the institution altogether, which would make nonsense of the sequel in Yahweh's acceding to the request. Rather it is to condemn the precipitate action of the people in pressing their desire, when Yahweh himself was able to do all that was necessary in order to ensure the people's salvation as the preceding Deuteronomistic narrative of the victory won by Samuel over the Philistines illustrates.[9]

Indeed, the portrait of kingship that Samuel paints appears to be an authentic description of the semifeudal Canaanite political structure as it existed prior to and during the time of Samuel.[10] He objects that having a king like "all the other nations" is not what Yahweh has in mind. Such an unchecked human institution will become militaristic, conscript Israelite men (even women!) into military service, confiscate property, and lead ultimately to enslavement (8:11–17).

The theme words of Samuel's warnings about kingship are "take" and "serve." Ancient Near Eastern kingship is "parasitic rather than giving," and Ahab's seizure of Naboth's vineyard (with Jezebel, of course) illustrates the truth of this warning all too well (1 Kings 21:7), as does David's seizure of Bathsheba (2 Sam. 11:2–5).[11] Nothing seems beyond the grasp of the king, whether children, personal property, or one's freedom. Kings take and take, and when everything is gone, they force you to serve. The final indignation, "you yourselves will become his slaves" (8:17b), is terminology used of

---

9. Ronald E. Clements, "The Deuteronomistic Interpretation of the Founding of the Monarchy in I Sam. VIII," *VT* 24 (1974): 398–410, esp. 406–7.

10. Despite the demurring of modern historians, Samuel's depiction of kingship probably fits better in the context of early Israel's history than the periods of exile or later. See I. Mendelsohn, "Samuel's Denunciation of Kingship in the Light of the Akkadian Documents from Ugarit," *BASOR* 143 (1956): 17–22, esp. 18; Anson F. Rainey, "Institutions: Family, Civil, and Military," in *Ras Shamra Parallels: The Texts from Ugarit and the Hebrew Bible*, Vol. 2, ed. Loren R. Fisher (AnOr 50; Rome: Pontifical Biblical Institute, 1975), 69–107, esp. 93–98. It is even possible to suggest that David's kingship had specifically Jebusite influences; see John Day, "The Canaanite Inheritance of the Israelite Monarchy," in *King and Messiah in Israel and the Ancient Near East: Proceedings of the Oxford Old Testament Seminar*, ed. J. Day (JSOT-Sup 270; Sheffield: Sheffield Academic Press, 1998), 72–90.

11. Youngblood, "1, 2 Samuel," 614; interesting also is Solomon's forced labor (1 Kings 4:6; 5:13–14; 9:15, 21).

enslavement by a conqueror.[12] The kind of kingship Israel is requesting has no redeeming qualities and is antithetical to Israelite faith and history.

Israel's Informed Decision (8:19–22)

ISRAEL CANNOT BE dissuaded; their course is set. Having heard what they can expect from such a king, they persist in their demand and elaborate on their motives. The desire to be "like all the other nations," is repeated (8:5, 20). To this is added, "with a king to lead us and to go out before us and fight our battles."[13] The lust for territorial security is stated in general terms here. But we can assume the long-standing Philistine threat has taken its toll on Israel. Later, in his farewell address, Samuel gives the further detail that the elders are concerned about Nahash the Ammonite, who comes into the story shortly after Saul becomes king (1 Sam. 11; see 12:12). This being the case, Israel is worried about the Ammonites to the east and the Philistines to the west. Their meager military resources are to be tested on two fronts. Apparently, the people of Israel have not learned sufficiently enough from the genuine repentance and glorious victory over the Philistines recorded in chapter 7.

After Yahweh confirms that he will indeed grant a king, Samuel dismisses the assembly and instructs the people to leave Ramah and return to their homes (8:21–22). This note prepares the reader for the action of 9:1–10:16 and for the next national assembly, which will take place at Mizpah (10:17–27) and at which time the nation will receive its king.

Bridging Contexts

MANY MODERN BELIEVERS live in nations governed without kings or queens. At any rate, none are like the ancient Canaanite and Israelite monarchies. Nor do we live in tribal confederations, such as Israel's judges period. In order to interpret this passage for today's church, we need to make the appropriate cultural "jumps" to our own political and social contexts. This text presents us with a vivid picture of Israel's longing and rebellion against God. In rejecting God's lordship, they forfeit its security and blessings and embrace instead a lesser model of God's governance.

As a paradigm for modern believers, Israel's desires, demands, and failures offer us opportunities to examine our own faith. How often modern Christians reject his loving rule, opting instead for some compromise. Regardless

---

12. Richard Schultz, "Servant, Slave," *NIDOTTE*, 4:1187.

13. Such terminology is used elsewhere to describe Yahweh's role as defender of Israel, illustrating again that Israel's request is tantamount to a rejection of Yahweh. See Gerbrandt, *Kingship*, 148.

of whether we live in a representative republic, in a constitutional monarchy, or under a dictatorship, God wants to rule among his people.

The text presents Israel's request for a king as shameless rebellion against God's will, reminiscent of her idolatrous behavior after the Exodus (8:8). God set out to create a nation in his image (Ex. 19:5-6), but now Israel wants to create a king in her image. There are at least three ways in which Israel's request for a king may be critiqued.

(1) The demand for a king is *sinful in its motives*. Israel's motivation is repeated twice in the text: They desire to be like "all the other nations" (8:5, 20). This motivation is stated in a most general way. There is certainly more involved emotionally, psychologically, and politically, as we learn elsewhere in this chapter and later in the book. But in general, this is the essence of the matter, and it is succinctly stated. They are tired of being who they are!

Like Adam and Eve in the Garden of Eden, the Israelites of Samuel's day attempt to cross over the divinely ordained boundaries in order to become something they were not created to be and are not supposed to be.[14] They are not satisfied with what God has done with them and where God has placed them. As Adam and Eve longed to become "like God" (Gen. 3:5), the elders of Israel long to become "like the other nations."

Again, like the first human family in the paradisiacal garden, Israel was a specially formed community. All of her needs were cared for and all her borders secure (esp. after the repentance and victory of ch. 7). God himself was Israel's Lord, protector, and provider. But Israel now chooses a new level of respect and acceptance among her neighbors, which she values as more desirable than her current status. Like Adam and Eve, the nation will learn too late how truly blessed her God-given position is (8:18).

(2) The demand for a king is *selfish in its timing*. Yahweh is not opposed to the concept of kingship in Israel. In fact, there are indications in the Pentateuch that this was his plan for Israel from the beginning.[15] When God confirmed his covenant with Abraham, he stated unequivocally, "I will make nations of you, and kings will come from you" (Gen. 17:6; cf. 17:16). In his deathbed blessing, Jacob appears to have referred to the coming Davidic line of royalty from the tribe of Judah, predicting the rise of the monarchy, the establishment of the Israelite empire, and perhaps even the coming of the Messiah himself (49:10).[16] And Balaam's fourth oracle also alludes to a

---

14. For some of these parallels with Gen. 2-3, see McCarter, *I Samuel*, 160-61.

15. On the structuring of Genesis with the early ancestry of the Davidic dynasty in view, see T. Desmond Alexander, *From Paradise to Promised Land: An Introduction to the Main Themes of the Pentateuch* (Grand Rapids: Baker, 1995), 6-18.

16. Note, however, that this is one of the most hotly debated verses of the Bible.

coming ruler from Israel who will bring military victory against all her enemies (Num. 24:17—19).[17]

The problem with Israel's demand in 1 Samuel 8 is not the *fact* that they want a king, but that they want a king *now!* They are wrongly motivated, but they are also selfishly driven to settle for something less than Yahweh's timing, even after Samuel's stern warnings about the consequences (8:11—17). It should be enough for believers to rejoice in what God has planned for the future, to enjoy his blessings vicariously through successors in the faith, and to live patiently in his grace for the moment. Awaiting the best God has to offer is always better than settling for something inferior. But saying "now" may be as disobedient as saying "no" to God. Impatience is a form of rebellion as much as any of Israel's sins in the desert after the Exodus (Isa. 40:31; James 1:4).

(3) The demand for a king is *cowardly in its spirit*. Israel suffered much during the judges period. Neighboring nations constantly threatened Israel, and these adversaries oppressed various tribes on many occasions (Judg. 2:14—15). But the source of their suffering was not the tribal political structure in the premonarchic period. Rather, the Bible states clearly that the source of their problems was their own apostasy from devotion to Yahweh and their propensity to worship the Canaanite gods of fertility (2:10—13).[18]

In fact, the book of Judges together with 1 Samuel 1—7 illustrates that the appointed judges were Yahweh's means of saving Israel from her enemies, and this tribal confederation had, at various times, been adequate for all her needs. But it demanded courage. It is difficult to trust in Yahweh alone when the enemy is threatening at the border. It seems so much more desirable to have a standing army supplied by an able monarch, someone you can see and trust as a tangible means of security. It takes courageous faith to trust in the judges system and to be willing to live without defenses until the need arises. Demanding a king is the easy way out, and it places blame on the political system rather than one's own religious unfaithfulness.

Samuel warns the Israelites about the consequences of the kingship they are requesting and gives them a chance to change their minds. But they are wrongly motivated from the beginning and will not back down now. It would take a courageous faith to continue to trust in the old judges system and patience to await Yahweh's time for the coming kingdom. But such faith Israel is unwilling to exercise. Likewise, the failure of modern Christians to exercise courageous and patient faith results in challenges to the lordship of Christ.

---

17. See also the law of kingship in Deut. 17:14—20, though, of course, this was a warning against precisely the kind of kingship Israel is now demanding.

18. Keil and Delitzsch, *Samuel*, 78—79.

JESUS IS LORD. Christians by definition embrace and celebrate the lordship of Christ. It is possible that the earliest of all Christian creeds was the simple affirmation, employing only the two Greek words *kyrios Iesous,* "Jesus is Lord." This affirmation appears to have been widely known among the early believers. Note Paul's statement in Romans 10:9: "If you confess with your mouth, 'Jesus is Lord,' and believe in your heart that God raised him from the dead, you will be saved" (see also 1 Cor. 12:3).

At first glance, such a brief affirmation may seem inadequate to characterize the early Christians. But the power of that assertion rests in the way in which the first-century Jews used and understood the Old Testament. Their Greek translation of the Hebrew Scriptures (the LXX) used *kyrios* ("lord, Lord") thousands of times to designate "Yahweh" (the name sometimes transcribed "Jehovah"), the personal name of God. In most modern English translations, God's sacred name becomes simply "the LORD," which continues the Jewish tradition of avoiding pronunciation of the name. So the profundity of the "Jesus is Lord" assertion is that the early followers of Jesus equated their Master with Yahweh of the Old Testament. The Creator of the universe and the covenant-making God of Israel was also Jesus of Nazareth, who came to give himself a ransom for many.

This earliest of creeds probably also lies at the heart of a passage sometimes called *carmen Christi* (Lat., "the song of Christ"; Phil. 2:6–11).[19] At the climax of this great passage, Paul describes the exaltation of Christ by asserting that God gave to Jesus "the name that is above every name" (2:9). Though the name he gave to his Son may have been "God" or "Jesus," it is more likely that Paul is referring to the title "Lord," the most superior name possible.[20] In a rousing climax of praise and adoration, Paul asserts that some day the entire universe will acknowledge what the tiny community of believers at Philippi already know, that "Jesus Christ is Lord," the great sovereign God of the universe.

J. R. W. Stott has explored the "intellectual dimension" of this simple creed and its radical commitment to discipleship. These words imply a degree of ownership, so that it was natural for an early Christian to refer to

---

19. Ralph P. Martin, *Carmen Christi: Philippians 2:5–11 in Recent Interpretation and in the Setting of Early Christian Worship,* rev. ed. (Grand Rapids: Eerdmans, 1983). Many scholars believe these verses constitute an early Christian hymn, adapted by Paul for his own special use. But for many reasons, this consensus is no longer tenable, and it is more likely that Paul composed the entire passage himself. See Frank Thielman, *Philippians* (NIVAC; Grand Rapids: Zondervan, 1995), 110–15.

20. Thielman, *Philippians,* 120–21.

himself as a "servant [slave] of Jesus Christ" (Rom. 1:1). This ownership must lay hold of the minds of modern believers, since, as Stott puts it, the intellect "is the central citadel of our personality and effectively rules our lives." He continues:

> Yet it is often the last stronghold to capitulate to the lordship of Jesus. The truth is that we rather like to think our own thoughts and ventilate our own opinions, and if they conflict with the teaching of Jesus, so much the worse for him![21]

Stott goes on to make the point that many modern Christians are so eager to respond relevantly to the contemporary world that they accommodate the world's way of thinking. Rather than becoming salt and light for the world, we often become like the world, in need of salt and light ourselves (Matt. 5:13−16).

I began exploring the contemporary meaning of this text by wistfully assuming Christians by their very natures "embrace and celebrate the lordship of Christ." Now I must confess that this is far from always true. All too often, Christians become more like Israel than we care to admit, forsaking the security of the lordship of God and grasping after a compromise authority in order to become something we were never meant to be. I know this to be true because I grew up in the church, later became a pastor in the church, and have seen it too often. Indeed, I have been guilty of such grasping myself more times than I care to admit. In our clearest and most honest moments, we all too often seek security by conforming to the *Zeitgeist*, the spirit of the times, rather than serving in the world as God's counterculture, as we were created to do. Like Israel, we tend to forfeit the lordship of God in order to become "like all the nations."

One of the greatest tragedies of the Second World War was the way some so-called German Christians accepted and even promoted the racial myths of Hitler's Third Reich.[22] This occurred because, as Helmut Thielicke concluded, the church failed to continue the debate between the gospel of Christ and the self-understanding of the age, between "eternity and time." He argued instead that true Christian faith believes *against* as well as *in;* that is, it self-consciously runs counter to the currents in the modern ideological stream.

---

21. John Stott, *The Contemporary Christian: An Urgent Plea for Double Listening* (Leicester, Eng.: Inter-Varsity Press, 1992), 86−98 (esp. 90−91).

22. However, other courageous Christians, such as Dietrich Bonhoeffer and his supporters, understood early on that Nazism was a brutal attempt to supplant God's rule on earth. These suffered, and some died in the resistance.

Thielicke speaks of the need for Christian theology's "polar structure." One pole is "a superior, eternal basis derived from revelation," while the other is "specific constellations of the spirit of the age."[23] But why does the church so often fail to be what Christ created her to be? Why do any of us fail to fulfill the high calling to which he has called us? Because our sinful motives and cowardly spirits drive us to grasp selfishly for a different sphere in life—in some cases, *any other* sphere in life. But like the Israelites, we only make it more difficult to follow the higher path God has for us.

One of those courageous German Christians who resisted the Nazi ideas was Dietrich Bonhoeffer. He saw clearly the paradox between losing one's life and finding it. Bonhoeffer himself lost his life on April 9, 1945, in the Flossenburg concentration camp, executed by special order of Himmler only a few days before the camp was liberated by the Allies. Bonhoeffer's tragic death makes the following quote, written by him in 1937, seem all the more poignant:

> Only the man who follows the command of Jesus single-mindedly, and unresistingly lets his yoke rest upon him, finds his burden easy, and under its gentle pressure receives the power to persevere in the right way. The command of Jesus is hard, unutterably hard, for those who try to resist it. But for those who willingly submit, the yoke is easy and the burden is light.[24]

Even in his martyrdom, Bonhoeffer taught that the yoke of Jesus is easy and that "its gentle pressure" gives power to persevere in a just cause. We are never *compelled* to accept the rule of God. But ultimately, God alone appoints the king, and we would do well to submit and find our rest.[25]

---

23. Helmut Thielicke, *Modern Faith and Thought*, trans. Geoffrey W. Bromiley (Grand Rapids: Eerdmans, 1990), 5–7; trans. of *Glauben und Denken in der Neuzeit* (Tübingen: J. C. B. Mohr/Paul Siebeck, 1983).

24. Bonhoeffer, *The Cost of Discipleship*, 40.

25. Baldwin, *1 and 2 Samuel*, 85.

1 Samuel 9:1–10:27

THERE WAS A BENJAMITE, a man of standing, whose name was Kish son of Abiel, the son of Zeror, the son of Becorath, the son of Aphiah of Benjamin. ²He had a son named Saul, an impressive young man without equal among the Israelites—a head taller than any of the others.

³Now the donkeys belonging to Saul's father Kish were lost, and Kish said to his son Saul, "Take one of the servants with you and go and look for the donkeys." ⁴So he passed through the hill country of Ephraim and through the area around Shalisha, but they did not find them. They went on into the district of Shaalim, but the donkeys were not there. Then he passed through the territory of Benjamin, but they did not find them.

⁵When they reached the district of Zuph, Saul said to the servant who was with him, "Come, let's go back, or my father will stop thinking about the donkeys and start worrying about us."

⁶But the servant replied, "Look, in this town there is a man of God; he is highly respected, and everything he says comes true. Let's go there now. Perhaps he will tell us what way to take."

⁷Saul said to his servant, "If we go, what can we give the man? The food in our sacks is gone. We have no gift to take to the man of God. What do we have?"

⁸The servant answered him again. "Look," he said, "I have a quarter of a shekel of silver. I will give it to the man of God so that he will tell us what way to take." ⁹(Formerly in Israel, if a man went to inquire of God, he would say, "Come, let us go to the seer," because the prophet of today used to be called a seer.)

¹⁰"Good," Saul said to his servant. "Come, let's go." So they set out for the town where the man of God was.

¹¹As they were going up the hill to the town, they met some girls coming out to draw water, and they asked them, "Is the seer here?"

¹²"He is," they answered. "He's ahead of you. Hurry now; he has just come to our town today, for the people have a sacrifice at the high place. ¹³As soon as you enter the town, you will find him before he goes up to the high place to eat. The

people will not begin eating until he comes, because he must bless the sacrifice; afterward, those who are invited will eat. Go up now; you should find him about this time."

[14]They went up to the town, and as they were entering it, there was Samuel, coming toward them on his way up to the high place.

[15]Now the day before Saul came, the LORD had revealed this to Samuel: [16]"About this time tomorrow I will send you a man from the land of Benjamin. Anoint him leader over my people Israel; he will deliver my people from the hand of the Philistines. I have looked upon my people, for their cry has reached me."

[17]When Samuel caught sight of Saul, the LORD said to him, "This is the man I spoke to you about; he will govern my people."

[18]Saul approached Samuel in the gateway and asked, "Would you please tell me where the seer's house is?"

[19]"I am the seer," Samuel replied. "Go up ahead of me to the high place, for today you are to eat with me, and in the morning I will let you go and will tell you all that is in your heart. [20]As for the donkeys you lost three days ago, do not worry about them; they have been found. And to whom is all the desire of Israel turned, if not to you and all your father's family?"

[21]Saul answered, "But am I not a Benjamite, from the smallest tribe of Israel, and is not my clan the least of all the clans of the tribe of Benjamin? Why do you say such a thing to me?"

[22]Then Samuel brought Saul and his servant into the hall and seated them at the head of those who were invited— about thirty in number. [23]Samuel said to the cook, "Bring the piece of meat I gave you, the one I told you to lay aside."

[24]So the cook took up the leg with what was on it and set it in front of Saul. Samuel said, "Here is what has been kept for you. Eat, because it was set aside for you for this occasion, from the time I said, 'I have invited guests.'" And Saul dined with Samuel that day.

[25]After they came down from the high place to the town, Samuel talked with Saul on the roof of his house. [26]They rose about daybreak and Samuel called to Saul on the roof, "Get ready, and I will send you on your way." When Saul got ready, he and Samuel went outside together. [27]As they were going

down to the edge of the town, Samuel said to Saul, "Tell the servant to go on ahead of us"—and the servant did so—"but you stay here awhile, so that I may give you a message from God."

¹⁰:¹Then Samuel took a flask of oil and poured it on Saul's head and kissed him, saying, "Has not the LORD anointed you leader over his inheritance? ²When you leave me today, you will meet two men near Rachel's tomb, at Zelzah on the border of Benjamin. They will say to you, 'The donkeys you set out to look for have been found. And now your father has stopped thinking about them and is worried about you. He is asking, "What shall I do about my son?" '

³"Then you will go on from there until you reach the great tree of Tabor. Three men going up to God at Bethel will meet you there. One will be carrying three young goats, another three loaves of bread, and another a skin of wine. ⁴They will greet you and offer you two loaves of bread, which you will accept from them.

⁵"After that you will go to Gibeah of God, where there is a Philistine outpost. As you approach the town, you will meet a procession of prophets coming down from the high place with lyres, tambourines, flutes and harps being played before them, and they will be prophesying. ⁶The Spirit of the LORD will come upon you in power, and you will prophesy with them; and you will be changed into a different person. ⁷Once these signs are fulfilled, do whatever your hand finds to do, for God is with you.

⁸"Go down ahead of me to Gilgal. I will surely come down to you to sacrifice burnt offerings and fellowship offerings, but you must wait seven days until I come to you and tell you what you are to do."

⁹As Saul turned to leave Samuel, God changed Saul's heart, and all these signs were fulfilled that day. ¹⁰When they arrived at Gibeah, a procession of prophets met him; the Spirit of God came upon him in power, and he joined in their prophesying. ¹¹When all those who had formerly known him saw him prophesying with the prophets, they asked each other, "What is this that has happened to the son of Kish? Is Saul also among the prophets?"

¹²A man who lived there answered, "And who is their father?" So it became a saying: "Is Saul also among the

prophets?" ¹³After Saul stopped prophesying, he went to the high place.

¹⁴Now Saul's uncle asked him and his servant, "Where have you been?"

"Looking for the donkeys," he said. "But when we saw they were not to be found, we went to Samuel."

¹⁵Saul's uncle said, "Tell me what Samuel said to you."

¹⁶Saul replied, "He assured us that the donkeys had been found." But he did not tell his uncle what Samuel had said about the kingship.

¹⁷Samuel summoned the people of Israel to the LORD at Mizpah ¹⁸and said to them, "This is what the LORD, the God of Israel, says: 'I brought Israel up out of Egypt, and I delivered you from the power of Egypt and all the kingdoms that oppressed you.' ¹⁹But you have now rejected your God, who saves you out of all your calamities and distresses. And you have said, 'No, set a king over us.' So now present yourselves before the LORD by your tribes and clans."

²⁰When Samuel brought all the tribes of Israel near, the tribe of Benjamin was chosen. ²¹Then he brought forward the tribe of Benjamin, clan by clan, and Matri's clan was chosen. Finally Saul son of Kish was chosen. But when they looked for him, he was not to be found. ²²So they inquired further of the LORD, "Has the man come here yet?"

And the LORD said, "Yes, he has hidden himself among the baggage."

²³They ran and brought him out, and as he stood among the people he was a head taller than any of the others. ²⁴Samuel said to all the people, "Do you see the man the LORD has chosen? There is no one like him among all the people."

Then the people shouted, "Long live the king!"

²⁵Samuel explained to the people the regulations of the kingship. He wrote them down on a scroll and deposited it before the LORD. Then Samuel dismissed the people, each to his own home.

²⁶Saul also went to his home in Gibeah, accompanied by valiant men whose hearts God had touched. ²⁷But some troublemakers said, "How can this fellow save us?" They despised him and brought him no gifts. But Saul kept silent.

IN THE PREVIOUS CHAPTER, Israel demanded a king, but Samuel warned that there would be consequences of having an Israelite monarchy patterned after a Canaanite model. This next unit (9:1–10:27) tells of the monarchy's actual initiation and public endorsement. We have here two sections, one that seems positive toward the monarchy (9:1–10:16) and one negative (10:17–27). The author appears to have assembled the available materials pertaining to the new institution without using extensive revision. It is as though the text presents an elaborate tapestry, weaving a number of different tapestries together that portray the Israelite kingship and the contrasting attitudes concerning it, and then hanging the various tapestries next to each other in a way that presents a complete history of the rise of Israel's new institution.[1] Through it all the fundamental question of 1 Samuel continues to be: What should be the nature of this new Israelite kingship?

Israel demanded a king like "all the other nations" (ch. 8). Yahweh both grants and denies that request. Israel receives Saul son of Kish as her first king. Yet he is not to become quite like the kings of the other nations. This is indeed the struggle portrayed in these chapters: Will Israel's king become like the kings of surrounding nations? In this unit, we read that Yahweh grants the king that Israel requests rather than the one he desires. Yet God is able to bless even this choice. It is the Old Testament's constant reminder of the love of God that he so often takes Israel's failures or compromises and turns them into opportunities for his grace.

Saul Looks for Donkeys and Finds a Kingdom (9:1–10:8)[2]

SAUL IS AN impressive young man. His father's lengthy genealogy implies the family has great wealth. Saul himself strikes an imposing figure, literally standing out in the crowd (9:2; 10:23–24). A future warning against putting too much value on the appearance or height of a particular candidate for the throne (cf. 16:7) may indicate that Saul's appearance is a major factor in his selection as king. From the present passage we know that God appoints Saul and blesses him with all that he needs to serve well. But it is also true that Saul is ultimately the people's choice. Yahweh grants as their first king "the man who in all Israel came nearest to fulfilling their idea of what a king should be."[3]

---

1. Vannoy, *Covenant Renewal at Gilgal*, esp. 198–225, where Vannoy surveys the history of criticism on 1 Sam. 8–12.

2. Similar to the title given this unit by Klein, "Asses Sought, a Kingdom Found" (*1 Samuel*, 80).

3. G. Coleman Luck, "The First Glimpse of the First King of Israel," *BibSac* 123 (1966): 60–66, esp. 61.

Saul and a servant set out to find a group of lost donkeys belonging to his father (9:3–4). They traverse the tribal territories of Benjamin and Ephraim but cannot find the lost animals. At the servant's suggestion, the two of them decide to inquire of a "man of God" at a certain town in the district of Zuph. The text does not mention the name of the town (probably Ramah) or the name of the man of God. Having thus built a satisfying amount of suspense, in verse 14 we learn, finally, that this is Samuel himself.

In a parenthetical paragraph, the author informs us that Yahweh has prepared Samuel the day before Saul's arrival (9:15–16). Thus, the prophet is prepared to anoint him as "leader" (*nagid*, "prince, ruler") over the nation Israel. This term is used in Samuel and Kings for the king-designate as the one officially chosen and appointed by Yahweh to rule his people Israel.[4] It emphasizes the primacy of Yahweh's choosing over any public acclaim. Saul is first "the one designated of Yahweh," which is a theological recognition of his selection. He will become "king" only at his public acclamation: "Long live the king!" (10:24).[5]

However, the term *nagid* likely connotes even more than the primacy of Yahweh's choosing. It seems probable that this word was initially a military term and may have referred to the "commander" of the national militia under the old tribal confederation. Thus, in this context, it limited the kingship of Saul by bearing certain traditions stemming from the tribal league's institutions. The choice of *nagid* rather that the common Hebrew word for "king" (*melek*) emphasizes the limited nature of Saul's kingship.[6] Perhaps *melek* is avoided here because *Yahweh* is Israel's king. It also seems likely that Saul's kingship is perceived as a conditional appointment or covenant. Saul will be king as long as the spirit of God moves him (see comments on 10:9–16) and as long as he does not violate the legal traditions of the tribal league.[7]

In 9:17–27, Saul and Samuel meet for the first time. Yahweh informs Samuel that this young visitor is the one who will "govern" Israel (9:17). There were much more common verbs available for "rule" or "reign," but here we have a verb that usually means "restrain" (ʿaṣar).[8] The other terms for

---

4. BDB, 617–18; Kenneth T. Aitken, "נָגִיד," *NIDOTTE*, 3:20–21; McCarter, *I Samuel*, 178–79. See also Roland de Vaux, "The King of Israel, Vassal of Yahweh," in *The Bible and the Ancient Near East*, trans. D. McHugh (Garden City, N.Y.: Doubleday, 1971), 153.

5. Hertzberg, *I and II Samuel*, 82.

6. Cross, *Canaanite Myth and Hebrew Epic*, 220.

7. Ibid., 221.

8. Shemaryahu Talmon and Weston W. Fields, "The Collocation משתין בקיר ועצור ועזוב and Its Meaning," *ZAW* 101 (1989): 85–112, esp. 104–5.

"rule" may have been avoided to indicate that this will be a governance under the strict lordship of Yahweh, thus again stressing the distinctiveness of Israelite kingship. Saul is to be a ruler-deliverer, who operates under the direct authority of Yahweh and his prophet.

Samuel immediately sets Saul's mind at ease about the missing donkeys. They have been found, and he should not worry about them again because they have bigger issues to discuss. Samuel then unexpectedly includes his guests in a banquet for that evening at the high place outside the town. Without warning, Saul becomes the center of attention, being given a place of honor and a specially designated portion of food. After dinner, Samuel and Saul engage in private conversation, which continues the next day.

In the morning, Samuel prepares Saul to receive a private word from God by asking that he send his servant on ahead of them (9:27). Once alone, Samuel anoints Saul with oil, kisses him, and announces that Yahweh has anointed him as the "leader" (*nagid*) over his people Israel. The use of oil is a symbol of the spirit of Yahweh in several Old Testament passages (Isa. 61:1; Zech. 4:14), and anointing with oil represents the empowerment of Yahweh.[9]

The sacramental act of anointing is a ritual of inauguration, which designates an individual for a specific office consecrated by Yahweh. By comparison with its use in other contexts of the ancient Near East, the practice of anointing appears to have had a contractual or covenantal significance when used to designate kings. When the people of Israel anoint David in 2 Samuel 2:4 and 5:3, they are likely pledging themselves to him and accepting an obligation to him, and David in turn is granting them a royal promise.[10] Prior to Samuel's anointing of Saul, the ritual was restricted in the Old Testament to the tabernacle and its priests.[11] This marks Israel's new monarchy as a divine institution, on a level of the priesthood. Here also, anointing stamps Saul with a special character and privilege because of a unique standing before God.[12]

The transformation of Saul from an unassuming youth to the king-designate is certainly a drastic change for him personally, but it is also revolutionary for the nation. Such radical claims and actions as Samuel has taken will require dramatic confirmation. In order to meet these needs, Samuel prophesies three events that will happen to Saul on his return home,

---

9. John N. Oswalt, "מָשַׁח," *NIDOTTE*, 2:1124–25.

10. Mettinger, *King and Messiah*, 137–50; see de Vaux, "The King of Israel, Vassal of Yahweh," 162–66.

11. On the likelihood of the great antiquity of traditions concerning priestly anointing, see Daniel Fleming, "The Biblical Tradition of Anointing Priests," *JBL* 117 (1998): 401–14.

12. Hertzberg, *I and II Samuel*, 84; Keil and Delitzsch, *Samuel*, 95.

---

which will confirm his selection at least privately (10:2–7). (1) At Zelzah near Rachel's tomb, two strangers will report to Saul that the lost donkeys have been located and that his father is worried about his safety (10:2). (2) Three men near Tabor will greet him and offer him bread (10:3–4). (3) At Gibeah he will be met by a group of prophets playing musical instruments.[13] The spirit of Yahweh will come upon him, he will join them in their prophesying, and he will be "changed into a different person" (10:6). Samuel concludes these signs of confirmation with a command to wait for seven days at Gilgal to receive further instructions. At that time, Samuel will sacrifice burnt offerings and fellowship offerings (10:8).

The consensus of critical scholarship is that 10:8 is not original in this context.[14] But whenever and however the verse may have been included is irrelevant to the current reading of this chapter.[15] The combination of 10:7 ("do whatever your hand finds to do") and 10:8 ("you must wait seven days until I [Samuel] come to you and tell you what you are to do") is not perceived by the author as contradictory.[16] Rather, these verses together establish for Saul the conditions for the new Israelite kingship.

In other words, despite the request of the elders of Israel in chapter 8, they are not receiving a Canaanite-like kingship. This is a highly circumscribed royal authority, a vassalship of Yahweh.[17] In a sense, this is a compromise. If Israel is to have a king, it will be a kingship unique in the ancient Near East. It will not be an absolute, divinely ordained monarchy, dropped out of heaven for the benefit of humankind, as perceived in Mesopotamia. Nor will the Israelite king be a semidivine potentate, like the pharaoh of Egypt. Instead, it will be a highly structured and restricted authority handed from God to prophet to king. Or, in the words of Matitiahu Tsevat, "the meaning of the kingship of God, according to the Bible, is the denial to [humankind] of the concentration and permanence of power."[18]

---

13. Gibeah is Saul's home and plays a significant role in his reign (see 10:26; 22:6). The identification of the site as Tell el-Ful has been widely accepted since the days of Albright. But an older identification of Gibeah as Geba (modern Jeba) has been suggested, which is gaining support in the scholarly community. See Patrick M. Arnold, *Gibeah: The Search for a Biblical City* (JSOTSup 79; Sheffield: JSOT Press, 1990).

14. For discussion, see McCarter, *I Samuel*, 183; Klein, *1 Samuel*, 85.

15. It is also possible that 10:7–8 together comprise a two-part commission, which attempts to circumscribe the new kingship to a military leadership subordinate to Yahweh and his prophet. See Long, *Reign and Rejection*, 58–66.

16. Either to an author who originally wrote both or to an editor who put them side by side.

17. Long, *Reign and Rejection*, 239.

18. Tsevat, "The Biblical Account of the Foundation of the Monarchy in Israel," 91.

"Is Saul Also Among the Prophets?" (10:9–16)[19]

SAUL WAS ON an innocent mission to find his father's lost donkeys. He was not looking for a kingdom. He appears humble, even mystified, by the honors being heaped on him (9:21). But as he turns to take his leave of the prophet, "God changed Saul's heart" (10:9). God is at work in Saul, and he will never be the same.

All three of the signs meant to confirm his anointing are fulfilled that very day. Only the third sign, however, is detailed in the text. When he reaches Gibeah, he meets the band of ecstatic prophets, as Samuel has prophesied. The spirit of God comes on him and empowers him to join the prophets, arousing the derision of the local inhabitants, who apparently know him and his family well.

The question "Is Saul also among the prophets" has several possible connotations.[20] It serves as a rhetorical question expecting a negative answer. In this light, the question affirms Saul's new spiritual gifts, not because he belongs naturally to the band of prophets but because he is the legitimate new ruler of Israel.[21] It affirms his anointing by Samuel, and he accepts his new role. This naturally provokes questions from his uncle (10:14–16). Saul's reticence to answer them is in keeping with the private nature of his encounter with Samuel and ensures that his selection by lot will be unsoiled. Concealment of God's work in one's life is attested elsewhere in the Old Testament (see Samson, Judg. 14:4, 6, 16).[22]

Coronation at Mizpah (10:17–27)

WHILE THE PREVIOUS paragraphs seemed positive and hopeful about the new monarchy, this concluding paragraph returns to the warnings of chapter 8 (as a counterpoint).[23] Fittingly, Samuel calls another national convocation at Mizpah, the site of Israel's humble repentance and victory (7:5–17). In stereotypical prophetic language, he reminds the people that Yahweh brought them out of Egypt and delivered them from its power. Now they have

---

19. It seems probable that 9:1–10:16 is a self-contained literary unit that may have originated in the lifetime of Saul. See Tomoo Ishida, *The Royal Dynasties in Ancient Israel: A Study on the Formation and Development of Royal-Dynastic Ideology* (BZAW 142; Berlin: de Gruyter, 1977), 43.

20. See McCarter, *I Samuel*, 183–84; Smith, *Samuel*, 70–71, for the possibilities.

21. Youngblood, "1, 2 Samuel," 627.

22. Some have even speculated this theme as the background to the messianic secret of the Gospel of Mark (see McCarter, *I Samuel*, 188).

23. Though even here there are hopeful signs. See Bruce C. Birch, "The Choosing of Saul at Mizpah," *CBQ* 37 (1975): 447–57.

rejected him by demanding a king for all the wrong reasons. Interestingly, the prophetic speech pattern used here is one well known throughout the Old Testament for announcing judgment. In fact, the selection of Saul is inserted at the very point where we would expect an announcement of judgment.[24] This being the case, Yahweh's act of providing a king for Israel is itself an act of divine wrath (see Hos. 13:11).

The people present themselves in successive order before Samuel so that the king may be designated by the casting of lots.[25] But when Saul is selected by a process of elimination, he is nowhere to be found. What has gone wrong? Is Saul hiding because of his humility or his cowardliness? In light of the fact that this king-designate has been prophetically anointed, has received three signs confirming his divine appointment (10:1–7), and has been empowered by the spirit of God, this hesitancy to take up the task reflects badly on Saul. "Such persistent reluctance can become reprehensible."[26]

Once located, Saul is presented to the people, who enthusiastically approve. The exultant "Long live the king!" has survived into modern times and universally implores health and success for a new monarch in the hopes that he might lead the people to better times. But this great "leader" has to be dragged before his subjects from behind the baggage, which does not bode well for the future.

THE PLACE OF THE MONARCH IN SALVATION HISTORY. Most Old Testament historical narratives are told on a number of levels.[27] This unit has much to teach us about the nature of Israelite kingship in general and its role in the overarching story of God's relationship with Israel. But on a more individualistic level, this text is also about Saul and the way God relates to him. In applying this text to our modern world, we must consider both levels of interpretation. We consider first the place of Israel's monarchy in biblical salvation history in general before turning to the issues involved in the anointing and preparation of Saul in particular.

The apostle Paul summarized God's work in ancient Israel in his address at Pisidian Antioch (Acts 13:17–22). The God of Israel elected the ancestors,

---

24. Westermann, *Basic Forms of Prophetic Speech*, 90–163; Long, *Reign and Rejection*, 240.

25. On the widespread use of lots in the Bible, see Baldwin, *1 and 2 Samuel*, 93; McCarter, *I Samuel*, 195–96.

26. Long, *Reign and Rejection*, 218.

27. Fee and Stuart, *How to Read the Bible*, 74; see also comments in the introduction to this commentary.

Abraham, Isaac, and Jacob. He prospered their descendants during a sojourn in Egypt, after which he delivered them "with mighty power" and endured their rebellious behavior for forty years in the desert. He overthrew the nations of Canaan and made his people Israel the new owners of the land. Then God appointed (lit., "gave") judges until the time of Samuel the prophet (Acts 13:20b). But "then the people asked for a king, and he gave [same verb] them Saul son of Kish" (13:21). After Saul, God raised up David as king, finding in him a man after his own heart (13:22). Finally, Paul concludes, God brought forth from David's line the Savior Jesus, as he had promised (13:23).

In this sweeping overview of the highlights of salvation history, we can see the role of Saul and the Israelite monarchy, which was a basic theme in God's plan of salvation. The new institution was a link from the ancestors to the coming of the Messiah.

Since this unit is the point at which Israel's monarchy is established for the first time, it is helpful to review in more detail the way in which kingship relates to other themes in the Old Testament.[28] Unlike neighboring cultures of the ancient world, the Bible does not make Israel's kingship an essential ingredient of creation. The Egyptians believed monarchy was rooted in the very order of nature, and the Mesopotamians thought it was necessary for human civilization. But the created order stands independent of Israel's need for a king, and the rule of any individual monarch was strictly granted as a means of God's grace.

Kingship, strictly speaking, was not essential to God's plans for salvation. However, God's promises to the ancestors of the book of Genesis found partial fulfillment in Israel's monarchy (Gen. 15:18–21; 17:6, 16; 49:8–12). Furthermore, the gift of land was linked to kingship in that any king who violated the land was in jeopardy of driving the people into exile. As we will see later in 1–2 Samuel, the central role of Jerusalem and ultimately the coming of the Messiah were also linked to Israel's kingship.

The preparation and anointing of Saul as king. This unit explains the mechanical means by which Israel got her first king. It narrates the divine selection, prophetic anointing, confirmation, and public acclamation of the new king. It is a *historical* narrative in that it tells us of Saul, the kingmaker Samuel, and the inauguration of Israel's monarchy. But like other historical narratives of the Bible, it is not *primarily* concerned with history per se. This is not a history of Israel's kingship. Rather, the narrator has a deeper interest. The story is first and foremost about Yahweh, not Saul or Samuel or even Israel. God is the guiding hand behind all that occurs in this passage.

---

28. For some of what follows, see Barth, *God with Us,* 190–91.

We get a sense of Yahweh's subtle but sovereign actions in a variety of ways. At first we learn about Saul and his mission to find his father's donkeys. But when we meet Samuel, the narrator tells us that Yahweh is in fact *sending* Saul to Samuel ("I will send you a man," 9:16). The Lord has also revealed to Samuel (9:15; lit., "uncovered Samuel's ear") precisely who is to become king, what his tribe of origin is, and how he is to anoint him as "leader." Such details drive the reader to conclude that Saul's journey to find the donkeys is not mere chance but the will of Yahweh.

The servant's insistence that they inquire of the man of God in the local city, Saul's encounter with Samuel, and all the details of the episode seem to be orchestrated, or at least utilized, by the unseen hand of God. And the denouement of the unit, the final step in the preparation of Saul for kingship, is Saul's change of heart, which is mediated and intensified by the spirit of Yahweh (10:6, 9—10). Thus, God is working through Israel's historical and political circumstances to accomplish his purposes for the nation.

Beyond the significance of Israelite kingship in biblical theology in general, this text also invites us to consider in particular the relationship between God's hand on our own lives and the influence of his Spirit in changing our characters. Saul becomes an example of what happens when an individual gets caught up in God's plan for his or her life. Of the three signs predicted to confirm Saul's status in Yahweh's new social order, only the one relating the coming of God's Spirit and the transformation of Saul's character is included (10:9—10). Here spiritual transformation is followed by new life under the authority of God's Spirit.

This is the earliest reference to the inner changes God works through the ministry of his Spirit. It is not accurate to speak in this case of conversion in the way Christians often use the term. Rather, this transformation of Saul realigns his worldview so that his former perceptions of himself and his role in national Israel are replaced with an openness for anything.[29] He is now prepared to follow whatever path Yahweh directs.

The coming of the spirit of Yahweh on Saul at Gibeah (10:6, 9—10) is parallel to a similar event from the time of Moses. While in the desert, the spirit of God rested on the seventy elders of Israel, who were to share responsibility with Moses for judging the people (Num. 11:16—18, 25). In both cases, persons not previously associated with the "prophets" were endowed with prophetic gifts temporarily, which probably confirmed their legitimacy.[30] We should not jump too quickly to a Christian, Trinitarian understanding of

---

29. Hertzberg, *I and II Samuel*, 86; Brueggemann, *First and Second Samuel*, 77.
30. Bergen, *1, 2 Samuel*, 130.

the spirit of the Lord or the spirit of God in the Old Testament. Such expressions are similar to saying a basketball team is infused with the spirit of its coach. The players display the coach's attitudes, character, and energy in the way they play the game.[31] One could say that because of this event, Saul sees things differently. He now shares Yahweh's perceptions of Israel and of himself as her new king. (For this reason, most translations of the Bible use a lowercase "s" for the expression "spirit of God.")

However, the coming of God's spirit here also accompanies an inner, spiritual transformation, turning Saul into "a different person" (10:6). The point is not that Saul becomes a prophet or merely receives a skill he does not have previously. Rather, by means of the spirit of God, Saul "became the Lord's possession and stood under the authority of Israel's true Savior."[32] By claiming ownership of Saul through his spirit, Yahweh also graciously dispenses a new inner unction that validates his anointing with oil. Though certainly not identical to the New Testament concept of the Holy Spirit, this passage is compatible with its teaching and at least illustrates the active presence of God in the affairs of individuals, to transform and empower them for his service.[33]

THIS UNIT HAS demonstrated how God is at work behind the scenes, bringing Samuel and Saul together miraculously, revealing his will to Samuel that he should anoint Saul, bringing dozens of other people into Saul's life as confirmation of his anointing, and finally changing Saul's character through his Spirit. God's unseen hand is touching and changing in order to empower Israel to fulfill her task in the world and to accomplish his purposes.

God at work in the world. God is still at work in the world today. Sometimes it is difficult for us to see or believe that he is, and it is often clear only to those who have eyes of faith. His work today is of a different nature from that of this biblical text only in that this story relates specifically how he moved and worked in Israel in order to bring salvation to the world. It is a particularly significant step in salvation history, since through Israel's monar-

---

31. I owe this analogy to John N. Oswalt, "John Wesley and the Old Testament Concept of the Holy Spirit," *Religion in Life* 48 (1979): 283–92, esp. 285; for the Spirit in the Old Testament, see M. V. Van Pelt, Walter C. Kaiser, and Daniel I. Block, "רוּחַ," *NIDOTTE*, 3:1075–78.

32. Barth, *God with Us*, 194.

33. For more on the Holy Spirit in the Old Testament, see comments on 16:1–13.

chy, God will eventually provide *the* great King, who will die for the sins of the whole world.

But God's work is not finished. The Bible continues to trace the story until the close of the age. The study of last things (i.e., "eschatology") examines how his work will come to fruition in the future. In the meantime, Christians believe that God is still at work on various levels, in many different ways, in order to accomplish a variety of purposes.

Not long ago, I heard a preacher whom I greatly respect use an illustration I found hard to believe. Later, when I asked his source for the story, he told me it had been published in *Reader's Digest*. When I could not find a reference to the story in recent years, I wrote to the magazine and asked for confirmation that they had published the story. They not only confirmed that they had published the story; they even sent me a faded copy of a 1949 edition of the magazine. I relate these events here as an illustration, humbly giving credit to the publisher for this extraordinary account.[34]

On January 10, 1948, just over two years after the conclusion of World War II, Marcel Sternberger got on a train in the Brooklyn subway he had never been on before. He normally took a different line, but he had changed his schedule in order to visit a sick friend that morning and was now boarding a noon train to get to work. The train was full. But just as he stepped in, one man jumped up and ran off, realizing he was about to miss his station. Sternberger quickly took the seat and sat down. Next to him was a man reading a Hungarian newspaper. Sternberger had been born in Hungary and though he would not normally strike up conversation with strangers in the subway, he felt compelled to say something. He looked over the man's shoulder and said in Hungarian, "I hope you don't mind if I glance at your paper." The man was surprised to be addressed in his native language, and during the half-hour ride to town, they became acquainted.

Sternberger's companion voluntarily shared his tragic story. His name was Paskin, and he had been a law student when the war started. He was eventually put into a labor battalion and sent to the Ukraine. Later he was captured by the Russians and put to work burying the German dead. After the war he covered hundreds of miles on foot, returned to his home in Debrecen, Hungary, and discovered his entire family gone. Strangers were living in the apartment once occupied by his father, mother, brothers, and sisters. When he reached the apartment he and his wife had shared, it also was occupied by strangers. Finally, he located old friends in Debrecen who had survived the war. They sadly informed him his entire family was dead. The

---

34. Paul Deutschman, "It Happened on the Brooklyn Subway," *Reader's Digest* (May 1949), 45–48.

Nazis had taken them and his wife to Auschwitz, where they were all presumably killed in the gas chambers.

Stunned by the news, the man fled Hungary, which had become a funeral land for him. He headed west toward Paris and emigrated to the United States in October 1947. As Sternberger listened, the story seemed somehow familiar. Suddenly he remembered why. He had recently met a young woman at the home of friends who had also been from Debrecen. She had been taken to Auschwitz but was then transferred to work in a German munitions factory. All her relatives had been killed in the gas chambers. After she had been liberated by the Americans, she was brought to New York in the first boatload of Displaced Persons in 1946. Sternberger had been so moved by her story he had written down her address and phone number, hoping to invite her to meet his family in order to help with her terrible loneliness and grief.

Sternberger thought it impossible that there could be a connection between these two people, but when he reached his station, he stayed on the train with his new friend. He asked as casually as possible, "Is your first name Bela?"

The man went pale as he said, "Yes! How did you know?"

Sternberger fumbled for his address book, as he asked, "Was you wife's name Marya?"

Looking as though he might faint, Paskin said, "Yes! Yes!"

Sternberger suggested they get off at the next station without explaining why. He took Paskin to a nearby phone booth. While Paskin stood there like a man in a trance, Sternberger dialed the number, and after a long delay, he had Marya Paskin on the line. Sternberger reminded her of their recent chance meeting, and she remembered him. Without explaining why, Sternberger asked Marya where she had lived in Debrecen before the war, and she told him the address. Sternberger turned to Bela and said, "Did you and your wife live on such-and-such a street?"

"Yes!" Bela exclaimed, as he turned white as a sheet and trembled.

Sternberger urged him to stay calm but then explained that something miraculous was about to happen to him. Then he handed Bela the phone, saying, "Here, take this telephone and talk to your wife!"

When Paskin realized he was really speaking with his Marya, he broke into uncontrollable crying. Sternberger sent him by taxi to the address to be reunited with his wife.

The article continues by describing the emotional reunion between the Paskins, each of whom thought the other was dead. Marya Paskin hardly remembers their reunion because of the sudden release of emotions.

> I remember only that when I left the phone, I walked to the mirror like in a dream to see maybe if my hair had turned gray. The next thing I

know a taxi stops in front of the house and it is my husband who comes toward me. Details I cannot remember; only this I know—that I was happy for the first time in many years. Even now it is difficult to believe that it happened. We have both suffered so much; I have almost lost the capability to be not afraid. Each time my husband goes from the house I say to myself, "Will anything happen to take him from me again?"

There are, of course, many possible explanations of what happened as a result of that subway ride one afternoon in 1948. Some would argue the Paskins were the beneficiaries of lucky coincidences. By contrast, this is how *Reader's Digest* ends the article.

Skeptical persons would no doubt attribute the events of that memorable afternoon to mere chance. But was it chance that made Sternberger suddenly decide to visit his sick friend, and hence take a subway line that he had never been on before? Was it chance that caused the man sitting by the door of the car to rush out just as Sternberger came in? Was it chance that caused Bela Paskin to be sitting beside Sternberger, reading a Hungarian newspaper? Was it chance—or did God ride the Brooklyn subway that afternoon?

An awareness that God is at work in the world today should make believers more sensitive to his unexpected and unseen influence in our everyday lives. Not that we should look for the spectacular and miraculous around every bend. But we should recognize and acknowledge his work in our own lives and in those around us. Saul and his servant were casually looking for his father's lost donkeys when God unexpectedly visited him through the prophet. Abraham was resting by the entrance to his tent when God paid him a visit (Gen. 18). Moses was pasturing sheep when God came and called him to service (Ex. 3). God does not miraculously send us a prophetic word every day or meet us in a burning bush. Nevertheless, we should learn to be faithful while attending to the routine, the ordinary, and the familiar. For in these, God often leads and directs his people.

God's Spirit at work. We should also take from this passage the means by which God leads his people. The anointing of Saul is parallel to another passage familiar to Christians because of its use by Jesus early in his ministry: "The Spirit of the Sovereign LORD is on me, because the LORD has anointed me to preach good news to the poor" (Isa. 61:1; Luke 4:18). Thus, our passage about King Saul has three features in common with this verse spoken by the Lord's Messiah (or "Anointed One"): Both were given the Spirit of the Lord; both were anointed; and both were commissioned for a specific task—

Saul to serve as Israel's first king and the Messiah to proclaim good news to the poor (an agenda spelled out more clearly in the rest of the Isaiah passage, Isa. 61:2–7). Anointing and reception of God's Spirit are indispensable for service in his kingdom.

Finally, Saul is one of the best biblical examples of personal transformation because of the work of God's Spirit in one's life, even though God eventually withdrew his approval and blessing from Saul. In this first unit introducing us to Saul, we learn of his anointing and confirmation as Israel's first king. But this passage lays special stress on Saul's change of character. One's personal conduct and moral character are central not only in one's standing before God but also for leadership among God's people. Furthermore, as the long and sordid story of Saul continues, we will see that God apparently does not long bestow his Spirit where there is no continued change of character.

1 Samuel 11:1–15

NAHASH THE AMMONITE went up and besieged Jabesh Gilead. And all the men of Jabesh said to him, "Make a treaty with us, and we will be subject to you."

²But Nahash the Ammonite replied, "I will make a treaty with you only on the condition that I gouge out the right eye of every one of you and so bring disgrace on all Israel."

³The elders of Jabesh said to him, "Give us seven days so we can send messengers throughout Israel; if no one comes to rescue us, we will surrender to you."

⁴When the messengers came to Gibeah of Saul and reported these terms to the people, they all wept aloud. ⁵Just then Saul was returning from the fields, behind his oxen, and he asked, "What is wrong with the people? Why are they weeping?" Then they repeated to him what the men of Jabesh had said.

⁶When Saul heard their words, the Spirit of God came upon him in power, and he burned with anger. ⁷He took a pair of oxen, cut them into pieces, and sent the pieces by messengers throughout Israel, proclaiming, "This is what will be done to the oxen of anyone who does not follow Saul and Samuel." Then the terror of the LORD fell on the people, and they turned out as one man. ⁸When Saul mustered them at Bezek, the men of Israel numbered three hundred thousand and the men of Judah thirty thousand.

⁹They told the messengers who had come, "Say to the men of Jabesh Gilead, 'By the time the sun is hot tomorrow, you will be delivered.'" When the messengers went and reported this to the men of Jabesh, they were elated. ¹⁰They said to the Ammonites, "Tomorrow we will surrender to you, and you can do to us whatever seems good to you."

¹¹The next day Saul separated his men into three divisions; during the last watch of the night they broke into the camp of the Ammonites and slaughtered them until the heat of the day. Those who survived were scattered, so that no two of them were left together.

¹²The people then said to Samuel, "Who was it that asked, 'Shall Saul reign over us?' Bring these men to us and we will put them to death."

¹³But Saul said, "No one shall be put to death today, for this day the LORD has rescued Israel."

¹⁴Then Samuel said to the people, "Come, let us go to Gilgal and there reaffirm the kingship." ¹⁵So all the people went to Gilgal and confirmed Saul as king in the presence of the LORD. There they sacrificed fellowship offerings before the LORD, and Saul and all the Israelites held a great celebration.

SAUL HAS NOT YET ACTED AS KING. He has been anointed by oil and the Spirit of God. He has been publicly acclaimed and confirmed as king. Even in this narrative, where he gets his first opportunity to function as king, he arrives from the fields looking every bit the farmer and hardly a reigning monarch ("returning from the fields, behind his oxen," 11:5). But now he rises to the occasion and functions as king splendidly. He becomes Israel's "savior" and delivers the nation from oppression and bondage. Indeed, this chapter revolves around the theme of deliverance.[1] Deliverance is the driving question of the elders of Jabesh Gilead at the beginning (11:3), is the promise of the new king at the center (11:9), and is the happy conclusion of the matter (11:13).

The Ammonite Threat (11:1–3)

ONE OF THE texts found among the scrolls of the Judean Desert (commonly referred to as the Dead Sea Scrolls) is important for the study of this chapter. 4QSamᵃ is a large scroll believed to have been copied during the first century B.C. and containing in fragmentary form parts of the books of Samuel. The scroll preserves a paragraph at the beginning of 1 Samuel 11, which is not present in either the Hebrew or Greek traditions of the Bible.[2] The missing paragraph provides background information about the Ammonite threat,

---

1. Brueggemann, *First and Second Samuel*, 82–83.

2. For translation and discussion, see McCarter, *I Samuel*, 198–99; Frank Moore Cross, "The Ammonite Oppression of the Tribes of Gad and Reuben: Missing Verses from 1 Samuel 11 Found in 4QSamuelᵃ," in *History, Historiography and Interpretation: Studies in Biblical and Cuneiform Literatures*, ed. H. Tadmor and M. Weinfeld (Jerusalem: Magnes, 1984), 148–58; Eugene C. Ulrich Jr., *The Qumran Text of Samuel and Josephus* (HSM 19; Missoula, Mont,.: Scholars Press, 1978), 166–70.

and most scholars believe it was original to the text. Perhaps future translations of the Bible will follow the lead of the NRSV, NEB, and NAB and include this paragraph at the beginning of chapter 11.[3]

The Qumran addition informs us that Nahash was "king" of the Ammonites, a detail curiously omitted until he is mentioned again in 12:12. He had oppressed the Transjordanian tribes of Gad and Reuben, gouging out the right eye of captured Israelite soldiers. Mutilation of captives was not uncommon in antiquity, but this may have also been a way of ensuring these troops would never again wage war by impairing their aim in battle.[4] The fragment from Qumran also informs us that seven thousand Israelite troops had retreated and escaped to the last Israelite stronghold, the city of Jabesh Gilead. Now, one month later, Nabash was threatening to take the city as well, which would give him uncontested control of much of Israel's entire eastern border.

During most of the history of the Israelite kingdoms (i.e., twelfth to sixth centuries B.C.), a Semitic people of the Transjordan maintained a rival state with a capital at Rabbath Ammon (modern Amman).[5] Occasionally allies but normally enemies, the Ammonites appear to have considered the east bank of the Jordan River as their own territory (Judg. 11:12–13). During the judges period, the Ammonites had threatened Israelite territory more than once (3:13; 10:6–9; 11:4). Claiming Jabesh Gilead, a city strategic in the defense of the east bank of the Jordan, would solidify Nabash's stranglehold on Gad and Reuben and constitute a further threat to all Israel in general. This comes at a time when Philistia was already a concern on Israel's western flank. Unable and unwilling to risk open warfare on two fronts, Israel must now deal decisively with this threat to the east before considering the more serious and long-term problem of the Philistines to the west.

The question that plagues the minds of the elders of Jabesh Gilead is whether there is anyone to "deliver" (NIV "rescue") them. The Qumran piece at the beginning of the chapter states that Nahash mutilated the captive Israelites in order to deny Israel a "deliverer."[6] Thus the text establishes the suspense. Will Israel's new king be up to the task, or will he fail to deliver, as the troublemakers of 10:27 suspect?

---

3. For more cautious voices, see Alexander Rofé, "The Acts of Nahash According to 4QSam^a," *IEJ* 32 (1982): 129–33; Robert P. Gordon, *I and II Samuel* (Grand Rapids: Zondervan, 1986), 63–64.

4. Baldwin, *1 and 2 Samuel*, 96. For other explanations, see Cross, "Ammonite Oppression," 148–58, esp. 156–57.

5. Randall W. Younker, "Rabbah," *ABD*, 5:598–600. Biblical tradition associates the Ammonites with the descendants of Lot's son Ben-Ammi (Gen. 19:36–38).

6. The NRSV for the Heb. *mwšyʿ*, though most of the word is reconstructed to fill in a break in the Qumran text.

Saul Defeats the Ammonites (11:4–11)

SAUL'S MILITARY VICTORY over the Ammonites is an important part of the extended narrative about his accession to royal authority. It follows the divine designation of 9:1–10:27 and precedes the confirmation of 11:15.[7] The account contains parallels with judges from Israel's premonarchic period and portrays Saul as a continuation of those who receive the Spirit of God, are roused into activity, and are used mightily to accomplish deliverance for God's people.

This passage is especially reminiscent of Judges 19–21.[8] In the earlier tragic episode, the Levite's concubine had been killed while he was spending the night in Gibeah of Benjamin. Out of desperation, he brought the crime to the attention of the Israelite tribes by dismembering her body and sending the pieces to the tribes for judicial decision. Saul appears to have intentionally mimicked this method when he kills the team of oxen and sends the pieces throughout Israel as a call to arms. When the tribes joined to take action against Benjamin for the crimes against the Levite's concubine, the inhabitants of Jabesh Gilead had not participated in the battles (Judg. 21:8). Reprisals were swift and severe (21:10–14). As a result, the inhabitants of the city probably have little reason now to hope that the tribes on the western side of the Jordan River will join together in order to defend them from the Ammonites. Their plea for seven days to find out if they have the support of their kindred tribes is not a ruse but a genuine question of concern (1 Sam. 11:3). Saul's ability to unite the tribes and lead them against the Ammonites in defense of a cause that is in doubt is an impressive beginning.

As in the previous passage, the "Spirit of God" comes on Saul to empower him (11:6; cf. 10:10). In chapter 10, the coming of the Spirit was a temporary blessing intended to confirm Saul as the anointed of Yahweh. He temporarily rejoiced with a local band of prophets. But in this passage, the text uses nearly identical phraseology as in Judges (Othniel, Gideon, Jephthah, Samson). The Spirit fills the judge with divine indignation and empowers him for military service. The earlier Spirit-empowerment of Saul was temporary, but this one is apparently more permanent, continuing until Samuel anoints David as Saul's replacement.[9] God's Spirit in the Old Testament empowers the recipient for leadership as prophet, king, or army general.

---

7. Edelman, "Saul's Rescue of Jabesh-Gilead," 195–209.

8. For more on what follows, see Robert Polzin, "On Taking Renewal Seriously: 1 Sam. 11:1–15," in *Ascribe to the Lord: Biblical and Other Studies in Memory of Peter C. Craigie*, ed. L. Eslinger and G. Taylor (JSOTSup 67; Sheffield: JSOT, 1988), 500–501.

9. Youngblood, "1, 2 Samuel," 637–38; Klein, *1 Samuel*, 107.

Saul's victory over the Ammonites follows immediately after the anointing and public acclamation of 9:1–10:27. Some interpreters assume this military victory in chapter 11 is the historical episode anticipated in the previous unit and that it stands in a certain degree of tension with the earlier narrative, both historically and literarily. But as noted earlier, we appear to have in chapters 8–12 a composite tapestry, which weaves together a number of different strands in order to portray the Israelite kingship in contrasting ways. If we assume this to be the case, then the Ammonite victory in chapter 11 functions as the "testing stage" for Saul's kingship.[10] In the overarching narrative of his rise to power, this victory is not the one pictured in his anointing and commissioning, which speaks instead of the Philistine threat (9:16; 10:5). Rather, this victory was Saul's first "test" and prepares for his final coronation at Gilgal.

Saul's victory over the Ammonites also endears him in the hearts of the eastern tribes, particularly the people of Jabesh Gilead long after his reign. We will see later how the city remains loyal to Saul until the bitter end (1 Sam. 31:11–13), and even after his death David must be concerned about incorporating the previous strongholds of Saul's support (2 Sam. 2:4–7).

Saul's Kingship Renewed (11:12–15)

EARLIER CERTAIN "WORTHLESS fellows" (NIV "troublemakers") doubted Saul's ability to deliver the nation and chose not to support him (10:27). After this spectacular victory over the Ammonites, it seems only logical to the people that they execute those who first opposed the Lord's anointed. Yahweh's judgment has been revealed. The troublemakers have despised and slandered Saul, who was Yahweh's anointed; therefore, they have despised Yahweh himself. The people of Israel ask for the death penalty because of their understanding of sacred justice.

But Yahweh has achieved a great deliverance on this day, which certifies his anointed king, Saul. Some have argued that this event portrays Yahweh's anointed as "the man who makes invalid the divine right of punishment, replacing it by the right of grace that is grounded in Yahweh's act of salvation for Israel."[11] Samuel himself did not have such authority. It is only the power and authority of Yahweh's anointed that pardons in such a way. As such, this little paragraph illustrates the role of the king as anointed or as messiah. The anointed one, whom Yahweh has publicly confirmed through victory, is the only one who has the ability to forgive crimes and abolish the demands of divine justice.

---

10. Long, *Reign and Rejection*, 183–89; also pp. 51–55.
11. Knierim, "Messianic Concept," 20–51, esp. 33–34.

MESSIAH AND DELIVERANCE. We find in 1–2 Samuel many contributions to Israel's understanding of Yahweh's "anointed one," a term that many centuries later will take on technical significance for Christians in the untranslated form "Messiah." We will see especially in the way these books present King David that these texts are central to the way later Judaism formulated their messianic expectations. This chapter in particular portrays the anointed one of Israel as the individual whom Yahweh has confirmed first by the Spirit of God, then by military victory over the enemy, and finally by the power to change the divine right of judgment into the divine right of grace. "This is the way the messiah looks when he appears in Israel."[12]

The chapter's emphasis on military deliverance is at the core of its contribution to Israel's messianism. The text opens with the need for deliverance from the Ammonites (11:3). It is the messianic figure of Saul who towers over everyone else, even Samuel, to assure that deliverance will in fact come (11:9). Even though Saul acknowledges that the victory was provided by Yahweh, the victory itself confirms Saul as Yahweh's anointed (11:13). Thus the passage demonstrates the soteriological function of kingship. Soteriology is the analysis and restatement in contemporary terms of all that salvation means to modern Christian faith.[13] Here, for the first time, the king of Israel, the anointed of Yahweh, is the means of salvation for his people (i.e., by means of rescue from hostile, threatening enemies).

The Israelite kingship was defined from the outset as an institution intended to provide deliverance. The elders of Israel understood it this way in their earliest requests for a king (8:20). Particularly important for this victory over the Ammonites is the way it functions between Saul's anointing and consecration in 9:1–10:27 and the renewal of the kingship in 11:14–15.[14] Without doubt the expectation, or at least the desperate hope, on the part of the people of Israel is that the king will provide military deliverance from their enemies. This is not outside Yahweh's plan for the king as well, though it will become clear later that he has a larger picture for the nature and function of the king.

Moved by God's Spirit. Of particular interest in this text is the spectacular success of Saul's new kingship and the manner in which it is accomplished. This, in fact, is Saul's one shining moment in history. Here he functions like the judges of old, like the charismatic leadership used of Yah-

---

12. Ibid., 34. One can argue that "the entire history of Saul . . . is designed out of a messianic theology" (28).

13. R. E. O. White, "Salvation," in *Evangelical Dictionary of Theology,* 967–69, esp. 969.

14. Edelman, "Saul's Rescue of Jabesh-Gilead."

weh to bring salvation and peace to Israel. When he turns his attention, however, to the Philistines in the west, things do not go so well. The key difference may be seen in the event described in 11:6. When Saul hears of the Ammonite threat, he is touched by the Spirit of God and is moved into action by God's initiative and in God's timing. Sadly, this is not what we will read of Saul in the future.

The Bible contains other examples of people moved at times by Yahweh to accomplish his purposes. We do not always have the same type of "Spirit language," and not all are messianic-type kings, but the implications are the same. When God's servants attempt to minister and serve in their own strength or in their own timing, the results are mixed at best. But when they are open to the prodding and inspiration of God, the results are uniformly effective.

For example, when Moses struck the Egyptian taskmaster and killed him, I believe he was attempting to achieve naturally the mission God had for him and for which God had prepared him from the beginning. He had been miraculously delivered at birth and raised in the pharaoh's court, yet nursed by his own mother and given the best education available in those ancient times (Ex. 2:1–10; Acts 7:22). In unique fashion, his childhood combined the best the world had to offer with the kind of religious training only his mother could provide. Unlike any other person alive, Moses was prepared to lead God's people out of Egypt and bring them into the Promised Land. He was being groomed from the beginning to function as Israel's "savior." But then he killed the Egyptian taskmaster and hid him in the sand. The next day he attempted to intervene in a fight between two Hebrew workers. This, too, ended in failure, though again Moses was attempting a good work—one that no doubt fit his calling and preparation. As a desperate failure he fled to Midian and tried to escape by changing everything about his life. He ran from the calling God had placed on his life (Ex. 2:11–22). As everyone knows, life for Moses after God met him in the burning bush was much different. From that point he functioned as God's messenger, accomplishing God's task in God's timing.

Similar problems arose for Jacob and his life in Haran with Laban prior to his encounter with the angel of Yahweh at Jabbok (Gen. 32). Some scholars suspect that Isaiah's ministry changed once he saw Yahweh "high and exalted ... [in] the temple" (Isa. 6:1).[15] This same pattern is, of course, evident

---

15. This is not to assume a strict chronological flow in Isa. 1–6 but to acknowledge that this chapter serves as the solution to the problems posed in chs. 1–5. The general literary relationship of Isa. 1–12 is, of course, complicated. See John N. Oswalt, *The Book of Isaiah: Chapters 1–39* (NICOT; Grand Rapids: Eerdmans, 1986), 171–76.

in the life of the Messiah. The parallel is incomplete since we cannot argue that Jesus attempted to serve in his own strength and failed. Rather, he dared not begin his ministry until he was confident he was working in the right time and the right manner. Once he was baptized by John and the Holy Spirit descended on him like a dove, Jesus immediately went to the desert to challenge Satan and then began his ministry by calling his disciples (Matt. 3:13–4:1; Mark 1:9–12).

Of course, you and I are not Jesus, and there are many differences here. But this simple spiritual truth is apparent even in his life and ministry. Effective ministry (even effective living!) requires the help of God, which he graciously bestows through his Holy Spirit on those who are sensitive and patient. If Jesus was open to the Holy Spirit and patient for God's timing and anointing, certainly today's Christians need the same openness and patience.

The simple truth of 1 Samuel 11 is that God's people need to be completely dependent on him for resources and strength and that he will miraculously multiply skills and talents in order to use them for his own purposes. The rest of the Saul narrative will unfortunately illustrate what happens when those who are prepared and called by God decide they no longer need to serve under the inspiration of God.

OPEN TO THE SPIRIT'S LEADING. I am sure all of us could illustrate from personal experience times of failure, when we were attempting to accomplish something worthy or noble but were working in our own power and relying on our own skills and talents. The hard truth, however, is that it is not always easy to know whether we are definitely moved by God's Spirit or by our natural instincts. It is easy to be confused about what we are supposed to do and when we are supposed to do it. In this text, we are presented with an Old Testament example of a chosen servant of God, prepared in many ways to fulfill God's mission for his life and also open and responsive to God's prodding, direction, and timing. We can learn much from such examples.

The denominational context in which I serve had its origins in the life and work of John Wesley. He and his brother, Charles, along with a colleague from their Oxford days, George Whitefield, were fervent in evangelism, Christian publishing and education, and social reform. Together they effectively reformed English society of the eighteenth century. Wesley himself was incredibly energetic. Excluded from the churches of his day because of his insistence on the Reformation theme of salvation by grace through faith, he was driven to open-air preaching. It has been estimated that during his ministry, he traveled approximately 250,000 miles on horseback through England, Scotland, Wales, and Ireland, preaching some forty thousand sermons.[16] He worked with fifteen languages, producing some six hundred pieces of written literature.

His work was remarkably effective. At the age of eighty-two in 1785, Wesley claimed that the number of those brought to God in the revival was perhaps greater than in any other age since the time of the apostles.[17] At his death in 1791, there were 72,000 members in his Methodist societies in Great Britain alone, not including those in North America and elsewhere.[18] The impact of the Wesleyan revival was dramatic in eighteenth-century England. The first half of the century witnessed a nation on the brink of moral disintegration. Many lost interest in the claims of the Christian faith, the social ills of the nation were becoming intolerable, and the nature of eighteenth-century Anglicanism made it weak and powerless to effect change.[19] Some historians and theologians believe the spiritual awakening led by the Wesleys and Whitefield was the single most important impetus in reforming the nation and saved England from the same bloody revolution witnessed in France during the same period.[20]

John Wesley's legacy is remarkable, and his mark on the history of Christianity is undeniable. He remained fiercely loyal to the Anglican Church all his life. After much reluctance, he ordained several of his preachers for the work in America, and Methodism was officially organized in Baltimore at the Christmas Conference of 1784. Soon after his death, Methodism became a separate denomination in England as well. But Wesley's significance transcends the reform of England and the birth of Methodism. His extraordinary accomplishments place him among other giants in Christian history. One historian has concluded that Wesley belongs to the whole church because the last of the major denominational bodies to develop in Christianity originated with him.[21]

---

16. R. G. Tuttle Jr., "Wesley, John," *Evangelical Dictionary of Theology*, 1164.

17. A. Skevington Wood, *The Burning Heart: John Wesley, Evangelist* (Exeter: Paternoster, 1976), 114.

18. Kenneth J. Collins, *A Real Christian: The Life of John Wesley* (Nashville: Abingdon, 1999), 158; Wood, *Burning Heart*, 114.

19. One scholar has mentioned esp. a lack of fervor in the pulpit, a distinct distrust of theology, a tepid morality unassociated with the evangelical truths of Christianity, and a lack of impact on the congregations (Wood, *Burning Heart*, 13–14).

20. Howard A. Snyder, *The Radical Wesley and Patterns for Church Renewal* (Downers Grove, Ill.: InterVarsity Press, 1980), 158.

21. Martin Schmidt, *John Wesley: A Theological Biography;* Vol 1. *From 17ᵗʰ June 1703 until 24ᵗʰ May 1738,* trans. Norman P. Goldhawk (Nashville: Abingdon, 1962), 9. Theologically this is true, e.g., of Wesley's doctrine of salvation, which has recently been shown to be a truly "conjunctive" theology belonging to the church universal. On this point esp. see Kenneth J. Collins, *The Scripture Way of Salvation: The Heart of John Wesley's Theology* (Nashville: Abingdon, 1997), 205–7.

But it was not always so clear for Mr. Wesley that he was being used of God in so mighty a fashion. In fact, at one point in his life, he considered himself an utter failure and incapable of sustaining a life of devotion. Having experienced what he would later call a "religious" conversion, he was ordained in 1725. After serving for a brief time as his father's curate and being elected Fellow of Lincoln College, Oxford, Wesley felt called to mission service in a new colony in America. Thus, in 1735, he arrived in Savannah, Georgia, to evangelize the Native Americans. Throughout this mission, Wesley proved an abysmal failure. He was appointed first chaplain to the governor of the new colony, General James Oglethorpe, and he managed to serve as priest to the colony's settlers. But his motives were all wrong: "My chief motive, to which all the rest are subordinate, is the hope of saving my own soul."[22]

His highly romantic notions about the Native Americans of Georgia would soon be shattered by the harsh realism of a failed mission. The few times he was actually able to make contact with Native Americans, they proved unresponsive to his ministry. Among the settlers, Wesley exercised an unyielding ecclesiastical discipline that was utterly out of place on the frontier. He withheld the sacrament of the Lord's Supper to one saintly pastor because the pastor had not been baptized by an episcopally ordained priest.[23] In another case, he was actually faced with legal proceedings. In 1738, he simply abandoned his responsibilities in Georgia and fled back to England as quickly as he could go. To make matters worse, he discovered on his trips across the Atlantic that he had a morbid fear of death.

He felt hopelessly defeated by these revelations and found himself forlorn and spiritually despondent: "I went to America to convert the Indians; but, oh, who shall convert me?"[24] He later confessed that up until this time, his entire spiritual journey had been a "refined way of trusting to my own works."[25]

This could easily have been the end of Mr. Wesley's ministry, and we would be all the poorer. But on the night of May 24, 1738, he went "unwillingly" to a meeting of Moravian Christians at Aldersgate Street in London. While listening to a reading from Luther's preface to his Romans commentary, Wesley felt his "heart strangely warmed."[26] Mere words now became real-

---

22. John Wesley, *The Works of John Wesley*, Vol. 25. *Letters I, 1721–1739*, ed. Frank Baker (Oxford ed.; Oxford: Clarendon, 1980), 439.

23. Collins, *A Real Christian*, 43; Wood, *Burning Heart*, 56.

24. John Wesley, *The Works of John Wesley*, Vol. 18. *Journal and Diaries I (1735–1738)*, ed. W. Reginald Ward and Richard P. Heitzenrater (Bicentennial ed.; Nashville: Abingdon, 1988), 211.

25. Ibid., 246.

26. Ibid., 250.

ities. This singular doctrine of the Protestant Reformation, "the change which God works in the heart through faith in Christ," seized Wesley's formidable mind and heart and transformed him from a self-absorbed and ill-tempered clergyman into a flaming evangelist. The "religious" conversion of his youth had become a genuine "evangelical" conversion.[27] He immediately launched a preaching, teaching, and writing ministry that occupied his next fifty years. His call to missionary service, which he took to mean ministry in Georgia, was now being fulfilled in his native country.

Not unlike King Saul, Wesley had learned that no amount of preparation or calling can substitute for an openness to the leading and empowerment of God's Spirit.

---

27. Wood, *Burning Heart*, 68.

1 Samuel 12:1–25

❧

S AMUEL SAID TO all Israel, "I have listened to everything you said to me and have set a king over you. ²Now you have a king as your leader. As for me, I am old and gray, and my sons are here with you. I have been your leader from my youth until this day. ³Here I stand. Testify against me in the presence of the LORD and his anointed. Whose ox have I taken? Whose donkey have I taken? Whom have I cheated? Whom have I oppressed? From whose hand have I accepted a bribe to make me shut my eyes? If I have done any of these, I will make it right."

⁴"You have not cheated or oppressed us," they replied. "You have not taken anything from anyone's hand."

⁵Samuel said to them, "The LORD is witness against you, and also his anointed is witness this day, that you have not found anything in my hand."

"He is witness," they said.

⁶Then Samuel said to the people, "It is the LORD who appointed Moses and Aaron and brought your forefathers up out of Egypt. ⁷Now then, stand here, because I am going to confront you with evidence before the LORD as to all the righteous acts performed by the LORD for you and your fathers.

⁸"After Jacob entered Egypt, they cried to the LORD for help, and the LORD sent Moses and Aaron, who brought your forefathers out of Egypt and settled them in this place.

⁹"But they forgot the LORD their God; so he sold them into the hand of Sisera, the commander of the army of Hazor, and into the hands of the Philistines and the king of Moab, who fought against them. ¹⁰They cried out to the LORD and said, 'We have sinned; we have forsaken the LORD and served the Baals and the Ashtoreths. But now deliver us from the hands of our enemies, and we will serve you.' ¹¹Then the LORD sent Jerub-Baal, Barak, Jephthah and Samuel, and he delivered you from the hands of your enemies on every side, so that you lived securely.

¹²"But when you saw that Nahash king of the Ammonites was moving against you, you said to me, 'No, we want a king to rule over us'—even though the LORD your God was your

king. ¹³Now here is the king you have chosen, the one you asked for; see, the LORD has set a king over you. ¹⁴If you fear the LORD and serve and obey him and do not rebel against his commands, and if both you and the king who reigns over you follow the LORD your God—good! ¹⁵But if you do not obey the LORD, and if you rebel against his commands, his hand will be against you, as it was against your fathers.

¹⁶"Now then, stand still and see this great thing the LORD is about to do before your eyes! ¹⁷Is it not wheat harvest now? I will call upon the LORD to send thunder and rain. And you will realize what an evil thing you did in the eyes of the LORD when you asked for a king."

¹⁸Then Samuel called upon the LORD, and that same day the LORD sent thunder and rain. So all the people stood in awe of the LORD and of Samuel.

¹⁹The people all said to Samuel, "Pray to the LORD your God for your servants so that we will not die, for we have added to all our other sins the evil of asking for a king."

²⁰"Do not be afraid," Samuel replied. "You have done all this evil; yet do not turn away from the LORD, but serve the LORD with all your heart. ²¹Do not turn away after useless idols. They can do you no good, nor can they rescue you, because they are useless. ²²For the sake of his great name the LORD will not reject his people, because the LORD was pleased to make you his own. ²³As for me, far be it from me that I should sin against the LORD by failing to pray for you. And I will teach you the way that is good and right. ²⁴But be sure to fear the LORD and serve him faithfully with all your heart; consider what great things he has done for you. ²⁵Yet if you persist in doing evil, both you and your king will be swept away."

Original Meaning

SAMUEL'S FAREWELL ADDRESS here corresponds to chapter 8. There the Israelites demanded a king. Samuel warned of the consequences of their request but eventually relented to Yahweh's directive (8:22): "Listen to them and give them a king." This chapter marks the changing of the guard, as Samuel announces in a verse that is central to the passage: "Now here is the king you have chosen, the one you asked for; see, the LORD has set a king over you" (12:13).

The Israelites have now accepted the new king (11:12–15). Samuel will no longer function as the leader of a theocracy but must redefine his role as a prophet in a new monarchy. Samuel's role as judge and prophet, at least under the old order, is officially over. At this crucial juncture in Israel's history, Samuel addresses the nation, and they finally come to understand that their demand for a Canaanite-style monarchy is sinful. But it is too late. Under the old system, Samuel had been more than fair in his treatment of the people (12:1–5), unlike future kings. With a sense of sin and loss, the Israelites now realize they have contributed yet another evil deed to their ancestors' long list of failures, and they plead with Samuel to intercede on their behalf.

Samuel's Faithful Ministry (12:1–5)

IT IS TIME for Samuel to clear the air. Under his tenure, things were fair and equitable. Before this national assembly of "all Israel," Samuel challenges the people to "testify against" him (12:3). Has he "taken" anything that was not rightfully his? Has he taken another's ox or donkey? Has he cheated or oppressed anyone in Israel? Has he been guilty of accepting bribes when pronouncing judgment? Having no accusers, Samuel is satisfied that he has been vindicated. Note the key term in this passage, "take" (*lqḥ*, four times in vv. 3–4, though obscured by NIV).

The claim that Samuel has not *taken* anything unlawfully or unjustly relates this speech with the one in 8:11–18.[1] There Samuel detailed "the way of the king," who would "take" everything they hold dear, including their freedom. The text also anticipates David's *taking* of Bathsheba, which is the ultimate portrait of the grasping king (2 Sam. 11:4). The contrast between the new kingship and the older prophetic leadership is clear. The older theocracy was better because it provided the same guidance and protection through faith. But the Israelites have received what they demanded.

Samuel has vindicated himself and his role in the former theocracy, which ruled the tribes of Israel during the judges period. But his speech has also emphasized the responsibility of the new king to maintain the same high standard of just and righteous leadership. The Israelites are to consider his faithfulness "in the presence of the LORD and his anointed" (12:3; see also v. 5). In Samuel's reference to the Lord's "anointed" (*mᵉšiḥo*, "his messiah"), he stresses the role of the new king to uphold Yahweh's rule among his people. Samuel is innocent of any wrongdoing, either in his leadership of the past or in his role as kingmaker. Now the burden rests on Saul.

---

1. McCarter, *I Samuel*, 218.

Samuel's Farewell Charge to the Israelites (12:6–15)

THE EXPRESSION "PRESENT YOURSELVES" (Heb. *hityaṣṣᵉbu*) in verses 7 and 16 mark these units as distinct (NIV "stand here" and "stand still"). Both usages prepare the audience to consider the mighty deeds of Yahweh. In the first (12:6–15), Samuel locates the people's recent demand for a king in the context of their national history and confronts them with a choice for the future. Their ancestors benefited from the "righteous acts" of Yahweh (12:7), even though they sinned against him. In the second (12:16–25), the venerable prophet performs a new "great thing" of Yahweh in order to demonstrate the prophetic ministry they have forfeited and urges them to be faithful in the future.

The familiar sequence of events from the Exodus, the Sinai covenant, and the conquest of the Promised Land came to function as a kind of "creed" for ancient Israel.[2] In this sermon, Samuel emphasizes in particular the judges period in order to show that regardless of how far short their ancestors fell, Yahweh never abandoned them. The cycle of sin, oppression, repentance, and judge-provided deliverance was oft repeated and had, in fact, preserved the nation. Now this current generation of Israelites has grown dissatisfied with the theocratic system, just as their ancestors had grown tired of the manna in the desert (Num. 11:4–6).

So Samuel drives home their choice. He forces them to face the reality of a human king as opposed to the divinely provided judge-deliverers. Verse 13 is the hinge or central theme of the chapter.[3] It is as if Samuel were saying, "Here! Here you are! This is the king you have chosen. You asked for him; you got him! Yahweh has given him to you." They have indeed received a king, but he comes with divine restrictions. He can never really be like a Canaanite ruler, which is not in their best interests anyway. Instead, this is the king that *Yahweh himself* has provided.

Then, to prove that this is no omnipotent monarchy, Samuel outlines the conditions for its success (12:14–15). Reminiscent of the old-covenant blessings and curses, Samuel offers Israel two ways. They *and their new king* can be faithful to Yahweh and be blessed, or they can fail to obey Yahweh and be no better off than their ancestors, king or no king. In other words, everything has changed—and nothing has changed. They have a new political structure, but they must continue to serve Yahweh. Even the king who reigns over them must follow Yahweh.

---

2. Baldwin, *1 and 2 Samuel*, 99.
3. Youngblood, "1, 2 Samuel," 643.

Samuel Redefines His Role As Prophet (12:16–25)

FOR THE SAKE OF FUTURE GENERATIONS, it is critically important for the Israelites to properly define and understand the role of the new king. But just as important is the role of prophets in the new government. In order to make a lasting impression on this point, Samuel calls for a thunderstorm at wheat harvest (12:16–18). This harvest in ancient Israel fell during May and June, and it scarcely ever rained during this time.[4] This demonstrates that Yahweh will continue to speak through prophets. Israel may have a new king and a new political structure, but they must never neglect the word of the servants of Yahweh, the prophets.

Samuel's words and the miraculous storm drive the people to repentance and to a plea for Samuel to intercede on their behalf (12:19). Samuel begins his answer by reminding the people that they themselves have demanded a king (12:20–22). They have acted wickedly, but they are not without hope. If they remain true to Yahweh, avoiding all idolatry, he will not reject them, because he was pleased to make Israel his own. Despite the new political system, Yahweh still wants the intimate relationship with Israel, but only under the old-covenant terms.

Having duly charged the people to remain faithful, the rest of Samuel's answer addresses his own responsibilities (12:23–25): "As for me...." Here Samuel inaugurates a new role for the prophet in Israel. To maintain the connections with the old covenant, Samuel's new role arises from his prophetic relationship with Yahweh. His service will now consist in two things. (1) He will intercede with Yahweh for the people. (2) He will instruct them in "the way that is good and right." In this way, Samuel becomes the paradigm for prophets as they appear later in Israel's history, who consistently serve "as the people's intercessor with Yahweh on the one hand and as the moral conscience of the kingdom on the other."[5]

TRANSITION SPEECHES. This chapter is commonly referred to as Samuel's "farewell address," and I have referred to it as such here. It is true enough that Samuel is bringing to a close his pivotal role as judge-deliverer (cf. 1 Sam. 7). But his death is not recorded until 1 Samuel 28, and he will continue to play an important role for some time to come, including the anointing of another king (David in ch. 16). Rather than a "farewell"

---

4. Keil and Delitzsch, *Samuel*, 120; Klein, *1 Samuel*, 118.
5. McCarter, *I Samuel*, 219.

speech, then, Samuel's sermon before the national assembly is the final step in making Saul king, and it prepares us for Saul's ultimate rejection in chapters 13–15. Samuel's speech contrasts his own faithfulness with the infidelity of Israel. They are responsible for having a king, and if that king proves to be a failure, it is their own causing. Furthermore, the chapter reconfigures Samuel's role as prophet and shapes all Israelite prophets to follow him. So Samuel's address is not as much a "good-bye" speech as it is a refocusing of God's covenant with Israel at this important transitional moment in their history.

In order for us to interpret this passage for our modern context, we must first consider its role in the larger scheme of biblical theology. This chapter serves an important role in the overall structure of the prophetic history extending from Deuteronomy and Joshua through 2 Kings (see comments on the Deuteronomistic Historian in the introduction).[6] The historian uses certain great speeches (or prayers) of Israel's most important figures to transition from one era to another. These passages serve as the organizational framework for the entire Deuteronomistic History. Thus Samuel's speeches in 7:2–8:22 and 12:1–25 serve as bookends for the section explaining the origins of the Israelite monarchy and interpreting its theological significance.[7]

Thus, the historian has given us great speeches or prayers to flag the major turning points in Israel's history. Some have concluded that Israel's history can be divided into five periods: the Mosaic period, the period of the Conquest, the age of the judges, the period of the united monarchy (considering together Saul, David, and Solomon), and the Israelite and Judean kingdoms. These periods were then tied together literarily with summary passages (speeches or prayers). In other words, Deuteronomy 1–4 are speeches of Moses on the plains of Moab, which illustrate the way Deuteronomy concludes the Mosaic period. Joshua 23–24 are speeches of Joshua, concluding the Conquest and initiating the judges period. Our passage in 1 Samuel 12 brings the judges period to a close and focuses attention on the new period of monarchy. As we will see, 2 Samuel 7 is a speech of another prophet (Nathan), which focuses on the Davidic dynasty and the city of Jerusalem.[8]

---

6. For more on what follows, see Noth, *The Deuteronomistic History*; Dennis J. McCarthy, "II Samuel 7 and the Structure of the Deuteronomic History," *JBL* 84 (1965): 131–38; Vannoy, *Covenant Renewal at Gilgal.*

7. Many today distinguish between pre-Deuteronomistic portions and genuine Deuteronomistic material in these chapters. See Bruce C. Birch, *The Rise of the Israelite Monarchy: The Growth and Development of 1 Samuel 7–15* (Missoula, Mont.: Scholars Press, 1976).

8. Though many since Noth (and including Noth himself) do not include 2 Samuel 7 in this list of summarizing and organizing speeches, the so-called "double redaction" school of thought on the Deuteronomistic Historian has returned it to the list (McCarthy, "II Samuel," 131–38).

Finally, the prayer of Solomon in 1 Kings 8 summarizes Israel's history to that date and initiates the period of temple worship.

This helps us put 1 Samuel 12 in broader perspective. Just as 1 Samuel 7–8 and 12 serve as bookends for the establishment of the monarchy, so on a larger scale, Joshua 23–24 serve together with 1 Samuel 12 as bookends for the narrative of the judges. Not surprisingly the farewell speeches of Joshua and Samuel have important features in common. They both look back at the Mosaic covenant at Mount Sinai as the anchor that will hold Israel securely during a time of historical transition. Joshua 23–24 reflect on the covenant's ramifications now that the Conquest is accomplished and life in the Promised Land begins. Samuel in 1 Samuel 12 likewise links the current generation of Israelites with the Mosaic covenant as he considers the end of the judges period and the beginning of life under the new monarchy.

In both cases, Joshua and Samuel are confident the old Sinai covenant will work in the circumstances of a new and uncertain situation. The old-time religion will certainly work for this new-fangled age. While Joshua and Samuel are confident of the Mosaic covenant, it is the people they have to worry about. The old-time religion is fine, as long as this new crowd is faithful.

The shared covenantal concerns of Joshua and Samuel have even led scholars to isolate a similar structure in their speeches (referring specifically to 1 Samuel 12:7–25 and Joshua 24:1–29).[9] (1) The people take their stance to hear the words of the covenant (1 Sam. 12:7; cf. Josh. 24:1). (2) The people hear a review of Yahweh's mighty acts on their behalf (1 Sam. 12:8–12; cf. Josh. 24:2–13). (3) The ancient covenant is related to the current momentous event (with the expression "and now," 1 Sam. 12:13; cf. Josh. 24:14). (4) The covenant's demands are listed for review (1 Sam.12:20b–21; cf. Josh. 24:14). (5) Finally, the conditions of the covenant are stated in terms of blessings and curses (1 Sam. 12:14–15, 24–25; cf. Josh. 24:20). Failure to keep covenant will result in disaster; faithfulness will bring success.

In a sense, Samuel's farewell address serves as a "second chance" for Israel. They have sinned, but God has incorporated their failure into his own plans. He is capable of overcoming their failure, of turning it into his means of salvation, and of giving them a new start. Each time Israel fails or begins a new venture, it seems Yahweh reestablishes the covenant and recommits himself never to abandon them. Whether it is their initial failure at Sinai (Ex. 32–35), the plains of Moab (Deut. 29:1), their new tribal confederation at Shechem (Josh. 24), or this covenant renewal at Gilgal (1 Sam. 12), Yahweh is their God and they are his people.

---

9. For more, see McCarter, *I Samuel*, 220–21.

GOD'S GRACE. God was constantly giving Israel second chances. This is fortunate for Israel because she was in constant need of a second chance. The covenant renewal at Gilgal combines with other covenant renewals in the Old Testament (esp. Ex. 32–35 and Deut. 29) to create a kind of mosaic—a collection of portraits of God's gracious goodness toward Israel. The nation seemed unable to maintain a faithful and loyal relationship with God. Yet as fickle and undependable as Israel was, God seemed just as determined to provide grace to forgive and restore.

Samuel's national assembly in 1 Samuel 12 illustrates two facets of the unmerited grace of God. (1) This episode highlights God's grace to forgive. Israel was not deserving of a second chance. But in point of fact, this was more of a third, fourth, or fifth chance for the nation. This was one of the points of Samuel's address in 12:7–13. Israel had rebelled under Moses and Aaron, they had failed to be faithful during the time of the judges, and now they had sinned again by demanding a king. At some point, one would wonder if God's grace might give out. When does one exhaust the mercy of God and begin to worry that God might withhold his forgiveness?

But once again we see that the Old Testament narratives illustrate a truth taught explicitly in the New Testament—what Philip Yancey has called "the new math of grace."[10] Yancey rightly highlights the answer Jesus gave to Peter's question about how many times we should forgive a brother who has sinned against us. Since current wisdom suggested three as the number of times one might be expected to forgive, Peter's proposal seemed magnanimous: "Up to seven times?" (Matt. 18:21). But Jesus' reply exposes the scandalous mathematics of God's grace. A translational ambiguity in Matthew 18:22 makes it impossible to say whether Jesus meant 77 times or 490 times, but it matters little. The number was astronomical, and the point was that forgiveness is not something one can track with a calculator. There is no limit to God's mercy.

The scandal of God's grace to forgive is also made apparent in 1 Samuel 12 in that Israel is seemingly unaware of her need to seek forgiveness. Until Samuel's address in verses 7–13, Israel seems oblivious to her need for grace, even though Samuel has warned against the demand for a king. So God's grace is evident here not only in his forgiveness but also in his willingness to send Samuel to Israel in the first place. God's grace to forgive takes shape first of all as grace to convict and uncover the hidden sinfulness of the human

---

10. Philip Yancey, *What's So Amazing About Grace?* (Grand Rapids: Zondervan, 1997), 59–72.

heart. Most Christians today stress only forgiveness as the ministry of God's grace. But here the hard words of the prophet, bringing awareness that one is in need of forgiveness, are also a gift of God's grace.

(2) The second facet of God's unmerited grace in 1 Samuel 12 is his grace to reconfigure and redeem. We often speak of God's grace, but we do so in too limited a fashion. We think of the grace of God to forgive, restore, empower, or even transform our lives into what they should be. These are obviously worthy topics, and in fact, they are features of what God's grace accomplishes in our lives. But this passage illustrates something beyond these. Here the sin of Israel, the very act of rejecting God's authority and demanding a new and worldly form of human rulership, is not only forgiven by God but is actually transformed by God into a new instrument of his grace. The very existence of a human king in national Israel—a result of Israel's sinful demands—is reconfigured into a savior. The institution of kingship paves the way for David, and his greater Son, Jesus. In the hands of God, even our failures and tragically sinful choices can be completely remade into something new and redemptive.

This principle, the reconfiguration of our sins into a means of redemption in God's gracious good hands, can be illustrated in the theme verse from the Joseph narrative. After the death of their father Jacob, the brothers of Joseph were afraid he would finally take his revenge on them for their betrayal so many years before. They threw themselves down before the mighty Joseph and begged forgiveness (Gen. 50:15–18). But Joseph reassured them that God had taken what they intended for evil and actually used it for good (50:20).

God indeed takes our frail attempts to serve him as well as our pitiable rebellions, and at times he reconstitutes and reconfigures them into a means whereby he saves us and others. His ultimate act of forgiveness and redemption for humankind was also the most hideous of sinful acts—the torturous execution of Jesus on a cross. We must learn to have great confidence that in the sovereign goodness of God, our meager service, no matter how flawed, can become a mighty ocean of love and grace in his hands (Rom. 8:28).

1 Samuel 13:1–22

SAUL WAS THIRTY years old when he became king, and he reigned over Israel forty-two years.

²Saul chose three thousand men from Israel; two thousand were with him at Micmash and in the hill country of Bethel, and a thousand were with Jonathan at Gibeah in Benjamin. The rest of the men he sent back to their homes.

³Jonathan attacked the Philistine outpost at Geba, and the Philistines heard about it. Then Saul had the trumpet blown throughout the land and said, "Let the Hebrews hear!" ⁴So all Israel heard the news: "Saul has attacked the Philistine outpost, and now Israel has become a stench to the Philistines." And the people were summoned to join Saul at Gilgal.

⁵The Philistines assembled to fight Israel, with three thousand chariots, six thousand charioteers, and soldiers as numerous as the sand on the seashore. They went up and camped at Micmash, east of Beth Aven. ⁶When the men of Israel saw that their situation was critical and that their army was hard pressed, they hid in caves and thickets, among the rocks, and in pits and cisterns. ⁷Some Hebrews even crossed the Jordan to the land of Gad and Gilead.

Saul remained at Gilgal, and all the troops with him were quaking with fear. ⁸He waited seven days, the time set by Samuel; but Samuel did not come to Gilgal, and Saul's men began to scatter. ⁹So he said, "Bring me the burnt offering and the fellowship offerings." And Saul offered up the burnt offering. ¹⁰Just as he finished making the offering, Samuel arrived, and Saul went out to greet him.

¹¹"What have you done?" asked Samuel.

Saul replied, "When I saw that the men were scattering, and that you did not come at the set time, and that the Philistines were assembling at Micmash, ¹²I thought, 'Now the Philistines will come down against me at Gilgal, and I have not sought the LORD's favor.' So I felt compelled to offer the burnt offering."

¹³"You acted foolishly," Samuel said. "You have not kept the command the LORD your God gave you; if you had, he would

have established your kingdom over Israel for all time. ¹⁴But now your kingdom will not endure; the LORD has sought out a man after his own heart and appointed him leader of his people, because you have not kept the LORD's command."

¹⁵Then Samuel left Gilgal and went up to Gibeah in Benjamin, and Saul counted the men who were with him. They numbered about six hundred.

¹⁶Saul and his son Jonathan and the men with them were staying in Gibeah in Benjamin, while the Philistines camped at Micmash. ¹⁷Raiding parties went out from the Philistine camp in three detachments. One turned toward Ophrah in the vicinity of Shual, ¹⁸another toward Beth Horon, and the third toward the borderland overlooking the Valley of Zeboim facing the desert.

¹⁹Not a blacksmith could be found in the whole land of Israel, because the Philistines had said, "Otherwise the Hebrews will make swords or spears!" ²⁰So all Israel went down to the Philistines to have their plowshares, mattocks, axes and sickles sharpened. ²¹The price was two thirds of a shekel for sharpening plowshares and mattocks, and a third of a shekel for sharpening forks and axes and for repointing goads.

²²So on the day of the battle not a soldier with Saul and Jonathan had a sword or spear in his hand; only Saul and his son Jonathan had them.

FIRST SAMUEL 13–15 deal with the early reign of King Saul. They serve as a bridge between the justification of kingship as an Israelite institution (chs. 8–12) and the rise of David, who is anointed in chapter 16. The point of these three chapters is Yahweh's rejection of Saul as king of Israel.¹

This chapter and the next are devoted to Saul's battles with the Philistines, who reappear now as Israel's main enemy. Saul had come to the throne for one main purpose: to lead Israel in battle (9:16; 10:5). The Philistines had precipitated the terrible crisis when they had captured the ark of the covenant (4:1b–7:1, see comments). Saul had fulfilled his duty by triumphing over the Ammonites to the east, and now he will have momentary successes

---

1. See the introduction on the unity of these three chapters.

against this greatest of Israel's enemies. But this is also the beginning of Saul's undoing. As is often the case in biblical history, the ultimate failure of our hero is not his inability to defeat the enemy. Rather, all is not right in his relationship with Yahweh. He ultimately loses his life in battle against the Philistines (ch. 31), which is merely a consequence of a deeper, more profound failure.

Philistine Wars Renewed (13:1–4)

THE OPENING VERSE has suffered textually, and it leaves us without the chronological details of Saul's reign. None of the textual witnesses give us his age at the beginning of his reign, and when we come to the question of the length of his reign, we are likewise in the dark. The Hebrew says only "two years," which is doubtlessly incomplete. It is also possible the historian has simply inserted the regnal formula for King Saul, choosing to omit the specifics because they are not known to him. In this case the lack of details would be intentional rather than because of textual corruption.[2] Regardless of the reason for the incomplete reference to Saul's reign in verse 1, it seems ironic that it heralds Saul's flawed reign.[3] The regnal formula introducing Saul is as defective as the king himself!

Jonathan appears for the first time with little fanfare. He is not identified specifically as Saul's son until verse 16. Yet he will play a significant role in the rest of 1 Samuel as the crown prince and expected heir to the throne. Here he is the brave and courageous commander of a military division and the one who initiates the war with the Philistines. His skirmish with a Philistine outpost escalates into the full-fledged war that everyone is expecting and for which Saul has been anointed king.

Saul Offers Up the Burnt Offering at Gilgal (13:5–15)

TENSIONS IN THE hills around Bethel mount, and war seems imminent.[4] When the Philistines muster what seems like insurmountable odds, many of Saul's troops begin to scatter (13:5–7). Saul has been directed by Samuel to wait seven days, after which the prophet will arrive, offer the appropriate sacrifices, and commission Saul and the troops to enter the battle (10:8).[5]

---

2. McCarter, *I Samuel*, 222–23.

3. Gordon, *1 and 2 Samuel*, 53.

4. For geographical details, see McCarter, *I Samuel*, 227, 237, and map at 231.

5. The chronology of these events and the relationship between this episode and 10:8 is in doubt. See Long, *Reign and Rejection*, 190–94; Bergen, *1, 2 Samuel*, 149, for survey of the pertinent issues.

Regardless of how we interpret Samuel's condemnation in verses 13–14, this episode illustrates the way Israelite kingship was intended to function. The king was not free to initiate warfare whenever and against whomever he wished. He had to answer to a higher authority. He could only receive marching orders from Yahweh and his prophet—in this case, Samuel. Thus, the text demonstrates the unique nature of the Israelite version of ancient Near Eastern monarchy as well as the unique nature of prophecy in Israel.[6] Standing beside every Israelite king was to be a prophet speaking God's word for the situation. The degree to which the king obeyed or rejected that prophetic word was the determining factor in the Bible's evaluation of his reign. In a sense, Yahweh remained Israel's king, represented by his prophet, who ordered Yahweh's anointed one.

Unable to hold his army together and desperate to get things underway, Saul offers the sacrifice himself (13:9). Both David and Solomon would later make similar sacrifices without receiving the slightest reprimand (2 Sam. 24:25; 1 Kings 3:15). So why the criticism of Saul here? Saul's offense is not the mere fact that he offers a sacrifice but that he disobeys God's word through the prophet Samuel.[7] No sooner has Saul finished than Samuel appears to announce his folly: "You acted foolishly" (13:13).

The prophet's speech contains an interesting wordplay centering on a verb that can mean both "command" and "appoint" in 13:13–14 (*ṣwh*). Yahweh *commanded* Saul to wait for Samuel. But now he will *appoint* a new king to take Saul's place. As McCarter has said, this subtle play on words in Samuel's final speech "unobtrusively but effectively directs our attention toward one central theme, viz. the relationship between kingship and obedience to Yahweh."[8] Saul has failed to keep his "appointment" (or command) as king, and therefore Yahweh will appoint a replacement.

It would be a mistake, however, to assume that this prophetic condemnation is a final rejection of Saul and his reign. Rather, Saul has lost the opportunity to establish an eternal dynasty. He himself will keep the throne, but it will not pass to his descendants and endure forever, as eventually will be promised to David (2 Sam. 7:15–16).[9] Instead, Yahweh will give the kingdom to "a man after his own heart" (1 Sam. 13:14).

---

6. Many scholars assume the account of Saul's battles with the Philistines originally lacked any reference to Samuel's rejection at Gilgal, which is alleged to have been a later prophetic redaction (esp. vv. 7b–15a). But recent investigations of literary method in biblical narrative have concluded that such assumptions are based on insubstantial evidence. See Long, *Reign and Rejection*, 43–66.

7. Youngblood, "1, 2 Samuel," 656.

8. McCarter, *I Samuel*, 228–29.

9. Keil and Delitzsch, *Samuel*, 129.

The term "heart" connotes "will" or "choice" in this context and emphasizes Yahweh's freedom in selecting a replacement for Saul rather than continuing Saul's line.[10] While this phrase primarily emphasizes Yahweh's choice of David, it also connotes something positive about David's character over against Saul's. The new king will genuinely act in accordance with Yahweh's wishes in a way that Saul does not. He will exhibit a certain "like-mindedness" with Yahweh.[11] Though both kings are said to have been chosen by Yahweh (David here and Saul in 8:22; 10:24), the circumstances of Saul's selection were clearly different, marred by the insolent demand of the people. The implication is that David is chosen on the basis of different criteria, that is, divine criteria unencumbered by the exigencies of human demands. "David was Yahweh's choice in a way that Saul, given in response to the people's request, was not."[12]

Philistine Strategic and Tactical Advantages (13:16—22)

THE PHILISTINES HOLD a decisive military superiority over the Israelites during this period. They substantially outnumber the troops of Saul and Jonathan.[13] They can afford the luxury of sending out detachments of "raiding parties" in different directions in order to seal off Saul's forces, preventing any Israelite reinforcements from the northern tribes.[14]

This personnel superiority is accompanied by a superiority in military equipment. By controlling a monopoly in metallurgical technology and technicians, the Philistines are able to limit Israel's arsenal.[15] While Philistine troops have the latest in advanced weaponry with finished metal products, Israel is restricted to weapons of wood and stone. The result is that on the day of battle, only Saul and Jonathan among the Israelites are armed with sword and spear (13:22). Presumably the Philistines know how inadequately Israel is prepared for war. It seems clear: Saul and his forces are in danger of annihilation.

---

10. There is an interesting parallel in the Babylonian Chronicles in which Nebuchadnezzar installs "a king of his own choice" (lit., "a king of his heart"), referring to his appointment of Zedekiah over Jerusalem as a vassal ruler in 597 B.C. See A. Kirk Grayson, *Assyrian and Babylonian Chronicles* (Locust Valley, N.Y.: Augustin, 1975), 102, chronicle 5, reverse 11–13; Alan Millard, "The Babylonian Chronicle," *COS*, 1.137:468. For discussion see Long, *Reign and Rejection*, 92–93; McCarter, *I Samuel*, 229.

11. Gordon, *I and II Samuel*, 134.

12. Long, *Reign and Rejection*, 93.

13. Though the numbers of the chapter are probably hyperbolic, they indicate a ten-to-one ratio of Philistine charioteers to Israelite foot soldiers (vv. 5, 15).

14. Bergen, *1, 2 Samuel*, 154.

15. James D. Muhly, "How Iron Technology Changed the Ancient World," *BAR* 8/6 (1982): 40–54.

THE ANATOMY OF SIN. The chapter contains the first of two confrontations between Saul and Samuel, in which the prophet announces Yahweh's rejection of Saul, first as father of an eternal royal dynasty (13:13–14) and then as king of Israel (15:10–35, esp. 15:23, 26). This text leaves the following questions begging for answer: What is Saul's sin? Does he have a chance, or is he ill-fated from the start?

Many biblical scholars have attempted to address the problem of the rejection of King Saul. Speculation on precisely why Saul is rejected has given rise to a number of different answers. In one recent attempt to address the question, David Gunn argues that Saul is not primarily responsible for his fate. Rather, his problems stem from a combination of "his own inner inadequacy as a human being" and his being "brought low essentially by external forces or circumstances."[16] Gunn suggests instead that Saul is "essentially an innocent victim of God," and that in this narrative we are encountering "the dark side of God."[17]

In a similar vein, Walter Brueggemann avers that Samuel himself appears unprincipled in this narrative and that the text raises questions about the character of Yahweh. Saul acts out of innocence and is simply a character in a narrative in which the cards are stacked in favor of David.[18] More recently, David Jobling has suggested that Saul's flaw is his inability to assert himself as king. He is incapable of freeing himself from the old order and therefore cannot be the bearer of the new order. Rather than being guilty of some sin per se, he is not allowed to function as a real king, partly because of his own ambiguity about kingship.[19]

These scholarly attempts to interpret 1 Samuel 13 are honestly trying to deal with difficult questions, primarily the way in which the chapter relates to other passages around it and the apparent inconsistency between offense and punishment. However, they fail to give due weight to the causes for Saul's rejection highlighted by the text itself, namely, the failure to keep the command of Yahweh. On the surface of the narrative, Saul's offense is a failure to wait for Samuel's arrival before consecrating battle. But more generally, this is tantamount to disobeying Yahweh's instructions as given through Samuel (see 13:13), which in turn exposes Saul's larger problem: He fails to

---

16. D. M. Gunn, *The Fate of King Saul: An Interpretation of a Biblical Story* (JSOTSup. 14; Sheffield: JSOT, 1981), 115.

17. Ibid., 123, 129.

18. Brueggemann, *First and Second Samuel*, 99–102.

19. David Jobling, *1 Samuel* (Berit Olam; Collegeville, Minn.: Michael Glazier, 1998), 79–88, esp. 85.

accept the structure of authority established for him by Yahweh and his prophet Samuel at the time of his appointment (13:14).[20] This unfortunately is a pattern that will be repeated in chapter 15.

Thus, Saul's guilt derives from his determination to usurp power rightly belonging only to Yahweh and his servant, Samuel. More generally, this text presents us with a portrait of Israel's first king, who has received all the blessing and empowerment any of us could hope to receive from God. Yet when pressed on every side by the approaching Philistine army, Saul is still inclined to disobey God's command.

It would be easy to illustrate this pattern from numerous parallels in biblical history. Indeed, in many respects, this is the anatomy of sin. First comes the tyranny of the urgent, the encroaching pressure from surrounding circumstances. This is followed by the insecurity and self-doubt arising from a lack of total reliance on God. Finally, there follows the rebellion itself—the pitiful human attempt to take matters into our own hands, which is tantamount to usurping, or at least presuming upon, the authority of God. This is the picture of sin demonstrated in the Garden of Eden as the paradigm of human failure, and as we all know too well, at least in our most honest moments, it is a pattern repeated many times in our own lives.

The results of Saul's failure are devastating. A quick glance back to 1 Samuel 11 highlights a striking contrast. In that text, the Israelites similarly confront a neighbor threatening military conflict, the Ammonites. There too we see Saul, leading his people in battle as he was prepared and anointed to do and serving his function as king of Israel. But in that conflict, Saul was empowered by the Spirit of Yahweh and led his people to a courageous and decisive victory (11:6–11). Here in 1 Samuel 13 we have no "Spirit-language." Though we are not told specifically that the Spirit of Yahweh has departed, one wonders about the "Ichabod" principle (1 Sam. 4:21). Has the glory of Yahweh departed? Has his Spirit been withdrawn?

Certainly in this initial conflict with the Philistines, the people act cowardly rather than with the bold aggressiveness of the Ammonite war (cf. 11:11 with 13:6–7). Saul himself is far from bold and assertive in his leadership. The text is clear in the value it places on obedience to Yahweh's word.

FAITHFUL OBEDIENCE. Modern Christians would do well to learn the subtle lessons of faithful obedience that lie just beneath the surface of this text. Saul was blessed with the Spirit of God and

---

20. Long, *Reign and Rejection*, 87–93.

was assured that he was "in the right place at the right time." He even exemplified God's power in his life during the war with the Ammonites, which was a similar situation as the one he faces here. But even all this is not enough to make him faithful in obedience to God's word through Samuel in the midst of the Philistine crisis. When threatened with apparent defeat and with his enemies pressing from every direction, he personally takes charge. He functions as a king would function in other nations in the ancient world. Against the explicit directives of God, he trusts his own ability to lead and to win the favor of God.

Consider the features of Saul's actions that contribute to what we have called the anatomy of sin. (1) Saul allows the circumstances of his current crisis to overtake him. He may have been tempted to trust in his army for defense of the country. But his troops are terrified, are hiding in caves and cisterns, and are running from the field of battle in the opposite direction (13:6–7). Saul realizes that "all the troops with him were quaking with fear" (13:7b), and it appears as if all is lost (13:11). But God's promise included victory over the Philistines. Indeed, Saul has been anointed as the prince who will deliver Israel from the power of this long-standing enemy (9:16). It is for just such a time as this that Saul has been made king. The circumstances of the moment swallow Saul and his vision of what God has in store for him.

(2) Saul commits himself to partial obedience. He fails to follow his commitments to God through to the end. He has been instructed to wait seven days for Samuel's arrival, at which time the prophet will make proper sacrifices to prepare for the war. Our text states explicitly that Saul "waited seven days, *the time set by Samuel*" (13:8). In this, Saul is obedient. But when Samuel does not arrive at the expected time, Saul proceeds to make other arrangements. He takes matters into his own hands in an attempt to ensure he will be victorious.

(3) Finally—and with this we arrive at the heart of the matter—when Samuel confronts Saul with this infraction, he fails to accept responsibility. He continues the kind of recrimination we have come to expect (and use ourselves!) since the Garden of Eden. He begins by trying to place partial blame on his troops and on Samuel himself (13:11): "When I saw that the men were scattering, and that you did not come at the set time. . . ." He finishes by maintaining that he had no alternatives: "I felt compelled" (13:12). This is an oft-repeated refrain: "I had no other choice, because you and others were not supportive!" Unfortunately this is the same defensive reaction Saul will use on other occasions when instead he should have admitted guilt and pled for mercy.

His punishment as announced by the prophet Samuel may seem harsh and unfair. But Samuel recognizes something in Saul that will recur in the subsequent narratives. Saul is content to depend on his own resources rather than lean on God's Word. This text is about learning to trust God when you see your own resources slipping away. But it is also about learning to trust God even when you think your resources are sufficient, when you think you can handle it alone. That is perhaps when we need to look to him more completely.

Wesley addressed the apparent inequity of the punishment with the question: But was it not hard to punish so little a sin so severely? In his answer, he states that disobedience to an express command, though in a small matter, is actually a great provocation. "And indeed, there is no little sin, because there is no little God to sin against. In general, what to [humans] seems a small offense, to him who knows the heart may appear a heinous crime."[21]

21. Wesley, *Wesley's Notes on the Bible*, 186.

1 Samuel 13:23–14:52

NOW A DETACHMENT of Philistines had gone out to the pass at Micmash. ¹⁴:¹One day Jonathan son of Saul said to the young man bearing his armor, "Come, let's go over to the Philistine outpost on the other side." But he did not tell his father.

²Saul was staying on the outskirts of Gibeah under a pomegranate tree in Migron. With him were about six hundred men, ³among whom was Ahijah, who was wearing an ephod. He was a son of Ichabod's brother Ahitub son of Phinehas, the son of Eli, the LORD's priest in Shiloh. No one was aware that Jonathan had left.

⁴On each side of the pass that Jonathan intended to cross to reach the Philistine outpost was a cliff; one was called Bozez, and the other Seneh. ⁵One cliff stood to the north toward Micmash, the other to the south toward Geba.

⁶Jonathan said to his young armor-bearer, "Come, let's go over to the outpost of those uncircumcised fellows. Perhaps the LORD will act in our behalf. Nothing can hinder the LORD from saving, whether by many or by few."

⁷"Do all that you have in mind," his armor-bearer said. "Go ahead; I am with you heart and soul."

⁸Jonathan said, "Come, then; we will cross over toward the men and let them see us. ⁹If they say to us, 'Wait there until we come to you,' we will stay where we are and not go up to them. ¹⁰But if they say, 'Come up to us,' we will climb up, because that will be our sign that the LORD has given them into our hands."

¹¹So both of them showed themselves to the Philistine outpost. "Look!" said the Philistines. "The Hebrews are crawling out of the holes they were hiding in." ¹²The men of the outpost shouted to Jonathan and his armor-bearer, "Come up to us and we'll teach you a lesson."

So Jonathan said to his armor-bearer, "Climb up after me; the LORD has given them into the hand of Israel."

¹³Jonathan climbed up, using his hands and feet, with his armor-bearer right behind him. The Philistines fell before Jonathan, and his armor-bearer followed and killed behind

him. [14]In that first attack Jonathan and his armor-bearer killed some twenty men in an area of about half an acre.

[15]Then panic struck the whole army—those in the camp and field, and those in the outposts and raiding parties—and the ground shook. It was a panic sent by God.

[16]Saul's lookouts at Gibeah in Benjamin saw the army melting away in all directions. [17]Then Saul said to the men who were with him, "Muster the forces and see who has left us." When they did, it was Jonathan and his armor-bearer who were not there.

[18]Saul said to Ahijah, "Bring the ark of God." (At that time it was with the Israelites.) [19]While Saul was talking to the priest, the tumult in the Philistine camp increased more and more. So Saul said to the priest, "Withdraw your hand."

[20]Then Saul and all his men assembled and went to the battle. They found the Philistines in total confusion, striking each other with their swords. [21]Those Hebrews who had previously been with the Philistines and had gone up with them to their camp went over to the Israelites who were with Saul and Jonathan. [22]When all the Israelites who had hidden in the hill country of Ephraim heard that the Philistines were on the run, they joined the battle in hot pursuit. [23]So the LORD rescued Israel that day, and the battle moved on beyond Beth Aven.

[24]Now the men of Israel were in distress that day, because Saul had bound the people under an oath, saying, "Cursed be any man who eats food before evening comes, before I have avenged myself on my enemies!" So none of the troops tasted food.

[25]The entire army entered the woods, and there was honey on the ground. [26]When they went into the woods, they saw the honey oozing out, yet no one put his hand to his mouth, because they feared the oath. [27]But Jonathan had not heard that his father had bound the people with the oath, so he reached out the end of the staff that was in his hand and dipped it into the honeycomb. He raised his hand to his mouth, and his eyes brightened. [28]Then one of the soldiers told him, "Your father bound the army under a strict oath, saying, 'Cursed be any man who eats food today!' That is why the men are faint."

[29]Jonathan said, "My father has made trouble for the country. See how my eyes brightened when I tasted a little of this

honey. ³⁰How much better it would have been if the men had eaten today some of the plunder they took from their enemies. Would not the slaughter of the Philistines have been even greater?"

³¹That day, after the Israelites had struck down the Philistines from Micmash to Aijalon, they were exhausted. ³²They pounced on the plunder and, taking sheep, cattle and calves, they butchered them on the ground and ate them, together with the blood. ³³Then someone said to Saul, "Look, the men are sinning against the LORD by eating meat that has blood in it."

"You have broken faith," he said. "Roll a large stone over here at once." ³⁴Then he said, "Go out among the men and tell them, 'Each of you bring me your cattle and sheep, and slaughter them here and eat them. Do not sin against the LORD by eating meat with blood still in it.'"

So everyone brought his ox that night and slaughtered it there. ³⁵Then Saul built an altar to the LORD; it was the first time he had done this.

³⁶Saul said, "Let us go down after the Philistines by night and plunder them till dawn, and let us not leave one of them alive."

"Do whatever seems best to you," they replied.

But the priest said, "Let us inquire of God here."

³⁷So Saul asked God, "Shall I go down after the Philistines? Will you give them into Israel's hand?" But God did not answer him that day.

³⁸Saul therefore said, "Come here, all you who are leaders of the army, and let us find out what sin has been committed today. ³⁹As surely as the LORD who rescues Israel lives, even if it lies with my son Jonathan, he must die." But not one of the men said a word.

⁴⁰Saul then said to all the Israelites, "You stand over there; I and Jonathan my son will stand over here."

"Do what seems best to you," the men replied.

⁴¹Then Saul prayed to the LORD, the God of Israel, "Give me the right answer." And Jonathan and Saul were taken by lot, and the men were cleared. ⁴²Saul said, "Cast the lot between me and Jonathan my son." And Jonathan was taken.

⁴³Then Saul said to Jonathan, "Tell me what you have done."

So Jonathan told him, "I merely tasted a little honey with the end of my staff. And now must I die?"

⁴⁴Saul said, "May God deal with me, be it ever so severely, if you do not die, Jonathan."

⁴⁵But the men said to Saul, "Should Jonathan die—he who has brought about this great deliverance in Israel? Never! As surely as the LORD lives, not a hair of his head will fall to the ground, for he did this today with God's help." So the men rescued Jonathan, and he was not put to death.

⁴⁶Then Saul stopped pursuing the Philistines, and they withdrew to their own land.

⁴⁷After Saul had assumed rule over Israel, he fought against their enemies on every side: Moab, the Ammonites, Edom, the kings of Zobah, and the Philistines. Wherever he turned, he inflicted punishment on them. ⁴⁸He fought valiantly and defeated the Amalekites, delivering Israel from the hands of those who had plundered them.

⁴⁹Saul's sons were Jonathan, Ishvi and Malki-Shua. The name of his older daughter was Merab, and that of the younger was Michal. ⁵⁰His wife's name was Ahinoam daughter of Ahimaaz. The name of the commander of Saul's army was Abner son of Ner, and Ner was Saul's uncle. ⁵¹Saul's father Kish and Abner's father Ner were sons of Abiel.

⁵²All the days of Saul there was bitter war with the Philistines, and whenever Saul saw a mighty or brave man, he took him into his service.

THIS TEXT IS ABOUT SAUL'S CONTINUED SUCCESSES against the Philistines. Yet even here, the narrative seems ambivalent at best about Saul.[1] Though he enjoys military successes, he seems a pious but confused king, "not so much wicked as foolish and frustrated."[2] After Jonathan's daring attack on the Philistine outpost at Micmash, God sends a panic against the Philistines, and the Israelites rout them decisively.

---

1. Many scholars assume chs. 13–14 rely on genuinely ancient materials that portrayed Saul originally in a positive light. These have been selected for inclusion because they could easily be used to contrast Saul with Jonathan and prepare for Saul's final rejection in ch. 15. See McCarter, *I Samuel*, 251. For a different approach, see Long, *Reign and Rejection*, 101–32.

2. David Jobling, "Saul's Fall and Jonathan's Rise: Tradition and Redaction in 1 Sam. 14:1–46," *JBL* 95 (1976): 367–76, esp. 368.

Nevertheless, Saul issues a foolish ban against eating during the battle, which weakens his troops and limits the extent of the victory.

This section stands as the middle of three devoted to the reign of King Saul (chs. 13–15). In the previous one, Saul failed to follow Samuel's instructions regarding the sacrifice before battle. The result was a prophetic rebuke, in which Saul was informed that his dynasty would not endure; another man would be appointed to succeed him instead of his own son (13:13–14). The great tragedy of that loss becomes apparent now in chapter 14. The narrative is essentially the story of Jonathan and his surpassing leadership qualities. What a fine king he would have been! The narrative describes and defends the rejection of Saul by means of analogy between Saul and Jonathan.[3] Father and son are contrasted in chapters 13 and 14 in order to condemn Saul.

Furthermore, chapter 14 portrays the progressive alienation of Saul so that by the end of the chapter, he is totally isolated from those around him. The effect of the text is to demonstrate that Saul's relationships with Jonathan and his troops are "outworkings of the more fundamental break in his relationship with Yahweh and his representative Samuel."[4]

Jonathan Attacks the Outpost at Micmash (13:23–14:15)

THE UNIT OPENS with the account of Jonathan's daring raid on the Philistine detachment at Micmash. Against all odds, he and his armor-bearer attack an outpost of Philistines. They are heavily outnumbered and at a strategic disadvantage. But Jonathan is unimpressed by the enemy's greater numbers and undeterred in his belief that Yahweh will deliver Israel from this dreaded enemy. His words to the armor-bearer reveal his character and commitment: "Nothing can hinder the LORD from saving, whether by many or by few" (14:6).

In fact, the Lord honors Jonathan's brave leadership. In this opening sortie, these two men alone kill around twenty Philistines in a small area (14:14). By implication the paragraph is showing what kind of king Jonathan would have been as his father's successor.[5] But alas, the text has already informed us that Jonathan will not be king because of Saul's unfaithfulness (13:13–14).

While Jonathan and his armor-bearer are on their secret mission, Saul is in Gibeah administering his kingdom in traditional Israelite fashion (cf. Judg.

---

3. Long, *Reign and Rejection*, 40–41; Gordon, *1 and 2 Samuel*, 57.

4. Long, *Reign and Rejection*, 131.

5. Indeed his unbounded enthusiasm for Yahweh's causes and his courage in the face of insurmountable odds anticipate another character in 1 Samuel (David before Goliath), who *will* in fact become Saul's successor (1 Sam. 17).

4:5).[6] The passing reference to Ahijah in 1 Samuel 14:3 is important for our reading of this unit. The presence of a royal chaplain with the Israelite troops might not be noteworthy in and of itself. He is wearing the priestly ephod with its Urim and Thummim and can be consulted in order to seek Yahweh's favor (Ex. 28). What is remarkable here is Ahijah's carefully phrased genealogy: "He was a son of Ichabod's brother Ahitub son of Phinehas, the son of Eli, the LORD's priest in Shiloh." The narrator has detoured from direct descent in the line of Aaron in order to highlight meticulously an uncle, Ichabod, thus recalling the checkered history of Eli, Phinehas, and Shiloh. In an important study of this chapter, David Jobling succinctly captures the importance of this reference:

> Saul is accompanied by Ahijah, a member of the rejected priestly house of Eli (14:3), and this first mention of an Elide after the disasters which befell Eli's family in chap. 4 triggers the response "rejected by Yhwh." Lest the point be missed, it is reinforced by the odd and needless genealogical reference to Ichabod, Ahijah's uncle, picking up on 4:21–22, and reminding the reader that "the glory has departed." His own royal glory gone, where else would we expect Saul to be than with a relative of "Glory gone"?[7]

The reference in verse 3 to the rejected priestly house thus stresses the rejection of Saul's royal house.[8] Moreover, it reveals something of the inner life of Saul, who has apparently lost the prophet Samuel as his spiritual advisor. Since Samuel announced the end of Saul's royal dynasty in 13:13–14, the prophet has apparently been replaced by a member of the rejected family of Eli. Saul has lost his way. He has turned from the legitimate counsel of Samuel to the discredited priestly line of Eli.

Saul and the Israelites Rout the Philistines (14:16–23)

THIS PARAGRAPH CONTINUES the contrast between Saul and Jonathan by illustrating how Jonathan is a leader who takes action, while Saul simply responds. When Saul sees what is happening, he calls for Ahijah to bring the ephod,[9] apparently in order to ask Yahweh whether he should join the battle with the Philistines or not. But inexplicably, Saul suddenly stops the inquiry and rushes

---

6. Bergen, *1, 2 Samuel*, 155.

7. Jobling, "Saul's Fall," 368.

8. Jobling, *1 Samuel*, 95.

9. The LXX has "ephod" here instead of the difficult Hebrew reference to the "ark of God," as in the NIV and most modern translations (see NIV text note). But see Keil and Delitzsch, *Samuel*, 140–41.

---

to the battlefield (14:19–20). Such sudden reversals expose Saul's uncertainty and remind the reader of his previous failure to wait for Samuel's arrival in order to offer sacrifice (ch. 13). This is but one decision of several others in this text that reveal Saul's "fatal impetuosity," and indeed this impetuosity begins to characterize his reign.[10] The battle appears to have been nearly won before Saul even arrives on the scene (14:20).

Saul's Foolish Ban Against Eating (14:24–46)

SAUL'S IMPETUOUS, EVEN careless, actions continue. The meaning of verse 24 is complicated by textual and literary problems (compare NIV and NLT with NRSV).[11] Whatever the original text may have been, apparently Saul places an unnecessary and unreasonable burden on his troops by disallowing them to eat food during the day of battle. He may have been motivated by a desire to create a "holy war" setting, which is reasonable in this context.[12] But however commendable his reasons for such a ban, the result is that his men are famished and exhausted.

This paragraph's unusual events illustrate again the contrast between Jonathan and Saul. Jonathan, unaware of his father's foolish ban, does not hesitate to refresh himself with honey. His "brightened" condition (14:27, 29) proves that he has better understood God's will for the troops than his father. He quickly condemns Saul's ban and accuses him of making trouble for Israel (14:29). Later, when Saul seeks divine guidance concerning a surprise night attack, there is no response from Yahweh.[13] This divine silence is tantamount to divine displeasure, and Saul begins an investigation to find the guilty party. When Jonathan proves to be the guilty party, Saul is faced with revolt in his own army.

Saul has gradually alienated himself first from Samuel, then from his army with the foolish ban against eating, and now finally from his own son (14:39). The result is a lost opportunity. The day that began with prospects of a final and decisive victory over the Philistines ends in a draw (14:46).

Summary of Saul's Reign (14:47–52)

THESE BRIEF NOTICES about Saul's reign are typical of the Deuteronomistic Historian (see "The Israelite Historians" in the introduction), who also provides

---

10. McCarter, *I Samuel*, 240.

11. Long, *Reign and Rejection*, 114–17; McCarter, *I Samuel*, 245.

12. Youngblood, "1, 2 Samuel," 665.

13. The phrase used here for seeking God's guidance will become an important theme later in 1 Samuel (see comments on 23:1–6).

royal summaries for David (2 Sam. 8) and commonly in the books of 1–2 Kings. It has been suggested that Saul's summary is more notable for what it does *not* say than for what it does say.[14] Unlike David's summary, for example, there is no mention of Yahweh. Twice, David is said to have been delivered wherever he went (2 Sam. 8:6, 14), whereas Saul is simply victorious wherever he turns (1 Sam. 14:47).

Especially important in light of Saul's failure to inflict a decisive blow against the Philistines in chapters 13–14 is the concluding verse: "All the days of Saul there was bitter war with the Philistines, and whenever Saul saw a mighty or brave man, he took him into his service" (14:52). The Philistine threat was Saul's reason for serving Israel as king (9:16). But the final subjugation of Philistia will have to await a greater king (2 Sam. 8:1, 12).

Bridging Contexts

DEPENDENCE ON GOD AND HIS WORD. In applying this text to our modern world, we must read this section in light of the larger context of chapters 13–15. These three chapters are devoted to Saul's reign and expose his inadequacies and his unsuitability to serve as Israel's king. The narrator does this on two levels. (1) He explicitly articulates Saul's rejection by Samuel in 13:13–14. Because Saul does not keep the command of Yahweh, his kingdom will not endure; that is, God will not establish Saul's royal dynasty forever. Instead, the crown prince, Jonathan, will be replaced by another prince, who is of God's own choosing. Such explicit rejection of Saul's posterity removes all suspense and only leaves the question of how Saul's own reign will conclude. It also drives the reader on to chapter 16 and the rest of the books of Samuel, which are devoted to Saul's successor, whose royal dynasty will in fact be established forever.

(2) The other level of Saul's rejection in the narrative is much more subtle than Samuel's condemnation in chapter 13. There is a "destructive darkness" in Saul's life that slowly but relentlessly wells up within the narrative itself.[15] Events gradually begin to work against Saul. He is not necessarily a fated leader, but he makes foolish and careless decisions at each step, which eventually take on greater consequences as the narrative unfolds. In essence, the extended narrative forms an answer to one of the book's leading questions: Who may serve suitably as Israel's king? Saul now begins to function as a negative answer to that question and becomes the foil for another king, who will be the ideal.

---

14. For this observation, see Long, *Reign and Rejection*, 130–31.
15. Brueggemann, *First and Second Samuel*, 106.

We discussed the specific nature of Saul's sin in our comments on chapter 13, and we will return to this question in chapter 15. But this chapter contributes to our understanding of his failures by contrasting Jonathan and Saul in many subtle ways. Jonathan is the bold and daring officer, who takes initiative and defends his fellow soldiers against his father's unwise ban on eating. By contrast, Saul is disengaged. He has no communication with Jonathan (14:1, 17, 27), and his ban against eating implies he is also detached from his army. It is also interesting that the prophet Samuel has no role to play in this chapter.

Some scholars have attempted to analyze Saul's personality traits, even to the extent of psychoanalyzing his behavior.[16] Whatever difficulties Saul may have experienced, the text emphasizes a deeper and more troubling development, a decaying spiritual character. In this episode in chapter 14, the contrast between Jonathan and Saul is most acute in the way they express their relationship to Yahweh. "Whereas Saul the commander publicly dishonored the Lord through fear-inspired disobedience, Jonathan the warrior would bring honor to the Lord through his fearless faith."[17]

Even beyond this military context, the text slowly drives the reader to the conclusion that Saul will never succeed as Israel's king because of a persistent refusal to accept Yahweh's word. Moreover, the absence of Samuel becomes important when we consider again the significance of the presence of Ahijah in verse 3. Samuel is gone, but this relative of Ichabod from Eli's discredited house is present. This implies that Saul has stopped listening to Samuel altogether, which has apparently been matched by Samuel's willingness to stop speaking (13:15). Saul is now looking to other sources for divine direction. God's word and direction for him have become dissatisfying or threatening, so he has turned to another way.

This illustrates the biblical truth that God's people are dependent on his Word for life and sustenance. But trouble comes when we choose to listen to other voices. It begins with Adam and Eve, who grew discontented with the simple prohibition, "You shall not eat," and exchanged it for the convoluted logic of a stranger in the garden. It continues with the Israelite nation, who grew weary of the words of the prophets and exchanged them for the favorable oracles of false prophets, who assured them the nation's history was secure (Jer. 27:16—22). It was true of the Lord's disciples, who could not accept his teaching about his messianic mission and tried giving it a military interpretation (Matt. 16:21—23; 26:47—51).

---

16. For example, R. K. Harrison has considered Saul's manic-depression and even suggested paranoid schizophrenia (*Introduction to the Old Testament* [Grand Rapids: Eerdmans, 1969], 715—16).

17. Bergen, *1, 2 Samuel*, 155.

Saul becomes another illustration of one of the truths of biblical salvation history: God's people are not capable of self-rule. Whether the nation Israel as a whole or individual believers, God's people have not been created for self-determination precisely because faith implies dependence on him, and any other source for guidance and direction will end in ruin. Those who love God are incapable of self-rule because by definition God's people are created to look beyond themselves for a word—a watchword from God—that will set their course. By definition, God's people are listening to *his* way, in the full conviction that no other will satisfy.

THE SAMUEL IN OUR LIVES. Implications of this text for modern culture flow from this concept that Saul's rejection occurs simultaneously with his own rejection of God's means of instruction and support. Saul has failed to give heed to Samuel, his spiritual adviser and source of instruction from God. The prophet was Saul's only legitimate means of learning what Yahweh wanted him to do and become. Once he stops listening to Samuel and the prophetic voice withdraws from Saul (as implied by 13:15), the "destructive darkness" of his life begins to become more apparent, and his course is set.

Most of us who live in the West accept as a rudimentary philosophical assumption the intrinsic freedom of the individual human. We generally assume also, however, that liberty and freedom are the same as the ability to "set our own course," to navigate our own affairs as we see fit. But herein is the conflict between Christian faith and the philosophies of the West. Christians are not supposed to navigate their own course. We must recognize that we are incapable of finding within our own beings the measure by which we must rule our lives. Just as Saul needed Samuel to direct and guide him, so we need God to shine his light on our paths (Ps. 119:105). As Saul was condemned once he turned from Samuel to find guidance in other sources, so modern believers must be warned against neglecting or abandoning God as the source of truth and light.

My brother-in-law, Joe Boggs, is a private pilot, meaning he flies occasionally for pleasure and for family trips. On the few occasions when he has managed to get me into his small four-passenger Cessna, I have been impressed with how many instruments it takes to fly the plane. Joe has instruments for measuring his altitude, his fuel supply, his horizontal equilibrium, and his air speed. Not knowing much about such things, I'm always grateful to God for all the instruments at Joe's disposal.

Joe explained to me one day that he has his "IFR" rating, which stands for "Instrument Flight Rules" (pilot-types love to sound military). This means that he can fly the plane without seeing the ground or horizon. If he is surrounded by thick clouds and can see nothing of the sky or ground, he can rely solely on the instruments of the plane to navigate. In order to qualify for his IFR rating, his instructor put a visor over his head blocking his view through the windshield. He had to prove he could fly in complete dependence on the instrument panel.

Christians need to have their IFR rating! Joe's dependence and faith in his instruments and their ability to keep him from crashing illustrate how Christians should rely on God as the source of direction in our lives. We first must believe that God is trustworthy. He is just and holy and wants what is best for us. This was the serpent's first lie in the Garden of Eden. He led Eve to believe that perhaps God was hiding something from her; perhaps God did not want what was best for her (Gen. 3:5). But just as Joe must believe his instruments are dependable and capable of keeping him from crashing, so Christians need to believe that God is worthy of our trust.

In addition, in order to fly the plane, Joe must physically commit himself. If his altitude is too high, Joe pulls back on the throttle to lower the plane. If his wings are not true to the horizon as indicated by the "artificial horizon" on his instrument panel, he adjusts the bank of the plane to the correct attitude. Thus, it is not enough simply to believe that God is trustworthy. We must act on that belief (James 2:19). Believers must commit themselves to God and his truth, and we must be willing to adjust quickly or change some sinful attitude or habit in our lives.

This text is compelling the reader to examine sources of authority in his or her life. It raises the question: Who is the Samuel in my life? Is God at liberty to communicate to me any message he needs me to hear in order to correct or admonish me? Or have I replaced Samuel with Ahijah? Have I turned from the dependable and true, which may be a harder word to hear? Have I turned instead to hear another word that is more pleasing or more attuned to my personal ambitions or desires? The Bible consistently shows the folly of turning to any other source.

Our guiding principles in life must be external to our own moral compass. All the instruments on Joe's Cessna are tied to something tangible and external to the plane itself. The plane's artificial horizon is tied to earth's gravitational pull, the altitude is based on external air pressure, the compass on earth's magnetic field, radio navigational instruments to radio signals, and so forth. Likewise, saving faith commits to a relationship with God, which establishes an objectifiable source of guidance external to the believer. Whether people look within to find the guiding principles of life or whether they look to the wisdom of other humans, anything short of divine counsel is self-destructive. Unfortunately, Saul's reliance on Ahijah is only the beginning of his search for another way.

The following is a shopworn story, but one that bears repeating. On his way to work every day, a man walked past a clockmaker's store. He would stop each day outside and synchronize his watch with the clock that stood in the window of the clockmaker's shop. Observing this routine, the clockmaker one day struck up a conversation with the man and asked him what kind of work he did. The man timidly confessed that he worked as the timekeeper at the nearby factory and that his malfunctioning watch necessitated daily readjustment. Since it was his job to ring the closing bell every day at 4:00 P.M., he synchronized his watch with the clock every morning to guarantee precision.

The clockmaker, even more embarrassed than the timekeeper, said, "I hate to tell you this, but my clock doesn't work very well either, and I have been adjusting it to the bell that I hear every afternoon from the factory at 4:00 P.M.!"[18] Saul in our text illustrates what happens to an individual who turns from God to find another opinion, which is like relying on a malfunctioning watch that is timed every day to a bad clock.

---

18. As narrated in Ravi Zacharias, *A Shattered Visage: The Real Face of Atheism* (Brentwood, Tenn.: Wolgemuth & Hyatt, 1990), 47–48.

1 Samuel 15:1–35

S AMUEL SAID TO Saul, "I am the one the LORD sent to anoint you king over his people Israel; so listen now to the message from the LORD. ²This is what the LORD Almighty says: 'I will punish the Amalekites for what they did to Israel when they waylaid them as they came up from Egypt. ³Now go, attack the Amalekites and totally destroy everything that belongs to them. Do not spare them; put to death men and women, children and infants, cattle and sheep, camels and donkeys.'"

⁴So Saul summoned the men and mustered them at Telaim—two hundred thousand foot soldiers and ten thousand men from Judah. ⁵Saul went to the city of Amalek and set an ambush in the ravine. ⁶Then he said to the Kenites, "Go away, leave the Amalekites so that I do not destroy you along with them; for you showed kindness to all the Israelites when they came up out of Egypt." So the Kenites moved away from the Amalekites.

⁷Then Saul attacked the Amalekites all the way from Havilah to Shur, to the east of Egypt. ⁸He took Agag king of the Amalekites alive, and all his people he totally destroyed with the sword. ⁹But Saul and the army spared Agag and "the best of the sheep and cattle, the fat calves and lambs— everything that was good. These they were unwilling to destroy completely, but everything that was despised and weak they totally destroyed.

¹⁰Then the word of the LORD came to Samuel: ¹¹"I am grieved that I have made Saul king, because he has turned away from me and has not carried out my instructions." Samuel was troubled, and he cried out to the LORD all that night.

¹²Early in the morning Samuel got up and went to meet Saul, but he was told, "Saul has gone to Carmel. There he has set up a monument in his own honor and has turned and gone on down to Gilgal."

¹³When Samuel reached him, Saul said, "The LORD bless you! I have carried out the LORD's instructions."

¹⁴But Samuel said, "What then is this bleating of sheep in my ears? What is this lowing of cattle that I hear?"

¹⁵Saul answered, "The soldiers brought them from the Amalekites; they spared the best of the sheep and cattle to sacrifice to the LORD your God, but we totally destroyed the rest."

¹⁶"Stop!" Samuel said to Saul. "Let me tell you what the LORD said to me last night."

"Tell me," Saul replied.

¹⁷Samuel said, "Although you were once small in your own eyes, did you not become the head of the tribes of Israel? The LORD anointed you king over Israel. ¹⁸And he sent you on a mission, saying, 'Go and completely destroy those wicked people, the Amalekites; make war on them until you have wiped them out.' ¹⁹Why did you not obey the LORD? Why did you pounce on the plunder and do evil in the eyes of the LORD?"

²⁰"But I did obey the LORD," Saul said. "I went on the mission the LORD assigned me. I completely destroyed the Amalekites and brought back Agag their king. ²¹The soldiers took sheep and cattle from the plunder, the best of what was devoted to God, in order to sacrifice them to the LORD your God at Gilgal."

²²But Samuel replied:

"Does the LORD delight in burnt offerings and sacrifices
    as much as in obeying the voice of the LORD?
To obey is better than sacrifice,
    and to heed is better than the fat of rams.
²³For rebellion is like the sin of divination,
    and arrogance like the evil of idolatry.
Because you have rejected the word of the LORD,
    he has rejected you as king."

²⁴Then Saul said to Samuel, "I have sinned. I violated the LORD's command and your instructions. I was afraid of the people and so I gave in to them. ²⁵Now I beg you, forgive my sin and come back with me, so that I may worship the LORD."

²⁶But Samuel said to him, "I will not go back with you. You have rejected the word of the LORD, and the LORD has rejected you as king over Israel!"

²⁷As Samuel turned to leave, Saul caught hold of the hem of his robe, and it tore. ²⁸Samuel said to him, "The LORD has torn the kingdom of Israel from you today and has given it to one of your neighbors—to one better than you. ²⁹He who is the Glory of Israel does not lie or change his mind; for he is not a man, that he should change his mind."

³⁰Saul replied, "I have sinned. But please honor me before the elders of my people and before Israel; come back with me, so that I may worship the LORD your God." ³¹So Samuel went back with Saul, and Saul worshiped the LORD.

³²Then Samuel said, "Bring me Agag king of the Amalekites."

Agag came to him confidently, thinking, "Surely the bitterness of death is past."

³³But Samuel said,

"As your sword has made women childless,
so will your mother be childless among women."

And Samuel put Agag to death before the LORD at Gilgal.

³⁴Then Samuel left for Ramah, but Saul went up to his home in Gibeah of Saul. ³⁵Until the day Samuel died, he did not go to see Saul again, though Samuel mourned for him. And the LORD was grieved that he had made Saul king over Israel.

THIS CHAPTER IS THE LAST OF THREE devoted to the reign of King Saul, all of which focus on his military efforts—first against the Philistines and then the Amalekites. As elsewhere in biblical historiography, the narrator is not really concerned to detail the brute facts of history. These chapters are intended rather to answer the question: Why did Yahweh reject Saul as king of Israel? His war with the Amalekites contributes to this explanation. It was a war divinely initiated, with strict regulations and restrictions. But Saul proves unwilling to accept Yahweh's restrictions and suffers prophetic condemnation as a consequence.

Before moving on to the prince after God's own heart (the anointing of David in ch. 16), we have this one final chapter on Saul's failure. In chapter 13, Saul lost his prospects for an enduring royal dynasty. In chapter 14, he lost an opportunity to rout the Philistines as well as the respect of his own people. Now he loses his kingdom. The rest of 1 Samuel narrates the circumstances of his gradual decline and the rise of another to take his place.

Saul's Victory over the Amalekites (15:1–9)

THE AMALEKITES WERE a seminomadic tribal group from the south and south-west.[1] They were the first people to oppose the Israelites after the Exodus (Ex. 17:8–16) and are portrayed as terrorists who preyed on weaker opponents, showing no regard for God (Deut. 25:17–18). Because of their cowardly tactics on an unsuspecting nation, Yahweh promised to extract vengeance against them in some future day when Israel was established in the Promised Land: "I will completely blot out the memory of Amalek from under heaven" (Ex. 17:14; cf. Deut. 25:19). Because of their opposition to God and his people early in biblical history, the Amalekites are consistently portrayed in the Old Testament as vigorous enemies of Israel and of Yahweh. They apparently came to represent any group or nation who defied Yahweh and his purposes.[2]

Samuel returns in this chapter (after a brief absence in ch. 14) to announce that now is the time to accomplish Yahweh's vengeance against Amalek (15:2–3), and Saul is the king to do this. The ambiguity of the text toward Saul is still apparent. He has lost all hope for an enduring dynasty—but he is still God's anointed one. Yahweh still has an important mission for him, and even now his destiny is uncertain. Who knows, good conduct might yield a divine change of mind.

Samuel's instructions for warfare are clear (15:3). The description given is familiar to us as what has become known as "holy war," though this terminology is not used in the Old Testament itself. In such wars, Yahweh himself initiates the conflict and ensures its success.[3] He is a "warrior" who graces the battlefield and Israel's war camp with his presence. Such wars become an act of worship, surrounded with appropriate sacrifices and cultic rituals, including at times spiritual preparation such as circumcision and Passover celebration. Sometimes the ark of the covenant is used to underscore the fact that Yahweh is present.[4] Typically when engaged in holy war, Israel is supposed to disregard the number of troops amassed in the enemy's ranks. Since Yahweh will fight the battles, the number of troops is not significant, whereas Israel's character and state of mind are central (Deut. 20:2–9).

Samuel's words in 15:3 are an important part of this "holy war" tradition: "Now go, attack the Amalekites and totally destroy everything that belongs

---

1. It is possible a northern group of Amalekites inhabited the hills of western Samaria. See Diane Edelman, "Saul's Battle Against Amalek," *JSOT* 35 (1986): 71–84.

2. Gerald L. Mattingly, "Amalek," *ABD*, 1:169–71; Debra Reid, "Amalek," *NIDOTTE*, 4:371–72.

3. Deut. 20 provides the regulation for such wars. For more on what follows, see Longman and Reid, *God Is a Warrior*; Miller, *The Divine Warrior in Early Israel*; Tremper Longman III, "חרם," *NIDOTTE*, 2:785–89.

4. See comments on Israel's futile attempt to force the issue in 4:1b–11.

to them." The term "totally destroy" (Hiphil of *ḥrm* or the noun *ḥerem*) occurs eight times in this chapter and is an important concept in understanding why Saul is rejected. The word denotes a special act of consecration to God; when related to warfare it designates the consecration of a city or its population to destruction.[5] The entire city of Jericho was devoted for destruction (Josh. 6:17). But when Achan disobeyed the ban, Israel lost a battle to the people of Ai, thus illustrating the importance of rigid obedience to Yahweh in time of holy war.

This paragraph ends on a note that Saul and his army are *selectively* obedient to Yahweh's instructions. They destroy completely only the weak and unwanted spoils but spare the best of the sheep and cattle, fat calves and lambs, in addition to Agag, the king of the Amalekites (15:9). Saul's motivation for sparing Agag has been much disputed, but it is apparently a vain attempt to display a royal slave—a common practice in the ancient Near East. The victory "monument in his own honor" (15:12) may support the idea that Saul saved Agag as a trophy of his triumph.[6]

Samuel Confronts and Condemns Saul (15:10–31)

PARTIAL OBEDIENCE IS really only *dis*obedience made to look acceptable. Saul obeys God's word to a degree in that he does in fact attack the Amalekites and win a great victory against them. But he convinces himself that he has satisfied the divine injunctions. Samuel is then sent to expose Saul's actions as unacceptable. The text then narrates an extended dialogue between the prophet and the king, in which Saul's sin gradually becomes insurmountable. The reader is forced to conclude that Saul must go! He can no longer serve as king of Israel.

Yahweh informs Samuel that he regrets making Saul king: "I am grieved that I have made Saul king" (15:11). This precipitates an encounter between Samuel and Saul, in which Saul first tries to deflect the blame, then tries to justify it, and finally tries to minimize its seriousness. All in all, we would say Saul fails to take responsibility for his actions.

When they first meet, Saul greets Samuel with the cheery "The LORD bless you! I have carried out the LORD's instructions" (15:13). Apparently he is oblivious to the extent of his crimes. He has replaced Samuel as his spiritual adviser (ch. 14), and now he has failed to fulfill the mission as defined by Yahweh. Samuel's blunt questions shatter the delusional world in which Saul is living: "What then is this bleating of sheep in my ears? What is this

---

5. Jackie A. Naudé, "חרם," *NIDOTTE*, 2:276.
6. Keil and Delitzsch, *Samuel*, 153; Long, *Reign and Rejection*, 140.

lowing of cattle that I hear?" (15:14). Saul has rationalized his sparing of Agag and the best of the cattle as a delay, a temporary suspension of God's instructions for holy war. This will give his soldiers time to offer the animals up as sacrifices to God and give Saul time to enjoy parading a captured royal prisoner! In Saul's mind, this is only a temporary postponement in fulfilling Yahweh's command. But Samuel's booming "What then is this bleating of sheep?" breaks into Saul's world and reveals his deception for what it truly is— a selfish rejection of God's message.

There was no denying it; there was a sound of livestock in the camp. Anyone could hear it. The very presence of live sheep and cattle (and king Agag) condemns Saul. Samuel has arrived on the scene merely to point out the obvious. The series of statements made by the king in his defense before Samuel in this passage reveals a pitiable soul who is sorry only that he has been caught. His instincts are to defend himself against his prophet accuser.

First, Saul tries deflection, hoping to divert the blame onto the soldiers (15:15, where the Hebrew has simply "the people," which at times means "army"). It is, after all, really the troops who have spared the best of the cattle, not strictly speaking Saul himself. Such recrimination is as old as the Garden of Eden, where the strategy of deflecting guilt onto someone else (anyone else!) was first tried (Gen. 3:12–13). But Saul is no more successful at averting guilt than Adam and Eve. Samuel reminds the king that it is Yahweh's command that made him king and that it is also Yahweh's command that he has now rejected (15:17–19).

Once deflection of blame fails, Saul's second strategy is argumentation ("But I did obey the LORD," 15:20–21). In his defense, Saul continues to insist it is really the soldiers who are to blame, since he himself went on the mission and accomplished the task. But the central issue in his argumentation is a redefinition of Yahweh's command. In one breath, Saul argues that he did in fact execute the terms of holy war (i.e., complete annihilation of the enemy) *and* brought back Agag the king! But this is a self-condemning contradiction. They cannot both stand as a fulfillment of Yahweh's command. His argument is flawed by a lame attempt to impose an alien definition on the otherwise clear command of God. This too is a common strategy for escaping condemnation. In the face of exposed disobedience, many have attempted to redefine what it actually means to obey.

Samuel's response is unequivocal (15:22–23). Yahweh desires obedience over everything else. Even sacrifice is unacceptable if it becomes only a ruse for real submission to God's will. Samuel announces the judgment of Yahweh, which is strictly commensurate with the nature of Saul's sin as illustrated in the play on the verb "rejected" (*m's*): "Because you have *rejected* the word of the LORD, he has *rejected* you as king" (15:23).[7] Now Saul has lost not only his dynasty (as in ch. 13) but his right to serve as king.

After hearing the irrefutable statement of rejection, Saul changes his strategy again and for the first time we hear something like a confession. This strategy might be called self-serving confession (15:24–25). Technically, he uses the right words: "I have sinned." But this is followed by many more words revealing the compulsory and obligatory nature of that confession. He intends to appease Samuel by mentioning yet again "the people" (or "army") and his fear of them. He further pleads with Samuel to appear with him before the people in order to save face. Even his confession, if it can honestly be called that, is contrived and motivated by self-interest. It is disingenuous, and Samuel responds by reaffirming Yahweh's rejection of Saul as king (15:26–29).

The unit concludes with a climactic "I have sinned," in which Saul acknowledges his guilt a second time (15:30). But again he follows this with more words calling into question the sincerity of his confession. His concern is again saving face before the people rather than finding forgiveness before God. The repetition of Saul's confession (15:24–25, 30) has led some modern interpreters to assume we have two narrative accounts combined into one, so that verses 24–29 are secondary. But recent literary studies have shown that repetition is common in Old Testament narrative as a technique for emphasis.[8] The differences in the second occurrence often reveal the main theme of the narrative.

In this text, the second confession serves a climactic role near the end of a unit and reveals the spirit of Saul's ploy. He has replaced "forgive my sin" with "honor me before the elders" (cf. vv. 25 and 30). Saul seems more concerned with *his* people than with *Samuel's* God.[9] Notice the pronouns in 15:30: "Honor me before the elders of *my* people . . . come back with me, so that I may worship the LORD *your* God." Saul's "confession" is really nothing more than an acknowledgment of wrongdoing. He displays no contrition and gives no indication that he will act differently in the future.

---

7. Our verb implies the formal repudiation of a relationship and is the legal opposite of "choose" (*bḥr*). Only Yahweh can reject Saul as king because he alone has "chosen" him (10:24). See McCarter, *I Samuel*, 268.

8. Meir Sternberg, *The Poetics of Biblical Narrative: Ideological Literature and the Drama of Reading* (Bloomington, Ind.: Indiana Univ. Press, 1987), 365–440; Adele Berlin, *Poetics and Interpretation of Biblical Narrative* (Sheffield: Almond, 1983), 72–80; Robert Alter, *The Art of Biblical Narrative* (New York: Basic Books, 1981), 88–113.

9. Long, *Reign and Rejection*, 37–38, 164.

Samuel and Saul Part Company (15:32–35)

IN THE CLOSING SCENE, Samuel executes the Amalekite king. The job unfinished by the king is now left for the prophet himself, who gave the original order (see 15:3). The public execution of Agag is itself an implicit rebuke of Saul, who allowed him to live in the first place.

The sad closing verses of chapter 15 effectively bring Saul's reign to an end. Samuel and Saul go their separate ways—the prophet to Ramah and Saul to Gibeah, their respective homes. They will not see each other again.[10] Their relationship is broken, which bodes only ill for Saul and his reign. Samuel was the king's approved source for divine authority, the legitimizing theocratic base of Israel's new monarchy. For all practical purposes, this statement of the loss of relationship with Samuel means Saul's reign has ended. He will technically continue as Israel's king for many years, but his legitimacy has eroded. He has disqualified himself as the representative of Yahweh.

Finally, there are words of sorrow. Samuel mourns for Saul, and Yahweh is grieved that he made Saul king.[11] Everyone seems full of sorrow and regret—except Saul. The text ends by implicitly emphasizing that Saul is unrepentant, showing no true remorse or contrition.

Bridging Contexts

THIS TEXT ON the rejection of Saul plays an important role in the biblical story line. It is strategically placed as a transition from Saul to David. Saul continues as king until his death (ch. 31), but his fate is sealed by his own sin. He is king in name only because his reign is illegitimate. In this chapter, the historian is less concerned to relate Saul's wars with the Amalekites than to explain his rejection. This is its central purpose. Along the way, we encounter two other important topics that bridge the contexts from ancient Israel's culture to our own: the prophetic perspective on sacrifice (15:22) and the nature of confession and repentance.

Saul's rejection. Saul's failure to execute the ban of holy war against the Amalekites is similar in many respects to his failure to wait for Samuel to make the sacrifice. Both are acts of disobedience of Yahweh's specific word given through the prophet. In both, we see the king's deep-seated rejection of Yahweh's structure of authority for human kingship in Israel. In chapter 15 especially, the narrative goes to great lengths in the dialogue between Samuel and Saul to generalize the king's crimes and expose their full nature and

---

10. Except for the brief encounter in 19:23–24 and the ethereal encounter in ch. 28.

11. The verb used for Samuel's emotion (*hitʾabbel* in 15:35) is often used to express grief over death, as if Saul were already dead.

significance. On a general level, Saul's failure constitutes a disregard of the word of Yahweh, and ultimately of the theocratic authority structure necessary for legitimate kingship in Israel.[12] He simply cannot continue as the anointed king of Israel because he has consistently repudiated the very structure that made his kingship possible.[13] His sin has knocked over the pillar that has supported his own rule.

This raises a question that continues to surface in Christian theology in our modern context: Was Saul fated from the start? Was he doomed to failure, or did he have choices before him that could have prevented this outcome? As we have seen, some contemporary interpreters have described Saul as an innocent victim who had no possibility of success.[14] He became king because of the nation's impertinence, while David his successor was God's own choice.[15] In these modern literary approaches, such scholars assume either the text of the Bible is biased against Saul, or else God's own character should be called into question. God made Saul king even though he never actually *approved* him as king, or else the text is simply pro-David and therefore takes great pains to explain why Saul had to be cast aside.

But for readers who take seriously the message of the text itself (esp. in its canonical shape), these are hardly options, since certain early passages are clear that Yahweh was behind Saul's leadership (review 9:15—17; 10:9—10, 24). In the two chapters especially devoted to explaining Saul's rejection, the blame is clearly placed on Saul himself (review 13:13 and 15:23, 26). God rejected Saul *because* Saul had rejected God.

But this emphasis of the text only pushes the question further back along the theological cause-and-effect continuum. Did God determine that Saul would be king and at the same time also determine that Saul would ultimately fail in his responsibilities as king? Or was Saul free to choose his own actions, so that he simply chose to reject Yahweh's word because of inner motives and states common to all of us in our human experiences? Or was he somehow both determined and free? Is it possible that Saul was free and responsible for his actions even though they were causally determined in a way that we do not fully understand?[16]

---

12. The matter of Saul's rejection has been described convincingly as a failure to accept the authority structure for human kingship (see Long, *Reign and Rejection*, 133—69 [esp. 167], 235—42).

13. Interestingly, Samuel compares Saul's sin to rebellion and arrogance tantamount to divination and idolatry (15:23).

14. See my summaries of Gunn and Brueggemann in the comments to ch. 13.

15. A point made by Gunn, *The Fate of King Saul*, 77—79.

16. These options can be conveniently summarized along the lines of "hard determinism," "libertarian freedom," and "soft determinism." See Scott R. Burson and Jerry L. Walls,

Christians of different theological and denominational traditions respond to these questions in varying ways. But we should all take seriously the Bible's emphasis on Saul's free moral responsibility. Samuel is clear that if Saul had kept God's command, God would have established his kingdom over Israel for all time (13:13). The wordplay on the verb "rejected" in 15:23 emphasizes the direction of the cause-and-effect relationship: "Because you have rejected the word of the LORD, he has rejected you as king."

Prophetic view of sacrifice. Besides clarifying the nature of Saul's sin, this text also brings into focus the prophetic view of sacrifice, which becomes an important theme elsewhere in the Bible.[17] "Does the LORD delight in burnt offerings and sacrifices as much as in obeying the voice of the LORD? To obey is better than sacrifice, and to heed is better than the fat of rams" (15:22). Samuel is not repudiating Saul's (and Israel's) use of animal sacrifices in general. Such could never be the case in light of the extensive commands and regulations for just such sacrifices in the Torah (especially Leviticus). Rather, this is a typical prophetic call to go beyond the physical act of sacrifice to consider matters of the heart. What are the motives for sacrifices?

Sacrifice is an external and physical phenomenon that reflects a spiritual reality between God and human. But if one's motives are impure or ungodly, then the sacrifice itself is meaningless. Worse, it becomes nauseating to God (Isa. 1:13). Religious ritual always becomes a burden unless it is accompanied by appropriate heartfelt repentance, love, and adoration for God.

Saul's response to prophetic correction. As I suggested in the introduction, Saul's loquacious answers to Samuel in this text must be read together with Israel's example in 7:6 and especially with David's brief and fitting response to Nathan when that prophet confronted David with his sins: "I have sinned against the LORD" (2 Sam. 12:13).[18] With David there was no evasion or argumentation. He did not attempt to defend himself or to offer a contrived confession that would in some way explain his virtual innocence. He was a broken man (2 Sam. 12:16–18; cf. also the traditional association of Ps. 51 to this event).

This is the appropriate answer for a king confronted by a prophet who exposes his sins rather than the avoidance tactics of Saul's self-defense. Taken together, these texts present negative and positive examples of confession,

---

C. S. Lewis and Francis Schaeffer: Lessons for a New Century from the Most Influential Apologists of Our Time (Downers Grove, Ill.: InterVarsity Press, 1998), 66–69.

17. Ps. 40:6–8; 51:16–17; Prov. 21:3; Isa. 1:11–17; Jer. 7:21–23; Hos. 6:6; Mic. 6:6–8; Matt. 12:7; Mark 12:33; Heb. 10:8–9.

18. Compare the introduction's comments on the trajectory of these three passages of 1–2 Samuel and the example of repentance and confession in each (pages 38–40, above).

forgiveness, and restoration. The Bible has many other passages that supplement David's confession and explain why his repentance was effective and why he became Israel's greatest king. But this passage on Saul is a rare picture of how *not* to confess! By way of contrast, Saul reveals the nature of "a broken and contrite heart" (Ps. 51:17) and gives us a glimpse into the kind of king Yahweh desires in the long survey of Israel's kings (anticipating 1−2 Kings).

THE NATURE OF TRUE CONFESSION. The various themes discussed in our Bridging Contexts section are related to each other. The fundamental lesson here is what happens when we disregard God's Word and reject his authority structures that make our very lives possible. Part of God's universal structure provides for forgiveness when we sin. But if we focus on externals and fail to grasp the internal realities of worship and confession, we forfeit the structures for forgiveness as well as his structures for authority. In other words, the nature of confession is related to the ritual-versus-reality contrast.

The life Adam and Eve enjoyed in the Garden of Eden before their fall was completely dependent on God's arrangement. The numerous trees produced plenty of food, and because Adam and Eve had free access to the tree of life, they never had to worry (Gen. 2:9). God's gracious structure for their world made their lives possible. But when they rebelled by disobeying his only command, they forfeited their access to the tree of life. In a similar way, Saul has rejected the very authority structure that made his kingdom possible. By rejecting it, he lost the possibility of continuing as king. Sin is always a rejection of that which makes life possible. It is self-destructive behavior.

This text illustrates how we only make our situation worse by failing to learn the true nature of worship and confession. Church attendance and tithing are worthless unless they come from the heart, just as the Old Testament sacrifices made Yahweh nauseous unless they were genuine. In our various denominations, we have many different types of rituals in our services. For some, worship involves high liturgy with robed pastors and choirs singing Bach and Beethoven, while for others it is praise bands leading Bible choruses in jeans and T-shirts. Regardless of whether we are comfortable with high and formal services or informal, contemporary praise, ritual remains an integral part of any worship service. And in either case, it is possible simply to "go through the motions" while neglecting the internal realities of our tortured souls. Samuel reminds us with his word to Saul that obedience is better than sacrifice. If we miss the reality of internal worship and confession, no amount of attention to externals, such as church attendance or involvement in Christian causes, will atone for disobeying God's Word.

This brings us again to the central theme of this chapter. Saul stands as a warning about the dangers of disregarding God's Word and thereby rejecting the structures he has provided to make our lives or our ministries possible. Samuel's opening salvo is a powerful wake-up call for all who have failed to obey God: "What then is this bleating of sheep in my ears?"[19] The old prophet of God vigorously stands before all who sin and raises the question that defies circumvention. The sheep are there, and anyone can hear them. The question itself presents the undeniable realities of sin. What remains is only our reaction: Will we react as Saul or as David?

The most dominant news item in the closing years of the twentieth century centered sadly around a United States president caught in immoral conduct. The press and his political enemies confronted the president with undeniable facts about his illicit relationship with a young intern. The ensuing drama that caught the nation's attention had all the ingredients of Saul's conversation with Samuel. The president or his surrogates attempted various forms of evasion, blaming everyone from the opposing political party, which they said was behind the charges, to the young intern herself, who was accused of being flirtatious and obsessed with the president.

There was also an attempt at argumentation or denial. In a now-famous speech on January 26, 1998, the President declared while pounding the podium, "I did not have sexual relations with that woman, Miss Lewinski." Then in August of that year, when it became politically necessary, the president admitted to an "inappropriate" relationship with the intern, details of which soon became available to the public via the Internet, and shortly afterward in book form. The president's many words of explanation reminds us of Saul's compulsory and obligatory confession. Here is another example of our ability as human beings to attempt to appease our accusers by acknowledging wrongdoing without actually taking responsibility for our actions. Such grudging and contrived remorse is expedient for a president, just as Saul's "confession" was in 1 Samuel 15.

I do not wish to reopen the debate over who was ultimately to blame, congressional accusers or presidential defenders. The tragic episode merely serves to illustrate the way all of us behave when confronted by the prophetic "What then is this bleating of sheep in my ears?" Unfortunately, we can all identify with King Saul and President Clinton, for we have all heard the undeniable accusation that we are guilty. The choice remains for us, however—as individuals and as a corporate body of Christ—to respond, either as Saul or as David.

---

19. Not unlike God's condemning question of Adam and Eve: "Where are you?" (Gen. 3:9).

1 Samuel 16:1–13

❦

THE Lord SAID to Samuel, "How long will you mourn for Saul, since I have rejected him as king over Israel? Fill your horn with oil and be on your way; I am sending you to Jesse of Bethlehem. I have chosen one of his sons to be king."

²But Samuel said, "How can I go? Saul will hear about it and kill me."

The LORD said, "Take a heifer with you and say, 'I have come to sacrifice to the LORD.' ³Invite Jesse to the sacrifice, and I will show you what to do. You are to anoint for me the one I indicate."

⁴Samuel did what the LORD said. When he arrived at Bethlehem, the elders of the town trembled when they met him. They asked, "Do you come in peace?"

⁵Samuel replied, "Yes, in peace; I have come to sacrifice to the LORD. Consecrate yourselves and come to the sacrifice with me." Then he consecrated Jesse and his sons and invited them to the sacrifice.

⁶When they arrived, Samuel saw Eliab and thought, "Surely the LORD's anointed stands here before the LORD."

⁷But the LORD said to Samuel, "Do not consider his appearance or his height, for I have rejected him. The LORD does not look at the things man looks at. Man looks at the outward appearance, but the LORD looks at the heart."

⁸Then Jesse called Abinadab and had him pass in front of Samuel. But Samuel said, "The LORD has not chosen this one either." ⁹Jesse then had Shammah pass by, but Samuel said, "Nor has the LORD chosen this one." ¹⁰Jesse had seven of his sons pass before Samuel, but Samuel said to him, "The LORD has not chosen these." ¹¹So he asked Jesse, "Are these all the sons you have?"

"There is still the youngest," Jesse answered, "but he is tending the sheep."

Samuel said, "Send for him; we will not sit down until he arrives."

¹²So he sent and had him brought in. He was ruddy, with a fine appearance and handsome features.

Then the LORD said, "Rise and anoint him; he is the one."
¹³So Samuel took the horn of oil and anointed him in the presence of his brothers, and from that day on the Spirit of the LORD came upon David in power. Samuel then went to Ramah.

 THE PREVIOUS CHAPTER represents the final and official rejection of Saul as Israel's anointed king. He has failed as the Lord's first designated king because he rejected the Lord's authority structure for Israel's unique kingship. The second messiah figure is the ideal anointed one because he accepts Yahweh's authority in principle and genuinely repents when he fails to accept it in practice.

The Lord sends Samuel to anoint David. The future king is anointed in private and is purely the choice of Yahweh. This chapter marks a turning point in this book. Prior to Saul's final rejection in chapter 15, he and Samuel have been the central figures in the book. From now on, David is central even though he does not become king until the early chapters of 2 Samuel.[1] In this text we finally meet the man after God's own heart (as foretold in 13:14), though here he is hardly more than a boy (16:11). He is to become the focus of the rest of our commentary. Indeed, he becomes the ideal king of Israel with whom all subsequent rulers will be compared and who paves the way for the coming of the Messiah.

Samuel Goes to Bethlehem to Anoint a New King (16:1–5)

THE PREVIOUS CHAPTER ended with a note that Samuel mourned over the loss of Saul as king. But Yahweh is a God of action, and he commands his prophet to move forward regardless of his sense of personal loss: "Fill your horn with oil and be on your way" (16:1). We learned earlier that Yahweh selected someone of his own choosing ("after his own heart," 13:14), someone better than Saul (15:28), to replace him as king. Now we learn that the chosen someone is from the family of Jesse of the city of Bethlehem.

Jesse is the grandson of Ruth and Boaz (Ruth 4:17–22) and comes from the tribe of Judah (Ruth 4:12; cf. Gen. 38). From this time forward, the name of Jesse, the city of Bethlehem, and the tribe of Judah will always be linked to Israel's Messiah.[2] The reference to "Jesse of Bethlehem" in 16:1 appears

---

1. McCarter, *I Samuel*, 270.
2. Isa. 11:1, 10; Mic. 5:2; Matt. 1:5–6; 2:4–6; Rom. 15:12.

again in 17:58 and serves as a literary envelope (a so-called inclusio) tying chapters 16 and 17 together.[3]

The last phrase of verse 1 contains a subtle but powerful statement about David, though the NIV's rendering obscures its significance: "I have chosen one of his sons to be king." The Hebrew stresses that David is Yahweh's own choice. A better translation is: "I have provided *for myself* a king from among his sons." This suggests a contrast with the circumstances surrounding Saul's selection, when Yahweh made a concession for the sake of the people: "Listen to them [i.e., the people] and give them a king" (8:22).[4]

Samuel is evidently aware of Saul's hostile intent toward him because he fears for his life if it were known that he has anointed David (16:2). But Yahweh assures Samuel that he will make known to the prophet what he should do. He consecrates Jesse and his sons and invites them (and presumably the elders of Bethlehem) to the sacrifice.

Samuel Anoints David (16:6–13)

WHEN SAMUEL MEETS JESSE'S SONS, he is impressed with the oldest, Eliab. He assumes that this firstborn son, so striking in appearance, is Yahweh's choice as king (16:6). This is not the first time Samuel has considered impressive physical appearance a criterion for ruling Israel as king (cf. 10:23–24). But looks are deceiving. Yahweh immediately tells Samuel that this young man is not to become king and that Samuel should not be unduly influenced by external features, such as Eliab's handsome appearance.

This is followed in 16:7 by a particularly memorable saying contrasting human abilities with God's ability. People and God do not perceive reality in the same way. Men and women are not God! Humans and Yahweh are not normally on the same page, looking at the same things. Humans are limited to the externals, the "outward appearance," but Yahweh "looks at the heart."[5] This assertion becomes an important theological concept in Scripture: What really counts in a person has more to do with the heart than with the eyes.[6] Despite the benefits of God-given favors, such as natural good looks, there is no substitute for a God-pleasing heart. In order to anoint the right son of Jesse, Samuel will have to overcome his human reliance on his own ability to see. He will soon meet the young man who has captured the heart of God (cf. 13:14).

3. Youngblood, "1, 2 Samuel," 682–83.

4. Baldwin, *1 and 2 Samuel*, 121.

5. Robert Alter has shown that "see" is a dominant thematic key word in 16:1–13, used to set up a "didactic ritual of true choice after false, true sight after false," which emphasizes the "vertical" perspective of the narrative (*The Art of Biblical Narrative*, 148–49).

6. 1 Kings 3:9; 8:39; Luke 16:15; John 7:24; 2 Cor. 5:16.

The other sons of Jesse parade before the great prophet, but none is the "chosen" one (16:8–10). The number seven is a number of fullness and completeness, indicating Samuel appears to have reached the total of sons available for service to Samuel.[7] No one feels it necessary to include the youngest son of Jesse. He is apparently so unlikely a candidate it hardly seems necessary to summon him from his work following the sheep (16:11). Once he is summoned, however, Yahweh quickly confirms his choice: "Rise and anoint him; he is the one" (16:12). Samuel immediately obeys and anoints David in this private setting. He will not be publicly anointed king until much later (2 Sam. 2:4; 5:3).

This is the second time Samuel has anointed a king for Israel. In 1 Samuel 10:1 he anointed Saul. As we noted there, the use of oil is symbolic of the Spirit of Yahweh and represents supernatural empowerment. Prior to Samuel's anointing of Saul and David, the act of sacramental anointing had been restricted to the tabernacle and its priests. It marks the inauguration of someone for a specific office consecrated by Yahweh.

Israel was one of the few nations of the ancient world that anointed kings.[8] It has been argued that the use of oil in business contracts, family law, and international diplomacy demonstrates a contractual or covenantal significance for its use in the anointing of kings. When the elders of the people anoint David in 2 Samuel, they are likely pledging themselves to him and accepting an obligation to him (2 Sam. 2:4; 5:3). He in turn grants them a royal promise (5:3). In this text, Yahweh is obligating himself to David and establishing a relationship with him that will eventually find expression in the Davidic covenant (2 Sam. 7).[9]

As in the case of Saul, anointing for kingship is accompanied by the arrival of the Spirit of Yahweh, empowering the king-designate for service (cf. 10:10). The passages describing the coming of God's Spirit on Saul and David use the same idiomatic expression for the onrushing of the divine breath or spirit. The idiom (verb *ṣlḥ* plus prepositions *ʿal* or *ʾel*) only occurs seven times and is stereotypical of godly inspiration, either in a sudden burst of heroic strength (Samson, Judg. 14:6) or in prophetic ecstasy (Saul, 1 Sam. 10:10).[10] The "Spirit of the LORD" is the vital force of God, which bestows the recipient with his invigorating power. Here, however, it also seems to denote the royal charisma that comes to mark Israelite

---

7. Philip P. Jenson, "שֶׁבַע," *NIDOTTE*, 4:34–35.

8. Hittite kings were anointed upon their ascent to the throne, and certain Egyptian officials were also anointed. See Mettinger, *King and Messiah*, 208–32; see also de Vaux, "The King of Israel," 162–66.

9. Mettinger, *King and Messiah*, 137–50.

10. Alex Luc, "צלח," *NIDOTTE*, 3:804–5.

kings and in fact distinguishes Israelite kingship from other monarchies of the ancient Near East.[11]

Bridging Contexts

DAVID'S ANOINTING IS a turning point in the books of Samuel (see Bridging Contexts section of 16:14–23). So far, we have learned that God's first and best plan was to rule Israel himself as her only king, just as he had done in her early history. But because of Israel's military and political needs and her selfish demands, God chose to rule Israel by means of human anointed ones (Heb. "messiahs"). The first anointed one failed because he refused to accept Yahweh's authority. The second anointed one will succeed and become an ideal figure for all future generations because he will enthusiastically and vigorously embrace Yahweh's authority.

In this text, we encounter the unexpected way in which God seeks people, or more precisely, the *kind* of person God seeks and what happens when he finds individuals who fit the bill. When we look for bridges from Israel's ancient context to our own, we are struck by a number of important features of this passage.

Yahweh's eyesight. The text emphasizes that Yahweh has superior eyesight! He is not limited or restricted by physical eyes, which may actually become hindrances to seeing reality. For the most part, we all acknowledge this to be true. We even have expressions to summarize this concept: "Looks aren't everything"; "looks can be deceiving"; "you can't judge a book by its cover." In a more profound way, our text applies this principle to Eliab's and David's personal commitments and spiritual qualities, which are not discernible to the human eye.

God announces to Samuel that he does not look at (or at least give much credence to) the things we humans behold (16:7). Rather than leaving Samuel in total confusion, God continues by establishing a contrast. While humans "look at" (or perhaps "are limited by") outward appearances, God has the superior vantage point of seeing the heart. Since we are not God, we cannot know who will answer his call and who will be effective in his service. This means both that we should be cautious about judging other people and their potential effectiveness in the kingdom of God, and also that we should not question our own abilities and gifts for service. We may feel that we do not have much to offer God—but that would be a superficial evaluation, based on our own limited perspective. If God calls, he also empowers.

---

11. Barth, *God with Us*, 193–94; on the role of the Spirit of God in the Old Testament, see Bridging Contexts section for 9:1–10:27, above.

Looks, indeed, can be deceiving, and often are. Samuel needs help in learning to see God's perspective regarding David. Likewise, we need a God-perspective in order to overcome our biases. We often fail to see the God-potential in others (or in ourselves) because we are easily impressed by the wrong indicators. David, who will become the ideal anointed figure, is an unassuming sort when we first meet him. He would not have naturally attracted attention as a potential savior of his people. He is too young, too inexperienced, and too insignificant in his family's birth order (see below). But David is also a precursor to one greater than he, to *the* Messiah, who also bore no especially striking physical characteristics:

> He had no beauty or majesty to attract us to him,
>   nothing in his appearance that we should desire him.
> He was despised and rejected by men,
>   a man of sorrows, and familiar with suffering.
> Like one from whom men hide their faces
>   he was despised, and we esteemed him not. (Isa. 53:2b–3)

When David's greatest Son finally did appear, the world did not recognize him because they saw him only with human eyes. But by the grace of God, some learn to perceive the deeper reality of his coming, to look beyond superficial appearances in order to discern the truth. To these the Messiah gives the privilege of becoming the children of God, not through physical birth but through spiritual rebirth (John 1:10–13).

The younger son. A second important feature of this text is the theme of the younger son displacing the firstborn. It apparently does not occur to anyone in Bethlehem that the little shepherd boy could possibly be God's choice. He is so unlikely to be used of God in so powerful a way that his own father does not see any reason to interrupt David's menial task of tending the sheep (16:11). But God often turns things upside down.

It is a common Old Testament theme that God often uses the least likely to accomplish his purposes.[12] When twins were born to Rebekah, it was the older who would "serve the younger" (Gen. 25:23). Among the sons of Jacob, Reuben was older and Judah stronger. But it was Joseph who acquired the right of firstborn (1 Chron. 5:1–2). Thus, the firstborn son is often displaced by the late-born, as with Abel and Cain, Isaac and Ishmael, Jacob and Esau. Likewise, in the stories of Ephraim and Manasseh, Moses and Aaron,

---

12. For what follows, see Bill T. Arnold, "בכר," *NIDOTTE*, 1:658–59. In the Old Testament, God tends to favor the late-born over the firstborn, just as Israel derives its royal and priestly lines from late-born sons rather than firstborn. See Jon D. Levenson, *The Death and Resurrection of the Beloved Son* (New Haven, Conn.: Yale Univ. Press, 1993), 69–81.

Solomon and Adonijah, it is regularly the younger who rises to prominence in God's economy. In addition, it is not only the youngest but often the weakest whom God chooses to use. God's salvation can come in the form of an infant (Isa. 7:14—16) or a suffering servant (52:13—53:12).

These first two features of our text are related to each other in that the son born late in time did not *appear* to have any significance. Those around David do not see his ability because they have limited eyesight. They cannot see beyond the external reality of his place in the birth order. In other words, human perception seldom sees beyond the limitations of one's birth-gifts. If someone does not seem particularly "gifted," others will fail to see potential that only God can see because his perception reaches the heart. But when God's perception is made clear, we can then respond in a way that cooperates with his grace. When the apostle Paul learned that God's power is made perfect in his weakness, he decided to accept his weaknesses so Christ's power could rest on him: "For when I am weak, then I am strong" (2 Cor. 12:9—10). In this way, Paul also learned to become a man after "God's own heart" (cf. 1 Sam. 13:14).

God's Spirit. A third feature of the text is the association of anointing with the arrival of God's Spirit. The anointed one, as the representative of Yahweh in ancient Israel, became the bearer of the Spirit of God, which was marked by the anointing of oil (16:13).[13] Saul also received the Spirit of God soon after his anointing (see comments on 10:6, 9—10). In his case, the arrival of the Spirit effected a change of perception. He joined the band of prophets and began to share Yahweh's perception of Israel and of himself as her new king. But the coming of the Spirit also accompanied an inner, spiritual transformation, turning Saul into "a different person" (10:6).

In David's case, the text says simply, "the Spirit of the LORD came upon David in power" (16:13). The impact of Yahweh's Spirit in David's life will become apparent in the subsequent narratives (see esp. ch. 17). As is often the case in Old Testament narratives, the stories of the heroes of faith are "largely narrated as a history of the Spirit of God with them."[14]

This passage also has implications for the role of God's Spirit in the Old Testament. It is not uncommon for Christians to claim that the saints of the Old Testament period experienced God's Spirit in a fundamentally different manner from that of New Testament believers or modern Christians. Many have relied on the specific idioms of the Old Testament to argue that the Holy Spirit only came *upon* people in the Old Testament but *into* people in the New Testament. Thus, the Holy Spirit was only bestowed temporarily, and then externally, to Old Testament believers as opposed to the permanent

---

13. Knierim, "The Messianic Concept," 31—32.
14. Hertzberg, *I and II Samuel*, 140.

indwelling of the early church. Such preaching and teaching drives a wedge between the Testaments, placing too much emphasis on disunity rather than on mutual interdependence between Old and New.[15]

This is an inadequate and incomplete understanding of the role of the Spirit in the Old Testament. Though the Spirit of God sometimes comes upon individuals in the Old Testament to empower for specific (and temporary) tasks, there can be no doubt that his role and function is also more extensive. He has an indwelling and transforming presence in Old Testament believers as well and is described as the animating feature that effects spiritual renewal.[16]

In his nighttime conversation with Nicodemus, Jesus assumed that a learned Jew of his stature should have understood better the transforming power of the Spirit of God (John 3:5–10). The new ministry of the Spirit on the Day of Pentecost was not an entirely new function of indwelling and transformation (Acts 2:1–4). Rather, at this point for the first time, the Spirit of God was welcomed and received by a significant number of people at the same time. With the inauguration of the church, the Spirit was now free to transform a whole body of God's people, as in fact had been the desired result in the Old Testament period. So the Spirit's role and ministry was not different, but rather the *extent* to which it became a reality was new.

THE KIND OF PERSON GOD SEEKS. The man after God's own heart turned out to be an unassuming boy! Looks can be so deceiving that we actually miss the very thing we are looking for. God sends Samuel to find a new king. But he would have missed David entirely because David does not look the part. Just as David as a new messianic ruler is easy to overlook, so *the* Messiah *was* overlooked because he did not appear as people were expecting.

But this text is especially concerned with the kind of person God seeks. When you and I consider the qualities of the people around us, we are inevitably (and inescapably) influenced by what we see with our eyes. But God sees things we miss. Because he has superior vision, we may often be

---

15. On the relationship between the Testaments, see David L. Baker, *Two Testaments, One Bible: A Study of the Theological Relationship between the Old and New Testaments*, rev. ed. (Downers Grove, Ill.: InterVarsity Press, 1991); Osborne, *The Hermeneutical Spiral*, 277; Bill T. Arnold and Bryan E. Beyer, *Encountering the Old Testament: A Christian Survey* (Grand Rapids: Baker, 1999), 475–76; G. Goldsworthy, "Relationship of OT and NT," *NDBT*, 81–89.

16. Daniel I. Block, "The Prophet of the Spirit: The Use of *rwḥ* in the Book of Ezekiel," *JETS* 32 (1989): 40–41; see also M. V. Van Pelt, Walter C. Kaiser, and Daniel I. Block, "רוּחַ," *NIDOTTE*, 3:1076–78.

surprised by the people he chooses to accomplish his purposes. In ancient Israel, it was often the surprising choice of the youngest son instead of the expected oldest. At various times of church history, believers have been surprised (or disturbed!) when God has called a woman to serve him in a role normally filled by a man. Such times may challenge the church's dogma and require revisiting our beliefs about such roles. God can also use an unassuming child to teach important lessons needed for a given time. He has used the uneducated, the poor, the disenfranchised. The fact is that you and I simply cannot see the human heart the way God does; thus, we may often be surprised by what God sees in others.

Early in my teaching ministry, I read and benefited from a little book by the nineteenth-century novelist George MacDonald entitled *The Curate's Awakening.*[17] The story illustrates in a graphic manner the lesson of this text: Appearances can be deceiving, especially regarding spiritual reality. Matters of the heart—the most important issues with which we deal—are often obscured because of physical impressions.

MacDonald describes a young Anglican curate settling into his first parish.[18] Like so many ministers of our day, the young Thomas Wingfold had chosen the ministry merely as a profession. While he was still trying to find his way in his new assignment, he met a skeptic in the community who shook his confidence with one little question about the Christian gospel he had been teaching: "Tell me honestly, do you really believe one word of all that?" Realizing he had nothing to answer, Wingfold begins to face genuinely the fact that he does not know what he believes. Through much soul-searching and agony, he considers finishing out his year with the congregation and then leaving the ministry.

But before this happens, he experiences another crisis. Wingfold's shallowness and spiritual malaise lead him to plagiarize his sermons. One day he receives a letter from a parishioner who has recognized one of his sermons as that of another clergyman, and the letter exposes him to potential shame. Wingfold writes back, acknowledging the truth and asking to meet the man in order to confess and ask for help. The astute parishioner turns out to be a certain Joseph Polwarth, a tragically deformed dwarf whose ghastly appearance draws mostly pity from the community and even disdain from a few. But as Wingfold gradually comes to know his unfortunate-looking new friend,

---

17. Originally published as *Thomas Wingfold, Curate* (London: Hurst & Blackett, 1876). The novel has been retold for today's reader and edited by Michael R. Phillips (Minneapolis: Bethany, 1985).

18. A curate in MacDonald's time was usually a very young clergyman appointed to smaller parishes, which were unable to maintain a full-time vicar. Curates performed the duties and services of the priest but did not hold the office themselves.

he discovers that in reality he is a giant of faith. Polwarth has insight and wisdom that comes only from years of reading Scripture and loving God. His conversations with Polwarth astound the young curate and cause Wingfold to consider the bankruptcy of his own soul. Eventually he comes to envy Polwarth instead of pitying him.

Early in their relationship, the two men share their stories in complete honesty. Mr. Polwarth narrates his painful childhood, of his being sent away to boarding school because he was an embarrassment to his family, and of the ways he learned to cope with the derision and jokes of the other children. As an adult he learned to deal with his deformities and get on with his life. But he remained dissatisfied with himself. Through a series of painful experiences, Polwarth confesses that he discovered his heart was filled with envy, vindictiveness, and conceit. He concludes: "I began to be aware that, heavy affliction as it was to be made so different from others, my outward deformity was but a picture of my inward condition."[19] That summer, Polwarth committed himself to a thoughtful reading of the New Testament, through which he became acquainted with the man Jesus.

By contrast, Wingfold confesses his miserable condition to his new friend:

> I was brought up for the church. I passed all my examinations with decency, distinguishing myself in nothing. I went before the bishop and became a deacon, after a year was ordained, and after another year or two of false preaching and parish work, suddenly found myself curate in charge of this grand old abbey church.[20]

The young clergyman confides that Christianity seems useless to him and he is utterly without direction, though he finds himself now pastoring this good little flock. In complete despair, he commits himself to meeting with Mr. Polwarth regularly for the purpose of reading and studying together. As the novel unfolds, the handsome young minister comes to respect and appreciate Joseph Polwarth more than anyone he has ever known. With his help, Wingfold moves from faith in an *idea* of God to faith in the living God.[21]

This fascinating novel illustrates the fundamental principle of our text: The truth about a person is a matter of the heart and not the eyes. The community in which Wingfold and Polwarth live accept the new minister as a spiritual leader with considerable commitment to Christian truth. But they continue to pity the misshapen dwarf as someone who should live alone quietly because he has so little to offer the world. How little they knew!

---

19. MacDonald, *Awakening*, 52.
20. Ibid., 49.
21. Ibid., 176.

1 Samuel 16:14-23

❧

NOW THE SPIRIT of the LORD had departed from
Saul, and an evil spirit from the LORD tormented him.

[15]Saul's attendants said to him, "See, an evil spirit from God
is tormenting you. [16]Let our lord command his servants here
to search for someone who can play the harp. He will play
when the evil spirit from God comes upon you, and you will
feel better."

[17]So Saul said to his attendants, "Find someone who plays
well and bring him to me."

[18]One of the servants answered, "I have seen a son of Jesse
of Bethlehem who knows how to play the harp. He is a brave
man and a warrior. He speaks well and is a fine-looking man.
And the LORD is with him."

[19]Then Saul sent messengers to Jesse and said, "Send me
your son David, who is with the sheep." [20]So Jesse took a
donkey loaded with bread, a skin of wine and a young goat
and sent them with his son David to Saul.

[21]David came to Saul and entered his service. Saul liked
him very much, and David became one of his armor-bearers.
[22]Then Saul sent word to Jesse, saying, "Allow David to
remain in my service, for I am pleased with him."

[23]Whenever the spirit from God came upon Saul, David
would take his harp and play. Then relief would come to Saul;
he would feel better, and the evil spirit would leave him.

"IT IS AN exciting moment in the biblical drama
when David first steps on stage."[1] As a means of
introducing us to David, 1 Samuel 16 has two
units. The first unit narrated his anointing by the
great prophet Samuel (vv. 1–13). This second unit explains how subsequent
events lead to David's introduction to the royal court of Saul. It is commonly
assumed that these two paragraphs were originally unrelated and came
together as part of the diachronic evolution of the text.[2] But literary sensi-

---

1. McCarter, *I Samuel*, 282.
2. Klein, *1 Samuel*, 159.

tivity to the many similarities between the units gives ample evidence that these paragraphs are closely related. Together they characterize David and prepare us for the rest of this book.[3] In verses 1–13, Yahweh intervened directly and commissioned Samuel to anoint David. Here the historian narrates events that show God's providential but less intrusive involvement.

With the assertion that the Spirit of Yahweh rushes upon David with power (16:13), the narrator proceeds to explain that an opposite effect has occurred in Saul's case (16:14): "The Spirit of the LORD had departed from Saul, and an evil spirit from the LORD tormented him." In so doing, the historian also explains how the young David came to be appointed to an important position in Saul's court and begins to show Spirit-empowerment in a way very unlike Saul.

Saul Needs a Harpist (16:14–18)

SAUL IS NOT a well man. Just as the arrival of the Spirit of Yahweh marked David as someone destined and supremely fitted to *become* king of Israel (16:13), so the departure of the Spirit from Saul marks him as destined not to *remain* king. The narrative explains further that the departure of God's Spirit is followed by the presence of "an evil spirit from the LORD," which overwhelms and terrifies Saul. This preternatural presence is variously denoted elsewhere in the narrative as "an evil spirit from God" (16:15, as in 18:10), or in abbreviated form as "spirit from God" or "the evil spirit" (both in 16:23). It is never, however, called "the Spirit of the LORD," as compared to that which has come on David and which has withdrawn from Saul.[4] The narrator has taken great pains to describe this spirit as *from* Yahweh, but which is not to be associated *as* Yahweh. The Spirit *of* Yahweh comes to bestow strength and power for service, while the evil spirit *from* Yahweh torments.

Many interpreters have speculated about the psychological particulars of Saul's ailment.[5] This is not totally inappropriate, since subsequent narratives display actions and behaviors that easily remind us of paranoia or bipolar illness. But Brueggemann warns against two polarized dangers when analyzing the pathology of Saul. Some attempt to explain Saul's problems in terms of a "supernatural theological verdict without reference to the experiential reality of life," while others reduce his ailment to psychology.[6] Rather,

---

3. Stanley D. Walters, "The Light and the Dark," in *Ascribe to the Lord: Biblical and Other Studies in Memory of Peter C. Craigie*, ed. L. Eslinger and G. Taylor (JSOTSup 67; Sheffield: JSOT, 1988), 569–73.

4. A point emphasized by Keil and Delitzsch, *Samuel*, 170.

5. So, e.g., R. K. Harrison suggested Saul suffered from paranoid schizophrenia (*Introduction to the Old Testament*, 715–16).

6. Brueggemann, *First and Second Samuel*, 124.

Saul's difficulties are both theological and psychological. His growing alien-ation is rooted in a theological disorder. This is, in fact, what most captures our narrator's attention, so that answering the question in terms of psychol-ogy contributes nothing to our understanding of the text's message.

The way in which this spirit from Yahweh is described as "evil" (*ra'ab*) is ambiguous. Perhaps the narrator intends us to assume demonic forces, though this would be unusual in early Israelite literature.[7] The term can also mean simply an "injurious" or "bad" spirit, as noted by the NIV translators, and may well denote a "bad mood" or "gloomy outlook." In this way, the spirit from Yahweh represents a foreboding sense that Saul is moving inescapably toward self-annihilation. As we will see, the attacks generated by this injurious spirit are not constant but are periodic. However we are to understand its precise nature, the text is clear. The ruinous spirit comes from Yahweh because of Saul's persistent and unrepentant stance, and it is the source of his problems, plaguing him throughout the rest of the narrative.

Saul's courtiers believe music is the answer. They offer to find an appro-priate harpist to smooth the ailing Saul whenever his fits occur. We can assume a significant passage of time between 16:14–23 and the previous paragraph of chapter 16, for David has now become well known, at least to this unnamed courtier. He uses several important descriptors for David: son of Jesse, harpist, brave warrior, eloquent, and fine-looking.[8] The most ironic and telling, however, is the last descriptor: "The LORD is with him." This expression is reminiscent of many other passages of Scripture[9] but is most important in this location because of the ominous beginning of the para-graph (16:14): "Now the Spirit of the LORD had departed from Saul." Thus, a contrast is established between Saul and David, which marks the extended narrative throughout the remainder of 1 Samuel: Yahweh is with David and has departed from Saul.

David Enters Saul's Service (16:19–23)

HERE SAUL AND David meet for the first time. The rest of 1 Samuel narrates Saul's fall and David's rise in interchanging fashion. Their stories are nar-rated in a crisscrossing pattern, at times intersecting and at other times going

---

7. Smith, *Samuel*, 147.

8. On this last descriptor, Youngblood comments, "The same Hebrew word is preceded by a negative particle in its description of great David's greater Son as one who had 'no beauty' (Isa 53:2)" ("1, 2 Samuel," 689).

9. The assurance of God's presence becomes an important part of the ancestral promises and the Joseph narrative in the book of Genesis, and therefore in the rest of the Bible (for references and discussion, cf. Arnold, *Encountering the Book of Genesis*, 200–205).

separate directions.[10] From this point forward, the rest of our commentary deals particularly with David. This little paragraph introduces three themes that will recur in 1 Samuel 17–31:[11] Saul is in decline, David prospers because "the LORD is with him," and Saul is deeply attached to David.

Bridging Contexts

THIS TEXT HAS been called the "literary, historical, and theological crux of 1 Samuel as a whole."[12] Not only is the chapter the symmetrical center of the book, but its transition at verses 13 and 14 is programmatic for other narratives on the anointed ones, Saul and David. In verse 13, David receives the Spirit of Yahweh, marking him as Saul's replacement. In verse 14 Saul loses the Spirit of Yahweh and begins to be tormented by his injurious outlook. As a central paragraph in 1 Samuel, this text narrates the shift of political and spiritual power from Saul to David. Possibly this is not only a transfer of the Spirit of God from Saul to David as the designated messiah to lead Israel, but it is also a reflection of God's disapproval of Israel's manner of establishing the monarchy.[13]

When considering a bridge from ancient Israelite culture to our own context, it is instructive to remember that Old Testament narratives are never content simply to chronicle political events. As a transitional text from Saul to David and a central text in the book of 1 Samuel, it is not possible to determine from this paragraph any details about the political forces that made Saul king and whether they have now turned against him. Rather, the Old Testament historian was more interested in the theological truths behind these events.

Thus, the gradual fall of Saul and the commensurate rise of David is explained in theological terms: The Spirit of God has departed Saul and now resides with David. Furthermore, Saul begins now to be plagued by the mysterious "evil spirit from the LORD." Then the narrative presents the seemingly mundane circumstances in which David comes to serve in Saul's court. By narrating these events immediately after the theological explanations, the text implies that the hand of Yahweh is involved in David's summons to join the royal court of Saul.

---

10. This intercalation is what Fokkelman terms "the crossing fates" (Jan P. Fokkelman, *Narrative Art and Poetry in the Books of Samuel: A Full Interpretation Based on Stylistic and Structural Analyses*, 4 vols. [Assen, The Netherlands: Van Gorcum, 1981, 1986, 1990, 1993], 2:17–21 and passim).

11. McCarter, *I Samuel*, 282–83.

12. Youngblood, "1, 2 Samuel," 682.

13. David M. Howard Jr., "The Transfer of Power from Saul to David in 1 Sam. 16:13–14," *JETS* 32 (1989): 473–83, esp. 477.

Evil spirit. Therefore, this text raises two interesting issues for us as modern Christian readers. First is the problem of the "evil spirit from the LORD." Even if we understand the concept here as "injurious spirit" (as in the NIV's footnote), it remains difficult for us to harmonize with our understanding of God. The difficulty arises partly from the cultural distance between us and the ancient Israelites and partly from a legitimate philosophical problem.

(1) The cultural distance has to do with our impulse to examine all historical events in a strictly cause-and-effect relationship. By contrast, the Israelites preferred to skip intermediary causes altogether. They chose to focus on ultimate causes, and when it was clear to them that God was at work in history, they saw no need to outline in detail the secondary causes. If God was the ultimate and primary force behind events, the Old Testament authors chose to acknowledge his involvement. As one scholar has put it, "the world of biblical perspective is a world without secondary cause."[14] Thus this injurious spirit, regardless of whether we define it as demonic or psychotic, is ultimately from Yahweh, because nothing is beyond his sovereignty.

(2) The philosophical aspect of this problem is not so easily settled. The fact remains, the injurious spirit comes *from* the Lord. Old Testament authors do not hesitate to name God as the origin of calamity or trouble, often described by the same term for "evil." For example, God sent a similar "evil spirit" between Abimelech and the citizens of Shechem (Judg. 9:23).[15] The Bible does not attempt to answer the questions, Why does evil exist, and, Where does evil come from? Instead, biblical authors attempt only to expose the nature of human sin, which they see as the ultimate origin of pain and suffering in the world.[16]

Thus in this context, the signs of mental illness appear only after Saul's confrontation with Samuel, at which point Saul's disobedience is exposed and condemned (15:10–31). Though modern readers may resist taking this injurious spirit as coming *from* God, the point of the text is to link Saul's illness to his own rebellion against God.[17] His problems from this point on are a result of his refusal to accept God's authority structures, so that God is justified in sending the injurious spirit.

Divine sovereignty and human freedom. The second issue raised is the relationship between the events of our everyday lives, the routine affairs of life, and the active involvement of God to guide and direct our lives. Put dif-

---

14. Brueggemann, *First and Second Samuel*, 125.

15. Note too the "lying spirit" sent by God to entice Ahab to attack the Syrians (1 Kings 22:19–22).

16. Arnold, *Encountering the Book of Genesis*, 37.

17. Baldwin, *1 and 2 Samuel*, 123.

ferently, this relates to the question of divine sovereignty and human free-dom. The church has often debated the role of "synergism" in our salvation, which is the attempt to reconcile God's sovereign work in our lives with our own moral responsibility.

In this text, God's Spirit is at work and is blessing David. But David also has a responsibility to follow Jesse's instructions and to serve a newly defined role in the royal court. The Bible often presents episodes in which God is so powerfully and obviously at work in the lives of biblical characters that we wonder how they could have missed his presence. However, the narrators often reflect on the events from the advantage of historical distance. It is always easier to recognize God's activity in retrospect. It is another matter to live and work in the assurance of God's protecting and guiding hand dur-ing the events themselves, when the outcome is in doubt, from our limited human perspective.

The passage before us is instructive because of the way it links the theo-logical explanations (the Spirit *of* Yahweh and the evil spirit *from* Yahweh) with subsequent events in David's life. The reader knows that the Spirit of the Lord has come upon David in power (16:13) and that God is with David (even the royal courtier knows as much, 16:18). As the reader moves through this paragraph, it becomes clear that God is positioning David in the royal court as a means of preparing him to fulfill Samuel's prophecy. Saul needs a gifted musician to help him deal with his problems. Providentially, one of Saul's attendants knows of David and extols his surpassing qualities, which qualify David far beyond his role as court musician. Ironically, Saul brings his own replacement as king into the court himself and becomes so attached to David that he insists he stay in the royal service permanently. Through these events, the new anointed one is on the rise, and the unfortunate Saul is begin-ning his decline. The die was cast; David will become king.

How much does David know? More to the point, how is David to respond to these events now that the prophet Samuel has anointed him as king? In this way, the text illustrates how God often works behind the scenes of the everyday affairs of a believer's routine activities in ways that are often indis-cernible except in retrospect.

EVERYDAY AFFAIRS OF LIFE. This passage illustrates the symbiotic way in which God's will and desire for our lives are worked out in the everyday affairs of life. We often go about our life's activ-ities without much thought to what God's desire might be in any given set of circumstances. As Christians, we are committed to the *idea* that God is at work in our lives—directing, guiding, and in some instances, cajoling. But we are not often *consciously aware* of the specifics of his involvement. We are not frequently reminded that God is working behind the scenes to enable us to fulfill his greatest and best for our lives. Furthermore, we are often confused about how it all fits together. How can God's call and purpose for my life possibly be related to the messy affairs around me, which often seem completely at odds with what we would expect God to be achieving in us?

Perhaps the best way to appreciate this interweaving of God's work and our own actions is to imagine what this episode from 1 Samuel must have been like for the shepherd boy of Bethlehem on a day-by-day basis. In what follows, I invite you, as a twenty-first-century reader, to speculate about the confusion and emotional turmoil that may have accompanied David's experiences those many centuries ago.[18]

David remembers well the day the venerable prophet Samuel anointed him. What a strange day it was! He had been called in from tending the flock, and there in the presence of his family, the old prophet poured oil on his head and seemed to rejoice that he had found David. What could it all mean? The same prophet had once anointed King Saul, and as everyone in the nation knows, Jonathan, the crown prince, was a worthy successor as the next king of Israel. And Jesse's family was not in the priestly tribe. It did not seem possible that Yahweh wanted David to be a priest. And yet, there was the eccentric prophet with his oil! Yahweh must have something special in mind for young David. But what could it be?

David is certainly willing to serve God in any capacity needed. After the bizarre day of anointing, David went back to shepherding his father's flocks. He contented himself with the knowledge that he was willing and ready to do whatever God wanted. If that meant staying in Bethlehem and working with his father and brothers, then David would be content. But he felt so restless. Now that Samuel had come with anointing oil, it must be that Yahweh has something great in store for his future. What should he do, and when should he do it? If Yahweh wills him to become a priest, a great military general, or even king of Israel, so be it. But how, and when? What is he to do now?

Finally, after what seems like an interminable wait, David receives strange instructions from his father. He has been summoned to the royal court to minister to the king, who is ill. He takes his father's gifts for the king, the goat and the donkey loaded with bread and wine, and sets out with the king's

---

18. Remember that such creative speculation is for instructional purposes and is only loosely based on the interpretation of the text itself, for which see my Original Meaning and Bridging Contexts sections, above.

messengers. But along the journey, David continues to question and ponder what it all means. It all seems so confusing. Sure, he is willing to serve God in any capacity. But what does entering into the royal service as a musician have to do with God's plans?

David knows that he loves playing the harp, and he is sure that however he eventually comes to serve Yahweh, he will continue to enjoy the musical talents God has given him. But to become a court musician! David never imagined his musical skill would result in this introduction to royal service. Maybe that is it; perhaps the anointing is simply to designate him a royal musician. But this is not what he has pictured for himself. Nevertheless, David tries to remind himself that the most menial of tasks are fulfilling if one can be assured they are Yahweh's will. He obeys his father and continues the journey, because David would rather be anywhere other than outside Yahweh's will for his life.

But what of the prophet's unusual actions? Perhaps it is all a big mistake. Perhaps by entering into the royal service now, David will be jeopardizing his chance to fulfill some other calling in his life later. Or perhaps Samuel has been mistaken. As David continues on the way to Saul's court, he wonders if perhaps Samuel has gotten it wrong. Perhaps he is only supposed to help Saul in his distress rather than serve some grander, more glorious role in Israel. At any rate, David determines to do the best he can, even while he is so confused about how these events fit into the big picture of Yahweh's will for his life.

It seems to work out for the best. David plays his harp, and it definitely helps the king. And King Saul seems grateful. Samuel's anointing on that strange day seems a long time ago now. And whatever it ultimately means, David is willing to accept this new role. Saul likes him, and it is comforting for David to know that Yahweh's anointed one appreciates the effort. When the king requests David to become his permanent musician to help him deal with the pressures of his burden, David is pleased that he can contribute in such a way.

Moreover, David very much enjoys the young crown prince, Jonathan. Surely David can be content with his own contribution to the people of God. Still, that day back at home when Samuel anointed him is all very confusing. In light of what has happened now, what does it all mean? Perhaps in his old age, David will understand it better. But in the meantime, he will be content serving as court musician and contemplating that strange day long ago when the prophet appeared suddenly in Bethlehem.

Of course, the text of 1 Samuel 16:14–23 does not provide any of this detail about the inner thought processes of David. It is not written to expose his emotions and doubts concerning his arrival at the royal court. But the tension between God's calling on our lives and our everyday experiences often cause confusion, and this exercise is merely a way of illustrating how often our own lives are meshed together with God's will. We may often be as confused and feel as uncertain as I have portrayed David. Little does he realize it is precisely through his musical talents that he will eventually gain access to the court and that the anointing oil designates something quite specific in God's will for David. All this will happen sooner rather than later in David's life. But he has to walk through these circumstances somewhat in the dark. He is left simply to do his best without having the big picture. So it often is with modern believers.

1 Samuel 17:1–58

OW THE PHILISTINES gathered their forces for war and assembled at Socoh in Judah. They pitched camp at Ephes Dammim, between Socoh and Azekah. ²Saul and the Israelites assembled and camped in the Valley of Elah and drew up their battle line to meet the Philistines. ³The Philistines occupied one hill and the Israelites another, with the valley between them.

⁴A champion named Goliath, who was from Gath, came out of the Philistine camp. He was over nine feet tall. ⁵He had a bronze helmet on his head and wore a coat of scale armor of bronze weighing five thousand shekels; ⁶on his legs he wore bronze greaves, and a bronze javelin was slung on his back. ⁷His spear shaft was like a weaver's rod, and its iron point weighed six hundred shekels. His shield bearer went ahead of him.

⁸Goliath stood and shouted to the ranks of Israel, "Why do you come out and line up for battle? Am I not a Philistine, and are you not the servants of Saul? Choose a man and have him come down to me. ⁹If he is able to fight and kill me, we will become your subjects; but if I overcome him and kill him, you will become our subjects and serve us." ¹⁰Then the Philistine said, "This day I defy the ranks of Israel! Give me a man and let us fight each other." ¹¹On hearing the Philistine's words, Saul and all the Israelites were dismayed and terrified.

¹²Now David was the son of an Ephrathite named Jesse, who was from Bethlehem in Judah. Jesse had eight sons, and in Saul's time he was old and well advanced in years. ¹³Jesse's three oldest sons had followed Saul to the war: The firstborn was Eliab; the second, Abinadab; and the third, Shammah. ¹⁴David was the youngest. The three oldest followed Saul, ¹⁵but David went back and forth from Saul to tend his father's sheep at Bethlehem.

¹⁶For forty days the Philistine came forward every morning and evening and took his stand.

¹⁷Now Jesse said to his son David, "Take this ephah of roasted grain and these ten loaves of bread for your brothers and hurry to their camp. ¹⁸Take along these ten cheeses to the

commander of their unit. See how your brothers are and bring back some assurance from them. [19]They are with Saul and all the men of Israel in the Valley of Elah, fighting against the Philistines."

[20]Early in the morning David left the flock with a shepherd, loaded up and set out, as Jesse had directed. He reached the camp as the army was going out to its battle positions, shouting the war cry. [21]Israel and the Philistines were drawing up their lines facing each other. [22]David left his things with the keeper of supplies, ran to the battle lines and greeted his brothers. [23]As he was talking with them, Goliath, the Philistine champion from Gath, stepped out from his lines and shouted his usual defiance, and David heard it. [24]When the Israelites saw the man, they all ran from him in great fear.

[25]Now the Israelites had been saying, "Do you see how this man keeps coming out? He comes out to defy Israel. The king will give great wealth to the man who kills him. He will also give him his daughter in marriage and will exempt his father's family from taxes in Israel."

[26]David asked the men standing near him, "What will be done for the man who kills this Philistine and removes this disgrace from Israel? Who is this uncircumcised Philistine that he should defy the armies of the living God?"

[27]They repeated to him what they had been saying and told him, "This is what will be done for the man who kills him."

[28]When Eliab, David's oldest brother, heard him speaking with the men, he burned with anger at him and asked, "Why have you come down here? And with whom did you leave those few sheep in the desert? I know how conceited you are and how wicked your heart is; you came down only to watch the battle."

[29]"Now what have I done?" said David. "Can't I even speak?" [30]He then turned away to someone else and brought up the same matter, and the men answered him as before. [31]What David said was overheard and reported to Saul, and Saul sent for him.

[32]David said to Saul, "Let no one lose heart on account of this Philistine; your servant will go and fight him."

[33]Saul replied, "You are not able to go out against this Philistine and fight him; you are only a boy, and he has been a fighting man from his youth."

³⁴But David said to Saul, "Your servant has been keeping his father's sheep. When a lion or a bear came and carried off a sheep from the flock, ³⁵I went after it, struck it and rescued the sheep from its mouth. When it turned on me, I seized it by its hair, struck it and killed it. ³⁶Your servant has killed both the lion and the bear; this uncircumcised Philistine will be like one of them, because he has defied the armies of the living God. ³⁷The LORD who delivered me from the paw of the lion and the paw of the bear will deliver me from the hand of this Philistine."

Saul said to David, "Go, and the LORD be with you."

³⁸Then Saul dressed David in his own tunic. He put a coat of armor on him and a bronze helmet on his head. ³⁹David fastened on his sword over the tunic and tried walking around, because he was not used to them.

"I cannot go in these," he said to Saul, "because I am not used to them." So he took them off. ⁴⁰Then he took his staff in his hand, chose five smooth stones from the stream, put them in the pouch of his shepherd's bag and, with his sling in his hand, approached the Philistine.

⁴¹Meanwhile, the Philistine, with his shield bearer in front of him, kept coming closer to David. ⁴²He looked David over and saw that he was only a boy, ruddy and handsome, and he despised him. ⁴³He said to David, "Am I a dog, that you come at me with sticks?" And the Philistine cursed David by his gods. ⁴⁴"Come here," he said, "and I'll give your flesh to the birds of the air and the beasts of the field!"

⁴⁵David said to the Philistine, "You come against me with sword and spear and javelin, but I come against you in the name of the LORD Almighty, the God of the armies of Israel, whom you have defied. ⁴⁶This day the LORD will hand you over to me, and I'll strike you down and cut off your head. Today I will give the carcasses of the Philistine army to the birds of the air and the beasts of the earth, and the whole world will know that there is a God in Israel. ⁴⁷All those gathered here will know that it is not by sword or spear that the LORD saves; for the battle is the LORD's, and he will give all of you into our hands."

⁴⁸As the Philistine moved closer to attack him, David ran quickly toward the battle line to meet him. ⁴⁹Reaching into his bag and taking out a stone, he slung it and struck the Philis-

tine on the forehead. The stone sank into his forehead, and he fell facedown on the ground.

⁵⁰So David triumphed over the Philistine with a sling and a stone; without a sword in his hand he struck down the Philistine and killed him.

⁵¹David ran and stood over him. He took hold of the Philistine's sword and drew it from the scabbard. After he killed him, he cut off his head with the sword.

When the Philistines saw that their hero was dead, they turned and ran. ⁵²Then the men of Israel and Judah surged forward with a shout and pursued the Philistines to the entrance of Gath and to the gates of Ekron. Their dead were strewn along the Shaaraim road to Gath and Ekron. ⁵³When the Israelites returned from chasing the Philistines, they plundered their camp. ⁵⁴David took the Philistine's head and brought it to Jerusalem, and he put the Philistine's weapons in his own tent.

⁵⁵As Saul watched David going out to meet the Philistine, he said to Abner, commander of the army, "Abner, whose son is that young man?"

Abner replied, "As surely as you live, O king, I don't know."

⁵⁶The king said, "Find out whose son this young man is."

⁵⁷As soon as David returned from killing the Philistine, Abner took him and brought him before Saul, with David still holding the Philistine's head.

⁵⁸"Whose son are you, young man?" Saul asked him.

David said, "I am the son of your servant Jesse of Bethlehem."

DAVID'S DRAMATIC VICTORY OVER GOLIATH has become a classic for the ages. It contains all the elements of great literature. Many of us became familiar with the details of the story in our early childhood, and with good reason. Who among us has not felt the terror caused by a bully like Goliath, the giant of a man who boasts as though he is invincible and appears to have the goods to back up his bravado? And who of us can resist the innocence of the young shepherd boy who simply cannot understand why this culprit is permitted to defy the armies of the living God? It is the story of sling and stones versus sword, spear, and javelin; of defiant military aggression versus purity and faith; of right versus might;

of tall versus short; and of youth versus maturity. This account has brought faith to millions over the centuries precisely because here purity and right are victorious over might, unlike so many of our own experiences.

Beyond the sheer power of the narrative, this famous chapter also plays an integral role in the message of 1 Samuel. It confirms implicitly the truths stated more explicitly in the previous chapter: The Lord has withdrawn his blessing from Saul, who is now king in name only. Because of his refusal to accept Yahweh's authority, Saul has forfeited his right to remain king of Israel. Now he is ineffectual and powerless to produce deliverance from the Philistines, which was the great promise of Israel's new monarchy. Saul and his army seem fearful and helpless and find themselves locked in a stalemate with the enemy. In the face of Goliath's defiance, Saul seems paralyzed. By contrast, the shepherd boy, David, appears to bear all the marks of Spirit-filled leadership. He seems motivated only by the impulse to defend the honor of Yahweh's name, and his victory mobilizes the Israelite army, resulting in a great rout of the Philistines. Just as the Lord has abandoned Saul, so he has blessed David (cf. 16:13—14).

Several features of this chapter have generated questions among scholars. These have to do primarily with the uneasy relationship of chapter 17 with chapter 16 and with the supposed composite structure of chapter 17 itself. (1) The account shows no awareness of details in chapter 16. It does not seem to be aware of David's anointing (16:1—13) or his service in Saul's court as a musician (16:14—23). Instead of a well-established royal courtier, he appears in this text as a simple shepherd boy, not the brave warrior he is said to be in 16:18. More striking still is the fact that Saul does not seem to be aware of David's identity (17:55—58), which is difficult to square with his great love and appreciation for David in 16:21—22.

(2) Textual evidence indicates that the oldest Greek translations we have of this chapter omitted large portions of chapter 17.[1] This has led to speculation that portions (esp. vv. 12—31, 41, 48b, 50, 55—58) were part of an alternative account that circulated independently and were later edited into the main narrative.[2] Thus many scholars conclude this chapter has a separate tradition history from chapters 16 and 18, and some assume it weaves together two or more accounts that originally existed separately.[3]

---

1. Emanuel Tov, *Textual Criticism of the Hebrew Bible* (Minneapolis/Assen: Fortress/Van Gorcum, 1992), 334—36; for helpful survey of the issue, see Klein, *1 Samuel,* 173—74.

2. It is possible that ch. 16 originated and circulated in Bethlehem, while ch. 17 was preserved among later military records of Jerusalem, recording encounters with the Philistines. See Baldwin, *1 and 2 Samuel,* 124.

3. See the influential explanations of McCarter, *I Samuel,* 284—309, esp. 306—9, and Gordon, *I and II Samuel,* 64—66.

(3) Nevertheless, a few scholars working recently on literary techniques of the canonical shape and form of these texts have been more impressed by the literary integrity of chapter 17 and have even argued for the unity of the text as it now stands. One can argue that the narrator has intentionally written a lengthy account with many quotations and extended descriptions (e.g., the details of Goliath's armor) as a means of giving this story special prominence in the overarching account of David's rise.[4] This would confirm the view that speculation about the history behind the present text of 1 Samuel 17 should not detract us from the main task, which is to expose the meaning of the text as we have received it.

(4) Along similar lines, scholars of ancient Hebrew narrative have explained the chronological inconsistencies in chapters 16 and 17 as an intentional technique for characterizing David as the important new figure in the narrative. The compiler of the book used both versions of David's introduction into the royal court as a means of characterizing him fully. David rose to power under the aegis of Saul in peacetime (ch. 16) and under that of God during wartime (ch. 17). Both accounts were necessary in order to render a full description of the horizontal and vertical dimensions of David's character and function in the rest of the story.[5]

Regardless of how the text came into its present form, our task is to consider what it communicates in its canonical shape. The ancient narrator was obviously less concerned with historical and chronological precision than with the theological significance of David's rise to power. The location of David's victory over Goliath, coming as it does immediately after chapter 16, is strategic in the unfolding narrative. By means of this specific historical example, the text confirms all the descriptions of David in chapter 16 (and even in 13:14).

Battle Lines at the Valley of Elah (17:1–3)

THE TRIBES OF Israel under Joshua's leadership had settled in the central highlands while the Philistines lived in five capital cities of the coastal plains in the southwest. In the intervening years of the judges period, the Philistines had been Israel's greatest military threat. Defeating them had been their principal reason for requesting a king (9:16). Saul's initial victory over them drove

---

4. Bergen, *1, 2 Samuel*, 187–88. See the various articles in Dominique Barthélemy, David W. Gooding, Johan Lust, and Emanuel Tov, *The Story of David and Goliath: Textual and Literary Criticism* (OBO 73; Fribourg/Göttingen: Editions Universitaires/Vandenhoeck & Ruprecht, 1986), esp. D. W. Gooding, "An Approach to the Literary and Textual Problems in the David-Goliath Story" (55–86); see also T. A. Boogaart, "History and Drama in the Story of David and Goliath," *Reformed Review* 38 (1985): 204–14.

5. Sternberg, *The Poetics of Biblical Narrative*, 231; Alter, *The Art of Biblical Narrative*, 147–53.

the Philistines out of Israel's central highlands and made this battle in the foothills between Israelite and Philistine territory inevitable (chs. 13–14). Much is at stake in the conflict, so much so that the peace and prosperity of Israel's future can be said to hang in the balances.[6]

The battleground between Socoh and Azekah places this event in the western foothills of Judah. The Valley of Elah (Valley of the Terebinth) separates the opposing armies, presumably with the Philistine troops on the southern slopes of the valley and the Israelite forces on the northern slopes.[7]

Description of Goliath and His Challenge (17:4–11)

PECULIAR TO THIS Israelite-Philistine battle is the appearance of a single infantryman who challenges Israel to match him in representative combat. In this way the issue of the war between the two nations might be settled in single combat: "Choose a man and have him come down to me" (17:8). Man-to-man combat as a substitute for full-fledged battle between opposing armies was possible in the ancient world as a means of settling disputes without recourse to extensive bloodshed.[8] Though examples are sometimes in dispute, it is possible to see the famous Babylonian creation account, known as the *Enuma Elish*, as such an example among the gods. The great Babylonian divine hero, Marduk, represented most of the deities against the terrifying Tiamat.[9] But in most of these examples, representative individual combat seldom succeeded as a means of limiting warfare. As in our text, the warring parties often continued with the battle after the contest between the designated representatives was over (17:52–54; cf. 2 Sam. 2:12–17).

The first item in the narrator's elaborate description of Goliath is the NIV's "champion" (*ʾîš-habbenayim* in 17:4; lit., "the man-in-between"; also in 17:23). The designation occurs only here in the Old Testament, but its plural appears frequently in the so-called *War Scroll* from ancient Qumran as "infantry-men."[10] It is possible that such representative contests were not known to the

---

6. On the history of Israelite-Philistine conflict, see Howard, "Philistines," 239–41.

7. Youngblood, "1, 2 Samuel," 694–95; Joe D. Seger, "Azekah," *OEANE*, 1:243.

8. Harry A. Hoffner Jr., "A Hittite Analogue to the David and Goliath Contest of Champions?" *CBQ* 30 (1968): 220–25.

9. Roland de Vaux, "Single Combat in the Old Testament," in *The Bible and the Ancient Near East*, trans. D. McHugh (Garden City, N.Y.: Doubleday, 1971), 124–35. De Vaux collects other possible examples from the Bible as well as numerous ones from classical Greek sources. See also Yigael Yadin, *The Art of Warfare in Biblical Lands in the Light of Archaeological Study*, trans. M. Pearlman; 2 vols. (New York: McGraw-Hill, 1963), 2:265–66.

10. Rare biblical expressions often find a different or more precise meaning in texts from the Judean Desert, and this is particularly true of military terms in the War Scroll. Jean Duhaime translates the plural ("the men-in-between") as "skirmishers" (see his "War Scroll"

Israelites and that the term connotes "one who enters into single combat between two armies."[11] This may be supported by the observation that it is always the Philistine champion who challenges Israel to representative combat, so that the practice may have been a Western custom imported by the Philistines, perhaps from their Aegean homeland.[12]

Goliath is not designated a "giant," as we might imagine from children's stories like "Jack and the Beanstalk." Rather, he is portrayed as an exceedingly tall warrior whose very height strikes terror in the hearts of his potential foes. The NIV's "over nine feet tall" represents the Hebrew text. A Greek translation preserves a reading that Goliath was six feet nine inches tall.[13] Regardless of the precise details, the narrative's description of Goliath's impressive stature reminds the reader of another impressive leader described as "head and shoulders above the rest" (10:23). In other words, Saul is the best match for Goliath. Indeed, there is an implicit condemnation of Saul in Goliath's description, since King Saul would be expected not only to motivate his troops but to lead them forth against the Philistines. But on hearing Goliath's words, "Saul and all the Israelites" are paralyzed with fear (17:11). How unlike the Saul of chapter 11.

Description of David (17:12–16)

THE ELABORATE DESCRIPTION OF GOLIATH THE WARRIOR in the previous paragraph makes a stark contrast with David, the shepherd boy, described here. Goliath is enormous, protected by impressive armor, armed with potent weapons, and accompanied by his own shield bearer for added protection. He must have looked overpowering, even invincible.

By contrast, David can hardly look more vulnerable and insignificant. His primary role is traveling back and forth between home and the battle-

---

in *The Dead Sea Scrolls: Hebrew, Aramaic, and Greek Texts with English Translations.* Vol. 2: *Damascus Document, War Scroll, and Related Documents*, ed. J. H. Charlesworth et al. [Tübingen/Louisville: Mohr/Westminster John Knox, 1995], 80–141, especially 1QM 1.14 and 3.1 on pp. 96–97 and 100–101, respectively). Another recent suggestion is "foot-soldiers" (Geza Vermes, *The Complete Dead Sea Scrolls in English* [New York: Penguin, 1997], 164–65).

11. De Vaux, "Single Combat," 124–25.

12. Ibid., 127.

13. McCarter, *I Samuel*, 286, 291 for discussion. It can be argued that the LXX preserves an original text and the Hebrew MT represents an exaggeration of the facts, or that the Greek text is a pious emendation intended to lend credibility to the tradition. The narrator's great interest in Goliath's armor supports the abnormal height recorded in the Hebrew tradition, and it is possible Goliath suffered from gigantism. Kellermann has argued that David took advantage of Goliath's affliction, which is often associated with visual problems (D. Kellermann, "Die Geschichte von David und Goliath im Lichte der Endokrinologie," *ZAW* 102 [1990]: 344–57).

field, tending his father's sheep at Bethlehem and taking rations to the soldiers on the front line, as we learn in the next section. Rather than describing impressive military gear or physical stature, the narrator is more interested in David's heritage as the son of Jesse the Ephrathite.[14]

The text further characterizes David by contrasting him with everyone else in the story. His oldest brothers are in Saul's military, stationed at the camp of the Israelites. Goliath is in the habit of taking his defiant stand morning and evening for forty days. The descriptions of David and Goliath in 17:4–16 subtly differentiate the powerful and defiant enemies of God in the world against the unassuming innocence of God's faithful shepherd boy from Bethlehem.

David Arrives at the Valley of Elah (17:17–30)

DAVID HAS BEEN given the menial task of carrying provisions to the commander of his brothers' unit. But one day, when David delivers the rations, he arrives just as the army is going forth to battle, and he personally witnesses Goliath's defiant challenge. In his subsequent conversations with the troops, David learns that there will be a substantial reward for the Israelite soldier powerful and brave enough to defeat the terrifying Philistine champion. His oldest brother, Eliab, rebukes David because he believes his kid brother is conceited and has come to the front lines only to criticize their lack of initiative in answering Goliath's challenge. But David has matured enough to speak for himself, and he ignores his brother's disapproval.

The central question of the paragraph is David's in verse 26: "Who is this uncircumcised Philistine that he should defy the armies of the living God?" It is possible to see an intentional contrast between the words of David here and those of the Israelite troops in verse 25. Rather than "this man," David sees an "uncircumcised Philistine." Where they describe Goliath as a man who comes out to "defy Israel," David sees him as defying "the armies of the living God." The Israelite troops see a terrifying and seemingly invincible warrior who brings reproach on all Israel. But David sees only an uncircumcised Philistine, who worships deities that are not even alive (as we know from the Dagon episode in ch. 5). This worshiper of dead idols has the audacity to reproach the armies of the living God. Thus the soldiers' words of resignation are contrasted with David's words of indignation.[15]

As I will suggest in the Bridging Contexts section, David has learned to see things others cannot see. Just as God told Samuel that God sees in a way unlike humans (16:7), now David has learned to see things from God's per-

---

14. Ephrathah (abbreviated "Ephrath") was the Judahite area surrounding Bethlehem. As the Davidic dynasty rose in importance, Ephrathah came to be identified with its royal village, Bethlehem. See Lamontte M. Luker, "Ephrathah," *ABD*, 2:557–58.

15. Boogaart, "Story of David and Goliath," 208–9.

spective. What God (and David!) see in the Valley of Elah is very different from the view of the Israelite soldiers.

David Volunteers and Prepares to Meet Goliath (17:31–40)

DAVID'S CONVERSATIONS WITH the troops contain an implicit offer to fight Goliath. Saul is at least willing to entertain the possibility. But when they meet and David volunteers to fight Goliath, Saul cannot accept the idea that this inexperienced youth could go up against Goliath.

David's explanation of how he might be able to prevail against the Philistine also reveals his profound faith in Yahweh. This uncircumcised Philistine is no more frightening than a lion or bear trying to eat one of the sheep from his father's flock. Just as David has rescued sheep, so now he will rescue the armies of the living God. Since the Hebrew word translated "paw" in verse 37 is the same for "hand" (*yad*), David is relating the hand/power of the Philistine with that of the lion or bear. Just as Yahweh delivered from the hand of the lion and bear, so he will deliver from the hand of Goliath. In young David's mind, all the enemies of God are reduced to the same level; they are nothing but dumb beasts. Regardless of size or strength, the Lord will provide victory over all. David has moved from reciting his own bravery and skill (17:34–36) to acknowledging that Yahweh is the source of deliverance (17:37).[16]

In one final paragraph of preparation before the battle, David chooses the familiar sling and stones in his shepherd's bag rather than the cumbersome but potentially life-saving armor of the king.[17] Almost as a secondary theme, the text also informs us that King Saul has his own armor! It is possible that Saul's offer for David to use his royal armor is a calculated effort to bind the two together in a way that will make it possible for Saul to take credit for David's victory, should he actually succeed in defeating the Philistine champion.[18] In any event, Saul appears all too willing to loan his fighting gear to someone else, since he is not prepared to use it himself, especially against Goliath.

David Kills Goliath (17:41–51)

THIS LONGER THAN usual narrative has drawn the reader slowly and deliberately to this moment of high tension, which it quickly resolves.[19] First we read

---

16. Brueggemann, *First and Second Samuel*, 130.

17. The simple sling was common as an instrument of warfare. As a shepherd, David apparently became proficient, like certain Benjamite soldiers who could sling a stone at a hair without missing (Judg. 20:16). After the bow and arrow, the slingshot was the weapon of choice for long-range combat in ancient Egypt (Alan R. Schulman, "Military Organization in Pharaonic Egypt," *CANE*, 1:289–301, esp. 291).

18. Youngblood, "1, 2 Samuel," 699–700.

19. Brueggemann, *First and Second Samuel*, 127.

of the Philistine champion, accompanied by his shield bearer, approaching closer to David. After getting a good look at this young Israelite challenger, Goliath is incredulous. Despising David's shepherd staff as a "stick," he curses David in the name of the Philistine gods and threatens to expose his corpse to the wild animals.

Now it is David's turn. In a beautiful speech that dramatizes the conflict between Israel and the enemy nations around her, David emphasizes that Goliath is trusting in his own superior military resources ("sword and spear and javelin"). In contrast, David comes against him only in the name of Yahweh, God of the armies of Israel, whom Goliath has defied. David repeats his theme by promising that everyone present, both Israelite and Philistine, will learn (they will "know," *yd*ᶜ) that Yahweh's salvation is not by means of sword or spear, because the battle already belongs to the Lord (17:47). The narrator returns to this theme to stress its centrality (17:50): "So David triumphed over the Philistine *with a sling and a stone;* without a sword in his hand he struck down the Philistine and killed him." David's speech has been called "a high water mark in the series of Old Testament utterances on the subject of faith."[20]

Goliath is not prepared for battle with David. Even if he knows how effective a simple sling and stone can be, he must have underestimated David's marksmanship. No doubt, this young shepherd boy is unlike any other warrior Goliath has ever seen. But superior strength and military resources are useless against the representative of Yahweh. The contest is over before it begins. David kills Goliath with one of his choice stones. Since he does the job "without a sword in his hand," Yahweh has been true to his word: He saved "not by sword or spear" (17:47).[21]

Decapitation is the decisive sign the battle is over (cf. 31:9). But David, of course, has no sword of his own. So while the dead Philistine champion lies face down in the dirt, David borrows his sword to finish the job. The Philistine army runs in shock and terror.

Israel Routs the Philistines (17:52–54)

GATH AND EKRON were two of the five capital cities of the Philistines, making up their pentapolis in southwestern Canaan.[22] With this great military victory, David is well on the way to becoming the messianic leader the people

---

20. Gerhard von Rad, *Old Testament Theology,* trans. D. M. G. Stalker; 2 vols. (New York: Harper & Row, 1965), 2:379.

21. The NIV's translation of verse 51 stretches to harmonize with this detail: "After he killed him, he cut off his head with the sword" (cf. NRSV).

22. Howard, "Philistines," 243; Trude Dothan and Seymour Gitin, "Miqne, Tel," *OEANE,* 4:30–35; Eliezer D. Oren, "Haror, Tel," *OEANE,* 2:474–76.

are expecting; as one scholar has put it, this episode describes his "transformation from being a shepherd of flocks to becoming a leader of people."[23]

Furthermore, the location of the account is a deliberate narrative technique in the book's structure. After Saul's anointing, the narrator recorded the new king's military victory over the Ammonites (10:1–2; 11:1–11). So here the text moves from David's anointing to this victory over Goliath and the Philistine nation generally (16:13 and ch. 17).[24] It seems important to illustrate in each case that Yahweh's chosen is qualified to lead Israel victoriously into battle. With the rout of the Philistines, the course for David seems certain. Though Saul is still technically the king, David has become Israel's leader.[25]

Victory over one's enemies was frequently followed in antiquity by plundering the enemy camp, cutting off the head of one's conquered foes, and putting them on public display.[26] The difficulty in 17:54, however, is that David displays Goliath's head in Jerusalem, which stays in Jebusite control until David conquers it much later (2 Sam. 5:6–10). The simplest explanation is probably that the skull, as a trophy of David's victory, was brought to Jerusalem later as a "relic."[27]

It was apparently also a custom to take the armor of one's enemies and deposit it in one's own cult sanctuary (1 Sam. 31:10; 2 Sam. 8:7, as the Philistines did with the ark of the covenant, 1 Sam. 5:2). Though we cannot be certain what is intended by "his own tent" at the end of 17:54, the next time we read about the "sword of Goliath" it is in the sanctuary of Yahweh at Nob (21:9). So, perhaps "his own tent" refers to the Israelite cult sanctuary at Kiriath Jearim (6:21–7:1; 2 Sam. 6:2).

Saul Determines David's Identity (17:55–58)

THE SCENE SHIFTS in this paragraph back to the moment when David went out to meet the Philistine challenger. In this way, the main verbs of the paragraph can be translated in the pluperfect, as in "Saul had said to Abner. . . . Abner had replied. . . ." In perplexing fashion, the narrative presents a Saul who does not seem to be aware of David's identity, which is difficult to square with

---

23. Youngblood, "1, 2 Samuel," 697.

24. Ibid., 693.

25. Klein, *1 Samuel*, 183.

26. Or other body parts and armor, as will happen with Saul's defeat (31:10).

27. Hertzberg, *I and II Samuel*, though it would not be necessary to assume that the mention of Jerusalem belies a kind of "idealization" of David that arose much later in the literature (McCarter, *I Samuel*, 296–97). See also John T. Willis, "The Function of Comprehensive Anticipatory Redactional Joints in I Samuel 16–18," *ZAW* 85 (1973): 294–314, esp. 302–5; Gordon, *I and II Samuel*, 158.

his great love and appreciation for David in 16:21–22. Some have speculated that Saul's unstable mental condition has resulted in a loss of memory (see 16:14), or perhaps Saul wants to know more about David's parentage because he had promised to give his daughter in marriage to the one who killed Goliath (17:25).[28] However, it is possible to interpret chapter 16 as Saul's initial pleasure with David as a court musician, while here he is interested in David as a warrior.[29] In any case, after this episode in the Valley of Elah, Saul will have no difficulty knowing who David is (18:7).

THUS FAR IN OUR WALK THROUGH 1 SAMUEL, we have learned that God's first and best plan was to rule Israel himself as its only king, just as God had done in Israel's early history. Because of the nation's military and political needs and its selfish demands, the Lord agreed to rule Israel through human anointed ones ("messiahs"). The first of these failed because he refused to accept Yahweh's authority (King Saul). In the previous chapter, David was anointed as Saul's successor. This military victory over Goliath and the Philistines validates David's anointing, just as Saul's victory over the Ammonites (11:1–15) validated his anointing (9:1–10:27).

Unlike Saul, David proves to be a king who embraces Yahweh's authority enthusiastically. Indeed, he demonstrates that he is a man after Yahweh's own heart (13:14), a description that emphasizes David as the Lord's choice for king and also implies a like-mindedness between God and king. Though David's victory over Goliath is merely the beginning of his rise to the throne, the die is cast. He has been anointed by the Lord's prophet and has now demonstrated his ability to lead Israel. The rest of 1 Samuel is devoted to tension caused by having two anointed ones in Israel's royal court.

Most readers today have little difficulty building a bridge between this text about David and Goliath and our contemporary culture in the early twenty-first century. This is perhaps the world's most beloved story illustrating God's ability to provide victory in the face of overwhelming odds. Many believers today identify immediately with David and take this text as a promise of victory against whatever problems seem overwhelming at the moment.

But we should ask if this is really the right bridge (or the only bridge). The task of bridging the distance between the biblical historian's account of victory over Goliath and our own times is in reality complicated precisely by

---

28. Gordon, *I and II Samuel*, 158–59.

29. For this possibility, see Youngblood, "1, 2 Samuel," 690, though such a proposal is not without its own difficulties.

the fact that this is probably the best-known story in the books of Samuel, and certainly a narrative that has a permanent place in world literature and art.[30] This familiarity helps with our task simply because the details of the episode are so well known. But it is also true that familiarity can actually hinder our ability to bridge the contexts, because we tend to prejudge the original meaning of the text and what its significance is for modern readers.

1 Samuel 16 and 17. We should begin by examining more closely the function of this famous story in the overall structure of the books of Samuel. The selection of David and his anointing as the next king of Israel (ch. 16) and his replacement of Saul form the backbone of the narrative from 1 Samuel 16 to the beginning of 2 Samuel.[31] As David's fortunes are rising, Saul's are declining—at times gradually, at times precipitously.[32]

One of the most important observations about the role and function of 1 Samuel 17 is its relationship with 1 Samuel 16. This is perhaps because of the chronological inconsistencies between the two units (see discussion above). But regardless of the diachronic development of these texts, we must learn to let the previous unit inform and shape our understanding of chapter 17. Together they tell us that David has been designated by God as Saul's replacement, that the Spirit of Yahweh has come upon David and departed from Saul, and that David has entered the royal service of the king and demonstrated his courage as a military leader capable of inspiring the Israelite troops. These two chapters complement each other in characterizing both David and Saul and preparing the reader for the rest of 1 Samuel.

Beyond this important role of chapters 16 and 17 as programmatic for the rest of the book, I believe there is a sort of conversation taking place between them in order to characterize David further. In chapter 16, we learn that spiritual reality is a matter of the heart, not the eyes. Yahweh does not consider things mortals see. Mortals look at the outward appearance, but Yahweh sees the heart (16:7, see comments). Spiritual reality has an internal dimension that can be easily overlooked or missed because of physical impressions. Human perception often misses truth because of an inability or unwilling-

---

30. As, e.g., Michelangelo's famous sculpture of David showing the young man moments before his encounter with Goliath.

31. David becomes king first of Judah and then over all Israel (2 Sam. 2 and 5 respectively). The fall of Saul and rise of David culminate in the important theological chapter of 2 Sam. 7, where Yahweh promises David that he is the first king of a royal dynasty, which will endure forever (7:16). There will always be a son of David on the throne of Israel.

32. An index of his fall is his visit with the witch of Endor (1 Sam. 28) and his ignoble death at Mount Gilboa (1 Sam. 31). In 2 Samuel his descendants gradually disappear until the only remaining trace is the pitiable Mephibosheth, who is graciously sustained at David's table (2 Sam. 9:13).

ness to penetrate beyond the externals to discern the truth. But God perceives and understands what cannot be discerned by the human eye.

Chapter 16 also tells us immediately that the Spirit of Yahweh came upon David (16:13). This is the nature of the narrative in chapter 16 as a stylized, "vertical" narrative that moves "from God above to the world below," in which God instigates all the action and even speaks to Samuel in order to reveal his intentions.[33] Chapter 17, by contrast, is a detailed "horizontal" view, in which David himself takes the initiative and delivers the most penetrating speeches.

In light of the way the narratives work together to characterize David, I believe it is especially striking that David sees and hears things that other characters do not. The Israelite troops, for example, see and hear an intimidating infantryman from the Philistine camp, who looks and sounds invincible. David, however, hears and sees only blasphemous defiance of the armies of the living God. Others see reasons for fear and hesitation, but David sees only reasons for taking immediate action. Others see despair, where David sees an opportunity for national vindication against the Philistines and personal advancement in the service of the king.

In other words, reading chapters 16 and 17 together suggests that David has learned (or is learning) not to be overly impressed with external physical appearances. He has learned the lesson taught to Samuel in 16:7: God sees beyond the superficial appearances to the realities of the heart. Thus, David sees beyond the hopelessness of the Valley of Elah. Rather than an uncertain situation in which others are frozen by fear, David sees clearly that Yahweh has given victory against such an enemy as this defiant Philistine, Goliath. Such a close reading of this text in light of the context of 1 Samuel (esp. ch. 16) helps us overcome our familiarity with the David and Goliath account.

Military language. Many readers today have another problem when it comes to bridging the context between this text and our own day. Some have difficulty learning the lessons we need to learn from the Old Testament in general because those lessons are so often couched in military terms. The significance of the conflict between Goliath (and his god) versus David (and Yahweh) can get lost in our contemporary aversion to militarism. We tend to forget that God has human enemies who oppose him. We tend to see them as ignorant and pitiable, whereas the Bible understands them as malevolent.

In order to grasp fully the significance of David's victory over Goliath, we must remember that ancient Near Eastern philosophy equated military strength with a nation's deity. Most polytheists in antiquity assumed any nation that conquered another nation did so because of a superior god. The

---

33. Alter, *The Art of Biblical Narrative*, 152.

famous *Enuma Elish* goes to great lengths to demonstrate exactly why Marduk, the god of Babylon, was superior to all other deities.[34]

Closer to home, Israel's enemies assumed that Yahweh was only a god of the hills and not a god of the valleys (1 Kings 20:23–28). They thought they could defeat Israel if they fought them in the valley, where their deity would be superior. As today's Christians reading the Old Testament, one of the most difficult adjustments we have to make is to learn to rejoice with national Israel when they witness Yahweh's salvation accomplished through military strength. This is especially meaningful when the military victory is won miraculously. Thus, for example, the sight of Egyptian corpses lying on the shore of the Red Sea symbolized Yahweh's gracious deliverance of a defenseless Israel against the greatest military power of that day (Ex. 14:30). The sight of dead Egyptian soldiers strengthened their faith (14:31) and led to worshipful singing and praise (15:1–21). Indeed, Yahweh's defeat of the Egyptian army became the concrete sign of his salvation and new life for Israel throughout the Old Testament.

So too in the account of David and Goliath, the narrator intends us to rejoice at the sight of the decapitated Philistine, lying motionless in the Valley of Elah (1 Sam. 17:51) or at the news that the Philistine dead are strewn along the road from Gath to Ekron after the great Israelite victory (17:52). Admittedly, these are not images we normally evoke when we are seeking to build Christian faith today. But this is part of the challenge of bridging the contexts between ancient Israelite narrative and modern application.

Especially is this true in the present narrative since the conflict has been carefully framed in theological images. Repeatedly we are told Goliath defies the ranks of Israel, which David interprets as defiance of "the armies of the living God" (17:26, 36). David's speech makes the point forcefully. Goliath relies on his military power ("sword and spear and javelin"), whereas David relies solely on the name of Yahweh (17:45). The episode demonstrates that Yahweh's salvation—though military in its effect—is not accomplished through military power but rather through simple trust and reliance on him (17:47). David was Yahweh's instrument of salvation with a sling and stone, "without a sword in his hand" (17:50).[35]

---

34. Bill T. Arnold and Bryan E. Beyer, eds. *Readings from The Ancient Near East: Primary Sources for Old Testament Study* (Grand Rapids: Baker, 2002), text #6 (pp. 31–50).

35. A more complete understanding of holy war (or Yahweh war) as a distinctively Old Testament way of expressing God's salvation for Israel is important for contemporary interpreters. Such victory is always accomplished by Yahweh on behalf of his people and becomes an act of worship and a reason for praise. Conversely, the nation Israel itself can become the victims of Yahweh's warfare when they rebel against him later in Old Testament history. For introduction to this topic, see Longman and Reid, *God Is a Warrior*, 31–60.

As I emphasized in the introduction, Old Testament narratives can have different levels of interpretation: universal, national, and individual.[36] Every individual narrative also plays some role in the greater national narrative of Israel's history and therefore also contributes to the ultimate narrative of God's redemptive plan in history. This remarkable passage is important on a number of levels, since it contributes to the collection of Davidic narratives that characterize him so precisely in 1 and 2 Samuel. Beyond this individual level, the present passage eventually came to be understood on the national level because of its contribution, along with other Old Testament texts, to the messianism of early Judaism.

Thus, we may speak in terms of the *general* and *specific* significance of this narrative in our attempt to bring this passage to our own day. Generally speaking, the narrative teaches about personal faith and the desire of God to accomplish mighty things through the simple faith and actions of his servant. But more specifically, the narrative also portrays David as the ideal shepherd leader for Israel; as such, it contributes to the larger body of texts that subsequently feed into the concept of the Messiah.

The development of messianism. The books of Samuel contain in germinal form the basic concepts that contributed to the development of messianism. There can be no doubt that the portrayal of David in these texts contributed several themes by which the New Testament authors attempted to define Jesus. In particular, the books of Samuel emphasize four main themes that contributed to the concept of the messiah, themes which run throughout both books.[37] (1) The anointed one is God's appointed ruler. (2) He trusts in God and is protected by him. (3) The anointed one of Yahweh leads Israel victoriously in battle against the nation's enemies. (4) The anointed one is a just ruler.

In light of these emphases, 1 Samuel 17 stands as a programmatic text at the center of the book. The previous chapter portrays David as Yahweh's appointed ruler (the first of these themes); now the present text quickly confirms and establishes David as the military savior of his people, as the anointed one of Yahweh, who leads God's people in battle (the third theme).[38] This is especially apparent in David's speech (17:45–47), where he becomes the "Yahweh confessor"—also a typical role for the messiah. As

---

36. Or in Fee and Stuart's terminology, top, middle, and bottom levels. Fee and Stuart, *How to Read the Bible*, 73–78.

37. For what follows here, see Satterthwaite, "David in the Books of Samuel," 42–47.

38. Subsequent victories over Israel's other enemies will develop this concept further (1 Sam. 27:8–12; 2 Sam. 5; 8; and 10). See Satterthwaite, "David in the Books of Samuel," 46.

Yahweh confessor, the messiah represents Israel in fighting for the nation and is confirmed through Yahweh's victory over her enemies.[39]

The power of faith. Beyond this specific contribution to the concept of messianism, this text speaks more generally to every generation of believers about the miraculous way in which God uses the faith of weak but determined servants to defeat overwhelming obstacles. What a striking picture of God's great salvation! The young David, undeterred by the fierceness of Goliath's appearance or taunting threats, boldly witnesses to his faith in God to deliver and then acts upon that faith. One eminent scholar of the books of Samuel observes that two factors make David's heroism possible: his zeal for the reputation of Israel's God ("the whole world will know that there is a God in Israel," v. 46) and his utter trust in God's ability to save him against all odds (vv. 37, 45–47).[40] David's energetic zeal and childlike faith as portrayed here are exemplary for all believers. We should all feel so deeply and act so boldly as David does.

Furthermore, as readers, we understand his zeal and faith better because the text has portrayed David as the man of God's own choosing (i.e., he is a man after God's own heart, 13:14) and as someone who has adopted God's own perception of reality (i.e., he now sees beyond superficial externals and is able to see Goliath's defiance for what it really is). The specific terms used to describe Goliath's defiance imply that the Philistine is arrogantly crowing about his own strength and virtue.[41] But because of David's zeal and faith, he understands the irony of the Philistine warrior scorning the armies of the God who is alive as opposed to Dagon, the lifeless Philistine deity. This is in fact what drives the passage forward to its inevitable conclusion. David's conviction that Yahweh is a living God means that Goliath deserves to die.

Finally, the general interpretation of this passage for all believers also emphasizes the way God uses the unlikely and unexpected to confound and defeat the more powerful enemies of his purposes. Certainly this becomes an important theme in many Israelite contexts, so that late in Old Testament history the great prophet Zechariah could teach that God's purposes are not achieved by might nor by power but by the Spirit of Yahweh (Zech. 4:6). Likewise, when the apostle Paul described the qualifications of the early believers in Corinth, he stated that God had chosen "the foolish things of the world to shame the wise" and "the weak things of the world to shame the strong" (1 Cor. 1:27).

---

39. Knierim, "Messianic Concept," 35–36.

40. Gordon, *I and II Samuel,* 153.

41. The NIV's noun and verb ("disgrace" and "defy") in v. 26 are from the same Hebrew root, which is a way of taunting or mocking one's weaker enemy. See John E. Hartley, "חרף," *NIDOTTE,* 2:280–81.

INTERPRETATION AND APPLICATION of this great story will suffer if we leap too quickly to "victory over our Goliaths" as a metaphor for whatever wistful ailments or emotional frailties we encounter in our regular, everyday experiences. Such applications will be anemic and will miss the grand and powerful themes of this text. But if we keep the issues that rise from the exegetical study before us, the metaphor becomes a useful one: David is an example of the faithful and brave servant of Yahweh, and through his faith and action God wins victory over his blasphemous enemies. In this sense, all of us benefit by learning from this text that God grants victory over his Goliaths and that our faith and action are keys to the battle.

Facing enemies. Christians should not be surprised when they encounter opposition to what God has called them to do. The Bible teaches in a variety of ways that there will often be challenges to God's sovereign rule in the world. Whether it is Amalekites attacking Israel's rearguard as they depart Egypt (Ex. 17:8–16), Amorite coalitions uniting against Joshua in the Promised Land (Josh. 9:1–2), imposing-looking Philistines screaming offensive challenges at Saul's troops, or enemies of Jesus plotting his destruction (Mark 3:6), the world has never lacked for enemies of God's people.

Beginning with the book of Judges, the entire Philistine-Israelite conflict provided historical opportunities for the Israelites to learn spiritual truths (e.g., review the ark narrative and the Ebenezer passages; see comments on 4:1–7:17). When they sinned and turned their backs on God, the Philistines defeated them militarily. When they repented and returned to God, he gave them victory over their enemies. In this text, the Philistines once again appear as the quintessential enemies of God. The newly anointed leader of Israel, who will eventually become the ideal messianic king, is confronted for the first time with the rebellious opposition of the world. The Philistine warrior's defiance of Yahweh offers all of us an opportunity to reflect on the nature and extent of opposition to Christian ideals and causes in our own setting.

Church history presents many examples of Christians who failed to interact redemptively with hostile surrounding cultures.[42] For example, the Christian community in Germany unfortunately responded to the rise of

---

42. A good model for such reflection is the well-known study entitled *Christ and Culture* by H. Richard Niebuhr (New York: Harper & Brothers, 1951). In what has become a classic study of Christian interaction with culture, Niebuhr offered a schematization of the different ways in which believers have interacted with their world: "Christ against culture," "the Christ of culture," "Christ above culture," "Christ and culture in paradox," and "Christ the transformer of culture."

nationalism and fascism in varied and often disingenuous ways. It is true that many members of the German Evangelical Church formed a Confessing Church movement that openly opposed Nazi racism and brutality, and its leaders were imprisoned, exiled, or executed (as in the case of Dietrich Bonhoeffer). But for the majority of the church in Germany, it was easier simply to look the other direction.

Nazi Germany is far removed from most contemporary Christians' context. For Christians living in North America, the act of professing Christian faith has not typically meant the believer needs to worry about blatantly aggressive opposition from the culture. Anti-Christian messages throughout the history of the United States have normally taken subtler forms. But that may be changing. The horrific school shootings plaguing the United States since 1998 have sometimes been laced with troubling anti-Christian rhetoric, which came to a tragic culmination with the death of Cassie Bernall, called by many a modern-day Christian martyr.[43] If such decidedly anti-Christian sentiments continue to grow in this country, the prevailing question for the church in coming years will be how we respond.

The German church failed to reject radical nationalism and to oppose vigorously the growth of Nazism in the early twentieth century. The church essentially failed to function as a transforming element of the culture.[44] The way in which today's Christians in North America respond to postmodernism and the growing possibility of anti-Christian sentiment may pose a discomfiting parallel. In the face of clear opposition to biblical truth, David's speech and courageous service in 1 Samuel 17 offer an example for today's church to emulate.[45]

Messianism and Jesus Christ. In keeping with our discussion in the preceding Bridging Contexts section, I would argue that 1 Samuel 17 must be applied to our day in two ways. First, the chapter's contributions to the intertestamental understanding of messianism should enable us to understand the nature and mission of Jesus Christ as the Messiah. David's victory over Goliath confirms him as the anointed one of God, as the Yahweh confessor, and as the one who seals victory for God's people. The New Testament affirms that Jesus was born of Abrahamic and Davidic lineage (Matt. 1:2–16; Luke 2:4–15). Such claims demonstrate that the coming of Jesus fulfilled the promises of both the ancestral covenant and the Davidic covenant, the latter of which contained a promise to provide a son of David to rule Israel (2 Sam. 7).

---

43. David van Biema, "A Surge of Teen Spirit," *Time* 153, no. 21 (May 31, 1999): 58–59.
44. Niebuhr's fifth pattern is "Christ the transformer of culture."
45. After his victory has been translated from its military garb, of course (see discussion above).

Thus, Jesus was the anointed one of God, the man of God's own choosing, as David had been centuries before. Jesus was also a "Yahweh confessor," as David had been. Just as the speech of David in 1 Samuel 17:42–47 represented the truth to the Philistines and the Israelites, so the sermons of Jesus were accepted by the disciples and the early church as the prophetic word of God (Matt. 7:29). And just as David's courageous actions won victory for his people, so the life, death, and resurrection of Jesus provide victory for those who love him and are identified with him in faith (1 Cor. 15:54–57; 1 John 5:4).

This brief survey hints at only a few of the many ways in which the New Testament defines the role of the Messiah and frames the significance of Jesus in light of these Old Testament themes. Our purpose here is to highlight the way 1 Samuel 17 contributes to our Christology. In the New Testament, Jesus is presented as the ultimate fulfillment of the promises concerning great King David's greater Son (2 Sam. 7). But he also fulfills other aspects of the Old Testament's longing for an ideal Davidide, including important aspects of the David-Goliath episode. So our text is part of a continuous trajectory throughout the Old Testament (and esp. so in the books of Samuel). This trajectory gradually and irrevocably points our attention to the work and majesty of Jesus of Nazareth. He is God's own Anointed, the Speaker of God's word, and the Victor over sin and death.

A second application of this text for today's church flows from the emphasis here on individual faith and responsibility in the face of opposition to God's work. In the Bridging Contexts section above, I highlighted three aspects of David's victory over Goliath that I believe contribute to our understanding of contemporary Christian faith. (1) David had divinely guided insight that others lacked. Because of the Spirit of God working within him, he saw things others did not see (16:13). His perception of Goliath was dominated by what he saw with his heart, not his eyes. This internal dimension was lacking in Saul and the Israelite army.

(2) David was motivated by his zeal for God and his faith in God's character. He was alone in his confidence that Goliath could be defeated, since apparently the entire Israelite army believed otherwise. His conviction that God would defeat the Philistine aggressor made it possible for him to stand alone in the face of overwhelming odds.

(3) David was aware of the means by which the victory would be accomplished. He understood that faith in Yahweh was the determining factor, and he was not dissuaded by the staggering power at the disposal of his enemy. David was not fooled by the majority opinion that "might makes right."

A woman who has become an American cultural icon in the closing years of the twentieth century provides an interesting parallel. One day in 1955, a forty-two-year-old African American seamstress riding a bus in Montgomery, Alabama, violated segregation laws by refusing to give up her seat to a white passenger. The enemy Rosa Parks faced must have looked like an invincible warrior. The governmental laws and cultural norms were all aligned against her, and she was arrested for her refusal to conform. But she perceived things that others did not see, and she was confident in the righteousness of her cause.

It is no accident that this simple act of an unassuming but disenfranchised woman became the spark igniting a movement led by Dr. Martin Luther King Jr. He and others in Montgomery organized African Americans in a boycott of the bus system, which eventually led to the desegregation of the buses in December 1956. This celebrated incident was only the beginning of a long struggle involving the entire nation. Regarding her role in the civil rights movement and her decision to refuse to give up her seat, Mrs. Parks would later say, "Knowing what must be done does away with fear. . . . It was time for someone to stand up—or in my case, to sit down."[46] Her perception, strength in weakness, and confidence are not unlike David's and his similar complaint (17:26): "Who is this uncircumcised Philistine that he should defy the armies of the living God?"

So Rosa Parks can serve as a modern illustration of the principles at work in David's defeat of Goliath, explained most eloquently by the apostle Paul, who reminds us that God chooses "the weak things of the world to shame the strong" (1 Cor. 1:27). David versus Goliath remains a vivid portrait of God's miraculous victories and should serve as an example for us of individual faith and responsibility in the face of strong opposition. Note what Wesley wrote on this text: "A little shepherd, come but this morning from keeping sheep, has more courage than all the mighty men of Israel! Thus does God often do great things for his people by the weak things of the world."[47] With such biblical and contemporary examples of courage and resolve, Christians can move forward with confidence to face the challenges of our era.

---

46. Rosa Parks, *Quiet Strength: The Faith, the Hope, and the Heart of a Woman Who Changed a Nation* (Grand Rapids: Zondervan, 1994), 17−18.

47. Wesley, *Wesley's Notes on the Bible*, 189.

---

1 Samuel 18:1–30

❧

AFTER DAVID HAD finished talking with Saul, Jonathan became one in spirit with David, and he loved him as himself. ²From that day Saul kept David with him and did not let him return to his father's house. ³And Jonathan made a covenant with David because he loved him as himself. ⁴Jonathan took off the robe he was wearing and gave it to David, along with his tunic, and even his sword, his bow and his belt.

⁵Whatever Saul sent him to do, David did it so successfully that Saul gave him a high rank in the army. This pleased all the people, and Saul's officers as well.

⁶When the men were returning home after David had killed the Philistine, the women came out from all the towns of Israel to meet King Saul with singing and dancing, with joyful songs and with tambourines and lutes. ⁷As they danced, they sang:

"Saul has slain his thousands,
    and David his tens of thousands."

⁸Saul was very angry; this refrain galled him. "They have credited David with tens of thousands," he thought, "but me with only thousands. What more can he get but the kingdom?" ⁹And from that time on Saul kept a jealous eye on David.

¹⁰The next day an evil spirit from God came forcefully upon Saul. He was prophesying in his house, while David was playing the harp, as he usually did. Saul had a spear in his hand ¹¹and he hurled it, saying to himself, "I'll pin David to the wall." But David eluded him twice.

¹²Saul was afraid of David, because the LORD was with David but had left Saul. ¹³So he sent David away from him and gave him command over a thousand men, and David led the troops in their campaigns. ¹⁴In everything he did he had great success, because the LORD was with him. ¹⁵When Saul saw how successful he was, he was afraid of him. ¹⁶But all Israel and Judah loved David, because he led them in their campaigns.

¹⁷Saul said to David, "Here is my older daughter Merab. I will give her to you in marriage; only serve me bravely and

fight the battles of the LORD." For Saul said to himself, "I will not raise a hand against him. Let the Philistines do that!"

¹⁸But David said to Saul, "Who am I, and what is my family or my father's clan in Israel, that I should become the king's son-in-law?" ¹⁹So when the time came for Merab, Saul's daughter, to be given to David, she was given in marriage to Adriel of Meholah.

²⁰Now Saul's daughter Michal was in love with David, and when they told Saul about it, he was pleased. ²¹"I will give her to him," he thought, "so that she may be a snare to him and so that the hand of the Philistines may be against him." So Saul said to David, "Now you have a second opportunity to become my son-in-law."

²²Then Saul ordered his attendants: "Speak to David privately and say, 'Look, the king is pleased with you, and his attendants all like you; now become his son-in-law.'"

²³They repeated these words to David. But David said, "Do you think it is a small matter to become the king's son-in-law? I'm only a poor man and little known."

²⁴When Saul's servants told him what David had said, ²⁵Saul replied, "Say to David, 'The king wants no other price for the bride than a hundred Philistine foreskins, to take revenge on his enemies.'" Saul's plan was to have David fall by the hands of the Philistines.

²⁶When the attendants told David these things, he was pleased to become the king's son-in-law. So before the allotted time elapsed, ²⁷David and his men went out and killed two hundred Philistines. He brought their foreskins and presented the full number to the king so that he might become the king's son-in-law. Then Saul gave him his daughter Michal in marriage.

²⁸When Saul realized that the LORD was with David and that his daughter Michal loved David, ²⁹Saul became still more afraid of him, and he remained his enemy the rest of his days.

³⁰The Philistine commanders continued to go out to battle, and as often as they did, David met with more success than the rest of Saul's officers, and his name became well known.

DAVID'S VICTORY IN THE VALLEY OF ELAH made a
national hero of him and entitled him to the hand
of Saul's daughter (17:25). But it also aroused feelings of jealousy in Saul (18:9), which set in
motion the events that fill the rest of 1 Samuel. Suddenly David is a threat
to Saul. Saul's jealousy drives a wedge between himself and David, and with
each passing unit of 1 Samuel 18–31, the distance becomes more severe.

This text begins to narrate the relational tension between Saul and David.
The narrator has chosen to characterize the two men with extreme subtlety,
by contrasting the way Saul's *family* relates to David with the way Saul himself
relates to him. So we begin with a paragraph on Jonathan, the crown prince,
and David (18:1–4), proceed to two paragraphs on Saul's ill-tempered feelings
of jealousy and his attempts to kill David (18:5–16), and conclude with two
paragraphs on Saul's daughters and their relationships with David (18:17–30).
The love of Saul's family for David serves as a contrastive foil for Saul's own jealousy, which oscillates between murderous hatred and gracious tolerance.

However, at the core of this text is not David's relationship with the royal
family but the narrator's explicit statement of theological causes behind the
historical realities. Events are moving ahead, irreversibly now, because Yahweh has abandoned Saul and is instead "with" David, a theme repeated three
times (see below). All of Saul's efforts to stop David's rise in popularity serve
only to propel David further into the limelight. When we come to the end
of the unit, the narrator informs us that Saul himself has now come to understand the two recurring elements of this text: Yahweh is with David and
Saul's family loves David (18:28).

Jonathan's Covenant with David (18:1–4)

THE RELATIONSHIP BETWEEN Jonathan and David that begins to unfold here
is one of the classic stories of deep and abiding friendship, and it plays an
important role in subsequent chapters of this book. Their relationship was
marked by unity ("one in spirit") and exceptional commitment ("he loved
him as himself").

Some scholars cite this passage, with its word "love" (vv. 1, 3), as evidence for a homosexual relationship between David and Jonathan.[1] Others
argue that Jonathan's role in this text is that of a woman; that is, the original
historian cast him in the image of David's other women. Jonathan, so they

---

1. Tom Horner, *Jonathan Loved David: Homosexuality in Biblical Times* (Philadelphia: Westminster, 1978), 20, 26–28, 31–39. Interpreters predisposed to such a reading frequently turn
to 1 Sam. 20:17; 2 Sam. 1:26 (see comments).

claim, is ahead of Michal (and later Abigail) in his love for David and in his practical ways of saving and helping him. In order to be crown prince, he must be male. But in order to be motivated to abdicate the throne, he must be like the women in David's life, who empty themselves for David's sake. The answer is to portray a homosexual relationship between David and Jonathan, in which Jonathan assumes a female role. This relationship, it is argued, was more transparent in the older form of the story. Interpreters who argue along these lines further contend that subsequently, the homosexual relationship between David and Jonathan was subverted by later editors because of cultural abhorrence of homosexuality.[2]

Today's pro-homosexual interpreters claim the text has forced an injustice on gay readers because the true homosexual nature of the relationship has been suppressed both by ancient editors and modern scholars because of homophobia. Surely, however, it is just as much an injustice to today's heterosexual readers to subvert the obvious face value of the canonical text and to deny that David and Jonathan should have had a loving commitment to each other that was nonsexual. Are heterosexual men incapable of such deep and abiding friendships? Such readings rob heterosexual men and deny them the right to have a loving, yet nonsexual relationship with other men. In ancient patriarchal cultures such as Israel's, a wife was a man's partner for raising the family but not necessarily his best friend.

Today, we recognize the imperfections of such patriarchal assumptions, and I would even argue that the ancient patriarchal societies lost the original codependent and egalitarian ideals of creation (Gen. 1:27). Furthermore, we have ancient, extrabiblical parallels for the intimacy of David's nonsexual relationship with Jonathan.[3] But beyond this point, perhaps it is more important to note that such pro-homosexual readings miss the intended significance of "love" and other covenantal terms in the text, to which we now return.

We now know that the specific verb for "love" used here (*'hb*) has important political overtones. So, for example, Saul loved David in 1 Samuel 16:21 (NIV has "liked"), and Hiram king of Tyre loved David in 1 Kings 5:1 (cf. NIV, "had always been on friendly terms"). Indeed, the relationship between David and Jonathan is a classic example of a covenant between individuals, and the language used to characterize that relationship is typical of ancient kinship and mutual kinship obligation.[4]

---

2. Danna Nolan Fewell and David M. Gunn, *Gender, Power, and Promise: The Subject of the Bible's First Story* (Nashville: Abingdon, 1993), 151; Jobling, *1 Samuel*, 161–65. But we have little or no evidence for such a preexisting story.

3. See comments on Gilgamesh and Enkidu at 2 Sam. 1:26.

4. Frank Moore Cross, *From Epic to Canon: History and Literature in Ancient Israel* (Baltimore: Johns Hopkins Univ. Press, 1998), 9.

J. A. Thompson has concluded that "love" is used here as an "ambiguous word" because it denotes more than natural affection, however deep and genuine.[5] The political overtones of Jonathan's love for David are thus marked by their "covenant" (*berit*, 18:3) and by Jonathan's extravagant gifts (18:4). Thompson further suggests that this paragraph is part of a larger motif in the extended narrative in which the greater, more powerful person surprisingly passes his weapons on to David. So King Saul offered his arms to the young David about to face Goliath (17:38–39), and Goliath's sword passed on to David (17:51; 21:9), as here Jonathan gave him his sword and bow.[6]

It is also possible that the specific idiom for "became one in spirit" has a similar kind of double meaning, inferring again the political nature of their relationship.[7] David's and Jonathan's immediate bonding and personal friendship apparently leads the crown prince to renounce his throne, and the gifts of verse 4 are symbolic of his commitment to defer to David's right to be king.[8] The last time they see each other, Jonathan confirms his resolve that David will be king and that he will himself play a secondary role in the kingdom (23:16–18).

Saul First Becomes Jealous of David (18:5–9)

THIS SECTION EMPHASIZES Saul's anger and jealousy of David. Recent literary studies in the David narratives have made us more aware of the amazing artistry through which the historian has characterized David throughout 1–2 Samuel.[9] The historian carefully sets up a screen around David's intimate responses to other characters and to events as they unfold by withholding from the reader David's thoughts or feelings. We learn what kind of person he is by his speeches, by his impressive military exploits, and by what other characters feel about him. But the narrator never makes statements about *David's* feelings or reveals his inner thoughts.

By contrast, the narrator exposes in this chapter the feelings and emotions of everyone around David. Jonathan is entirely motivated by love and

---

5. J. A. Thompson, "The Significance of the Verb *Love* in the David-Jonathan Narratives in 1 Samuel," *VT* 24 (1974): 334–38 (quote on p. 336); see also William L. Moran, "The Ancient Near Eastern Background of the Love of God in Deuteronomy," *CBQ* 25 (1963): 77–87.

6. Thompson, "Significance of the Verb *Love*," 335.

7. Peter R. Ackroyd, "The Verb Love—*'āhab* in the David-Jonathan Narratives—A Footnote," *VT* 25 (1975): 213–14.

8. Gunn, *The Fate of King Saul*, 80.

9. For introduction to what follows here, see Alter, *The Art of Biblical Narrative*, 114–30. Alter believes that David is "the most complex and elaborately presented of biblical characters" (115).

devotion for David. The general populace are motivated by admiration for David (the military officers are pleased when he is promoted, and the women celebrate his victories). Saul is motivated by fear, anger, and jealousy. Michal, like Jonathan, is motivated by her love for David (18:20). All of these emotions are stated flatly by the narrator. But David's inner life is revealed more opaquely and is held in suspense throughout most of the narratives. This technique focuses our attention squarely on David as the central figure, as everyone around him seems likewise focused.[10]

Saul Attempts to Kill David (18:10–16)

SAUL OBVIOUSLY HAS deep psychological problems.[11] This chapter contains the first of several references to his fits of jealousy over David's popularity, and Saul is afraid. But as always in biblical narrative, the historian is more interested in the theological causes than historical details. Here the narrator's voice is clear about the theologically significant forces at work in the events he describes. By exposing Saul's inner life, the narrator puts the other events of this chapter in theological perspective.

The omniscient narrator knows who loves whom (Jonathan and Michal love David) and who is jealous of whom (Saul is jealous of David). More impressively, the writer knows that an injurious spirit from God comes upon Saul, that Yahweh is with David, and that Yahweh has abandoned Saul. The theme of the paragraph is repeated twice: Yahweh is with David, and Saul is afraid of David (18:12, 14–15; cf. 18:28–29). These statements form the theological centerpiece of the chapter and give the narrator's underlying foundations for what is happening historically in the family of Saul and in Saul himself.

In the Bridging Contexts section for chapter 14 we noted the destructive darkness in Saul's life that slowly but relentlessly wells up within the narrative. From 1 Samuel 15 on, events begin to move against Saul, gradually at first but then more and more rapidly. In this paragraph, what begins as anger and jealousy (18:8–9) moves to murderous and irrational fear.

The text is also clear about the causal connection between Saul's fear and David's successes. Yahweh is with David in order to make successful everything he attempts, and therefore Saul is afraid (18:12, 14–15). The irony that plays out in the subsequent narrative is that David will not himself raise a hand

---

10. Alter (ibid., 125–30) believes that Israel's unique way of characterizing leading figures in the Bible is ultimately related to the monotheistic revolution. Unlike the specific narration of Greek historiography, Israelite narratives are more conscious of singular divine direction and esp. the free moral agency of human nature.

11. As we noted earlier, some have speculated about the possibility of paranoid schizophrenia (Harrison, *Introduction to the Old Testament*, 715–16).

against Yahweh's anointed, Saul.[12] But the king is past understanding that David will be loyal. His anger and jealousy have given birth to such bouts of resentment and terror that he can only think of bringing David's life to an end.

Saul's Daughters, Merab and Michal (18:17–30)

THE REST OF the chapter relates Saul's attempts to rid himself of David, whom he comes to view as the singular threat to his reign and to the continuation of his dynasty through Jonathan. First he offers in marriage his oldest daughter to David, which is the expected reward for the warrior who defeated Goliath (17:25). But this offer is a ruse, because in exchange for Merab, Saul also seeks David's commitment to continue the military struggle against the Philistines. Saul's motive is revealed in 18:17, where his inner speech betrays his desire to let the Philistines kill David. But Saul changes his mind and gives Merab to another man, whose children suffer terribly (see 2 Sam. 21:8–9).

When Saul learns of Michal's love for David, he sees it as another opportunity to ensnare the young rival (1 Sam. 18:21). This time using more diplomacy, he persuades David to earn the right to Michal's hand by acquiring "a hundred Philistine foreskins" as a bride-price. Saul hopes such a requirement will actually cost David his life. The irony of the text is clear in the repetition of the expression "he was pleased" in 18:20 and 26.[13] Saul is pleased because he sees Michal's love for David as another opportunity for entrapment of David, but David is pleased because he sees it as an opportunity to become the king's son-in-law. This ironic twist illustrates the nature of Saul's relationship with David. "Everything Saul does to thwart David's rise works ironically to David's advantage; every opportunity Saul attempts to seize for himself turns in the end into an opportunity for David."[14]

Bridging Contexts

YAHWEH RULES OVER Israel, though he has chosen to do so through human anointed ones. The perplexing problem that drives the rest of 1 Samuel is the presence of *two* anointed ones in Israel—Saul and, since chapter 16, David. How will this be resolved? Which of these two anointed ones will ultimately lead God's people? Since the historian has already

---

12. The Heb. also contains an interesting wordplay that makes this point forcefully. The last word of verse 12 is in Heb. the same as the first verb in verse 13: Yahweh has turned aside (the verb *swr* in the Qal) from Saul [NIV "had left Saul"], and therefore, Saul drives David away (*swr* in the Hiphil [NIV "so he sent David away from him"]).

13. For what follows, see McCarter, *I Samuel*, 315–18.

14. Ibid., 318.

told us that David is God's choice and that Saul has been rejected (chs. 13–15), it remains only to narrate the details of the fall of Saul and the rise of David.

The text takes us through many twists and turns in a way that beautifully demonstrates God's sovereign work in the world among humans who are free to follow or resist. Furthermore, the ever-present contrast between Saul and David addresses one of the driving questions of 1–2 Samuel: Who may serve suitably as Israel's king? Any future kings who become like Saul will be illegitimate; all of Israel's kings should be like David.

Spirit *of* and *from* God. The central theological idea of this chapter is the coming of the "evil spirit from God" upon Saul, a theme originally introduced in 16:14 (see also 19:9).[15] As in that earlier reference, the arrival of an injurious spirit *from* God is preceded by (and becomes a consequence of) the departure of the Spirit *of* God: "The LORD was with David but had left Saul" (18:12; see comments on 16:14–18). The Spirit *of* God comes to bestow success on David, while the pernicious spirit *from* God continues to torment Saul.

The withdrawal of God's Spirit is reminiscent of another episode in this book, in which the glory of God departed Israel. Eli's daughter-in-law went into labor and gave birth when she heard the ark of the covenant had been captured. Because she understood that the glory of God had departed Israel, she named her newborn son Ichabod, "no glory," implying no hope for success or future (see comments on 4:19–22). Saul is certainly portrayed as an Ichabod figure, since the Spirit of God has departed and an injurious spirit from God has taken its place.

By contrast, the Lord is "with David" (18:12, 14, 28). He is the source of David's success and the cause of Saul's torment.[16] Moreover, David is God's choice as the next anointed one of Israel. God moves in and through these events in order to place David at the head of his people. As Saul is an Ichabod figure, so David is an Immanuel figure.[17] The Spirit has departed from Saul and rests on David. God is at work in David and in the circumstances around him in order to accomplish his purposes for his people. History is marching forward in its inexorable way, and Saul is helpless to stop it. God and most everyone else in the text are *with* David, while Saul is firmly set against him.[18] The more vigorously Saul opposes God's actions, the more successful God's servants become in accomplishing God's call on their lives.

---

15. Cf. NLT, "a tormenting spirit from God."

16. For other examples of God's presence "with" someone for comfort and strength, see Moses (Ex. 3:12) and Joshua (Josh. 1:5, 17); for this theme in Genesis, see Arnold, *Encountering the Book of Genesis*, 200–202.

17. "Immanuel" is the Hebrew name meaning "God with us." It becomes Isaiah's preferred name for the ultimate Son of David (Isa. 7:14; see Matt. 1:23).

18. Brueggemann, *First and Second Samuel*, 136.

Reverse returns. In our desire to bring this text into our contemporary world, it is helpful to remember that the Bible contains many such parallels to demonstrate and confirm the pattern: The more God's enemies resist his will, the more success God's children experience. Perhaps we can call this the biblical principle of "reverse returns" for those who oppose God's work. Those who oppose a servant of God, someone who has God "with" him or her, merely serve to propel the purposes of God further against their own wishes.

The brothers of Joseph, for example, intended to harm him, but instead they became instruments for accomplishing God's will for him (Gen. 50:20).[19] The pharaoh of the Hebrew oppression, because of fear and greed, enslaved the Israelites in order to control their population growth. But the result exacerbated his problem: "The more they were oppressed, the more they multiplied and spread" (Ex. 1:12). Pharaoh then tried infanticide as a means of controlling the Israelites. But God responded to the civil disobedience of the Hebrew midwives, and "the people increased and became even more numerous" (1:20).

Similarly, the pharaoh of the Exodus hardened his heart against Moses and the Israelite request to let God's people leave Egypt, and he thereby became a cause for the ten plagues, by which God delivered Israel (Ex. 3:19–20). Then there is Daniel and his three friends, who were captured and deported to Babylonia to serve in the king's court (Dan. 1). But such aggression merely placed Daniel and his friends in a position to receive an education in Babylonia and put them into Nebuchadnezzar's service, which prepared them further (esp. Daniel) to serve a significant role in God's next phase of salvation history (Dan. 2–12).

The ultimate example of this principle of reverse returns is Jesus. He was opposed by many people for a variety of reasons, and this opposition led to his ignoble death on a cross (Luke 22:1–6). But it is through that very death that Israel, and through Israel the nations, experience divine redemption.[20] The cross is the ultimate opposition to God's work, but in this most dramatic of all reversals, it has become the instrument of God's redemption and the eternal symbol of his love for the world. Far from preventing Jesus from

---

19. There may well be a formal relationship between 1 Sam. 18 and Gen. 39. See Alter, *The Art of Biblical Narrative*, 117.

20. According to the Gospels, Jesus foresaw his suffering and death and gave his crucifixion a "suffering Messiah" interpretation. This made it possible for Jesus and his earliest followers to hold together his elevated status as Messiah with his shameful death; it further made possible the acceptance of the efficacy of his death in redemption. See Joel B. Green, "The Death of Jesus and the Ways of God: Jesus and the Gospels on Messianic Status and Shameful Suffering," *Int* 52.1 (1998): 24–37.

accomplishing his mission, his adversaries provided the means through which Jesus fulfilled his mission.

Moreover, Jesus understood and taught his disciples that such persecution was cause for rejoicing (Matt. 5:11–12). Not that Christian faith should be masochistic or derive some sort of maniacal pleasure from suffering and persecution. Rather, Christians have the assurance that God's will cannot be thwarted by opposition; in fact, he often reverses the expected returns by turning opposition into the means of victory. The early church demonstrates this truth when the early Jewish believers were scattered throughout the Roman world because of persecution (Acts 8:1–4). Rather than halting the spread of Christianity, such persecution served as a means of introducing the gospel to the entire world (11:19–21).

THE CONTEMPORARY CHRISTIAN can take great comfort from the central ideas of this chapter. Even when an enemy of God, motivated by anger, jealousy, or hatred, attempts to intervene forcibly against the progress of what God is accomplishing, that very intervention itself can be used by God to further his purposes. This principle has been illustrated in American history in the second half of the twentieth century in the civil rights movement, thanks largely to the use of Christian principles in the civil disobedience of the movement's leadership.

Victory through persecution in the civil rights movement. A vivid illustration of this comes from the remarkable life and ministry of Dr. John M. Perkins, founder and leader of Voice of Calvary Ministries in Jackson and Mendenhall, Mississippi. Dr. Perkins testifies that an episode in 1970 taught him that love is stronger than hate. One horrible night in February, he was beaten nearly to death by white police officers. He later stated that God used this experience to give him a real compassion for whites. His story sheds light on how vicious opposition can actually strengthen a righteous cause in its resolve and effects.[21]

During the evening of February 7, two vans were returning African American students to Tougaloo College near Jackson from Mendenhall, where they had participated in a civil rights march. In Plain, Mississippi, a few miles after the vans rolled over the line separating Simpson County from Rankin County, a highway patrol car from Mendenhall pulled over one of the vans. Perkins received a call that the students had been taken to the Brandon jail

---

21. For what follows, see John Perkins, *With Justice for All* (Ventura, Calif.: Regal Books, 1982), 97–99.

in Rankin County. He and two pastor friends headed for the jail to set bail for the group. On the way, Perkins admits it occurred to him that this could be a trap. Why else would they arrest only one of the vans? Was it possible they were setting a trap for the leadership of the march?

As they arrived at the county courthouse and jail, a highway patrolman showed them where to park. They were then met by a dozen highway patrolmen in the parking lot. The policemen searched and arrested the three clergymen and immediately began beating them. They were then taken inside the jail, where the nightmare only continued. The local sheriff, five deputy sheriffs, and nearly a dozen patrolmen began beating them. In the subsequent court trial, Perkins described the scene in the jail that evening:

> "When I got to the jail and saw the people in jail, of course I was horrified as to why we were arrested and when I got in the jail Sheriff Jonathan Edwards came over to me right away and said, 'This is the smart nigger, and this is a new ballgame. You're not in Simpson County now; you are in Brandon.' ... He began to beat me, and from that time on they continued beating me."[22]

Perkins explains how he attempted to defend himself without retaliating. At one point, he describes how one of the policemen stabbed him with a fork as he continued stomping on and hitting him. Falling in and out of consciousness, Perkins could recall the looks of his attackers' faces, which he said were so twisted with hate they looked like white-faced demons. This was a turning point in his ministry, as he later reflected on the significance of the event:

> For the first time I saw what hate had done to those people. These policemen were poor. They saw themselves as failures. The only way they knew how to find a sense of worth was by beating us. Their racism made them feel like "somebody." When I saw that, I just couldn't hate back. I could only pity them. I said to God that night, "God, if you will let me get out of this jail alive ... I really want to preach a gospel that will heal these people, too." Well, although the students who watched over me through the night in that jail cell were sure for a while that I was dead or about to die, I came out alive—and with a new call. My call to preach the gospel now extended to whites.[23]

---

22. Ibid., 98.
23. Ibid., 99. He states further (p. 102): "At Brandon God showed me how racism had psychologically damaged whites just as much as it had blacks. Through those sick men, God showed me the need to take a gospel of love to whites filled with hate."

Perkins explains further that for the first time in his life, while he was being battered in that Mississippi jail, he had seen how the white man was a victim of his own racism. For the first time he wanted to bring a gospel that could set him free as well. But he contends that this was only a start, because now he saw the deep-seated bitterness he harbored in his own heart against whites for what they had done to him and his family.

Persecution in this case only intensified and strengthened the very movement the attackers wanted to stop. As Perkins's testimony illustrates, persecution served a purifying role in broadening his own ministry and made him more effective. For the leadership of the civil rights movement, where civil disobedience was practiced, opposition served only to propel the movement to new accomplishments. This is a story that could be repeated in other contexts, especially in cultures where the church is persecuted by imposing political forces at work.

Christians are called to refuse retaliation and to live in such a way as not only to *overcome* but *transform* the oppressors.[24] Though Saul had set his course and would not allow himself to be deterred, David was faithful to what God placed before him, and God was "with" David. As Christians, we must bear testimony to God's grace in our lives in good times and in bad, and we must remember that a loving response to opposition can transform our enemies, and as Dr. Perkins testifies, transform ourselves as well.

---

24. J. Christiaan Beker, *Suffering and Hope: The Biblical Vision and the Human Predicament* (Grand Rapids: Eerdmans, 1987), 85–91; Stanley Hauerwas, *The Peaceable Kingdom: A Primer in Christian Ethics* (Notre Dame, Ind.: Univ. of Notre Dame Press, 1983).

1 Samuel 19:1–17

SAUL TOLD HIS SON JONATHAN and all the attendants to kill David. But Jonathan was very fond of David ²and warned him, "My father Saul is looking for a chance to kill you. Be on your guard tomorrow morning; go into hiding and stay there. ³I will go out and stand with my father in the field where you are. I'll speak to him about you and will tell you what I find out."

⁴Jonathan spoke well of David to Saul his father and said to him, "Let not the king do wrong to his servant David; he has not wronged you, and what he has done has benefited you greatly. ⁵He took his life in his hands when he killed the Philistine. The LORD won a great victory for all Israel, and you saw it and were glad. Why then would you do wrong to an innocent man like David by killing him for no reason?"

⁶Saul listened to Jonathan and took this oath: "As surely as the LORD lives, David will not be put to death."

⁷So Jonathan called David and told him the whole conversation. He brought him to Saul, and David was with Saul as before.

⁸Once more war broke out, and David went out and fought the Philistines. He struck them with such force that they fled before him.

⁹But an evil spirit from the LORD came upon Saul as he was sitting in his house with his spear in his hand. While David was playing the harp, ¹⁰Saul tried to pin him to the wall with his spear, but David eluded him as Saul drove the spear into the wall. That night David made good his escape.

¹¹Saul sent men to David's house to watch it and to kill him in the morning. But Michal, David's wife, warned him, "If you don't run for your life tonight, tomorrow you'll be killed." ¹²So Michal let David down through a window, and he fled and escaped. ¹³Then Michal took an idol and laid it on the bed, covering it with a garment and putting some goats' hair at the head.

¹⁴When Saul sent the men to capture David, Michal said, "He is ill."

¹⁵Then Saul sent the men back to see David and told them, "Bring him up to me in his bed so that I may kill him." ¹⁶But when the men entered, there was the idol in the bed, and at the head was some goats' hair.

¹⁷Saul said to Michal, "Why did you deceive me like this and send my enemy away so that he escaped?"

Michal told him, "He said to me, 'Let me get away. Why should I kill you?'"

THIS UNIT CONTINUES THE MAIN THEMES of chapter 18. Saul's children, Jonathan and Michal, love David, but Saul attempts to kill him. Saul is plagued by injurious forces that cloud his thinking and lead to irrational suspicion of David. But for all his efforts to the contrary, Saul only contributes to David's rapid rise in popularity. There are many features of repetition between chapters 18 and 19 (for comments and application of these repetitions, see ch. 18).

Chapter 19 contains what some scholars have considered inconsistent references, leading them to postulate at least two competing sources for many of these stories; some have concluded these events are not narrated in chronological sequence.[1] Whether any of these scholarly suggestions is true is difficult to determine. But for our purposes it is more beneficial to notice the literary technique of intercalation as a means of heightening the suspense and emotions of the narrative. The narrator intercalates, or interchanges, the positive and negative responses to David (similar to ch. 18). The paragraph on Jonathan's love and support for David (19:1–7) is followed by Saul's pernicious attempt to kill David (19:8–10), which is followed by Michal's loving insistence on helping David escape (19:11–17). This literary device magnifies especially Saul's senseless opposition to David, which stands at the center of the unit.

Beyond reinforcing the previous themes, we may also allow this unit to raise some pertinent ethical issues for our day. Jonathan is secretive, if not duplicitous in his attempts to bring about reconciliation between his father and his friend. But Michal appears wholly dishonest in her speech to Saul. The text seems to present these events in an approving manner. We will consider their behavior in our attempt to apply this text to our contemporary lives.

---

1. On the literary sources, see Hertzberg, *I and II Samuel*, 163–64; for the historical sequence, see Klein, *1 Samuel*, 194–95.

Jonathan Attempts Reconciliation (19:1–7)

THE OPENING VERSE of the text states laconically that Saul now resolves to draw others into his conspiracy against David. But just as succinctly the narrator reminds us that Jonathan is "very fond of David" (19:1b; see NRSV "took great delight in David"). Because of his friendship and commitment to David (see 18:1–4), Jonathan arranges to serve as an intermediary in order to accomplish a reconciliation with his father. The fact that David is within earshot of the meeting and yet needs a summary of the conversation has led some to theorize that the narrative is a composite text of two earlier sources. But it is perhaps more likely that Jonathan's advice is intended to give David a convenient view of the meeting so that he can assess Saul's attitude for himself. Jonathan will elaborate any details.[2]

Jonathan has carefully planned what he will say. In persuasive fashion, he makes his case before Saul, with David waiting in the wings. He argues that David is in fact innocent of any wrongdoing. On the contrary, his actions have been of great benefit to the king. With disregard for his personal safety, David killed Goliath, at which time Yahweh achieved a great victory and made the king himself rejoice. Jonathan's closing question poignantly emphasizes that killing an innocent man for no reason is itself a wrongdoing. His logic and eloquence win the day, and his father and friend are reconciled. But the peaceable relations are short-lived.

Saul's Second Attempt on David's Life (19:8–10)

THE RETURN OF CONFLICT with the Philistines requires all the military skills that David displayed on previous occasions. The brief mention of war means that David is propelled once more into the forefront of national attention. But more military glory for David results again in more problems with Saul. As before, his victories ignite jealousy in Saul, which leads to yet another spontaneous and unexpected attempt on David's life (cf. 18:6–11). "Flight and escape were to be the facts of David's life while Saul lived, and the word 'fled' becomes a recurring motif in the subsequent narrative."[3]

Michal Helps David Escape (19:11–17)

WE MOVE NOW TO ANOTHER PARAGRAPH in which Saul's child saves David, though this time the break seems permanent. Reconciliation looks hopeless after this episode.

2. Gordon, *I and II Samuel*, 163.

3. Baldwin, *1 and 2 Samuel*, 132.

Michal's ruse shows just how morbid and insane Saul's preoccupation with David is. When troops are dispatched to put David under surveillance with the intent of killing him in the morning, she helps him escape during the night. She anticipates the soldiers may search the house and so places an "idol" (*teraphim*) in David's bed with appropriate disguise. The precise nature of such an idol in the Old Testament is much disputed, and it is apparently only here that one appears large enough to pass for a human under bed coverings. The narrative may contain a subtle derisive tone, suggesting such idols are really good for nothing, though they occasionally come in handy for use in tricks.[4]

The ruse works, giving David time to escape. But when Saul realizes what Michal has done, he becomes angry with her. In order to calm the unpredictable Saul, she deceives him, now for a second time (her "He is ill" was the first). Michal appears to have no hesitation about the deceptions, and the narrator relates the events in an apparently approving tone.[5] Saul's obsession is so severe and irrational that lies contrived between daughter and father seem justifiable. The reader is left with the sad but undeniable realization that Saul is hell-bent on destroying David. In chapter 18, Yahweh was with David. Here Saul is *after* David.

OUR STORY SEEMS to have degenerated into a soap opera. Jonathan has deceived and disobeyed his father for David's sake. Michal shamelessly tricks her father and then lies to cover it up. David has endured the humiliating escape through a window and is now on the run, never to appear in Saul's court again. Brueggemann's comments on this passage are apropos:

> There is nothing here of God or God's will or God's coming kingdom. We are treated to calculating human actions that do not conform to our expectations. Something is deeply awry when a future king must crawl through a window, when the wife of a coming king must lie to the father who is still king. The evil spirit of Saul has infected the whole scene.[6]

---

4. Their use in Gen. 31:19, 34–35 may also reveal a narrator's contempt for the objects. See Judith M. Hadley, "תְּרָפִים," *NIDOTTE*, 4:339; McCarter, *I Samuel*, 326.

5. Klein, *1 Samuel*, 198; see the brief comment in Keil and Delitzsch, *Samuel*, 196: "This prevarication she seems to have considered perfectly justifiable."

6. Brueggemann, *First and Second Samuel*, 144.

Thus this passage confirms, especially when read together with chapter 18, that Saul is no longer fit to serve as Israel's anointed one. He has been placed aside, though the events have yet to bear it out.

Ethical considerations. In the midst of such sordid details, this text also raises certain ethical considerations. The Bible often relates stories of deception and intrigue, but not often as approvingly as our historian does here. Jonathan disobeys his father, and more strikingly, Michal lies to him. In both cases, the narrator assumes they are motivated by just causes, and they are not condemned for their actions. This raises the question often asked by Christian philosophers: Is there any room for justifiable falsehood? Is lying justified or even morally required under certain conditions?

Interestingly, deception can be portrayed in contrasting ways in the Bible. Rachel and Jacob deceive the elderly Isaac, but their ruse plays an important part in the narrative of Genesis to characterize them both as manipulative and conniving (Gen. 27:1–29). Jael pretended to offer protection for Sisera, commander of the Canaanite army from Hazor, who was running from the Israelite forces. But the narrative seems to rejoice in the way she lulled Sisera to sleep and then assassinated him, and the text characterizes Jael as a woman of courage and resourcefulness (Judg. 4:17–21; see 4:9). So in one context, deception is condemned. But in others such behavior is praised.

Take, for example, Shiphrah and Puah, the Hebrew midwives of Exodus 1:15–21. The Egyptian pharaoh tried to control Israelite population growth by demanding that the midwives in charge of Hebrew births kill the boys, allowing only the girls to live. But because the midwives were God-fearing women, they refused to obey the king and allowed the boys to live as well. When the pharaoh demanded to know why they did not obey him, they simply lied (1:19): "Hebrew women are not like Egyptian women; they are vigorous and give birth before the midwives arrive." In this case, the midwives were blessed for their actions. God rewarded them with families of their own because they feared him more than the Egyptian king and chose to risk lying rather than kill the newborn Hebrew boys. Likewise Rahab certainly told a lie to the king of Jericho to save the two Israelite spies (Josh. 2:4–6), and New Testament authors unanimously praise her actions as works of faith (Heb. 11:31; James 2:25).

When we compare these disparate episodes, a certain biblical ethic begins to emerge, which is supported by our text in 1 Samuel 19. Rather than a monolithic prohibition against all lying and deception, the Bible offers a general principle, modified with several exceptions. The general principle is most notably stated in the ninth commandment, which contains a statement against lying in a court of law (Ex. 20:16). Elsewhere the Bible generally disdains all falsehood (Prov. 11:3) and portrays Satan as the "father of lies" (John

8:44; Eph. 4:25). But then we have exceptions such as the Hebrew midwives, who chose to embrace the guilt of deception in order to preserve the lives of the newborns. They unselfishly put themselves at risk before the pharaoh rather than fulfill his gruesome orders.[7]

Jonathan and Michal seem to be in the same category as the Hebrew midwives and Rahab. These biblical characters choose the higher good and are willing to accept the consequences of their choices, even if it puts them at personal risk in order to help an innocent person. Many Christian scholars through the centuries have agreed. Thomas Aquinas distinguished three classes of lies: *officious lies*, or helpful lies of necessity; *jocose lies*, told in jest; and *mischievous lies*, or malicious lies told to harm another person or to save face personally. Only the third category constitutes a sin in Aquinas's view.[8]

I would agree with Aquinas, but I would also warn that the lie of necessity is only morally justified (even morally required?) under certain circumstances, such as rare situations where it is clear that innocent lives are at stake. In this biblical ethic, lying and deception are wrong and to be avoided. However, the actions of Jonathan and Michal, the Hebrew midwives, and others suggest there are times when believers should choose to accept the guilt of lying in order to accomplish a higher good, as they believe it to be defined by God. Thus, we recognize deception as always bad but sometimes desirable in extenuating circumstances.

THE DILEMMA OF TRUTH AND FALSEHOOD. Christian application of the concept of justifiable falsehood is more difficult today than at any time in modern history. The reason is because of the emerging postmodern culture in North America, in which truth claims are no longer simply evaluated as true or false but are subjected to reinterpretation. By definition, our postmodern culture assumes what is "true" for one person may not be "true" for another.[9] Precision is impossible, and the definition of justifiable falsehood is therefore blurred.

---

7. On the various ethical issues involved in the ninth commandment, see Walter C. Kaiser Jr., *Toward Old Testament Ethics* (Grand Rapids: Zondervan, 1983), 222–34.

8. Luther agreed and conveniently categorized these as the humorous, the helpful, and the harmful. However, in this position, Aquinas and Luther demurred from Augustine, who rejected the idea of the so-called "lie of necessity." For this discussion, see Michael G. Moriarty, *The Perfect Ten: The Blessings of Following God's Commandments in a Post-Modern World* (Grand Rapids: Zondervan, 1999), 191–92.

9. Ibid., 192–93. It has been recently argued that the truly healthy individual can change identities. As the mythical Proteus could quickly change shapes, so the postmodern

Perhaps the most obvious and alarming example is President Bill Clinton's deceptions in 1998, which led one social critic to call him the nation's first "postmodern president," who did not feel bound by objective standards of truth.[10] Since truth is conditioned by circumstances, it is capable of being reshaped for the needs of the present situation. The president was able to tell the nation emphatically in a famous quote, "I did not have sexual relations with that woman, Miss Lewinsky," because he redefined the word "sex."[11] In our postmodernist environment, it is impossible to lie because there is no truth.

In such an environment, it may be dangerous for Christians to explore times when falsehood is acceptable because we may find ourselves vulnerable to the postmodern myth concerning truth. Rejecting this aspect of postmodernism, Christians will assert that truth is undivided and that we are still under mandate to be honest and truthful. However, we also must ask if there are times when modern believers would be justified in deceiving intentionally, just as Jonathan and Michal and other biblical characters are praised for doing.

There are plenty of examples in which the answer appears to be yes. Not surprisingly, the best examples come from the experiences of World War II, because in this period believers were faced with the most striking conflict between good and evil and were forced to make the most difficult choices in life. So, for example, an Allied agent might be cooperating with the French resistance in preparations for the great invasion of Normandy on June 6, 1944. If he were captured by the Nazis and asked for information about the invasion, his answers could cost thousands of lives and tip the scales of the war in favor of the Nazis. But a simple lie could lead the Axis forces to make calculated mistakes in their preparations and help the Allied cause immensely. As it turned out, an elaborate system of lies did in fact deceive Hitler, who assumed the invasion would be at another time and place and refused to believe the news when the invasion finally occurred.

---

individual is not restricted by a single set of beliefs, relationships, or character traits. Rather, the possibility always exists to "reinvent" oneself. The truly dysfunctional individual is inflexible and dogmatic about a particular belief system, implying that submission to a particular belief system is tantamount to mental illness. See Robert Jay Lifton, *The Protean Self: Human Resilience in an Age of Fragmentation* (New York: Basic Books, 1993).

10. Josef Joffe, "The First Postmodern President," *Time International Magazine* 148, no. 15 (October 7, 1996), n.p. Online: http://www.time.com/time/international/1996/961007/essay.html. Most appear to be relying on Lifton (*Protean Self*), who long before the scandals of 1998 had praised President Clinton as a man unencumbered by ideology and as one to reinvent himself. On the ease with which many today accept chameleon-like shifts—and in some cases even seek them—see Kenneth J. Gergen, "The Self in the Age of Information," *The Washington Quarterly* 23 (2000): 201–14, esp. 207–8.

11. He was later to do the same thing in his deposition regarding the word "is."

Perhaps a better example is that of Corrie Ten Boom, who was faced with similarly hard choices when hiding Jews in her home during the Nazi occupation of the Netherlands. Jews who were captured were often sent to Amsterdam and from there to Germany, where they were almost never heard from again. Corrie and her family were not in agreement on whether it was justifiable to lie to the Nazi officers in order to protect Jews hiding in their home. Corrie's sister Nollie, for example, insisted on rigid adherence to the concept of truth-telling. She believed that if a Jew were captured because she had answered truthfully, God would nevertheless protect him or her simply because she had been faithful and honest. On at least one occasion, Nollie's refusal to lie resulted in the arrest of a young Jewish woman in their charge.[12]

But Corrie felt the Nazi occupation created exceptional circumstances and that deception was justifiable. She referred to her sister's position as "rigid honesty."[13] Most of the family agreed with Corrie, and they even practiced lying in different scenarios to prepare for occasions when the Gestapo might question their activities.[14] Though they did not approve of deception, it was better to accept the guilt of lying and to ask forgiveness quickly than to turn Jews over to the Nazis. Such responses seem to be completely congruous with the biblical evidence.

It should be stated clearly that such extreme ethical dilemmas are rare for today's American Christians. We should be careful here and not assume that in our context we have frequent situations in which it would be desirable to mislead or deceive another person. Such extreme steps are required only when we are confronted with life-threatening choices. Saul was obsessed with killing David, so that Jonathan and Michal were justified in their actions. Likewise Corrie Ten Boom was justified in her actions when confronted by the policies of another madman, that of Hitler during the Nazi occupation.

---

12. Corrie Ten Boom, *The Hiding Place*, with John and Elizabeth Sherrill (Washington Depot, Conn.: Chosen Books, 1971), 88. Corrie's sister believed that God would not allow the young Jewish woman to suffer because she had obeyed God by being truthful. When the young woman escaped along with thirty-nine other Jews while still in Amsterdam, Corrie wondered if perhaps her sister was right after all (see pp. 105–6).

13. Ibid., 105. Corrie felt it was "dreadfully easy" to lie to the Nazis (p. 66).

14. Ibid., 108–9.

1 Samuel 19:18-24

WHEN DAVID HAD fled and made his escape, he went to Samuel at Ramah and told him all that Saul had done to him. Then he and Samuel went to Naioth and stayed there. ¹⁹Word came to Saul: "David is in Naioth at Ramah"; ²⁰so he sent men to capture him. But when they saw a group of prophets prophesying, with Samuel standing there as their leader, the Spirit of God came upon Saul's men and they also prophesied. ²¹Saul was told about it, and he sent more men, and they prophesied too. Saul sent men a third time, and they also prophesied. ²²Finally, he himself left for Ramah and went to the great cistern at Secu. And he asked, "Where are Samuel and David?"

"Over in Naioth at Ramah," they said.

²³So Saul went to Naioth at Ramah. But the Spirit of God came even upon him, and he walked along prophesying until he came to Naioth. ²⁴He stripped off his robes and also prophesied in Samuel's presence. He lay that way all that day and night. This is why people say, "Is Saul also among the prophets?"

Original Meaning

DAVID WILL NEVER RETURN to the royal court of Saul. The break is real and final, and he must now begin to make other plans. This text tells what happens when David flees from Saul and goes to meet with Samuel at Ramah.

This episode should be read together with 10:1-12, which relates the first time the Spirit of God came mightily on Saul, and he prophesied among the band of prophets.¹ The contrast between the two passages contributes to the extended narrative's growing condemnation of King Saul. The distance between the two anointed ones, David and Saul, continues to increase. As surely as David is certain to become Israel's king, Saul is just as certainly running to his own destruction.

---

1. It is not necessary to take this passage as a later adaptation of the same event, as in Smith, *Samuel*, 181.

Saul Sends Men to Capture David at Ramah (19:18–21)

HAVING FLED FROM SAUL'S WRATH and having no place else to go, David returns to Samuel, whose center for operations is at Ramah (7:17).[2] Though we have not heard anything from Samuel since David's anointing (16:13), he is evidently active as the leader of a band of prophets at Ramah. The irony of David's presence in Ramah with Samuel should not escape us. Though the text of 1 Samuel 10 does not say so explicitly, it appears that this is the place where God led Saul and Samuel to meet for the first time and where the old prophet anointed Saul king of Israel (10:1–8).[3] If so, this is also where Saul first received the promise of the Spirit of God and where his heart was transformed (10:6, 9). Now, however, the tide has turned, and it is David who meets Samuel at Ramah.

Samuel takes David to "Naioth at Ramah" (19:18–19). The Hebrew word translated "Naioth" is probably not a proper noun (as in NIV) but rather a reference to "camps," or remote country dwelling places, which could become the residences of shepherds and could be associated with the dwelling place of God.[4] Perhaps Samuel's prophetic group lives in these camps and is accustomed to meeting God there. When Saul's espionage sources tell him where David is, he sends three detachments to these camps at Ramah to capture David. But in all three instances, his envoys become enamored with the feverish worship, and they also prophesy in the spirit of God and are thereby distracted from their unworthy errand.

Saul Prophesies at Ramah (19:22–24)

FINALLY, OUT OF FRUSTRATION AND DESPERATION, Saul goes himself to the camps at Ramah. But before he even reaches the group, the "Spirit of God" comes, and he begins prophesying as the others before him. It is possible to interpret this "Spirit of God" as the same evil spirit *from* God that had plagued Saul (16:14; 18:10; 19:9).[5] Others have suggested that only Saul lies before Samuel "all that day and night," in this ecstatic state of external unconsciousness. The soldiers who prophesy do so only a short time, their consciousness returning earlier than Saul's. In this reading, the text is condemning Saul irrevocably as someone who has resisted God's grace and opposed God's purposes with regard to David.[6] The soldiers who prophesy under the Spirit's

---

2. On the terminology used here connecting this unit with chs. 20–21, see comments on 20:1–23.

3. Baldwin, *1 and 2 Samuel*, 133.

4. For details, see *HALOT*, 2:679, and Gerald H. Wilson, "נוה," *NIDOTTE*, 3:54–56.

5. Klein, *1 Samuel*, 198.

6. Keil and Delitzsch, *Samuel*, 197–98.

influence are not detained so long because they are mere emissaries on Saul's behalf. In any case, Saul's prophetic ecstasy before Samuel lasts an entire day, giving David plenty of time to escape.

The question closes the chapter, "Is Saul also among the prophets?" Its earlier use in 10:11 implied a positive evaluation of Saul. But here, the question, which must have been used in earliest times to characterize Saul, can only imply a negative evaluation. The irony of the question challenges the genuineness of Saul's prophetic behavior and thus also his legitimacy as king of Israel.[7]

WHEN BOTH SAUL and David were anointed with oil and marked as messianic leaders of God's people, they received the "Spirit" of God (cf. 10:1–13; 16:1–13; see comments). In both cases, the terminology implies a sudden burst of heroic strength or prophetic ecstasy, which empowers them for service (10:10; 16:13). In Saul's case, the arrival of the Spirit changed his heart, and he became a different person (10:6, 9). In David's case, the Spirit simply came "in power," and the effects became evident when he defeated Goliath (16:13; ch. 17).

In order to move from the original context of this account to contemporary meaning, it is necessary to read this paragraph in light of these previous arrivals of God's Spirit, especially Saul's first experience with divine inspiration recorded in 10:1–13. Though the terminology here is only slightly different, the context and results of God's inspiration are *considerably* different. Just as the first Spirit-anointing signaled the beginning of Saul's career, this one signals the end. Rather than baptizing Saul at the inception of his reign and empowering him to rule with peace and justice, the Spirit now constrains him from harming David. "The spirit of Yahweh now haunts him rather than helps him."[8]

In the first inspiration of Saul, he joins the band of ecstatic prophets as a welcomed guest. Here, however, he is an unwelcome enemy. In this sense, the recurrence of the question ("Is Saul also among the prophets?") may be interpreted as a sarcastic piece of irony. When we read them together, these two occurrences of the question may reflect opposing evaluations of Saul when compared to the ecstatic prophets. On the first occasion they are not fit company for him; now he is not fit company for them.[9]

---

7. Youngblood, "1, 2 Samuel," 717.
8. McCarter, *I Samuel*, 329.
9. W. McKane, *I and II Samuel* (Torch Bible Commentaries; London: SCM, 1963), 122.

THE APPLICATION OF this text takes the form of two simple observations. (1) God's empowering Spirit is a two-edged sword. The victory that God inspires for one is in fact a defeat for another. The same divine intervention that makes it possible for David to kill Goliath now prohibits Saul from killing David. The difference is human responsibility and faithfulness. The tragedy here is that Saul had been the beneficiary of that intervention, whereas now he has become the victim. The extended narrative is not blaming God as capricious or whimsical. The blame rests solely on Saul as a king who has become unfit for ruling. Brueggemann has summarized this well:

> The pitifully embarrassing scene is that of this once great man, still tall but no longer great, exhausted by demanding religious exercise (verse 24), clearly not in control, shamed, now rendered powerless in a posture of submissiveness. This episode is an act of dramatic de-legitimation of Saul.[10]

(2) This picture of Saul leads naturally to our second observation. The presence of God's empowering Spirit is no *guarantee* of future blessing. Gifted persons and inspired leaders often begin to feel invincible. The evangelical church in the last quarter of the twentieth century saw several of its most visible leaders stumble or even completely lose their ministries (e.g., Gordon MacDonald, Jimmy Swaggart, and Jim Bakker). There is innate danger in the heresy that Spirit-led ministry is invincible, irrespective of continued faithfulness.

This, of course, has implications for all of us as individuals, since we cannot live today on the spiritual blessings of our childhood or early adulthood. But the wider implications for the church are also obvious. No generation can afford to enjoy the spiritual benefits of their ancestors without giving any thought to their own responsibility in service and ministry. The church is always only one generation from extinction.

---

10. Brueggemann, *First and Second Samuel*, 145.

1 Samuel 20:1-42

THEN DAVID FLED FROM NAIOTH at Ramah and went to Jonathan and asked, "What have I done? What is my crime? How have I wronged your father, that he is trying to take my life?"

2"Never!" Jonathan replied. "You are not going to die! Look, my father doesn't do anything, great or small, without confiding in me. Why would he hide this from me? It's not so!"

3But David took an oath and said, "Your father knows very well that I have found favor in your eyes, and he has said to himself, 'Jonathan must not know this or he will be grieved.' Yet as surely as the LORD lives and as you live, there is only a step between me and death."

4Jonathan said to David, "Whatever you want me to do, I'll do for you."

5So David said, "Look, tomorrow is the New Moon festival, and I am supposed to dine with the king; but let me go and hide in the field until the evening of the day after tomorrow. 6If your father misses me at all, tell him, 'David earnestly asked my permission to hurry to Bethlehem, his hometown, because an annual sacrifice is being made there for his whole clan.' 7If he says, 'Very well,' then your servant is safe. But if he loses his temper, you can be sure that he is determined to harm me. 8As for you, show kindness to your servant, for you have brought him into a covenant with you before the LORD. If I am guilty, then kill me yourself! Why hand me over to your father?"

9"Never!" Jonathan said. "If I had the least inkling that my father was determined to harm you, wouldn't I tell you?"

10David asked, "Who will tell me if your father answers you harshly?"

11"Come," Jonathan said, "let's go out into the field." So they went there together.

12Then Jonathan said to David: "By the LORD, the God of Israel, I will surely sound out my father by this time the day after tomorrow! If he is favorably disposed toward you, will I not send you word and let you know? 13But if my father is inclined to harm you, may the LORD deal with me, be it ever so severely, if I do not let you know and send you away safely. May the LORD be with you as he has been with my father. ¹⁴But show me unfailing kindness like that of the LORD as long as I live, so that I may not be killed, ¹⁵and do not ever cut off your kindness from my family—not even when the LORD has cut off every one of David's enemies from the face of the earth."

¹⁶So Jonathan made a covenant with the house of David, saying, "May the LORD call David's enemies to account." ¹⁷And Jonathan had David reaffirm his oath out of love for him, because he loved him as he loved himself.

¹⁸Then Jonathan said to David: "Tomorrow is the New Moon festival. You will be missed, because your seat will be empty. ¹⁹The day after tomorrow, toward evening, go to the place where you hid when this trouble began, and wait by the stone Ezel. ²⁰I will shoot three arrows to the side of it, as though I were shooting at a target. ²¹Then I will send a boy and say, 'Go, find the arrows.' If I say to him, 'Look, the arrows are on this side of you; bring them here,' then come, because, as surely as the LORD lives, you are safe; there is no danger. ²²But if I say to the boy, 'Look, the arrows are beyond you,' then you must go, because the LORD has sent you away. ²³And about the matter you and I discussed—remember, the LORD is witness between you and me forever."

²⁴So David hid in the field, and when the New Moon festival came, the king sat down to eat. ²⁵He sat in his customary place by the wall, opposite Jonathan, and Abner sat next to Saul, but David's place was empty. ²⁶Saul said nothing that day, for he thought, "Something must have happened to David to make him ceremonially unclean—surely he is unclean." ²⁷But the next day, the second day of the month, David's place was empty again. Then Saul said to his son Jonathan, "Why hasn't the son of Jesse come to the meal, either yesterday or today?"

²⁸Jonathan answered, "David earnestly asked me for permission to go to Bethlehem. ²⁹He said, 'Let me go, because our family is observing a sacrifice in the town and my brother has ordered me to be there. If I have found favor in your eyes, let me get away to see my brothers.' That is why he has not come to the king's table."

³⁰Saul's anger flared up at Jonathan and he said to him, "You son of a perverse and rebellious woman! Don't I know

that you have sided with the son of Jesse to your own shame and to the shame of the mother who bore you? ³¹As long as the son of Jesse lives on this earth, neither you nor your kingdom will be established. Now send and bring him to me, for he must die!"

³²"Why should he be put to death? What has he done?" Jonathan asked his father. ³³But Saul hurled his spear at him to kill him. Then Jonathan knew that his father intended to kill David.

³⁴Jonathan got up from the table in fierce anger; on that second day of the month he did not eat, because he was grieved at his father's shameful treatment of David.

³⁵In the morning Jonathan went out to the field for his meeting with David. He had a small boy with him, ³⁶and he said to the boy, "Run and find the arrows I shoot." As the boy ran, he shot an arrow beyond him. ³⁷When the boy came to the place where Jonathan's arrow had fallen, Jonathan called out after him, "Isn't the arrow beyond you?" ³⁸Then he shouted, "Hurry! Go quickly! Don't stop!" The boy picked up the arrow and returned to his master. ³⁹(The boy knew nothing of all this; only Jonathan and David knew.) ⁴⁰Then Jonathan gave his weapons to the boy and said, "Go, carry them back to town."

⁴¹After the boy had gone, David got up from the south side of the stone and bowed down before Jonathan three times, with his face to the ground. Then they kissed each other and wept together—but David wept the most.

⁴²Jonathan said to David, "Go in peace, for we have sworn friendship with each other in the name of the LORD, saying, 'The LORD is witness between you and me, and between your descendants and my descendants forever.'" Then David left, and Jonathan went back to the town.

DAVID IS ON THE RUN. When it became obvious that Saul had ill intentions toward him, he ran first to Samuel, perhaps in order to confirm his anointing and divine favor (19:18–24). In this text he runs to Jonathan for another attempt at reconciliation with Saul. Earlier Jonathan showed a willingness to act as mediator between David and Saul (19:1–7). David was earnestly willing and ready to try any means necessary to resolve the conflict between himself and Saul, as the subsequent narratives reveal repeatedly. This is one more attempt of his to give reason and calm a chance, and he hopes Jonathan will be able to help.

At the beginning of this text, Jonathan appears unconvinced that Saul really intends to do harm to David, and only the events at the New Moon festival persuade him that he must take action to protect David. The chronological relationship between this chapter and the previous two is confusing.[1] Saul has already attempted to kill David on two occasions (18:10–11; 19:9–10). Jonathan has been aware of Saul's desire to kill David, at least in part (19:1), and David has had to run for his life (19:11–17). It seems unlikely that David and Jonathan need further convincing about Saul's intentions or that David will be an expected guest at Saul's table for the New Moon festival.

But as we have stated elsewhere, this historian is not concerned with historical precision (see comments in the introduction).[2] The kerygmatic or homiletical agenda of our historian means he subordinates the details of the history in order to make greater impact on the reader. Legitimizing David's right to kingship and understanding his and Jonathan's characters are more central to the story than narrating the correct sequence of events. In this case, the historian has reserved this emotional and extended text for the conclusion of the unit that explains why David must leave Saul's service and say farewell to his trusted comrade, Jonathan.

The event is presented in three scenes. The New Moon festival (20:24–34) is framed by two conversations between Jonathan and David (20:1–23 and 35–42).

Jonathan and David Devise a Plan (20:1–23)

THIS ACCOUNT BEGINS with an expression that connects 19:18–21:15 as a series of "flight" stories. Four sequential units begin with almost identical expressions to describe David's departure from one location to another (Heb. *wayyabo'*, lit., "and he went"; see 19:18; 20:1; 21:1; 21:10); three of these are additionally modified by another verb, "flee" (Heb. *brḥ*). First, David fled from Saul's approaching soldiers and went to Samuel at Ramah (19:18). Then he flees Naioth at Ramah and goes to Jonathan, presumably back in Gibeah (20:1). Next, David goes to Nob, that is, to the priest Ahimelech (21:1). Finally, he flees Saul and goes to Achish, king of Gath (21:10). Together, these four units illustrate the desperate circumstances in

---

1. For discussion, see Hertzberg, *I and II Samuel*, 171–72; McCarter, *I Samuel*, 343; Klein, *1 Samuel*, 204–5.

2. The mention of "Naioth at Ramah" in v. 1 may imply the chapter is chronological after all; see Youngblood, "1, 2 Samuel," 719.

which David meets with Jonathan. He needs safety and support. He needs to know who his friends are.

Jonathan had earlier established a covenant with David and had essentially abdicated his right to succeed Saul as king of Israel (18:1–4). David therefore feels he can trust Jonathan to act surreptitiously in order to learn the true disposition of the king and to help determine what he should do next. They agree on the ruse at the next day's New Moon festival as a test case for Saul's true intentions. The first day of the lunar month was designated as a day of rest and feasting, and specific sacrifices were prescribed according to Numbers 28:11–15.

The elaborate speeches of Jonathan (1 Sam. 20:12–15, 16, 18–23) contain more than a simple plan to determine Saul's intentions toward David. Acknowledging that David will certainly one day be king, Jonathan confirms his covenant commitment to David and desires to protect his own children when David in fact becomes king. He also speaks frankly and prophetically about David's future international rule, which is a new theme in the books of Samuel. These speeches of Jonathan have been called "the thematic centerpiece of the story of Jonathan," for they legitimize David's rule as the rightful successor to the throne of Israel and underscore the future relationship between the house of Saul and the house of David (20:15–16, NIV's "family" in v. 15 is "house" in Heb.).[3]

Saul's New Moon Festival (20:24–34)

AT FIRST GLANCE, David's absence at Saul's table seems like no more than a simple gaffe in social etiquette, though it could also represent a preference for David's ancestral line over the rightful place of Saul's royal lineage ("our family is observing a sacrifice in the town," 20:29).[4] Such an explanation may indicate that David's absence betrays his own royal aspirations, or so Saul may have assumed.

Whatever the implications, the reader is hardly prepared for the violent reaction of Saul in verse 30. He refers three times to David as "the son of Jesse" (20:27, 30, 31), which is perhaps derogatory.[5] But after hearing the full explanation for David's absence (20:28–29), Saul erupts into a full-fledged tirade in which he insults Jonathan personally, which one scholar has called "a burst of foul-mouthed anger."[6] Some of the modern translations concur with the

---

3. Bergen, *1, 2 Samuel*, 214–15.

4. Baldwin, *1 and 2 Samuel*, 135–36.

5. Assumed to be so by most commentaries. But see Gordon, *I and II Samuel*, 168.

6. Hertzberg, *I and II Samuel*, 175. Hertzberg is correct in stating that the reproach of Jonathan's mother is not actually against her but Jonathan himself, as in one such familiar reproach in English.

NIV's "You son of a perverse and rebellious woman!" as an English euphemism for a more graphic insult intended by the original (as in NLT's "You stupid son of a whore!" and NJB's "Son of a rebellious slut!").

Saul's shocking outburst reveals a new element in his obsession with David and helps explain why Jonathan and David finally realize they must abandon all hopes of reconciliation with Saul. In verse 31, Saul's suspicion of David (which has been prominent in his obsession; see 18:12, 14–15, 28–29) becomes a conviction that David's rapid rise not only threatens Saul personally, but also Jonathan and the hopes of a Saulide dynasty in Israel. Saul says to Jonathan, "As long as the son of Jesse lives on this earth, neither you nor your kingdom will be established." It is no longer enough to drive David away from the royal court at Gibeah, because Saul sees him as a threat to the dynasty even after Saul's death.

It has now become necessary, in Saul's mind, to take David's life in order to protect his own heritage. His fear and jealousy of David have grown into an irrational obsession with eliminating him as a means of ensuring his own future through Jonathan. This establishes the pattern of episodes that follow in 1 Samuel.[7] David has been driven from Saul's court at Gibeah, but the king will not stop there. Saul is convinced he must pursue David and take his life at almost any cost. He finishes his speech to Jonathan with the command, "Now send and bring him to me, for he must die!"

When Jonathan tries yet again to defend David's motives, Saul reaches for his spear to kill even Jonathan![8] One scholar has argued that Jonathan's role throughout these chapters has oscillated "between close identification with David and an emptying of himself into David," showing a readiness to be replaced by David as Saul's successor.[9] So here Saul threatens to impale Jonathan as he previously attempted to impale David (18:11; 19:10). "The identification of Jonathan and David is total: an act directed at one is an act directed at the other."[10] Jonathan is sure of Saul's resolve to kill his friend. Sadly, the time has come for Jonathan and David to part company. Jonathan must remain with Saul; David cannot.

Jonathan and David Say Farewell (20:35–42)

JONATHAN MEETS HIS friend at the predetermined location and communicates the bad news by the agreed-upon ruse. The boy used as a means of clan-

---

7. McCarter, *I Samuel*, 345.

8. The LXX supports a different vowel reading for the Hebrew, which implies that Saul *raises* his spear against Jonathan without actually going so far as *hurling* at him (as in NIV). See McCarter, *I Samuel*, 339; Smith, *Samuel*, 194; Gordon, *I and II Samuel*, 168. This interpretation is also possible for 18:11.

9. Jobling, *1 Samuel*, 93–98 (quote is from 96).

10. Ibid., 98.

destine communication is unaware of his role and goes back to Gibeah without a care (20:40). Jonathan, however, returns to the city burdened with problems that appear to have no resolution (20:42 [MT 21:1]).[11]

After the youngster is sent away, the two bid farewell in an emotional scene. One might ask if it is safe to meet in such a fashion, why was it necessary to use the elaborate ruse in the first place? But David and Jonathan have no way of knowing in advance if they will be able to speak face to face, and the secretive way of communicating seems wise. Further, this may be an example of strong emotions, so vividly expressed in the text, overcoming their better wisdom.[12]

Once alone and aware that circumstances have worked against them, they are overcome with emotion. Characterized as it is by physical signs of respect, mutual devotion, and sorrow (bowing, embracing, and weeping), this text powerfully illustrates the depth and profundity of the relationship between Jonathan and David. In this tearful good-bye, it is Jonathan who recognizes their only recourse: "Go in peace." This he follows with one last reminder that their oath of loyalty is witnessed by Yahweh himself, which Jonathan hopes will assure peaceable relations between his descendants and David's. This text, of course, creates a tension throughout the rest of 1 and 2 Samuel, resolved finally in David's relationship with Jonathan's son, Mephibosheth (2 Sam. 9; 21:1–14). After this scene, David and Jonathan will only see each other on one other occasion (1 Sam. 23:16–18).

IN BRIDGING THE DISTANCE from this ancient text to our own day, we have several options. The text has a decidedly forward-looking feature. Jonathan is convinced that David will one day rule Israel, and throughout the narrative he is keenly aware of what this could mean for his family. He knows that most ancient Near Eastern kings feel obligated to exterminate the descendants of other pretenders to the throne, and indeed most ancient readers would assume that David would execute all of Saul's children. In his speeches to David, Jonathan is careful to emphasize his covenant-based relationship with David in the hopes that David will preserve his children, regardless of what happens in the future (20:14–15, 42). Thus, we could explore the messianic themes that surround David's rise to the throne and the gracious way in which he kept faith with Jonathan's family once he became king.

---

11. The last phrase of the NIV ("Then David left, and Jonathan went back to the town") is 21:1 in the Heb. text, leaving a one-verse difference between English translations and Hebrew throughout ch. 21.

12. Gordon, *I and II Samuel*, 169.

But this text also has a decidedly retrospective feature. In the central and most dramatic moment of the narrative, Saul is once again moved by his anger and jealousy to curse his own son and to reveal to Jonathan (and to the reader) that he is indeed bent on destroying David (20:30–31). Thus, we could explore again the results of unchecked anger, jealousy, and fear in the life of Saul, which relates further to his failure as Yahweh's first king for his people Israel.

The ḥesed relationship. However, these two themes are developed more fully elsewhere in 1 Samuel. What really holds chapter 20 together is the relationship between David and Jonathan. That relationship drives them to find together solutions to their problems with Saul. When it becomes clear that no solutions are available to them, their tenacious relationship drives them again, this time to make future commitments to each other that have implications for the rest of 1 and 2 Samuel. It is Jonathan's commitment to David that partially makes it possible for David to survive and replace Saul as king. And it is David's faithfulness to Jonathan that leads him to preserve Mephibosheth in order to honor Jonathan's name, as we will see (2 Sam. 9:7; 21:7).

Using this passage, we could explore the simple virtues of friendship in general. But our text has considerably more to teach us. The essence of that relationship between David and Jonathan is a covenant that involves promises of mutual protection. They are committed to looking out for each other. Jonathan will do all he can to protect David; likewise, David will look after Jonathan. But the whole arrangement depends completely on the covenant relationship with its fierce loyalty. What holds the unit together is the prospects of relational faithfulness.

The specifics of this are detailed in two speeches, one of David's and one of Jonathan's. Both appeal to the covenant or relational loyalty of the other in order to motivate each other to fidelity in their relationship (cf. NIV's "kindness" in 20:8, 14–15). The term used in these verses has many important theological connotations and is important for reading the Old Testament in general (ḥesed, variously translated "loyalty, faithfulness, kindness, love, mercy," etc.).[13] It can have either human or divine features, since it is used to characterize God's relationship with humans or human relationships with each other.[14]

---

13. BDB, 338–39; DCH, 3:277–81. There have been several important monographs written on the term, notably Gordon R. Clark, *The Word Ḥesed in the Hebrew Bible* (JSOTSup 157; Sheffield: Sheffield Academic Press, 1993); Nelson Glueck, *Ḥesed in the Bible*, trans. Alfred Gottschalk (Cincinnati: HUC Press, 1961); Katharine D. Sakenfeld, *The Meaning of Ḥesed in the Hebrew Bible: A New Inquiry* (Missoula, Mont.: Scholars Press, 1978). For general survey of the issues and more bibliography, see David A. Baer and Robert P. Gordon, "חסד," *NIDOTTE*, 2:211–18. Also see Katharine D. Sakenfeld, *Faithfulness in Action: Loyalty in Biblical Perspective* (Philadelphia: Fortress, 1985).

14. Sakenfeld has defined it as "a responsible keeping of faith with another with whom one is in a relationship" (*Meaning of Ḥesed*, 233).

The preponderance of the 246 uses of *ḥesed* refer to God's beneficent actions expressed toward humans. In essence, *ḥesed* is the life-sustaining grace of God that makes it possible for humans to have a loving relationship with him. Opinions differ, but it appears that the *ḥesed* relationship is characterized by bilateral commitment, meaning the parties involved are mutually obligated, regardless of relative status. When used to describe Yahweh's relationship to his people, his *ḥesed* becomes the essence of the covenant itself. Because of his prior commitment or covenant with his people, God's boundless *ḥesed* is evident in his salvation from disaster or oppression. It is God's *ḥesed* that makes it possible for his people to relate to him at all. But even in Israel's covenant relationship with Yahweh, there is a reciprocity assumed, a mutual commitment on their part that requires faithful service and obedience.

Besides the covenant relationship between Yahweh and Israel, the Old Testament also has covenants between humans. The concept of *ḥesed* is central to these relationships as well, regardless of the status of the individuals involved. Moreover, *ḥesed* in such human relationships is frequently something one *does* or *performs*. It is not simply an abstraction. If it is genuine, *ḥesed* exhibits concrete expression of the underlying attitude through one's actions to another. This is frequent in the formulaic expression "show [lit., do] kindness to someone."[15]

These details provide important background for our passage, since David's plea is for Jonathan to "show kindness" because of their previous covenant (20:8; cf. 18:1–4). Most scholars agree that such kindness implies one member in the relationship is in a position to render help or aid to the other, who is for one reason or another in need and unable to help himself.[16] Furthermore, the help is performed simply because of the deep and enduring relationship between the two friends, which is sometimes also sealed by covenant, as is the case here. It is natural to emphasize the need for *ḥesed* in situations where its performance is in question, where it seems unnatural, or where future circumstances may render it unlikely that one friend will help the other.

Thus, David recognizes that Jonathan will undoubtedly come under incredible pressure to support Saul and to abandon their covenant relationship, with its attendant commitments of loyalty. Saul will certainly require Jonathan to hand David over to him. He pleads for Jonathan to remain loyal to their relationship (i.e., show *ḥesed*). The alternative? "If I am guilty, then kill

---

15. BDB, 338, I.1; *DCH*, 3:278–79.
16. See esp. Clark, *The Word Ḥesed*, 267.

me yourself!" (20:8). Sadly, David's fears quickly come to fruition in the next scene, when Saul takes up the spear to threaten his own son, revealing that he will certainly attempt to kill David (20:33).

Likewise, Jonathan pleads with David to "show kindness" and never "cut off" his *hesed* to Jonathan's descendants (20:14–15). Jonathan looks beyond the current crisis with Saul to its unseemly, but apparently unavoidable, continuation in the future. Their roles are reversed now in that the crown prince is asking David for favors. When David replaces Saul as king, Jonathan is concerned that David will remain loyal to him and preserve the life of his children. Thus, in both cases, one friend has a way to aid the other in services no other friend can perform. Jonathan can help David with Saul now, and David can help Jonathan with the crisis of the future.

Furthermore, Jonathan's use of the formulaic "show kindness" in verse 14 combines the human and divine uses of *hesed* because he asks for the "kindness of Yahweh" (NIV "unfailing kindness like that of the LORD"). Scholars have debated the significance of this "*hesed* of Yahweh," but it is probably a covenant oath claiming Yahweh as a witness or an idiomatic way of expressing the superlative, "the greatest possible kindness."[17] Besides the intersection of divine and human features of this important term, Jonathan's "*hesed* of Yahweh" also provides a link between this passage and 2 Samuel 9, where "*hesed* of Elohim [God]" occurs (2 Sam. 9:3; NIV's "God's kindness").[18] Jonathan's plea anticipates David's kindness or loyalty to Jonathan's son, Mephibosheth (2 Sam. 9:1; see 21:7).

Perhaps more significantly, Jonathan's plea is a bold and confident assertion about David's future. David is asking for help in his attempt to run for his life. In such uncertain circumstances his good friend says, as it were, "No, but it is I who should be asking favors from you." Jonathan is certain that David will be king, and though the present circumstances are not favorable, his concern turns to his role and that of his family in David's future kingdom. Hertzberg has summarized the situation eloquently.

> David is on the brink of flight, he is now dependent, and will soon be an outlaw; in the foreseeable future he will have to make decisions such as those now made by Saul and Jonathan, royal decisions. The Lord's plans are firmly and clearly contrasted to the present moment. The man shortly to be exiled will nevertheless become a king.[19]

---

17. BDB, 338, I.1; *DCH*, 3:279; Baer and Gordon, "חסד," 2:212.
18. Youngblood, "1, 2 Samuel," 722.
19. Hertzberg, *I and II Samuel*, 174.

FIDELITY AND LOYALTY. What drives this text forward is the question of fidelity in the covenanted relationship between David and Jonathan. Will Jonathan remain loyal to David even in the face of the harshest opposition from his father? Will he look for compromise and try to placate his father's fears while trying to keep David in the fold? The answer comes in verse 34, when Jonathan storms out of Saul's presence without eating because of his disgust at his father's treatment of his friend. It is Jonathan's faithfulness that also permeates the closing scene, when he protects David and urges him to flee.

But the closing lines turn the whole relationship around, when Jonathan reminds David that their covenant relationship should also mean peace between their descendants (20:42). Jonathan pleads for David's help in the future, as David has needed his help in the present. Just as the question of Jonathan's fidelity drives 1 Samuel 20, the question of David's fidelity will become a central question in the chapters to follow and well into 2 Samuel.

The message of fidelity in covenanted relationships speaks as powerfully today as it did in the biblical context. Especially compelling is the *permanency* of the commitment between David and Jonathan, which grew out of their covenant relationship rooted in love (20:17). The relevance of this discussion on faithfulness for contemporary culture in North America should be readily apparent and applicable on several levels. Our society today longs for models of such permanency or lasting commitment in relationships.

Generally, Christians today bemoan what is happening in our culture concerning the abandonment of children by parents, the crumbling of traditional marriages, and the broken and dishonorable way in which business is conducted in today's marketplace. The concept of *ḥesed*-faithfulness in this text holds up a discernible model that teaches about advanced decision-making and mutual dependence. Thus the Bible opens up a whole different perspective into the potential of human relationships. Against much of modern pop culture, this text teaches that it is possible for humans to build relationships that are durable and employable in God's plan for the future.

Larger social issues. Most Christians are content with applying these biblical principles to a limited number of selected issues. We are often satisfied to address family values without tackling the larger social problems. Certainly the lessons of 1 Samuel 20 are applicable to the needy marriages and parent-child relationships of our generation. It teaches us that it is possible to be so radically committed to each other that our families can survive and grow into healthy, unbreakable relationships even when change and external pressures attack. But does the David and Jonathan friendship covenant have anything to say to the larger social issues?

For example, many Christians today are slow to explore the way greed and materialism in American society affect the poor. We generally abhor all forms of communism and are quick to teach that the collapse of Soviet communism in the closing decades of the twentieth century is a lesson that Marxism in general is an exhausted and vanquished ideology. There is no question that the form of liberation theology that was so influential from 1965 to 1990 is a decaying system and is in crisis at the moment in many Third World countries.[20] But it will also not be sufficient to appeal to a simple market-driven capitalism as the only true alternative. True democratic capitalism must be tempered and held in check, in a way that has never been successfully accomplished, by Christian ideals, such as faithfulness in relationships with fellow humans.

This text illustrates those Christian ideals. It is Christianity itself that made democracy and free-market capitalism possible, through its emphasis on human freedom.[21] But it is also Christianity that teaches us about ḥesed relationships. We must be committed to our fellow human beings so that *all* can enjoy our economic prosperity, not just those who look and sound like us. We are called to live in ḥesed loyalty with those less fortunate than we are, which, as we have seen, implies a determination to help a brother or sister who is unable to provide such aid for themselves. While embracing the concept of free enterprise, John Perkins reminds us that greed and exploitation create a system that is just as oppressive as communism is ineffective.

> Free enterprise, as it now exists, falls far short of God's standard. It has failed to distribute the earth's resources equitably. And when Christianity should have been calling the American free enterprise system to account for its immoral stewardship, it was instead "baptizing" the system, adopting free enterprise as an implicit "article of faith." Free enterprise has become almost a religious doctrine that justifies our greed and substitutes token charity for real economic justice. It enables us to blame the victims of oppression for their own poverty and lets us feel little responsibility to redistribute our wealth to the needy. The result of such a system is predictable—increasing production by the rich, but continuing poverty for the oppressed.
>
> . . . While some economic systems are better than others, no system will serve the people well as long as those who control it are motivated by greed. We as Christians must champion an alternative.

---

20. Humberto Belli and Ronald Nash, *Beyond Liberation Theology* (Grand Rapids: Baker, 1992).
21. Ibid., 97–114.

... Despite its serious failures I don't want to throw out the free enterprise system. The freedom which many use to satisfy their greed can also be used to develop economic enterprises not based on greed. The free enterprise system gives us the freedom to create businesses designed to serve, rather than to exploit.[22]

The *ḥesed* loyalty illustrated in 1 Samuel 20 provides a basis for our understanding of such commitment to our fellow human beings. A fully Christian application of covenant relationships will consider not only how this informs our family relationships and our church partnerships, but also our larger commitments to the social structure in which we live. As David and Jonathan were faithful in their responsibilities to each other, so may today's church be faithful in her responsibilities to the world.

---

22. John Perkins, *With Justice for All* (Ventura, Calif.: Regal Books, 1982), selections from 168–70.

1 Samuel 21:1–22:23

DAVID WENT TO NOB, to Ahimelech the priest. Ahimelech trembled when he met him, and asked, "Why are you alone? Why is no one with you?"

²David answered Ahimelech the priest, "The king charged me with a certain matter and said to me, 'No one is to know anything about your mission and your instructions.' As for my men, I have told them to meet me at a certain place. ³Now then, what do you have on hand? Give me five loaves of bread, or whatever you can find."

⁴But the priest answered David, "I don't have any ordinary bread on hand; however, there is some consecrated bread here —provided the men have kept themselves from women."

⁵David replied, "Indeed women have been kept from us, as usual whenever I set out. The men's things are holy even on missions that are not holy. How much more so today!" ⁶So the priest gave him the consecrated bread, since there was no bread there except the bread of the Presence that had been removed from before the LORD and replaced by hot bread on the day it was taken away.

⁷Now one of Saul's servants was there that day, detained before the LORD; he was Doeg the Edomite, Saul's head shepherd.

⁸David asked Ahimelech, "Don't you have a spear or a sword here? I haven't brought my sword or any other weapon, because the king's business was urgent."

⁹The priest replied, "The sword of Goliath the Philistine, whom you killed in the Valley of Elah, is here; it is wrapped in a cloth behind the ephod. If you want it, take it; there is no sword here but that one."

David said, "There is none like it; give it to me."

¹⁰That day David fled from Saul and went to Achish king of Gath. ¹¹But the servants of Achish said to him, "Isn't this David, the king of the land? Isn't he the one they sing about in their dances:

"'Saul has slain his thousands,
    and David his tens of thousands'?"

¹²David took these words to heart and was very much afraid of Achish king of Gath. ¹³So he pretended to be insane in their presence; and while he was in their hands he acted like a madman, making marks on the doors of the gate and letting saliva run down his beard.

¹⁴Achish said to his servants, "Look at the man! He is insane! Why bring him to me? ¹⁵Am I so short of madmen that you have to bring this fellow here to carry on like this in front of me? Must this man come into my house?"

²²:¹David left Gath and escaped to the cave of Adullam. When his brothers and his father's household heard about it, they went down to him there. ²All those who were in distress or in debt or discontented gathered around him, and he became their leader. About four hundred men were with him.

³From there David went to Mizpah in Moab and said to the king of Moab, "Would you let my father and mother come and stay with you until I learn what God will do for me?" ⁴So he left them with the king of Moab, and they stayed with him as long as David was in the stronghold.

⁵But the prophet Gad said to David, "Do not stay in the stronghold. Go into the land of Judah." So David left and went to the forest of Hereth.

⁶Now Saul heard that David and his men had been discovered. And Saul, spear in hand, was seated under the tamarisk tree on the hill at Gibeah, with all his officials standing around him. ⁷Saul said to them, "Listen, men of Benjamin! Will the son of Jesse give all of you fields and vineyards? Will he make all of you commanders of thousands and commanders of hundreds? ⁸Is that why you have all conspired against me? No one tells me when my son makes a covenant with the son of Jesse. None of you is concerned about me or tells me that my son has incited my servant to lie in wait for me, as he does today."

⁹But Doeg the Edomite, who was standing with Saul's officials, said, "I saw the son of Jesse come to Ahimelech son of Ahitub at Nob. ¹⁰Ahimelech inquired of the LORD for him; he also gave him provisions and the sword of Goliath the Philistine."

¹¹Then the king sent for the priest Ahimelech son of Ahitub and his father's whole family, who were the priests at Nob, and they all came to the king. ¹²Saul said, "Listen now, son of Ahitub."

"Yes, my lord," he answered.

¹³Saul said to him, "Why have you conspired against me, you and the son of Jesse, giving him bread and a sword and inquiring of God for him, so that he has rebelled against me and lies in wait for me, as he does today?"

¹⁴Ahimelech answered the king, "Who of all your servants is as loyal as David, the king's son-in-law, captain of your bodyguard and highly respected in your household? ¹⁵Was that day the first time I inquired of God for him? Of course not! Let not the king accuse your servant or any of his father's family, for your servant knows nothing at all about this whole affair."

¹⁶But the king said, "You will surely die, Ahimelech, you and your father's whole family."

¹⁷Then the king ordered the guards at his side: "Turn and kill the priests of the LORD, because they too have sided with David. They knew he was fleeing, yet they did not tell me."

But the king's officials were not willing to raise a hand to strike the priests of the LORD.

¹⁸The king then ordered Doeg, "You turn and strike down the priests." So Doeg the Edomite turned and struck them down. That day he killed eighty-five men who wore the linen ephod. ¹⁹He also put to the sword Nob, the town of the priests, with its men and women, its children and infants, and its cattle, donkeys and sheep.

²⁰But Abiathar, a son of Ahimelech son of Ahitub, escaped and fled to join David. ²¹He told David that Saul had killed the priests of the LORD. ²²Then David said to Abiathar: "That day, when Doeg the Edomite was there, I knew he would be sure to tell Saul. I am responsible for the death of your father's whole family. ²³Stay with me; don't be afraid; the man who is seeking your life is seeking mine also. You will be safe with me."

AFTER THEIR EMOTIONAL FAREWELLS at the end of the previous chapter, Jonathan goes back to Gibeah, but David simply goes away (NIV "left," 20:42b).¹ The fact is, Jonathan has some place to go whereas David is now officially alone in exile. He is in desperate need to

---

1. The grammar of the Hebrew would support a translation such as "David rose and departed, but Jonathan went back into the city." This phrase is actually the first verse of ch. 21 in the Heb. text, leaving a one-verse difference between English translations and Hebrew throughout the chapter.

escape the murderous intentions of Saul. These two chapters begin the unit on David's permanent estrangement from Saul, which continues through the end of 1 Samuel. The first portion of this unit (21:1–15) introduces three new characters who will play important roles in future narratives and explains David's relationship to each: Ahimelech the priest, Doeg the Edomite, and Achish the Philistine king. The second section (22:1–23) shows the risks involved in helping David.

The geographical features of these chapters illustrate David's flight from Saul's service in the royal court. Saul was originally from Gibeah of Benjamin, which became the location of his rule and therefore became known as the "Gibeah of Saul" (1 Sam. 11:4; 15:34; 2 Sam. 21:6; see also 1 Sam. 10:26; 13:2, 15–16; 14:2, 16; 22:6; 23:19).[2] In the early period of David's association with Saul, he was presumably free to come and go in Gibeah as he pleased (cf. 1 Sam. 16–18). But then David fled to Samuel at Ramah, just north of Gibeah (19:18–24).[3] Next he escaped Ramah and went to Jonathan, who was presumably back in Gibeah (20:1).

Now David finds it necessary to flee to the priest Ahimelech at Nob, just two and one-half miles southeast of Gibeah and slightly north of Jerusalem (21:1). His flight from Saul eventually takes him to Achish, king of Gath, which is significantly farther away (about twenty-three miles southwest of Nob, 21:10). When that fails to be beneficial, David escapes to the cave of Adullam (approximately ten miles east of Gath, which is sixteen miles southeast of Jerusalem, 22:1). The identifications for Mizpah of Moab and the forest of Hereth are not possible (22:3, 5).

All of these references follow David's journeys as he moves farther and further from central royal power at Gibeah and into the fringes of Judahite society. These references create suspense in the extended narrative, as the reader sees David forced through no fault of his own to move farther from God's anointing purposes and call on his life (16:1–13). David is the man after God's own heart and the chosen replacement for Saul. Through these circumstances, he is being forced in the opposite direction. How will these tensions be resolved?

David Flees to Ahimelech the Priest (21:1–9)

WE KNOW FROM other references that Ahimelech the priest was the son of Ahitub (22:9, 11, 20), who was in turn the son of Phinehas, son of Eli (14:3).

---

2. On the extensive scholarly debate surrounding the identification of this city and its relationship to Geba of Benjamin, see Patrick M. Arnold, *Gibeah*, 39–54.

3. On the terminology tying these "flight" stories together, see comments on 20:1–23. For a helpful map of these locations, see McCarter, *I Samuel*, 352–53.

These many years after the death of Eli and his sons (4:17–18), the priestly responsibilities were continued by Eli's great-grandson and eighty-five surviving members of the priestly family (22:18) in the city of Nob, in the vicinity north of what would become Jerusalem.[4] David is uncertain he can confide openly in the priest, so he uses subterfuge to avoid revealing the entire situation.[5] He receives aid from Ahimelech, though the real purpose for his presence in Nob may have been to "inquire" of Yahweh, which is only revealed later (22:10, 15). The sad consequences of Ahimelech's involvement with David will only be revealed in the next chapter.

You can learn a lot about a person by seeing where they turn in times of trouble. When David first found it necessary to run from Saul, he went to Samuel at Ramah (19:18–24). The prophets at Ramah were unable to guarantee his safety for any extended time, so he went back to Gibeah to seek Jonathan's intercession (20:1–42). Now officially on the run, David is in immediate need of food, arms, and shelter. In desperation he goes to Ahimelech, the priest at Nob, where he receives "the bread of the Presence" of Yahweh and the sword of Goliath, reminding him of his reliance on Yahweh at other times of conflict and crisis. He enthusiastically accepts Goliath's sword, which is unique in its ability to prompt images of strength and victory in Yahweh's cause: "There is none like it; give it to me."[6]

Earlier he received the aid of the old prophet Samuel; now he gets the assistance of a priest of Yahweh in the old traditions of the tabernacle at Shiloh. The reminder of the military victories of his youth in the name of Yahweh (referred to twice here, 21:9, 11), together with his contacts with prophet and priest, helps David turn to the faith of his childhood. In his greatest hour of need, David is reminded that Yahweh has been his help in time of trouble (Ps. 34; 52; 56 are tied to this period in David's life by the Jewish tradition contained in their superscriptions).

David Flees to King Achish of Gath (21:10–15)

HAVING BENEFITED ALL he could and not wishing to endanger further the gracious priests at Nob, David needs to continue to distance himself from Saul.

---

4. The town must have been in close proximity to Jerusalem, though the exact location is unknown (Isa. 10:32). See Jeffries M. Hamilton, "Nob," *ABD*, 4:1133.

5. Whether David shrewdly avoids exposing his plight or intentionally deceives the priest is a matter of interpretation (Youngblood, "1, 2 Samuel," 727–28). In any event, David later accepts full responsibility for the death of the priests (22:22).

6. Having only a sling and stones, David had used Goliath's own sword to cut off the warrior's head in the Valley of Elah, and he had kept the sword briefly in his home (17:51, 54). It is possible he subsequently offered the sword as a gift to the tabernacle in honor of Yahweh (see Keil and Delitzsch, *Samuel*, 184–85).

This paragraph narrates his failed attempt to join himself to the Philistines, though it foreshadows the important coalition to be formed later with Achish (chs. 27–29).

Interestingly, the servants of Achish identify David as "king of the land," which probably means they think of him as a local chieftain or ruler, while they still recognize Saul as king of the Hebrews.[7] At any rate, they must not have realized his real status as a refugee on the run from Saul. Their acknowledgement of David as "king" of *any* kind is ironic, in that such an identification on the lips of Israel's inveterate enemies underlines "the fact that the divine plan is inviolably bound up with David."[8]

The paragraph is also a humorous indictment of the Philistines, who can be so easily duped by the quick-thinking David. Not only was Achish gullible, but by his own admission, the city of Gath is so full of crazy men they have no use for any more![9]

David at Adullam and Mizpah (22:1–5)

BEING DRIVEN OFF by the Philistines, David now withdraws to Adullam, where he is met by family members and four hundred malcontents, who join forces with him in a loosely organized army. Those men who are drawn to David are unhappy with the way things are going for one reason or another. They are oppressed (NIV "in distress"), in debt, or otherwise embittered by their circumstances. It is from this motley band of men that David begins to form a fiercely loyal inner circle of followers, which is to become a personal army. This group will grow into at least six hundred (see 23:13) and become an important ingredient of the rest of his rule over Israel (see 2 Sam. 23:8–39).

While on the run, David's famous father and the rest of his family will likely also be threatened. When it becomes necessary to seek refuge outside of Saul's reach and therefore outside the borders of Judah, it seems logical to turn to the homeland of Jesse's grandmother, Ruth the Moabitess (Ruth 4:17).

The Slaughter of the Priests of Nob (22:6–23)

THE NARRATIVE NOW returns to the priestly family at Nob. The account is only briefly interrupted in order to detail accounts of David's flight from Saul, including his sojourns in Gath, Adullam, and Moab.

As the scene opens, Saul is surrounded with all the trappings of power: seated on a hill in the royal city, spear in hand, powerful officials all around

---

7. McCarter, *I Samuel*, 356–57.

8. Hertzberg, *I and II Samuel*, 183.

9. Klein, *1 Samuel*, 217.

(22:6).[10] Yet the point of the narrative is that he is in fact powerless to do anything about David, no matter how outrageous and abhorrent his attempts. When Saul accuses his court officials of conspiring against him to conceal Jonathan's support of David, only Doeg the Edomite responds. This character was introduced in passing as "one of Saul's servants" in 21:7, where he happened to observe David's activities in Nob. Doeg, being an Edomite and having no compulsion about sparing David or the priests at Nob, sees this as an opportunity to turn his good fortune into political advantage. He informs Saul about Ahimelech's aid for David, and Saul promptly condemns the priests to death, despite Ahimelech's denial of participation in a conspiracy. When the Israelite officials uniformly refuse to carry out Saul's death sentence, Doeg is conscripted to perform the ghastly service for Saul.

Only one member of the priestly family escapes, Abiathar. When he runs to David with the news, David takes full responsibility for the terrible consequences of his relationship with Ahimelech. However, the reader knows that which David can only surmise. The real causes for the disaster are Saul's irrational pursuit of David and the treachery of Doeg the Edomite.[11]

Interpreters usually comment on Saul's slaughter of the priests of Nob as legally unjustified and morally outrageous, explicable only as the desperate actions of a madman. But recent investigations of legal and cultural conventions from the ancient Near East challenge this interpretation, making it possible to see Saul's actions as based on conventional ancient practice, though still an act of desperation.[12] Specifically, oracular priests and diviners were sometimes required to take oaths of loyalty to the king, committing themselves to serve in essence as informants if they learned of any rebellion in the land. By Ahimelech's own admission, he made oracular inquiry on David's behalf rather than Saul's and failed to inform Saul of David's activities, implicating himself and his fellow priests as coconspirators in rebellion (22:15; also 22:10). The result of such sedition was usually the death penalty. Thus Saul's actions can be understood as a rational act, though still a desperate and evil attempt to maintain power by relying on human power structures.

David implores Abiathar to remain with him where he will be safe, so that David becomes the protector of the last surviving priest. As a result, king-elect and priest-elect join forces as fellow fugitives, and they forge a relationship that will last throughout David's reign.[13]

---

10. Gibeah was Saul's home and played a significant role in his reign (see 10:5, 26; 22:6). On its identification as Geba (modern Jeba), see Arnold, *Gibeah.*

11. Klein, *1 Samuel,* 222.

12. For details, see J. J. M. Roberts, "The Legal Basis for Saul's Slaughter of the Priests of Nob (1 Samuel 21–22)," *JNSL* 25 (1999): 21–29.

13. Youngblood, "1, 2 Samuel," 737.

THE PRIMARY POINT OF THIS PASSAGE may not be immediately apparent or necessarily easy to relate to our contemporary context. Our work is complicated since there are supplementary themes that we could also develop. The primary concept that we should develop first is the historian's concern for prophecy and fulfillment, which is supplemented by issues related to human power structures and their dismal role in human history.

Prophecy and fulfillment. The main narration of the text is the encounter between David and Ahimelech in 21:1–9 and the slaughter of Ahimelech and his fellow priests in 22:6–23.[14] The first prepares for the other, and together they represent the author's main focus, which is to relate the death of the priests of Eli's line as fulfillment of the prophecy in 2:31–36. The narration also characterizes Saul as someone hopelessly committed to evil intentions, while it characterizes David as someone surrounded with his childhood faith in the midst of crisis.

When we read this text in light of several others earlier in 1 Samuel, we realize our historian has carefully recorded a double fulfillment of prophecy. In 2:27–36, an anonymous "man of God" appeared to Eli and announced the entire Elide house would suffer the consequences of his family's wickedness.[15] Eli himself would be the last elderly priest of the line (2:22); all others would die young. The initial fulfillment of the prophecy occurred when Eli's sons, Hophni and Phinehas, died on the same day, which also resulted in the pitiable end of Eli's life (4:11–18). Now many years later, we learn of the violent deaths of eighty-five priests in the family line of Eli, which means the curse has been fulfilled again. But even here, one escapes (Abiathar) and joins David in his flight from Saul. The ultimate fulfillment of this prophecy awaits Solomon's early reign, when he replaces Abiathar with Zadok (1 Kings 2:26–27, 35).

The biblical historian's concern for tying together prophecy with its fulfillment is clear in the reference to the original prophecy (1 Kings 2:27): "So Solomon removed Abiathar from the priesthood of the LORD, fulfilling the word the LORD had spoken at Shiloh about the house of Eli." In this way the Old Testament historians emphasize the sovereign rule of God over Israel. He is indeed king of Israel, and he is faithful to what he prophesies. Even during the dark days of Saul's worst crimes, God is fulfilling his word to Israel and accomplishing his purposes for David.

---

14. Between them are miscellaneous episodes concerning David's flight from Saul, which further prepare the reader for the rest of 1 Samuel.

15. The curse was confirmed through the boy Samuel in 3:11–14.

Interpreters approach biblical prophecy in one of at least three ways. (1) Some take a strictly *historical* approach to prophecy, meaning they assume the oracles relate only to the past and that whatever fulfillment can be expected has already occurred. (2) Others take a *dispensational* approach, which assumes that each prophecy has one and only one fulfillment. In this way, a specific prophecy can be said to await future fulfillment if it can be shown that it has not taken place in history. (3) Others assume a *progressive fulfillment* approach, in which it is assumed that prophecies may have meaning in two or more events.[16] This is not to say a prophecy has multiple meanings but that it has both near future and distant future applications.

The prophecy in 2:27–36 has a near future application in the deaths of Eli, Hophni, and Phinehas. It has subsequent applications in the deaths of Ahimelech and his fellow priests at Nob and in the displacement of Abiathar. This text and its relationship to others on Eli's family give us a perspective on biblical prophecy that helps us see it as finding fulfillment in partial and incomplete ways at various points in history before an ultimate fulfillment in the distant future.

The faithfulness of God. The fact that God is faithful to fulfill his prophetic word concerning Eli also has implicit significance for these narratives on Saul and David. As we have said, emphasizing the fulfillment of an ancient prophetic word is one way of highlighting the faithfulness of God. He is still at work to accomplish his purposes, even in these gruesome and hopeless circumstances. And there are prophetic words hovering over the actions of Saul and David. Saul has been rejected as king (15:28), while David has been designated to replace him (16:1–13). In both cases, the prophecy has been announced by the ideal prophet, Samuel himself. By implication we are being taught that just as certainly as God fulfilled his word concerning Eli's family, so his words concerning David and Saul will be fulfilled.

Saul, in his desperate grasping after power and his dependence on *Realpolitik*, or human power structures, is a pathetic and doomed figure. His paranoia and suspicion have isolated his own officers, and his insidious obsession with David has now cost the lives of Ahimelech and the innocent priests of Nob. By contrast, David has turned to the familiar faith of his childhood in his time of crisis and has sought help from priests, prophets, and strangers alike. The two—Saul and David—are traveling in opposite directions. The reader gets the impression in both cases that God will fulfill his word to them, as God has now fulfilled his word concerning Eli's family in these awful events at Nob.

---

16. Willem A. VanGemeren, *Interpreting the Prophetic Word* (Grand Rapids: Zondervan, 1990), 80–83.

FULFILLMENT OF THE PROPHETIC WORD. This text illustrates that in the worst of times and under the most calamitous circumstances, people go in opposite directions seeking extreme solutions. But God is still at work behind the scenes accomplishing his purposes. The most obvious way in which God is at work in this text is by bringing his prophetic word to fruition. While David finds protection and provisions in exile, Saul gives the ludicrous command to execute the priests at Nob. Though this looks like the desperate act of a godless king, we know from our book-level reading that in fact, this is fulfillment of God's Word. God had foretold the execution of the Elide priesthood many years before.

The effective ministry of God's Word in the world is a recurring theme in the books of Samuel.[17] Just as this text narrates how God brought the prophecy concerning the Elide priesthood to fulfillment, other texts emphasize the saving power of God's Word. The prophetic call of Samuel in 1 Samuel 3 emphasized three facets of that Word (see comments there). (1) The Word of God is certain and true, whether for good or ill. God sets the standard, and his Word announces the verdict. His Word finds fruition in the lives of those for whom his voice is intended. (2) His Word is evocative, calling the hearer (reader?) to service and submission. It is intended to arouse us from our lethargy, as it aroused the young Samuel from his early morning sleep. (3) God's Word is transformative, changing all who respond to his call. Thus, it has a ministry of both information and transformation, which can be illustrated in many biblical texts.

This text serves to illumine all three facets of God's Word. The overarching theme of the text is that God's Word is certain and true, as illustrated in the death of the Elide priests at Nob. Certainly our world needs to hear precisely this message. In previous decades many attacked the validity of the Bible and challenged the trustworthiness of God's Word. In today's emerging postmodernism, we are faced with a different challenge. The postrationalistic nature of our emerging generation rejects the idea that truth is absolute and purely rational.[18] Many today dethrone human intellect altogether and turn instead to other paths of truth besides reason, such as the emotions and intuition. Though there are positive aspects of such a shift, it is still necessary to communicate this simple truth of the gospel: God will be

---

17. This is true for most of the Old Testament historical books generally, leading many to assume these books have their origins in the prophets (as per Jewish tradition, Talmud, *b. B. Bat.* 14b).

18. Grenz, *A Primer on Postmodernism*.

faithful to his Word. This message comes as comfort to the believer and cause for alarm for the unbeliever.

This last phrase raises another challenge for our generation, namely, the lack of concern for the Bible's message of condemnation. Our culture has so tainted the Bible's portrait of God that we hear little talk of the consequences of rebellion. Yet this text clearly shows that God was faithful to his oracle of judgment against the Elide priests and that he will therefore be faithful to his oracles against Saul. We can infer from this that God will be faithful to his oracles of eternal judgment for those who continually rebuff his grace.

The second and third facets of God's Word were that it is evocative and transformative. Misery is the natural and inevitable consequence for those who choose not to be rightly related to God and his Word. It is only logical to conclude that we cannot believe in God without also believing in a destiny for those who do not want God.[19] C. S. Lewis emphasized that no one goes to heaven deservingly, and no one ever goes to hell unwillingly:

> There are only two kinds of people in the end: those who say to God, "Thy will be done," and those to whom God says, in the end, "*Thy* will be done." All that are in Hell, choose it. Without that self-choice there could be no Hell. No soul that seriously and constantly desires joy will ever will it. Those who seek find. To those who knock it is opened.[20]

David and Saul illustrate the two types of people identified in the quote by Lewis. David illustrates the person who responds to God's call and begins the lifelong process of transformation. Saul is the contrastive figure, who shows the natural and inevitable consequences of refusing God's call. In this text, the two are going in opposite directions. The narrator has driven a wedge between Saul and David, and the distance is greater with each passing chapter.

The contrast between these two cannot be more acute than in their reactions to the priests of Nob. David regretfully accepts blame for the massacre, while ironically Saul seems resolute in his condemnation of the priests. Saul is ultimately responsible for their deaths, though David humbly accepts the blame. Saul is slowly and gradually self-destructing, while David is successively growing in strength and self-assurance. This process will continue until Saul is dead and David is king. This much we know because God's Word has proclaimed it so.

---

19. Walls, *Hell*, 157–59. Walls argues in general that heaven is for sinners who want to spend eternity with God, while hell is for sinners who want to spend eternity apart from God.

20. C. S. Lewis, *The Great Divorce* (New York: Macmillan, 1946), 72–73.

1 Samuel 23:1–29

WHEN DAVID WAS told, "Look, the Philistines are fighting against Keilah and are looting the threshing floors," ²he inquired of the LORD, saying, "Shall I go and attack these Philistines?"

The LORD answered him, "Go, attack the Philistines and save Keilah."

³But David's men said to him, "Here in Judah we are afraid. How much more, then, if we go to Keilah against the Philistine forces!"

⁴Once again David inquired of the LORD, and the LORD answered him, "Go down to Keilah, for I am going to give the Philistines into your hand." ⁵So David and his men went to Keilah, fought the Philistines and carried off their livestock. He inflicted heavy losses on the Philistines and saved the people of Keilah. ⁶(Now Abiathar son of Ahimelech had brought the ephod down with him when he fled to David at Keilah.)

⁷Saul was told that David had gone to Keilah, and he said, "God has handed him over to me, for David has imprisoned himself by entering a town with gates and bars." ⁸And Saul called up all his forces for battle, to go down to Keilah to besiege David and his men.

When David learned that Saul was plotting against him, he said to Abiathar the priest, "Bring the ephod." ¹⁰David said, "O LORD, God of Israel, your servant has heard definitely that Saul plans to come to Keilah and destroy the town on account of me. ¹¹Will the citizens of Keilah surrender me to him? Will Saul come down, as your servant has heard? O LORD, God of Israel, tell your servant."

And the LORD said, "He will."

¹²Again David asked, "Will the citizens of Keilah surrender me and my men to Saul?"

And the LORD said, "They will."

¹³So David and his men, about six hundred in number, left Keilah and kept moving from place to place. When Saul was told that David had escaped from Keilah, he did not go there.

¹⁴David stayed in the desert strongholds and in the hills of the Desert of Ziph. Day after day Saul searched for him, but God did not give David into his hands.

¹⁵While David was at Horesh in the Desert of Ziph, he learned that Saul had come out to take his life. ¹⁶And Saul's son Jonathan went to David at Horesh and helped him find strength in God. ¹⁷"Don't be afraid," he said. "My father Saul will not lay a hand on you. You will be king over Israel, and I will be second to you. Even my father Saul knows this." ¹⁸The two of them made a covenant before the LORD. Then Jonathan went home, but David remained at Horesh.

¹⁹The Ziphites went up to Saul at Gibeah and said, "Is not David hiding among us in the strongholds at Horesh, on the hill of Hakilah, south of Jeshimon? ²⁰Now, O king, come down whenever it pleases you to do so, and we will be responsible for handing him over to the king."

²¹Saul replied, "The LORD bless you for your concern for me. ²²Go and make further preparation. Find out where David usually goes and who has seen him there. They tell me he is very crafty. ²³Find out about all the hiding places he uses and come back to me with definite information. Then I will go with you; if he is in the area, I will track him down among all the clans of Judah."

²⁴So they set out and went to Ziph ahead of Saul. Now David and his men were in the Desert of Maon, in the Arabah south of Jeshimon. ²⁵Saul and his men began the search, and when David was told about it, he went down to the rock and stayed in the Desert of Maon. When Saul heard this, he went into the Desert of Maon in pursuit of David.

²⁶Saul was going along one side of the mountain, and David and his men were on the other side, hurrying to get away from Saul. As Saul and his forces were closing in on David and his men to capture them, ²⁷a messenger came to Saul, saying, "Come quickly! The Philistines are raiding the land." ²⁸Then Saul broke off his pursuit of David and went to meet the Philistines. That is why they call this place Sela Hammahlekoth. ²⁹And David went up from there and lived in the strongholds of En Gedi.

THE CONTRAST BETWEEN SAUL AND DAVID increases as we progress through 1 Samuel 21–31. The previous two chapters illustrated the process. As David fled away in order to put *physical* distance between himself and Saul, the narrator highlighted the *symbolic* distance between them. Saul teaches the reader the natural and inevitable consequences of refusing God's call, while David shows what happens when one responds to God's call and begins the lifelong process of transformation. At the book level, the text continues to contrast Yahweh's two anointed ones. The first has rejected Yahweh's authority and is running headlong to his own destruction. The second is the ideal messianic figure and continues to make choices motivated only by loyalty and reliance on God's strength. These two are moving in opposite directions.

This text continues the contrast between Saul and David by relating the events surrounding the Philistine attack on the city of Keilah and the subsequent events in the southern deserts of Judah. The previous chapter related the destruction of the priestly city of Nob by Saul, who killed the priests, their families, and the inhabitants of the city (22:19). Ironically, David now takes actions to save a Judahite city, though its citizens appear to have no particular feeling of support for him (23:12).

These events provide the narrator with background information to highlight a contrast of greater significance between Saul and David, namely, the way the two men make important decisions. David consistently inquires of Yahweh before making any important moves, whereas Saul is dependent on rumors and espionage. David seems keenly aware of God's guidance and leadership in his life, while Saul seems out of touch and indifferent to divine guidance. In sum, this text is a case study in contrasting approaches between someone who is seeking to *perform* God's will and someone who is seeking to *avoid* God's will.

David Saves Keilah (23:1–6)

THE PHILISTINE THREAT, which played a role in the rise of the monarchy itself, has receded into the background of the narrative tracing David's rise to power. Now these people are once again threatening the borders of central Judah. The city of Keilah is located in the low-lying hills of the west, known as the Shephelah, approximately eight miles northwest of Hebron.[1] Its location in the hills between Judah and Philistia make it particularly vulnerable to various raids, such as the one described here on the threshing floors. Such

---

1. LaMoine F. DeVries, "Keilah," *ABD*, 4:13–14.

agricultural locations would not have been heavily defended, but the loss of grain would have created a burden for the inhabitants.

David's reliance on the Lord is accented here. He uses Abiathar the priest to discern Yahweh's will concerning whether he should go to Keilah or not. When his men balk because of Philistine superior strength in the area, David checks again in order to confirm the message from God. The technical phrase used here for discerning God's will (NIV "inquired of the LORD," 23:2, 4) becomes an important theme in this chapter and elsewhere in the David narratives. The phrase in Hebrew is literally to "ask of Yahweh" (the verb *š'l*, used with the preposition *b* denoting the one being asked).[2] This phrase is a technical expression for inquiring an oracle of God when a simple affirmative or negative response can be anticipated.[3]

The reference to Abiathar and the priestly ephod ties these events together with the previous episode (22:20–23) and presumably means David's inquiries are answered by means of the sacred lots, the Urim and Thummim stored in the ephod (Ex. 28:30; Lev. 8:8; Num. 27:21). The specifics of how these worked is not clear, but they served as a form of divinely sanctioned lot-casting, which may have functioned something like our "heads" or "tails."[4] Since Abiathar is now with David permanently, he can easily inquire of the Lord before taking any serious action.

This important feature of David's relationship with God is central in the contrast between Saul and him. Yahweh has long since stopped answering Saul's inquiries, presumably because Saul has made up his mind before asking (14:36–37). This silence of Yahweh for Saul persists until the very end of his life (28:6). By contrast, Ahimelech earlier inquired of Yahweh on David's behalf (22:10, 13, 15), which may be when David learned the value of such inquiries. Other narratives in David's rise to kingship emphasize the importance he attaches to seeking such information from God (see, e.g., 30:8; 2 Sam. 2:1; 5:19, 23; 16:23).

---

2. Usually this is "Yahweh," but "God" occurs in the expression in 14:37; 22:13, 15; also 2 Sam. 16:23.

3. John A. Beck, "שאל," *NIDOTTE* 4:7–10.

4. The words "urim" and "thummim" have been taken to mean "accursed" and "acquitted," or else words to symbolize the first and last letters of the Hebrew alphabet. Their appearance has been guessed as small pebbles, dice, or more likely, sticks. They apparently ceased to be used after the time of David. See Roland de Vaux, *Ancient Israel: Its Life and Institutions* (New York: McGraw-Hill, 1965), 353; J. Lindblom, "Lot-Casting in the Old Testament," *VT* 12 (1962): 164–78. For a different opinion on the nature of the Urim and Thummim, see Cornelis Van Dam, *The Urim and Thummim: A Means of Revelation in Ancient Israel* (Winona Lake, Ind.: Eisenbrauns, 1997); for an Assyrian parallel using black and white stones, see Victor Hurowitz, "A Psephomancy Ritual from Assur," *COS*, 1.127:444–45.

In one important passage near the end of 1 Samuel, however, Saul becomes so desperate because Yahweh has refused to give any answer, either by dreams or Urim or prophets, that he contacts a medium (28:6, see comments). The contrast between Saul and David continues, as David consistently and faithfully inquires of Yahweh while Saul gets no answer.[5] Saul may appear to have the upper hand politically, but David has God's guidance.

David Escapes Keilah (23:7–14)

SAUL SHOULD HAVE REJOICED in the deliverance of Keilah from the Philistines. But his only thoughts are of how much easier it will be to trap David in a city "with gates and bars" than in the open country. David is still painfully aware of his role in the tragic deaths of the citizens of Nob (22:6–23), and he fears the same will happen now at Keilah, as his prayer reveals (23:10): "Saul plans to come to Keilah and destroy the town on account of me." It is a shocking fact that Saul is mustering his troops to capture *David* rather than to take advantage of the victory to pursue the Philistines further.[6] The citizens of Keilah would be anxious to avoid the same fate as Nob, regardless of how grateful they may be to David. They would be compelled to surrender David to Saul. In order to avoid more innocent bloodshed, David and his men escape into the desert of Ziph, a city of Judah approximately five miles southeast of Hebron.[7]

As Saul's hostility against David intensifies, the narrator informs us that "God did not give David into his hands." This reminder keeps before us the question of royal authority in Israel. While the two anointed ones, Saul and David, are trudging through these military and political circumstances, playing their deadly game of hide-and-seek, Yahweh, the true king of Israel, is in charge, and ultimately his plan will be accomplished.

Jonathan Reassures David (23:15–18)

DAVID'S LOCATION is further identified as "Horesh," which appears to be located approximately two miles south of Ziph, though some take it to mean "wood" or "wooded height."[8] As in other texts where Jonathan and David appear together, the crown prince acknowledges the future greatness of David, though this statement is the most explicit of all (cf. 18:1–4;

---

5. Fokkelman, *Narrative Art and Poetry in the Books of Samuel*, 2:430.

6. As implied by the word order of v. 9; see Klein, *1 Samuel*, 230.

7. The identification of the site is in some dispute. See H. Darrell Lance, "Ziph," *ABD*, 6:1104.

8. LaMoine F. DeVries, "Horesh," *ABD*, 3:288.

20:11–17). Jonathan's intent is to strengthen David's hand in God (NIV "helped him find strength in God," 23:16b), which implies encouragement. David is no doubt encouraged by their long-standing friendship, but perhaps more by Jonathan's certainty and optimism about the future (23:17): "You will be king over Israel, and I will be second to you." Ironically, this is the last time they see each other.

Saul Pursues David Farther South (23:19–29)

SAUL CONTINUES HIS PURSUIT OF DAVID with the help of the Ziphites. The city of Maon is approximately eight miles south-southeast of Hebron and just over four miles south of Ziph.[9] These geographical references are used somewhat imprecisely, not because the narrator is confused about their locations but because many of these events occur in the open fields and hills between occupied cities. David is being forced to find refuge in the remote cracks and crevices of the southern deserts of Judah.

The narrator has already informed us that God did not give David into Saul's hands (23:14). The same Yahweh who delivered the Philistines into David's hands now protects David from the hand (i.e., the power) of Saul.[10] The irony here is again the role of the Philistines. Just as Saul is closing in on David and feels he has him trapped at long last, word comes of another Philistine raid, forcing Saul to abandon his pursuit of David. The hand of Yahweh is clearly behind these events, since he is free to use any means necessary to protect David, even the perennial threat of the Philistines.

The text also contributes to the extended narrative's emphasis on the contrast between Saul and David. Saul's pathetic reliance on rumors and reconnaissance missions is a reminder that Yahweh has ceased answering his pleas for help (see 14:36–37; cf. 28:6). Saul has long since stopped seeking messages from Yahweh, depending instead on his own political and strategic decision-making abilities. In this chapter, he receives word that David is in Keilah, and he immediately concludes, "God has handed him over to me" (23:7). Again, the inhabitants of Ziph approach him and inform him of David's presence among them, and Saul responds with a request for more intensive espionage and reconnoitered information (23:19–23). In his desperate obsession with killing David, he is completely dependent on his own wisdom and whatever information he can gather from informants. All of this while the king should have been concerned instead about the Philistines.

---

9. LaMoine F. DeVries, "Maon," *ABD*, 4:512–13.

10. On the importance of the repetition of "hand" in chs. 23–24, see Youngblood, "1, 2 Samuel," 738.

By contrast, David is himself inflicting losses on the Philistines and doing so with the help of Abiathar. This text presents us with two occasions when David consults the priestly ephod for guidance. The first is when David needs divine direction concerning the Philistine threat against Keilah, and the second when he needs guidance in his attempt to escape the clutches of his father-in-law, King Saul. This practice of consulting Yahweh becomes David's standard modus operandi throughout much of his reign. By contrast, Saul has executed the priests who could have helped him, and he seems incapable of hearing God's word.

THE NEED FOR DIVINE GUIDANCE. David here receives guidance about his actions through divine disclosure (Abiathar's ephod) and human confirmation (Jonathan's encouragement). Yahweh answers his queries through the approved priestly means, and Jonathan voluntarily confirms the larger picture of God's plan for David's life. Saul's activities are recorded as a foil for the narrator's ideal picture of David. In contrast to David, Saul relies on espionage and subterfuge, which leaves him helpless and vulnerable to attack by the Philistines. Saul fails to inquire of Yahweh until it is too late (28:6), and even then he is wrongly motivated and the means he uses are ill-advised (i.e., the medium of Endor).

The need for divine guidance is an undeniable link between believers of Bible times and today. The contrast in this text between David and Saul thus offers us timeless truths about reliance on God alone for the important decisions of life. Indeed, the Bible has much to say about receiving and acting on divine guidance.

The ancestral narratives of Genesis have many examples of hearing and receiving messages from God—from Abram's original call (Gen. 12:1–4) to Jacob's stairway dream (28:10–22). Though we can never be quite certain of the exact means of God's communication to Abram (audible voice, inner impression, writing in the sky?), we know that his "promises" became central in the Abrahamic story, and indeed in the book of Genesis.[11] There were many subsequent occasions when God repeated these promises to Abraham, Isaac, and Jacob. Even when we are not certain of how that ancestral "voice of God" was communicated, it is clear that God provided guidance and protection for his children.

With the provision of Moses and the Sinai covenant, God continued to offer guidance. Whether through a burning bush (Ex. 3–4), pillars of cloud

---

11. For details, see Bill T. Arnold, *Encountering the Book of Genesis*, 72–73, 200–202.

and fire (13:21–22; Num. 9:15–23), or a theophany complete with thunder and lightning and trumpet blast (Ex. 19:16), God was clearly guiding his people. The covenant itself came complete with a written word from God, which included the Ten Commandments and many applications of the law (Ex. 24:4; Deut. 31:9, 24). This written expression of God's will quickly became the primary means by which God communicated with his people, though he also made provisions for the priestly ephod with its Urim and Thummim for special occasions (as illustrated in this text).

The means of divine guidance changed as biblical revelation progressed. After the rise of Old Testament prophecy, God relied on specific, designated individuals in order to communicate with his people. In many situations, the prophets did not reveal something entirely new but rather interpreted the older written traditions for a current situation. The word of God revealed through the Sinai covenant needed interpretation for each new period of Israel's history, so the prophets were mediators and enforcers of the old covenant for each new situation.[12]

During and after the Babylonian exile, the Jews turned more and more to the written word as God's divinely approved means of guidance and direction. As "the people of the book," they were the immediate predecessors of the earliest Christians, who likewise turned to the sacred pages of the Old Testament for divine guidance. Thus, the authors of the New Testament went to great lengths to base their message on the Old Testament, as is illustrated by the New Testament's sheer mass of quotations of or allusions to the Old Testament.[13]

In the New Testament two passages are especially pertinent to the question of divine guidance. The apostle Paul emphasized the transformation of the Christian's mind in contrast to conformity to the wisdom of the world. As a result, believers can discern God's will, which is good and pleasing and perfect (Rom. 12:2). Similarly, James promises that anyone who lacks wisdom can ask of God, who gives generously to everyone, and it will be granted (James 1:5). In the tradition of the Old Testament, "wisdom" is knowledge that deepens one's relationship with God and makes clear the course of action that is pleasing to God and life-sustaining for the believer. Here and elsewhere in the New Testament, it is assumed that the believer can know and perform God's will for his or her life.

---

12. Israel's psalms and wisdom literature also speak about divine guidance (see, e.g., Ps. 25:8–9, 12; 32:8; Prov. 3:6).

13. The authors of the New Testament made 295 explicit references to the Old Testament, comprising some 352 verses of the New. See Roger Nicole, "Old Testament Quotations in the New Testament," in *Hermeneutics*, ed. Bernard L. Ramm (Grand Rapids: Baker, 1971), 41–42.

The result of the Bible's emphasis on divine revelation is an expectation that God will indeed provide direction and guidance for his people. Whether through whirlwind (Job 38–41), human-like theophany (Josh. 5:13–15), a gentle whisper (1 Kings 19:12), or a consistent prophetic voice, we can be assured that God desires to communicate with his people. But for most contemporary believers, this is precisely the problem! The conviction that God communicates with us leaves us with the question, Precisely *how* does God guide and direct today? How does he guide *me* in my Christian pilgrimage? Most Christians today struggle with this "not because they doubt that divine guidance is a fact, but because they are sure it is."[14] They are convinced that God has promised to guide every believer, but they are uncertain of their own receptiveness to the guidance of God. This leads us to the application of this text.

THIS IS A TIMELESS TRUTH of Scripture: God speaks to his people and desires to guide them in their pilgrimage. The contrast between David and Saul in 1 Samuel 23 offers opportunities to modern believers to consider which character we are like. Are we sensitive to God's guidance, like David, or are we presumptuous about God and dependent on human wisdom, like Saul?

Divine means of communication. Before we can address this question, we must consider a prior one. We can all agree that God is a speaking God and that he still speaks today to his people. The question becomes: Precisely *how* does God speak today? We no longer have David's advantage of priestly ephod with its Urim and Thummim (though we would all admit to longing for such techniques at critical junctures of our lives). Nor do most of us today experience the means of God's communication in days of old, such as cloud and fire, bush and mountain, whirlwind and audible voice. In the history of biblical revelation, such dramatic and obvious messages from God became more rare as prophecy became the primary means of revelation. As much as we might long for sensational messages from God written in the sky, the truth is for today's believers, it is not always easy to discern God's will. So what are the primary methods by which God communicates today?

Without denying a role for modern prophets or the *possibility* of audible voices or some other dramatic means of communication, we must begin by stating that God's *primary* means of communication today is through Scripture. As we saw in the Bridging Contexts section, our identity as Christians

---

14. J. I. Packer, *Knowing God* (Downers Grove, Ill.: InterVarsity Press, 1973), 209.

means we are a people of the book—more specifically, sixty-six books divided into Old and New Testaments. The words that God inspired in these texts are not a dead letter, but they are alive and active, "sharper than any double-edged sword" (Heb. 4:12).

In seeking the guidance of God we should never separate the work of the Holy Spirit from the role of Scripture, because the Bible is "the sword of the Spirit" (Eph. 6:17). The texts of the Old and New Testaments comprise the primary weapon the Holy Spirit uses to accomplish his purposes in our lives. Through these ancient texts, God speaks to our contemporary world. "He speaks through what he has spoken."[15]

Like David or like Saul? We can now return to this question. In answering it, we should consider present Christians corporately and individually. *Corporately,* the church today tends to be much more like Saul than we care to admit. Most mainline denominations make unwarranted assumptions about God's will and rely too often on human wisdom. Consequently, many churches today have ambivalent records on important moral and social issues such as poverty, abortion, ecology, violence, and homosexuality. The pressures of our age and the changing opinions of human "experts" have swayed many into changing long-held social principles of Christianity. For the most part, mainline churches do not hold Scripture in high enough esteem to refute the changing values of our society. Like Saul we seem unconcerned with seeking God's will and more enamored with human perceptions.

Unfortunately, the record of evangelical denominations has also been more like Saul than David. In the heat of the greatest moral crisis of our generation—the civil rights movement of the 1960s—most evangelicals chose to sit on the sidelines.[16] And evangelicals have not typically been at the vanguard of social change regarding poverty or matters of race relations.

With regard to *individual* application of this text, it is helpful to distinguish between the *general* and the *particular* will of God.[17] (1) The general will of God is the desire he has for all his people everywhere and at all times. In this sense his will has been revealed to us in Scripture and cannot be missed by thinking readers. God wants us to "be conformed to the likeness of his Son" (Rom. 8:29), to become Christlike in all our behavior. Most of us are painfully aware of our failures here, and we can only strive to allow the

---

15. John Stott, *The Contemporary Christian: An Urgent Plea for Double Listening* (Leicester: Inter-Varsity Press, 1992), 105.

16. Yancey, *What's So Amazing About Grace?* 248. See throughout Yancey's book for painful admissions of the failure of the evangelical church to serve as dispensers of God's grace.

17. For part of this discussion, see Stott, *Contemporary Christian*, 129–40; Packer, *Knowing God*, 212–15.

Holy Spirit's work to bring to completion what he has begun in us (Phil. 1:6; 1 Thess. 5:23–24).

(2) The particular will of God has more to do with the important "vocational" choices we must all make in life: choices of occupation, of spouse, of church, of the best use of time and energy, and so on. Individual Christians certainly desire to be like David in this regard: to discern God's will and to obey it quickly. But we often fail because of a mistaken notion about the nature of "divine guidance." Since our vocational questions, for example, cannot be settled by a simple recourse to Scripture, many Christians are guilty of believing that guidance is essentially an inward prompting of the Holy Spirit apart from the written Word. They are more prone to rely on subjective impulses or vague "impressions" rather than probing the biblical text for principles of divine direction.[18]

Yet even in these issues where we are left without explicit biblical mandate, the basic method in which God guides and directs us is through a rational understanding of the principles of Scripture. These principles establish the parameters in which we then must seek to discern the specifics of his will. "The Spirit leads within the limits which the Word sets, not beyond them."[19] Having thus committed ourselves to God's Word, we then may become his sheep, who know only his voice and follow wherever he leads (John 10:3–5).

---

18. For comical extremes of Christians listening for the inward voice of the Spirit to direct one's every action, see Packer, *Knowing God*, 213–14. For a thorough discussion of the issues involved in following God's will, see Jerry Sittser, *Discovering God's Will* (Grand Rapids: Zondervan, 2002).

19. Packer, *Knowing God*, 215.

1 Samuel 24:1–22

❧

FTER SAUL RETURNED FROM PURSUING THE PHILISTINES, he was told, "David is in the Desert of En Gedi." ²So Saul took three thousand chosen men from all Israel and set out to look for David and his men near the Crags of the Wild Goats.

³He came to the sheep pens along the way; a cave was there, and Saul went in to relieve himself. David and his men were far back in the cave. ⁴The men said, "This is the day the LORD spoke of when he said to you, 'I will give your enemy into your hands for you to deal with as you wish.'" Then David crept up unnoticed and cut off a corner of Saul's robe.

⁵Afterward, David was conscience-stricken for having cut off a corner of his robe. ⁶He said to his men, "The LORD forbid that I should do such a thing to my master, the LORD's anointed, or lift my hand against him; for he is the anointed of the LORD." ⁷With these words David rebuked his men and did not allow them to attack Saul. And Saul left the cave and went his way.

⁸Then David went out of the cave and called out to Saul, "My lord the king!" When Saul looked behind him, David bowed down and prostrated himself with his face to the ground. ⁹He said to Saul, "Why do you listen when men say, 'David is bent on harming you'? ¹⁰This day you have seen with your own eyes how the LORD delivered you into my hands in the cave. Some urged me to kill you, but I spared you; I said, 'I will not lift my hand against my master, because he is the LORD's anointed.' ¹¹See, my father, look at this piece of your robe in my hand! I cut off the corner of your robe but did not kill you. Now understand and recognize that I am not guilty of wrongdoing or rebellion. I have not wronged you, but you are hunting me down to take my life. ¹²May the LORD judge between you and me. And may the LORD avenge the wrongs you have done to me, but my hand will not touch you. ¹³As the old saying goes, 'From evildoers come evil deeds,' so my hand will not touch you.

¹⁴"Against whom has the king of Israel come out? Whom are you pursuing? A dead dog? A flea? ¹⁵May the LORD be our

judge and decide between us. May he consider my cause and uphold it; may he vindicate me by delivering me from your hand."

¹⁶When David finished saying this, Saul asked, "Is that your voice, David my son?" And he wept aloud. ¹⁷"You are more righteous than I," he said. "You have treated me well, but I have treated you badly. ¹⁸You have just now told me of the good you did to me; the LORD delivered me into your hands, but you did not kill me. ¹⁹When a man finds his enemy, does he let him get away unharmed? May the LORD reward you well for the way you treated me today. ²⁰I know that you will surely be king and that the kingdom of Israel will be established in your hands. ²¹Now swear to me by the LORD that you will not cut off my descendants or wipe out my name from my father's family."

²²So David gave his oath to Saul. Then Saul returned home, but David and his men went up to the stronghold.

AFTER SAUL'S PROBLEMS with the Philistines recede again into the background, he resumes his pursuit of David. At En Gedi, David unexpectedly and ironically finds himself in a position where he can kill his adversary and move to take the kingdom for himself. But his exemplary reverence for the Lord and for the Lord's anointed restrains him, and he therefore restrains his men from taking action. The episode ends with speeches in which David argues his innocence and Saul confesses David's right to be king.

According to this passage, David is not maliciously intent on taking Saul's life and is not culpable for Saul's demise. On the contrary, he seems motivated only by a genuine devotion to Yahweh and to the office of Israel's king. The idea of taking Saul's life is unthinkable to him. By contrast, Saul is characterized as a monarch obsessed with destroying his (perceived!) enemy, David, irreverently pursuing him instead of protecting the people of Israel from the Philistines. This pattern only heightens David's legitimacy as Saul's successor.

This text is often compared to chapter 26, where David is again unwilling to take Saul's life when presented unexpectedly with the opportunity. Many assume the two chapters are alternate memories of one event. It is also possible that the similarities between the two accounts are better understood by allowing a significant degree of assimilation between the narratives early in their transmission history.[1] Regardless of how we view the relationship between chapters 24 and 26, their present arrangement in 1 Samuel is intended to trace the development in David's character, as we will see in our discussion of chapter 26.

Chance Encounter in a Cave near En Gedi (24:1–7)

SAUL'S DESPERATE STATE of mind is illustrated by his willingness to deploy a significant military contingent (three thousand infantrymen) to pursue David, even while the Philistine threat still looms in the shadows. En Gedi is located on the western shore of the Dead Sea, approximately thirty-five miles southeast of Jerusalem. It was one of several spring-fed oases between the lower slope of the cliffs of the desert in Judah and the Dead Sea's coastline.[2]

Saul's purpose for entering the cave is clear from the Hebrew's euphemistic phrase "to cover his feet," which is used in other contexts for "to defecate" (NIV "to relieve himself").[3] Seeking privacy and thinking he is alone, he has no idea David and his men are "far back" in the same cave (24:3 [MT 24:4]).[4] The assumption on the part of David's men that Yahweh has miraculously provided this opportunity to kill Saul is only natural. They refer to a previous prophecy in which Saul would be delivered up to David (24:4). Though we have no such specific promise recorded in the Bible, they may have been offering their own interpretation of the episode of David's anointing (16:13), of Jonathan's abdication of his right to rule (18:1–4), or of Jonathan's assertion that David will certainly become king (23:15–18).[5]

At any rate, this seems to David's men like a divine moment; God has delivered Saul into David's "hands." The idiom "to give over/deliver into the hands" is common in the Old Testament in military settings to connote abandonment of a person into the power of another.[6] In fact, the expression "the gods delivered (someone or something) into my hand" is used by kings of the ancient Near East to signify divine approval, especially of a military victory.[7]

---

1. Contrast the approaches of Gordon, *I and II Samuel*, 178, 187, with Klein, *1 Samuel*, 236–38, and McCarter, *I Samuel*, 385–87.

2. Jeffries M. Hamilton, "En-gedi," *ABD*, 2:502–3.

3. *HALOT*, 2:754, BDB, 697; cf. Judg. 3:24.

4. The last phrase of ch. 23 (NIV "And David went up from there and lived in the strongholds of En Gedi") is 24:1 in the Heb. text, leaving a one-verse difference between English translations and the Heb. throughout ch. 24.

5. The NIV's footnote offers an alternative interpretation: "Today the LORD is saying. . ." In this way, the men are assuming God is accomplishing his purposes through this unexpected turn of events.

6. Michael A. Grisanti, "נתן," *NIDOTTE*, 3:205–11, esp. 210.

7. Bertil Albrektson, *History and the Gods: An Essay on the Idea of Historical Events As Divine Manifestations in the Ancient Near East and in Israel* (ConBOT 1; Lund: C. W. K. Gleerup, 1967), 38–39.

It is also possible that this text is intentionally linked with the previous chapter by a frequent recurrence of "hand" as a *Leitwort* or theme word, which occurs eleven times in this chapter and nine times in chapter 23.[8] Its recurring emphasis in chapter 23 seems to highlight the proper use of power, while here it draws attention to the restraint of power rather than to its use.[9]

David's cutting a corner of Saul's robe is probably more than a means of proving his goodwill toward Saul.[10] True enough, he will shortly hold high the piece of robe in order to prove that he has refused to kill Saul when he could easily have done so. But one's robe in the ancient Near East often bore symbolic significance (Heb. *mᵉᶜil*).[11] Placing a garment before a newly anointed king could signify one's submission to him (2 Kings 9:13), and the tearing of a garment could symbolize a torn kingdom (1 Sam. 15:27–28; 1 Kings 11:30–31).[12] In 1 Samuel 18:4, Jonathan removed his robe and gave it to David, apparently as a symbol that he was giving up his right to royal succession and bestowing it on David.

It seems likely here that David's cutting of the hem of Saul's garment has enormous symbolic significance, denoting perhaps not only that Saul's hold on the kingdom is over but that David's has now begun.[13] So David takes a portion of Saul's garment rather than his life. Though it looks merciful at first sight, we learn immediately that David is conscience-stricken by his deed. "The fact that he immediately regrets this violation of Saul's robe strongly suggests that his initial motivation was not so high-minded, and differed only in degree from the more primitive stirrings in his men."[14]

As we have seen in 1 Samuel, the anointed of Yahweh is endowed with Yahweh's Spirit and is therefore considered sacrosanct (10:6, 10; 16:13). The act of anointing itself imparts something of the sanctity of Yahweh to

---

8. Youngblood, "1, 2 Samuel," 738, 745.

9. Peter D. Miscall, *1 Samuel: A Literary Reading* (Bloomington, Ind.: Indiana Univ. Press, 1986), 139.

10. The problem of *how* David could have surreptitiously cut the hem of Saul's garment is easily solved by the suggestion that Saul has removed it and placed it to one side while he is indisposed. See Keil and Delitzsch, *Samuel*, 235.

11. *HALOT*, 2:612. As early as the Middle Bronze Age, kings of Old Syrian city-states are depicted in the iconography wearing a garment with thick fringes, which probably distinguished the ruler from other citizens. See Othmar Keel and Christoph Uehlinger, *Gods, Goddesses, and Images of God in Ancient Israel*, trans. Thomas H. Trapp (Minneapolis: Fortress, 1998), 39–48.

12. Though not the same Hebrew term in every case.

13. Victor H. Matthews, *Manners and Customs in the Bible* (rev. ed.; Peabody, Mass.: Hendrickson, 1991), 119; see Robert P. Gordon, "David's Rise and Saul's Demise," *TynBul* 31 (1980): 37–64.

14. Gordon, *I and II Samuel*, 179.

---

the anointed one, and the idea of striking such a one is repulsive to David. Even in the case of Saul, from whom the Spirit of Yahweh has departed, David's act symbolizing the transfer of power (even if only in theory at this point) is in a sense lifting the hand against Yahweh's anointed. For this reason David does not permit his men to go any further with the plans to harm Saul. It is not enough to glean from this text that David has a magnanimous spirit toward Saul. "It is more important that he complies with the will of God where it is unmistakably clear. What appears to the others as the will of God seems to him to be a temptation from which God will 'preserve' him."[15]

Saul Acknowledges David's Right to Rule (24:8–22)

THE REST OF this text consists of speeches by David and Saul. A typical feature of Old Testament narrative is its use of "contrastive dialogue" to differentiate characters. As we have seen, the contrast between Saul and David grows in intensity as we move through the final section of 1 Samuel (chs. 21–31). Both are anointed ones. But Saul has become an Ichabod figure (cf. 4:19–22; 16:14), meaning the Spirit of Yahweh has been withdrawn from him, while David grows in the strength and Spirit of Yahweh in each narrative. David's long eloquent speech in 24:9–15 is juxtaposed with Saul's "choked cry" in 24:16–21.[16] Saul's speech culminates in an admission that David is in the right and will in fact be king. Nothing legitimizes David's reign more than a confession on the lips of Saul himself that David is the legitimate anointed one (24:20).

David is respectful of Saul's position, both in terminology ("my lord the king!" 24:8) and body language (bowing humbly before him).[17] He persuasively details his case. He is innocent regardless of the false rumors Saul has been receiving (24:9). He is loyal to King Saul, which is proven by the piece of robe in his hand. He pleads for divine intervention, asking that God may vindicate him before Saul (24:14–15).

In response, Saul can only evoke the awkward question reminiscent of their earlier close relationship: "Is that your voice, David my son?" (24:16). After acknowledging that David is in the right, Saul makes the profound confession: "I know that you will surely be king and that the kingdom of Israel will be established in your hands" (24:20).[18] Here there is no recrimination as we have come to expect from Saul (cf. 15:10–31). He seems

---

15. Hertzberg, *I and II Samuel*, 196.
16. For more on "contrastive dialogue," see Alter, *The Art of Biblical Narrative*, 72–73.
17. We may assume at a safe distance, as in 26:13.
18. The Heb. infinitive absolute makes this emphatic: "You will certainly be king."

genuinely to understand that he will be placed aside in favor of David, but his admission is too late.

Having nothing else to say, Saul seeks to ensure that David will not exterminate his family once he replaces Saul as king of Israel (24:21). His confession and request for protection for his descendants is similar to that of Jonathan (20:14–15; 23:17). In fact, as the narrative progresses, there is a growing consensus that David will be king. First, Samuel (ch. 16), then Jonathan, and now Saul come to realize that David will become king and that a Saulide dynasty is impossible. The reader, too, gradually comes to accept the inevitability of David's reign and becomes convinced of his innocence and legitimacy.

The relationship between David and Saul's descendants is an important theme throughout the extended narrative on David's rise to power. Jonathan made this part of his covenant relationship with David (20:14–15, 42), which is understandable since usurpers routinely wiped out any family of the previous king who might make future claims on the throne. Here Saul expresses the same concern, leading David to take an oath that he will not exterminate Saul's family when he becomes king (24:21–22).

Most of Saul's sons are eventually killed by the Philistines (31:2) and the Gibeonites (2 Sam. 21:1–14). The historians responsible for the final books of Samuel want the reader to understand that David does keep his promises to Jonathan and Saul. He shows kindness to Mephibosheth, the son of Jonathan (2 Sam. 9:7), which is part of the historian's justification of David. It *may* have been convenient that all of Saul's children except for one crippled son are killed. But David *himself* has nothing to do with this; he is innocent of any wrongdoing. Unlike most ancient monarchs, David shows a God-pleasing, compassionate magnanimity toward his enemies; in this sense, he is truly a man after God's own heart.

DAVID HAS EVERYTHING Saul wants. Saul wants an opportunity to kill David; here David receives just such an opportunity to kill Saul. Saul is king, yet he strives for legitimacy; David is not yet king, but he is the legitimate anointed one.

Revering God. The central theme of the text revolves around David's temptation to take advantage of the situation in the cave. His men advance the idea of executing Saul and bringing their misery (and David's) to a swift conclusion. At first it appears that David agrees. He moves stealthily upon Saul without being detected ("David crept up unnoticed"), and the reader can only assume he is about to kill Saul. But then the narrative takes an odd twist when the sentence concludes, "and cut off a corner of Saul's robe" (24:4). David's speech to his men reveals his motives, as elsewhere in speeches in Old Testament narratives. He reveres Yahweh and Yahweh's anointed too much to strike Saul. David is repulsed by the prospects of killing the anointed one, however advantageous it may appear to him personally.

Some have speculated that David is aware of setting a negative precedent. If he raises his hand to slay Saul, perhaps someone in the future will raise his hand against other anointed ones, even against David himself. That is, he is protecting himself against future coup attempts, guarding against the possibility of his own murder later.[19] But the text knows nothing of this. David is singularly and simply motivated by his reverence for Yahweh and his devotion to Yahweh's anointed. He will eventually have the throne of Israel, but as a gift of God rather than as a result of his grasping and maneuvering.[20]

Two psalms are connected by their superscriptions to this event (Ps. 57 and 142). Though the tradition of these superscriptions may not be dependable,[21] both psalms contain emotional expressions appropriate to David in this episode. Psalm 57 particularly illustrates his reverence for God and his reliance on him to fulfill David's purposes for his life.

> Have mercy on me, O God, have mercy on me,
>> For in you my soul takes refuge.
> I will take refuge in the shadow of your wings
>> until the disaster has passed. (Ps. 57:1)

While taking refuge in a cave from his ravenous enemies (Ps. 57:4), David knows his true refuge is God. Irrespective of this psalm's connection to 1 Samuel 24, it illustrates the spirit of David while in the cave. He refuses to trust in the wisdom of his men and in his own ability to kill his adversary. Rather, he trusts in God to accomplish his purposes for his life.

> I cry out to God Most High,
>> to God, who fulfills his purpose for me. (Ps. 57:2)

---

19. Robert Polzin, *Samuel and the Deuteronomist: A Literary Study of the Deuteronomic History*, Part 2: *1 Samuel* (San Francisco: Harper & Row, 1989), 210.

20. Brueggemann, *First and Second Samuel*, 174.

21. Over the past two hundred years, scholars have become increasingly more skeptical about the trustworthiness of psalm titles. Recent interpreters have tended to recognize them as important information "within the framework of a history of the transmission and collection of the Psalms" (Hans-Joachim Kraus, *Psalms 1–59: A Commentary*, trans. H. C. Oswald [Minneapolis: Augsburg, 1988], 31–32; see also 65–68, where Kraus theorizes about the development of the titles during the Second Temple period by priests at the temple of Jerusalem). At the very least, the titles furnish the earliest commentary on the psalms.

David is willing to trust patiently in God, who will eventually deliver him from Saul. His salvation will be complete because it will include repudiation of Saul.

> He sends from heaven and saves me,
> rebuking those who hotly pursue me;
> God sends his love and his faithfulness. (Ps. 57:3)

Thus, this text is about revering God and his anointed one. David's words in 1 Samuel 24:6, "The LORD forbid that I should do such a thing," capture the spirit of his respect and illustrate the nature of reverence and obedience in the Bible. This text stands in a long line of Old Testament passages about reverence for God and dependence on him during a crisis or temptation. Whether it is Joseph declaring that adultery with Potiphar's wife is tantamount to "sin against God" (Gen. 39:9), or Joshua lying prostrate before the commander of the Lord's army (Josh. 5:14), or the proverbial instruction on "the fear of the LORD" (Prov. 1:7), the message is the same. Reverence for God and all things godly is a chief characteristic of Old Testament saints.

 REVERENCE AND TRUST IN GOD. The application of this text is simpler than many others because the timeless message of reverence and trust in God is needed today and always. While few Christians today are faced with hiding in caves because of the wrath of an insane monarch hell-bent on destroying them, it is nonetheless true that many believers around the globe continue to suffer for their faith. The solution for them is, as it was for David while Saul pursued him, reverence for the Lord and for his anointed one.

Even for believers living in cultures not openly hostile to Christian faith, the text's message of reverence and trust speaks volumes. The danger is that we might not apply the message of this text in broad enough strokes. Reverence for God is more than respect for the pastor and the church. If we want to mimic the attitude of David in this passage, it has to be more than focusing on the way we speak about God or avoiding certain explicatives with "God" in them. David in this text exemplifies a radical reverence for God that controlled his thoughts and actions. He refused to succumb to a bloody resolution to his problems, even while his trusted allies around him assured him it was "God's will" that he kill Saul. This is vital reverence resulting in obedience, even when it is unclear which action is the obedient action to take.

David revered all that God stood for and all that rightly stood for God. Saul was God's anointed one, period! Even though Saul had forfeited his right to reign, for David it was a closed issue. He could not bring himself to show hostility or ill will of any kind to the anointed one of God. Somewhere along life's journey, David had been taught never to challenge God's plan or God's *timing*. He was willing to wait on God's timing to become king, even though it meant taking the risk and prolonging the time during which Saul could attempt to end David's life. This is radical reverence coming to fruition in obedience to God during a crisis of uncertainty and danger. It is the type of reverence taught elsewhere in Israel's wisdom literature (Prov. 1:7) and law (esp. in the combination of "love" and "fear" in Deuteronomy, as in Deut. 10:12).

Addressing postmodernism. For Christians living in North America, the emphasis on reverential obedience is especially needed. The emerging postmodern worldview of our society marks a pervasive paradigm shift that has affected every aspect of our lives. Since the primary assumption of the new worldview is that truth is relative (being neither rational nor objective), everyone's view is equally valid.[22] Tolerance is the only accepted doctrine. With this development, which took place gradually during the closing decades of the twentieth century, the influences of the Judeo-Christian heritage in the United States have begun to wane.

In this new context, the central truths of Christianity are being challenged. The culture redefines Jesus as a good and moral teacher who points us to God, a sort of "God-light," one among many others who direct us to God. Jesus, as is assumed in this new paradigm, built an earthly kingdom (the church) based on his understanding of God as forgiving Father (or doting grandfather?) and on the brotherhood of all humankind united in love. So Christianity is defined as believing in God, respecting Jesus, and living by the Golden Rule.[23]

But orthodox Christianity teaches that Jesus is more than a "God-light." He is in reality God himself, the Anointed One. The concepts of sin, incarnation, and redemption are ridiculed as vestiges of an older and outmoded European cultural system, which was marred by ethnocentrism and an instinctive drive for political dominance. Orthodox Christianity itself, with its truth-based self-claims, is automatically ruled out as "intolerant" and therefore bigoted. Reverential obedience to God and his Word seems irrelevant or misguided, not because it is wrong (what difference would this make?) but because it seems unnecessary. Since there are other, more tolerant avenues

---

22. For description and critique of these developments, see Grenz, *A Primer on Postmodernism*.

23. Benton Johnson, Dean R. Hoge, and Donald A. Luidens, "Mainline Churches: The Real Reason for Decline," *First Things* 31 (March 1993): 13–18, esp. 15.

to God, the Christian God has been placed aside by the communally defined truth of humankind.

In an essay written in 1948 on the task of evangelizing modern unbelievers, C. S. Lewis spoke with his characteristic brilliance about the place God holds in the minds of modern people compared to ancient times:

> The ancient man approached God (or even the gods) as the accused person approaches his judge. For the modern man the roles are reversed. He is the judge: God is in the dock [or "defendant's seat"]. He is quite a kindly judge: if God should have a reasonable defence for being the god who permits war, poverty and disease, he is ready to listen to it. The trial may even end in God's acquittal. But the important thing is that Man is on the Bench and God in the Dock.[24]

Lewis's words, true enough in his own day, seem almost prophetically written for our times. The truth of God has been displaced in postmodernism by a communally contrived understanding of religion, or better, spirituality. Truth has become a concept difficult to define; it becomes whatever you believe it is, as long as you believe it sincerely. In this context, the idea of taking on oneself personal risk and discomfort for the sake of faithfulness to an idea one holds as "true" will become more and more of a rarity.

But we are left with this portrait of David. He allows Saul to walk away unharmed from the cave at En Gedi because he believes in the sacredness of Saul's anointing and in the holiness of Saul's God. Such ideals and values are likely to become more rare in our culture as postmodernism continues to evolve, making our example of David useful for all who look to Christ as the author and perfecter of our faith (Heb. 12:2).

---

24. C. S. Lewis, "God in the Dock," in *God in the Dock* (Grand Rapids: Eerdmans, 1970), 240–44, the quote is from 244.

1 Samuel 25:1–44

❧

NOW SAMUEL DIED, and all Israel assembled and mourned for him; and they buried him at his home in Ramah.

Then David moved down into the Desert of Maon. ²A certain man in Maon, who had property there at Carmel, was very wealthy. He had a thousand goats and three thousand sheep, which he was shearing in Carmel. ³His name was Nabal and his wife's name was Abigail. She was an intelligent and beautiful woman, but her husband, a Calebite, was surly and mean in his dealings.

⁴While David was in the desert, he heard that Nabal was shearing sheep. ⁵So he sent ten young men and said to them, "Go up to Nabal at Carmel and greet him in my name. ⁶Say to him: 'Long life to you! Good health to you and your household! And good health to all that is yours!

⁷"'Now I hear that it is sheep-shearing time. When your shepherds were with us, we did not mistreat them, and the whole time they were at Carmel nothing of theirs was missing. ⁸Ask your own servants and they will tell you. Therefore be favorable toward my young men, since we come at a festive time. Please give your servants and your son David whatever you can find for them.'"

⁹When David's men arrived, they gave Nabal this message in David's name. Then they waited.

¹⁰Nabal answered David's servants, "Who is this David? Who is this son of Jesse? Many servants are breaking away from their masters these days. ¹¹Why should I take my bread and water, and the meat I have slaughtered for my shearers, and give it to men coming from who knows where?"

¹²David's men turned around and went back. When they arrived, they reported every word. ¹³David said to his men, "Put on your swords!" So they put on their swords, and David put on his. About four hundred men went up with David, while two hundred stayed with the supplies.

¹⁴One of the servants told Nabal's wife Abigail: "David sent messengers from the desert to give our master his greetings, but he hurled insults at them. ¹⁵Yet these men were very good

to us. They did not mistreat us, and the whole time we were out in the fields near them nothing was missing. ¹⁶Night and day they were a wall around us all the time we were herding our sheep near them. ¹⁷Now think it over and see what you can do, because disaster is hanging over our master and his whole household. He is such a wicked man that no one can talk to him."

¹⁸Abigail lost no time. She took two hundred loaves of bread, two skins of wine, five dressed sheep, five seahs of roasted grain, a hundred cakes of raisins and two hundred cakes of pressed figs, and loaded them on donkeys. ¹⁹Then she told her servants, "Go on ahead; I'll follow you." But she did not tell her husband Nabal.

²⁰As she came riding her donkey into a mountain ravine, there were David and his men descending toward her, and she met them. ²¹David had just said, "It's been useless—all my watching over this fellow's property in the desert so that nothing of his was missing. He has paid me back evil for good. ²²May God deal with David, be it ever so severely, if by morning I leave alive one male of all who belong to him!"

²³When Abigail saw David, she quickly got off her donkey and bowed down before David with her face to the ground. ²⁴She fell at his feet and said: "My lord, let the blame be on me alone. Please let your servant speak to you; hear what your servant has to say. ²⁵May my lord pay no attention to that wicked man Nabal. He is just like his name—his name is Fool, and folly goes with him. But as for me, your servant, I did not see the men my master sent.

²⁶"Now since the LORD has kept you, my master, from bloodshed and from avenging yourself with your own hands, as surely as the LORD lives and as you live, may your enemies and all who intend to harm my master be like Nabal. ²⁷And let this gift, which your servant has brought to my master, be given to the men who follow you. ²⁸Please forgive your servant's offense, for the LORD will certainly make a lasting dynasty for my master, because he fights the LORD's battles. Let no wrongdoing be found in you as long as you live. ²⁹Even though someone is pursuing you to take your life, the life of my master will be bound securely in the bundle of the living by the LORD your God. But the lives of your enemies he will hurl away as from the pocket of a sling. ³⁰When the

LORD has done for my master every good thing he promised concerning him and has appointed him leader over Israel, ³¹my master will not have on his conscience the staggering burden of needless bloodshed or of having avenged himself. And when the LORD has brought my master success, remember your servant."

³²David said to Abigail, "Praise be to the LORD, the God of Israel, who has sent you today to meet me. ³³May you be blessed for your good judgment and for keeping me from bloodshed this day and from avenging myself with my own hands. ³⁴Otherwise, as surely as the LORD, the God of Israel, lives, who has kept me from harming you, if you had not come quickly to meet me, not one male belonging to Nabal would have been left alive by daybreak."

³⁵Then David accepted from her hand what she had brought him and said, "Go home in peace. I have heard your words and granted your request."

³⁶When Abigail went to Nabal, he was in the house holding a banquet like that of a king. He was in high spirits and very drunk. So she told him nothing until daybreak. ³⁷Then in the morning, when Nabal was sober, his wife told him all these things, and his heart failed him and he became like a stone. ³⁸About ten days later, the LORD struck Nabal and he died.

³⁹When David heard that Nabal was dead, he said, "Praise be to the LORD, who has upheld my cause against Nabal for treating me with contempt. He has kept his servant from doing wrong and has brought Nabal's wrongdoing down on his own head."

Then David sent word to Abigail, asking her to become his wife. ⁴⁰His servants went to Carmel and said to Abigail, "David has sent us to you to take you to become his wife."

⁴¹She bowed down with her face to the ground and said, "Here is your maidservant, ready to serve you and wash the feet of my master's servants." ⁴²Abigail quickly got on a donkey and, attended by her five maids, went with David's messengers and became his wife. ⁴³David had also married Ahinoam of Jezreel, and they both were his wives. ⁴⁴But Saul had given his daughter Michal, David's wife, to Paltiel son of Laish, who was from Gallim.

AFTER THE BRIEF REFERENCE TO SAMUEL'S DEATH, this text relates the conflict between Nabal and David, in which Nabal's noble wife intercedes to prevent a violent conclusion. In the end, however, God himself intercedes to vindicate David's actions and to confirm in David the lesson he has learned from the episode: Patience and restraint are the path to Yahweh's best plan.

The unit is unique in that two of the main protagonists of 1 Samuel so far are not present. The narrator chooses this point in the story to announce Samuel's death (see comment on 25:1), which removes permanently this spiritual giant for Israel.[1] Saul is also absent. Abigail alludes to the king in her reference to David's pursuers (25:29), but Saul is not mentioned by name until the last verse in a closing comment (25:44). With literary subtlety, this narrative substitutes Nabal for Saul. His stance and demeanor toward David are the same as Saul's (25:10–11), and his sudden death prefigures Saul's death, after which David receives the spoils of both his adversaries.[2]

The Nabal episode confirms David's actions of the previous chapter, in which he refused to take Saul's life in the cave at En Gedi. But the question remains: Will David take vengeance against his enemies in his own power and become king by his own hands, or will he wait patiently for God's timing? Nabal provides a test case for David. How he responds here will reveal how he will bear up under similar but even more drastic circumstances. This text is really about David and his evolution from young exile to ideal king. He is in transition, on his way to becoming Yahweh's ideal anointed one, someone suitable to serve as king of Israel.

As we have seen elsewhere in 1 Samuel, the first anointed one failed because he refused to accept Yahweh's authority. The second is the ideal anointed one because he accepts Yahweh's authority in principle and is willing to put that authority into practice. Yahweh is still king over Israel. But in David he has found an anointed one through whom he can rightly govern his people. This is a story about the preparation and maturation of Israel's greatest king.

The Death of Samuel (25:1)

IT MAY SEEM perplexing that the great prophet, whose name is attached to this book, has been mostly unheard of since chapter 16 (except the brief

---

1. At least until Saul unadvisedly revives Samuel one last time in ch. 28.

2. Gunn, *The Fate of King Saul*, 96–103; see also Gordon, "David's Rise and Saul's Demise," 37–64.

appearance in 19:18–24). Since the anointing of David, the narrative has been singularly focused on the conflict between the two anointed ones, tracing the rise of David and the fall of Saul.

The venerable prophet's death is recorded here in passing, and it appears at first sight to have little to do with the context of the surrounding chapters.[3] But it is not insignificant that the reference to Samuel's death follows immediately on the heels of Saul's confession in 24:20–21, which was a public announcement accepting Samuel's judgment on him. Saul has now come to see the truth of what Samuel predicted concerning him and his reign, though it is too late for Saul (chs. 13–15).

The loss of Samuel must have been a terrific blow for David. Indeed, the whole nation mourns his death, because "since the days of Moses and Joshua, no man had arisen to whom the covenant nation owed so much as to Samuel."[4] But who owes more to the great prophet than Saul and David? His death comes now just as Saul realizes too late the truth of his message and just as David needs his guidance more than ever. Having what appears to be one more reason for despair, David turns to journey farther into the desert and farther away from Saul.

Nabal Rejects David's Request (25:2–13)

DAVID NOW TURNS to the Desert of Maon, which was the scene of Saul's previous pursuit of David.[5] Here we encounter for the first time Nabal, who is wealthy but boorish. His name in Hebrew means "foolish," which becomes an ironic part of the narrative (25:25). In reality, this may be an intentional distortion of his real name or only a nickname, though the historian may also have suppressed his actual name "in order to give him a name indicative of his character."[6] However, as rude and unsavory as Nabal is, his wife Abigail is "intelligent and beautiful" (25:3). Her name means "my father is joy(ous)," and her beauty is more than skin deep.[7]

---

3. Some early commentaries concluded that it in fact has *no* connection with the surrounding texts (see Smith, *Samuel*, 220). The death notice is repeated in 28:3, but the NIV's pluperfect there is probably correct.

4. Keil and Delitzsch, *Samuel*, 238.

5. See comments on 23:19–29. Maon is the LXX reading of 25:1, presumably because the Hebrew tradition of "Paran" (as in the NIV note) seems too far south (for its location see Jeffries M. Hamilton, "Paran," *ABD*, 5:162). However, "the historical improbability of David's going so far into the wilderness is not a sufficient reason for changing the text" (Smith, *Samuel*, 220).

6. Jon D. Levenson, "I Samuel 25 As Literature and As History," *CBQ* 40 (1978): 11–28, esp. 13–14.

7. Baldwin, *1 and 2 Samuel*, 147.

David's request for food and assistance takes on the appearance of a Mafia-style racket: promising protection (euphemistic for a promise not to harm Nabal) in return for payment.[8] But David's delegation asks for no more than payment for protection they have voluntarily rendered earlier. Indeed, ancient Near Eastern customs of hospitality and Old Testament laws suggest that Nabal, who is more than able to provide such modest provisions, is under obligation to aid David. It is even possible that David, knowing Nabal's character (had his reputation preceded him?) is looking for an opportunity to dispose of him, assuming he is hated by the general populace of Judah. Not unlike David's habit of killing Judah's enemies and sending the booty to the inhabitants back home (30:26), he would endear himself to the people by killing Nabal.[9]

Nabal's response brings a swift reaction. David's command "Put on your swords!" leaves no doubt about his intentions. Verse 13 contains the word "sword" three times in the Hebrew, revealing a dependence on armed force we have not seen in David before.[10] Certainly in his youth he did not rely on the sword, as we know from that earlier, more famous battle with Goliath, another surly protagonist even more threatening than Nabal. On that day his words were as profound as his aim was true: "It is not by sword or spear that the LORD saves" (17:47). Here David acts impetuously and violently, which does not bode well for his future as ruler over Israel.

Abigail Intercedes (25:14–35)

NABAL'S SERVANTS FEEL it useless to try to reason with him directly ("He is such a wicked man that no one can talk to him"). Instead, one of them goes immediately to his remarkable wife, Abigail. She recognizes the seriousness of the situation at once and takes decisive action. Her gift is suitable in light of what David's men are asking, and she is shrewd enough to carry out her mission without her husband's knowledge. Just as she and David approach each other, David is premeditating the vengeful action he is about to take. He swears he will not "leave alive one male of all who belong" to Nabal, because Nabal has paid him evil for good (25:21–22). His intentions are clear and his mind is set.

Abigail's speech shows remarkable wisdom and skill (25:24–31). Indeed, the narrator has so emphasized her speech and character that some

---

8. Levenson, "1 Samuel 25 As Literature," 19.

9. Baldwin, *1 and 2 Samuel*, 148.

10. The NIV's "and David put on his" obscures the third occurrence of "sword." Some of the Greek traditions have omitted the third occurrence, but this is probably a result of textual error. See McCarter, *I Samuel*, 393.

commentators have argued the chapter is a "narrative analogy," presenting a "proleptic glimpse" of Bathsheba and 2 Samuel 11. In contrast to Bathsheba, Abigail is the "ideal woman," whose "rhetorical genius" prevents David from killing her husband.[11]

Abigail softens David first with her "present" and then addresses him as a superior ("My lord ... let your servant speak to you," 25:24). In a speech full of subtleties and polite innuendo, she flatters and cajoles in order to prevent David from bringing bloodguilt on himself. She recognizes that David will one day be king and seems more conscious than he that such bloodguilt would be unworthy of the anointed one of Yahweh. She fully expects the Lord to work out a better way, and she urges David to return good for evil, as he has consistently done to Saul. In verse 29, she makes passing reference to Saul, who still torments him even now in the different form of Nabal, and to Goliath, over whom David won a great victory with the Lord's help.[12]

Abigail has made it nearly impossible for David to extract his revenge on this beautiful and gifted woman, who so humbly and persuasively intervenes on behalf of her master's servants and herself. More importantly, she has reminded David of who he is and stays his hand from unnecessary violence, preparing an important lesson that he will need in the future. As the legitimate anointed one, he must continue to live by faith and wait patiently for God's way and timing. The young king-in-waiting learns his lesson well. David recognizes that Abigail has saved him from wrongdoing and that Yahweh himself is at work in these events to prevent the guilt of bloodshed (25:32–34). He has learned that consistent personal restraint makes a way for Yahweh to work, whereas violence only gives way to more violence.

Here David faces a danger related to that in the cave at En Gedi, when he was tempted to kill Saul (ch. 24). Perhaps this violent instinct to extract vengeance with his own hands is even more serious! Abigail's speech hints that taking such violent action will abrogate his responsibility before Yahweh and result in forfeiting his place in Yahweh's plan. "Through Abigail, the Lord saves David from a danger different from that in the cave with Saul, but none the less great. It consists ... in the possibility that David may take matters into his own hand and thus make himself master of his fate, instead of letting it be guided by the Lord."[13] To do so would be to become like Saul.

---

11. In contrast to Bathsheba, whose acquiescence leads to the death of her husband. Levenson ("I Samuel 25 As Literature," 23–24).

12. Abigail's comment that Yahweh will hurl away the lives of David's enemies as from "the pocket of a sling" is probably a veiled reference to the David and Goliath episode, which would remind David of the way in which Yahweh wins battles. Contra McCarter, *I Samuel*, 399.

13. Hertzberg, *I and II Samuel*, 204.

Nabal Dies and Abigail Becomes David's Wife (25:36–44)

THIS FINAL SECTION demonstrates how Yahweh preserves, protects, and teaches David. But he does much more than that. God also uses David's compliance to turn the trouble with Nabal into an opportunity for blessing and salvation.[14] As usual, God turns a negative into a positive. Not only does Nabal's death suddenly confirm David's actions, but it makes the way clear for this remarkable woman, Abigail, to become David's wife. Her wisdom and strong character make her a suitable partner for David, and she is in many respects his equal.[15]

The political significance of his marriage should not be missed.[16] David's exile from Saul's court means he has lost his power base in Gibeah, where he was hailed as a military hero (18:6–7). Similarly, the loss of Saul's daughter Michal to another man gives David one less claim to royal lineage (25:44). His marriages to Abigail and Ahinoam give him ties to the Hebron and Jezreel areas, perhaps giving him a new power base among the inhabitants of Judah.[17] Nabal has apparently been a prominent member of the leading clan of Hebron (since he was identified as a "Calebite," 25:3), and it is interesting that David first becomes king at Hebron (2 Sam. 2:1–4).

The Bible nowhere presumes that David is involved in a calculated and deliberate plan to overpower Saul and lead a political coup against the Saulide dynasty. Rather, David is simply one participant (along with Abigail and the unfortunate Nabal) in Yahweh's overarching plan. David's compliance and teachability are turned to good use in the movement toward a new kingdom, so that once again the Lord hammers out his will on the anvil of human circumstances.

Bridging Contexts

PATIENCE AND TEACHABILITY. Superficially, this text appears to contribute little to the extended narrative on the history of David's rise (1 Sam. 16–2 Sam. 5). One could explain its presence as a historical explanation of how Abigail came to be David's wife since the text ends in the etiology about David's wives (1 Sam. 25:42–44). But upon

---

14. Keil and Delitzsch, *Samuel*, 238.

15. Youngblood, "1, 2 Samuel," 754.

16. See Jon D. Levenson and Baruch Halpern, "The Political Import of David's Marriages," *JBL* 99 (1980): 507–18, esp. 511–12.

17. Hebron of course is well-known in Judah, but the identity and location of Jezreel is uncertain though probably somewhere southwest of Hebron. See Melvin Hunt, "Jezreel," *ABD*, 3:850.

closer examination, the Nabal episode plays an important literary function because of its location between chapters 24 and 26, and it is this literary function that helps us bridge this text with our own contemporary context. As we will see in the next chapter, David has learned much since the robe-cutting episode in the cave at En Gedi—and that learning takes place here in chapter 25.

David's speech near the end shows he has discovered that patience and restraint are the path to Yahweh's best plan (25:39), and Abigail's speech explains that taking the long-term view is more beneficial than yielding to one's immediate impulses (25:30–31). In terms of modern discipleship, we may speak of "delayed gratification"; as one scholar put it, Abigail explains "the long-term advantages of a clear conscience over any momentary gain from self-indulgence."[18]

This text gives us a glimpse of David on his way to becoming the ideal king. He is evolving from the young exile who acts impetuously out of fear and anger to becoming Yahweh's anointed one, who is patient enough and faithful enough to wait out God's timing. The encounter with Nabal is his test case. With Abigail's speech to guide David (indeed, they appear to be a team even before their marriage), David navigates a course through the murky relationship with Nabal that is God's choice for him. David learns not to seek revenge or seize power with his own hand, but rather to depend on God and on God's timing. This is the lesson he learns from Abigail and the outcome of the Nabal conflict, and it is a lesson he will put to good use in the next chapter.

Another theme in this text is David's teachability. Before he is confronted by Abigail, his mind is made up, and he is determined to take violent action (25:21–22). But after her persuasive plea, he not only changes his mind but also acknowledges that God is the source of her instruction (25:32). Though the Hebrew words for "repent" and "repentance" do not occur in this text, the message is similar. Upon hearing new instruction from God, David immediately changes his mind and takes a decidedly different course of action from that planned. He is capable of correction. He is flexible enough to learn new principles and to quickly put them into action.

This text illustrates a fundamental characteristic present in all the great exemplary saints of the Old Testament, a personal trait that in fact made it possible for God to use them powerfully in his salvation-history plan. Whether we consider Abraham's departure from his homeland (and his ancestral religious traditions), or Jacob at Peniel, or Moses at the burning bush, they had the capacity for change—some more than others and some quicker than

---

18. Gordon, *1 and 2 Samuel*, 64.

others. But eventually they were individuals with a capacity for correction and modification. Unlike Nabal and Saul, David could hear an entirely unexpected word from God that corrected his understanding, and he could respond accordingly.

DISCIPLESHIP. THE ISSUES we have discussed in the previous section have really to do with discipleship. The nature of Christian discipleship involves "learning," since a disciple is, after all, a "learner" and the rabbi is a "teacher."[19] This text serves as a reminder that disciples must be teachable; they receive the word of God and must act on it, adjusting their lives accordingly. David had been anointed king; according to ancient Near Eastern practices, it would not be out of the question for him to demand provisions from the wealthy Nabal. But he learns a different course of action. He learns that patience and personal restraint are a better way, a God-pleasing way of acting as king. Thus, he quickly changes his mind.

All of us are on a journey to somewhere; all of us are in the process of becoming someone. Christian discipleship adopts a certain understanding of the nature of growth in grace. In one sense, growth does not really change the nature of the thing itself or, in this case, the essential nature of the person. An oak seedling simply cannot grow into a mature pine or maple tree, no matter how much growth occurs. So a new believer, immature in faith at first, should grow naturally into a mature believer.

Growth enlarges what is there in germinal form. A babe in Christ should move inexorably toward maturity, becoming (it is hoped) a giant in the faith (cf. 1 Cor. 3:1–2; Heb. 5:11–14). Conversely, it is unnatural *not* to grow. A babe in Christ who does not grow will in time become stunted, a diminutive Christian. In another sense, however, growth requires many changes, not of the essence of the thing (or person) but of many other features. To continue our botanical analogy, the oak seedling experiences many changes as it becomes a mature oak tree. Its roots move deeper and farther away from the center as it requires more and more nutrients, it develops thicker kinds of bark, and the trunk itself becomes larger with each annual ring. Likewise, the growth that is natural for a maturing Christian requires many changes. As one becomes more mature in faith, one discovers areas of change needed in one's life that may be unexpected.

---

19. The New Testament word "disciple" (Gk. *mathetes*) signifies such personal commitment and attachment that English words such as "pupil" or "learner" are inadequate.

David illustrates this principle well. He at first thought it only natural and reasonable to exact revenge on Nabal because of the rude and unfair treatment he had received ("He has paid me back evil for good," 25:21). But after learning of a better way, he quickly changes. Again David shows himself to be the legitimate anointed one of Israel. His essential nature as a man after God's own heart (13:14) is what the anointed one should be. He resists the use of violence to accomplish his goal, even though he knows the goal is, after all, the very thing God wants for him. Instead, he waits patiently for God's plan and timing and for God's means of accomplishing the goal.

In this sense, David prefigures another Anointed One, who also resisted the use of violence to accomplish God's plan. He also waited patiently for God's means of accomplishing the plan, even when the whole world expected a different method. Jesus, the "Son of David," is also the legitimate Anointed One, who like his ancient ancestor, refused to resort to human power structures to accomplish the will of the one who sent him.

1 Samuel 26:1–25

THE ZIPHITES WENT to Saul at Gibeah and said, "Is not David hiding on the hill of Hakilah, which faces Jeshimon?"

²So Saul went down to the Desert of Ziph, with his three thousand chosen men of Israel, to search there for David. ³Saul made his camp beside the road on the hill of Hakilah facing Jeshimon, but David stayed in the desert. When he saw that Saul had followed him there, ⁴he sent out scouts and learned that Saul had definitely arrived.

⁵Then David set out and went to the place where Saul had camped. He saw where Saul and Abner son of Ner, the commander of the army, had lain down. Saul was lying inside the camp, with the army encamped around him.

⁶David then asked Ahimelech the Hittite and Abishai son of Zeruiah, Joab's brother, "Who will go down into the camp with me to Saul?"

"I'll go with you," said Abishai.

⁷So David and Abishai went to the army by night, and there was Saul, lying asleep inside the camp with his spear stuck in the ground near his head. Abner and the soldiers were lying around him.

⁸Abishai said to David, "Today God has delivered your enemy into your hands. Now let me pin him to the ground with one thrust of my spear; I won't strike him twice."

⁹But David said to Abishai, "Don't destroy him! Who can lay a hand on the LORD's anointed and be guiltless? ¹⁰As surely as the LORD lives," he said, "the LORD himself will strike him; either his time will come and he will die, or he will go into battle and perish. ¹¹But the LORD forbid that I should lay a hand on the LORD's anointed. Now get the spear and water jug that are near his head, and let's go."

¹²So David took the spear and water jug near Saul's head, and they left. No one saw or knew about it, nor did anyone wake up. They were all sleeping, because the LORD had put them into a deep sleep.

¹³Then David crossed over to the other side and stood on top of the hill some distance away; there was a wide space

between them. ¹⁴He called out to the army and to Abner son of Ner, "Aren't you going to answer me, Abner?"

Abner replied, "Who are you who calls to the king?"

¹⁵David said, "You're a man, aren't you? And who is like you in Israel? Why didn't you guard your lord the king? Someone came to destroy your lord the king. ¹⁶What you have done is not good. As surely as the LORD lives, you and your men deserve to die, because you did not guard your master, the LORD's anointed. Look around you. Where are the king's spear and water jug that were near his head?"

¹⁷Saul recognized David's voice and said, "Is that your voice, David my son?"

David replied, "Yes it is, my lord the king." ¹⁸And he added, "Why is my lord pursuing his servant? What have I done, and what wrong am I guilty of? ¹⁹Now let my lord the king listen to his servant's words. If the LORD has incited you against me, then may he accept an offering. If, however, men have done it, may they be cursed before the LORD! They have now driven me from my share in the LORD's inheritance and have said, 'Go, serve other gods.' ²⁰Now do not let my blood fall to the ground far from the presence of the LORD. The king of Israel has come out to look for a flea—as one hunts a partridge in the mountains."

²¹Then Saul said, "I have sinned. Come back, David my son. Because you considered my life precious today, I will not try to harm you again. Surely I have acted like a fool and have erred greatly."

²²"Here is the king's spear," David answered. "Let one of your young men come over and get it. ²³The LORD rewards every man for his righteousness and faithfulness. The LORD delivered you into my hands today, but I would not lay a hand on the LORD's anointed. ²⁴As surely as I valued your life today, so may the LORD value my life and deliver me from all trouble."

²⁵Then Saul said to David, "May you be blessed, my son David; you will do great things and surely triumph."

So David went on his way, and Saul returned home.

THIS IS THE LAST MEETING between the competing anointed ones, the last time Saul and David will see each other. Saul continues his pursuit of David, taking once again a large contingent of troops into the southern desert of Judah to find and kill David. With the miraculous intervention of Yahweh, David is able to humiliate the king and his commanding general. The encounter ends with Saul's confession of guilt, though he falls short of promising to let David live.

This text emphasizes the continuing active role of Yahweh in David's rise to the throne and in Saul's downfall (26:12; see comments below). As we have seen elsewhere in 1 Samuel, Yahweh is sovereign. He himself rules over Israel, though he has chosen to use human surrogates, or anointed ones, to govern the nation. The failure of Saul as Yahweh's anointed one is sure, a fact that David himself has learned in a new way (26:10). Moreover, David's legitimacy as anointed one is becoming more obvious and is clear from this text because of his reliance on Yahweh, in stark contrast to Saul.

As we noted in chapter 24, this passage has much in common with that chapter. The following features seem parallel. Saul receives a report concerning David's whereabouts (26:1; cf. 24:1). He pursues David with three thousand chosen men (26:2; cf. 24:2). David finds himself with an opportunity to kill Saul and end the conflict (26:7; cf. 24:3). Those around him urge him to perform the deed (or allow them to do it; 26:8; cf. 24:4). David refuses to kill Saul because of his profound respect for the anointed of Yahweh (26:9–11; cf. 24:6). The episode ends with a dialogue involving Saul and David, with Saul admitting his guilt (26:21; cf. 24:17).

Rather than alternate memories of a single event, it is likely that these two narratives tended to assimilate early in their transmission history, which explains their similarity in content and structure. It is also possible that the narratives have been intentionally placed in close proximity in order to trace the development in David's character as he responds to the same set of circumstances. The Nabal episode of chapter 25 has left David more resolved than ever to avoid harming Saul.[1]

David in Saul's Camp (26:1–12)

THE ZIPHITES WERE SAUL'S INFORMANTS once before concerning David's location (see comments on 23:19–29). They were apparently spying out David's movements throughout their areas of southern Judah in order to gain the favor of King Saul.

---

1. Gordon, *I and II Samuel*, 178, 187; see also Keil and Delitzsch, *Samuel*, 247–49.

Saul once again expends a significant corps of troops to chase David. The latter is at a five-to-one disadvantage with only six hundred loyal soldiers. But David also has the capacity to reconnoiter Saul's location. When he learns that Saul has camped in a vulnerable location, he daringly enters the camp with Abishai. With the aid of a "deep sleep" from Yahweh, the two are able to slip into the midst of the camp and take Saul's spear and water jug (26:12). The spear symbolized the king's royal status, as is most evident from the scene in 22:6, where Saul appears seated under a tamarisk tree on a hill at Gibeah, with his royal court around him and with "spear in hand."[2] David makes off with Saul's spear, just as the king suspects he is trying to do with the kingdom generally.

The Old Testament has other occasions when a "deep sleep" (*tardemah*, 26:12) fell on a person in order to allow God to perform his work without interference. Most notably, the Lord God caused the first man to fall into a deep sleep, and while asleep, God took one of his ribs for use in the creation of Eve (Gen. 2:21; see Isa. 29:10). At other times, this type of trance-like sleep became the occasion for a special revelation from God (Gen. 15:12; Job 4:13; Dan. 8:18).[3]

It is no mere tribute to David's and Abishai's furtiveness as soldiers that they are able to draw so near to the king. Rather, it is made possible through the active participation of Yahweh himself. Saul was once before supernaturally hindered from finding David, when the Spirit of God seized him and prevented him from apprehending David (19:23–24). Now Saul and his entire regiment are unaware of David's presence because of God-induced sleep. In both episodes, the text emphasizes Yahweh's personal and active involvement in David's rise to power.

When Abishai wants to take advantage of Saul's vulnerability, David's reaction is similar to that in the cave of En Gedi (cf. 26:9–11 with 24:6). He is repulsed by the idea of striking the anointed of Yahweh. Such arrogance can only result in guilt for the one who raises a hand against Yahweh's anointed one.[4] Only God himself has a right to take the life of such a divinely sanctioned leader.

But there is also significance in the variety of ways in which David suggests Saul might meet his end: "The LORD himself will strike him; either his

---

2. Cf. also 14:2; 1 Kings 22:10; and the Ugaritic parallel in the Danel Epic (*CTU* 1.17 v 4–8 and *CTU* 1.19 i 19–25). For translation and commentary of the Ugaritic parallel, see Dennis Pardee, "The ʾAqhatu Legend," *COS*, 1.103:343–56, especially 346 (v 4–8) and 351 (i 19–25). The significance of the water jug is not clear.

3. William C. Williams, "רדם," *NIDOTTE*, 3:1057.

4. An attitude David no doubt hopes to instill in the people around him once he becomes king.

time will come and he will die, or he will go into battle and perish" (26:10).[5] The idea that Saul might die in battle anticipates chapter 31. But David has also learned his lesson from the Nabal episode (ch. 25), that the Lord might directly strike his adversary with untimely death. With the recent events of that chapter in mind, David is more resolved than ever to allow God to work out the details in his own timing. He has learned well the lesson of his relationship with Nabal and Abigail; patience and restraint are the path to Yahweh's best plan, while violence only gives way to more violence.

David's and Saul's Last Meeting (26:13–25)

HAVING ABSCONDED WITH Saul's spear and water jug, David now confronts Saul with the irrationality and injustice of his vile pursuit (cf. 24:8–22). He begins by chastising Abner, the general of the army, for failing to protect adequately Yahweh's anointed (26:15–16). In the ensuing dialogue, David pleads his innocence and implores the king to consider how irrational is his obsession with capturing David. He argues that whether the source of his delusional actions is divine or human, there are other more reasonable means of handling them (26:19–20).

David again implies that the king's reckless pursuit is useless because he, David, is harmless and trivial as a "flea" (26:20; cf. 24:14).[6] The reference to himself as "a partridge in the mountains" seems obscure. But David uses an interesting wordplay on Abner's desperate question in 26:14, "Who are you who calls to the king?" The Hebrew for "partridge" is literally "he who calls on the mountains," which is ironically appropriate for David who calls to Saul and Abner on a mountain (26:13–14). David is drawing the analogy because the fate of the partridge (or "calling-bird") was to be pursued relentlessly by the fowler, just as Saul is pursuing David.[7]

Saul admits his guilt and makes more concessions than he has before: "I have sinned ... surely I have acted like a fool and have erred greatly" (26:21). David ignores Saul's invitation to return to the royal court and his promises not to attack David again. It is simply too late. David merely returns Saul's spear and expresses his faith that God will honor his actions and deliver him

---

5. The NIV assumes the first clause is the general statement and the last two are particular ways in which the Lord may "strike" Saul, through natural causes or military defeat. But the text may actually intend three possibilities: premature death by disease, natural death, or death in battle. See Youngblood, "1, 2 Samuel," 769, for discussion of the translation possibilities.

6. Certain LXX traditions support the reading, "the king of Israel has come out to seek my life." Contrast the RSV with the NRSV.

7. McCarter, I Samuel, 408–10.

from trouble (26:24).[8] David concludes it is safer to rely on Yahweh for protection, even in exile in the desert, than to trust Saul and his unpredictable temperament.

Saul's parting words, "You will do great things and surely triumph," are more prophetic than Saul could have known and certainly more than he intends. This is to be the last meeting between the two anointed ones. David "went on his way" with the blessing and protection of Yahweh. Saul "returned home," a king in name only.

Bridging Contexts

CHAPTERS 24–26 CONTRIBUTE to the extended unit's emphasis on the growing distance between Saul and David. The history of David's rise (1 Sam. 16–2 Sam. 5) demonstrates the logical outcome of 1 Samuel 16:13–14. At that critical juncture of the book, Samuel anointed David with oil, and he received the Spirit of God. By contrast, the Spirit of Yahweh departed from Saul, who was henceforth plagued by a tormenting spirit from the Lord.

The two episodes in which David spares Saul's life are narrated in close proximity, separated only by the Nabal–Abigail object lesson, in order to help us "measure the development in David's character as he reacts to basically the same set of data."[9] David matures and becomes more confident in his role as king-in-waiting; Saul is rejected. The distance between the two messianic figures continues to increase. As surely as David is certain to become Israel's king, Saul is just as certainly running to his own destruction.

In chapter 24, we commented on some of the issues in this text. Especially important is the recurrence of reverential respect for Yahweh's anointed one (cf. 24:6; 26:9–11). David has once again acted on his conviction that it is not acceptable to execute justice through wrongdoing. In other words, the end does not always justify the means.[10] Though God had anointed David and repeatedly confirmed that he would replace Saul, David knows he must never raise a hand against Saul himself. It would be wrong to kill Saul, even though God condemned him.

Portrait of David. However, there are two subtle comments in this text that contribute to our expanding portrait of David; these should inform our

---

8. Returning the spear may indicate that Yahweh himself is the only one who can legitimately take Saul's kingdom away.

9. Gordon, *I and II Samuel*, 187.

10. Our ethical formulations, however, must allow for exceptions upon rare occasions. For example, on the possibility of justifiable deception, see comments on 19:1–17 and 27:1–12.

application of this text. (1) The first comment is David's reason for not allowing Abishai to kill Saul in 26:9–11. A comparison of these verses with 24:6 reveals a David who has grown significantly in his understanding of his own role in these events—and more importantly, of Yahweh's active involvement. In both passages, of course, the central objection to harming Saul is that he is the anointed of Yahweh. But in chapter 26, David adds the various ways in which Saul might die, either by natural causes or in battle (see comments above). Either way, it must be Yahweh's doing, not David's.

In chapter 24, David was sorely tempted to kill Saul in the cave at En Gedi (see comments). After he took a piece of the royal robe, David felt strong remorse (24:5). But in chapter 26, his answer to a similar opportunity is unequivocal. Having learned from Nabal's sudden death, which benefited him so unexpectedly, David has learned that it is *always* better to wait patiently for God's timing and methods. Thus, Saul will eventually die by some other means, not by David's hand. This is a much more mature and confident David.

(2) Note too the historian's passing cause-and-effect comment in 26:12b: "They were all sleeping, because the LORD had put them into a deep sleep." As we saw in the Original Meaning section, the term for "deep sleep" is used elsewhere in the Old Testament for a God-induced, trance-like sleep, which made it possible for God to perform his work without interference. In most of the other occurrences, that type of sleep falls on a single individual or a small group of persons (Isa. 29:10 and Job 4:13 may be exceptions). Here God causes three thousand soldiers to fall into the stupor, making it possible for David and Abishai to slip into the camp, discuss what they are going to do, take the royal spear and canteen, and make an undetected escape. Do David and Abishai think it is because of their own skills they are able to avoid detection? Are they even aware of the miraculous nature of the event? Historically we have no way of knowing, but theologically the narrator is clear: Yahweh is personally involved to protect and defend David.

Perhaps the most intriguing aspect of this text is the way in which the human and divine interact. David is growing in confidence that God is at work in the events to bring Saul's reign to a conclusion and to bring him to the throne in Saul's place. But he is apparently unaware of the specifics of Yahweh's involvement *in this text*. The comment about Yahweh's "deep sleep" is between the narrator and the reader. David is more convinced than ever of the general truth of God's activity, though he is unaware of the specifics.

This may be a convenient profile of faith. David negotiates his way through the gritty details without always being aware of God's participation. So it is with all believers. We walk through life with the conviction that God loves us and is involved in the details of our lives. But only on rare and wonderful occasions do we actually become conscious of God's abiding hand.

To ask for more is to expect more than was possible even for Israel's ideal anointed one, the king after God's own heart.

Contemporary Significance

THE NATURE OF FAITH. The issues that we can apply to our own times grow out of the two comments just discussed. The concept of David's growth and maturation is dealt with in the comments on chapter 25, where Christian discipleship was discussed. Here I will make only a brief comment on the nature of faith as "being sure of what we hope for and certain of what we do not see" (Heb. 11:1).

David will not always be exemplary as a paragon of faith. But at least in this text, he is convinced of God's guidance, even if he does not have immediate confirmation. This is also a natural part of Christian discipleship. As we grow and mature in our faith (our first emphasis from this text), we also become more confident about God's guidance, and we spend less time seeking constantly for evidence of his moving.

Unfortunately in our modern context, the opposite development is taking place. As Christians become more comfortable in the conviction that God is at work in the details of life, the world around us has made less and less room for God. The premise that God exists and that he defines human moral responsibilities has been an underlying principle for two millennia of Western civilization. But in the closing decades of the twentieth century, Western cultures have been experimenting with the prospects of defining our responsibilities without the benefit of God. Modern humankind has learned to live without God.

One leading sociologist describes American values today as "utilitarian individualism."[11] We are mostly driven by the need for personal success and vivid personal feelings. Marriage becomes an instrument for personal development, work becomes a vehicle for personal advancement, and the church a means for personal fulfillment. We simply live as though God were not there.

A number of years ago, a close friend gave me a copy of an magazine article entitled "The Mice in the Piano."[12] The article invites us to imagine a family of mice who live all their lives in a large piano, just as you and I live our lives in our fragment of the universe. To the mice in their piano-world came the music of the instrument, filling all the dark spaces with sound and

---

11. Robert N. Bellah et al., *Habits of the Heart: Individualism and Commitment in American Life* (Berkeley and Los Angeles: Univ. of California Press, 1985), 142–63.

12. *His* (April, 1982), 33.

harmony. At first the mice were much impressed by it. They drew comfort and wonder from the thought that there was Someone who made the music—though invisible to them, yet close to them. They loved to think of the Great Player whom they could not see.

Then one day a daring mouse climbed up part of the piano and returned very thoughtful. He had discovered how the music was made. Wires were the secret—tightly stretched wires of graduated lengths that trembled and vibrated. They must revise all their old beliefs. None but the most conservative could any longer believe in the Unseen Player. Later, another explorer carried the explanation further. Hammers were now the secret, numbers of hammers dancing and leaping on the wires. This was a more complicated theory, but it all went to show that they lived in a purely mechanical and mathematical world. The Unseen Player came to be thought of as a myth.

I particularly liked the way the article concluded with one brief sentence, "But the pianist continued to play the piano." Regardless of the astounding advances in science that improve our understanding of the universe and give us greater appreciation for its beauty and symmetry, there is still the question of ultimate causes. The Christian faith holds firmly to the conviction that God is that Ultimate Cause. He is actively involved in the universe in general and in the particulars of our lives, though we are not often conscious of his direct participation.

1 Samuel 27:1–12

BUT DAVID THOUGHT to himself, "One of these days I will be destroyed by the hand of Saul. The best thing I can do is to escape to the land of the Philistines. Then Saul will give up searching for me anywhere in Israel, and I will slip out of his hand."

²So David and the six hundred men with him left and went over to Achish son of Maoch king of Gath. ³David and his men settled in Gath with Achish. Each man had his family with him, and David had his two wives: Ahinoam of Jezreel and Abigail of Carmel, the widow of Nabal. ⁴When Saul was told that David had fled to Gath, he no longer searched for him.

⁵Then David said to Achish, "If I have found favor in your eyes, let a place be assigned to me in one of the country towns, that I may live there. Why should your servant live in the royal city with you?"

⁶So on that day Achish gave him Ziklag, and it has belonged to the kings of Judah ever since. ⁷David lived in Philistine territory a year and four months.

⁸Now David and his men went up and raided the Geshurites, the Girzites and the Amalekites. (From ancient times these peoples had lived in the land extending to Shur and Egypt.) ⁹Whenever David attacked an area, he did not leave a man or woman alive, but took sheep and cattle, donkeys and camels, and clothes. Then he returned to Achish.

¹⁰When Achish asked, "Where did you go raiding today?" David would say, "Against the Negev of Judah" or "Against the Negev of Jerahmeel" or "Against the Negev of the Kenites." ¹¹He did not leave a man or woman alive to be brought to Gath, for he thought, "They might inform on us and say, 'This is what David did.'" And such was his practice as long as he lived in Philistine territory. ¹²Achish trusted David and said to himself, "He has become so odious to his people, the Israelites, that he will be my servant forever."

THIS TEXT BEGINS A FIVE-CHAPTER UNIT that narrates David's sojourn in Philistia (1 Sam. 27–31). While running from Saul, David earlier attempted to find refuge with Achish of Gath, but that episode did not end well (cf. 21:10–15). Now he is accepted by the Philistine overlord, presumably because Achish wants to exploit the conflict between Saul and David. Since Saul has pursued David so persistently, Achish could only have assumed the breach is irreparable.

Chapters 29–30 continue the narration of David's life as a mercenary soldier with the Philistines, especially his revenge against the Amalekites and his covert battles on behalf of various cities of Judah. The conflict with Saul is placed aside for these stories, and Saul is hardly an important figure. However, David's sojourn in Philistia is momentarily interrupted by chapter 28, which returns to Saul in one final episode to illustrate the pathetic and pitiable state to which he has fallen. The concluding chapter of 1 Samuel relates the battle of Mount Gilboa, in which Samuel's prophecy is fulfilled and Saul's life comes to an end.

David's sojourn with the Philistines accomplishes two objectives. (1) He seeks and finds protection because Saul is still trying to kill him. Having passed up two opportunities to kill Saul (chs. 24 and 26), David has now forsaken hope that Saul will give up the chase. He realizes it cannot continue indefinitely; eventually Saul will be successful (27:1). But David also knows that Saul cannot afford to expend entire regiments of Israelite troops deep into Philistine territory simply to pursue him (as he did in southern and central Judah). (2) The second objective is less obvious. While in Philistia, David devotes himself to warring against the potential enemies of Judah while convincing Achish that he is fighting the enemies of the Philistines. Thus he endears himself to both the Philistines *and* the citizens of Judah, whom he will someday rule as king.

This text relates how David comes to live peaceably among the Philistines, how he settles in Ziklag (which eventually becomes a royal city), and how he outwits Achish—again! Besides important historical background for the rest of the extended narrative, we also learn here that David is politically daring and shrewd.

David Flees to Gath and Receives Ziklag (27:1–7)

THIS IS DAVID'S most desperate hour. He realizes his only lasting means of escaping Saul's evil intentions is to go into exile in Philistia (27:1). David implied in his last dialogue with Saul that the king's irrational pursuit would necessitate living beyond Saul's reach in a land where Yahweh is not worshiped (26:19). He is being driven from Yahweh's presence and forced to live where pagan gods are served. As David once fled from Gibeah and the royal court (19:18–24), now he is forced to flee from the desert recesses of southern Judah. This is David's last resort, his only hope of survival.[1]

We have encountered Achish before (21:10–15).[2] His city, Gath, is one of the five principal cities of the Philistines, governed in a so-called pentapolis. Each of these cities is ruled by a Philistine "lord" (*seren*, often simply "ruler" in the NIV) or (occasionally) "king" (cf. Achish in 27:2).[3] Gath is an inland city, situated among the low-lying hills known as the Shephelah; it is the closest Philistine city to Judah in the east.[4] David's stratagem works. The narrator laconically notes that when Saul receives the news David is in Gath, he no longer searches for him.

It is not to David's advantage to settle actually *in* the city of Gath. Since it is a "royal city," meaning it is the seat of power for Achish, and since David is called "king of the land" of Judah by Achish's own servants, it is only natural for David to need his own headquarters. As we will learn, David must operate somewhat independently of Achish's close observation. It is also possible that Achish is more than happy to consign David and his six hundred men and their families to a less conspicuous location, thereby free from the burden of feeding and caring for them.

Achish has the authority to grant landed property.[5] Though Ziklag was allocated to the tribe of Judah by Joshua, it was never successfully conquered (Josh. 15:31). It appears to be ideal for David's purposes, though it is vulnerable to attack from marauders from the south, as we will see. In verse 6 the narrator gives a hint at the success with which David occupies Ziklag: "So on that day Achish gave him Ziklag, and it has belonged to the kings of Judah ever since."

---

1. The historian is also careful to make sure we understand David is not committing treason. He has no intention of becoming disloyal to Judah, but he has no choice because of Saul's activities. As we will see, this sets up a suspenseful scenario, which is only resolved gradually in the narrative.

2. For background and historical details, see Duane L. Christensen, "Achish," *ABD*, 1:55–56.

3. Howard, "Philistines," 243–44.

4. Its precise location is still debated. The best options include Tel ʿErani and Tel Haror (see Baruch Brandl, "ʿErani, Tel," *OEANE*, 2:256–58; Eliezer D. Oren, "Haror, Tel," *OEANE*, 2:474–76). See also Joe D. Seger, "Gath," *ABD*, 2:908–9; Anson F. Rainey, "A Problem in Source Analysis for Historical Geography," *ErIsr* 12 (1975): 63–76.

5. McCarter, *I Samuel*, 414.

David's Campaigns and His Deception of Achish (27:8–12)

DAVID'S CUSTOM DURING THE SIXTEEN MONTHS he lives in Philistia (27:7) is to conduct raids against Judah's desert neighbors, thereby providing a measure of security for his homeland. The Geshurites are inhabitants of the southern territory, north of the Egyptian border and south of the Philistine coastal plain.[6] The Girzites are mentioned only here; their identity is disputed, though they appear also to have occupied territory between Philistia and Egypt.[7]

Saul himself had earlier conducted a campaign against the Amalekites (15:1–9, see comments). They were traditional enemies of Israel because of their vicious and unprovoked attack shortly after the Exodus (Ex. 17:8–16). Biblical tradition associates them initially with Edom, but they were nomadic or seminomadic and were evidently scattered across a vast territory of the ancient world.

These military successes on the geographical fringes of Judah would certainly endear David to the citizens of Judah. Later we learn that at times David even shares the booty of these campaigns with the cities of Judah (30:27–31). While living in Philistia on the run from King Saul, he has actually become a defender of Judahite causes. He is Judah's protector against desert marauders. At the same time, by deceiving Achish, he is also able to endear himself to the Philistine king, leading him to think David is fighting Philistia's enemies. David has it both ways: the inhabitants of Judah and the Philistine king love him.

Upon returning to King Achish, undoubtedly to share portions of the goods mentioned in verse 9, David reports on his campaigns. But he consistently deceives Achish about the targets of his raids. Instead of the enemies of Judah, David tells his host he is attacking the southern districts of Judah itself: the "Negev of Judah," the "Negev of Jerahmeel," or the "Negev of the Kenites" (27:10).[8] The location of Jerahmeel was probably in Judah's southeastern desert basin, south of Beersheba.[9] The Kenites were a non-Israelite group frequently associated with the desert near Sinai but also located in the northeastern desert basin near Judah's border with Edom.[10]

---

6. Josh. 13:2 says the Geshurites were unsubdued by the conquering Israelites. Diana Edelman, "Tel Masos, Geshur, and David," *JNES* 47 (1988): 254–55. See also Gerald J. Petter, "Geshurites," *ABD*, 2:996–97.

7. Edelman, "Tel Masos, Geshur, and David," 254.

8. *Negev* is the Heb. word for "south country," or area south of another place. Usually in the Old Testament it refers to the desert south of the Judean hills.

9. Jack R. Lundbom, "Jerahmeel," *ABD*, 3:683.

10. Baruch Halpern, "Kenites," *ABD*, 4:17–19.

Achish believes David is raiding areas of southern Judah itself, when in reality he is assaulting enemies who are troublesome to Judah. The Philistine ruler naively believes David has burned his bridges, irreparably alienating himself from his own people. He accepts David's word and assumes the citizens of Israel must hate him so much by now that David will have no choice but to remain loyal to his new Philistine colleague (27:12).

Throughout the books of Samuel, the Philistines are consistently treated with derision. In the Ark Narrative a sort of dour humor was used to ridicule their idolatry (4:1b—7:1). Later, in David's first encounter with Achish, he outwitted him by feigning madness, and Achish appeared almost comical in the assertion that his city was so full of crazy men he had no use for any more (21:15). In this text, the reader is reassured of David's uncompromising loyalty to his homeland of Judah. But above and beyond that, the repetition of the story must have brought pleasure to the ancient readers of this text as they picture David thrashing Israel's enemies, all while Achish thinks David is actually double-crossing his own tribe. In keeping with the book's treatment of the Philistines elsewhere, Achish is portrayed as gullible and easily outfoxed.

As I NOTED in the introduction to this chapter, Saul is momentarily placed aside by the narrator. He has practically no role here. In the previous chapter, David and Saul parted ways for the last time. David has been forced to abandon all hopes of reconciliation and is now driven into the arms of Israel's enemies. Samuel is absent as well, his death being recorded in 25:1. More strikingly, God is absent in this chapter, by which I mean God is not mentioned. The narrator uses neither the generic word "God" or his intimate personal name, "Yahweh." David is alone! He and his family, along with six hundred loyal soldiers, have moved together to enemy territory. But the family and troops are all dependent on David. He must now lead on his own initiative alone. He has neither venerable prophet nor cherished crown prince (Jonathan) to guide him.[11] Instead, David enters into a sort of filial relationship with Achish of Gath (who deduces, "he will be my servant forever," 27:12).

God's guidance. The absence of overt reference to God's direction or guidance seems appropriate in a passage devoted to describing the way David negotiates his way through tricky circumstances, without the obvious assurance of God's guidance. He must now move on faith, remembering past

---

11. We may assume that Abiathar the priest is still at his disposal, though he is not mentioned here (23:7—14).

times of God's faithfulness. As such, this text illustrates ways in which believers are often forced to make important decisions without the benefit of a specific word from God. At other times David has had the approved means of "inquiring of Yahweh" about important decisions. Earlier, for example, he was able to consult the priestly ephod with its Urim and Thummim to discern God's will for him (see 23:1–6 and comments).[12] Though these may have been available to David during his Philistine sojourn (as in 30:7–8), this text makes no mention of them. Instead, the chapter may be divided into three paragraphs illustrating the way David makes his decisions.

(1) Verses 1–4 portray David in deliberation, a sort of self-conversation in which he speaks to himself with the determination to take action. He concludes that the current crisis cannot continue and that the best thing he can do is flee from Judah altogether. Using his best judgment, David settles on doing what he thinks is logical. Though not stated by the narrator, we may assume from the characterization of David elsewhere that he takes action in the assumption that God will intervene on his behalf. Such a subtle narrative gives us insight into the divine-human interchange and the guidance of God.

We know from several other texts in the extended narrative that Yahweh was actively supporting David as Saul's successor. Thus, it comes as no surprise that David's actions, though taken on his own initiative, are effective. Here we are simply informed that his plan works: "When Saul was told that David had fled to Gath, he no longer searched for him" (27:4). David is doing what seems logical, walking through the doors open to him. God honors what he does.

(2) In verses 5–7 a similar process seems to be at work. David decides to approach Achish about occupying Ziklag. He uses logic and diplomacy to persuade his host that he should be allowed to move to the country and live in another city. Again the narrator gives indirect indication that David's stratagem works; note 27:6b: "[Ziklag] belonged to the kings of Judah ever since." The city that should have been a possession of Israel from the beginning (Josh. 15:31) now goes into David's hands and eventually becomes a royal city of Judah. Once again, God honors David's decisions.

(3) Verses 8–12 relate David's military campaigns during his Philistine sojourn. In this also David acts on his own God-given instincts. We may be tempted to label the events of this paragraph as "disreputable" and to deplore David's use of deception in his dealings with Achish.[13] But the text

---

12. See also 22:10, 13, 15; 30:7–8; 2 Sam. 2:1; 5:23. By contrast, Yahweh stopped responding to Saul's inquiries (1 Sam. 14:36–37; 28:6).

13. As is done by Gordon, *I and II Samuel*, 191. Others comment laconically that the Bible reports such episodes without condoning them.

is not included as a means of critiquing David's actions, no matter how questionable those actions seem to us today. Rather, in typical ancient Near Eastern fashion, the text celebrates the shrewdness of our protagonist and his ability to ingratiate himself to both his own people and to the Philistine overlord.

In fact, the Old Testament has other examples of justifiable deception (see 19:11–17, and our discussion there in the Bridging Contexts and Contemporary Significance sections; also 20:1–34). There are many occasions when the Bible actually honors those leading characters who are able to outwit their pagan foes (cf. the book of Judges). Here too the text reports David's actions and, by implication, approves of his methods. We are told simply that David's decisions work. Achish "trusts" David and believes they have formed a lasting political and martial relationship that will benefit them both (27:12).

There are many other examples of Old Testament characters who make decisions and take actions on their own, but who trust God through it all to guide their steps (e.g., Joseph in Gen. 37–50). Rarely do the saints of the Old Testament have direct confirmation of their actions, though they hold resolutely to the belief that God is involved. Such examples remind us to submit our entire decision-making process to God and trust him to enlighten our God-given reason and logic and to guide us in our important decisions in life.

LOOKING FOR GOD'S GUIDANCE. Some time ago, I heard Dr. Susan Muto speak in a seminary chapel service on the mystery of the divine-guided life. She said, "God writes straight in crooked lines."[14] I do not know if I understood her comment precisely as she intended it. But it struck me as a good way to describe my own experience in Christian faith. Normally we only see the specific ways in which God has led us as we look back on it after the passage of time. Only then can we trace God's special guidance, and do that through very crooked lines, meaning unexpected or even unwanted events. Yet through all of it, we can see that God has indeed written straight. What he writes, he writes well—just as Joseph looked back across time at the cruelty of his brothers and said, "You intended to harm me, but God intended it for good to accomplish what is now being done, the saving of many lives" (Gen. 50:20; cf. the New Testament equivalent in Rom. 8:28). Certainly the circuitous route Joseph took to lead Egypt in the famine would have appeared as if God writes straight, albeit in crooked lines.

---

14. Chapel at Ashland Theological Seminary, January 23, 1995.

Reflecting on the important decisions of life after the fact is easy. Making those decisions at the time, however, and determining the "right" decision can leave us with a most helpless feeling. David presents us here with an example of carefully making thoughtful decisions with the best critical faculties we have been given by God, while trusting him to guide us along the way. Here we find the principles of deliberation and consultation before taking decisive action, and these are steps that God often honors.

In my own experience, as with most others it seems, such guidance came at a pivotal juncture in my life. Months before I was to graduate from seminary, my wife and I faced an important decision that would clearly have implications for the shape and form of our future ministry together. I had planned for the pastoral ministry for four or five years. I had been ordained, and my denominational official was offering a church that looked exciting. Indeed, he believed it was an excellent beginning and claimed to be looking for the best ways to launch my career.

But in the closing semesters of my seminary training, I had felt interested in pursuing graduate studies in the field of Old Testament and Semitic languages. I had studied the various schools available and consulted with respected teachers in my seminary. We were left with these two choices: I could make application to the graduate school of my choice and wait to see if I would be accepted, or I could simply accept the denomination's assignment and begin my pastoral ministry full time. After careful consideration, prayer, and consultation with my professors, I made application to the graduate school. The official of my denomination agreed to wait until we heard from the school before making a final decision.

For months we waited on the proverbial "pins and needles." We were both excited about the church possibility and would have been quite happy to accept it. But the more we dreamed of graduate studies and a career in teaching, the more we both felt "led" in that direction. The question (as always) was, Is this what God wants for us? We were torn between the two and prayed for "guidance" to know what to do.

One day during this agonizing period, I realized that God was also working something new in my life spiritually. It was at this time of uncertainty, when my whole life seemed to hang in the balances, God spoke clearly—not about the specifics of whether I should go here or there, but about my willingness to do either. He was interested more in my *availability* than in my *ability*. He wanted me to seek first his will, not my own interest in what could satisfy my desires best. You may ask, But how do you know that is what God wanted? The answer is that he used the reason and clear logic of a particular prayer during a Eucharist service at the seminary. It was intended to commission graduating seniors and send them into the world for ministry. As part of the service, we read this prayer from John Wesley's covenant-renewal service:[15]

> I am no longer my own, but Thine. Put me to what Thou wilt, rank me with whom Thou wilt; put me to doing, put me to suffering; let me be employed for Thee or laid aside for Thee, exalted for Thee or brought low for Thee; let me be full, let me be empty; let me have all things, let me have nothing; I freely and heartily yield all things to Thy pleasure and disposal.

I realized slowly and painfully that I could not pray that prayer honestly. At various times in my young Christian experience, I had become too concerned about my own personal success, career, or attainment of academic status. I had not been concerned first and foremost about being employed for God or laid aside for God's sake. I had not learned the freedom that comes from caring not whether I was exalted or humbled, full or empty, having all things or having nothing. I had not learned fully the joy of yielding to God's good pleasure.

This text presents us with examples of David's taking decisive action that affect the role he will play in God's plans for the future. He bases his decisions on the logical and rational circumstances around him and appears to have simply trusted God to guide the process. Because we often lust for the tangible and the safety of the discernible, this type of trust is usually difficult for us. This type of trust can be illumined by one of my favorite quotes from Blaise Pascal: "Faith certainly tells us what the senses do not, but not the contrary of what they see; it is above, not against them."[16]

As we negotiate our own way through life's circumstances, it is our perception of those circumstances that often guides us in the decision-making process. But as believers, we understand there is a higher plane involved. Our faith helps us discern God's guidance in and through the circumstances, and we understand that he can, and we are not surprised when he actually does, intervene to change the circumstances or alter our decisions.[17]

---

15. Wesley's source for the service was Richard Alleine's *Vindiciae Pietatis* (see Marion A. Jackson, "An Analysis of the Source of John Wesley's Directions for Renewing Our Covenant with God," *Methodist History* 30 [1992]: 176–84). A copy with some modest updating of the English can be found in *The United Methodist Book of Worship* (Nashville: United Methodist Publishing, 1992), 291–94.

16. Blaise Pascal, *Pensées*, trans. A. J. Krailsheimer (London: Penguin, 1995), number 185.

17. Pascal's observation has many other implications—e.g., on the relationship between faith and science. But I think one implication of his insight relates to making decisions without discernible guidance from God.

1 Samuel 28:1–25

IN THOSE DAYS the Philistines gathered their forces to fight against Israel. Achish said to David, "You must understand that you and your men will accompany me in the army."

²David said, "Then you will see for yourself what your servant can do."

Achish replied, "Very well, I will make you my bodyguard for life."

³Now Samuel was dead, and all Israel had mourned for him and buried him in his own town of Ramah. Saul had expelled the mediums and spiritists from the land.

⁴The Philistines assembled and came and set up camp at Shunem, while Saul gathered all the Israelites and set up camp at Gilboa. ⁵When Saul saw the Philistine army, he was afraid; terror filled his heart. ⁶He inquired of the LORD, but the LORD did not answer him by dreams or Urim or prophets. ⁷Saul then said to his attendants, "Find me a woman who is a medium, so I may go and inquire of her."

"There is one in Endor," they said.

⁸So Saul disguised himself, putting on other clothes, and at night he and two men went to the woman. "Consult a spirit for me," he said, "and bring up for me the one I name."

⁹But the woman said to him, "Surely you know what Saul has done. He has cut off the mediums and spiritists from the land. Why have you set a trap for my life to bring about my death?"

¹⁰Saul swore to her by the LORD, "As surely as the LORD lives, you will not be punished for this."

¹¹Then the woman asked, "Whom shall I bring up for you?"

"Bring up Samuel," he said.

¹²When the woman saw Samuel, she cried out at the top of her voice and said to Saul, "Why have you deceived me? You are Saul!"

¹³The king said to her, "Don't be afraid. What do you see?"

The woman said, "I see a spirit coming up out of the ground."

"What does he look like?" he asked.

"An old man wearing a robe is coming up," she said.

Then Saul knew it was Samuel, and he bowed down and prostrated himself with his face to the ground.

¹⁵Samuel said to Saul, "Why have you disturbed me by bringing me up?"

"I am in great distress," Saul said. "The Philistines are fighting against me, and God has turned away from me. He no longer answers me, either by prophets or by dreams. So I have called on you to tell me what to do."

¹⁶Samuel said, "Why do you consult me, now that the LORD has turned away from you and become your enemy? ¹⁷The LORD has done what he predicted through me. The LORD has torn the kingdom out of your hands and given it to one of your neighbors—to David. ¹⁸Because you did not obey the LORD or carry out his fierce wrath against the Amalekites, the LORD has done this to you today. ¹⁹The LORD will hand over both Israel and you to the Philistines, and tomorrow you and your sons will be with me. The LORD will also hand over the army of Israel to the Philistines."

²⁰Immediately Saul fell full length on the ground, filled with fear because of Samuel's words. His strength was gone, for he had eaten nothing all that day and night.

²¹When the woman came to Saul and saw that he was greatly shaken, she said, "Look, your maidservant has obeyed you. I took my life in my hands and did what you told me to do. ²²Now please listen to your servant and let me give you some food so you may eat and have the strength to go on your way."

²³He refused and said, "I will not eat."

But his men joined the woman in urging him, and he listened to them. He got up from the ground and sat on the couch.

²⁴The woman had a fattened calf at the house, which she butchered at once. She took some flour, kneaded it and baked bread without yeast. ²⁵Then she set it before Saul and his men, and they ate. That same night they got up and left.

SAUL HAS NOT functioned as the legitimate anointed one. The best evidence of this is the continued presence of Israel's perennial threat, the dreaded Philistines. They played a significant role in the rise of the monarchy (chs. 8–12), becoming the main raison d'être for the institution of kingship in Israel (9:16). Yet the Philistines have not been much heard from in the extended narrative on the history of David's rise. Soon after David's anointing, he led a decisive victory against them, thanks to his spectacular defeat of Goliath (ch. 17). The Philistines reappeared in an attempt to capture the city of Keilah, threatening the borders of central Judah (ch. 23). Again, it was David and not Saul who saved the people from the Philistines. At the conclusion of the Keilah episode, Saul was obsessed with pursuing David at the expense of defending the nation against the Philistines (23:19–29).

Rather than trace the details of the Philistine conflict, our historian has devoted himself to characterizing the two anointed ones, David and Saul, and outlining the contrasts between them. But the Philistines have never been far away. With the opening words of chapter 28, the Philistine threat once again comes to the foreground as the most important historical context for these events. This time the conflict serves as the backdrop for the defeat and death of King Saul and Israel's crown prince, Jonathan. This conflict will dominate the remainder of 1 Samuel.

Few would argue with the appraisal of this text as one of the most unusual in the Bible. In a desperate attempt to determine God's plan (in distinction to discerning God's *will*), Saul goes to a necromancer, or spiritual medium, in order to conduct a séance in which he converses with the deceased Samuel. With the Philistine and Israelite armies facing off in the Jezreel Valley, the traditional place for combat, Saul is seized by terror. In his moment of despair, he resorts to an illegitimate and forbidden substitute for prophecy. In a way that surprises most modern readers, the Bible describes the specter, or the ghost of the departed Samuel, in conversation with Saul.

Today's readers might be tempted to dismiss the reality of this episode as a vestige of primitive, superstitious shamanism or as a literary invention to describe Saul's character, having little to do with reality.[1] But the biblical text is unapologetically consistent in its assertion that the event described here

---

1. In fact, scholars through the centuries have tried a great variety of interpretations for the event. See K. A. D. Smelik, "The Witch of Endor: I Samuel 28 in Rabbinic and Christian Exegesis till 800 A.D.," *Vigiliae christianae* 33 (1979): 160–79.

is historical.[2] Today's readers would do well to admit that there remains much we do not understand about death and the afterlife, and we should not easily dismiss the face value of the text.

Renewed War with the Philistines (28:1–2)

FOR ACHISH, RENEWED HOSTILITIES WITH ISRAEL present a test of David's loyalty to his new Philistine allies.[3] But for the narrator, the situation presents a dilemma for the anointed one, who has been guided and protected by God until now. David is now in an impossible situation. Achish joins his fellow Philistine overlords in mustering their forces against Israel's heartland (namely, Aphek, cf. 29:1), and it is time for David to "fish or cut bait." If he refuses Achish, he belies his true loyalty to his native Israel and makes an enemy of Achish more dangerous than Saul. But to fight against his own people, whom he is anointed to rule, is equally impossible.

David's response seems carefully crafted to be noncommittal, though it satisfies Achish. The Philistine ruler is remarkably trusting, even naïve. Perhaps his affection for David has dimmed his memory of the younger shepherd boy who once decapitated another Philistine from Gath (ch. 17).[4] David's dilemma is suspended until chapter 29, where it reaches resolution. For now, the narrator switches to the *other* anointed one, Saul, in order to relate the nadir in his tragic downfall.

Circumstances of Saul's Final Humiliation (28:3–6)

THIS PARAGRAPH PROVIDES essential background elements for reading what follows. The narrator moves succinctly from older events that need to be foregrounded because of their relevance (28:3) to recent and current events that make it possible for the reader to critique Saul's actions in the rest of the text (28:4–6).[5]

The first piece of older information is a detail recorded earlier, namely, the death of Samuel (see 25:1).[6] Thus, we remember that Saul has lost his

---

2. "There is no indication that anyone [among the biblical tradents] regarded the apparition of Samuel as a fraudulent fiction perpetrated by the woman. Both the earlier account and the Deuteronomistic compiler are convinced that Samuel was really present" (Hertzberg, *I and II Samuel*, 220–21).

3. These verses assume the events of ch. 27 (see comments; also see comments at 21:10–15 for the identity of Achish).

4. Achish's statement in v. 2, "I will make you my bodyguard" (lit., "watcher of my head") may be an ironic wordplay on Goliath's head (see Miscall, *1 Samuel*, 167).

5. The NIV's pluperfects in verse 3 are appropriate in comparison to the simple past verbs in verses 4–6.

6. The statement in v. 3a is nearly verbatim from 25:1, which I argued is also strategic in its location there.

prophetic source of divine guidance. But by implication we also recall that Samuel rests among the shades of the underworld, which means he can still be consulted through the practice of necromancy.[7]

The additional information from the past is new to us: Saul had banished all "mediums and spiritists" from Israel. The narrator anticipates the witch's initial objections (28:9). But more importantly, the phrase highlights an important detail that aids the reader in critiquing Saul's actions. Even Saul himself, at some point earlier in his reign—perhaps under the direction of Samuel—had forbidden the use of necromancy. By expelling "mediums and spiritists," Saul had obeyed Pentateuchal law (Lev. 19:31; 20:27; Deut. 18:10–11).[8] But as we will soon see, driving the specific sin of necromancy from Saul's land did not drive the roots of that sin from his heart.

The narrator now moves to current events. The battle lines are being drawn in the fateful Jezreel Valley, where armies often gathered for battle. In the northern reaches of the valley, the Philistines are encamped at Shunem (approximately nine miles east-northeast of Megiddo). The very presence of the Philistine army so far north indicates Saul's weakness and the likelihood that they are attempting to isolate Saul from the Israelite tribes farther to the north.[9] On the opposite side of the valley to the south lies the Gilboa ridge, approximately ten miles south-southeast of Shunem.[10] The two armies are facing off for battle. Saul's position on Mount Gilboa places him strategically on a type of observation deck so he can observe the outcome.

The narrator prepares us further for what follows by exposing Saul's inner life. At the sight of the Philistine army, "terror filled his heart" (28:5). The statement that he "inquired of the LORD" is significant in light of this phrase's other occurrences in 1 Samuel (see comments at 23:1–6). The extended narrative has contrasted Saul and David by showing that David often "inquired of Yahweh," and this feature will continue to characterize him in 2 Samuel. Even when this particular means of seeking divine guidance is not employed (for whatever reason), David continues to depend on God's direction for his decisions (see comments on ch. 27). By contrast, Saul has killed the priests of Nob and forfeited the means of consulting Yahweh (22:6–23). Now the

---

7. Theodore J. Lewis, *Cults of the Dead in Ancient Israel and Ugarit* (HSM 39; Atlanta: Scholars Press, 1989), 112.

8. The terms used here (ʾob and yiddᵉʿoni) have to do with communicating with the spirits of the dead and either refer to types of necromancers (male and female?) or simply form a hendiadys to necromancy in general (see ibid., 113–14). Note that Saul's obedience of Pentateuchal law was only partial since such people were to be put to death.

9. Baldwin, *1 and 2 Samuel*, 158; Gordon, *I and II Samuel*, 194.

10. Yohanan Aharoni and Michael Avi-Yonah, *The Macmillan Bible Atlas* (New York: Macmillan, 1977), 64. Mount Gilboa is always associated with Saul's death.

contrast comes to a climax, because Saul *finally* "inquires" but receives no answer. The text anticipates 30:7–8, where David again inquires before avenging the war crimes at Ziklag.

For Saul, it is too late. Verse 6 catalogs the acceptable methods by which an Israelite can seek God's guidance: dreams, lots (NIV "Urim"), and prophecy.[11] But Yahweh has long since stopped answering Saul since the king is more inclined to make up his mind before asking (see 14:36–37). When his "foxhole" prayer brings no satisfaction, he becomes desperate to discern the plan of God. His next action represents the lowest point of his troubled reign as king over Israel.

Saul Consults the Medium at Endor (28:7–14)

IN A DESPERATE move, Saul asks his attendants to help him locate a medium who can communicate with the dead. The town of Endor has not been conclusively located, but according to all the biblical data, it is likely located in the southern portion of the Jezreel Valley, near the Kishon River.[12]

This text clearly illustrates what some Israelites believed about ancestor worship and cults of the dead.[13] Materials from Ugarit and elsewhere in the ancient Near East have illumined the biblical evidence, and in recent decades scholarly investigations have come to new understandings of ancestor worship and related death rituals in popular religion during the Old Testament period.[14] Against the wishes of the prophets and the leaders of normative religion in ancient Israel, some Israelites apparently persisted in the Canaanite custom of necromancy and other death rituals.[15] In such rituals, actions were directed to the deceased in an attempt to appease the dead or to secure favors from them. This text, then, represents a vestige of the customs and religious practices of Canaanites and of some Israelites, despite the disapproval of normative Old Testament religion.[16]

---

11. McCarter, *I Samuel*, 420; see our commentary at 23:1–6 on Urim and Thummim.

12. Diana V. Edelman, "En-dor," *ABD*, 2:499–501.

13. This is the *locus classicus* for any examination of necromancy in the Old Testament, though there are others. For details and for more on the understanding of the text presented here, see esp. Lewis, *Cults of the Dead*, 104–17.

14. For overview of this topic, see Bill T. Arnold, "Religion in Ancient Israel," in *The Face of Old Testament Studies*, ed. David W. Baker and Bill T. Arnold (Grand Rapids: Baker, 1999), 414–15. For a contrary approach, see Philip Johnston, "The Underworld and the Dead in the Old Testament," *TynBul* 45 (1994): 415–19.

15. Necromancy is a form of divination, which calls upon the dead for communication of knowledge. Verse 8b demonstrates that some people (Saul included) believed the dead had knowledge not available to the living.

16. Others have argued that interest in the dead developed first in the Neo-Assyrian Empire and entered Israel only in the late eighth and seventh centuries B.C. because of

The terminology of verse 8 may reflect certain aspects of the ritual. Saul's visit at night may have been a simple military necessity. But nighttime may also have been the approved time for such séances, the darkness of night being the appropriate time to communicate with those who live in darkness.[17] Saul's specific imperative (*qos°mi*, "consult") is a technical verb for divination, which is not limited to necromancy but applies to all forms of divination.[18] His intention is narrowed to necromancy here by the qualifying phrase, "a spirit for me." The idea that Saul needs the medium to "bring up" someone reflects the concept of Sheol as a place for the dead beneath the earth's surface, to which people descend at death.[19]

Ironically, the medium is hesitant.[20] He who wanted to eliminate necromancy from the land (28:3) has come to her with just such a request, and she who communicates with the dead is worried about joining them prematurely: "Why have you set a trap for my life to bring about my death?" Once Saul guarantees her safety, the medium is ready to hear the name of the departed individual whom Saul wishes to contact. Now we learn for the first time that it is Samuel (though the reference in v. 3 prepared us for this news).

As on the day of Yahweh's judgment, when his people who have rejected his Word will endure a famine of the prophetic word and search everywhere for that life-sustaining power but not find it (Amos 8:11–12), so Saul desperately wants to hear the word of Yahweh once again. The voice of his prophetic mentor has long been silenced by Saul's persistent rebellion. But as the noose closes in around his neck on this night before his death, he who is king in name turns one final time to Israel's kingmaker, Samuel. This great prophet has been Saul's source of the life-sustaining word of Yahweh. Unfortunately for Saul, the die is cast.

Much to the surprise of the medium (not to mention the modern reader!), she successfully conjures up Samuel. At his appearance, the woman shrieks and immediately recognizes that her client is King Saul himself (28:12). At this point in the narrative, we are left with unanswered questions. Why

---

Assyrian influence. See Brian B. Schmidt, *Israel's Beneficent Dead: Ancestor Cult and Necromancy in Ancient Israelite Religion and Tradition* (Tübingen: J. C. B. Mohr, 1994). However, in order to explain the evidence of ch. 28, Schmidt is forced to argue for its late or post-Deuteronomistic origins (201–20).

17. Job 10:21–22; see Lewis, *Cults of the Dead*, 114.

18. Malcolm J. A. Horsnell, "קסם," *NIDOTTE*, 3:945–51.

19. Eugene H. Merrill, "שאול," *NIDOTTE*, 4:6–7; see Philip S. Johnston, "'Left in Hell?' Psalm 16, Sheol and the Holy One," in *The Lord's Anointed: Interpretation of Old Testament Messianic Texts*, ed. P. E. Satterthwaite, R. S. Hess, and G. J. Wenham (Carlisle: Paternoster, 1995), 213–22 (esp. 216–21).

20. "It is ironic that a woman who can see into the underworld has not been able to this point to see through Saul's disguise" (Lewis, *Cults of the Dead*, 115).

precisely should the woman be shocked at the apparition if she were accustomed to such séances? Does her surprise indicate that she does not really have the power to raise the dead and is therefore shocked at her own success? Or does Samuel's appearance differ significantly from other specters? Why does she suddenly discern Saul's identity? Some have argued that the woman does not actually have the ability to conjure up the dead, so that her alarm indicates her own lack of control of the situation.[21]

Without becoming sidetracked with questions that are finally unanswerable, we can state that the essentials are clear.[22] Samuel appears to Saul one last time and communicates with him through this medium. Saul himself is not able to see Samuel, at least not initially, since he has to ask the medium about Samuel's appearance (28:14). Convinced by her description that it is indeed Samuel, the king prostrates himself before the venerable prophet and prepares for the encounter.

The medium's description of Samuel requires comment: "I see a spirit coming up out of the ground" (28:13). The NIV's "spirit" is the ordinary word for "God" or "gods" (*ʾĕlohim*), and it has long been recognized that it can stand simply for "godlike being" or "celestial spirit."[23] But work done in recent decades on ancestor worship in other ancient cultures has confirmed that the dead could be referred to as "gods" in an attempt to describe some type of transcendent character. These individuals existed beyond the natural realm, so that we might describe them as "preternatural."[24] Furthermore, Samuel is described as arising out of the "ground" (*haʾareṣ*), which in Hebrew as well as in cognate Near Eastern languages can designate the netherworld or the realm of the dead.[25] Thus the medium explains to Saul that she is observing a preternatural being coming up from the underworld.

Samuel's Answer and Its Result (28:15–25)

GIVEN AN AUDIENCE WITH HIS FORMER MENTOR, Saul summarizes his situation succinctly and factually: The Philistines are threatening and God has

---

21. David F. Payne, *I and II Samuel* (Philadelphia: Westminster John Knox, 1982), 145.

22. For the history of interpretation of the many perplexing facets of this text, see Smelik, "The Witch of Endor," 160–79.

23. Keil and Delitzsch, *Samuel*, 263.

24. I.e., they are *beyond* or different from that which is natural, as opposed to the "supernatural," which is *above* what is natural (Lewis, *Cults of the Dead*, 49–50, 115–16).

25. *HALOT*, 1:91; *Ahw*, 245. Hence the "land of the living" is often contrasted with the underworld (Isa. 38:11; 53:8, etc.; see Magnus Ottosson, "אֶרֶץ," *TDOT*, 1:390–404, esp. 399–400). On the underworld receiving the dead, see F. M. Cross Jr. and F. N. Freedman, "The Song of Miriam," *JNES* 14 (1955): 237–50, esp. 247–48; William L. Holladay, "*ʾereṣ*– 'Underworld': Two More Suggestions," *VT* 19 (1969): 123–24.

withdrawn (28:15). Saul's concluding explanation reveals his desperate and hopeless condition: "I have called on you to tell me what to do." The matter-of-fact tone Saul uses seems to imply that he and Samuel can return to the early years of Saul's kingdom. Saul is hoping to turn back the clock to better days. It is as though he wants Samuel to forget all that has happened—as if he is saying: "Please ignore this medium standing here and the illicit way I have contacted you, or your various condemnations of my character in the past, or the way I have recklessly sought to kill David while neglecting the Philistines all these years. Please tell me what to do now."

Samuel's reply has no advice concerning the impending battle with the Philistines (28:16–19). The message of the deceased Samuel was the same as the living Samuel. He simply reiterates the divine judgment against the king announced when he was alive. Yahweh is no longer with Saul; rather, he has been faithful to his word by becoming Saul's enemy. He has torn the kingdom from him and given it to David. As in chapter 15, all of this relates to Saul's failure in the war against the Amalekites. The great old prophet (as eloquent in death as in life) has condensed the entire narrative of chapters 16–28 into the fulfillment of his earlier condemnations of Saul (13:13–14; 15:22–29).

> Samuel tells Saul no more than he should already know, i.e., why ask me, since you already have the word of the Lord? Or, with a slight twist, why ask me, since I am dead and can only tell you what you already know?[26]

Though there is no advice concerning the Philistines, there is this: "The LORD will hand over both Israel and you to the Philistines, and tomorrow you and your sons will be with me." Samuel ignores the sin of necromancy and the presence of the medium. He makes no more speeches decrying Saul's shameful disregard for Yahweh's word. He speaks only of "today" and "tomorrow."[27] The time of Saul's judgment has arrived.

First Samuel has narrated the anointing of two kings and has traced the conflict between the two. The theme of Yahweh's rejection of the first anointed one, Saul, arrives at a climax in 28:20 (and is substantiated in ch. 31). Saul falls "full length on the ground," overcome with fear because of the message from Samuel. We have come a long way from the depiction of Saul as head and shoulders above the crowd, the man of God's own choosing (10:23–24).

Saul's lack of food has variously been explained as a necessity of war because food was not easily accessible or as a result of his emotional state. But

---

26. Miscall, *1 Samuel*, 169.
27. Ibid., 170.

it seems probable that fasting was a requirement of the ritual involved in necromancy.[28] He has gone without food "all that day and night" in preparation for his night visit to the medium at Endor. Now he is exhausted, finished. His kingdom is over, and he himself as good as dead. The woman feeds him his last meal, a banquet fit for a king who will not be king much longer.[29]

Bridging Contexts

WHERE TO TURN IN A CRISIS. During the darkest days of David's exile, when Saul had turned all his energies to the sole task of killing him, David sought help wherever he could find it. As we noted in our comments on chapter 21, you can learn a lot about a person by seeing where he or she turns in a time of trouble. David turned first to Samuel (while he was still alive) at his hometown, Ramah (19:18–24). When it became obvious the prophets at Ramah could not protect David indefinitely, he fled back to Gibeah to seek the help and advice of his good friend Jonathan (20:1–42). Finally, convinced he could not secure reconciliation with Saul and being in need of arms and shelter, David went to Ahimelech the priest at Nob (21:1–9). In his greatest hour of need, David returned to the sources of his childhood faith and was reminded that Yahweh had always been his help.

This text obviously tells us a lot about Saul by relating where he turned in *his* darkest hour. The historian's contrast between Saul and David thus builds to a climax in these closing chapters of 1 Samuel. Saul's nocturnal trip to Endor marks his final departure from faith in Yahweh, from the faith that Samuel had stood for in life. Now in death, as in life, Samuel proclaims once again the judgment of the Lord against Saul. This episode along with the report of Saul's ignoble death at Mount Gilboa (ch. 31) marks the final events in the fall of the king.

As David ascends to new heights, Saul is stooping to new lows. In 2 Samuel, Saul's descendants gradually disappear until the only remaining trace is the pitiable Mephibosheth, who is graciously sustained at David's table (2 Sam. 9:13). The Chronicler's brief treatment of Saul cites this event as evidence that Saul deserved the punishment that befell him (1 Chron. 10:13–14): "Saul died because he was unfaithful to the LORD; he did not keep the word of the LORD and even consulted a medium for guidance, and did not inquire of the LORD. So the LORD put him to death and turned the kingdom over to David son of Jesse."

---

28. Lewis, *Cults of the Dead,* 114.
29. Brueggemann, *First and Second Samuel,* 196.

Magic arts and prophecy. The Old Testament preserves vestiges of necromancy in other texts, indicating that necromancy continued to be a temptation for the Israelites for centuries.[30] According to the Pentateuch, official Yahwism condemned cults of the dead (Lev. 19:26–32; 20:6, 27; Deut. 14:1; 18:9–11; 26:14). But several references in the historical books imply that individual Israelites continued to succumb to the idea that such practices were beneficial. David's vigil over the imminent death of his son seems to engage in a ritual descent to the underworld (2 Sam. 12:15–24). David's son Absalom apparently engaged in some sort of cult of the dead in a funerary ritual for his deceased sons (14:27; 18:18). The story of the bones of Elisha reviving a dead man may well reflect the belief, known also from Mesopotamian texts, that the bones of the deceased could be utilized for curative purposes (2 Kings 13:20–21). The biblical authors condemned Manasseh's evil as including consultation with mediums (21:6), and Josiah's reform specifically targeted forms of divination, including necromancy (23:24).

Israel's ban on magic was a unique characteristic of the nation's overarching worldview. All other nations in the ancient Near East believed in and practiced a wide variety of magical arts. They believed formulaic recitations and imitative acts could manipulate and exploit the powers of the deities and thereby procure benefits for themselves that were otherwise impossible. By implication, the gods were viewed as subservient to supernatural forces beyond their control. Israel's monotheism and concepts of the transcendence and sovereignty of Yahweh made such views an impossibility. The Creator God is not subservient to any manner of supernatural force beyond his control and cannot be manipulated under any circumstances. Israel's theology simply made the use of magic forbidden.

Significantly, however, the Old Testament's ban on magic is not based on the assertion that magic is ineffective. On the contrary, magic is banned precisely because it *does* work. As monotheists, the biblical authors did not believe magic was connected to other gods but depended on self-operating forces. They attributed a reality to magical power that was independent of the gods, though they seldom attempted a more specific definition of that power. Magic, therefore, was tantamount to human rebellion that unlocked divine secrets, making humanity equal with God.[31]

Two issues, therefore, help bring this passage into our century: magic and prophecy. Saul turns to the illegitimate use of magic as a means of seeking guidance while closing his eyes to the prophetic word. The result, ironically,

---

30. For full discussion of these and several other texts, see Lewis, *Cults of the Dead*, 99–170.

31. Kaufmann, *The Religion of Israel*, 7–121; Mark W. Chavalas, "Magic," *EDBT*, 502.

is that the magic he uses actually confirms the prophetic word he has scorned. Samuel's speech (28:16–19) makes this clear. The prophecies about Saul and David have been fulfilled, and these cannot be rescinded or ignored; they are only confirmed by Saul's use of necromancy.

Thus, these closing chapters of 1 Samuel illustrate who can suitably serve as the anointed one. David, the legitimate anointed one, turns to Yahweh for guidance, either through the officially approved means of priestly ephod with its Urim and Thummim (22:10, 13, 15; 23:1–6; 30:8; 2 Sam. 2:1; 5:19, 23; 16:23) or through rational dependence on Yahweh's guiding spirit (1 Sam. 27). By contrast, Saul has driven the priestly ephod away from his service because of his maniacal preoccupation with killing David and must now turn to magic to seek guidance. Magic and prophecy are related to each other as opposite sides of the same coin. They are mutually exclusive, and the anointed of Yahweh must choose between them. The use of magic will bring prophetic condemnation, while reliance on the prophetic word will result in the expulsion of magic from the land. In either case, the question is how one relates to the Lord and whether one will allow the Lord to direct one's paths.

 CONTEMPORARY INTEREST IN MAGIC. There are certain obvious ways in which we can relate this text to our contemporary setting. Not many years ago, the practice of magic and participation in the occult were rare in North American society and were definitely seen as emanating from the fringes of society. All of that has changed with the rise of postmodernism and especially in the emphases of the New Age movement. A positive side of postmodernism is a renewed hunger and desire to experience the supernatural. But wherever Christianity has been slow or unprepared to meet the need, the New Age movement has rushed in to fill the gap with beliefs in channeling, crystals, horoscopes, paranormal psychology, and reincarnation.

Saul in this text represents a paradigm of the individual who turns away from legitimate sources of relating to God and relies instead on illicit ways of manipulating God through magic. In many ways, this relates to the way New Agers offer our culture an array of services to assist people in their search for the supernatural as a means of self-fulfillment. The church needs to be consistent in condemning all uses of magic as tools for manipulating God and other less obvious strands, such as those put forward by the New Age movement.

Subtle magic. But there are more subtle ways in which this text applies. It would be simplistic for us to limit the application of this text to blatant heretical practices such as the occult and magical incantations. Rather, we should also consider how easy it is to use good things in a magical way in an attempt to manipulate God. For example, consider the magical use of prayer, church attendance, and tithing among modern believers. Saul's reliance on a nonbiblical worldview needs to be applied to such cases in which perfunctory observance of the standard means of grace can come to represent the means by which we exact God's good favor. In other words, some believers come to expect good things from God, even believe that God *owes* them something, because they (we!) have fulfilled certain obligations. One's relationship with God can be quickly reduced to a sort of previously arranged agreement, a sort of quid pro quo, in which all we have to do is keep our end of the bargain and God will be forced to keep his.

I once served for a period of time as an intern chaplain in a prison while I was in training for ministry. One day I met Mr. Smith (not his real name). He was in prison for embezzlement, was serving a light term, and was expecting to be released soon. In one of our sessions, Mr. Smith began explaining how God would eventually bring him great success in his business ventures; in fact, he said God *owed* him success. When I tried delicately to ask about the particulars of that assumption, Mr. Smith acted surprised that I did not follow his logic. You see, God owed him success in business because he, Mr. Smith, had been so faithful to return a tithe of his profits to the church. He even quoted Scripture to prove his point (Luke 6:38): "Give, and it will be given to you. A good measure, pressed down, shaken together and running over, will be poured into your lap." When I tried to suggest that this may be a misapplication of that verse and that, in fact, the Bible has other things to say about stewardship and our responsibilities in the world, Mr. Smith simply refused to listen to me. After all, I was only a young seminary student.

Later in my ministry, I realized Mr. Smith is no exception. In fact, his views on the use of money are in many ways symptomatic of other believers I have known, though his unmitigated avarice and unsophisticated hermeneutic made it easier to explain how he could arrive at such conclusions. What I have found more frustrating and less explainable is how believers who seem mature in every other respect and who have been actively involved in the life of the church for many years develop similar assumptions.

Indeed, many Christians today in the North American context implicitly view church attendance as a sort of deposit in their spiritual account. It is an investment they believe will pay benefits in the future. So with Bible reading, or tithing, or befriending the unchurched, or visiting shut-ins—all become a means to an end instead of a means of expressing our love for, adoration of, and thanks to God. Church attendance in such a view is transformed from a regular custom of worship to a means of ingratiating ourselves to God, a way of purchasing God's favor. Such abuses of the means of grace are just as misguided as Saul's trip to Endor.

Capitalizing on our faith. Another way in which to apply this text is to stress the inconsistency in Saul's actions. Our Bridging Contexts section emphasized the two options available to Saul for divine communion: magic and prophecy. They are mutually exclusive, representing competing world-views. Saul had rightly banned all mediums and spiritists from his kingdom (28:3), but he had not replaced them by nurturing and supporting the proper replacements for such mediums.

In other words, Saul had not fostered a close relationship with the legitimate means of divine communication, the prophets and priests of Yahweh, who should naturally have filled the void left by the departure of the mediums and spiritists. In fact, in Saul's irrational pursuit of David, he had killed the majority of the priests and marginalized the prophets (cf. 22:6–23; 19:18–24). When the Philistine crisis came, Saul was unprepared because he had not consistently nurtured his relationship with God. He had not replaced the magicians with prophets. The trip to Endor reveals that he had not replaced his own personal reliance on magicians with a vital relationship with God.

One astute theologian who can help us understand this is Helmut Thielicke, who was forced to hammer out his theology on the anvil of Hitler's Third Reich. Plagued by the realization that many of Germany's Christians had accepted and even defended Nazism's racial lies, Thielicke later explored theology's "polar structure."[32] He contended that one pole of theology stems from "a superior, eternal basis derived from revelation," while the other stems from "specific constellations of the spirit of the age." As a result, Christian faith "believes *against* as well as *in*," because it will always involve opposition to the *Zeitgeist*, or the spirit of the age. Using Saul as the example, we could argue that it is not enough to believe *against* (as Saul banned the mediums and spiritists). We must believe *in* as well, replacing our mediums and spiritists with prophets and priests of the Lord.

We stated earlier that you learn a lot about people by observing where they turn in times of trouble.[33] When David's life was in jeopardy, he turned first to Samuel, next to Jonathan, and then to Ahimelech the priest. David consistently returned to the sources of his childhood faith. By contrast, Saul's visit to Endor in *his* darkest hour represents his final departure from faith in Yahweh. Any severe crisis heightens the sense of what one really believes.

---

32. Helmut Thielicke, *Modern Faith and Thought*, trans. Geoffrey W. Bromiley (Grand Rapids: Eerdmans, 1990), 5–7.

33. See Bridging Contexts section above; also comments on ch. 21.

During World War II, combat soldiers in Belgium on Christmas Day were involved in the Battle of the Bulge, one of the most brutal and gruesome battles in the history of the United States Army. Even though there was no general cease-fire, the troops spoke of an "urge to go to church," which resulted in a few strange services in which civilians sat with soldiers in full combat fatigues and weapons.[34] My father was a sergeant in the 83rd Infantry Division on the northwest flank of the bulge. Under intense artillery fire when several men in his squad lost their lives, he testifies to an overwhelming sense of God's presence, which drove him back to his own childhood faith and resulted in commitments that lasted the rest of his life.

We caricature the "foxhole prayer" as a commitment tossed heavenward in desperation and one that seldom lasts. But I have met veterans who are convinced that their own crisis was life-changing, while other men in the same situation never gave God a thought. The crisis has a way of bringing to the surface what one really believes. Saul's trip to Endor belied the king's real commitments and revealed that his failure to nurture his relationship with Yahweh during his lifetime meant he was unprepared for his life to end. Christians must attend to that most important of all relationships so that in our own moment of crisis, which is inevitable for us all, we can face God with confidence and hope.

---

34. Stephen E. Ambrose, *Citizen Soldiers: The U.S. Army from the Normandy Beaches to the Bulge to the Surrender of Germany, June 7, 1944–May 7, 1945* (New York: Touchstone, 1997), 236.

1 Samuel 29:1–30:31

◟

THE PHILISTINES GATHERED all their forces at Aphek, and Israel camped by the spring in Jezreel. ²As the Philistine rulers marched with their units of hundreds and thousands, David and his men were marching at the rear with Achish. ³The commanders of the Philistines asked, "What about these Hebrews?"

Achish replied, "Is this not David, who was an officer of Saul king of Israel? He has already been with me for over a year, and from the day he left Saul until now, I have found no fault in him."

⁴But the Philistine commanders were angry with him and said, "Send the man back, that he may return to the place you assigned him. He must not go with us into battle, or he will turn against us during the fighting. How better could he regain his master's favor than by taking the heads of our own men? ⁵Isn't this the David they sang about in their dances:

"'Saul has slain his thousands,

and David his tens of thousands'?"

⁶So Achish called David and said to him, "As surely as the LORD lives, you have been reliable, and I would be pleased to have you serve with me in the army. From the day you came to me until now, I have found no fault in you, but the rulers don't approve of you. ⁷Turn back and go in peace; do nothing to displease the Philistine rulers."

⁸"But what have I done?" asked David. "What have you found against your servant from the day I came to you until now? Why can't I go and fight against the enemies of my lord the king?"

⁹Achish answered, "I know that you have been as pleasing in my eyes as an angel of God; nevertheless, the Philistine commanders have said, 'He must not go up with us into battle.' ¹⁰Now get up early, along with your master's servants who have come with you, and leave in the morning as soon as it is light."

¹¹So David and his men got up early in the morning to go back to the land of the Philistines, and the Philistines went up to Jezreel.

³⁰:¹David and his men reached Ziklag on the third day. Now the Amalekites had raided the Negev and Ziklag. They had attacked Ziklag and burned it, ²and had taken captive the women and all who were in it, both young and old. They killed none of them, but carried them off as they went on their way.

³When David and his men came to Ziklag, they found it destroyed by fire and their wives and sons and daughters taken captive. ⁴So David and his men wept aloud until they had no strength left to weep. ⁵David's two wives had been captured—Ahinoam of Jezreel and Abigail, the widow of Nabal of Carmel. ⁶David was greatly distressed because the men were talking of stoning him; each one was bitter in spirit because of his sons and daughters. But David found strength in the LORD his God.

⁷Then David said to Abiathar the priest, the son of Ahimelech, "Bring me the ephod." Abiathar brought it to him, ⁸and David inquired of the LORD, "Shall I pursue this raiding party? Will I overtake them?"

"Pursue them," he answered. "You will certainly overtake them and succeed in the rescue."

⁹David and the six hundred men with him came to the Besor Ravine, where some stayed behind, ¹⁰for two hundred men were too exhausted to cross the ravine. But David and four hundred men continued the pursuit.

¹¹They found an Egyptian in a field and brought him to David. They gave him water to drink and food to eat—¹²part of a cake of pressed figs and two cakes of raisins. He ate and was revived, for he had not eaten any food or drunk any water for three days and three nights.

¹³David asked him, "To whom do you belong, and where do you come from?"

He said, "I am an Egyptian, the slave of an Amalekite. My master abandoned me when I became ill three days ago. ¹⁴We raided the Negev of the Kerethites and the territory belonging to Judah and the Negev of Caleb. And we burned Ziklag."

¹⁵David asked him, "Can you lead me down to this raiding party?"

He answered, "Swear to me before God that you will not kill me or hand me over to my master, and I will take you down to them."

¹⁶He led David down, and there they were, scattered over the countryside, eating, drinking and reveling because of the great amount of plunder they had taken from the land of the Philistines and from Judah. ¹⁷David fought them from dusk until the evening of the next day, and none of them got away, except four hundred young men who rode off on camels and fled. ¹⁸David recovered everything the Amalekites had taken, including his two wives. ¹⁹Nothing was missing: young or old, boy or girl, plunder or anything else they had taken. David brought everything back. ²⁰He took all the flocks and herds, and his men drove them ahead of the other livestock, saying, "This is David's plunder."

²¹Then David came to the two hundred men who had been too exhausted to follow him and who were left behind at the Besor Ravine. They came out to meet David and the people with him. As David and his men approached, he greeted them. ²²But all the evil men and troublemakers among David's followers said, "Because they did not go out with us, we will not share with them the plunder we recovered. However, each man may take his wife and children and go."

²³David replied, "No, my brothers, you must not do that with what the LORD has given us. He has protected us and handed over to us the forces that came against us. ²⁴Who will listen to what you say? The share of the man who stayed with the supplies is to be the same as that of him who went down to the battle. All will share alike." ²⁵David made this a statute and ordinance for Israel from that day to this.

²⁶When David arrived in Ziklag, he sent some of the plunder to the elders of Judah, who were his friends, saying, "Here is a present for you from the plunder of the LORD's enemies."

²⁷He sent it to those who were in Bethel, Ramoth Negev and Jattir; ²⁸to those in Aroer, Siphmoth, Eshtemoa ²⁹and Racal; to those in the towns of the Jerahmeelites and the Kenites; ³⁰to those in Hormah, Bor Ashan, Athach ³¹and Hebron; and to those in all the other places where David and his men had roamed.

THIS TEXT IS PART of an extended unit on David's sojourn in Philistia (chs. 27–31). Chapter 27 relates how David, realizing that reconciliation with Saul was impossible, came to live peaceably with Achish of Gath and settled in Ziklag. The narrative is interrupted by chapter 28, which portrays the pitiable Saul before the specter of Samuel and the medium at Endor. The present chapters return to David's life as a mercenary soldier in Philistia and relate first how he is delivered from participating in the war between his Philistine hosts and his native people, and then how the insidious Amalekites raid Ziklag in David's absence and how he, led by the Lord, exacts vengeance against them. Finally, we learn details of David's support of key cities of his homeland in anticipation of the day when he will rule them as king.

The account of Saul's nocturnal visit to the medium at Endor has settled once and for all the outcome of the narrative with regard to Saul. He can only come to ruin, and that in an ignoble death in the imminent battle with the Philistines. But we as readers are left with unanswered questions. When we left David in chapter 27, he was enjoying amiable relations with the Philistines, though he had deceived Achish and had surreptitiously become the protector and defender of Judah against desert marauders. As long as Achish does not know the true nature of David's military campaigns, David will continue to gain favor with the people of Judah while endearing himself further to this Philistine master.

But this is a dangerous game. The single development David can ill afford is renewed hostilities between the Philistines and Saul's armies. In such a conflict, David will be trapped. If he joins his Israelite brothers by turning against his Philistine allies, he will forfeit the protection he has found in Gath and will once again be at the mercy of Saul. But if he fights against the Israelites, he will certainly jeopardize the God-given promise of becoming their king.[1]

We were told earlier that the two armies were facing off for battle (28:1–2), which left us uncertain about David's future. Saul is as good as dead, since he is dying from the inside out. But how will David's dilemma be resolved? Will he be able to escape the consequences of his successful but dangerous doublecrossing of Achish? We have placed great hope and confidence in David thus far. But now his future as the anointed king of Israel is once again in jeopardy.

---

1. As we will see, after David becomes king over Judah, he has difficulty winning over the northern tribes, who are fiercely loyal to the idea of a Saulide dynasty (2 Sam. 3:1). Had David been associated with the death of Saul and Jonathan at Mount Gilboa, the history of Israel may have been very different.

David Is Rejected by the Philistine Rulers (29:1–11)

THE GEOGRAPHICAL REFERENCES of 29:1 indicate that this is a resumptive sentence, meaning it picks up the earlier narrative strand temporarily set aside after 28:1–2. A comparison with the geographical references at 28:4 reveals that the episodes narrated in chapters 28 and 29–30 are out of chronological sequence.[2] The city of Aphek was located in the coastal plain of Sharon, which served as an assembly area for Philistine troops before moving up to Jezreel (cf. 4:1).[3]

Thus the actual order of these events is as follows. The Philistine forces are mustered at Aphek, in preparation for moving farther north to confront the Israelites in the Jezreel Valley. There, the Philistine generals object to David's presence, and the events narrated in chapters 29–30 occur. Subsequently, the Philistines move into the Jezreel Valley, where they encamp at Shunem.[4] On the opposite side of the valley to the south lies the Gilboa range, where Saul deploys his forces to meet the Philistines. Saul's visit to the medium at Endor occurs on the evening immediately before the battle (see comments on 28:3–6).[5]

As I stated in the introduction, the historian responsible for the materials in 1 and 2 Samuel was not concerned with brute facts or with history for history's sake.[6] So here it seems likely that the intent is to heighten the contrast between Saul and David. Saul is helpless and frightened and turns to the illicit resources of the medium at Endor. He has been irrevocably abandoned by Yahweh. By contrast, David is providentially delivered from a predicament that he cannot avoid, and in his vengeance against the Amalekites appears fully capable of leading his people. The narrator wants Samuel's reference to Saul's failure against the Amalekites (28:18) to come just prior to David's dismissal by Achish and return to Ziklag, where he finds it necessary to pursue and punish the Amalekites. Once again, David succeeds where Saul has failed.

---

2. S. R. Driver, *Notes on the Hebrew Text and the Topography of the Books of Samuel* (Oxford: Clarendon, 1912), 213–14 (repr., Winona Lake, Ind.: Alpha Publications, 1983); see also Jeffries M. Hamilton, "Gilboa, Mount," *ABD*, 2:1019.

3. Rafael Frankel, "Aphek," *ABD*, 1:276.

4. Verse 11 makes it esp. clear that David is turned back from joining the Philistines *before* they arrive in Jezreel, thus confirming that ch. 28 is out of chronological sequence.

5. However, some of the older commentators mistakenly assumed the existence of another Aphek in the Jezreel Valley near Shunem, thereby alleviating the need to assume these chapters are out of chronological sequence. See, e.g., Keil and Delitzsch, *Samuel*, 270; Smith, *Samuel*, 243.

6. We will also see chronological materials in 2 Samuel rearranged literarily to make a theological point.

As the Philistines muster for war, David and his men are organized as the rearguard. But the Philistine commanders object, quoting the famous Israelite ditty that memorialized David's great military victories.[7] The generals are aware of the danger of mixed loyalties during the strain of combat, and they apparently have experience with Hebrew soldiers who easily switched from one army to another (see 14:21). They insist that Achish send David away.

David's questions in verse 8 feign shock and disappointment. Particularly his third question seems to contain an ironic ambiguity: "Why can't I go and fight against the enemies of my lord the king?" Achish would naturally assume that he himself is the king David refers to, but the reader must assume, in light of the context, that David is loyal only to Saul and the Israelite troops.[8] For David, the real "enemies" *are* the Philistines, and "my lord the king" must refer to Saul. This question implies that if David were forced to join the battle, he would indeed turn on the Philistines, showing that the concerns of these generals are well founded.

Achish is truly enamored with David. He has enjoyed a lucrative relationship with him over the last sixteen months (cf. 27:7). His simile of David as "an angel of God" probably connotes an ability on David's part to make right decisions—that is, to discern right from wrong, to decide correctly between two difficult options (see 2 Sam. 14:17; 19:27, where the expression is used in this way). He appears to be concerned that David might try to force himself on the generals and demand that he fight in the battle. So he urges him to "get up early" (which always indicates determination to take action) and go back as soon as possible (1 Sam. 29:10).

The irony of Achish's speech is impressive. David's worst-case scenario has developed, and he appears to have no means of avoiding the battle. Now ironically one of the Philistine rulers praises David's character and reluctantly *prohibits* him from staying. Achish thinks he is disappointing David by driving him away. In reality, he has become God's instrument for delivering David from an impossible lose-lose situation.

The manner in which David is disencumbered from this trap leaves us breathless. We marvel at the providential care but also at the ironic, almost humorous way David "comes out smelling like a rose," as we might say. In a single turn, his predicament, which seemed to have no solution, becomes an opportunity to avoid conflict with either Saul or the Philistines. As the next paragraphs show, it is providential that the Philistine generals have rejected David, for he has other business to attend to at Ziklag.

---

7. The "rulers" of v. 2 are distinct from the "commanders" of v. 3, who are the military generals.

8. McCarter, *I Samuel*, 427.

The Amalekite Raid of Ziklag (30:1–6)

WE HAVE MET THE AMALEKITES BEFORE.[9] Their role in biblical history is clear because of their vicious and unprovoked attack on Israel shortly after the Exodus (Ex. 17:8–16). They are portrayed as terrorists who took advantage of weaker opponents. As a result Yahweh promised Israel he would extract vengeance against them at some future time: "I will completely blot out the memory of Amalek from under heaven" (Ex. 17:14; Deut. 25:17–19).

The importance of David and his rule over Israel is demonstrated in this fact: David is the instrument of Yahweh's vengeance against Amalek. Saul's early victories over the Amalekites were taken as a sign of his legitimacy as king of Israel (see 1 Sam. 14:48). But it was ultimately his failure to execute the holy war ban against Amalek that revealed his spiritual failure and resulted in Samuel's condemnation (15:10–31, fittingly mentioned by Samuel again in 28:18). Thus, the contrast between David and Saul is highlighted again in the way they deal with the Amalekites.

In this episode David exacts vengeance because of the Amalekite raid of Ziklag. In the historian's summaries of David's military victories, the Amalekites are listed among those whom the great king subdued (2 Sam. 8:12; cf. 1 Chron. 18:11). But this is getting ahead of the story. In this paragraph, the Amalekites have once again acted ruthlessly, plundering David's adopted city and taking alive all the women and children of his men, including David's own two wives, Ahinoam and Abigail.

As if this were not enough, David's own men for the first time question his leadership (1 Sam. 30:6). Their bitterness over losing their families is so severe that they now talk of stoning David. This brings us to another crisis in David's life, which is narrated in such a way as to heighten the contrast between him and Saul. Like Saul in chapter 28, David is now surrounded with trouble. Saul was pressed all around by the Philistines with little hope of victory, while David is surrounded by his own grieving men and likewise appears to have no hope of retrieving their families. Both men are at their lowest ebb. Reading these texts together intensifies the contrast between the two anointed ones. Saul's actions prove beyond question that he has become unsuitable as king, while David's actions will illustrate again why he will become the ideal king of Israel.

The contrast between Saul and David becomes most apparent in the closing phrase of 30:6: "But David found strength in the LORD his God." In Saul's greatest moment of crisis, he had tried to inquire of Yahweh but found that the Lord had abandoned him (28:6). In desperation he turned to illegitimate

---

9. See comments above at 15:1–9 and 27:8–12.

means to discern God's will and ironically evoked only a confirmation of his own doom. His defeat at the hands of the Philistines is a foregone conclusion, as announced by the narratively resuscitated Samuel (28:19). The narrator has withheld nothing except the actual account of Saul's defeat and death, which comes soon enough in chapter 31.

By contrast, David strengthens himself in Yahweh at the moment of his greatest crisis. The verb translated by the NIV as "found strength" involves a reflexive element (cf. NRSV "David strengthened himself in the LORD his God").[10] This expression emphasizes David's personal faith—and does so in a way that illustrates the synergistic nature of faith. That is, faith requires a human response, though it is enabled by God (cf. Eph. 2:8). Even though God graciously makes faith possible, it is up to us to respond to his grace. Here David musters up his strength in his greatest moment of crisis. The full significance of this strength is in the phrase "in the LORD his God." The means by which David is strengthened during his crisis is Yahweh himself. The added "his God" stresses the personal relationship between Yahweh and David.

Saul's weakness as the first anointed one must be seen ultimately in this light. He has no faith-based personal relationship with Yahweh. In his moment of utter despair, he is incapable of relying on Yahweh for deliverance. By contrast, David is the ideal anointed one. His long-standing relationship with Yahweh makes it only natural to seek strength once again from Yahweh in his moment of need.

David Avenges the Amalekite Raid (30:7–25)

THE IMPORTANT ASSERTION of David's faith in 30:6 is a general statement in which the narrator reveals David's inner life and emphasizes his spiritual reliance on Yahweh. Now we learn the specifics. David calls for Abiathar to bring the priestly ephod containing the Urim and Thummim, the divinely sanctioned and approved means of seeking divine guidance. David's faith finds expression in concrete actions that will reverse this seemingly hopeless situation.

The particular terminology used in 30:7–8 refers to the practice of "inquiring" (lit., "asking") of Yahweh, that is, seeking his will in specific situations.

---

10. BDB, 305; *DCH*, 3:190; *HALOT*, 1:304. The Hithpael of חזק should be taken here as a reflexive-factitive, echoing the reflexive/reciprocal nature of the verbal stem in which the verb describes the production of a state (in this case, the state of being strong). See Bruce K. Waltke and M. O'Connor, *An Introduction to Biblical Hebrew Syntax* (Winona Lake, Ind.: Eisenbrauns, 1990), 429–32; Ronald J. Williams, *Hebrew Syntax: An Outline* (2d ed.; Toronto: Univ. of Toronto Press, 1992), 29. As such the verb connotes the human dimension of David's faith. David brings about within himself the condition of strength, which is the factitive use of the verb.

As we have seen elsewhere in 1–2 Samuel, this phrase is a technical expression for inquiring an oracle of God when a simple affirmative or negative response can be anticipated.[11] Inquiries could be answered by means of the sacred lots, the Urim and Thummim, stored in the ephod (Ex. 28:30; Lev. 8:8).[12] The good priest Ahimelech had earlier inquired of Yahweh on David's behalf, which may have been when David learned the value of such inquiries (1 Sam. 22:10, 13, 15). David's rise to kingship is characterized by the importance he attached to seeking guidance from God (see 23:2, 4; also 2 Sam. 2:1; 5:19, 23; 16:23).

In fact, the narrative uses this practice of David to continue the contrast between Saul and David. Yahweh has stopped answering Saul's inquiries, presumably because Saul has made up his mind before asking (14:36–37). As we saw in the preceding chapter, the silence of Yahweh persists until the end for Saul (28:6). By contrast, David faithfully inquires of Yahweh and continues to receive guidance.

The victory over the Amalekite marauders is narrated in such a way as to highlight an important feature of David's character: He is a leader who shows magnanimity to individuals in vulnerable situations, especially if they are soldiers loyal to him (cf. 2 Sam. 10:2–5). He identifies with people and understands their needs. First Samuel 30 highlights two such episodes. (1) David is generous and gracious in his treatment of an Egyptian who had been an Amalekite slave (30:11–15). David obviously wants to use him as an informant, who can lead him to the Amalekite camp. But he has been abandoned by the Amalekite master when he became ill and was left in a field to starve to death. In contrast, David and his men feed and nurse him to health.

(2) David intervenes in a dispute among his followers concerning the distribution of their plunder. He magnanimously decides to include those too exhausted to make the journey to the Amalekite encampment and opted to stay with the supplies. David thus establishes the principle of equality that lasts throughout his reign (30:24): "Share and share alike!"

The reversal of David's losses at the hands of the Amalekites is a stunning victory. "On their return from Aphek, David and his men had faced their ruined and abandoned homes; everything seemed lost, and David was in danger of being stoned to death."[13] But through his faith in Yahweh and his resolve to avenge his losses and those of his men, he turns an impossible and hopeless situation into a great victory. Only four hundred of the Amalekite men are able to escape on camels (30:17), and David and his men

---

11. See comments on 23:1–6.

12. For opinions on the nature of the Urim and Thummim, see Van Dam, *The Urim and Thummim*, 9–103.

13. Baldwin, *1 and 2 Samuel*, 169.

retrieve their families. While Saul is preparing for his final battle, which is doomed to failure, David is leading his meager forces in victory against one of Israel's greatest enemies. While Saul has proven himself ill-equipped and inadequate for leading God's people, David seems perfectly suited for the task.

David Supports the Cities of Judah (30:26–31)

DAVID HAS BEEN spared the impossible choice of fighting his own people or turning on his Philistine overlord, Achish (ch. 29). But he continues to play a dangerous game. One of David's objectives during the time he lived in Ziklag was to strengthen Judah's position by fighting her traditional enemies in the south. He managed to convince Achish that his regular raids in the south were against southern Judah itself, when in reality he was assaulting enemies troublesome to Judah (see comments at 27:10–12). This victory over Amalek is certainly good news for Judah and even fulfills Yahweh's promise to avenge Israel's early losses by eventually subduing the Amalekites altogether. With this victory, David now takes the daring step of sharing the spoils with his "friends" in Judah. By giving them portions of "the plunder of the LORD's enemies" (30:26), David continued to endear himself to the citizens of Judah, whom he will soon rule as king. Presumably many of these "friends" are the same who will shortly anoint him king "over the house of Judah" at Hebron (2 Sam. 2:4).

The list of localities in the southern portion of the hill country around Hebron may have constituted the initial holdings in a Hebron-based state of Judah.[14] The first city mentioned in the paragraph is Ziklag, where David was an independent leader of a small band of men and from where he sends the gifts to Judah. The last city mentioned is Hebron, where David will soon become king of Judah.[15]

 *Bridging Contexts*

THE TRUTHS OF this unit of Scripture may be summarized by exploring two central concepts. (1) The first continues the contrast between David and Saul that the historian has emphasized since chapter 16. The two anointed ones are very different in their relationship to God and to his people. This text continues that contrast and moves

---

14. On the identification and location of these sites, see Youngblood, "1, 2 Samuel," 795–96. Though the timing is in question, an attempt to unite these towns and villages may have been a fledgling step in establishing a state that rivaled Saul's in the north. The biblical historian, however, makes it clear that David is made king only *after* Saul's death. See Edelman, "Tel Masos, Geshur, and David," 253–58, esp. 255.

15. Miscall, *1 Samuel*, 181.

us closer to its denouement. (2) David is described as one who "found strength in the LORD his God" (30:6). These two concepts can serve as trusses to construct a bridge from the ancient text to our contemporary context.

Contrast between Saul and David. The historian has adroitly contrasted David and Saul in several ways since David's anointing in chapter 16. The main question addressed in these narratives is, Who can serve suitably in the new Israelite institution of kingship? The book has emphasized that Yahweh must always remain Israel's king. In the new world of Israel's monarchy, all of the old religious and political institutions must be transformed or reconfigured (priesthood, tabernacle, ark of the covenant, and judges system of governance). In their new forms, they will continue to be symbols of Yahweh's kingship in Israel, though now he will rule through a designated viceroy or deputy. The human appointee will be anointed by Yahweh's prophet with oil and will be guided by Yahweh's Spirit. But even these signs of divine designation are no guarantee that an anointed leader of Israel will represent Yahweh suitably. Much of 1 Samuel has been devoted to the differences between Saul and David in an attempt to explain why Saul is unacceptable and David is ideal.

On the surface there are many reasons for this. Saul is unable to subdue Israel's greatest enemies, the Philistines and the Amalekites. It may be closer to the truth to say Saul is *uninterested* in subduing them. From the outset, David has great success against both, from the spectacular defeat of Goliath the Philistine immediately after his anointing (ch. 17) to his divinely guided victory over the Amalekites in this text (30:8, 23).

Saul, by contrast, is portrayed as a self-absorbed, inconsistent, and unpredictable despot, more concerned with his public image than with heeding the advice of his prophetic mentor, Samuel. David, it is true, is impetuous, but only in a way that seems endearing. He is passionate about defending Yahweh's honor before the Philistine oppressors and is more concerned about the welfare of his soldiers and the inhabitants of Judah than his own safety. At times, David risks everything in order to follow a path he believes is right, while Saul is only willing to risk everything in his efforts to kill David. In short, the first anointed one consistently rejects Yahweh's authority as sovereign in Israel while the second anointed one is committed to nothing but Yahweh's authority. Saul follows his own instincts without regard for divine approval while David is satisfied with nothing less than God's approval.

This contrast between Saul and David comes to a climax in these closing chapters of 1 Samuel. Saul's utter humiliation in chapter 28 and David's astounding victory in chapters 29–30 set the stage for Saul's death in the last chapter and for David's coronation in 2 Samuel. These texts contrast their two ways of life—irrational tyrant versus passionate God-pleaser. One takes the road to Endor; the other seeks the counsel of Abiathar, priest of Yahweh. This is the story of black magic versus divine revelation, of subterfuge versus submission, of deceit versus dependence.

As we noted in the introduction to this section, the chronological arrangement of chapters 28 and 29–30 have most likely been reversed for dramatic literary effect. One scholar has suggested David and Saul are even seeking Yahweh's guidance on the very same day, though for different reasons and obviously through different means. If so, this only heightens the contrast between them. Thus, "Saul sought help from a medium and received the promise of death; David sought help through an Aaronic priest using the ephod and received the promise—later fulfilled—of life and blessing."[16]

David's inner life. The fact that "David found strength in the LORD his God" (30:6) combines David's personal involvement in mustering his strength with an emphasis on Yahweh as the means by which he is strengthened. This is no passive faith, no faith without works (James 2:17). It is appropriate to associate this phrase with Paul's two-part statement, "continue to work out your salvation with fear and trembling, for it is God who works in you to will and to act according to his good purpose" (Phil. 2:12–13). One scholar has stated that this phrase in verse 6 anticipates Paul in this way and goes on to say: "David counts heavily on God's being at work. At the same moment David is boldly at work on the rescue mission."[17] In this light, David becomes a historical illustration of the truth Paul teaches and urges on his Philippian readers.

David's personal faith-based relationship with Yahweh finds expression in several ways here. His utter reliance on God in a moment of crisis is evident in his "inquiry," that is, in his use of Abiathar's ephod and the sacred means of communicating with God. Beyond this obvious example, the narrator subtly reveals the results of David's faith in other ways. David's political predicament is described in chapter 27. He cannot afford to fight *for* the Philistines *against* Israel, or *against* the Philistines *for* Israel. He is hopelessly trapped, caught between cat and mouse and with commitments to both. Without overt descriptions of divine intervention or miraculous revelation, the historian describes the solution to this dilemma (29:1–11). Though not stated in blatant terms, this text must be read together with chapter 27, which leaves the reader in awe of the providential care that protects and guides David.

David's faith also finds expression in the decisive and persistent action he takes to avenge his losses to the Amalekites. Once he is clear on Yahweh's promise for deliverance (30:8), he immediately sets out to recapture his

16. Bergen, *1, 2 Samuel*, 276.
17. Brueggemann, *First and Second Samuel*, 202.

family and those of his troops. Nor is he deterred by difficulties such as fatigue among his men, the seemingly impossible task of locating the Amalekite encampment, or the superior numbers of his enemy. We see further manifestations of his faith in Yahweh in his empathy and generosity. He is gracious to the lost and sick Egyptian, the fatigued men in his entourage who cannot continue in the pursuit, and his "friends" of the cities of Judah.

All of David's actions after 30:8 are decisive, confident, gracious, and resolute. His bold steps are taken without hesitation because he accepts readily the divine word of assurance: "You will certainly overtake them and succeed in the rescue." In a time of great crisis, David seeks God's word, and having found it he never looks back. All in all, this text portrays David as a great leader whose strength arises from a deep reservoir of personal faith and a conviction that Yahweh will win his victories for him.

THIS TEXT HAS MANY POSSIBLE APPLICATIONS. One useful approach would be to consider the ways in which David can serve as an example of godly leadership. He resolutely leans on God for deliverance while working diplomatically to find his own way through difficulties (ch. 29). His unswerving faith is the wellspring of all other actions, which shows him to be persistent, sympathetic, decisive, and full of integrity (ch. 30). In this way, David can serve as the paradigm for constructing a vision of ideal Christian leadership for our churches.

Guidance in time of need. However, if we limit the application of this text to our cultural infatuation with achieving successful "leadership," we will miss what the text has to teach us about the broader themes of faith and life. In truth, this text taken together with the larger context in 1 Samuel 16–31 draws attention to the two ways between which all of us must choose. It raises the largest of all questions about revelation, authority, and faith itself. Specifically it raises the issue of how each of us must look beyond ourselves for direction and guidance, and the text draws our attention to the all-important question: Where do we turn for help in our time of need? As modern believers, we seek the face of God through the portals of his written Word. Being convinced by the truth in his Word, we must seek to act boldly on it, with confidence and hope.

One prominent Christian philosopher, Emile Cailliet, speaks of the "basic incompatibility between the Living God of Christianity and the gods that have not made the heavens and the earth."[18] Differences between, for exam-

---

18. Emile Cailliet, *Journey into Light* (Grand Rapids: Zondervan, 1968), 34.

ple, the Greek perceptions of the universe and the worldview taught in the Bible are fundamentally the differences between naturalism and supernaturalism, between paganism and Christianity. Greek views of history are disassociated from religious truth, whereas Christianity is essentially a historical religion. Cailliet continues:

> In his *City of God*, Augustine would give full scope to the implications of this purposeful Hebrew-Christian overall view. Indeed, it is to this view that we owe the best of our notion of a philosophy of history—that of meaningful duration. From the Stoic's vantage point, on the other hand, a wise man was not concerned with time. How could he be, in view of the Greek outlook? In the context of Aristotle's *Meteors* (I,ii,2,339) the tumult of meaningless cycles of history glittered endlessly.[19]

Cailliet has dramatically distinguished Aristotle and Augustine to illustrate in general the contrast between naturalism and Christianity. This fundamental distinction can be illustrated in diverse ways, including the two thieves on the cross. One was open and accepting of truth, the other intolerant of truth, even in his direst moment of need.

Our text offers another way of illustrating this distinction. We present-day believers must choose between paths that lead either to the medium of Endor or to Abiathar, son of Ahimelech! By the living of our everyday lives, we establish patterns of seeking advice and help, either from Endor or from Abiathar—that is, finding answers in naturalism (or postmodernism, or New Age gurus, etc.) or from the God of heaven and earth, who has revealed his truth in Scripture. These are really the only two options. In time, we will become like Saul, incapable of making right decisions, or we will become like David, who makes right decisions almost instinctively.

This text illustrates especially well David's pursuit of God's will in a time of extreme need. He serves as a model for relying exclusively on God's truth just as Saul is an illustration of what happens when we reject God's truth (ch. 28). These are the choices in life: Endor or Abiathar, the witch or the godly priest. Each of us must choose. Most of us go through our lives without giving it much thought. We step on one path or the other without considering which paradigm we are following or who is even defining the paradigms. Or worse, we attempt to redefine them ourselves. In rather pathetic ways, we often try to find new and innovative ways to the truth when the old and proven ones work just as reasonably well. Then the crisis comes, as it came for Saul and David, and we learn what we really believe.

---

19. Ibid., 34–35.

G. K. Chesterton begins the book *Orthodoxy* by relating the comical story of the English yachtsman who slightly miscalculated his course and discovered England under the impression that it was a new island in the South Seas. He describes the scene of the man coming ashore armed to the teeth and talking by signs in order to plant the British flag on that barbaric temple, which turned out to be the Pavilion on Brighton (a prominent city on the southern coast of England). Chesterton explores further the emotions the man felt upon learning his mistake:

> What could be more delightful than to have in the same few minutes all the fascinating terrors of going abroad combined with all the humane security of coming home again? What could be better than to have all the fun of discovering South Africa without the ... necessity of landing there? What could be more glorious than to brace one's self up to discover New South Wales and then realize, with a gush of happy tears, that it was really old South Wales?[20]

Chesterton explains that in a real sense, *he* is the man who with the utmost daring discovered what had been discovered before. He fancied he was the first to set foot in Brighton, and then found that he was in fact the last. The book *Orthodoxy* is itself an account of his "elephantine adventures in pursuit of the obvious."[21] In it, he confesses he tried to be some ten minutes in advance of the truth, and found instead that he was eighteen hundred years behind it. In an attempt to be original, he succeeded in inventing all by himself an inferior copy of the existing traditions of civilized religion. Chesterton concludes that he accepts Christianity because it has not merely told this truth or that truth, but it has revealed itself as a truth-telling system.

> All other philosophies say the things that plainly seem to be true; only this philosophy has again and again said the thing that does not seem to be true, but is true. Alone of all creeds it is convincing where it is not attractive.[22]

In seeking to find truth and to stake our lives on it, today's Christians follow in the steps of David and his reliance on the words of Abiathar. This is a story that could be repeated often, for it is the same principle illustrated in Noah, Abraham, Joseph, Joshua, Daniel, Peter, Paul, and Augustine. To turn from this tradition is to attempt to discover what has already been discovered and has been graciously revealed to us as perfectly "obvious," as Chester-

---

20. Gilbert K. Chesterton, *Orthodoxy* (New York: John Lane, 1909), 14–15.
21. Ibid., 18.
22. Ibid., 291.

ton would put it. Saul's ultimate failure is his inability or unwillingness to accept God's authority as the basis for his reign over Israel (see comments on ch. 15). By contrast, David not only accepts God's authority but refuses to proceed until he is certain of it. In this he serves as an example for all contemporary believers as well as a suitable forerunner of his greater Son, the Messiah.

1 Samuel 31:1–13

NOW THE PHILISTINES fought against Israel; the
Israelites fled before them, and many fell slain on
Mount Gilboa. ²The Philistines pressed hard after
Saul and his sons, and they killed his sons Jonathan, Abinadab
and Malki-Shua. ³The fighting grew fierce around Saul, and
when the archers overtook him, they wounded him critically.

⁴Saul said to his armor-bearer, "Draw your sword and run
me through, or these uncircumcised fellows will come and
run me through and abuse me."

But his armor-bearer was terrified and would not do it;
so Saul took his own sword and fell on it. ⁵When the armor-
bearer saw that Saul was dead, he too fell on his sword and
died with him. ⁶So Saul and his three sons and his armor-
bearer and all his men died together that same day.

⁷When the Israelites along the valley and those across
the Jordan saw that the Israelite army had fled and that Saul
and his sons had died, they abandoned their towns and fled.
And the Philistines came and occupied them.

⁸The next day, when the Philistines came to strip the dead,
they found Saul and his three sons fallen on Mount Gilboa.
⁹They cut off his head and stripped off his armor, and they
sent messengers throughout the land of the Philistines to proclaim the news in the temple of their idols and among their
people. ¹⁰They put his armor in the temple of the Ashtoreths
and fastened his body to the wall of Beth Shan.

¹¹When the people of Jabesh Gilead heard of what the
Philistines had done to Saul, ¹²all their valiant men journeyed
through the night to Beth Shan. They took down the bodies
of Saul and his sons from the wall of Beth Shan and went
to Jabesh, where they burned them. ¹³Then they took their
bones and buried them under a tamarisk tree at Jabesh, and
they fasted seven days.

THIS TEXT RELATES THE TRAGIC EVENTS on Mount Gilboa and informs us of the fate of Israel's first anointed one. Saul dies in battle against the very enemies he was supposed to subdue, the Philistines (cf. 9:16). His body is dismembered and desecrated in a way that seemed especially appalling to ancient peoples. Finally, Saul's remains are burned and given an ignoble burial. Thus the book ends with an emphatic answer to the question: Who may serve suitably as Israel's king? Certainly not Saul, and the anointed of Yahweh must never again be anyone like him!

Some have suggested that the reason for ending 1 Samuel with the death of Saul was in order to bring the book into conformity with other books that conclude with the death of a major figure: Jacob and Joseph at the end of Genesis, Moses at the end of Deuteronomy, and Joshua at the end of the book of Joshua.[1] This may be so. However, the death of Saul also brings to a close one of the main themes of the book. The second half of 1 Samuel has contrasted Saul and David, Israel's first and second royal anointed ones. As David's fortunes rose both politically and spiritually, Saul continued in a downward spiral, beginning with chapter 15 and ending here.

Saul has rejected Yahweh's authority as the true king of Israel, refusing to accept his own role as a limited viceroy. His actions have manifested a character unacceptable in Israel's king, and the narrative makes this more and more apparent. His visit to the medium of Endor is an index of his fall (ch. 28), and his ignoble death at Mount Gilboa removes any doubt about this anointed one. He was unfit as king and serves as an example for future Israelite rulers about the dangers of self-reliance and self-sufficiency. As the account continues in 2 Samuel, we learn that Saul's descendants gradually disappear altogether until the only remaining trace is the unfortunate Mephibosheth, who is graciously sustained at David's table (2 Sam. 9:13).

The Deaths of Saul and Jonathan (31:1–6)

THE REFERENCE TO Mount Gilboa picks up the strand of 28:4. The conflict between Israel and the Philistines had been set aside temporarily to explain what was happening to David (chs. 29–30).[2] Death was always preferable to

---

1. McCarter, *I Samuel*, 3. We would add: Ahab and Jehoshaphat (1 Kings), and David (1 Chronicles).

2. See our comments on geography and chronology in the Original Meaning section for 29:1–11. On the nature of the circumstantial clause of 31:1 as resuming the account from 28:4, see Keil and Delitzsch, *Samuel*, 278. The resumption may also be implied by the pluperfect anterior construction of 28:2–3 (Ziony Zevit, *The Anterior Construction in Classical Hebrew* [SBLMS 50; Atlanta: Scholars Press, 1998], 27).

being captured where the Philistines were concerned (cf. Judg. 16:21). Saul's fears that the enemy would "abuse" him (or "sport with him mischievously," cf. NRSV) were well founded.

The description of Saul's death brings the contrast between David and Saul to a climax.[3] Chapter 30 has just related David's great success against the Amalekites; he rescued Ziklag and saved the lives of everyone associated with him. By contrast, Saul and everyone associated with him die in this losing battle with the Philistines. Saul had been commissioned as king specifically to provide victory against the Philistines (9:16), which makes his death at their hands especially ironic and provides "the measure of his failure."[4]

The Philistines Desecrate Saul's Body (31:7–10)

THE RESULT OF THE DEBACLE at Mount Gilboa is devastating for Israel. The subsequent evacuation of the towns in the area leaves the Philistine military in control of Israelite territory. Saul's decapitated body is fastened "to the wall of Beth Shan," a city that stands impressively over the junction of the Jezreel and Jordan valleys, guarding access to both.[5] It had never been conquered and held by the Israelites (Josh. 17:11, 16; Judg. 1:27) and therefore provided a natural stronghold for Philistine occupation. Saul's armor is placed in "the temple of the Ashtoreths," which may refer to the goddess Astarte worshiped principally at Sidon but is more likely a derogatory reference to the unnamed principal goddess of Beth Shan.[6]

Philistine occupation of territory so far north of Philistia and so central to Israel marks a nadir in Israel's national history. Of course, the biblical historian is less concerned to narrate the details of the national tragedy. We might have expected more detail about the battle itself and the social and military repercussions. Instead, the narrator moves quickly over those details and emphasizes the personal and theological consequences of Saul's disappointing rule.

Saul's worst fears of bodily desecration at the hands of the Philistines become a reality. Moreover, his defeat and death become occasions for proclamation of glad tidings in the temples of foreign idol gods, implying the victory of those gods over Yahweh in the minds of the Philistines. The

3. The details of Saul's death narrated here differ significantly from the Amalekite's report in 2 Sam. 1:7–10 (see comments).

4. Baldwin, 1 and 2 Samuel, 170.

5. Patrick E. McGovern, "Beth-shan," ABD, 1:693–96; Amihai Mazar, "Beth-Shean," OEANE, 1:305–9.

6. "Ashtoreths" can also refer in general to any foreign goddess, being equivalent to "other gods" or "foreign gods." See Judith M. Hadley, "עַשְׁתֹּרֶת," NIDOTTE, 3:562–63; see further the Original Meaning section for 7:2–4.

national tragedy, painful though it is, serves merely as the backdrop for Saul's failure to vigorously defend and honor the name of Yahweh.

Citizens of Jabesh Gilead Bury Saul's Remains (31:11–13)

EVEN IN THIS DREARY MOMENT, the anointed of Yahweh cannot be left in such degrading circumstances. The residents of Jabesh Gilead never forgot how Saul rescued them from the Ammonites (ch. 11). Indeed, his triumph over Nahash the Ammonite and rescue of the citizens of Jabesh Gilead in the Transjordan was Saul's one shining moment, in which his role as the anointed of Yahweh was clearly manifested.[7] Now they will repay his kindness with their loyalty. Their actions paid homage not to the king of Israel as fallen hero but to the king of Israel as the anointed one of Yahweh. This is no rejection of God's judgment on Saul but of the atrocities of the victorious Philistines in their jubilant celebration.[8]

Because the Old Testament custom was burial rather than cremation, a few scholars have followed the suggestion that the term "burned" in 31:12 has the meaning "anointed with spices."[9] But it seems more likely that the extenuating circumstances demanded extreme measures. The advanced state of decomposition because of the Philistines' mistreatment of Saul makes it necessary to prevent contagion from the plagued corpses. Furthermore, the citizens of Jabesh Gilead may be fearing that the Philistines will return and inflict more humiliation on the fallen warriors.[10] Regardless of the details of their actions, their kindness in return for Saul's kindness provides the king some dignity in his otherwise ignoble death.

 **Bridging Contexts**

OLD TESTAMENT HISTORICAL BOOKS do not attempt simple history. They never trace historical cause-and-effect connections simply for the sake of explaining the past and how it relates to the present. Rather, these are theological treatises, which use history to illustrate primarily cause-and-effect connections that concern God and Israel. These are vertical narratives rather than horizontal narratives. The

---

7. This action also anticipates the revenge of the Gibeonites (see 2 Sam. 21:12–14).

8. Keil and Delitzsch, *Samuel*, 282.

9. Proposed by G. R. Driver, "A Hebrew Burial Custom," *ZAW* 66 (1954): 314–15, and followed by P. R. Ackroyd, *First Book of Samuel* (CBC; Cambridge: Cambridge Univ. Press, 1971), 229; J. Mauchline, *1 and 2 Samuel* (NCB; London: Marshall, Morgan & Scott, 1971), 193; and Hertzberg, *I and II Samuel*, 233. Interestingly, the parallel account in Chronicles omits the reference to cremation (1 Chron. 10:12).

10. For these and other possible interpretations, see Robin Wakely, "שרף," *NIDOTTE*, 3:1285–86.

cause-and-effect relationships in biblical history are those that demonstrate the benefits of relating rightly to God or to each other. Conversely, they also demonstrate the consequences of relating wrongly to God or to each other. It is in this sense that the story of Saul's death contributes eternal truths that are applicable to today's believers. This text illustrates tragically the consequences of relating wrongly to God and others.

The national level. It should be remembered that Old Testament historical narratives have different levels of interpretation: universal, national, and individual.[11] Each individual narrative plays a role in the greater national narrative of Israel's history and therefore also contributes to the ultimate narrative of God's redemptive plan in history. This mournful episode contributes on the national level to the book's answer to the question: Who can serve suitably in the new Israelite institution of monarchy?

In the earlier portion of the book, the prophet Samuel devoted a large portion of his ministry to defining the new institution of kingship (chs. 8–12). Though the monarchy will be constituted as a human institution, Yahweh remains the king of Israel, and he will rule through human anointed ones. These anointed ones will be his viceroys on earth. They will be anointed with oil by Yahweh's prophets and be guided by Yahweh's Spirit. But their success will depend entirely on their acceptance of Yahweh's authority as true king and acceptance of their own role as mere viceroy. In this way, they will not be like other kings of the ancient Near East.

Saul then serves as the first anointed one. Unfortunately, he becomes an example of the kind of king who may *not* serve suitably as Yahweh's viceroy. The contrast between him and David since 1 Samuel 16 has built to this point. Whereas David is trusting and depends on God, Saul is manipulative and vindictive. Saul fails to accept the authority of Yahweh as true king, whereas David recognizes the source of his royal authority and is quick to rely on Yahweh for guidance and deliverance.

In the previous unit, God's guidance for David was both defensive and offensive. He intervened in David's dealings with Achish and the Philistines to prevent him from fighting against Israel, but he also intervened against the Amalekites to provide a much-needed military victory. By contrast, Saul is quickly turned over to the Philistines and decapitated after his death, and his body is left exposed to the elements. Saul failed to accept Yahweh as king, so Yahweh rejected Saul as king.[12] Future anointed ones should be like David, not like Saul.[13]

---

11. See our introduction; also Fee and Stuart, *How to Read the Bible*, 73–78.

12. A vivid reversal of Gen. 15:6, where Abram accepted God's word as true and God accepted Abram as righteous.

13. Ultimately we have the New Testament to explain that *the* Messiah was like David in many ways—and certainly not like Saul.

The individual level. The passage also contributes to biblical theology on an individual level. Ultimately this is a story of divine judgment. King Saul reaps in death what he sowed in life. His words and actions on Mount Gilboa only arouse pity in the reader, as it did for the good citizens of Jabesh Gilead. Saul is in these final moments free of his paranoia and paralyzing distrust. He is simply trying to do his best as the anointed of Yahweh.[14] But Yahweh has departed, and the prophecy of Samuel through the medium at Endor is coming true. Saul is soon to die. In one fatal battle he loses his kingdom, his life, his sons, and—despite his suicide—his dignity. "In this ignominious fate of Saul there was manifested the righteous judgment of God in consequence of the hardening of his heart."[15]

Divine judgment is a central concept in biblical thought. It appears early in the Old Testament story when Abraham asked (Gen. 18:25): "Will not the Judge of all the earth do right (*mišpaṭ*)?" In the last pages of the Bible, it is God's penultimate act at the conclusion of human history (Rev. 20:11–15). Throughout both Testaments, God is the God of *mišpaṭ* ("justice/judgment"). Judgment is essential to his character (Deut. 32:4; Ps. 97:2; Isa. 40:14; Jer. 8:7). Sometimes modern believers think of judgment only as forward looking, some distant "day of judgment" in which God will make right all the wrongs of this world. And so it can be in both Testaments (Ps. 96:13; Rom. 3:5–6; Heb. 6:1–2; Rev. 20:11–15).

But often divine judgment becomes a reality in the present life. In Old Testament contexts, believers have no fully developed concept of eternal bliss or eternal punishment. As a result, one suffers the consequences of one's sins in this life.[16] Even in the New Testament, Paul's description of God's judgment on pagans of past generations is contained in the three occurrences of "God gave them over" (Rom. 1:24–32). Setting aside for the moment the nature of the final judgment in the end times, the present text reminds us that all of us suffer the consequences of our actions in this present life. Judgment is not an abstraction imposed on the sinner. Rather, it grows from within the created cosmos itself, governed by the universal principles of life established by God.

So the book of 1 Samuel ends in a cemetery near Jabesh, with a group of faithful and loyal subjects paying homage to the fallen king. But the book also

14. A point made by Klein, *1 Samuel*, 290.

15. Keil and Delitzsch, *Samuel*, 282.

16. This is esp. pertinent in the Old Testament's emphasis on "retribution theology," which had such an important role in the theological framework of the historical books. See Hans Walter Wolff, "The Kerygma of the Deuteronomic Historical Work," in *The Vitality of Old Testament Traditions*, ed. W. Brueggemann and H. W. Wolff (Atlanta: John Knox, 1975), 83–100.

ends in expectation. We are not left on this theme of judgment, having no hope. There is a quiet waiting, an anticipation, which finds fulfillment in 2 Samuel. The narrator has carefully prepared us for the second anointed one, who is ready to fulfill his role in history and in God's plan. "The narrator would not have us believe that Saul's death nullifies the hope of Hannah."[17]

The expectation at the conclusion of 1 Samuel is met with the triumphant and joyful account of David in 2 Samuel 1–9. Likewise, present-day believers should read this account of the divine judgment of Saul with an eye to the New Testament. Just as this text anticipates the coming of the anointed one who *is* suitable to serve as king of Israel, so it also anticipates the coming of his greater Son. Just as the first readers of this text waited in expectation for the next chapters leading to the coronation of King David, so we today celebrate the coming of the Messiah, who comes to forgive and restore.

APPLICATION OF THIS TEXT can draw on both the individual and national levels of interpretation. On the individual level, the death of Saul draws our attention to the experience of death itself and its relationship to the way we live our lives. On the national level, this text completes the contrast between David and Saul and contributes to our understanding of the nature and role of the Messiah.

The experience of death. Death unifies all humanity. It is the one experience we all share in common, regardless of our race, creed, heritage, or station in life. In this singular event "we leave behind everything we have and take with us everything we are."[18] In the Old Testament generally, an ignoble or untimely death implies the deceased was sinful or somehow deserving of death (Deut. 19:6; 21:22; Jer. 26:11, 16).

In the case of Saul's death, the message is clear because of the line of reasoning followed by the narrator since 1 Samuel 9: Saul's suicide is the result of the tragic choices he made in life.[19] He had been anointed by Yahweh's prophet, and the Spirit of Yahweh had come upon him powerfully to guide

---

17. Brueggemann, *First and Second Samuel*, 209–10.

18. Ravi Zacharias, *A Shattered Visage: The Real Face of Atheism* (Brentwood, Tenn.: Wolgemuth & Hyatt, 1990), 94.

19. Saul was mortally wounded and therefore chose to die rather than face the certain abuse that would come at the hands of his captors, not unlike the suicide of Abimelech (Judg. 9:54). The armor-bearer, however, committed suicide purely out of horror and devotion to Saul. Other cases to compare are Ahithophel (2 Sam. 17:23), Zimri (1 Kings 16:18), and Samson (Judg. 16:29–30).

and direct him as the new king of Israel (10:1, 10). God had transformed him into a better man (10:9), and he initially had great military success in defeating the enemies of God's people (ch. 11). But he slowly came to despise the very man who anointed him as king, making it impossible to follow God's instructions for the nation. Ultimately he rejected God's authority as king of Israel, and his life degenerated into pathetic bickering and jealousy. Rather than saving the people from the Philistines, Saul devoted himself to denying the kingdom to David. His charismatic gifts and divine blessings had deteriorated into madness.[20] Saul's ignoble death is due to his ignoble life.

Woody Allen said of death, "It's not that I'm afraid to die, I just don't want to be there when it happens."[21] It is one thing to have no fear of death, but quite another to want to escape the undeniable uncertainty of it all. As we saw in the Bridging Contexts section, this text is about the judgment of God. Christians often postpone justice until that final day in the end times. But Saul's death brings us face to face with the realization that there is more to divine justice/judgment than "pie in the sky," which makes the Christian gospel bigger than any simple "turn or burn" message. We all suffer in this life because of the sins we commit. Conversely, the Christian gospel offers more than reward in the hereafter. Correctly formulated and communicated, the gospel offers hope and peace in this life. By rightly relating to God in the here and now, we prepare for loving him eternally in the hereafter.

C. S. Lewis has reminded us that we are all in the same boat and that any of us could end like Saul:

> When any man comes into the presence of God he will find, whether he wishes it or not, that all those things which seemed to make him so different from the men of other times, or even from his earlier self, have fallen off him. He is back where he always was, where every man always is. *Eadem sunt omnia semper* ["Everything is always the same"]. Do not let us deceive ourselves. No possible complexity which we can give to our picture of the universe can hide us from God: there is no copse, no forest, no jungle thick enough to provide cover.... It may happen to any of us at any moment. In the twinkling of an eye, in a time too small to be measured, and in any place, all that seems to divide us from God can flee away, vanish leaving us naked before Him, like the first man, like the only man, as if nothing but He and I existed. And since that contact cannot be avoided for long, and since

---

20. W. Lee Humphreys, "The Tragedy of King Saul: A Study of the Structure of 1 Samuel 9–31," *JSOT* 6 (1978): 18–27, esp. 25.

21. Quoted in Zacharias, *Shattered Visage*, 94.

> it means either bliss or horror, the business of life is to learn to like it.
> That is the first and great commandment.[22]

The way we die is related to the way we live. As Lewis implies, we have no greater or more urgent task in this life than to learn how to die well.

The Messiah. Another lesson to be learned from Saul's death grows out of the national level of interpretation, through which this text contributes to our understanding of the Messiah. The first anointed one's death is described here in succinct and shocking tones. In a matter-of-fact way, the narrator relates Saul's despair, as he sank lower into the shadows of loneliness, abandonment, and desperation. Perhaps the ultimate contrast between Saul and David is the fact that David "rested with his fathers," meaning he was buried in the family tomb (1 Kings 2:10).[23] His death came after a long and successful rule over Israel, and he died surrounded by his family, with his son Solomon on the throne (though not without great difficulty because of Adonijah, see 1 Kings 1). Saul's sons died with him, his body was dismembered, and his bones were given a modest disposal by the people of Jabesh. Death overwhelms Saul as an unwanted but irresistible foe. David met death as the timely and natural outcome of life. Thus, David becomes the ancestor of *the* Messiah, who will be victorious over sin and death, confirmed by his resurrection.

Death is not the end of our story. Contemporary believers should read 1 Samuel 31 in a way that leads to hope for the future. Just as ancient Israelite readers would have read this text in anticipation of the coronation of David and the rule of the ideal anointed one, so we know there is more to the story. The coming of David's greater Son has given us reason to hope that a new day will dawn in which death will no more claim its wretched price (1 Cor. 15:54–57).

---

22. C. S. Lewis, "Dogma and The Universe," in *God in the Dock*, 38–47, the quote is from 47.

23. William C. Williams, "שכב," *NIDOTTE*, 4:102.

2 Samuel 1:1–27

AFTER THE DEATH of Saul, David returned from defeating the Amalekites and stayed in Ziklag two days. ²On the third day a man arrived from Saul's camp, with his clothes torn and with dust on his head. When he came to David, he fell to the ground to pay him honor.

³"Where have you come from?" David asked him.

He answered, "I have escaped from the Israelite camp."

⁴"What happened?" David asked. "Tell me."

He said, "The men fled from the battle. Many of them fell and died. And Saul and his son Jonathan are dead."

⁵Then David said to the young man who brought him the report, "How do you know that Saul and his son Jonathan are dead?"

⁶"I happened to be on Mount Gilboa," the young man said, "and there was Saul, leaning on his spear, with the chariots and riders almost upon him. ⁷When he turned around and saw me, he called out to me, and I said, 'What can I do?'

⁸"He asked me, 'Who are you?'

"'An Amalekite,' I answered.

⁹"Then he said to me, 'Stand over me and kill me! I am in the throes of death, but I'm still alive.'

¹⁰"So I stood over him and killed him, because I knew that after he had fallen he could not survive. And I took the crown that was on his head and the band on his arm and have brought them here to my lord."

¹¹Then David and all the men with him took hold of their clothes and tore them. ¹²They mourned and wept and fasted till evening for Saul and his son Jonathan, and for the army of the LORD and the house of Israel, because they had fallen by the sword.

¹³David said to the young man who brought him the report, "Where are you from?"

"I am the son of an alien, an Amalekite," he answered.

¹⁴David asked him, "Why were you not afraid to lift your hand to destroy the LORD's anointed?"

¹⁵Then David called one of his men and said, "Go, strike him down!" So he struck him down, and he died. ¹⁶For David

had said to him, "Your blood be on your own head. Your own mouth testified against you when you said, 'I killed the LORD's anointed.'"

¹⁷David took up this lament concerning Saul and his son Jonathan, ¹⁸and ordered that the men of Judah be taught this lament of the bow (it is written in the Book of Jashar):

¹⁹"Your glory, O Israel, lies slain on your heights.
    How the mighty have fallen!

²⁰"Tell it not in Gath,
        proclaim it not in the streets of Ashkelon,
    lest the daughters of the Philistines be glad,
        lest the daughters of the uncircumcised rejoice.

²¹"O mountains of Gilboa,
        may you have neither dew nor rain,
        nor fields that yield offerings of grain.
    For there the shield of the mighty was defiled,
        the shield of Saul—no longer rubbed with oil.
²²From the blood of the slain,
        from the flesh of the mighty,
    the bow of Jonathan did not turn back,
        the sword of Saul did not return unsatisfied.

²³"Saul and Jonathan—
        in life they were loved and gracious,
        and in death they were not parted.
    They were swifter than eagles,
        they were stronger than lions.

²⁴"O daughters of Israel,
        weep for Saul,
    who clothed you in scarlet and finery,
        who adorned your garments with ornaments of gold.

²⁵"How the mighty have fallen in battle!
        Jonathan lies slain on your heights.
²⁶I grieve for you, Jonathan my brother;
        you were very dear to me.
    Your love for me was wonderful,
        more wonderful than that of women.

²⁷"How the mighty have fallen!
        The weapons of war have perished!"

WITH THIS REPORT OF SAUL'S DEATH, we begin a new unit in the books of Samuel continuing through 2 Samuel 5:10. The twelve tribes of Israel do not univocally declare David king after the death of Saul. In general, David controls the south, particularly Judah and its politically important central city, Hebron. But Saul's son Ish-Bosheth becomes king of the northern tribes, often referred to simply as "Israel." For an indefinite period of time (probably two years, see 2:10), the nations are embroiled in civil war between the house of Saul and the house of David.[1] In a sense, the contrast between Saul and David that was so central in 1 Samuel 16–31 continues in the form of the civil war between David and Ish-Bosheth.

It has been said that the books of Samuel are organized along a complex succession of three overlapping trajectories centered on its leading characters: Samuel, Saul, and David.[2] With the death of Saul recorded in 1 Samuel 31, David's is the lone trajectory to follow, though it takes several years (and nearly five chapters!) to find him ruling over a unified nation Israel. After years of running from Saul, we might expect to find David rejoicing at the news that his old antagonist is dead. But as we saw in previous episodes, David has the greatest respect for the Lord's anointed and is willing to wait patiently for the Lord to fulfill his word in due course.

Second Samuel 1 makes its point in two ways. (1) The report of Saul's death comes to David and his men at Ziklag. The narrative reveals in graphic, even shocking ways, how deeply David feels the pain of losing Saul and Jonathan. (2) The concluding elegy expresses the same ideas in moving poetry.

The Report of Saul's death (1:1–10)

THE ACCOUNT OF the Amalekite messenger appears incongruous with the narrative given in 1 Samuel 31, as any cursory reading of the two chapters together will show. Some scholars have explained the differences by assuming this paragraph is a composite of two different accounts.[3] Others have

---

1. For the history in general, John Bright, *A History of Israel* (4th ed., Louisville: Westminster John Knox, 2000), 195–98; J. Maxwell Miller and John H. Hayes, *A History of Ancient Israel and Judah* (Philadelphia: Westminster, 1986), 168–74. For anthropological and sociopolitical background, see Carol Meyers, "Kinship and Kingship: The Early Monarchy," in *The Oxford History of the Biblical World*, ed. M. D. Coogan (New York: Oxford Univ. Press, 1998), 165–205.

2. Nelson, *The Historical Books*, 116.

3. For such approaches and my critique, see Bill T. Arnold, "The Amalekite's Report of Saul's Death: Political Intrigue or Incompatible Sources?" *JETS* 32 (1989): 289–98.

attempted to portray David as an uncompromising religious extremist who victimizes the truthful Amalekite.[4] It seems more logical that the historian has placed these two chapters together intentionally to portray the Amalekite as a liar. His account in general agrees with 1 Samuel 31 except for 2 Samuel 1:7–10, where he enhances his own involvement in order to win the favor of David (clear from David's subsequent reference to this event in 2 Sam. 4:10). Furthermore, deception is an important motif in the books of Samuel, and the idea that the messenger lies in order to gain favor with the new king-designate is congruous with other literary features of these books.[5]

The reference to David's recent military campaign against and defeat of the Amalekites not only places this text in historical perspective but prepares us for the irony of what follows (1:1; review 1 Sam. 30). Though precise chronology is impossible, David's return and the conclusion of the battle on Mount Gilboa are roughly contemporaneous.[6]

The messenger is not identified as an Amalekite until his speech to David (2 Sam. 1:8). Even as a resident alien in the borders of Israel, his identity as an Amalekite would automatically raise suspicion among David's men and call into question his role in the events on Mount Gilboa. Not only were the Amalekites among David's worst enemies; they are also portrayed consistently as terrorists who never fail to take advantage of weaker opponents.[7] This messenger is not likely to arouse sympathy among those who have just rescued their families from the Amalekites and have only two days before returned to homes destroyed by the Amalekites (1 Sam. 30:1–2). And, unlike the reader (1 Sam. 31), they have no independent report with which to compare that of the Amalekite.

How the royal insignia of crown and armlet come to be in David's possession is an important issue to clarify (1:10). Whether or not the poor Amalekite messenger realizes it, he is delivering these important items to the very person prepared by Yahweh to wear them. Yet David's association with the Philistines, his possession of the royal insignia, and the fact that he has much to gain from Saul's death might implicate him in the tragic events at Gilboa. Perhaps many in Israel suspect David has in fact killed Saul and Jonathan.

One of the important subthemes of our narrative is the legitimacy of David and his innocence in Saul's downfall. By explaining the chronology,

---

4. Mauchline, *1 and 2 Samuel*, 197.

5. Harry Hagan, "Deception As Motif and Theme in 2 Sam. 9–20; 1 Kgs 1–2," *Bib* 60 (1979): 301–26; Arnold, "The Amalekite's Report," 297–98.

6. The Heb. of 1:1 makes David's return from the defeat of the Amalekites a circumstantial clause, and we could translate with the pluperfect: "Now David had returned from defeating the Amalekites and had stayed in Ziklag two days." See Keil and Delitzsch, *Samuel*, 285.

7. See comments at 1 Sam. 15:1–9; 27:8–12; 30:1–6.

the narrator has made it clear that David is probably just returning from the Amalekite campaign while the debacle at Mount Gilboa is taking place. He simply could not have killed Saul and Jonathan because he could not have been in two places at once. More importantly, as the text will soon show, David could never have taken such actions against Saul because his loyalties have always been with Yahweh's anointed one and his son Jonathan.

David Mourns Saul and Kills the Amalekite Messenger (1:11–16)

SOME MAY HAVE EXPECTED DAVID and his men to rejoice at the death of Saul. After all, he has been forced to run for protection and has for months been living as an exile among the Philistines. His hopes of returning to his family are not good, much less his dreams of fulfilling his God-given mission of becoming king over Israel. It could be argued that Saul has ruined his life. Why not rejoice? It might have been a dramatic scene, even a celebration of God's confirmation, had David and his men broken forth in songs of praise and thanksgiving.

But instead of rejoicing, David and his men show signs of catastrophic grief, and they are unanimous in their mourning and sorrow (1:11–12). All of this proves for the reader that David has remained loyal to Israel and God's people. He was forced to flee from Saul's wrath and live among the Philistines, but he never lost his love and faithfulness for Israel.

Furthermore, his execution of the Amalekite messenger manifests an important theological point that also motivates David. He has the highest reverence for the sanctity of the Israelite king, the anointed one of Yahweh. He himself passed up more than one opportunity to kill Saul (see 1 Sam. 24 and 26). That which he refused to do out of respect for the king, this "foreigner, a man belonging to the nation of the Amalekites, Israel's greatest foes, had actually done for the sake of gain, or at any rate had pretended to have done."[8] Unlike the narrator and the reader, David does not know the Amalekite is lying. It makes no difference; he has confessed to a terrible crime ("Your own mouth testified against you," 1:16). Far from rejoicing at the news and rewarding the messenger, David is full of grief, which now comes to fruition in song.

David's Lament for Saul and Jonathan (1:17–27)

IN THE EVENT that any reader could conceivably doubt David's sincerity in mourning for Saul and Jonathan, the text now moves to an elegy in which

---

8. Keil and Delitzsch, *Samuel*, 288.

David's deepest emotional responses are expressed lyrically. Old Testament tradition assumes that David was a man especially gifted in music and song (1 Sam. 16:18, 23; 18:10; 2 Sam. 23:1; Amos 6:5; often in the Psalms, where seventy-two individual psalms are associated with his name). Many have noted that at various levels this poem implies that David himself is the composer, and the burden of proof lies with anyone denying this assertion.[9] The poetry has a lofty quality; "only a rare spirit deeply moved by an event of great moment is likely to have produced a little masterpiece like this."[10]

In one of the most emotional and moving scenes of the Bible, David's genuine pain comes through with singular clarity. In a series of vocatives, David addresses first the nation Israel, then the specific geographical location of the fateful battle (Mount Gilboa), and finally the "daughters of Israel" (1:19, 21, and 24). The theme of the dirge is clear from the phrase repeated three times (vv. 19, 25, and 27): "How the mighty have fallen!" This simple phrase (only three words in Hebrew) powerfully captures the depth of David's emotions and serves as a literary marker for the structure of the poem.[11]

Just before the end of the poem, we have a verse that is at the heart of one of the great ethical debates of our times. In verse 26, David becomes intensely personal in his lament for Jonathan:

> I grieve for you, Jonathan my brother;
>> you were very dear to me.
> Your love for me was wonderful,
>> more wonderful than that of women.

We have already seen how the narrator of 1 Samuel emphasizes the love between David and Jonathan (see comments on 1 Sam. 18:1–4). Some modern interpreters take this statement as evidence that David and Jonathan had a homosexual relationship.[12] Thus, certain aspects of the narrative of 1 Samuel

---

9. Ackroyd, *Second Book of Samuel*, 24; esp. P. Kyle McCarter Jr., *II Samuel* (AB 9; New York: Doubleday, 1984), 78–79.

10. Gordon, *I and II Samuel*, 210. It is also possible to see this poem as the conclusion of the trajectory in the books dealing with Saul's career and life and the end of David's exile. Conceivably whoever in the Middle Ages divided the Heb. book of Samuel into two books could have ended 1 Samuel with this dirge instead of the narrative account in 1 Sam. 31 (Jan P. Fokkelman, *Narrative Art and Poetry in the Books of Samuel*, 2:17).

11. The repetition of the phrase in vv. 19 and 27 creates an inclusio, a sort of literary frame for the poem. Many also assume a more complete chiastic structure in the poem, though there is little agreement about details. For two approaches, see William H. Shea, "Chiasmus and the Structure of David's Lament," *JBL* 105 (1986): 13–25; Youngblood, "1, 2 Samuel," 810.

12. For an early example of this interpretation, see Tom Horner, *Jonathan Loved David: Homosexuality in Biblical Times* (Philadelphia: Westminster, 1978), 20, 26–28, 31–39. See also

are thought to have been subverted by later editors because of cultural abhorrence of homosexuality, while other aspects such as Saul's irrational outbursts against David (1 Sam. 20:30–34) are explained as the senseless rage that accompanies homophobia.[13]

However, this interpretation should be rejected for the following reasons. (1) The noun for "love" used here (*ʾabᵃbah*, and its verb *ʾhb*) has important political and diplomatic connotations.[14] Since David's and Jonathan's relationship has already been marked as a covenant sealed by their love (same word), this part of the poem is referring to the depth of that covenant relationship (1 Sam. 18:3). By contrast, the standard Old Testament verb for sexual activity, whether homosexual or heterosexual, is "know" (*ydᶜ*), and it is never used to describe the relationship between David and Jonathan.

(2) David's comparison of his relationship with Jonathan with that of women is probably a subtle reference to the promise of 1 Samuel 17:25, when the young David learned that whoever killed Goliath would receive the king's daughter as reward. But David did not immediately receive Saul's daughter. Instead, he won the immediate admiration and love of Jonathan (1 Sam 18:1–4). The love and covenant relationship between David and Jonathan has been referred to in the text elsewhere (19:1; 20:17); now upon the occasion of Jonathan's death, David returns to the theme. He realizes that his covenantal relationship with Jonathan, which had nothing to do with sexual activity, proved more meaningful to him than his relationships with women.

(3) We possess an interesting parallel in the greatest literary piece from ancient Babylonia, the "Gilgamesh Epic."[15] The hero of the story, King Gilgamesh, is informed in a dream that a friend will come into his life who will match him in strength and whom he will love like a woman. The account explains how Enkidu soon arrives on the scene. They engage in a titanic battle, in which Gilgamesh and Enkidu prove to be of equal strength. Instead of one prevailing over the other, they become close friends, and the epic continues with a series of adventure themes involving both of them. Most scholars agree that it would be a misinterpretation of the story to assume this has

---

David M. Gunn, *The Story of King Saul* (Sheffield: Univ. of Sheffield Press, 1980), 93; Fewell and Gunn, *Gender, Power, and Promise*, 148–51.

13. Jobling, *1 Samuel*, 161–65.

14. Cross, *From Epic to Canon*, 9; Thompson, "Significance of the Verb *Love*," 334–38; Ackroyd, "The Verb *Love*," 213–14.

15. For introduction, see William Moran, "The Gilgamesh Epic: A Masterpiece from Ancient Mesopotamia," *CANE*, 4:2327–36. For translations, see Stephanie Dalley, *Myths from Mesopotamia: Creation, the Flood, Gilgamesh, and Others* (Oxford: Oxford Univ. Press, 1989), 39–153; Danny P. Jackson, *The Epic of Gilgamesh* (Wauconda, Ill.: Bolchazy-Carducci, 1992).

anything to do with homosexuality. The phrase is merely a rhetorical expression of the great depth of friendship experienced between Gilgamesh and his friend, Enkidu.[16]

(4) Homosexual acts were unequivocally condemned in Israelite law (Lev. 18:22; 20:13). It would be incongruous for a narrative so devoted to portraying David in positive light to describe him engaged in homosexual love with Jonathan.

In short, the controversy surrounding verse 26 is more a reflex of our modern society's impulse to defend and justify homosexual activity than it has to do with accurate exegesis of this text.[17] The controversy itself also illustrates an unfortunate contrast between modern Western culture and that of the ancient Near East. Ancients (and some moderns of the Middle East) refer to and display affection between members of the same sex easily without implying homosexual attraction. Conversely, public displays of affection between men and women are scandalous in the Middle East today.[18]

Bridging
Contexts

WITH THE DEATH of Saul and his three sons at Mount Gilboa, the text now raises the question of succession. Ish-Bosheth is still alive and will reign among the northern tribes, though we have not yet been told of him (see comments on 2:8–9). The books of Samuel are partially intended to answer the question: Who will reign suitably as king of Israel? Saul has shown himself patently unsuitable, and his ignoble death confirms the fact that future kings must be different from this first anointed one. By contrast, our historian has related the anointing of David and the remarkable way in which God has prepared and protected him. He is without question suitable as Saul's successor.

David and Saul's fate. Old Testament scholarship has long recognized that an important subplot in the books of Samuel is the desire to legitimize

---

16. Nissinen concedes that "homoeroticism is certainly not a central theme in the *Epic of Gilgamesh*" (Martti Nissinen, *Homoeroticism in the Biblical World: A Historical Perspective* [Minneapolis: Fortress, 1998], 20–24, esp. 23).

17. Nissinen speaks of David and Jonathan as an example of ancient oriental homosociability, "which permits even intimate feelings to be expressed" between same-sex friends without sexual implications. Ancient literature has other examples of male relationships of intimate affection and companionship, which are often strong in societies in which men's and women's worlds are segregated. He mentions especially Achilles and Patroclus in Homer's *Iliad* and Gilgamesh and Enkidu. See Nissinen, *Homoeroticism*, 53–56. See also Martti Nissinen, "Die Liebe von David und Jonatan als Frage der modernen Exegese," *Bib* 80 (1999): 250–63.

18. An ironic point made by Steven L. McKenzie, *King David: A Biography* (Oxford: Oxford Univ. Press, 2000), 85.

David as king of Israel against charges that he was guilty of collusion. Did he undermine a vulnerable King Saul and manipulate circumstances to take the throne when it was not rightly his? Did he in fact collaborate with the dreaded Philistines to end Saul's life (and reign)? Could he be charged indirectly with the murder of Saul? This historian has gone to great lengths to answer these questions with an emphatic "no." David has in no way attempted to bring about Saul's demise. He has, on the contrary, remained faithful and loyal to Saul and to the apparent crown prince, Jonathan, to the bitter end. David is where he is solely because of Yahweh, who has anointed him and prepared him for the task.

This text continues that emphasis. When the deceptive Amalekite arrives at Ziklag, he presumably expects to receive a reward for bringing the good news to Saul's evident successor. Thus, the misguided messenger assumes what others in ancient Israel must have assumed—David will rejoice at the death of Saul. But he (and any ancient readers who made the same assumption) quickly learns that David is a bigger soul, who is less interested in personal gain than in proper respect for Yahweh's anointed one. The Amalekite unintentionally becomes "the instrument by means of which Yahweh proleptically 'crowned' the future king of Israel."[19] The last portion of this text records David's moving dirge, which brings the point home. This great lyrical lament shows that David is in fact incapable of leading a coup d'état against Saul. His love and admiration for the anointed one and for Jonathan have precluded any such subversive behavior. It is simply impossible to blame David for Saul's fate.

The faithfulness of David—and of Yahweh. Beyond the concern to legitimize David as king, this chapter highlights the faithfulness of David generally. Rather than seizing by force the kingdom promised to him, David remains devoted to the royal family and to the vision of God to provide a stable monarchy. David as portrayed here is not grasping or avaricious but broken by grief. His bereavement at the loss of Saul and Jonathan as expressed in his moving eulogy is undeniable, and he commands all the inhabitants of Judah to share in his mourning (1:18).

Indirectly, our text also emphasizes the sovereign action of Yahweh. God had promised to deliver David from Saul and to make him king in Saul's place. But instead of seeing these promises fulfilled immediately, David was forced to flee Judah and live as an exile in Philistia. During this long interval the question has been: How and when will God bring about his promises? Now Saul's death has come prematurely because of the way he lived. Saul's death prepares the way for a new beginning in Israel.

---

19. A. A. Anderson, *2 Samuel* (WBC 11; Dallas: Word, 1989), 10.

David has been faithful and hence is well qualified and well prepared to be king. But God also has been faithful. His faithfulness is manifested in premature death for Saul and in new possibilities and new beginnings for David. Another way of saying this is that God has been faithful to his prophetic word by seeing that Saul's obstinate rebellion has been answered with justice and that David is positioned to become the next king in Israel.

THE POWER OF SONG. Pivotal moments in Israel's history are often marked by song. Just as Moses and Miriam sang after the crossing of the Red Sea (Ex. 15) and the women of Israel sang in celebration after Saul and David's military victories (1 Sam. 18:7), so this tragic moment is preserved in mournful lament. The narrative of the report of Saul's death is a historical prelude to David's funeral dirge. Together, the narrative and the poem explore the depths of national and personal sorrow, even as God's will is becoming a reality for David and Israel.

The joyful song of Israel's women singing and dancing in Saul's honor was that "Saul has slain his thousands" (1 Sam. 18:7). He led the nation in glorious victory over God's enemies and was rightly hailed as God's instrument of peace and deliverance. But now that chorus has changed to the phrase so prevalent in David's lament, "How the mighty have fallen!" The unthinkable has occurred. The hymn of victory and celebration has turned into a funeral dirge, using the richness of Hebrew poetry to measure the depths of sorrow and death rather than the rapturous chords of celebration.

How has it happened? Why has it happened? As we have seen, Saul was dissatisfied with his "thousands" when David was praised for slaying his tens of thousands. Saul was unable to accept God's role for him in the new kingdom. He presumed upon the grace of God by misappropriating royal power. He made too many assumptions about the power inherent to his new role as king and the nature of God's new kingdom in Israel.

The anointed of Yahweh. The Amalekite messenger in our text is a warning about the same issues. He also presumed too much about power and the nature of God's new kingdom. Being an Amalekite, he naturally accepted power as a means of getting what one wants. The Amalekites attacked the helpless ex-slaves from Egypt as they crossed the Sinai (Ex. 17:8–16; Deut. 25:17–18) and raided a defenseless Ziklag while David was away (1 Sam. 30:1–6). So this Amalekite presumes he can lie to seize power in David's new kingdom. But he does not know David and has no idea what it means to be an anointed of Yahweh.

More tragically, even Saul did not understand what it meant to be an anointed of Yahweh. The funeral portrait in this chapter is so tragic for precisely this reason. Saul never learned to revel in God's grace and enjoy his favor. Why have the mighty fallen so tragically? Why has the poetry of victory been turned into the poetry of sorrow? Because Saul took his position of power personally. He abused his role as king in order to persecute David, and he lost sight of his mission and God's calling on his life.

But David understands what it means to be Yahweh's anointed one. Not only does he twice refuse to strike down Saul; he also refuses to condone someone else who struck him down. He is intolerant toward the enemies of God. David is passionate about the things of God. Opportunities for personal gain cannot possibly be framed in terms of losses for God's people, and he refuses to play power politics. The Amalekite learns too late what David believed about God and God's anointed.

Power and its (ab)use. Sociologists and philosophers speak in terms of *Realpolitik* or the abuse of human power structures in social groups.[20] There is nothing more heartbreaking than the abuse of political power in Christian institutions, whether they are churches, parachurch organizations, or educational institutions. Some of the most harmful and hurtful consequences for the Christian gospel I have witnessed have been brought about by individuals *within* the church who abuse their roles in the power structures.

Yet power among all social groups, including churches, is inevitable. Power itself is not inherently evil, but the way people use it often is. The Bible has much to teach us on this point. At this transitional chapter in the books of Samuel, it is appropriate to consider Saul's abuse of power as narrated in 1 Samuel, and this chapter serves to demonstrate the results. Conversely, David has served in 1 Samuel as an example of the right use of power, and he will continue to serve this way in the next few chapters. Unfortunately, however, David will not be so exemplary throughout all of 2 Samuel.

---

20. Paul Tillich, *Love, Power, and Justice: Ontological Analyses and Ethical Applications* (New York: Oxford Univ. Press, 1954), 72–106; see Niebuhr's distinction between the moral and social behavior of individuals and that of social groups (national, racial, and economic), necessitating "political policies which a purely individualistic ethic must always find embarrassing" (Niebuhr, *Moral Man and Immoral Society*, xi, 1–22).

2 Samuel 2:1–7

‌

I‌N THE COURSE of time, David inquired of the LORD. "Shall I go up to one of the towns of Judah?" he asked.

The LORD said, "Go up."

David asked, "Where shall I go?"

"To Hebron," the LORD answered.

²So David went up there with his two wives, Ahinoam of Jezreel and Abigail, the widow of Nabal of Carmel. ³David also took the men who were with him, each with his family, and they settled in Hebron and its towns. ⁴Then the men of Judah came to Hebron and there they anointed David king over the house of Judah.

When David was told that it was the men of Jabesh Gilead who had buried Saul, ⁵he sent messengers to the men of Jabesh Gilead to say to them, "The LORD bless you for showing this kindness to Saul your master by burying him. ⁶May the LORD now show you kindness and faithfulness, and I too will show you the same favor because you have done this. ⁷Now then, be strong and brave, for Saul your master is dead, and the house of Judah has anointed me king over them."

WE HAVE REACHED A TURNING POINT in the account of the rise of David. With the death of Saul and Jonathan, it is time for David to become king, first in Judah in the south and subsequently over all Israel (5:1–5).

Though the way for David to proceed is clear in theory, it is also fraught with danger. The Philistines have demonstrated their superiority in the north (as far as Mount Gilboa and Beth Shan; see 1 Sam. 31) in addition to their traditional strongholds in the southwest. We will soon learn of Saul's son Ish-Bosheth, who has legitimate claims from a human perspective (over the northern tribes especially). If David is to become king of a unified Israel, he will need more wisdom than he can conjure on his own. This text explains how Yahweh's guidance works together with David's best human political diplomacy to effect the first step in David's coronation as king of Israel.

David Becomes King at Hebron (2:1–4a)

THE OPENING PHRASE ("In the course of time," 2:1) is a Hebrew idiom used as a transition marker, especially in 2 Samuel (see 8:1; 10:1; 13:1; 15:1; 21:18).[1] Here this phrase introduces the public anointing of David by the people of Judah. Earlier, Samuel had anointed David (1 Sam. 16:13). Now that David's predecessor Saul proved himself unworthy and is dead and properly buried, it is time for this private and prophetic anointing of David to be repeated in public. Now is the time for David to move into action and claim the promises of God.

But as so often happens, it is difficult to know when one should take action and when one should wait upon God's guidance. Fortunately for David, he does not have to rely on his own instincts and intuition, as valuable as they are. The expression "David inquired of the LORD" (2:1) tells it all. Occasionally in the history of David's rise, we have seen him "inquire" of Yahweh as a means of discerning God's will and determining what his next course of action should be. David learned the importance of inquiring of Yahweh from the good priests of Nob (1 Sam. 22:10, 13, 15). When the priest Abiathar managed to escape the slaughter that took place at that unfortunate city, he found refuge with David. Thereby David gained the benefits of obtaining the Urim and Thummim, the divinely sanctioned and approved means of seeking God's guidance.[2] On numerous occasions, David called for the priestly ephod containing the Urim and Thummim in order to seek God's will (1 Sam. 22:10; 23:2, 4; 30:7–8; 2 Sam. 5:23; cf. 1 Sam. 22:13, 15). This dependence on Yahweh for guidance characterizes David and is partly what the text refers to when it describes him as the ideal king of Israel.

Moreover, the narrator has highlighted this phrase in several places in order to contrast David with Saul. Yahweh eventually stopped answering Saul's inquiries, presumably because Saul summarily made up his mind before asking (1 Sam. 14:36–37). Near the end of his life, the silence of Yahweh was an ominous indication of the depth of Saul's despair (28:6). By contrast, David is the faithful leader who learns from the priest how to listen to God.

The contrast in the technical terminology for seeking God's will continues to manifest itself in David and Saul's son Ish-Bosheth. David inquires before taking a step, but Ish-Bosheth becomes king as a result of political machinations in the north (2:8–11). David is portrayed as relying only on

---

1. Randall Bailey, *David in Love and War: The Pursuit of Power in 2 Samuel 10–12* (JSOTSup 75; Sheffield: JSOT, 1990), 56–57; C. Conroy, *Absalom Absalom! Narrative and Language in 2 Sam. 13–20* (AnBib 81; Rome: Biblical Institute Press, 1978), 41–42.

2. On the nature of the Urim and Thummim and general discussion of the phrase "inquire" of Yahweh, see comments at 1 Sam. 23:1–6 above.

the power and timing of Yahweh, while Ish-Bosheth will be introduced as a puppet in the hands of human power structures. David patiently inquires of the Lord before he takes any action. This is no "power play" on David's part. Instead, this is "faith play," and the significance of the contrast between David and Ish-Bosheth will dominate the next few chapters.

David's move to Judah is permanent; he has no intentions of returning to Philistia, as is evident by the reference to his entire company of people: the men with him, their families, and David's own two wives (2:2–3). Ahinoam and Abigail were prominent women from the surrounding countryside. Their presence aids David in his transition from ally in a foreign land to recently returned candidate for the throne.[3]

With God's guidance revealed clearly through the Urim and Thummim, surrounded by his retinue of family and personal troops, David is finally ready to be anointed king by the inhabitants of Judah. Gathering at Hebron, they use the traditional Israelite custom of anointing as a means of formalizing the royal status of David (2:4). Prophetic anointing indicates divine approval and is symbolized by the coming of the Spirit of Yahweh and the bestowal of supernatural empowerment (see comments on 1 Sam. 16:6–13). Here, however, anointing is by the people, which represents the public acceptance of David as king. Most likely it symbolizes a pledge of loyalty to David on the part of the inhabitants of Judah; for his part, David is granting them a royal promise.[4]

David's Proposal to Jabesh Gilead (2:4b–7)

THIS PARAGRAPH IS ALL ABOUT LOYALTY. There had been a special relationship between Saul and the citizens of Jabesh Gilead ever since early in Saul's reign when he, as the first king of Israel, delivered the city from the hands of the Ammonites (1 Sam. 11:1–11).[5] At the end of his reign, the citizens of Jabesh Gilead heroically demonstrated their loyalty to Saul in their efforts to save him and his sons from the disgrace of exposure after their deaths in battle

---

3. In fact, it has been argued that these marriages were politically motivated from the start, deliberate steps to prepare for David's move to take the throne (see Levenson and Halpern, "The Political Import of David's Marriages," 507–18). It is even possible that Ahinoam was first the wife of Saul, so that David's marriage to her was tantamount to a claim to the throne (Levenson, "I Samuel 25 As Literature," 27).

4. Mettinger, *King and Messiah*, 175. Frank Moore Cross considers this pledge of loyalty a "covenant of kingship," though the term *covenant* is not used. In the south, royal ideology involved an eternal decree as distinct from the northern tribes, which assumed the conditional and covenantal character of kingship. Cross, *Canaanite Myth and Hebrew Epi*, 219–73. Note that "covenant" *is* used when David becomes king of the north (2 Sam. 5:35).

5. Jabesh Gilead was strategically located on the east bank of the Jordan (see comments on 1 Sam. 11:1–3).

(1 Sam. 31:11–13). David, realizing the need to have supporters in the north (esp. in the difficult-to-hold Transjordan), offers himself as the logical and convenient successor to Saul. The loyalty of the people of Jabesh Gilead is a significant confirmation of David's right to rule the whole of Israel rather than Judah only.

David's offer draws on their loyalty to Saul. He implies that God's blessing and favor on their city are parallel to his own goodwill toward Jabesh Gilead (2:6). Ironically, he suggests that in light of the tragic king's death, their loyalty to Saul will best find fruition in loyalty to David. Central to his claim is the emphasis on showing "kindness" (*ḥesed*), which again emphasizes loyalty in human relationships.[6] To "show/do kindness" to someone is to provide needed help or aid to the other party, who for one reason or another is unable to help himself or herself. Such help is performed not out of a hope for reciprocation or advantage but purely on the basis of prior relationship and commitment.[7]

Thus, when Saul needed their help, the citizens of Jabesh Gilead responded by jeopardizing their own lives to provide him a proper burial (2:5). Now both Yahweh and David will come to the city's aid (2:6), since presumably the rise of the Philistines and Saul's death will once again threaten Jabesh Gilead (perhaps at the hands of the Ammonites again). David's proposal is that the good people of Jabesh Gilead should strengthen themselves for the decision to be loyal to David in the full knowledge that Saul is dead and buried and that he, David, has been made king in Judah. Their loyalty to Saul must now be transformed to David (2:7).

DAVID'S MOTIVES. From the perspective of the modern historian, David's actions immediately before and after his coronation at Hebron may hint at crude political manipulation.[8] After all, he has shared the plunder from his raid against the Amalekites with these same inhabitants of Judah (1 Sam. 30:26–31), perhaps considering it a bribe or a down payment on his future royal claims. The wives mentioned in verse 2, Ahinoam and Abigail, are both from the area around Hebron and provide David with significant familial connections to the south, perhaps also preparing for his seizure of political power.[9] His diplomatic overtures

---

6. BDB, 338 (sec. I.1); DCH, 3:278–79; see also Bridging Contexts discussion of 1 Sam. 20.

7. Clark, *The Word Ḥesed in the Hebrew Bible*, 267.

8. McCarter, *II Samuel*, 89–90.

9. Ackroyd, *Second Book of Samuel*, 30; Levenson and Halpern, "The Political Import of David's Marriages," 507–18.

to the people of Jabesh Gilead in the north (2:4b–7) look like calculated attempts to undermine the authority of his counterpart Ish-Bosheth, who has laid claim to these same regions (2:9). David is certainly shrewd and deliberate in his decisions, but is it also possible to interpret him as cold and insidious in his quest for the throne? Perhaps his coronation at Hebron is the result of nothing more than rapacious ambition, and David is no more than a driven politician seizing power after the death of his unfortunate opponent.

However one might answer this question is mere speculation because we cannot delve into the motives of David beyond the indications of the text. Besides, this is the wrong question to ask. Whether David is savagely opportunistic or simply naïve may be a question for today's historians, but this is not the point of our text. The narrator has been clear from the outset: This anointed one, unlike Saul, is driven only by the promises of Yahweh and takes action under Yahweh's leadership. Thus, our narrative explains that David takes the throne of Judah at God's invitation and promptly offers to rule the unified nation by extending an olive branch to Jabesh Gilead.

David is no doubt politically shrewd, and perhaps he *is* ambitious. But our task as Christian readers of the Bible is not to reconstruct David's psychological motivations. Rather, we are looking for the central message of this text, from which we can build a bridge to today's world. This paragraph is an important step in the extended narrative's concern with this question: Who can serve suitably as king of Israel? Irrespective of the psychoanalytical realities of David's character, David is primarily galvanized by his zeal for Yahweh and is completely dependent on Yahweh for guidance and strength. In short, David is suitable as Israel's king in a way that Saul was not—and now Ish-Bosheth is not.

Inquiring for God's will. However, it is precisely that suitability that gives us difficulty. It is David's faithful and persistent dependence on the will of God that makes him suitable as Israel's king. We want to be faithful too, but God's will can seem all too elusive. Wherever we encounter the phrase "inquire of the LORD" (2:1) in the history of David's rise, we as twenty-first-century readers must address the question: How does one inquire of God today?[10]

The need for divine guidance is an undeniable link between believers of Bible times and today. The Bible is clear that God communicated to Israel's ancestors, but we are not often told the precise *means* through which he did so. The Lord simply "said" to Abraham that he must leave Ur of the Chaldeans

---

10. Review my Bridging Contexts sections for 1 Sam. 23:1–29 and 29:1–30:31.

and travel to an unknown land (Gen. 12:1). The ancestral narratives contain many such examples of hearing and receiving divine messages, though rarely are we told how the revelation is mediated. Jacob's stairway dream is one exception, as is also his encounter with the mysterious night visitor at Peniel (Gen. 28:10–22; 32:22–32).[11]

With the arrival of the Mosaic covenant, we read of a variety of divine communications, including the burning bush, pillars of cloud and fire, and theophanic trumpet blasts. But with Moses, the divine communication was given a permanency because of the written word of God, which included the Ten Commandments and applications of the law (Ex. 24:4; Deut. 31:9, 24). This new form of divine communication quickly became primary over other expressions of God's will. The Mosaic law made provisions for the Urim and Thummim for special communications in the future (Ex. 28:30; Lev. 8:8; Num. 27:21), but the written covenantal law was clearly on a different level as an expression of divine will. During subsequent periods of Old Testament history, the prophets arrived to interpret and explain the significance of the law, and Jewish believers of the Exile accepted the written Word as God's divinely approved means of guidance and direction.

Christians generally believe that God is still a communicating God and that he desires to communicate with us in clear and discernible ways. But we no longer have David's advantage of priestly ephod with its Urim and Thummim. We should recognize that we stand in a great historical line of believers that stretches back to biblical times. As God's revelation progressed, the means of communicating his guidance and direction changed. Like faithful Jewish believers before us, we Christians are "people of the book." Without denying the possibility of audible voices or dramatic writing in the sky, we must admit that God's *primary* means of communicating today is through Scripture. Any spectacular revelation that contradicts Scripture is wrong. Through Scripture, we believe God still communicates and teaches us, just as he communicated and instructed in Old Testament days.

The portrait of David in this paragraph is not complete, however, with only the seeking and finding of Yahweh's will. Perhaps the most impressive words of the text are those that open verse 2: "So David went up there...."[12] Having heard God's voice through the Urim and Thummim, David acts in accordance with that revelation. This is what makes him a suitable king for Israel as much as his persistence to inquire of Yahweh. This king, unlike

---

11. The fact that Jacob needs special forms of divine encounter may itself be an indictment of his character.

12. It is even possible to see emphasis in the Hebrew word order on the little word "there," placing stress on David's obedience.

Saul, will obey the direction of Yahweh. Certainly this raises questions for readers who know and anticipate the surprising and disappointing events of 2 Samuel. But those events are yet to be, and we must not get ahead of our narrator.

Looking back and looking ahead. When considering how to build a bridge from this text to our context, we should also note that our paragraph has a distinctively retrospective dimension. There are interesting intertextual reverberations between David as Israel's king and Israel's ancestors narrated in Genesis 12–50. When David became king of Judah and eventually of all Israel (see 5:1–3 below), he fulfilled the promises of God to Abraham and Sarah, the parents of the nation of Israel ("kings will come from you," Gen. 17:6, 16).[13] David is perhaps also the fulfillment of Jacob's blessing to Judah (49:10): "The scepter will not depart from Judah, nor the ruler's staff from between his feet, until he comes to whom it belongs and the obedience of the nations is his."[14]

Similarly, the surprise ending to the story of Ruth and Boaz transforms the message of that book. Instead of an interesting little narrative about a young woman who was fortunate to find a new life in Bethlehem, the book becomes a profound statement about God's direction in history (Ruth 4:13–22). God intervened in the lives of faithful Israelite commoners in order to prepare for the coming of Israel's ideal king. Our little paragraph in 2 Samuel now brings the great-grandson of Ruth and Boaz to the throne of Judah. These intertextual echoes bind this narrative with much of what precedes and demonstrate God's faithfulness to his promises through his guidance in establishing the united monarchy.

But if this text exhibits a retrospective dimension, it is also decidedly forward-looking. After all, Samuel had anointed David king of *Israel* (1 Sam. 16:1). This paragraph brings us only to David's rule over Judah, but for the fulfillment of Yahweh's promise we must await the outcome of a bloody civil war and his anointing by "all the tribes of Israel" (2 Sam. 5:1). So our text is part of a trajectory that goes through a subsequent coronation, which itself is part of a larger mosaic, contributing finally to intertestamental expectations of a Messiah. Just as David appears here as a patient servant who is completely reliant on God for direction and strength, so the trajectory of Scripture leads us eventually to David's greater Son, the Messiah, who illustrates for us the ultimate reliance on his Father for direction and strength.

---

13. Just as the conquest of the Promised Land under Joshua was a fulfillment of Gen. 15:18–21. On the ancestral connections, see Barth, *God with Us*, 191.

14. The prominence of the city of Hebron in this paragraph as well as Mahanaim in the next may also have ancestral overtones. See Baldwin, *1 and 2 Samuel*, 183–84.

DAVID SOUGHT, FOUND, and obeyed the will of God. In the process, God fulfilled his promises to him and made him king of Judah. The timeless truth of this text becomes clear for us when we realize that David serves as the paradigm for the ideal king of Israel and secondarily as a paradigm for any believer.

Obedience. Perhaps you have heard it said (or have said yourself): If only I could have the same kind of experience with God as Moses (or David, or X-biblical saint), then surely I would be as faithful as they were. In reality, we have the advantage over these biblical saints because of where we stand in relation to God's redemptive acts in history and because we have in our possession the entire Bible. Benjamin Disraeli once remarked, "As a general rule the most successful [person] in life is the [one] who has the best information."[15] If this is true, you and I have the potential to be more faithful than these great biblical characters. Whereas David relied on the priestly ephod, with its Urim and Thummim, to "inquire of the LORD," you and I have far superior resources. Instead of limited "yes" or "no" answers from God, we have the complete and full revelation of his overarching plan, which is clear and perspicuous in its essential details.

We also have a seemingly limitless number of recent translations of the Bible, stores full of wonderful tools for Bible study, and computer software programs to save us time in our quest for God's truth. David sought the voice of God in the primitive use of Urim and Thummim; you and I have God's inspired Word in so many forms we are forced to choose which to use. Whether all of these advantages have made today's church any more effective in its witness is debatable. Perhaps it is even presumptuous to talk about seeking, finding, and obeying the will of God as David did. In reality, we have the potential to seek and find much easier than believers of any other generation before us. Obedience is the final frontier.

In a famous journal entry entitled "The Tame Geese," Søren Kierkegaard imagined a land in which geese could talk. Not only could they talk, but it was also their habit to waddle off to church every Sunday, where one of the ganders preached. The sermons were essentially the same: The geese had been given a lofty destiny and a high goal by the Creator (and every time the Creator was mentioned, the geese all curtsied and the ganders bowed their heads). "By the aid of wings, the geese could fly away to distant regions, blessed climbs, where properly they were at home, for here they were only

---

15. Quoted in Robert H. Waterman Jr., *The Renewal Factor: How the Best Get and Keep the Competitive Edge* (New York: Bantam Books, 1987), 24.

strangers." And so it was Sunday after Sunday. But Kierkegaard noted the unfortunate truth that each Sunday after such eloquent sermons, "as soon as the assembly broke up each waddled home to his own affairs," rather than attempted to fly. All the while, the geese "throve and were well-liked, became plump and delicate—and then were eaten . . . and that was the end of it."[16]

In this text, David not only sought and found God's will, but having found it, he obeyed ("So David went up," 2:2). When applying this text, it would be easy (and convenient!) to dwell on the legitimate and all-too-difficult task of rightly discerning God's will for our lives. True, it is often difficult to discern what we should do in specific situations. But we must go beyond this to the obedience of Israel's ideal king. Though we may occasionally be in need of clarification and may not always feel we understand God's direction in our lives, we should devote ourselves to living up to the light we have received while praying and waiting for further clarification.

I have heard it said that God is looking for the kind of person he can afford to bless. As a paradigm for all believers, David *is* the kind of person God can afford to bless! More specifically, this text relates to 1 Samuel in demonstrating the kind of ruler God is pleased to bless in contradistinction to Saul (the text's retrospective dimension, see above). The text also contributes to Israel's encompassing messianic consciousness by illustrating why David is the ideal king and why he will ultimately become the standard by which all future kings of Israel will be measured (forward-looking dimension). David understands that as king of Israel he will be merely a viceroy. He knows who *really* rules Israel, which is why he continues to "inquire" of Yahweh.

---

16. Robert Bretall, ed., *A Kierkegaard Anthology* (Princeton, N.J.: Princeton Univ. Press, 1951), 433.

2 Samuel 2:8–4:12

MEANWHILE, ABNER SON of Ner, the commander of Saul's army, had taken Ish-Bosheth son of Saul and brought him over to Mahanaim. ⁹He made him king over Gilead, Ashuri and Jezreel, and also over Ephraim, Benjamin and all Israel.

¹⁰Ish-Bosheth son of Saul was forty years old when he became king over Israel, and he reigned two years. The house of Judah, however, followed David. ¹¹The length of time David was king in Hebron over the house of Judah was seven years and six months.

¹²Abner son of Ner, together with the men of Ish-Bosheth son of Saul, left Mahanaim and went to Gibeon. ¹³Joab son of Zeruiah and David's men went out and met them at the pool of Gibeon. One group sat down on one side of the pool and one group on the other side.

¹⁴Then Abner said to Joab, "Let's have some of the young men get up and fight hand to hand in front of us."

"All right, let them do it," Joab said.

¹⁵So they stood up and were counted off—twelve men for Benjamin and Ish-Bosheth son of Saul, and twelve for David. ¹⁶Then each man grabbed his opponent by the head and thrust his dagger into his opponent's side, and they fell down together. So that place in Gibeon was called Helkath Hazzurim.

¹⁷The battle that day was very fierce, and Abner and the men of Israel were defeated by David's men.

¹⁸The three sons of Zeruiah were there: Joab, Abishai and Asahel. Now Asahel was as fleet-footed as a wild gazelle. ¹⁹He chased Abner, turning neither to the right nor to the left as he pursued him. ²⁰Abner looked behind him and asked, "Is that you, Asahel?"

"It is," he answered.

²¹Then Abner said to him, "Turn aside to the right or to the left; take on one of the young men and strip him of his weapons." But Asahel would not stop chasing him.

²²Again Abner warned Asahel, "Stop chasing me! Why should I strike you down? How could I look your brother Joab in the face?"

²³But Asahel refused to give up the pursuit; so Abner thrust the butt of his spear into Asahel's stomach, and the spear came out through his back. He fell there and died on the spot. And every man stopped when he came to the place where Asahel had fallen and died.

²⁴But Joab and Abishai pursued Abner, and as the sun was setting, they came to the hill of Ammah, near Giah on the way to the wasteland of Gibeon. ²⁵Then the men of Benjamin rallied behind Abner. They formed themselves into a group and took their stand on top of a hill.

²⁶Abner called out to Joab, "Must the sword devour forever? Don't you realize that this will end in bitterness? How long before you order your men to stop pursuing their brothers?"

²⁷Joab answered, "As surely as God lives, if you had not spoken, the men would have continued the pursuit of their brothers until morning."

²⁸So Joab blew the trumpet, and all the men came to a halt; they no longer pursued Israel, nor did they fight anymore.

²⁹All that night Abner and his men marched through the Arabah. They crossed the Jordan, continued through the whole Bithron and came to Mahanaim.

³⁰Then Joab returned from pursuing Abner and assembled all his men. Besides Asahel, nineteen of David's men were found missing. ³¹But David's men had killed three hundred and sixty Benjamites who were with Abner. ³²They took Asahel and buried him in his father's tomb at Bethlehem. Then Joab and his men marched all night and arrived at Hebron by daybreak.

³:¹The war between the house of Saul and the house of David lasted a long time. David grew stronger and stronger, while the house of Saul grew weaker and weaker.

²Sons were born to David in Hebron:

His firstborn was Amnon the son of Ahinoam of Jezreel;

³his second, Kileab the son of Abigail the widow of Nabal of Carmel;

the third, Absalom the son of Maacah daughter of Talmai king of Geshur;

⁴the fourth, Adonijah the son of Haggith;

the fifth, Shephatiah the son of Abital;

⁵and the sixth, Ithream the son of David's wife Eglah.

These were born to David in Hebron.

⁶During the war between the house of Saul and the house of David, Abner had been strengthening his own position in the house of Saul. ⁷Now Saul had had a concubine named Rizpah daughter of Aiah. And Ish-Bosheth said to Abner, "Why did you sleep with my father's concubine?"

⁸Abner was very angry because of what Ish-Bosheth said and he answered, "Am I a dog's head—on Judah's side? This very day I am loyal to the house of your father Saul and to his family and friends. I haven't handed you over to David. Yet now you accuse me of an offense involving this woman! ⁹May God deal with Abner, be it ever so severely, if I do not do for David what the LORD promised him on oath ¹⁰and transfer the kingdom from the house of Saul and establish David's throne over Israel and Judah from Dan to Beersheba." ¹¹Ish-Bosheth did not dare to say another word to Abner, because he was afraid of him.

¹²Then Abner sent messengers on his behalf to say to David, "Whose land is it? Make an agreement with me, and I will help you bring all Israel over to you."

¹³"Good," said David. "I will make an agreement with you. But I demand one thing of you: Do not come into my presence unless you bring Michal daughter of Saul when you come to see me." ¹⁴Then David sent messengers to Ish-Bosheth son of Saul, demanding, "Give me my wife Michal, whom I betrothed to myself for the price of a hundred Philistine foreskins."

¹⁵So Ish-Bosheth gave orders and had her taken away from her husband Paltiel son of Laish. ¹⁶Her husband, however, went with her, weeping behind her all the way to Bahurim. Then Abner said to him, "Go back home!" So he went back.

¹⁷Abner conferred with the elders of Israel and said, "For some time you have wanted to make David your king. ¹⁸Now do it! For the LORD promised David, 'By my servant David I will rescue my people Israel from the hand of the Philistines and from the hand of all their enemies.'"

¹⁹Abner also spoke to the Benjamites in person. Then he went to Hebron to tell David everything that Israel and the whole house of Benjamin wanted to do. ²⁰When Abner, who had twenty men with him, came to David at Hebron, David prepared a feast for him and his men. ²¹Then Abner said to David, "Let me go at once and assemble all Israel for my lord

the king, so that they may make a compact with you, and that you may rule over all that your heart desires." So David sent Abner away, and he went in peace.

²²Just then David's men and Joab returned from a raid and brought with them a great deal of plunder. But Abner was no longer with David in Hebron, because David had sent him away, and he had gone in peace. ²³When Joab and all the soldiers with him arrived, he was told that Abner son of Ner had come to the king and that the king had sent him away and that he had gone in peace.

²⁴So Joab went to the king and said, "What have you done? Look, Abner came to you. Why did you let him go? Now he is gone! ²⁵You know Abner son of Ner; he came to deceive you and observe your movements and find out everything you are doing."

²⁶Joab then left David and sent messengers after Abner, and they brought him back from the well of Sirah. But David did not know it. ²⁷Now when Abner returned to Hebron, Joab took him aside into the gateway, as though to speak with him privately. And there, to avenge the blood of his brother Asahel, Joab stabbed him in the stomach, and he died.

²⁸Later, when David heard about this, he said, "I and my kingdom are forever innocent before the LORD concerning the blood of Abner son of Ner. ²⁹May his blood fall upon the head of Joab and upon all his father's house! May Joab's house never be without someone who has a running sore or leprosy or who leans on a crutch or who falls by the sword or who lacks food."

³⁰(Joab and his brother Abishai murdered Abner because he had killed their brother Asahel in the battle at Gibeon.)

³¹Then David said to Joab and all the people with him, "Tear your clothes and put on sackcloth and walk in mourning in front of Abner." King David himself walked behind the bier. ³²They buried Abner in Hebron, and the king wept aloud at Abner's tomb. All the people wept also.

³³The king sang this lament for Abner:

"Should Abner have died as the lawless die?
³⁴   Your hands were not bound,
        your feet were not fettered.
    You fell as one falls before wicked men."

And all the people wept over him again.

³⁵Then they all came and urged David to eat something while it was still day; but David took an oath, saying, "May God deal with me, be it ever so severely, if I taste bread or anything else before the sun sets!"

³⁶All the people took note and were pleased; indeed, everything the king did pleased them. ³⁷So on that day all the people and all Israel knew that the king had no part in the murder of Abner son of Ner.

³⁸Then the king said to his men, "Do you not realize that a prince and a great man has fallen in Israel this day? ³⁹And today, though I am the anointed king, I am weak, and these sons of Zeruiah are too strong for me. May the LORD repay the evildoer according to his evil deeds!"

⁴:¹When Ish-Bosheth son of Saul heard that Abner had died in Hebron, he lost courage, and all Israel became alarmed. ²Now Saul's son had two men who were leaders of raiding bands. One was named Baanah and the other Recab; they were sons of Rimmon the Beerothite from the tribe of Benjamin—Beeroth is considered part of Benjamin, ³because the people of Beeroth fled to Gittaim and have lived there as aliens to this day.

⁴(Jonathan son of Saul had a son who was lame in both feet. He was five years old when the news about Saul and Jonathan came from Jezreel. His nurse picked him up and fled, but as she hurried to leave, he fell and became crippled. His name was Mephibosheth.)

⁵Now Recab and Baanah, the sons of Rimmon the Beerothite, set out for the house of Ish-Bosheth, and they arrived there in the heat of the day while he was taking his noonday rest. ⁶They went into the inner part of the house as if to get some wheat, and they stabbed him in the stomach. Then Recab and his brother Baanah slipped away.

⁷They had gone into the house while he was lying on the bed in his bedroom. After they stabbed and killed him, they cut off his head. Taking it with them, they traveled all night by way of the Arabah. ⁸They brought the head of Ish-Bosheth to David at Hebron and said to the king, "Here is the head of Ish-Bosheth son of Saul, your enemy, who tried to take your life. This day the LORD has avenged my lord the king against Saul and his offspring."

⁹David answered Recab and his brother Baanah, the sons of Rimmon the Beerothite, "As surely as the LORD lives, who has delivered me out of all trouble, ¹⁰when a man told me, 'Saul is dead,' and thought he was bringing good news, I seized him and put him to death in Ziklag. That was the reward I gave him for his news! ¹¹How much more—when wicked men have killed an innocent man in his own house and on his own bed—should I not now demand his blood from your hand and rid the earth of you!"

¹²So David gave an order to his men, and they killed them. They cut off their hands and feet and hung the bodies by the pool in Hebron. But they took the head of Ish-Bosheth and buried it in Abner's tomb at Hebron.

Original Meaning

SAUL AND JONATHAN ARE DEAD AND BURIED, and now David is king in Judah. The narrator next takes us into an extended unit that begins and ends with a new character, the unfortunate Ish-Bosheth, son of Saul. He becomes king over the northern kingdom of Israel at the beginning of this unit (2:8) and is assassinated at its conclusion (4:5–12). The events narrated here take place while Ish-Bosheth is king in the north and David is king over Judah in the south.

We are told little about Ish-Bosheth himself. In a sense he serves as a foil to highlight David's rise. The history of David's rise (1 Sam. 16–2 Sam. 5) has driven us inexorably forward in contrasting the ideal anointed one (David) and the tragic first king of Israel (Saul). That contrast continues in this unit, which collects the materials related to Ish-Bosheth's brief rule over the northern kingdom. As we will see, this text is more interested in legitimizing David's rule and highlighting his rise to power over all Israel than in detailing the reign of Saul's son.

The narrative ties the Ish-Bosheth materials together with brief summary statements (2:10–11, 17, 30–31; 3:1, 6, 36–37; 4:1). These parenthetical inserts give the unit focus and prepare the reader for important events to follow in the rest of 2 Samuel.¹ These summary statements will be highlighted below in this Original Meaning section.

---

1. There is much scholarly discussion about this unit's relationship to the surrounding narratives. I take it as part of the history of David's rise, though David Gunn has argued that the bulk of 2 Sam. 2:8 (or 2:12) to 5:3 should be considered the true beginning of the court history of David (2 Sam. 9–20 and 1 Kings 1–2). See David M. Gunn, *The Story of King David: Genre and Interpretation* (JSOTSup 6; Sheffield: JSOT, 1978), 65–84.

Rival Monarchies (2:8–11)

DAVID'S OFFER TO BECOME KING in the north (2:4b–7) is no match for a genuine son of Saul in the light of Israel's new impulse toward dynastic succession. Events in the north quickly move against David, and his hopes for a peaceful transition of power over a unified Israel are not to be realized. This paragraph leaves us with competing royal houses and illustrates that union between north and south was always a tenuous proposition in ancient Israel.

For the first time, our historian tells us of "Ish-Bosheth son of Saul" (2:8). His name means "Man-of-Shame" and is probably a euphemistic substitution for Ish-Baal, "Man-of-Baal" (referring to the Canaanite fertility god Baal).[2] Ish-Bosheth is not referred to elsewhere in the Bible outside this unit.[3] The only time he speaks in this passage, he wrongly accuses his most loyal supporter (Abner) and consequently drives him into the camp of his rival, David (3:7). The only time he appears to function as king, he pathetically gives an order to return Michal, the daughter of Saul (i.e., his half-sister), to David. Thus, his only royal action is an act of acquiescence to David's demands (3:13–16). Descriptions of his inner life are characterized by fear (3:11; 4:1), and his death is ignominious in the same way his father's was (4:5–12).

Abner we have met before as the commander of Saul's army. He is identified as Saul's cousin when first introduced as the military general (1 Sam. 14:50–51). Abner was also present when the young shepherd boy David killed Goliath (17:55, 57). He apparently sat regularly at King Saul's table (20:25), and he was present when David spared Saul's life (26:5, 7, 14–15). He was one of the most powerful men in Saul's kingdom, and this text is clear that Abner was the real power behind Ish-Bosheth's kingship. All hopes for a lasting Saulide dynasty in the north rested with this rugged military man. This is strikingly clear in the Hebrew causative verb of 2 Samuel 2:9 ("He made him king"), which is the same terminology used when Samuel the prophet made Saul king over Israel (1 Sam. 8:22; 12:1).[4] Make no mistake about it, Abner is the power behind the new king in the north! We might call

---

2. Most scholars assume the word *bošet* ("shame") was substituted by scribes to defame the pagan deity. This assumption has been seriously challenged by Tsevat, who believes certain Akkadian parallels support the idea that the name originally had much more positive overtones. See Matitiahu Tsevat, "Ishbosheth and Congeners: The Names and Their Study," *HUCA* 46 (1975): 71–87. His interpretation is disputed by McCarter, *II Samuel*, 85–86.

3. His name appears in its presumed authentic form (Esh-Baal) in Saul's genealogy in 1 Chron. 8:33 and 9:39. The element "Baal" (or "lord") may have been an accepted epithet for Yahweh during the judges period, but in the early monarchy it came to be used only for the Canaanite storm god.

4. Hiphil of the denominative verb *mlk* ("to be king"; see *HALOT*, 2:590–91; BDB, 574).

Ish-Bosheth's rise to power in Israel "an inside job," which has all the trappings of hardcore political intrigue and conspiracy.[5]

Mahanaim is located along the Jabbok River in the part of the Transjordan known as Gilead. The Hebrew name probably means "two camps," which played an important role in the narrative of Jacob's wrestling with God and the naming of Peniel (Gen. 32:2, 7–10, 22–30). The city probably served as a gateway to the iron resources of the area and seems to have functioned as the administrative seat for Gilead in Saul's day and throughout most of the early monarchy.[6] If Abner wants Ish-Bosheth to claim the throne of Israel, his power play may have a better chance if based in this municipal center far away from political and social forces in the south.[7]

So Ish-Bosheth has become king in the north by means of an auspicious confluence of factors. He has the support of the powerful general of his father's army, and he has staked his claim using a strategically important Transjordanian city far from southern control. Our text portrays this move as a calculated power play. It is a daring maneuver, but one that Abner and Ish-Bosheth take boldly when they assert control over "all Israel" (2:9). Unfortunately for these conspirators, the house of Judah follows David (2:10).

The specific phraseology used in this paragraph seems intentional in order to underscore the contrast between David and Ish-Bosheth (esp. in light of David's coronation in Judah in the preceding paragraphs). Unlike David's rise to power, there is no mention here of divine direction or of seeking divine approval (cf. 2:1). Nor is there mention of public anointing or popular support. Ish-Bosheth is part of a political power move, planned and executed by a military strongman. He is a puppet in Abner's hands. By contrast, David rises to power through sensitivity to Yahweh's guidance and timing. He seeks direction from no human but from God alone. Once he has Yahweh's message in hand, he moves forward with no hesitation or timidity. David's is no power play; rather, his is a "faith play."

---

5. Brueggemann, *First and Second Samuel*, 221.

6. Diana V. Edelman, "Mahanaim," *ABD*, 4:473.

7. The chronological references in 2:10–11 are difficult to resolve. Either David reigned in Judah five and a half years while Ish-Bosheth and Abner were gaining support in the north (Youngblood, "1, 2 Samuel," 824 and Alter, *David Story*, 204), or David established his state five and a half years before Saul's death, which would imply Judah existed as a rival state to Israel while Saul was still king (David N. Freedman, "Early Israelite History in the Light of Early Israelite Poetry," in *Unity and Diversity*, ed. H. Goedicke and J. J. M. Roberts [Baltimore: Johns Hopkins Univ. Press, 1975], 16; repr. in *Pottery, Poetry, and Prophecy: Studies in Early Hebrew Poetry* [Winona Lake, Ind.: Eisenbrauns, 1980], 131–66, esp. 155–56; Edelman, "Tel Masos, Geshur, and David," 255).

Thus, we can expect the contrast between Saul and David to continue, even now that Saul is dead. Ish-Bosheth, the hapless son of Israel's first king, simply takes his father's place as the antithesis of David. Authority and power in the northern kingdom are located in Abner and in his ability to thwart David's armies. By contrast, authority and power in the southern kingdom are located solely in Yahweh and in David's faithfulness to Yahweh's command. In sum, Ish-Bosheth is not a suitable king, any more than his father was suitable to reign over Yahweh's people. But David continues to reveal what it means to be a man after God's own heart, a ruler of God's own selection, who exhibits like-mindedness with God (see comments at 1 Sam. 13:14).

At the outset of these two reigns, we learn that in Israel there is a right way and a wrong way to become king. Like the Amalekite of 2 Samuel 1, Abner and Ish-Bosheth fail to understand how the Israelite monarchy is to be unique from other kingdoms. The Amalekite who brought the news of Saul's death to David at Ziklag assumed that by bearing the news he could enter into the power-sharing structure of the new kingdom. If he could be quick enough and smart enough to beat others to the draw, perhaps he could position himself to benefit from the distribution of power in David's new kingdom. But he failed to grasp the uniqueness of the Israelite monarchy, and he paid with his life. Likewise, Abner and Ish-Bosheth understand only the *wrong* way to become king. David continues to illustrate the *right* way one becomes king.

War Between the Rival Monarchies (2:12–32)

THE ACCOUNT OF the civil war between the house of David in the south and the house of Ish-Bosheth in the north is held together literarily by the march of the generals with their armies from their respective capitals to Gibeon (2:12–13) and by their return after the conflict (2:29–32).

The first section records an example of the ancient custom of representative combat, in which man-to-man fighting substituted for full-fledged battle between opposing armies in an effort to settle disputes without recourse to extensive bloodshed.[8] It is hoped that the standoff at the pool of Gibeon (2:13) might be resolved by such representative combat, in this case involving twelve infantrymen from each army. But the twenty-four champions are all killed, and no side can claim an undisputed victory (2:14–16).

As a result, the hostilities continue, and the blood-letting becomes severe. Our historian summarizes the events of that day with the words (2:17):

---

8. Not unlike David's battle with Goliath (1 Sam. 17:4–11, where see our discussion of representative combat in general). Here see particularly F. Charles Fensham, "The Battle Between the Men of Joab and Abner As a Possible Ordeal by Battle?" *VT* 20 (1970): 356–57.

"Abner and the men of Israel were defeated by David's men." Joab's presence at Gibeon in Benjamin, the home tribe of Saul, may indicate Joab's army had made successful advances north into Ish-Bosheth's territory.[9] Abner's proposal to use representative combat may have been an attempt to impede Joab's advance.

The episode between Abner and Joab's brother Asahel serves two purposes in the narrative (2:18–28). (1) In the immediate context it explains how the death of Asahel sickens both sides ("every man stopped when he came to the place where Asahel had fallen," 2:23). It is a turning point in the conflict between soldiers who know each other and feel a certain bonhomie for each other. As a result, both sides lose the heart and will for warfare and declare a truce (2:28). (2) In the larger narrative, the episode explains why hostility between Joab and Abner continues. This vendetta will continue to characterize David's and Solomon's military, not only in 3:26–27 but also soon after David's death (1 Kings 2:28–35).

Summary of the War Years (3:1–5)

RATHER THAN RECOUNT further gruesome details of the civil war, the text merely states that it goes on "a long time" (3:1) and that David gradually gains strength while Ish-Bosheth grows weaker. The summary statement substantiates the casualty count for the fateful battle near Gibeon (see 2:30–31): twenty of David's men (including Asahel) versus 360 Benjamites of Abner's army.

The inclusion of a list of David's sons seems curious here. Apparently, the historian has this list before him and wants to incorporate it with other materials from the Hebron years of David's rule. But there is surely more to it than that.[10] In light of the emphasis on the growing strength of David contrasted with the waning strength of Ish-Bosheth in the immediately preceding verse (3:1), most likely this list of David's sons born while he rules from Hebron is intended to intensify the contrast.[11]

The text includes the list of David's impressive wives, some of whom have political significance. This may further contrast David with Ish-Bosheth, whose tenuous claim to his father's throne is apparent in the next verses, where he suspects Abner of asserting his own claim to Saul's throne by sleep-

---

9. It is also possible that the inhabitants of Gibeon are sympathetic to David rather than Saul's son. See McCarter, *II Samuel*, 95.

10. The idea that the list is intended to portray David as obedient to the Pentateuch's mandate to "be fruitful and multiply" is a case of forcing a larger schematic framework onto an unsuspecting pericope (though the framework itself is fruitful; Bergen, *1, 2 Samuel*, 305).

11. Youngblood, "1, 2 Samuel," 830.

ing with Saul's concubine. In addition, these verses prepare the reader for an important topic elsewhere in 2 Samuel: Who will succeed David as king?

Death of Abner (3:6–39)

BEFORE MOVING ON to David's coronation over all Israel, the biblical historian relates two more details from this period of civil war: the deaths of Abner and Ish-Bosheth. Together these accounts substantiate the summary conclusion that "the house of Saul grew weaker and weaker" (3:1), and they effectively put to rest once and for all the prospects of a Saulide dynasty. They illustrate without stating explicitly that there is now no opposition to David's reign as king over all Israel.

Abner, the general of Ish-Bosheth's army, has grown in political influence and strength in the house of Saul (3:6). In light of 3:1, this means he has become stronger and stronger in an increasingly weak kingdom. The passage also confirms that Abner is the real power in the northern kingdom. He has influence with the army, the "elders of Israel," and "the Benjamites" to sway the entire northern kingdom into David's camp (3:9–10, 12, 17–21).

As we have seen elsewhere, sexual relations with a king's wife or concubine in the ancient world was tantamount to a claim to that king's throne.[12] In his weakness, Ish-Bosheth suspects Abner will use his strength to take the throne of the northern kingdom. But Abner defiantly proclaims that he has been stubbornly "loyal" (ḥesed, "kind, faithful," 3:8) to the house of Saul but has decided to turn all of Israel over to David, "from Dan to Beersheba" (3:10). He then defects to David, making a covenant-agreement (berit) with him. Abner moved quickly to exert his influence on the elders of Israel and specifically the tribe of Benjamin, so that he effectively lays the foundation for David to become king of a unified Israel.

Historians might speculate about Abner's motivations here. Perhaps he sees he has been supporting a candidate who cannot win and expects to earn a prestigious position in a united monarchy ruled by David or at least to be well rewarded monetarily. But we should limit ourselves to what the narrator describes about Abner. He becomes "very angry" and is insulted by Ish-Bosheth's accusation against him (3:8). Abner expresses twice his decision to do for David what Yahweh has sworn (NIV "promised") to do, that is, to transfer the house of Saul into David's hands (3:9, 18). Abner does not offer ulterior motives. The narrator and we as readers are aware that David is the one suitable to serve as king of Israel. But Abner has no such

---

12. Matitiahu Tsevat, "Marriage and Monarchical Legitimacy in Ugarit and Israel," *JSS* 3 (1958): 237–43; Levenson and Halpern, "The Political Import of David's Marriages," 508. See also 2 Sam. 16:20–22 and 1 Kings 2:13–25.

privileged position. He appears to be doing the best he can in a nearly impossible situation.

In narrating Joab's murder of Abner, the narrator goes to great lengths to emphasize David's innocence. He painstakingly repeats the refrain that David sent him away "in peace" (three times in 3:21–23). When Joab summons Abner with the clearly premeditated intent to kill him, we are told explicitly, "David did not know it" (3:26). Finally, David personally leads the throng at the funeral, weeps aloud, sings a lament for Abner (as he had for Saul and Jonathan), and fasts all that day (3:31–35). In another important summary statement, the text explains that all the people of Israel accept David's innocence and are greatly pleased by everything he has done. They understand (as the narrator hopes the reader will) "that the king had no part in the murder of Abner son of Ner" (3:36–37).

Death of Ish-Bosheth (4:1–12)

THE BRUTAL END for Ish-Bosheth seems inevitable. As long as he had Abner in his camp, there was hope. But once he insulted the general's loyalty and drove him into an agreement with David, this tragedy seems unavoidable.

Our passage's final summary statement emphasizes the reactions of Ish-Bosheth and his people to the loss of Abner (4:1): "He lost courage, and all Israel became alarmed."[13] It remains only for Baanah and Recab to strike the *coup de grâce*. The decapitation of Ish-Bosheth's body is reminiscent of Saul's own death (1 Sam. 31:8–9), bringing full circle the punishment of Saul's crimes upon his unfortunate scion. As in the narration of Abner's death, the biblical historian is concerned to document David's innocence. Any hint that Ish-Bosheth's murder was engineered by David could hinder the king's attempt to win the loyalty of the northern tribes.[14] So David's quote reminds us there is a right way and a wrong way to become king, and the cruel murder of "an innocent man in his own house and on his own bed" is not the right way (4:9–11).

David seems to be the only one in the narrative to understand this. Citing the precedent of the deceptive Amalekite who announced Saul's death as though it were good news (4:10; cf. 1:1–16), David determines that the two assassins of Ish-Bosheth should also be executed. They have made the wrong assumptions about kingship in Israel. They have no perception of a divine mandate for the role of the king, and their use of power and violence

---

13. The expression "lost courage" literally states that Ish-Bosheth's "hands grew weak." Hands symbolize strength and courage in Heb.; Robert Alter compares this idiom to our colloquial "lost his grip" (*David Story*, 217).

14. Gordon, *I and II Samuel*, 222.

is self-incriminating. Once again, David is innocent of violent acts that nonetheless benefit his rise to power. He alone illustrates who may rightly serve as king of Israel.

Note the reference to Mephibosheth in 4:4, which at first blush seems out of place here (hence NIV's parentheses).[15] This is the first time we meet Jonathan's son, and the intrusion here prepares the reader for his role later in the court history of David (see 9:6–8, 10–13; 16:1–4; 19:24–30). Although it is true that this verse disrupts the flow of the present narrative, its inclusion highlights the pitiable end of Saul's progeny. In addition to Ish-Bosheth (whose life is about to end), there remains another descendant of Saul—but is crippled. Just as impressive physical features confirmed the right of Saul and David to rule (1 Sam. 9:2; 10:23; 16:12), so Mephibosheth's disability makes him an unlikely candidate in a time of political uncertainty.[16]

Since no one else of royal blood remains, David is the only option as king of Israel. The way has been cleared for his coronation at 5:1. Furthermore, 4:4 echoes the old prophet's pronouncement against Saul (1 Sam. 13:14): "Your kingdom will not endure; the LORD has sought out a man after his own heart and appointed him leader of his people, because you have not kept the LORD's command." This mention of crippled Mephibosheth reminds us that David's coming rule over all Israel has a corresponding truth: Saul's descendants will *not* rule Israel.

TWO QUESTIONS. As we have seen, the books of Samuel are primarily interested in two questions. (1) What is the acceptable nature of the new Israelite monarchy? First Samuel illustrated the deficiencies of the older tribal confederation with its center at Shiloh and its priestly leadership. We learned there that kingship is necessary in Israel and, if rightly constituted, even desirable. Gradually a nation is formed, with a monarchy that is similar to, yet also different from, the monarchies among Israel's neighbors. Unlike Canaanite rulers, the powers of Israel's new king are circumscribed by the unique configuration of Israel's monarchy. The king is not free to initiate warfare whenever and against whomever he wishes, nor can he confiscate property or conscript an army without just cause or usurp

---

15. On his name, see comments on 2 Sam. 9.

16. For a similar assumption, see Keil and Delitzsch, *Samuel*, 309. On the nature of his debilitating condition, see John H. Walton, Victor H. Matthews, and Mark W. Chavalas, *The IVP Bible Background Commentary: Old Testament* (Downers Grove, Ill.: InterVarsity Press, 2000), 326.

the power of the priesthood (not to mention prophets!). This is truly a different kind of kingship.

(2) A further reason why Israel's king is different is because of the answer to the second question addressed in the books of Samuel: Who may serve suitably as king of Israel? Yahweh alone is king of Israel, and he governs his people through his chosen anointed ones, who are merely viceroys under his command. The first anointed one, Saul, failed because he refused to accept Yahweh's authority. The second anointed one, David, is ideal because he accepts Yahweh's authority in principle and genuinely repents when he fails to accept it in practice.

As readers of the accounts of Saul and David in 1 Samuel, we have a privileged position as we approach the text. We have already learned that David is the legitimate replacement for Saul rather than Saul's own son Ish-Bosheth. David has been anointed with oil by the venerable prophet Samuel, and at his anointing the Spirit of the Lord came upon David in power (1 Sam. 16:1–13). Saul, by contrast, has been irrevocably condemned by Samuel and has forfeited the right to establish an eternal dynasty (13:5–15).

The second half of 1 Samuel describes the transfer of political and spiritual power from Saul to David and with agonizing clarity narrates Saul's tragic self-destruction. While Saul was permitted to maintain his hold on the throne of Israel for a while, the prophet Samuel was clear that kingship would not pass to his descendants (1 Sam. 13:13–14). The promise of a lasting dynasty will eventually be given to David (2 Sam. 7:15–16). Ish-Bosheth is thus a tragic figure like his father. He is made king by human power structures, is mostly silent, and comes quickly to a violent end. Saul's dynasty is truly over. Yet this unit also informs us of a son of Jonathan, who will become important later in the extended narrative (4:4).

As I have noted elsewhere in this commentary, Old Testament narratives can have different levels of interpretation: universal, national, and individual.[17] Every individual narrative also plays some role in the greater national narrative of Israel's history and thus also contributes to the ultimate narrative of God's redemptive plan in history. This present unit of Scripture contributes on a number of levels to legitimize and explain David as the rightful successor to Saul. The individual accounts of the civil war between David and Ish-Bosheth illustrate the national drama, as summarized by the historian (3:1): "David grew stronger and stronger, while the house of Saul grew weaker and

---

17. See the introduction. To use Fee and Stuart's terminology, top, middle, and bottom levels (Fee and Stuart, *How to Read the Bible*, 73–78). See also John Barton, *Reading the Old Testament: Method in Bible Study* (rev. ed.; Louisville: Westminster John Knox, 1997), and Odil Steck, *Old Testament Exegesis: A Guide to the Methodology* (Atlanta: Scholars Press, 1995).

weaker." This collection of individual narratives create trajectories moving in opposite directions: Ish-Bosheth's leading inexorably down and David's steadily up.

The ideal anointed one. I have also emphasized the growing messianism in 1 and 2 Samuel. On the universal level of interpretation, this unit makes its own contribution to Israel's understanding of the ideal anointed one. The books of Samuel emphasize four main themes that contributed to the concept of messiah.[18] (1) The ideal anointed one is God's appointed ruler. (2) He trusts in God alone, who protects him. (3) The anointed one leads Israel to victory in battle against the nation's enemies. (4) He is a just ruler.

In the previous passage (2:1–7), we saw how David faithfully trusted God alone for direction. This unit continues to illustrate that David is God's appointed ruler, but it does so in different ways. It shows Yahweh's protection and guidance being worked out in the political and military realms. David and his army are victorious in battle and only grow stronger as the war continues. Furthermore, David is innocent of any wrongdoing in the vicious murders of Abner and Ish-Bosheth. In fact, the narrator is careful to portray David as a just ruler in executing Ish-Bosheth's assassins and eventually in avenging Joab's bloody revenge (1 Kings 2:5–6, 32–34). In other words, David is portrayed as victorious in battle and just in his actions, contributing further to the messianic ideal for Israel's future.

Roadblocks. However, today's Christian readers often stumble over a number of roadblocks, obstructing their ability to apply principles just cited. (1) Many struggle with the amount of warfare and bloodshed in Old Testament narratives. This unit is particularly brutal, and several subsequent passages in 2 Samuel will raise the same question. (2) This unit also contains examples of political conspiracy that result in murder but also play a role in Yahweh's plan to bring David to power. (3) The role of women in the Old Testament often seems offensive to today's readers. Note how Saul's unnamed concubine becomes a political pawn (3:7–8) and how Michal, the daughter of Saul, is treated as a royal object to be bartered for (3:13–16). Such difficulties may make it difficult to build a bridge from the ancient context to our own.

In addressing these difficulties, we should begin with a reminder about the nature of biblical revelation. God has revealed his nature and his ways of dealing with human brokenness through inspired, sacred texts. We are not built up in faith and nurtured in Christian understanding *primarily* through an exploration of ancient history, even sacred biblical history. Such exploration will contribute to our understanding of God, but historical research is not

---

18. Satterthwaite, "David in the Books of Samuel," 42–47.

sacred Scripture. Rather, the means of God's grace in our lives is the text of Scripture itself, and when we read the Old Testament historical books, we must be aware of the special concerns and worldview represented there. These biblical books relate the events of the past in order to build our faith. They select, organize, and explain the past as a kerygmatic treatise (see the introduction on this point). It is not the ancient historical events themselves that make us stronger in faith. Rather, it is the text's explanation of those actions and its interpretation of their significance that the Holy Spirit uses to strengthen our own experience with God.

In other words, obviously modern Christians are not to mimic the Old Testament's understanding of warfare and seek to participate in murderous political conspiracy, any more than we would view and treat women as they are treated in this narrative. It is not the actions narrated that serve as Christian Scripture but the text's selection, organization, and explanation that we need to heed. And the main point of this unit is Yahweh's faithfulness to his anointed servant David, even in the nitty-gritty, everyday affairs of his political and military life. Through time, all the messy affairs of Ish-Bosheth's rival monarchy in the north are resolved, and in Yahweh's timing the way becomes clear for David to become king of all Israel (5:1–25). Navigating carefully through the cultural peculiarities of the ancient Near East and reading this unit in light of the surrounding narrative make it possible to see the message of the rise of Israel's ideal king.

Let us now make a few comments on each of the difficulties mentioned above. (1) With regard to warfare in the Old Testament, one of the most difficult adjustments we must make is to learn to rejoice with national Israel when they witness Yahweh's salvation accomplished through military strength.[19] The sight of Egyptian corpses lying on the shore of the Red Sea symbolized Yahweh's gracious deliverance of a defenseless Israel against the greatest military power of that day (Ex. 14:30). The sight of dead Egyptian soldiers strengthened their faith (14:31) and led to worshipful singing and praise (15:1–21). Indeed, Yahweh's defeat of the Egyptian army became the concrete sign of his salvation and new life for Israel throughout the Old Testament.

In the account of David's defeat of Goliath, the text invited us to rejoice at the sight of the decapitated Philistine, lying motionless in the Valley of Elah (1 Sam. 17:51), or at the news that the Philistine dead were strewn along the road from Gath to Ekron after the great Israelite victory (17:52). Obviously, these are not images we normally evoke when seeking to build Christian faith today, but they are important and powerful images in biblical revelation.

---

19. Salvation in the Old Testament is intimately tied to Yahweh as warrior, who fights for and saves his people. See Miller, *The Divine Warrior*, 173.

We need to remember that ancient Near Eastern philosophy equated military strength with a nation's deity. Victory in battle authenticated a deity's superiority; this was part and parcel of the world in which ancient Israel moved. We must accept their cultural constraints without condemning their views, while learning the truths of the theological explanations given in Scripture.[20] Thus, David's and Joab's victories are here expressions of Yahweh's power and faithfulness.

(2) Similar cultural conditioning is necessary to understand the conspiracies and murders reported here. Joab's treachery against Abner is not reported in order to serve as an example for us. Rather, the text clearly condemns his actions (through the words of David), and such actions eventually result in Joab's own death (1 Kings 2:5–6, 32–34). Likewise, the collusion to assassinate Ish-Bosheth is condemned—again through the words of David. These episodes are not narrated as Yahweh's will, but they do illustrate that Yahweh is at work to accomplish his promises to David, even through such villainous and inane actions.

(3) Michal and Saul's concubine are certainly mistreated in this passage. Royal women particularly were often trapped in the political struggles of the ancient world, because they were believed to legitimize one's claim to the throne.[21] The injustices of ancient Near Eastern culture are often reflected in the sacred biblical texts. That is not to say the text condones those injustices, even when there is no explicitly stated condemnation. Again, we must read these texts in light of the theological explanation of the extended unit. Ish-Bosheth's rash accusation about the concubine (3:7) illustrates his growing weakness and his inevitable failure as king. It is not a laudatory acceptance of the way royal concubines were treated. Likewise, Michal's return to David has points of contact with 1 Samuel and later in 2 Samuel, all illustrating David's legitimacy as Saul's successor.

Thus, we read these texts for what they teach us about God's faithfulness to David and the Davidic dynasty, not as a means of critiquing contemporary views of warfare or the roles of women in society. There are other biblical texts (both Old and New Testament) for that. There are many indications, in fact, that the Old Testament's view of women in general was consistently at odds with its ancient Near Eastern matrix and that it began a process (continued in the New Testament) of liberating women from the injustices of cultural mores.

Having attempted to overcome these obstacles, the reader should not miss the importance of the summary statement at 3:1: "The war between the

---

20. Further, review the Contemporary Significance section on holy war at 1 Sam. 4:1b–11, as well as the comments on 15:1–9.

21. Levenson and Halpern, "The Political Import of David's Marriages," 507–18.

house of Saul and the house of David lasted a long time. David grew stronger and stronger, while the house of Saul grew weaker and weaker." Like looking through a lens and adjusting the focus for a better view, this verse gives us a sharp picture of David as the anointed one who received the Spirit of the Lord in power (1 Sam. 16:13). Soon after his anointing, strangers around him recognized that the Lord was with him in a unique way (16:18). The biblical historian has followed this theme, illustrating that Yahweh is the moving force behind the historical events (18:14, 18).

Our summary statement at 2 Samuel 3:1 propels us forward to that day when David will become king of all Israel because of God's powerful presence with him: "And he became more and more powerful, because the LORD God Almighty was with him" (5:10). All of the battles and intrigue narrated in here illustrate that God is with David. Old Testament historical books often teach by showing rather than by telling. By showing how these problems were resolved, this text illustrates again that God is blessing and preparing David, his ideal king of Israel.

JUST AS THERE was a right way and a wrong way to become king in ancient Israel, so there is for believers a right and wrong way to fulfill the promises of God in our lives. And just as the righteous way illustrated in this text by David leads to strength and the wrong way illustrated by Ish-Bosheth to weakness, so there are consequences to the way we choose.

Corporate significance. This understanding of our text has a corporate significance. In the case of the early church, Christian believers waited patiently in prayer as instructed by Jesus for the promised Holy Spirit of God to become a reality (Luke 24:49; Acts 1:4, 14). This devotion was not unlike David's patiently waiting for God's time and place to fulfill his promises. Sadly, the church has not always been so patient or, for that matter, so obedient to God's call. At times the body of Christ on earth has been more like Ish-Bosheth than David.

For example, Pope Urban II devised a plan to rescue the Holy Sepulchre in Jerusalem from the hands of the Turks, who had closed the city to Christian pilgrims. On November 26, 1095 A.D., at the council in Clermont, the pope urged Christians to capture the Holy Sepulchre by force, wresting it "from the wicked race" in order to subject it again to Christendom.[22] He

---

22. Kenneth Scott Latourette, *A History of Christianity*, 2 vols. (New York: Harper & Row, 1975), 1:410–11. See next note for some of the details related here.

shamelessly offered remission of sins and eternal life to anyone who took up the sword. The prospects of military conquest and unlimited spoils of war generated religious hysteria throughout France and Germany, and the first of the Crusades was under way.

In the spring and summer of 1096, soldiers began moving through the Rhine Valley, where thousands of Jews were victimized by the madness. Rumors spread that the Jews were aiding the cause of Islam. Approximately five thousand Jews were slaughtered at Worms, Mainz, and Cologne. More Jews would die with the thousands of Muslims who lost their lives later.[23] This is without question the wrong way to make God's promises a reality and to usher in the kingdom of heaven. The right way—the way of patience, trust, and hope—is illustrated by the early church and by King David. But the Crusaders replaced it with the way of Ish-Bosheth and Abner, a way of brute force and military power.

Individual significance. Beyond the corporate significance, this text also has individual significance. The Bible portrays two important gardens, where individuals typify the right way and the wrong way to fulfill God's purposes in our lives. In the Garden of Eden, Eve recognized that the forbidden fruit would make her wise like God (Gen. 3:5). Of course, she and Adam had been created in God's image and were as much like God as creatures could be. But she accepted the serpent's view of reality and believed she could forge a better way than that planned by God.

By contrast, an individual praying fervently in the Garden of Gethsemane presents a different portrait (Matt. 26:36–46; Luke 22:39–46). Faced with the supreme trial ("cup" is a metaphor for calamity and death), Jesus affirms his essential orientation around God's will, for good or ill. The structure of his prayer itself emphasizes his obedient submission to that will,[24] culminating in his resolute embrace of the right way: "Yet not what I will, but what you will" (Mark 14:36). These individuals, these two gardens, exemplify the choices before us as we too seek to make God's purposes a reality in our lives.

Universal significance. This portrait of Jesus embracing his divine vocation leads to yet another level of significance beyond the corporate and individual. The figure stooped in prayer in the Garden of Gethsemane fulfills for the Christian reader the messianic themes we have identified in the books of Samuel. David is celebrated in these texts as the ideal king, who willingly submits to God's timing and direction and consistently repudiates

---

23. Chaim Potok, *Wanderings: Chaim Potok's History of the Jews* (New York: Fawcett, 1978), 400–401.

24. Joel B. Green, *The Gospel of Luke* (NICNT; Grand Rapids: Eerdmans, 1997), 780.

the way of power politics and force. Jesus fulfills all that was right about David. Like David, he could have chosen the wrong way to accomplish his divine mission. In fact, Satan even tempted him with that (Matt. 4:1–11). But Jesus is the ideal king of Israel because he became king in the right way, through submission to his divine vocation as the Son of David and through patient waiting and service.

2 Samuel 5:1–6:23

A LL THE TRIBES of Israel came to David at Hebron and said,
"We are your own flesh and blood. ²In the past, while
Saul was king over us, you were the one who led Israel
on their military campaigns. And the LORD said to you, 'You will
shepherd my people Israel, and you will become their ruler.'"

³When all the elders of Israel had come to King David at
Hebron, the king made a compact with them at Hebron
before the LORD, and they anointed David king over Israel.

⁴David was thirty years old when he became king, and he
reigned forty years. ⁵In Hebron he reigned over Judah seven
years and six months, and in Jerusalem he reigned over all
Israel and Judah thirty-three years.

⁶The king and his men marched to Jerusalem to attack the
Jebusites, who lived there. The Jebusites said to David, "You
will not get in here; even the blind and the lame can ward you
off." They thought, "David cannot get in here." ⁷Nevertheless,
David captured the fortress of Zion, the City of David.

⁸On that day, David said, "Anyone who conquers the
Jebusites will have to use the water shaft to reach those 'lame
and blind' who are David's enemies. "That is why they say,
"The 'blind and lame' will not enter the palace."

⁹David then took up residence in the fortress and called it
the City of David. He built up the area around it, from the
supporting terraces inward. ¹⁰And he became more and more
powerful, because the LORD God Almighty was with him.

¹¹Now Hiram king of Tyre sent messengers to David, along
with cedar logs and carpenters and stonemasons, and they
built a palace for David. ¹²And David knew that the LORD had
established him as king over Israel and had exalted his kingdom for the sake of his people Israel.

¹³After he left Hebron, David took more concubines and
wives in Jerusalem, and more sons and daughters were born to
him. ¹⁴These are the names of the children born to him there:
Shammua, Shobab, Nathan, Solomon, ¹⁵Ibhar, Elishua,
Nepheg, Japhia, ¹⁶Elishama, Eliada and Eliphelet.

¹⁷When the Philistines heard that David had been anointed
king over Israel, they went up in full force to search for him,

but David heard about it and went down to the stronghold.
¹⁸Now the Philistines had come and spread out in the Valley
of Rephaim; ¹⁹so David inquired of the LORD, "Shall I go and
attack the Philistines? Will you hand them over to me?"

The LORD answered him, "Go, for I will surely hand the
Philistines over to you."

²⁰So David went to Baal Perazim, and there he defeated
them. He said, "As waters break out, the LORD has broken out
against my enemies before me." So that place was called Baal
Perazim. ²¹The Philistines abandoned their idols there, and
David and his men carried them off.

²²Once more the Philistines came up and spread out in the
Valley of Rephaim; ²³so David inquired of the LORD, and he
answered, "Do not go straight up, but circle around behind
them and attack them in front of the balsam trees. ²⁴As soon
as you hear the sound of marching in the tops of the balsam
trees, move quickly, because that will mean the LORD has
gone out in front of you to strike the Philistine army." ²⁵So
David did as the LORD commanded him, and he struck down
the Philistines all the way from Gibeon to Gezer.

⁶:¹David again brought together out of Israel chosen men,
thirty thousand in all. ²He and all his men set out from Baalah of
Judah to bring up from there the ark of God, which is called by
the Name, the name of the LORD Almighty, who is enthroned
between the cherubim that are on the ark. ³They set the ark of
God on a new cart and brought it from the house of Abinadab,
which was on the hill. Uzzah and Ahio, sons of Abinadab, were
guiding the new cart ⁴with the ark of God on it, and Ahio was
walking in front of it. ⁵David and the whole house of Israel were
celebrating with all their might before the LORD, with songs and
with harps, lyres, tambourines, sistrums and cymbals.

⁶When they came to the threshing floor of Nacon, Uzzah
reached out and took hold of the ark of God, because the
oxen stumbled. ⁷The LORD's anger burned against Uzzah
because of his irreverent act; therefore God struck him down
and he died there beside the ark of God.

⁸Then David was angry because the LORD's wrath had broken out against Uzzah, and to this day that place is called
Perez Uzzah.

⁹David was afraid of the LORD that day and said, "How can
the ark of the LORD ever come to me?" ¹⁰He was not willing to

take the ark of the LORD to be with him in the City of David. Instead, he took it aside to the house of Obed-Edom the Gittite. ¹¹The ark of the LORD remained in the house of Obed-Edom the Gittite for three months, and the LORD blessed him and his entire household.

¹²Now King David was told, "The LORD has blessed the household of Obed-Edom and everything he has, because of the ark of God." So David went down and brought up the ark of God from the house of Obed-Edom to the City of David with rejoicing. ¹³When those who were carrying the ark of the LORD had taken six steps, he sacrificed a bull and a fattened calf. ¹⁴David, wearing a linen ephod, danced before the LORD with all his might, ¹⁵while he and the entire house of Israel brought up the ark of the LORD with shouts and the sound of trumpets.

¹⁶As the ark of the LORD was entering the City of David, Michal daughter of Saul watched from a window. And when she saw King David leaping and dancing before the LORD, she despised him in her heart.

¹⁷They brought the ark of the LORD and set it in its place inside the tent that David had pitched for it, and David sacrificed burnt offerings and fellowship offerings before the LORD. ¹⁸After he had finished sacrificing the burnt offerings and fellowship offerings, he blessed the people in the name of the LORD Almighty. ¹⁹Then he gave a loaf of bread, a cake of dates and a cake of raisins to each person in the whole crowd of Israelites, both men and women. And all the people went to their homes.

²⁰When David returned home to bless his household, Michal daughter of Saul came out to meet him and said, "How the king of Israel has distinguished himself today, disrobing in the sight of the slave girls of his servants as any vulgar fellow would!"

²¹David said to Michal, "It was before the LORD, who chose me rather than your father or anyone from his house when he appointed me ruler over the LORD's people Israel—I will celebrate before the LORD. ²²I will become even more undignified than this, and I will be humiliated in my own eyes. But by these slave girls you spoke of, I will be held in honor."

²³And Michal daughter of Saul had no children to the day of her death.

HAVING NOW ARRIVED AT THE ZENITH of David's rise to power, the biblical historian devotes this next unit to the consolidation of that power. These two chapters narrate his coronation as king over all Israel (5:1–5) and the formation of a new state through political and religious innovations (5:6–6:23). The history of David's rise (typically viewed as an original narrative source ending at 5:10) is now supplemented with other materials related to David's reign.[1] The original source was ostensibly written in order to legitimize David's rule. Ancient Israelite readers unfamiliar with the story would need to know how David from the tribe of Judah, a man not in the genealogical line of the Benjamite Saul son of Kish, became king of Israel. Was this legitimate? Should David have been allowed to become king?

But the canonical text goes further by idealizing David and his time as king. Original sources and other materials have been combined to answer the question: Who may serve suitably as king of Israel? The result is not merely the legitimizing of David but his exaltation. He is held high as an example for emulation. All future kings of Israel should look like this!

Monarchy came relatively late in Israel's history. Compared to the important early roles of priest and judge (and even prophet) in Israel, the concept of "king" is in process of definition. This text establishes both the king and his royal city firmly in the psyche of Israel for the rest of biblical history. These images are among the most powerful in ancient Israel's worldview. This text narrates the *sociopolitical* and *religious* developments related to their entry onto Israel's stage.

David Becomes King over All Israel (5:1–5)

THE IMPORTANCE OF THIS PART in our story is highlighted by the presence of "all the tribes of Israel" with David at Hebron. Also here are the "elders of Israel," who deal directly with "King David," an appellative that takes on new meaning from this point forward (5:3).[2] The elders assert something

---

1. The unit on the history of David's rise is thought to have included at least 1 Sam. 16:14–2 Sam. 5:10 (see introduction).

2. David is called "King David" only once before in the narrative, at 2 Sam. 3:31. The parallel use of "elder" and "tribe" probably implies the twelve tribes of Israel are present symbolically in the persons of their representatives, not in any literal sense. On the power of the "elders" in this period, see Hayim Tadmor, "Traditional Institutions and the Monarchy: Social and Political Tensions in the Time of David and Solomon," in *Studies in the Period of David and Solomon and Other Essays*, ed. Tomoo Ishida (Winona Lake, Ind.: Eisenbrauns, 1982), 239–57.

equally significant: "We are your own flesh and blood." This expression in the Old Testament connotes more than biological kinship, though that is involved. That is, these "two parties have long stood together in strength (bone) and in weakness (flesh)."[3] The tribes of Israel, through their representative elders, present themselves to David at Hebron and are ready to commit to his rule over a united monarchy if he is willing to include the northern tribes.

This is a high-water mark to which the narrative has been building since 1 Samuel 16. David now reigns as king over all Israel. Today's historian is often dissatisfied with the Bible's explanations of how David rose to power over all Israel. Since he was not the legitimate or obvious heir to Saul's kingdom and his reign involved sociopolitical and religious innovations often difficult to explain, we might be tempted to speculate about a variety of factors giving rise to David's power. But as always in biblical narrative, the text is less interested in tracing historical events in a strictly cause-and-effect relationship. The Bible tends to skip intermediary causes and focus on ultimate causes. Wherever it was clear that God was at work in history, biblical historians saw no need to outline in detail the secondary causes.

The biblical explanation for David's rise to power identifies many factors. David is king of all Israel because *historically* Abner has paved the way for the northern tribes to support him and Ish-Bosheth was an ineffectual ruler.[4] *Sociologically* the northern tribes enter into a covenant agreeing to the terms of David's kingship. *Psychologically* David is a powerful figure who commands the loyalty of the people. Beyond these important factors, however, the books of Samuel argue for the legitimacy of David because of *theological* causation: Yahweh has chosen him. In the biblical worldview, this is most important, and there is nothing incompatible about these perspectives.

The northern tribes express three reasons for supporting David. (1) As a descendant of Jacob, he is a blood-relative of all the tribes, including the ones in the north. (2) Even when Saul was still king, David was the one leading the nation in military campaigns. (3) Yahweh himself has called David to be the "shepherd" and "ruler" over Israel (5:2).[5] This is the first time shepherd imagery is used to describe David as leader of God's people. David's childhood calling as a shepherd may have made the metaphor particularly

---

3. Brueggemann, *First and Second Samuel*, 237. Thus, the expression is not unlike our "in sickness and in health," or "through thick and thin."

4. Recall that it was Abner's political savvy and acumen behind Ish-Bosheth's ill-fated reign (2:8–9).

5. Keil and Delitzsch, *Samuel*, 313–14.

appropriate (1 Sam. 16:11), though it is standard royal ideology in the ancient Near East.[6] Elsewhere in the Old Testament, this imagery is widely used for the role of national leadership, especially of the Israelite king. Beyond human leadership, shepherd imagery also comes to illustrate the character of Yahweh himself in one of the most endearing images of God in the Old Testament (see Ps. 23).[7]

The new king makes a "covenant" with the elders of Israel at Hebron (5:3; *b^erit*, NIV "compact").[8] This agreement likely specifies the rights and obligations of each party. Once terms have been agreed to and the *b^erit* ratified, the elders of Israel anoint David king over all Israel. We have noted earlier that Israel was one of the few nations of the ancient world to use oil in anointing its kings.[9] The practice appears to have been used in the ancient Near East in business and legal contexts for contractual or covenantal purposes. Here the people of Israel pledge themselves to David and accept an obligation to him. He, in turn, grants them a royal promise.[10]

This paragraph teems with intertextual reverberations tying it to the important law of Israelite kingship in Deuteronomy 17:14–20.[11] The prophet Samuel had attempted to clarify "the regulations of the kingship" (1 Sam. 10:25). Now the elders of Israel are attracted to David because he best fulfills those regulations. Yahweh has designated him as "shepherd" and "ruler" (*nagid*), and he is related by blood (Deut. 17:15–16).[12] David has become king by both divine appointment and popular acclaim. His first anointing (by Samuel, 1 Sam. 16:6–13) marked him as Yahweh's choice and highlighted his future potentiality. His two public anointings (2:1–4a and here) make that potentiality a public and political reality.

The rest of this unit details a number of David's accomplishments, by which he brings his national goals to realization. In order to put these events in perspective, several scholars have applied to the evidence the work of

---

6. Hammurabi boasts of his role as "shepherd" in the prologue to his famous Law Code. See Martha T. Roth, "The Laws of Hammurabi," COS, 2.131:335–53, esp. 336 (i.50–53).

7. "Sheep, Shepherd," *DBI*, 782–85.

8. This illustrates the conditional and covenantal nature of kingship in northern ideology as compared to Judah, which thought in terms of an eternal decree. David's dual monarchy was a tenuous arrangement. See Cross, *Canaanite Myth and Hebrew Epic*, 230.

9. Review the Original Meaning sections for 1 Sam. 9:1–10:8; 16:6–13; 2 Sam. 2:1–4a.

10. Mettinger, *King and Messiah*, 175.

11. Evans, *1 and 2 Samuel*, 159.

12. Of course the reverberations are stronger in 1 Kings 11 with regard to Solomon. It is possible the Deuteronomic stipulation that the king be near in kinship resulted from Abimelech's attempt to rule (Judg. 8), since he was in fact, half-Canaanite. See Gordon, *I and II Samuel*, 355, note 4.

modern political science dealing with imperial systems. They conclude that David built an empire by applying a "grand strategy," which involved planning, specific aims, and a long-range perspective.[13] This approach allows us to discern five distinct levels of political interrelationships, which can be compared to five concentric circles in progression: (1) tribal kingdom, (2) national kingdom, (3) consolidated territorial state, (4) multinational state, and (5) empire.

Thus, we read here of David's capture and transformation of Jerusalem into a new capital city, his construction of a palace, his expulsion of the Philistines from Judah's heartland, and his religious reforms in the new capital city. By means of these activities, David moves Judah out of the first phase of sociopolitical development (tribal kingdom). His covenant agreement with the elders of the northern tribes moves Israel into the national kingdom phase. Breaking the Philistine stranglehold on the central highlands makes Israel a consolidated territorial state. The final two stages of David's empire will be narrated in 2 Samuel 8.

For now the narrative is clear that David has produced "an entirely new political order."[14] He is forging a new empire where one has not existed previously. The land now controlled by David had previously been a buffer region, caught between Egypt and imperially minded peoples to the north.[15] With the Iron Age collapse of Egyptian dominance in Syria-Palestine, the Philistines considered themselves the rightful heirs to Egyptian rule and seemed to be on the path to making that a reality. But David's rise to power makes Israel the rising star in the region.

---

13. Such a strategy drives "policy execution" and, as defined by political scientists, involves military, political, economic, and psychological factors. For more on what follows here, see Abraham Malamat, "A Political Look at the Kingdom of David and Solomon and Its Relations with Egypt," in *Studies in the Period of David and Solomon and Other Essays*, ed. Tomoo Ishida (Winona Lake, Ind.: Eisenbrauns, 1982), 189–204; Carol Meyers, "David As Temple Builder," in *Ancient Israelite Religion: Essays in Honor of Frank Moore Cross*, ed. P. D. Miller Jr., P. D. Hanson, and S. D. McBride (Philadelphia: Fortress, 1987), 357–76, esp. 360–61.

14. Malamat, "Political Look," 194. A socioanthropological approach identifies chiefdom, early state, and mature state as three stages of state formation. In this schema, the biblical evidence portrays Saul's reign as an early chiefdom, David's as transitional, and Solomon's as an early state. See Elman Service, *Origins of the State and Civilization* (New York: W. W. Norton, 1975), for introduction and a useful summary; William M. Schniedewind, *Society and the Promise to David: The Reception History of 2 Samuel 7:1–17* (New York: Oxford Univ. Press, 1999), 22–24. See also J. W. Flanagan, "Chiefs in Israel," *JSOT* 20 (1981): 47–73; for critique, see Schäfer-Lichtenberger, "Sociological and Biblical Views," 88–89.

15. First the Mitanni and later the Hittites. The central hills of southern Syria-Palestine had long been dominated by this "bipolar" power structure. Malamat, "Political Look," 191.

David Captures Jerusalem (5:6–10)

THE SPECIFIC DETAILS of this paragraph are obscure (see commentaries).[16] For example, we have little idea what the "water shaft" was (5:8), and the significance of the apparently etiological references to "the blind and the lame" escape us (5:6, 8). But the main points of the narrative are clear. David cannot rule a newly unified nation incorporating especially the northern tribes from a southern base at Hebron. Jerusalem is ideal for its natural defenses, central location, and lack of previous attachment to the tribes of Israel (though it was in the territory of Benjamin).[17] David cleverly devises a means of attack and turns the venerable old "fortress of Zion" into his own possession, the "City of David." He takes up personal residence in the new capital and strengthens its defenses further.

The narrative concludes with an affirmation of David's increasing power, which is attributable to the guidance and sustaining presence of "the LORD God Almighty" (lit., "Yahweh, God of hosts").[18] One of the driving theological convictions of our historian is that Yahweh is "with David," and David therefore succeeds because he is the legitimate anointed one who serves suitably as Israel's king (cf. 1 Sam. 16:18; 18:12, 14, 28; 2 Sam. 3:1; 7:3, 9).

Without doubt, Jerusalem is the most important city of the Bible. It is mentioned over eight hundred times in the Bible. The name "Jerusalem" itself is known from Egyptian texts as old as the nineteenth century B.C., hundreds of years before David's time.[19] Apparently, the Canaanites referred to the city as Jebus prior to David's conquest (Josh. 15:8; 18:28; Judg. 19:10). The name "Zion" occurs over 150 times in the Old Testament and refers originally to the southeast hill of the city, which is equated in our text with the "City of David." Like Jerusalem, the etymological meaning of Zion is unclear, but it comes to be used as a synonym of Jerusalem and takes on enormous theological significance in Psalms, Isaiah, and elsewhere.[20]

The rest of 2 Samuel 5–6 centers on David's activities in and around Jerusalem. David builds a new palace in Jerusalem (5:11–12), he increases his family there (5:13–16), he defends the new capital city against the Philistines in the immediate area (5:17–25), and he brings the ark of the covenant there

---

16. McCarter believes an archaic account, which became obscure to a later audience, has been enlarged here in verses 6–10 (*II Samuel*, 137).

17. McCarter refers to it as "a city located between two states but belonging to neither" (*II Samuel*, 141).

18. A fitting conclusion to what is believed by many to be the last verse in the history of David's rise (see introduction).

19. Philip J. King, "Jerusalem," *ABD*, 3:747–66; Terry L. Brensinger, "Jerusalem," *NIDOTTE*, 4:772–76; Dan Bahat, "Jerusalem," *OEANE*, 3:224–38.

20. Jon D. Levenson, "Zion Traditions," *ABD*, 6:1098–1102.

(6:1–19). From this point forward in biblical thought, Jerusalem becomes a powerful symbol of Israel's belief that God rules over the earth and that he has established the Davidic dynasty as his human agency for governing the world. By bringing the ark of the covenant into the city, Jerusalem becomes more than a center of human monarchical power; it becomes also the seat of God's kingship (Ps. 78:68; 132:13–18).[21] As the location of divine and human kingship, Jerusalem comes to stand for the nation as a whole, and its fate is synonymous with that of God's people (Isa. 2:2; Amos 2:5; Mic. 4:1).

A Palace for David in Jerusalem (5:11–12)

WITH THE AID of the powerful king of Tyre, who later helps Solomon in the construction of the temple (1 Kings 5:7), David now receives a palace in Jerusalem. This is vivid confirmation that Yahweh himself has established David as king for the sake of the people of Israel. The NIV's "and David knew" can be translated "and David realized" (NASB) or "David then perceived" (NRSV). As a result of these blessings, David now grasps fully his indebtedness to Yahweh.

The historical synchronism with Hiram of Tyre and his subsequent relationship with Solomon, along with other references, make it clear that the events narrated in this section are not given in chronological sequence.[22] The biblical historian has collected events topically in this unit in order to produce the full impact of David under the blessing of Yahweh (5:10). Just as these historical developments serve to confirm in David's mind that God has blessed him and established his kingdom (5:12), so they serve the same role for the readers.

David's Children Born in Jerusalem (5:13–16)

DAVID HAD CHILDREN BORN TO HIM at Hebron (3:2–5); now the historian reports the children born during his Jerusalem years. Though the extended narrative portrays David under the blessing of Yahweh, there may be hints of future trouble here. The new king has taken more wives and concubines in direct violation of the royal law of Deuteronomy 17:17. The expression "concubines and wives" is reversed from the normal "wives and concubines"

---

21. "Jerusalem," *DBI*, 436–37.

22. Keil and Delitzsch, *Samuel*, 318–19; McCarter, *II Samuel*, 145. Our historian has most likely used the literary device of association to coalesce David's goals and achievements as king and to group them together near the beginning of his reign. Such a practice was common for Assyrian scribes, who attributed to their kings' accession year all the achievements and accomplishments of their reigns. Most of the events narrated in chs. 5–8 probably occur late in David's declining years. See Eugene H. Merrill, "The 'Accession Year' and Davidic Chronology," *JANESCU* 19 (1989): 101–12.

elsewhere in the Old Testament, and some suspect the narrator has put "concubines" in an emphatic position in order to critique David's tendency to accept the trappings of a typical Near Eastern king.[23] Even in this unit emphasizing the blessing of Yahweh on David, troubled times lie ahead.

Two Victories over the Philistines (5:17–25)

AS LONG AS ISRAEL WAS DIVIDED into two competing nations, southern Judah and northern Israel, the Philistines could tolerate an anointed King David in the south. But the idea of a united Israel with David as king is a threat they attempt to prevent (5:17): "When the Philistines heard that David had been anointed king over Israel, they went up in full force to search for him." These paragraphs narrate two battles against the Philistines, who attack Judah's heartland in an apparent attempt to drive a wedge between David's two constituencies.[24] As we have seen throughout this unit, the events are reported thematically, not in chronological sequence.[25] These two battles against the Philistines are among the last recorded in the books of Samuel.[26] Together they contribute to the narrative's growing confidence in David as the anointed of Yahweh, whose primary purpose is deliverance from the dreaded Philistines (1 Sam. 9:16).

The Valley of Rephaim was a plain just southwest of Jerusalem, a portion of which lay on the border between Benjamin and Judah.[27] By attempting to cut David off from his new northern supporters, the Philistines present a critical moment early in David's rule. The Philistines have been warring against the northern tribes (note Saul's death on Mount Gilboa). On the one hand, should David fail in these battles, it would give the northern tribes reason to reconsider their allegiance to David. Moreover, failure to drive the Philistines from this location in the very interior of David's southern kingdom would galvanize the Philistines to strike for a final blow. On the other hand, victory now would mean a quick consolidation of his forces and the realization of David's dream for a consolidated territorial state.[28]

---

23. Keil and Delitzsch, *Samuel*, 322; Youngblood, "1, 2 Samuel," 859.

24. McCarter, *II Samuel*, 158.

25. These battles probably occurred in the interval of time between David's anointing (vv. 1–5) and his conquest of Jerusalem (vv. 6–10). See Merrill, "The 'Accession Year' and Davidic Chronology," 101–12, esp. 108; Keil and Delitzsch, *Samuel*, 323. But note the reservations of Robert P. Gordon (*I and II Samuel*, 229).

26. They warrant a summary statement in 8:1 and are retrospective references in 2 Samuel 21 and 23.

27. Gershon Edelstein, "Rephaim, Valley of," *ABD* 5:676.

28. To use the terminology of modern political science. See Malamat, "Political Look," 194–95.

Little wonder, then, that our narrator has included these brief military reports in a unit showing how God's hand blesses all that David does. By driving the Philistines "from Gibeon to Gezer" (5:25), David liberates the Israelite territory occupied since the battle of Ebenezer (1 Sam. 4:1b–11).[29] One British scholar has speculated that these victories were so dramatic and so emotional for David and the Israelites that they can be compared to the Battle of Trafalgar in the British psyche. Or better, she goes on to say, it must have been like "the awesome sense of God's overruling associated with the evacuation from Dunkirk, the Battle of Britain, and the D-Day landings during the Second World War."[30] Even though the events Baldwin describes occurred more than a half century ago, they continue to represent vivid and dramatic turning points in British and American history. Thus, it is difficult to overstress the joy and celebration in the narrator's voice in reporting these Israelite triumphs over the Philistines.

The significance of these victories is further highlighted by subtle references in the text. (1) The idea that the Philistines abandon their idols, which are subsequently captured by David and his men (5:21), is a powerful image. It was customary in the ancient world for victors to carry off the "gods" of the defeated enemy, which were thought to ensure the deity's succor in battle.[31] This reference also conjures up the horrifying shadows of the first battle of Ebenezer, when the Philistines captured the ark of the covenant (1 Sam. 4:1b–11). David's glorious victory is an apt reversal of those misfortunes.

(2) The Israelites in that earlier battle with the Philistines had recklessly attempted to create the circumstances of holy war (see comments on 1 Sam. 4:1b–11). Here, however, the terminology and imagery of divine armies marching in the balsam trees and Yahweh's "going forth" in front of Israel's army is reminiscent of ancient theophanic poetry, in which Yahweh and his celestial armies come to help in holy war.[32] Where earlier attempts failed, David succeeds.

(3) Finally, the repeated information that "David inquired of the LORD" is a familiar theme (5:19, 23; see comments at 1 Sam. 23:1–14; 30:7–25; 2 Sam. 2:1–4a). David's rise to kingship is characterized by the importance he attaches to seeking guidance from God—in contrast to Saul, who sometimes made up his mind in advance or failed to ask altogether. Now that David is king, he defeats the hated foe of God. But he continues to take steps that are directed and guided by Yahweh's loving response. Here again, David becomes the portrait of the ideal king of Israel.

---

29. McCarter, *II Samuel*, 157.
30. Baldwin, *1 and 2 Samuel*, 203.
31. Miller and Roberts, *The Hand of the Lord*, 9–16.
32. Miller, *The Divine Warrior*, 132.

David Brings the Ark to Jerusalem (6:1–23)

AT ONE TIME, the scholarly consensus held this chapter to be a concluding literary unit for the ark narrative.[33] But others have argued that the earlier narrative on the ark (1 Sam. 4:1b–7:1) and this chapter are singular compositions corresponding to disparate ancient Near Eastern genres. The ark narrative proper is comparable to texts on the capture in battle and eventual return of divine images. This chapter, by contrast, is more comparable to narratives relating ceremonies at the introduction of national gods to new royal cities.[34] Thus, many today believe that this chapter has been included in this unit (5:11–8:18) in order to contribute to the growing picture of David as the legitimate and blessed king of Israel.[35]

Regardless of its literary history, this chapter's location is significant in light of the immediately preceding paragraphs. David has captured Jerusalem and transformed the city into a political force by driving the Philistines back to their traditional borders and unifying the tribes of Israel at their new capital city. The new political role for Jerusalem is now supplemented by a new religious significance. The entrance of the ark of the covenant into the city is the culmination of a long and painful sojourn since the fall of Shiloh and the loss of a central cult center (see comments at 1 Sam. 4:12–22). Now, after "a long time" in Kiriath Jearim (1 Sam. 7:2), the ark is restored to a prominent role in the nation's religious life.[36] Thus the chapter's location builds on the political and military accomplishments of David in 5:6–25 by narrating an event of substantial religious significance.

"Baalah of Judah" is an alternate name for Kiriath Jearim (6:2). Some scholars have speculated that Baalah was the ancient Canaanite name meaning "wife" or "lady," denoting the city's devotion to one of the Canaanite goddesses. If so, it may be that the Israelites "demythologized" the place by giving it a new name, Kiriath Jearim (roughly equivalent to "Woodsville").[37]

The unusual designation for the ark in 6:2 calls for comment in the text: "the ark of God, which is called by the Name, the name of the LORD Almighty, who is enthroned between the cherubim that are on the ark." Such

---

33. For summary, see Campbell, *The Ark Narrative*, 28–54. See also the introduction and comments on 1 Sam. 4:1b–11.

34. Miller and Roberts, *The Hand of the Lord*, 9–16, 22–26.

35. McCarter, *II Samuel*, 182–84; Gordon, *I and II Samuel*, 22–24. For another opinion, see Campbell, *The Ark Narrative*; Anderson, *2 Samuel*, 99–100.

36. The "twenty years" of 1 Sam. 7:2 probably refers to the interval between the capture of the ark by the Philistines and the battle reported in 7:7–13. In light of Saul's forty-year reign, it seems likely the ark languished in exile more than sixty years. Youngblood, "1, 2 Samuel," 867.

37. Carl S. Ehrlich, "Baalah," *ABD*, 1:555.

a long and cumbersome designation probably indicates the use of a formal cult-related title for the ark and indirectly for the God of Israel. The full name of the ark appears to have been "the ark of the covenant of the LORD Almighty, who is enthroned between the cherubim" (see 1 Sam. 4:4). The ark was the divine throne itself, and the cherubim flanking the throne may reflect Canaanite royal thrones in which winged sphinxes were used. The expression "who is enthroned between the cherubim" is a sacred epithet used of God by the early Israelites in worship (lit., "Yahweh of armies who is 'Seated-between-the-Cherubim'").[38]

The care with which the narrator identifies the ark (and the God it stands for) denotes the significance of David's actions. This was truly a momentous event in Israel's life.

The full impact of David's bringing the ark into Jerusalem is felt when we remember that the written word (or even the spoken word) was necessarily limited in the ancient world. Other forms of communication were extremely important, especially visual symbols, or iconography.

> Both verbal and visual modes of communication stressed that dynastic power derived its legitimacy from its close connection with divine sovereignty.... A religious text could convey that sanction to a privileged, literate audience; a religious symbol or edifice could provide that message to a wider public.[39]

The ark of Yahweh was the most important symbol of God's approval among the unified tribes of Israel. Its presence in Jerusalem, in "the tent that David had pitched for it," represented the most powerful sign of God's support for David and his new capital city.

While the theological import of this move of the ark to Jerusalem seems central, it clearly has political significance as well. Shiloh was an important Israelite religious center prior to the rise of the monarchy (cf. 1 Sam. 1–3). David is most likely attempting to transfer the former authority and power of Shiloh, now sadly lost for decades, to the newly designated capital city. The use of this powerful iconographic symbol will go a long way to accomplishing that purpose. But we should also take care not to become cynical

---

38. Cross, *Canaanite Myth and Hebrew Epic*, 69–70. Rather than a simple ban on all iconic representations of God, early Israel was probably "aniconic." That is, God could be visually represented but without pictorial images, whether human or animal. Thus, for example, standing stones or stone pillars could represent God as "material aniconism," or the use of a throne or pedestal could represent God's presence (as with the ark of the covenant), which is an example of "empty-space aniconism." See Mettinger, *No Graven Image*, esp. 18–20; Lewis, "Divine Images and Aniconism in Ancient Israel," 36–53.

39. Meyers, "David As Temple Builder," 362.

about David's actions. The text is clearly celebrating David's kingship and praising the new king for his devotion to God. "That his devotion brought him advantages should not occasion any surprise, nor is a cynical and self-regarding interpretation of David's action appropriate."[40]

David must have meant well, but the process of bringing the ark into the city is disastrous. Note that on the second attempt no cart is used, for we read that the ark is carried rather than riding on a cart (6:13).[41] This detail is not missed by the later Chronicler, who suggests the reason for the disastrous first attempt, as explained by David himself to the priests in charge (1 Chron. 15:13): "It was because you, the Levites, did not bring it up the first time that the LORD our God broke out in anger against us."[42]

In a way that seems especially foreign to present-day readers, the unfortunate Uzzah illustrates the holiness of God present in the ark. "To touch the ark is to impinge on God's holiness, to draw too close and presume too much."[43] The Israelites have not taken his power and holiness seriously enough, and now David is left with the question (6:9): "How can the ark of the LORD ever come to me?" The text implies that the ark (and hence God's presence) can and will come into David's life, but his power and holiness come with it. Such warnings are healthy, indeed needed, in order to protect God's people from tendencies to trivialize God's holiness.

Finally, we must make a comment about the difficult references to Michal. It is possible, of course, to analyze her motives psychologically, as though she were reacting against her hard life since marrying David or dealing with the loss of her father, Saul, and brother Jonathan. But the text does not invite us into such psychoanalytic speculation. Instead, it leaves subtle literary hints to consider. Note that Michal is identified in her first appearance in this unit as the "daughter of Saul" rather than the "wife of David." In her objections and demeanor, she manifests her father's disposition rather than her husband's.[44] While nation and king celebrate the joyous occasion, Michal sulks as though *Saul* would have done better. She has forgotten that Saul had neglected the ark (and God!) and refused to heed the warnings of the prophet Samuel.

Whatever the details of Michal's objections may have been, she functions in this text as a remnant of the old Saulide line. The closing phrase of the unit

---

40. Baldwin, *1 and 2 Samuel*, 212.

41. A point made by Gordon, *I and II Samuel*, 231.

42. David speaks also of transporting the ark "in the prescribed way," which according to Gordon seems to have in view the pertinent Pentateuchal stipulations (Ex. 25:12–15; Num. 4:15; 7:9; Deut. 10:8; see Gordon, *I & II Samuel*, 231).

43. Brueggemann, *First and Second Samuel*, 249.

44. Keil and Delitzsch, *Samuel*, 336; Alter, *David Story*, 228.

implies her childlessness is her punishment. Thus, the narrative makes its point: Saul's house was to have "no ongoing part in the kingship of Israel."[45] Every offshoot of that branch has been torn off and abandoned. Saul, Jonathan, and Ish-Bosheth are dead; Mephibosheth is crippled; Michal is barren.

THE IMAGES OF KING AND CITY are among the most powerful in ancient Israel's worldview. This unit establishes both King David and Jerusalem/Zion, describing the political and religious developments that usher them into existence. The first step in our bridge-building process will be to consider the significance of these concepts (king and city) in Old Testament thought.

Zion theology. Old Testament theologians have long realized that ancient Israelites believed strongly in what has been called "Zion theology." Variously expressed in the Old Testament, this theology can be summarized as the conviction that Yahweh is the great king and that he has chosen Jerusalem as his dwelling place.[46] We have seen in 1 Samuel that the early Israelites held dearly to the idea that Yahweh was their king. Long before the controversy regarding whether God's people should have a human king, the Israelites praised Yahweh as their king: "The LORD will reign for ever and ever" (Ex. 15:18; cf. Num. 23:21; Deut. 33:5).

Indeed the lateness of the development of human kingship in Israel may be a result of their rejection of human monarchs in general as part of an oppressive political structure. They had suffered as slaves under Egyptian kingship, and therefore no such human structure would be tolerated in Israel. Fittingly, then, the metaphor of Yahweh as king served as a forceful argument against human kingship.

When 1 Samuel addressed the question of the nature of the Israelite monarchy, it was not in the context of relinquishing Yahweh's role as king. Instead, the new human king was to serve as his viceroy. Yahweh was the real king, while the human king was his representative or regent, chosen by God to carry out his earthly tasks. As Yahweh's vicegerent, David's military victories gave new insight into Yahweh's status as king. Now it became clear that Yahweh was sovereign over the Philistines as well as the Israelites (and, as we will see in ch. 8, over all Israel's near neighbors). He is the great king, the sovereign of all the universe, who rules as suzerain over the vassal states of earth (Ps. 2:1–3; 47).

---

45. Evans, *1 and 2 Samuel*, 164.
46. For what follows, see Roberts, "Zion," 93–108, esp. 94–104.

Further, Zion theology holds that Yahweh, the great king, has chosen Jerusalem for his dwelling place. Like other deities of Syria-Palestine, it was believed that Yahweh had his abode upon a high mountain.[47] Comparative studies between Israel and other Syro-Palestinian cultures reveal a common belief in a *cosmic mountain*, by which is meant a mountain with cosmic potencies and characteristics. Such a mountain has universal scope. It is the center of the universe, the meeting place of heaven and earth, where effective decrees are issued and conflicting natural forces engage in battle.[48]

Yahweh's original mountain abode appears to have been Mount Sinai, sometimes known as Horeb, the "mountain of God" (Ex. 3:1; 18:5; 24:13; Num. 10:33). He eventually departed Mount Sinai and took up his abode in Canaan (Deut. 33:2; Judg. 5:4; Hab. 3:3). At times Yahweh seemed to settle in the central hills of Syria-Palestine (Ps. 78:54). But once David captured Jebus and moved the ark to the new capital, Mount Zion became Yahweh's chosen mountain (Ps. 78:68–69).[49] Zion therefore becomes the fulcrum for the universe.

> Zion as the place from which the world was created, as the point from which the primal ray of light emanated, and as the only mountain to stand above the deluge, is also the highest point in the highest land, the center of the center, from which all the rest of reality takes its bearings.[50]

Thus, Yahweh is king, and he lives in Zion. Humans who live in the city with God must meet his standards of holiness (Ps. 24:3–4; Isa. 33:13–16), but they can also count on a secure and abundant life in his presence.[51] This "Zion theology," so ubiquitous in the Old Testament, gets its beginning here. David's coronation and his transformation of Jerusalem into Israel's capital city (and the relocation of the ark) become benchmark events for theological reflection. Their narration in the text before us already reflects an understanding of Zion theology; in fact, it lays the foundation for that theology.

---

47. Ugaritic mythological texts, e.g., portray Baal, the Canaanite storm god, as inhabiting the mountain Zaphon, located near the mouth of the Orontes River in northern Syria.

48. Richard J. Clifford, *The Cosmic Mountain in Canaan and the Old Testament* (HSM 4; Cambridge, Mass.: Harvard Univ. Press, 1972).

49. Jon D. Levenson, *Sinai and Zion: An Entry into the Jewish Bible* (San Francisco: HarperCollins, 1985), 111–37.

50. Ibid., 135.

51. Other features of Zion theology are developed in Psalms and prophetic literature, particularly the idea of a life-giving stream or river flowing from the presence of God on the mountain and the security that God's presence in the city provides through his defeat of hostile enemies. See Roberts, "Zion," 100–104.

The past and the future. Thus, within the Old Testament itself, this text is oriented toward both the past and the future. It looks backward across the pages of the books of Samuel to God's promise to make David ruler of all Israel. Ever since that fateful day when the venerable old prophet appeared in Jesse's home and anointed his youngest son as the future king (1 Sam. 16:1–13), David has been living with this conviction—sometimes confidently, sometimes in confusion. Even further back, beyond David's own personal promises (and beyond the pages of Samuel), this text looks back to God's promises to Israel's ancestors. Among the blessings that David fulfilled were the promise that kings would come from Abraham's line (Gen. 17:6, 16; 35:11) and that royal authority would arise from Judah (49:8–12).

But this text looks beyond its own pages to a future time as well. Once David is anointed king (5:1–5), the text moves inexorably toward the glory of Yahweh's kingdom and its capital city, Jerusalem. The city is captured and defended, and a royal palace built. And David has sons in Jerusalem, one of whom will succeed him as king. Then the most important symbol of Yahweh's presence with his people, the ark of the covenant, is brought into the city, only to sit in a makeshift "tent" (which is, of course, only temporary). After the construction of David's palace and the return of the ark, the next development must necessarily be a "house" for Yahweh (hence ch. 7). By looking forward to the grandeur of the kingdom and a new temple, this text drives us onward in a way that ultimately becomes eschatological.

The next step in the bridge-building process is to trace this trajectory through and beyond other Old Testament passages and into the New Testament. As God's salvation plan unfolds, the Davidic line and Jerusalem/Zion become prominent symbols of Israel's belief that God will ultimately rule over all the earth. Their central significance in the prophetic literature can hardly be overstated. As a corporate representative for God's people, Jerusalem illustrates that the city (i.e., the people of God) will enjoy salvation after a period of punishment for sin.[52] Eventually, after the Exile, Jerusalem/Zion will once again become the religious center of a restored holy land (Ezek. 45:1–6), and Mount Zion will receive the gifts and adoration of many peoples (Isa. 18:7; Zech. 8:22–23). In such passages, God's word issues forth from Jerusalem (Isa. 2:3), peoples gather to honor him (Jer. 3:17), and the messianic king will appear victoriously (Zech. 9:9–10).

Sometimes the temporal dimensions of these oracles of salvation blur or are not distinguishable, resulting in pronouncements that are reserved for the

---

52. For what follows, see Bill T. Arnold, "City, Citizenship," *New Dictionary of Biblical Theology*, ed. T. Desmond Alexander and Brian S. Rosner (Leicester, England/Downers Grove, Ill.: InterVarsity Press, 2000), 414–16.

distant future. In that age to come, Yahweh's rule will be firmly established in Jerusalem (Isa. 24:23; 65:18–19). The city will finally become a holy city and will never again be conquered by foreign nations (Joel 3:17 [Heb. 4:17]). In these prophetic passages, Jerusalem comes to symbolize the final and ultimate consummation of Yahweh's plan of salvation.

Much more could and should be said about the trajectory of David and Zion in the Old Testament (esp. regarding Isaiah and selected Psalms such as 68, 76, and 78).[53] But this eschatological movement of the prophets leads us to consider the New Testament appropriation of David and Zion. As we have seen elsewhere in this commentary, the books of Samuel contribute much to the messianism of the intertestamental period and thereby lay an important foundation for New Testament theology. But the same can now be said for the role of Jerusalem/Zion. Jesus identified his ministry with the inauguration of the kingdom of God (Matt. 4:17; Mark 1:15; Luke 4:14–20, 42–43). In light of the Old Testament and later Jewish messianism, this kingdom could only be realized with Jerusalem as the center of the divine and Davidic kingship. Jesus sheds tears and is sorrowful because he knows Jerusalem is no longer legitimate as the symbol of God's covenant with his people (Luke 19:41–44). His triumphal entry symbolized the victorious return of the Davidic kingship to Jerusalem (Luke 19:38).

Despite the eventual destruction of Jerusalem, its symbolic role in establishing the kingdom of God continued. The author of the letter to the Hebrews instructs readers that faith means they have not approached a physical mountain like Mount Sinai, with its fearful and awesome presence. Rather, they have "come to Mount Zion, to the heavenly Jerusalem, the city of the living God" (Heb. 12:22). The result is that on this earth we have no enduring city, "but we are looking for the city that is to come" (13:14). In this we Christians have Abraham as our example. While he, Isaac, and Jacob were living in tents in Canaan, they were actually seeking the "city with foundations, whose architect and builder is God" (11:10).

Abraham's seminomadism was rewarded beyond his comprehension. While he expected to inherit the cities of Canaan, which were difficult to defend and vulnerable to aggressors, he was rewarded with a far greater city—"the heavenly Jerusalem," the city of the living God, the capital of an unshakable kingdom (Heb. 12:22–23, 28). So Christian eschatological hopes are attached to a new Jerusalem, a city that will transcend the glory of its earthly counterpart.

The trajectory of future hope in David and Zion, begun in the Old Testament, arrives at its pinnacle in the closing chapters of the Bible. Although the book of Revelation is devoted primarily to a description of persecution

---

53. See, e.g., Barth, *God with Us*, 234–303.

and death (Rev. 6–20), chapters 21–22 move from time into eternity as they foretell the glorious outcome of God's redemptive plan. The first paragraph (21:1–8) describes in general terms the new heaven and new earth, relying largely on images from the prophecy of Isaiah (Isa. 65:17; 66:22). The old creation has passed away, making room for this new creation, including "the Holy City, the new Jerusalem, coming down out of heaven from God" (Rev. 21:2). The inhabitants of this new city will enjoy unhindered fellowship with God, thanks to the new Davidic king, Jesus (21:3–4).

The second literary unit describes the new Jerusalem in more detail (Rev. 21:9–21). The holy city will be the new home for God's people. It is described as perfectly symmetrical and radiant like pure jewels.

Revelation ends with a glimpse of life in the eternal city (Rev. 21:22–22:5). The new Jerusalem will be marked by the absence of things taken for granted as necessary in the former city. It has no temple, for the temple represented the presence of God in the midst of Jerusalem. Instead, God himself will be the temple in the new city (21:22). It has no sun or moon, for it will have the glory of God (21:23), and no night, because the Lord God will be light for its inhabitants (21:25; 22:5). Life in the new city will surpass the experiences of the first couple in the Garden of Eden, for this city has "the river of the water of life" and "the tree of life" (22:1–2).

This magnificent portrait is the culmination of Jerusalem imagery throughout the Bible. "The New Jerusalem represents the time when the reign of God will be fully actualized on earth through the vice-regency of the great Son of David."[54] Thus the closing chapters of the Bible tie king and city together—David and Jerusalem, bound together in the hope of every Christian.

Such theological significance for king and city makes the message of our text critically important for present-day believers. The obstacles involved in bridging the contexts to our contemporary setting are simple: These are not our images! King and city do not serve well as theological constructs in the postmodern world. This is especially true in more democratic North American contexts, but they are hardly applicable anywhere in the twenty-first century. In America we have no kings. We have many cities, but none with innate theological significance. Building a bridge to the contemporary setting requires a sensitivity to the overarching biblical picture we have attempted to provide here. We must explore the way this text looks back to Israel's past and forward to the future. Attention to this Janus characteristic of the text will make it come alive for today's reader.[55]

---

54. "Jerusalem," DBI, 437.

55. Janus in Roman mythology was the patron god of beginnings and endings. In iconography, his statue has two faces—one looking forward, the other back.

Contemporary Significance

THE SIGNIFICANCE OF THIS TEXT for today is clear when we consider its place in biblical thought as a benchmark for theological reflection. As we have seen, the text is *retrospective* in that it fulfills the promises of God to David, and before him, to Israel's ancestors. Our text is also *prospective* in that it drives us forward into the salvific significance of David and Jerusalem. The first of these aspects summons from the reader confidence in the faithfulness of God and in the character of his servant, David. The second aspect summons faith itself.

Retrospective: faithfulness. The retrospective aspect emphasizes God's faithfulness to Abraham, to Israel in general, and to David in particular. The long journey from the ancestral promises of a royal descendant, continuing through Israel's agonizing request for a king "as all the other nations" (1 Sam. 8:5), finally comes to an end here with David as kingdom builder. In sum, God has been faithful to his Word. Abraham's descendants have become a nation (on the way to becoming "a great nation," Gen. 12:2), and David has become their king. This is David's third anointing as king. His private anointing by Samuel was the divine stamp of approval on his life (1 Sam. 16:13). The public anointing by the elders of Judah was a partial fulfillment of God's promise (2 Sam. 2:4). But with this text, we have arrived at the full blessing of God.

Beyond the confidence this engenders in God's faithfulness, this aspect of the text also portrays David as the patient servant waiting on God's timing and direction. As a fugitive running from the deranged Saul, his life looked bleak indeed. But as a fugitive he learned to depend on God completely (review how often he "inquired of the LORD"[56]). This text contributes to the extended narrative's concern to portray David as a man after God's own heart (1 Sam. 13:14).

Prospective: faith. The prospective aspect assumes preknowledge on the part of the reader concerning the importance of David and Zion. When this text portrays David as kingdom builder, the informed reader realizes he is not building simply another earthly nation but Yahweh's kingdom. The Christian reader recognizes at once that David's accomplishments are truly cosmic, nothing less than laying the foundation for the Lord's Zion, the city of all future salvation.

The eschatological dimension of the text calls for faith on the part of the reader. By affirming Christian faith and becoming a member of the community, one joins in the journey to Zion. Like Abraham we march to a celestial

---

56. 1 Sam. 23:1–14; 30:7–25; 2 Sam. 2:1–4a; and here, 5:19, 23.

city, "whose architect and builder is God" (Heb. 11:10). Having the rest of the story gives today's Christian readers an appreciation for David's anointing and his building of Jerusalem. We know the consummation of these events in their glorious finality. With Christ before us as the Son of David and his eternal city as our destination, we march onward in faith. These two—king and city—symbolize our "hope of glory" in that we expect to participate in King Jesus' resurrection glory, a hope kept alive in us by his presence within (Col. 1:27).

Already–not yet. One further note on eschatology will help round out the contemporary significance of this text. The eschatological thrust of the passage is only apparent when we read it holistically with the rest of the canon. But even with this proviso, a warning is appropriate lest we read too much specific "end-times" reasoning into the narrative. The danger creeps into our work when we fail to grasp the Bible's concept of time. Time in the Bible is not cyclical, in which case eschatology refers to the completion of the cycle. Nor is it strictly linear, in which case eschatology refers to the termination of time. Rather, the Bible conceives of a recurring pattern in which judgment and salvation interact until the pattern "attains its definitive manifestation."[57]

Thus, eschatology may refer to the culmination of God's purpose without necessarily referring to the end of the world or of history. As the Davidic dynasty failed, Old Testament eschatology developed a futuristic expectation about the ultimate fulfillment of the promises to David. But these are only partially fulfilled in the first coming of Jesus.

Another way to express this is in the New Testament's tension between the "already" and the "not yet." Such "realized eschatology" emphasizes an endurance of faith during the overlapping of ages. The kingdom of God is certainly here, for Jesus proclaimed it so. But the kingdom is not here in all its fullness.

This observation ties together both the retrospective and prospective aspects of our text. David had lived faithfully during the interval, between the already and the not yet. He had been anointed king, but he was not yet king. In this way, he becomes an example for us as we consider the prospective, or eschatological, significance of the text. We too have the promise of king and city, but we continue to hold it as a great expectation, even after the King has arrived. David in this text becomes our example of how to live

---

57. F. F. Bruce, "Eschatology," in *Evangelical Dictionary of Theology*, ed. W. A. Elwell (Grand Rapids: Baker, 1984), 362–65, quote from 362. See also Ben Witherington III, *Jesus, Paul, and the End of the World: A Comparative Study in New Testament Eschatology* (Downers Grove, Ill.: InterVarsity Press, 1992), 15–48.

in the interval, even while he also establishes the "not yet" by building Zion. While we move toward that eternal city in hope, we also look back at David in the assurance that the victory is won.

Thus biblical eschatology always has an ethical thrust. Rather than becoming overly fixated on speculative details of interpretation concerning the end times (such as whether we should be pre-, a-, or post-millennialists or whether the temple must be rebuilt physically), today's Christian readers should emphasize this ethical dimension. With our eyes focused on our Davidic king, we should march to Zion in a way worthy of his example (Heb. 12:1–3).

One noted theologian has compared this tension between the "already" and the "not yet" to events in the European theater of operations during World War II.[58] The successful invasion of Normandy on D-Day by the Allied nations essentially sealed the fate of the Axis nations in the minds of many historians. That invasion began on June 6, 1944. There remained yet almost a year of hard fighting before the Axis nations surrendered on VE-Day, May 8, 1945. The Christian life is like living between D-Day and VE-Day. The victory is secure, but the battle is not won. Thus, David and Zion stand before us, and their victory is certain. The call, then, is for faithfulness along the journey.

---

58. Oscar Cullmann, *Christ and Time: The Primitive Christian Conception of Time and History*, trans. F. V. Filson (London: SCM, 1951), 84.

2 Samuel 7:1–29

FTER THE KING was settled in his palace and the LORD had given him rest from all his enemies around him, [2]he said to Nathan the prophet, "Here I am, living in a palace of cedar, while the ark of God remains in a tent."

[3]Nathan replied to the king, "Whatever you have in mind, go ahead and do it, for the LORD is with you."

[4]That night the word of the LORD came to Nathan, saying:

[5]"Go and tell my servant David, 'This is what the LORD says: Are you the one to build me a house to dwell in? [6]I have not dwelt in a house from the day I brought the Israelites up out of Egypt to this day. I have been moving from place to place with a tent as my dwelling. [7]Wherever I have moved with all the Israelites, did I ever say to any of their rulers whom I commanded to shepherd my people Israel, "Why have you not built me a house of cedar?" '

[8]"Now then, tell my servant David, 'This is what the LORD Almighty says: I took you from the pasture and from following the flock to be ruler over my people Israel. [9]I have been with you wherever you have gone, and I have cut off all your enemies from before you. Now I will make your name great, like the names of the greatest men of the earth. [10]And I will provide a place for my people Israel and will plant them so that they can have a home of their own and no longer be disturbed. Wicked people will not oppress them anymore, as they did at the beginning [11]and have done ever since the time I appointed leaders over my people Israel. I will also give you rest from all your enemies.

"'The LORD declares to you that the LORD himself will establish a house for you: [12]When your days are over and you rest with your fathers, I will raise up your offspring to succeed you, who will come from your own body, and I will establish his kingdom. [13]He is the one who will build a house for my Name, and I will establish the throne of his kingdom forever. [14]I will be his father,

and he will be my son. When he does wrong, I will punish him with the rod of men, with floggings inflicted by
men. ¹⁵But my love will never be taken away from him,
as I took it away from Saul, whom I removed from
before you. ¹⁶Your house and your kingdom will endure
forever before me; your throne will be established forever.'"

¹⁷Nathan reported to David all the words of this entire
revelation.

¹⁸Then King David went in and sat before the LORD, and
he said:

"Who am I, O Sovereign LORD, and what is my family, that you have brought me this far? ¹⁹And as if this
were not enough in your sight, O Sovereign LORD, you
have also spoken about the future of the house of your
servant. Is this your usual way of dealing with man, O
Sovereign LORD?

²⁰"What more can David say to you? For you know
your servant, O Sovereign LORD. ²¹For the sake of your
word and according to your will, you have done this
great thing and made it known to your servant.

²²"How great you are, O Sovereign LORD! There is
no one like you, and there is no God but you, as we
have heard with our own ears. ²³And who is like your
people Israel—the one nation on earth that God went
out to redeem as a people for himself, and to make a
name for himself, and to perform great and awesome
wonders by driving out nations and their gods from
before your people, whom you redeemed from Egypt?
²⁴You have established your people Israel as your very
own forever, and you, O LORD, have become their God.

²⁵"And now, LORD God, keep forever the promise
you have made concerning your servant and his house.
Do as you promised, ²⁶so that your name will be great
forever. Then men will say, 'The LORD Almighty is God
over Israel!' And the house of your servant David will be
established before you.

²⁷"O LORD Almighty, God of Israel, you have
revealed this to your servant, saying, 'I will build a
house for you.' So your servant has found courage to

offer you this prayer. ²⁸O Sovereign LORD, you are
God! Your words are trustworthy, and you have
promised these good things to your servant. ²⁹Now be
pleased to bless the house of your servant, that it may
continue forever in your sight; for you, O Sovereign
LORD, have spoken, and with your blessing the house of
your servant will be blessed forever."

DAVID HAS BEEN crowned king and transformed
Jerusalem into a new capital city. The narrator of
2 Samuel was prominent in that narration, using
speeches sparingly. The content of 2 Samuel 7,
however, is comprised almost entirely of speeches: one lengthy oracle of
Yahweh to Nathan (and subsequently to David), and one prayer of David in
response. This is a very different type of literary unit, in which the narrative
takes a long pause to consider the magnitude of these developments.[1] It is as
though, having arrived at the summit of the story line (i.e., the placement of
throne and ark in Jerusalem), we now are invited to pause and reflect on the
significance of David and his dynasty in the Bible's salvation story.

Most scholars believe there were two primary sources about David used
to compose the sections of the books of Samuel relating to David: "The History of David's Rise" (1 Sam. 16:1–2 Sam. 5:10) and "The Court History"
(2 Sam. 9–1 Kings 2).[2] If this is correct, the majority of the previous unit, this
chapter, and chapter 8 fall between these two sources as independent materials collected to further characterize David's reign.[3] The force of these

---

1. Robert Alter has referred to this chapter as a major cesura in the David story, marked
by ideological reflections on the future (*David Story*, 231). Although Martin Noth himself
did not include this chapter among the other important discoursive blocks used in the composition of the Deuteronomistic History, subsequent scholarship often has, following the
suggestion of D. J. McCarthy ("II Samuel 7 and the Structure of the Deuteronomic History,"
JBL 84 [1965]: 131–38). See Cross, *Canaanite Myth and Hebrew Epic*, 241–58; John Van Seters,
In Search of History: Historiography in the Ancient World and the Origins of Biblical History (New
Haven, Conn.: Yale Univ. Press, 1983), 271–77.

2. Review our introduction. The exact parameters of these sources continue to vex
scholars, but the references suggested here are still the consensus.

3. James Flanagan's analysis of the order of these materials between the primary sources
is forced, though I think on the right path. See James W. Flanagan, "Social Transformation
and Ritual in 2 Samuel 6," in *The Word of the Lord Shall Go Forth: Essays in Honor of David Noel
Freedman in Celebration of His Sixtieth Birthday*, ed. C. L. Meyers and M. O'Connor (Winona Lake,
Ind.: Eisenbrauns, 1983), 361–72. For scholarship on the literary history of ch. 7 per se, see
McCarter, *II Samuel*, 210–31.

materials is to illustrate the concluding statement of "The History of David's Rise" (2 Sam. 5:10): "And [David] became more and more powerful, because the LORD God Almighty was with him." Chapter 7 makes the same point but in a different way. Here we learn the extent to which God was *with* David. The truth of Yahweh's eternal commitment to David is powerful, even difficult to believe—which was David's own humble response.

This is one of the most important chapters of the Bible.[4] Here the Lord speaks through his servant Nathan the prophet to King David. Through this oracle (7:4–17), God establishes a covenant with David (though the term *covenant* does not occur here; see the Bridging Contexts section). God's promise to establish David's dynasty in Jerusalem eternally takes its place alongside the Abrahamic covenant and the Sinaitic (or Mosaic) covenant as critical links in the Bible's story line of salvation. In subsequent Israelite thinking, this chapter became a constitutional text. It expressed an ideology (and became a document) "through which Israel would define itself as a nation, as a people, and as a religion."[5] It has been compared to the Magna Carta or the United States Declaration of Independence, texts that inspire a whole people and engender a national identity. Not surprisingly, then, this text also has profound significance for present-day Christian readers, as we will see.

David's Intentions to Build a Temple (7:1–3)

WITH A CHAPTER mostly speeches, we have little in the way of plot. In this first paragraph, the writer provides all the narrative skeleton necessary for the important speeches to follow.[6] David intends to build a temple for Yahweh in his new capital city, and Nathan the prophet supports the plan.

The mention of David's "palace" in 7:1 assumes knowledge of the capture of Jerusalem (5:6–9) and the building of a royal palace with Phoenician help (5:11). The statement that Yahweh had given David rest from all the enemies around him assumes David's success at driving the Philistines out of Israelite territory (5:17–25). David's complaint that "the ark of God remains in a tent" (7:2) recalls the ark's arrival into Jerusalem and its deposition in a temporary tent (6:1–23). Thus, the previous chapters have been preparing us for this

---

4. The scholarly secondary literature on this chapter is immense. See Lyle Eslinger, *House of God or House of David: The Rhetoric of 2 Samuel 7* (JSOTSup 164; Sheffield: Sheffield Academic Press, 1994); Schniedewind, *Society and the Promise to David*, esp. 30–33.

5. Schniedewind, *Society and the Promise*, 3. Schniedewind's book vividly shows the impact of 2 Sam. 7 on subsequent Israel. For the role it plays in the Deuteronomistic History, see Halpern, *Constitution of the Monarchy*, 19–20.

6. Jan P. Fokkelman, *Narrative Art and Poetry in the Books of Samuel*, 3:207; see 207–54 for sensitive exposition of the literary features of the entire chapter.

moment in the extended narrative. With these sentences we have arrived at a critical juncture in 2 Samuel.

Beyond the immediate context, these verses are also reminiscent of Deuteronomy 12:10–11, where the command was given: Once the Israelites had settled in the Promised Land and enjoyed "rest" from all their "enemies," they were to worship at "the place the LORD your God will choose as a dwelling for his Name."[7] The Lord has blessed the Israelites with land and peace, and the entrance of the ark of the covenant seems to confirm that the new capital of Jerusalem is that "place" God chose.[8] Surely this is a propitious time for the new energetic king to build a permanent structure for God's dwelling.

With the reference to David's "palace" in 7:1, the narrator introduces a theme word for the chapter—*bayit* ("house"), which occurs fifteen times in the chapter. It will recur several times in the next few verses, all referring to a physical structure, either a royal palace (as here in v. 1) or a temple. David's complaint in 7:2 contrasts the "house" he lives in (NIV "palace") with the tent where the ark of God resides. To David's thinking, the time seems right to build a permanent structure to house the ark of God.[9] Nathan concurs and encourages David to fulfill his dream. As substantiation, Nathan repeats the sentiment that is an important theme of the extended narrative (7:3): "The LORD is with you" (see also 7:9).

The Lord's Alternate Plan (7:4–17)

BUT DURING THE night, Yahweh reverses the plan. The characteristic "word of the LORD came to . . ." is the formal announcement of prophetic oracle. It immediately raises the specter of Saul, and this question surfaces in the minds of the reader: Will David hear Nathan's prophetic voice any differently from how Saul heard Samuel's voice? Will David refuse to hear the divine oracle

---

7. For the convincing semantic links between this paragraph and Deut. 12:10–11, see Satterthwaite, "David in the Books of Samuel," 53.

8. God's choice of a place for his name to dwell (Deut. 12:11; 2 Sam. 7:13) refers simply to God's reputation, not to some mystical hypostasis of God's presence, as is often assumed in Old Testament scholarship since the nineteenth century. See Sandra L. Richter, "The Deuteronomistic History and the Place of the Name" (Ph.D. diss., Harvard University, 2001).

9. The chapter is not a condemnation of David's desire to build a temple. He is simply doing what any good ancient Near Eastern monarch would do after succeeding at war. See Avigdor Hurowitz, *I Have Built You an Exalted House: Temple Building in the Bible in Light of Mesopotamian and Northwest Semitic Writings* (JSOTSup 115; Sheffield: JSOT Press, 1992), 171–223; on the connections between temple projects and dynastic promises in the ancient Near East in general, see Ishida, *The Royal Dynasties in Ancient Israel*, 86–92.

as Saul did, or will he submit to Yahweh's will? This chapter, more than any other, answers these questions irrevocably: David is not like Saul. He is as much an ideal ruler of God's people as Saul was an inadequate one.

Yahweh's objection to David's plan (7:5) has historical reasons (7:6–7). He has not needed a physical home since the time of the Exodus until the day of David. Furthermore, Yahweh has not requested such a house. Temples were for deities who were tied down. Israel's God cannot be manipulated or contained in a temple, a point made carefully when the temple *was* eventually built (see 1 Kings 8:27). The use of "cedar" (7:2, 7) imagines an extravagant temple corresponding to David's lavish new palace. But for now, "Yahweh will not be bought off, controlled, or domesticated by such luxury. Yahweh has been a free God and will continue to be. The royal apparatus is not able to make Yahweh its patron."[10]

Instead, Yahweh has an alternate plan (7:8–17).[11] The plan is stated first generally (7:8–11a) and then specifically (7:11b–17). The general statement emphasizes the special relationship Yahweh has with David, signaled at the outset by the epithet "my servant David" (7:5, 8). In essence, God has done *everything* for David. He took David "from the pasture and from following the flock" to make him ruler of the people. Yahweh has been *with* David wherever he went. God himself thus states what the books of Samuel have been emphasizing throughout the extended narrative, that he has been with David. One of the driving theological convictions of the history of David's rise has been that David succeeds where Saul fails because Yahweh has blessed David with his divine presence (see 1 Sam. 16:18; 18:12, 14, 28; 2 Sam. 3:1; 5:10; 7:3). David is the legitimate anointed one who suitably rules God's people because he is the Immanuel figure; God is with him.

Yahweh promises, furthermore, to continue these blessings in the future. He will make David's name great, "like the names of the greatest men of the earth."[12] Such a word is an astounding promise to make David famous long after his death and to ensure a permanent place for him in history. Moreover, through David, Yahweh will provide security for all Israel and will "give [them] rest" (*beniḥoti*, 7:11) from their enemies.

The promise of rest in the land is an important unifying theme throughout the Deuteronomistic History (Deut. 12:9–10). It was partially fulfilled

---

10. Brueggemann, *First and Second Samuel*, 254.

11. Scholars are perplexed by seeming inconsistencies here. Most assume an older oracle that was opposed to building the temple (7:1–7) and another oracle that was pro-temple (7:11b–16). It is assumed the middle section was a Deuteronomistic linkage (7:8–11a). See Cross, *Canaanite Myth and Hebrew Epic*, 241–57. For overview of other approaches, see McCarter, *II Samuel*, 209–31.

12. Cf. how God promised to make Abraham's "name great" (Gen. 12:2).

in the conquest of Joshua but eventually came to be linked to the central worship of Yahweh in his chosen place.[13] Now that Jerusalem has been established, this chapter introduces the theme of a temple for Yahweh, which means the long-awaited "rest" is possible. This text's references to "rest" (7:1, 11) reveal that this rest has now been secured in David and will be ensured by his perpetuating dynasty.[14]

But all of these wonderful blessings are given in place of David's desire to build the temple. Why is David not allowed to build it? We must look elsewhere to learn the specific reasons, since 2 Samuel 7 is silent on this matter. The Bible suggests two separate reasons. (1) David is too busy waging war with Israel's enemies to build the temple, which presumably means his desire expressed in 7:2 is naïve (see 1 Kings 5:3). (2) David's role as a warrior who is accustomed to shedding blood makes him inappropriate as the temple builder (1 Chron. 22:8; 28:3).[15] As David's response indicates (2 Sam. 7:18–29), he completely accepts Yahweh's verdict regarding the temple. The Chronicler relates David's detailed plans and provisions for the construction of the temple, which David believes Solomon will build (1 Chron. 22–29).

Next, Yahweh details his plan more specifically for David (7:11b–17). At this point, the chapter's theme word returns to carry the message. Rather than David's building a "house" for Yahweh, God declares he instead will build a "house" for David (7:11b). The message of the oracle revolves around a wordplay on "house" (*bayit*). The fifteen occurrences of the term in this chapter have either a literal or a metaphoric denotation: physical building (either palace or temple) or extended family, clan, or tribe.[16] The wordplay creates meaning by mixing these uses. David intends to build a physical

---

13. McCarter, *II Samuel*, 204, 217–20.

14. The phrase "I will provide a place for my people Israel" (7:10) may be a rare idiom for Yahweh's sacred mount or temple precinct, which casts a protective shade over the people who dwell beneath it. See David Vanderhooft, "Dwelling Beneath the Sacred Place: A Proposal for Reading 2 Samuel 7:10," *JBL* 118 (1999): 625–33.

15. It is possible to argue that David was well on his way to constructing the temple himself before a severe plague created unfavorable economic conditions. See Meyers, "David As Temple Builder," 357–76. However, there are other plausible historical explanations (see Meyers's note 47; Schniedewind, *Society and the Promise*, 49–50).

16. It is physical building (palace or temple) in vv. 1, 2, 5, 6, 7, and 13. But the chapter uses it in wordplay to denote David's tribal family (in the past) or his royal dynasty (in the future) in vv. 11, 16, 18, 19, 25, 26, 27, and 29 (2x). The term is common in Aramaic and Akkadian to designate the name of a tribe of descendants of the same person. Thus we have Bit-Adini ("House of Adini") or Bit-Yakin ("House of Yakin") as names of Aramaic tribes. Likewise, Assyrian royal inscriptions refer to the northern kingdom of Israel as "the house of Omri," and the Bible itself refers to the "house of Isaac" (Amos 7:16) and the "house of Eli" (1 Sam. 3:14).

house for Yahweh, but he is not the right person for that job. Then the oracle contains this surprise. In an ironic twist, Yahweh announces he himself will build an enduring house (read "royal dynasty") for David because of his special relationship with the new king. David will be succeeded by a son, thus establishing the first royal dynasty in Israel. That son will build the temple (7:13).

But this is only part of the promise. David's line will be established "forever" (7:13, 16). More sons will follow, so that David's line will not end. Yahweh will be a father to them, and they will be his sons (7:14).[17] When they sin, Yahweh will graciously restrict his punishment to that appropriate for humans, but he will never withdraw his steadfast covenant love as he withdrew it from Saul (7:14b–15). Saul's progeny will not last; David's is forever! The wonderful and surprising promises end with the emphatic sentence (7:16): "Your house and your kingdom will endure forever before me; your throne will be established forever."

David's Prayer (7:18–29)

YAHWEH HAS REJECTED the plan to build a temple, but he does not reject David. He has something greater in store for him. The rest of the chapter presents David's response—at first in thanksgiving and praise (7:18–24) and then in supplication (7:25–29).[18] He humbly expresses a sense of overwhelming unworthiness, but he also prays that Yahweh will fulfill his promises. His prayer of grateful deference and bold demand "manages both to yield and to insist at the same time. It is this marvelous blend of yielding and insistence that marks David's faith and Israel's prayer at its best."[19]

Perhaps here more than anywhere else we see the contrast between David and Saul. Put simply, David acquiesces to "the word of the LORD" (7:4), whatever it may portend for him, whereas Saul always looked to negotiate. Consider David's relationship with Nathan compared to Saul's with Samuel. Our text has the first reference to Nathan the prophet, but it will not be the last (see 2 Sam. 12; 1 Kings 1). And wherever he appears beside David to pronounce God's word, he is a welcomed guest, someone whose voice is treasured and obeyed. By contrast, once Saul became king, he began to see

---

17. This phrase in v. 14a is seen by some as a Canaanite formula of divine sonship of the king, which here stands in the place of the covenant formula. See Cross, *Canaanite Myth and Hebrew Epic*, 257–58, and Bridging Contexts section below.

18. Keil and Delitzsch, *Samuel*, 350; Matitiahu Tsevat, "The Steadfast House: What Was David Promised in 2 Samuel 7?" in *The Meaning of the Book of Job and Other Biblical Studies: Essays on the Literature and Religion of the Hebrew Bible* (New York: Ktav, 1980), 110.

19. Brueggemann, *First and Second Samuel*, 259.

Samuel as an unwanted intruder (1 Sam. 13; 15; 28). So again the books of Samuel teach that the king who suitably rules Israel will value Yahweh's prophetic word and obey it faithfully. All future anointed ones will prosper only insofar as they live in consonance with Yahweh's word.

In response to Nathan's oracle, David enters in and sits before the Lord, presumably inside the temporary tent before the ark of the covenant (cf. 6:17). David's opening question admits that his tribal family has no legitimate dynastic expectations (7:18): "Who am I, O Sovereign LORD, and what is my *family*, that you have brought me this far?"[20] David has been thinking of building a physical temple for Yahweh, but his blessing is far more than he expects or feels he deserves. Yahweh will make David's house stand forever, and David is greatly humbled by the promise.

David's opening question is also reminiscent of Saul's: "Am I not a Benjamite, from the smallest tribe of Israel?" (1 Sam. 9:21). But the similarity ceases there. Saul's humility soon turns to defensive self-preservation, while David's drives him to further dependence on Yahweh. Saul's humility is mixed with genuine self-doubt, while David has great confidence in what he and Yahweh can accomplish *together*. Of course the contrast is most evident in the fact that Saul's house does not last, but David's will last forever.

In this part of the prayer, David is driven from humility to adoration of God's greatness (7:22–24). He rightly understands that this promise to establish a permanent Davidic dynasty is related to God's great saving acts of old, his deliverance of Israel from Egypt and the conquest of the Promised Land (7:23). Israel has become Yahweh's people, and he is her God (7:24), which is covenant language again emphasizing the continuity of this promise to David with God's mighty acts of the past (Deut. 29:12–13; cf. 2 Sam. 7:14, above).

As we will note in the Bridging Contexts section, this important promise to David came to be understood in biblical thought as a covenant on a par with the covenants to Abraham and Moses. The historical continuity of the covenants shows that they may be developed and adapted, but they are not superseded. "God's choice of David and his house stands alongside God's choice of Israel. This God was able to deliver Israel and can therefore be trusted to deliver David."[21]

David closes with supplication. As elsewhere in the Old Testament, Israel's prayers, when at their best, call on God to be fully God in their lives and base the request on God's own reputation and character (7:26): "so that your name

---

20. The NIV's "family" is our theme word *bayit* ("house"), which stands here for David's tribal family (cf. NRSV).

21. Evans, *1 and 2 Samuel*, 169.

477

will be great forever."[22] By making this promise to David a reality, Yahweh will demonstrate his great faithfulness to Israel and show himself different from the whimsical gods of the ancient Near East.

GOD HAS REVEALED HIMSELF at different times and places in different ways according to the needs and circumstances of the recipients of his revelation. But one constant is that revelation in a fallen and sinful world has a redemptive character. God often begins his redemptive self-revelation to Israel's ancestors by revealing an important attribute or divine name. For example, God is a "shield," or his name is El Shaddai, or Yahweh (respectively, Gen. 15:1; 17:1; Ex. 3:14). He appeared to Moses and the Israelites at Sinai in shaking mountain, fire, and smoke (Ex. 19–24). Later God allowed his "goodness" to pass before Moses (Ex. 33:19), because revealing an attribute in that particular instance was more important than another pyrotechnic appearance.[23] To Elijah God appeared not in the windstorm, earthquake, or fire, but in "a gentle whisper" (1 Kings 19:11–12). These are just a few of the ways God has revealed himself in Old Testament times, but they demonstrate the merciful and gracious way in which he has condescended to the specific needs of his people over the centuries.[24]

Covenant. One of the most important ways (some would say *the* most important way) God reveals himself in the Bible is by defining his relationship with his people in terms of a "covenant." The text before us is the *locus classicus* of the Davidic covenant and is thus one of the most important chapters of the Bible. But this identification raises a number of questions. Is this chapter really about a covenant? Does it even establish such a binding relationship between Yahweh and David, since the word "covenant" does not appear in this chapter? If we conclude it *is* a covenant, why is it so different from previous covenants in the Old Testament? How does it relate to the other covenants of the Bible? In order to bridge the distance between ancient Israel's understanding of this text and today's believing reader, we must address these questions.

---

22. This emphasis on "name" (*šem*, 7:9, 13, 26) is another wordplay in the chapter, linked to the wordplay on "house." Yahweh will make David's *name* great, but it is through both Solomon's *house* (temple) and David's *house* (dynasty) that the *names* of both Yahweh and David will be built up. See Richter, "Place of the Name," 72–79.

23. Brevard S. Childs, *Exodus* (OTL; Philadelphia: Westminster, 1974), 596.

24. For introduction to the nature of our self-revealing God and his revelation in the Bible, see William Dyrness, *Themes in Old Testament Theology* (Downers Grove, Ill.: InterVarsity Press, 1979), 25–38.

(1) Does 2 Samuel 7 really establish a covenant between Yahweh and David? After all, the term *bᵉrit* ("covenant") occurs nowhere in the chapter. Furthermore, we have nothing here of the characteristic outline used in Exodus 20–24, Deuteronomy, and Joshua 24, which is paralleled in the well-known Hittite suzerainty treaties.[25] Other passages of the Old Testament take this chapter to be a covenant (see below), but it must be admitted that little in the text of 2 Samuel 7 itself insists that it be so.

Most commentators appeal to the terminology in 7:15: "My love will never be taken away from him." The term translated "love" in the NIV is steadfast relational loyalty (*ḥesed*), which presumes an already existing relationship.[26] At the very least, Yahweh's *ḥesed* for David in this verse denotes "the supportive power by which God maintains the family line on the throne."[27] But there seems to be more here, since this is standard Old Testament covenant terminology. God's *ḥesed* is his life-sustaining grace that makes the covenant possible between Yahweh and Israel. Because of his covenant with Israel, God's boundless *ḥesed* is evident in his salvation from disaster or oppression. It is the essence of the covenant itself, and its use here hints at a new covenant between Yahweh and David. In addition, the adoption formula of 7:14 ("I will be his father, and he will be my son") is known elsewhere in the ancient Near East as characteristic of political alliances. Its use here may also hint at a covenant commitment on Yahweh's part toward David.[28]

Whatever doubt may remain that 2 Samuel 7 establishes a covenant between Yahweh and David is removed by innerbiblical exegesis. That is, later passages of the Old Testament that expound on 2 Samuel 7 clearly see this passage as establishing a covenant between Yahweh and David. Particularly important is the poetic adaptation of 2 Samuel 7 in Psalm 89:1–4:[29]

---

25. The Mosaic (or Sinaitic) covenant in its various permutations reflects a specific outline known from Hittite treaties as early as the mid-second millennium B.C. See Arnold and Beyer, *Encountering the Old Testament*, 148–51. On the inadequacy of the English "covenant" for the Hebrew *bᵉrit*, which connotes both "promise and commandment," see Roland de Vaux, "The King of Israel, Vassal of Yahweh," in *The Bible and the Ancient Near East*, trans. D. McHugh (Graden City, N.Y.: Doubleday, 1971), 157, 160. The breadth of this Hebrew term may explain why other biblical authors so easily applied "covenant" to the promises of 2 Sam. 7.

26. See Bridging Contexts for 1 Sam. 20:1–42.

27. Sakenfeld, *Meaning of Ḥesed*, 144. Elsewhere she states that it is Yahweh's "provision" for continuing his relationship with David (145).

28. Youngblood, "1, 2 Samuel," 892.

29. See further vv. 19–37 of this psalm, as well as Ps. 132:11–18 and 1 Chron. 17. For careful exegesis of the pertinent passages on the Davidic covenant, see Gary N. Knoppers, "David's Relation to Moses: The Contexts, Content and Conditions of the Davidic Promises," in *King and Messiah in Israel and the Ancient Near East: Proceedings of the Oxford Old*

I will sing of the LORD's great love forever;
  with my mouth I will make your faithfulness known through all generations.
I will declare that your love stands firm forever,
  that you established your faithfulness in heaven itself.
You said, "I have made a covenant with my chosen one,
  I have sworn to David my servant,
'I will establish your line forever
  and make your throne firm through all generations.'"

Based on textual interplay between Psalm 89 and 2 Samuel 7, it seems probable that the historical narrative was written first and constituted the base for Psalm 89.[30] Here we are beyond doubt. The poet sings of Yahweh's great *ḥesed*-love and faithfulness (*ʾemunah*) and celebrates Yahweh's "covenant" (*bᵉrit*) with David (89:3). In fact, these terms are repeated often, with "covenant" recurring in 89:28, 34, and 39. There are, of course, important differences between the emphases of 2 Samuel 7 and Psalm 89. But the nature of the relationship between Yahweh and David is covenantal; about that there is no question.[31]

(2) Why is this covenant so different from previous covenants in the Old Testament? Particularly, why are there no stipulations, which are so central to the Mosaic covenant? This has led some scholars to debate whether the Davidic covenant was unconditional whereas the Mosaic covenant was clearly conditional because of the elaborate stipulations attached to it (i.e., the Pentateuchal legal materials).

This debate stems partly from the Bible itself, which displays an ambivalent stance on these issues. On the one hand, the term "forever" in 7:13, 16 gives the promises of Yahweh to David a permanence, a certain unconditional quality.[32] Shockingly, even when David's descendants disobey (7:14), Yahweh will not withdraw his *ḥesed*-love from them as he withdrew it from Saul

---

Testament Seminar, ed. John Day (JSOTSup 270; Sheffield: Sheffield Academic Press, 1998), 91–118, esp. 111–14 for Ps. 89. To these texts we should add 2 Sam. 23:1–7; 1 Chron. 22:9–10; Ps. 2; Isa. 42:1, 6; 55:3; perhaps Jer. 31:31–34.

30. Psalm 89 appears to be an interpretation of a genuinely early form of 2 Sam. 7:1–17 dated from or close to the united monarchy, contra those who argue that this psalm is an earlier tradition behind a late 2 Sam. 7. See Nahum Sarna, "Psalm 89: A Study in Inner Biblical Exegesis," in *Biblical and Other Studies*, ed. A. Altmann (Cambridge, Mass.: Harvard Univ. Press, 1963), 29–46; Ishida, *The Royal Dynasties in Ancient Israel*, 82.

31. See further David's own affirmation of Yahweh's "everlasting covenant" in 2 Sam. 23:5.

32. Though it must be admitted that the term "forever" may mean simply a limited time span, the endurance of something within its natural limits (see Tsevat, "Steadfast House," 106–7).

(7:15). But elsewhere, continuance of the Davidic dynasty is clearly conditional (esp. in 1–2 Kings; e.g., 1 Kings 8:25; 9:4–5; see also Ps. 132).

Beyond the ambivalence of such biblical references, the debate is often intensified by the differences among theological schools of thought. Systems committed to a form of determinism (such as soft determinism, sometimes called compatibilism) are inclined to assume all covenants are unconditional. Theological systems committed to a form of libertarian freedom are more inclined to consider some or all of the covenants as conditional (esp. the Mosaic covenant).[33]

In my view, however, the discussion cannot advance as long as we continue to use words such as "conditional" and "unconditional," which force us to oversimplify the issues. All of the Old Testament covenants we will discuss below have certain promissory features that are unconditional. These promissory features are more prominent in the Abrahamic and Davidic covenants and less so in the Mosaic covenant, which is largely defined by stipulations required for continuance of the covenant. Moreover, all of these covenants are conditioned on stipulations, whether explicitly stated or not. Thus for 2 Samuel 7, it is incorrect to assume that because there are no conditions mentioned, it must be an unconditional covenant. Later biblical references make it painfully clear that continued succession of Davidic kings was contingent upon obedience (esp., as we said, in the books of Kings).[34]

More importantly, this argument can be turned around and viewed from a canonical or metanarrative perspective. Many scholars from a compatibilist position assume the text is unconditional until proven otherwise (as in "guilty until proven innocent"). In other words, conditions would need to be specifically stated in order to make the covenant conditional. But such an approach is foreign to ancient Israelite perceptions of their monarchy. Nothing in 2 Samuel 7 (or Ps. 89) implies that the king is somehow exempt from the stipulations of the Mosaic covenant. Indeed, any such concept would be

---

33. For more on these distinctions, see Scott R. Burson and Jerry L. Walls, *C. S. Lewis and Francis Schaeffer: Lessons for a New Century from the Most Influential Apologists of Our Time* (Downers Grove, Ill.: InterVarsity Press, 1998), 66–69.

34. It is also helpful to define *covenant* simply as "a formal agreement involving two or more parties," while at the same time acknowledging they are always bilateral, either symmetrical or asymmetrical. So certain covenants emphasize the obligation of one party more than the other. Some stress the promises of the more powerful party, while others the responsibilities and commitments of the weaker party. The Davidic covenant is asymmetrical, meaning it highlights the promises of the stronger party. Conversely, the Mosaic covenant highlights the commitments of the weaker party. But both contain an implicit mutuality, as all such covenants do. See Gary N. Knoppers, "Ancient Near Eastern Royal Grants and the Davidic Covenant: A Parallel?" *JAOS* 116 (1996): 670–97, esp. 696.

anathema to ancient Israelites. On the contrary, the reverse should be assumed: David and his descendants are all committed to keep the Mosaic covenant as part of their responsibility as kings, and certainly as a citizen of Israel. In this way, the Davidic covenant is built on the earlier covenants and assumes their continuing validity (much as the New Testament is built on the Old Testament and assumes its lasting value).[35]

So as to the question why this covenant is so different, we must look to progressive revelation for the answer. The covenants of God first with Abraham and then with Moses comprised a program of revelation bound to the people of Israel.[36] With the Davidic covenant, God has now committed himself to the line of David and to the royal family. But I believe the Bible assumes the Mosaic covenant, with its stipulations and conditions, is just as pertinent for the royal family as for anyone else. Sinai has not been superseded, merely complemented. "There is no text in the Hebrew Bible that holds that the Davidic *replaces* the Sinaitic. But within the national covenant lies another, restricted to one family, the royal house of David."[37] The Davidic covenant is therefore different because the situation in which God has revealed himself is different. In his grace God condescends to our needs and specific circumstances.

(3) All of this naturally leads to a third question raised by the Davidic covenant: What is the nature of the specific relationship between the Davidic covenant and other covenants in the Old Testament? In describing how Christians have answered this question, we may consider a spectrum with continuity on one extreme and discontinuity on the other. Many positions have been taken at the extremes, and some have attempted to compromise somewhere toward the center.[38]

---

35. Note that God's *eternal* promise ("forever") to Eli's priestly family was also conditioned on their character. The Lord withdraws his favor with the pregnant phrase (1 Sam. 2:30): "Those who honor me I will honor, but those who despise me will be disdained."

36. On the essentially revelatory nature of the covenants, see John H. Walton, *Covenant: God's Purpose, God's Plan* (Grand Rapids: Zondervan, 1994), 24–46 and throughout.

37. Levenson, *Sinai and Zion*, 99, and generally 187–217.

38. So-called "covenant theologians" assume an organically unified character of the biblical covenants (O. Palmer Robertson, *The Christ of the Covenants* [Phillipsburg, N.J.: Presbyterian & Reformed, 1980], 28). By contrast, classic dispensationalism assumes a number of distinct dispensations (often seven), each governed by its own covenant (Robert L. Saucy, *The Case for Progressive Dispensationalism: The Interface Between Dispensational and Non-Dispensational Theology* [Grand Rapids: Zondervan, 1993], 24–27). John H. Walton has taken something of a mediating position in his provocative book, *Covenant*, 47–62, 179–80. Also for some of what follows, consult Dyrness, *Themes in Old Testament Theology*, 113–26; Christopher J. H. Wright, *Knowing Jesus Through the Old Testament* (Downers Grove, Ill.: InterVarsity Press, 1992), 77–102.

(a) The Bible's first occurrence of the word "covenant" describes God's commitment to Noah (Gen. 6:18; 9:1–17).[39] The essence of Noah's covenant was a solemn promise from God first to deliver Noah and his family from the Flood and then to refrain from such devastating floods in the future. The latter promise was marked for all time by the rainbow, which becomes a "sign" of the covenant. As the first covenant of the Bible, Noah's is universal in scope. It is not limited to Noah and his family but extends to all creation. In this sense, the covenant of Noah establishes God's program of general revelation for all humankind and provides a context for the other covenants of the Old Testament, which will introduce more specific, special revelation.[40]

(b) The next covenant is that established between God and Abraham (Gen. 15 and 17). The covenant proper was preceded by the call of Abraham to leave his homeland and journey to an unknown land (Gen. 12:1–3; see Heb. 11:8–19).[41] God comforted Abraham with promises of descendants and habitable land and assured him he would protect him and make him an instrument for blessing the world.[42] After Abram (his original name)

---

39. It is often asserted that God entered into a covenant with Adam and Eve, variously called a covenant of creation or the Edenic covenant. Though the term "covenant" does not occur in the opening chapters of Genesis, these scholars argue the elements of a covenant (as we come to know them later in the Bible) are present, primarily referring to the promise of eternal life and marked by the blessing, "Be fruitful and increase in number" (Gen. 1:28). But this is a theological construction imposed on the biblical text, often in order to support a preconceived notion of "dispensations." Ironically, the same mistake was made by Julius Wellhausen for very different reasons (*Prolegomena to the History of Ancient Israel* [Gloucester, Mass.: Peter Smith, 1983], 338–39; repr. of *Prolegomena to the History of Ancient Israel*, trans. J. Sutherland Black and Allan Enzies [Edinburgh: Adam & Charles Black, 1885]; trans. of *Prolegomena zur Geschichte Israels* [2d ed.: Berlin: G. Reimer, 1883]). See the critique of Frank Moore Cross (*Canaanite Myth and Hebrew Epic*, 295–96).

40. This first covenant also establishes the specific idioms and linguistic formulae characteristic of the other covenants in the Pentateuch. Frank Moore Cross posits a convincing pattern in which the Pentateuch has been intentionally organized by such rubrics, including most importantly a system of 3 covenants (those of Noah, Abraham, and Moses) standing as transition markers between four ages (*Canaanite Myth and Hebrew Epic*, 293–300).

41. Bill T. Arnold, *Encountering the Book of Genesis*, 91–98.

42. The promissory element connects the Abrahamic and Davidic covenants, as emphasized esp. by Robert P. Gordon (*I and II Samuel*, 235–42). Moshe Weinfeld identified the Abrahamic and Davidic covenants as "promissory" covenants based on ancient Near Eastern royal grants, as opposed to the "obligatory" Mosaic covenant based on political treaties. The former obligated the master to the servant, while the latter was an obligation of the servant (vassal) to the master. Moshe Weinfeld, "The Covenant of Grant in the Old Testament and in the Ancient Near East," *JAOS* 90 (1970): 184–203. It is better to view all the biblical covenants as asymmetrical and to take the Abrahamic and Davidic as covenants stressing the promises of the powerful party (God), while the Mosaic stresses the responsibilities of the weaker party (Israel). See Knoppers, "Ancient Near Eastern Royal Grants" 696.

responded by obeying this call, God establishes a covenant with him. Genesis 15 confirms the promises and records a solemn ritual through which "the LORD made a covenant with Abram" (15:18).

In Genesis 17:1–22, the term covenant (*bᵉrit*) occurs thirteen times. Here God changes Abram's name to Abraham and gives circumcision as the sign of the covenant (as the rainbow had been the identifying marker of Noah's covenant).[43] Both of these covenants contained promissory elements that sound unconditional: God will not again flood the earth, and he will make Abraham exceedingly fruitful, which is three times labeled "an everlasting covenant" (Gen. 17:7, 13, 19). But unlike the earlier universal covenant, Abraham's relationship with God clearly contains stipulations ("walk before me and be blameless," 17:1; see also 17:9–14).

(c) Abraham's covenant "was at once deeper and narrower" than Noah's, meaning more was revealed to fewer.[44] The universal scope was replaced with the individual concerns of a wandering nomad. But the ancestral covenant of Genesis 12–50 also foreshadows and prepares for the third covenant mentioned in the Bible, the Mosaic covenant, where the scope becomes national (Exodus–Deuteronomy). While the progression from Noah to Abraham was a narrowing process, that from Abraham to Moses is a broadening one. The principles of the ancestral family covenant are now applied to the nation Israel. These covenants (ancestral and Sinaitic) are more organically bound together than either was to the universal covenant of Noah (Ex. 2:24; 3:6, 15).

The Mosaic covenant is more clearly conditioned on elaborate stipulations.[45] This relationship between Yahweh and Israel is a confirmation and, in a sense, a fulfillment of the promises to Abraham. Having redeemed Israel from slavery, God reveals more of his nature to them, establishes a unique relationship with them, and promises to fulfill the land promise (Ex. 6:6–8). In addition, God defines Israel's essential nature as a missionary nation, since they are called to become a priestly kingdom serving as mediators between God and the nations, thereby fulfilling the final promise to Abraham (Gen. 12:2–3). The Mosaic covenant's final program of curses and blessings emphasizes the conditions for perpetuating their relationship with God (Deut. 27–28).

---

43. Abram, "father is exalted" became Abraham, "father of a multitude," though we may also be dealing here with a dialectical variant of an older name.

44. Cross, *Canaanite Myth and Hebrew Epic*, 296.

45. The use of a secular international treaty form to express the covenant only heightens the conditionality of the covenant, since the laws were placed where the treaties have requirements for the vassal nation.

(d) Finally we return then to the Davidic covenant of 2 Samuel 7. Again we see a narrowing from the national covenant of Moses to the royal family. God condescends again to Israel, this time in light of the new sociopolitical context of monarchy. In the Mosaic covenant, Yahweh was portrayed as the sovereign suzerain, the overlord of the vassal nation, Israel. Now with the reality of a king, royal court, and standing army, God deepens and furthers his promises to Abraham and confirmed by the Mosaic covenant. Only this time the concept of a kingdom is dominant, implying that God will guarantee the continuance of the new kingdom by assuming responsibility for it. "God seems to say that he will take David's throne for himself and make it his own to ensure its permanence (2 Sam. 7:16)."[46]

Some scholars make a sharp contrast between the Davidic and Mosaic covenants. The well-known historian of the Old Testament period, John Bright, is often cited in this regard, but there are many other examples.[47] Few have driven a wedge between David and Moses as sharply as David Jobling. He refers to the Davidic covenant as a new, everlasting, unconditional covenant in contrast to the older, conditional Mosaic covenant. The older Mosaic covenant had been in operation through the extended "book of Judges," by which Jobling means Judges plus 1 Samuel 1–12. Because this chapter establishes what he considers to be a different kind of covenant, Jobling refers to 1 Samuel 13–2 Samuel 7 as "The Book of the Everlasting Covenant."[48]

But this approach merely repeats the mistake of many Israelites living at the time of Jeremiah—namely, that of allowing one covenant to supersede another.[49] If we elevate the promises to David over the stipulations of Moses, we have a skewed understanding of how God sought to relate to the Israelites. We need to learn to read the idiosyncratic features of each covenant in light of the new situation each addresses. From prehistoric flood plains to ancestral individuals, from national legislation to royal charters, God sought to reveal himself to Israel and through that revelation to establish relationship. We must read the differences in the covenants in light of the historical developments, all the while recognizing a basic organic unity to the program of

---

46. Dyrness, *Themes in Old Testament Theology*, 121.

47. Bright believed the Davidic covenant pushed the Mosaic covenant into the background, setting up a tension between the two for much of the rest of the Old Testament. Bright, *History of Israel*, 227.

48. Jobling, *1 Samuel*, 78–79.

49. Jeremiah fought against a Zion theology that elevated David over Moses, or Zion over Sinai. See Walter Brueggemann, *To Pluck Up, To Tear Down: A Commentary on the Book of Jeremiah 1–25* (ITC; Grand Rapids: Eerdmans, 1988), 5–7. For a more nuanced explanation of the problems Jeremiah addressed, see Levenson, *Sinai and Zion*, 165–69.

revelation God has established. Part of our problem (and one that can stand in the way of building a bridge from this text to our culture) is a misconception of "covenant" as an abstract, changeless idea. But this brief survey has demonstrated that the concept has assumed forms that are at one and the same moment different but similar.

In sum, the Bible seems to relate the Davidic covenant to others in the Old Testament in an organically unified way while recognizing their genuine differences, which are due largely to historical and functional reasons. These are differences of degree rather than of kind. As one scholar has put it, "the voice of Sinai is heard on Zion," so that David depends on, builds on, and complements Moses and Abraham.[50] This scholar adds: "The traditions correct each other. Each is fulfilled only in the presence of the other. The whole is greater than the sum of its parts."[51] I believe this is also a helpful way to relate Old and New Testaments.

(4) One final question remains as part of our bridge-building exercise: How does this Davidic covenant relate to the New Testament? Verse 14a contains an especially important promise in this regard, when Yahweh says of David's offspring: "I will be his father, and he will be my son." Though opinions differ, this expression, which is parallel to the covenant phrase "I will be your God" (Gen. 17:7; Ex. 6:7, etc.), denotes adoption rather than begetting.[52] Henceforth, Israelite kings (or, more specifically, Judahite kings) will be thought of as sons of Yahweh (Ps. 2:7; 89:26). For Christian readers, God's father-son relationship with the Son of David reverberates throughout the gospel story, beginning with the baptism of Jesus (Matt. 3:17).[53] This text is clearly programmatic for New Testament authors when defining Jesus as the Son of David (or, relying on 2 Sam. 7:14a, as the Son of God, see Heb. 1:5).

The New Testament's messianic use of our text is possible not simply because of the predictive, forward-looking nature of the chapter, but also because of the way other Old Testament texts build on the themes here[54] and

---

50. The quote is from Levenson, *Sinai and Zion*, 207; see de Vaux, "King of Israel," 159.

51. Levenson, *Sinai and Zion*, 209. In general I find Levenson's treatment extremely helpful (see especially "The Manifold Relationships Between Sinai and Zion," 185–217), though his assertion that the Davidic covenant displaced the Sinaitic in the New Testament is overstated due largely to a misreading of Paul's statements concerning the law (216).

52. Whatever vestigial links this concept may have had in Canaanite divine kingship, it functions here as the language of adoption. See Cross, *Canaanite Myth and Hebrew Epic*, 257–58; McCarter, *II Samuel*, 207; Gordon, *1 and 2 Samuel*, 76.

53. In the third Gospel, the connection is made by Gabriel even before Jesus is born (Luke 1:30–35). Joel B. Green, *Beginning with Jesus: Christ in Scripture, the Church, and Discipleship* (Nashville: Cokesbury and Bristol House, 2000), 23–24.

54. See, e.g., Ps. 89; Jer. 23:5–8; Ezek. 37:21–23; Hag. 2:21–22; Zech. 3:8–10; 12:10–13:1.

because of the tradition of messianic understanding of 2 Samuel 7 in Second Temple Judaism.[55] Indeed, building on the powerful Jerusalem/Zion concepts of the previous chapters, 2 Samuel 7 constitutes an "ideological summit" for the Old Testament as a whole.[56]

To continue the summit metaphor, from this peak we are able to look back and reflect on great themes leading up to this height while at the same time turning to look forward to the culmination of these promises. When future Davidic kings failed to serve Yahweh as David had done, the conviction grew in ancient Israel that another Son of David could be expected who would deliver the nation (Isa. 11:1; Mic. 5:2). "We shall not be exaggerating the importance of the Nathan oracle, therefore, if we see it as the matrix of biblical messianism."[57]

THIS TEXT SPEAKS as powerfully to our contemporary world as it did in its ancient Israelite context. But as we have seen in the Bridging Contexts section, the significance of the passage is multifaceted, and in order to explore all the possible applications we will have to consider a number of features of its message.

The nature of evangelical faith. This text illustrates through the life of David once again the nature of evangelical faith.[58] By this I mean the way the narrative has blended into its portrayal of David a desire to serve and please God with a complete reliance on God's revealed word. As elsewhere in the extended narrative (1 Sam. 16–2 Sam. 8), this text shows David to be a paragon of virtue and a model of faith. In this text as elsewhere, he is in close relationship with the people and institutions that become God's means of communication and direction in his life. He listens to Nathan and quickly

---

55. 4 Ezra 12:31–32; *Psalms of Solomon* 17–18; 1QM 11:1–18; 4QFlor 1:11–14; 4QTest 9–13. For more on the eschatological interpretation of 4QFlorilegium, see Schniedewind, *Society and Promise*, 158–60.

56. Gordon, *I and II Samuel*, 235.

57. Ibid., 236. For the importance of 2 Sam. 7 in establishing the book's tension between promises and unfulfilled reality, thereby creating a messianic expectation, see Satterthwaite, "David in the Books of Samuel," 52–56, 64–65. On this chapter's messianic thrust in light of the structure of the books of Samuel, see Childs, *Introduction to the Old Testament*, 276–77.

58. Or, as Brueggemann says, this "utterance is the root of evangelical faith in the Bible: that is, faith that relies on the free promise of the gospel" (Brueggemann, *First and Second Samuel*, 257). Though I find Brueggemann's bifurcation of Davidic and Mosaic promises problematic, his discussion on this point is, as always, stimulating.

acquiesces to the prophetic word. When he feels overwhelmed by God's response, he enters in before the ark of the covenant and prays.

Even David's prayer is a model of yielding to God while at the same time boldly imploring that God truly be God, keeping faithfully his promises. Likewise, present-day believers must avail themselves of every opportunity to receive the grace of God: church attendance, Bible study, prayer, involvement in missions and outreach, commitment to serve the poor, and so on. Just as David lived close to the established means of God's grace, so must today's believers learn to revel in the different ways in which God speaks today. The historian of the books of Samuel has offered David as an example for future kings through the narrative thus far. As such he functions as a model for all of us who worship the Son of David today.

Covenant. This chapter brings to the foreground the role and significance of the concept of covenant in our Christian faith. As we have seen, the scholarship on David's covenant is often preoccupied with the questions of conditionality or unconditionality and its relationship with the Mosaic covenant. These were important questions that we had to address before considering application. But if we limit our application strictly to these concerns, we will miss what I believe are the broader themes more central to the Davidic covenant as understood by the biblical authors. From the beginning of 2 Samuel 7, the historian has much more in view than simply the question of dynastic succession and David's legacy. The historical retrospection of Nathan's oracle summarizes the deliverance from Egypt and God's life with Israel since the Exodus (7:5–7), and then the oracle turns to Israel's future (7:8–16). The promises involve military victory and security in the land and construction of the temple, as well as the Davidic dynasty.

We saw in the Bridging Contexts section that the terms *conditional* and *unconditional* are inadequate for the discussion. The Davidic covenant clearly contains promissory features that are unconditional at the same time the covenant itself is dependent on the previous Mosaic covenant with its obvious conditionality.[59] The Israelite authors simply did not think in these categories (or, we should say, these categories were inadequate for their thinking).

Furthermore, the relationship of the Davidic covenant with the Mosaic (and others) is multifaceted and interdependent. The editors of biblical texts

---

59. The Chronicler's primary version (1 Chron. 17) of the Davidic covenant is more unconditionally stated than it is in 2 Sam. 7. But elsewhere, the Chronicler incorporates expressions of the covenant that are clearly conditioned on obedience (1 Chron. 22:12–13; 28:7–10; 2 Chron. 6:16–17; 7:17–18). See Knoppers, "David's Relation to Moses," 101–6, 115–18. This may be explained partly by his overarching purpose of comforting the exiles with assurances of Yahweh's continued blessing and enduring relationship with them.

linked them together irrevocably so that together they provide the skeletal frame for the Bible's salvation history and create a trajectory of such covenantal relationships for the future. Indeed as Christian readers, we accept the new covenant as the fulfillment, culmination, and extension of the Abrahamic-Mosaic-Davidic chain of covenants. The New Testament embraces Jesus as the heir to the Davidic promises and makes us heirs to the blessings and richness of all the covenants.

If, then, we limit our interpretation of 2 Samuel 7 to questions of Davidic succession, conditionality, or relationship to Moses, we miss the grand picture before us. The interrelated themes of the Davidic covenant include the long-awaited rest in the land, peace and security, the political stability provided by an eternal dynasty, and the construction of a permanent temple for Yahweh's great name. Moreover, by imbedding this text in the historical narrative of 2 Samuel, and especially coming immediately after the turning of Jebus into Zion, the city of David (5:1–6:23), the Davidic covenant interrelates with even more of Israel's broad themes: the resplendent Zion and the security of Jerusalem, the ark of the covenant with its *mysterium tremendum*, the sovereignty of Yahweh in holy war, and many other important theological themes.

All of these become part of our own rich heritage as believers in Jesus, the Son of David. Simply put, we too have a covenant with God. It is not different from, nor does it supersede, the Davidic, Mosaic, or Abrahamic covenants. Our *new* covenant is organically related as the same binding relationship, though made new by our different social and historical circumstances.

Yahweh's anointed one. This text gives clearer definition to our understanding of Yahweh's anointed one so crucial to our Christian faith. As we have seen, this text together with the preceding unit (5:1–6:23) gave shape to messianism in early Judaism and Christianity.[60] The previous unit established king and city and linked them together irrevocably. This text now establishes David's line as the only legitimate successor to that throne, which brings us again to one of the central questions addressed in the books of Samuel: Who will serve suitably as king of Israel? To this question we now have a new answer: *Only* a true son of David may serve as king.

In our reading from the perspective of the New Testament, we admit that David could not have fully understood the extent of that blessing. No matter how majestically he thought of God, David could not exhaust the breadth and depth of this promise. He only thought of building a temple.

---

60. For a helpful summary of the pitfalls of assuming a unified "Jewish expectation of a Messiah" in the first century, see Green, *Beginning with Jesus*, 20–26; Craig A. Evans, "Messianism," *Dictionary of New Testament Background*, ed. Craig A. Evans and Stanley E. Porter (Downers Grove, Ill.: InterVarsity Press, 2000), 698–707.

But God surprised him with blessings he could not imagine. God shows himself over and again to be the God who "is able to do immeasurably more than all we ask or imagine, according to his power that is at work within us" (Eph. 3:20). In other words, you and I, when reading the Old Testament in light of the New, now understand that the kingship envisioned is grander than David imagined and that the Son of David promised here is more majestic than David could have thought.

In this sense, we have the advantage of a chronological perception, which bears also the burden of faith. Like David, we may wish to do something for God, to contribute to his causes, to build something for him. But if that is not in God's timing or will, also like David, we must learn to acquiesce and be grateful.

So Jesus came announcing that the kingdom of David (i.e., the kingdom of God) had arrived (Matt. 4:17, 23; Mark 1:15). As the Son of David, Jesus fulfilled the Old Testament's yearnings for a king like David. But David's kingdom has also been transformed into a grand metaphorical design— again, far beyond anything David could have imagined. It is a kingdom of subjects who, like David himself, are redeemed sinners submitting and acquiescing to God's decrees. It is the kingdom of David because it fulfills all the Davidic grandeur.

Yet this claim also evokes division (Matt. 12:30; Luke 11:23): "He who is not with me is against me, and he who does not gather with me scatters." The royal decree of this king is "an invitation to a kingdom-spirituality, invoking the power of the king to liberate those held in Satan's bondage."[61] Our kingdom task is clear: Living a life of submission to this king, this Son of David, is a life in covenant with God, a life marked with *ḥesed*-love and marked also with commitment to his causes. It means taking up his causes and planting the flag of his kingdom in territory currently occupied by contesting claimants.

> You commit yourself to the work of healing and liberation, both actual and symbolic. You commit yourself to freeing slaves, to loosening the bonds of debt, to bringing good news to the poor. And you commit yourself to doing those things, not as a grand social action which you will implement by your own energy and ingenuity, but in the power, and with the weapons, of the kingdom of God: by prayer and fasting, by truth and righteousness, by the gospel of peace, by faith, by salvation, by the word of God.[62]

---

61. N. T. Wright, *The Way of the Lord: Christian Pilgrimage Today* (Grand Rapids: Eerdmans, 1999), 53.

62. Ibid., 53–54.

---

2 Samuel 8:1–18

IN THE COURSE OF TIME, David defeated the Philistines and subdued them, and he took Metheg Ammah from the control of the Philistines.

²David also defeated the Moabites. He made them lie down on the ground and measured them off with a length of cord. Every two lengths of them were put to death, and the third length was allowed to live. So the Moabites became subject to David and brought tribute.

³Moreover, David fought Hadadezer son of Rehob, king of Zobah, when he went to restore his control along the Euphrates River. ⁴David captured a thousand of his chariots, seven thousand charioteers and twenty thousand foot soldiers. He hamstrung all but a hundred of the chariot horses.

⁵When the Arameans of Damascus came to help Hadadezer king of Zobah, David struck down twenty-two thousand of them. ⁶He put garrisons in the Aramean kingdom of Damascus, and the Arameans became subject to him and brought tribute. The LORD gave David victory wherever he went.

⁷David took the gold shields that belonged to the officers of Hadadezer and brought them to Jerusalem. ⁸From Tebah and Berothai, towns that belonged to Hadadezer, King David took a great quantity of bronze.

⁹When Tou king of Hamath heard that David had defeated the entire army of Hadadezer, ¹⁰he sent his son Joram to King David to greet him and congratulate him on his victory in battle over Hadadezer, who had been at war with Tou. Joram brought with him articles of silver and gold and bronze.

¹¹King David dedicated these articles to the LORD, as he had done with the silver and gold from all the nations he had subdued: ¹²Edom and Moab, the Ammonites and the Philistines, and Amalek. He also dedicated the plunder taken from Hadadezer son of Rehob, king of Zobah.

¹³And David became famous after he returned from striking down eighteen thousand Edomites in the Valley of Salt.

¹⁴He put garrisons throughout Edom, and all the Edomites became subject to David. The LORD gave David victory wherever he went.

[15]David reigned over all Israel, doing what was just and right for all his people. [16]Joab son of Zeruiah was over the army; Jehoshaphat son of Ahilud was recorder; [17]Zadok son of Ahitub and Ahimelech son of Abiathar were priests; Seraiah was secretary; [18]Benaiah son of Jehoiada was over the Kerethites and Pelethites; and David's sons were royal advisers.

AFTER THE SPEECHES that comprised the previous chapter, our narrator returns to the story. In staccato-like repetition, chapter 8 narrates David's military successes in the Transjordan and in the north (even the Philistines in the southwestern plain appear again briefly, 8:1, 12). This text is a "catalogue of victories" organized thematically rather than chronologically.[1]

The historian who compiled 2 Samuel was working from two main sources relating to David: the history of David's rise (1 Sam. 16:1–2 Sam. 5:10) and the court history (2 Sam. 9–1 Kings 2).[2] As we have seen, the materials included since 5:10 have linked together several themes of particular interest to our historian: the role of Jerusalem as the city of David, the ark of the covenant, Yahweh's temple, and the permanence of David's reign. These materials since 5:10 have been used effectively to narrate further David's glorious rule.

This text appears to have been an independent historical source that the narrator has adapted to round off the story of David's rise before turning to the court history (beginning in ch. 9). One scholar has even identified the underlying source (convincingly, I believe) as an Israelite "display inscription," a genre of which we have numerous examples from the ancient Near East, particularly from Assyria (esp. Tiglath-Pileser).[3] Such inscriptions typically listed victories of the reigning monarch, and did so topically or geographically rather than chronologically. We have every reason to believe the original was written early in David's reign and accurately reflects the territorial gains David made in the Transjordan and more modest gains in the north.[4]

---

1. McCarter, *II Samuel*, 251–52. On the achronological, thematic details, see Baruch Halpern, "The Construction of the Davidic State: An Exercise in Historiography," in *The Origins of the Ancient Israelite States*, ed. V. Fritz and P. R. Davies (JSOTSup 228; Sheffield: Sheffield Academic Press, 1996), 54–55.

2. See the introduction and the critical commentaries in the bibliography for details.

3. For what follows, see Halpern, "Construction of the Davidic State," 44–75.

4. Halpern even speculates that the specific display inscription this chapter is based on was referred to in the chapter itself (Halpern, "Construction of the Davidic State," 70). This

Like the display inscriptions of the ancient Near East, this chapter is remarkably reserved in its explicit claims for David's reign, yet grandiose in its implications.[5] But it is the implications that are so significant. Halpern further describes the writing techniques used by the authors of 2 Samuel or its sources:

> They suggested, implied, insinuated that David's achievements were a great deal more extensive than in reality they were. But they did not openly prevaricate, on this subject at least. Their method was a good deal more subtle than outright forgery, and very much at home in the historiographic traditions of the chanceries of the ancient Near East.[6]

Thus, through subtle adaptation of the underlying source, our narrator illustrates how David's reign has fulfilled the promises and purposes of Yahweh. As a capstone to David's great reign,[7] this text stands together with the capture of Jerusalem (ch. 6) and the dynastic promise (ch. 7) to produce a portrait of an Israelite kingdom that captures the imagination of subsequent generations. As such, our text makes a significant contribution, albeit in a very different way, to the biblical understanding of David as the ideal king.

Catalogue of Defeated Nations (8:1–6)

THE OPENING PHRASE (NIV "In the course of time") is an idiom used frequently as a transition marker in 2 Samuel (see comment on 2:1; see also 10:1; 13:1; 15:1; 21:18). It is a distinctive temporal introduction, which at one and the same time separates and links this chapter with what has gone before.[8] After the important speeches of David's covenantal promise in chapter 7, this text again picks up the refrain of David's military successes as a demonstration that those promises are in fact becoming a reality.

As we have seen, the original source known as "The History of David's Rise" had a recurring phrase: Yahweh was with David.[9] The overarching theological conviction of the narrative was that Yahweh's presence with David

---

interpretation assumes a translation of v. 3 very different from the NIV: "David also struck down King Hadadezer son of Rehob of Zobah, as he went to *restore his monument* at the river Euphrates" (NRSV; cf. NEB, NJPS, and McCarter, *II Samuel*, 247–48). This aspect of Halpern's theory remains speculative, but the overall connection with display inscriptions is impressive and supports his conclusion that much of the biblical material relating to the united monarchy comes from roughly contemporary sources.

5. Halpern, "Construction of the Davidic State," 71.

6. Ibid.

7. Ibid., 54.

8. Jan P. Fokkelman, *Narrative Art and Poetry in the Books of Samuel*, 3:257.

9. See 1 Sam. 16:18; 18:12, 14, 28; 2 Sam. 3:1; 5:10; cf. 2 Sam. 7:3, 9.

caused him to succeed where Saul failed and verified David's legitimacy as the true anointed one. Now we have another recurring phrase, making the same point in a more specific manner (8:6, 14): "The LORD gave David victory wherever he went." This phrase serves not only as the theme of the chapter but also as the literary marker for our three units (standing as it does at each transition, 8:1–6, 7–14, 15–18).

This recurring phrase refers in 8:1–6 to military victory.[10] The Philistines have been Israel's perennial enemy (see 1 Sam. 14:52; 19:8; 23:1–5; 31:1).[11] After the collapse of the Egyptian Empire in Syria-Palestine at the close of the Late Bronze Age (around 1200 B.C.), the Philistines inhabited the southwest coastal plains while the Israelites were in the central hills. They often fought each other to a standstill, but the Philistines began to dominate Israel and occupied much of the Israelite countryside because of their monopoly on iron weaponry (1 Sam. 13:19–21). Saul's failure as king may be defined in human, historical terms as his failure to drive the Philistines from Israelite territory. His death and mutilation at the hands of the Philistines was a stunning indictment on his impotency as king (1 Sam. 31).

But the Philistines are unable to continue encroaching on Israelite territory once David is anointed king over a unified Israel. As we have seen, shortly after his coronation, David drove the Philistines from Judah's heartland and confined them to the coastal plains (5:17–25). The victory mentioned here probably indicates that he reclaims disputed territory and almost completely subjugates them (8:1).[12]

The rest of the paragraph lists David's victories over enemies in the Transjordan (Moab) and the north (the Arameans of Zobah and Damascus). His cruel treatment of Moabite prisoners of war is surprising in light of his Moabite ancestry and the fact that the Moabites had helped his parents during their enforced exile (Ruth 4:21–22; 1 Sam. 22:3–4). Attempts to explain the execution of two-thirds of the captives as merciful seem forced, though there may have been an economic basis for his actions that benefited Israel.[13]

---

10. Our text is marked by recurring verbs denoting military action. See Youngblood, "1, 2 Samuel," 901–2.

11. Howard, "Philistines," 231–50.

12. The NIV's "Metheg Ammah" in 8:1 is controversial, since this expression is not known elsewhere as a place name. Several commentators assume it is an idiom indicating truce or possibly surrender (Yoshitaka Kobayashi, "Methegh-Ammah," ABD, 4:800). Others assume it indicates that David exercises supremacy over the Philistines (Anderson, 2 Samuel, 131; Fokkelman, Narrative Art and Poetry in the Books of Samuel, 3:257).

13. Bergen, 1, 2 Samuel, 347; Evans, 1 and 2 Samuel, 172. Similarly, David's motivation for hamstringing the enemy's horses is contested but may have had military roots. See Anderson, 2 Samuel, 132–33.

As the opening temporal clause of the paragraph ties chapters 7 and 8 together, the "taut series of military success reports in ch. 8 is the fulfilment of the proleptic or promising clauses" of chapter 7.[14] Yahweh had given David "rest" from his enemies in the past (7:1), and in his oracle through Nathan the prophet, Yahweh reassured David he would give "rest from all your enemies" (7:11). With the final subjugation of the Philistines to the southwest, the Transjordanian nations to the east, and Arameans to the north, this chapter illustrates Yahweh's great faithfulness to David. The covenantal promises of chapter 7 are becoming a reality.

David Collects the Spoils of War (8:7–14)

THE RECURRING PHRASE that gives structure to chapter 8 ("the LORD gave victory," vv. 6 and 14) referred to military victory in 8:1–6. Here it relates to collections of the spoils of war. The narrative's literary structure makes 8:7–12 the "chapter's centre of gravity" and brings into focus what David does with the booty in Jerusalem.[15] His response to Yahweh's victory becomes the central theme in the narrative, in that David consistently "dedicated" (*hiqdîš*, v. 11 ["consecrated, sanctified"]) the captured articles to Yahweh. Once again in contrast to Saul, we learn who may suitably serve as Israel's king (cf. 1 Sam. 15:1–31). When God blesses, the true anointed one gives thanks and obeys.

The inclusion of "Amalek" in 8:12 may be another subtle reminder that David is the legitimate king. We have encountered the Amalekites before in 1–2 Samuel (see comments on 1 Sam. 30:1–6). As ruthless enemies of Israel since the Exodus, Yahweh promised to destroy them (Ex. 17:14; see Deut. 25:17–19). He intended to use the monarch of Israel to fulfill this promise, and Saul's early victories over the Amalekites served to validate his own legitimacy (1 Sam. 14:48). But when Saul failed to execute the holy-war ban against Amalek, Samuel exposed his failure as spiritual and announced Yahweh's rejection of Saul as Israel's legitimate king (15:10–31). By contrast, David executes God's judgment against the Amalekites (here and 1 Sam. 30:7–25) and thus proves himself to be the legitimate king of Israel.

Several scholars have studied David's realm from the perspective of modern political science dealing with imperial systems (see the Original Meaning section for 5:1–5). In this view, the five distinct levels of political interrelationships are: (1) tribal kingdom, (2) national kingdom, (3) consolidated

---

14. Fokkelman, *Narrative Art and Poetry in the Books of Samuel*, 3:257.
15. Ibid., 255.

territorial state, (4) multinational state, and (5) empire.[16] Thus far in 2 Samuel, the historian has described the transformation of Jerusalem into a new capital city, the construction of a royal palace, the expulsion of the Philistines from Judah's heartland, and union between Judah in the south and Israel in the north. These advances have moved the fledgling nation through the first three stages of sociopolitical development.

This text now claims that David has reached a point where he can turn his attention to Israel's perennial foes to the east and south (Edom, Moab, and Ammon), which he must have subdued sequentially in a sort of "domino theory."[17] In the schema of modern political scientists, this moves Israel into the "multinational state" stage of development (the fourth level). Moreover, the Arameans of Zobah in the north have achieved a similar status as a "great power," so that David's victories over them moves Israel into the final, true "empire" stage of state formation. By means of this analysis, one can conclude that David's expansion of Israel "dwarfed every previous political entity established in the Palestinian sphere, even exceeding the extent of the Egyptian province in the second millennium B.C."[18]

David's Officials (8:15–18)

WITH THIS LIST of royal officials, the historian has taken us a step further in understanding the new Israelite institution of monarchy. The organization of the state under the new institution is considerably different from the tribal organization operative at the beginning of 1 Samuel under the able leadership of the prophet Samuel. The previous social stratification based on kinship has given way to a structure based more on skill and ability. So in this list of royal officers, a series of functional roles (generals, recorders, priests, secretaries, and advisers) has replaced the elders of Israel and Judah as the power structure.[19]

The new monarchy under David is different from the older tribal confederation in one other way. In a summarizing sentence, the narrator assesses David's monarchy (8:15): "David reigned over all Israel, doing what was just

---

16. Malamat, "Political Look," 191–97. For a slightly more nuanced approach based on a wide array of sociological factors, see Schäfer-Lichtenberger, "Sociological and Biblical Views," 78–105, esp. 90–105.

17. Malamat, "Political Look," 195.

18. Ibid., 196.

19. Abraham Malamat, "Organs of Statecraft in the Israelite Monarchy," *BA* 27 (1965): 34–65. Differences in this list compared to the one in 2 Sam. 20:23–26 may insinuate a continued role for kinship-based organization for local administration outside the capital early in David's reign. But this changed after the north's attempt to secede from David's political union (ch. 20). See Schäfer-Lichtenberger, "Sociological and Biblical Views," 102–3.

and right for all his people." The NIV may be a bit misleading here if we miss the concept of David serving as administrator of justice and equity for Israel. Whether or not David actually "took over the supreme office of judge,"[20] he has certainly centralized the judicial and administrative systems, perhaps for the first time in Israel. In this sense, he has not only provided "rest" for Israel, but he has reconfigured the internal government as well, providing "all his people" an equitable security.

This is, of course, the picture the narrator wants us to see. David is the embodiment of Yahweh's rule on earth. He is Yahweh's chosen, anointed one, who rules as Yahweh himself wants his people to be governed. David becomes the example for all future kings—the standard by which they will be judged. But as we will see in the rest of 2 Samuel, this is not the whole story.

Bridging Contexts

THIS LITTLE CHAPTER contains greater theological import than we might think on a surface reading. In the context of the extended narrative of 2 Samuel, it plays an illuminating role. We have witnessed much. David has become king, first of Judah, then of all Israel. He has established Jerusalem as a new capital for the united kingdom, has brought the ark of the covenant into the city with great pomp and ceremony and has been blessed by Yahweh's promise to keep his dynasty in perpetuity. As readers we are prepared to learn of David's great success as Israel's ideal king, and indeed the text before us serves as a capstone of the narrative of David's royal career.[21] The force of the narrative prepares for more successes, which makes David's reversals in the court history more shocking. But that is getting ahead of the story.

The thrust and function of the text before us is clear exegetically, thanks to the narrator's transparent use of the recurring theme: "The LORD gave David victory wherever he went" (8:6, 14). As we have seen above, the chapter is most likely based on a source produced early in David's reign, and its claims are historically reasonable. I suspect the historian has supplemented the earlier source by adding this catchphrase at key junctures to conveniently divide the materials and make the point unequivocally: God himself, not King David, is the Savior of Israel.

Stumbling blocks. Though the message of the text is clear exegetically, there are at least three stumbling blocks that may make application difficult for present-day believers. The first of these is a cultural difficulty because of

20. Hertzberg, *I and II Samuel*, 293.
21. Halpern, "Construction of the Davidic State," 54.

the enormous gulf separating modern believers from ancient Israelite culture, while the others are more subtle theological difficulties.

(1) We cannot help but notice the militaristic nature of chapter 8. If it were not for the recurring theme of verses 6 and 14 and the mention that David consecrated the war loot to Yahweh (v. 11), we might conclude that a strictly secular military report has been mistakenly included in the Bible. Not only so, but David's treatment of prisoners of war and captured war horses would by today's standards make him guilty of war crimes, and rightly so. Many contemporary readers have difficulty reading this text and making the application intended.

But herein lies part of the problem. Our interpretive mistake lies in our attempt to evaluate David's treatment of prisoners and animals *by today's standards*. David did not live in a time remotely similar to today's Western culture, and his actions in warfare should not be judged by current mores.[22] Perhaps more importantly, the true significance of his actions is revealed by the text itself, which the recurring theme in verses 6 and 14 emphasizes. Wherever David went, he was successful. Whether he was fighting the Philistines, Moabites, Arameans, and so on, or taking riches from Israel's enemies, God was with David so powerfully that he always enjoyed victory. The sometimes brutal excesses that make this text difficult for present-day Christian readers are the same features that for the original readers help emphasize the king's God-given successes. David was so totally successful that he was unencumbered in his treatment of war prisoners and extravagant in his distribution of his victims' plunder. This is an anointed king who cuts and slices through God's enemies without restraint because God is powerful through him.

(2) The second stumbling block is the degree of subtlety used in the extended narrative, which links this text with the immediately preceding chapter. Chapter 7 recorded the covenant God established with David and its many promised blessings. While chapter 8 solidifies the kingdom of God firmly in David's hands, it appears also to fulfill (partially) the promises of God to David recorded in chapter 7.

At the beginning of that unit, God had granted rest from Israel's enemies so that David enjoyed a modicum of peace in Jerusalem (7:1). The glorious promises of chapter 7 included a much broader and all-encompassing picture, however. As part of a package of promises (continued divine presence, making David's name great, and establishing his dynasty forever), God also promised to give a more complete and lasting "rest" from all Israel's enemies

---

22. On a Christian response to war in general, see the Contemporary Significance section of 1 Sam. 4:1b–11.

(7:11). By placing our text directly after chapter 7, the historian illustrates that Yahweh fulfills his covenant promises to David, beginning immediately with spectacular military successes and unprecedented war booty.

By implication, this text also illustrates the truth of the broader program of divine blessing given in chapter 7. If the promise of rest is fulfilled so quickly and definitively, so must also the other promises of chapter 7 be believed, even if their fulfillment is for the future. David's name *will* become great, God *will* be with him wherever he goes, and in fact, David's dynasty *will* be established forever. By weaving chapters 7 and 8 together carefully, the historian has given the reader reason to pause and celebrate the covenant-making and promise-keeping God. But if we fail to read the chapters together, we will miss the connections.

(3) The third stumbling block is the way some present-day Christians (especially in North America) hear the refrain so central to a balanced reading of the chapter: "The LORD gave David victory wherever he went." The difficulty has to do not so much with the distance between that day and our own as with the hollowness of so-called "success theology" rampant among parts of the church today. Some readers take the chapter and its theme verse out of context and assume it means God will give victory to his children no matter what the contravening and accompanying circumstances. Does this text teach that King David will always and only enjoy success?

Once again, in order to avoid this stumbling block we must remember the extended narrative and carefully read the text in light of that context. Did David's covenant relationship with Yahweh mean he was free to do whatever he pleased? Would he always enjoy success despite all circumstances? Certainly not! In fact, the immediately preceding chapter, in which that covenant relationship was solidified, contains an imposing stipulation: David is not permitted to build the temple of Yahweh, ever! That has been precluded by his military service (1 Chron. 22:8; 28:3). The king may enjoy consistent military success in chapter 8, but he does not get everything he wanted in chapter 7.

Unlike much of the success theology plaguing the church in North America today, David is not promised he will always avoid difficulties and defeats. Rather, he is promised God's abiding presence and the assurance that God will be sufficient to empower him to fulfill his mission as king in providing rest for the nation Israel.

Reading this chapter with an eye to the extended narrative also reminds us that David has not always enjoyed success. He has lived through the agonizing and dangerous years in which King Saul wanted him dead. At first David lived on the fringes of Judahite society as a fugitive, running from Saul, then in exile among the Philistines. He had to fight the Amalekites on the one hand and worry about Saul's insidious jealousy on the other. Though

God was with David through all those days, they also contained times of uncertainty. The rest of 2 Samuel will illustrate further that God's blessings in military victory in chapter 8 are no guarantee that David will avoid difficult circumstances.

Finally, the NIV's "victory" (*yošaʿ*) in 8:6, 14 is almost misleading. Though it certainly does denote military victory in this text, its general use elsewhere in the Old Testament implies help for someone in the midst of trouble rather than a general rescue from the trouble itself.[23] In other words, this phrase does not mean David is somehow guaranteed success just because he is David. Nor does it mean his future will be full of only success after success. Rather, it means that David's special relationship with God makes it possible for him to serve as the suitable anointed one for Israel, and as such, God will be with him. In general, God provides a way out of trouble, but it does not mean there will be no more trouble for David.

Our relationship with God, as his adopted sons and daughters, is certainly no guarantee that we will always meet with success, especially as defined from today's human perspective. Rather, God will empower us to fulfill the mission to which we have been called, as David was able to become Israel's ideal king through the power of Yahweh's Spirit. But the image of unmitigated victory and good fortune is a figment of human imagination, not the paradigm of our lives with God.

"THE Lord GAVE David victory wherever he went." What would it mean for today's believers to have victory wherever we go? David's military victories were God's blessings for him as the legitimately anointed and suitable king of Israel. But since today's believers are no longer called upon to engage in holy war (and none of us is called to lead national Israel as a righteous king!), what contemporary significance can this text have for us?

Fulfilled promises of God. As we have seen, reading chapter 8 in light of the extended narrative of the books of Samuel creates a portrait of the fulfilled promises of God, including the strength and gifts to fulfill the calling we have in God's kingdom. This chapter's link with the preceding promise to David (2 Sam. 7) gives it significance as the partial fulfillment of those promises. Beyond the immediate context, this text takes its place in the overarching interests of the Deuteronomic History, one of which is the promised

---

23. Robert L. Hubbard Jr., "יָשַׁע," *NIDOTTE*, 2:556–62, esp. 556.

"rest" God will provide his people in the land (Deut. 12:9–10). Samuel's farewell speech had implicitly linked security in the Promised Land with Israel's new institution of monarchy (1 Sam. 12:6–15), and God had promised such a rest to David (2 Sam. 7:11). Solomon would need such "rest" in order to build the temple (1 Kings 5:4–5). Our text illustrates that it is through David that the promised "rest" has now become a reality.[24]

Our faith is indeed rooted and grounded in the promises of God. The covenant with Noah was marked by the promise not to destroy humankind again by means of a flood (Gen. 9:11). The Abrahamic covenant was distinctively characterized by promises of land, descendants, and blessing (12:1–3).[25] Those promises began to take shape among Abraham's descendants in the Sinai covenant (Ex. 19–20; 24). The Davidic covenant was marked by promises of land and eternal dynasty (2 Sam. 7:11–13). Eventually, Jeremiah will promise that God will implement a new, spiritual covenant based on an internalized law (Jer. 31:31–34). The New Testament asserts that the coming of Jesus of Nazareth fulfills the divine promises made to Abraham and David (Luke 1:68–79; Acts 13:23). The account of David's military victories in 2 Samuel 8 takes its place in the long litany of biblical texts emphasizing the faithfulness of God to his Word.

A promise, of course, is only as good as the promise-giver. Those of us who have children can well understand how important it is to keep our word, once it has been promised. To fail to "keep" a promise reflects poorly on Mommy or Daddy. A little one is not as likely to accept a parental promise in the future if promises have been "broken" in the past. By contrast, this text and hundreds of others in the Bible speak to the faithfulness of God to his Word.

> The faithfulness of God is a datum of sound theology, but to the believer it becomes far more than that: it passes through the processes of the understanding and goes on to become nourishing food for the soul.... Upon God's faithfulness rests our whole hope of future blessedness. Only as He is faithful will His covenant stand and His promises be honored. Only as we have complete assurance that He is faithful may we live in peace and look forward with assurance to the life to come.[26]

---

24. On this chapter as an "editorial catalogue" placed immediately after the Davidic covenant chapter in order to conclude David's rise and bring to fulfillment the promised "rest" of Deut. 12:9–10, see McCarter, *II Samuel*, 219, 251.

25. Alexander, *From Paradise to the Promised Land*, 39–40.

26. A. W. Tozer, *The Knowledge of the Holy: The Attributes of God, Their Meaning in the Christian Life* (New York: Harper & Row, 1961), 86–87.

This chapter illustrates that God is faithful to his Word and strengthens his servants for the task to which he has called them. So what can it mean for today's believers to have victory wherever we go? It means that God has already won the victory and has promised to strengthen us for the tasks we are called to perform in the church and in the world. As David defeated Israel's enemies, so today's believers can expect to accomplish successfully our God-given and God-ordained tasks, with the help of his Holy Spirit. This catalogue of military victories should inspire confidence in all believers that God is at work fulfilling his Word through his people.

2 Samuel 9:1–13

DAVID ASKED, "IS THere anyone still left of the house of Saul to whom I can show kindness for Jonathan's sake?"

²Now there was a servant of Saul's household named Ziba. They called him to appear before David, and the king said to him, "Are you Ziba?"

"Your servant," he replied.

³The king asked, "Is there no one still left of the house of Saul to whom I can show God's kindness?"

Ziba answered the king, "There is still a son of Jonathan; he is crippled in both feet."

⁴"Where is he?" the king asked.

Ziba answered, "He is at the house of Makir son of Ammiel in Lo Debar."

⁵So King David had him brought from Lo Debar, from the house of Makir son of Ammiel.

⁶When Mephibosheth son of Jonathan, the son of Saul, came to David, he bowed down to pay him honor.

David said, "Mephibosheth!"

"Your servant," he replied.

⁷"Don't be afraid," David said to him, "for I will surely show you kindness for the sake of your father Jonathan. I will restore to you all the land that belonged to your grandfather Saul, and you will always eat at my table."

⁸Mephibosheth bowed down and said, "What is your servant, that you should notice a dead dog like me?"

⁹Then the king summoned Ziba, Saul's servant, and said to him, "I have given your master's grandson everything that belonged to Saul and his family. ¹⁰You and your sons and your servants are to farm the land for him and bring in the crops, so that your master's grandson may be provided for. And Mephibosheth, grandson of your master, will always eat at my table." (Now Ziba had fifteen sons and twenty servants.)

¹¹Then Ziba said to the king, "Your servant will do whatever my lord the king commands his servant to do." So Mephibosheth ate at David's table like one of the king's sons.

¹²Mephibosheth had a young son named Mica, and all the members of Ziba's household were servants of Mephibosheth. ¹³And Mephibosheth lived in Jerusalem, because he always ate at the king's table, and he was crippled in both feet.

WITH THE LIST of David's officials concluding the previous chapter (8:15–18), we now have a complete picture of the king firmly established on the throne in his new capital, surrounded by his royal retinue. David has a new capital and a new palace, and God has given the promised "rest" to Israel by subduing his enemies in neighboring territories. The interesting little narrative before us is transitional in that it lays aside the themes of chapters 5–8, in which David built and consolidated the kingdom. Now David directs his attention to the family of Saul in order to finish some old business. This text relates the new king to the old one, reminding us of the familiar contrast between Saul and David and implicitly raising the question of dynastic succession.

Most scholars believe this transitional narrative is the beginning of one of the most important original sources behind the books of Samuel, the so-called "Court History."[1] The idea that 2 Samuel 9–1 Kings 2 were originally a single narrative unit consisting of traditions about the Davidic court and the accession of Solomon has long commanded an impressive consensus among Old Testament scholars. Literary observations that seemed characteristic of these chapters as a unit included style, worldview, theme, plot, and intercalation of subject matter. Moreover, a concluding editorial comment at 1 Kings 2:46 appears to give the whole a cohesive underlying motive: "The kingdom was now firmly established in Solomon's hands."

However, over the past couple of decades, questions have been raised about the precise boundaries of the narrative. While there is widespread agreement that 1 Kings 2 marks the *end* of the narrative, there is considerable disagreement about its *beginning*.[2] While it is impossible to determine whether our text served as the beginning of an earlier original source, this poses no problem in our interpretation of the passage.

---

1. Sometimes also known as the "Succession Narrative" or "Court Narrative"; see the introduction.

2. For a summary of the issues, see Peter R. Ackroyd, "The Succession Narrative (So-called)," *Int* 35 (1981): 383–96; Gunn, *The Story of King David*, 65–84. Gunn argues on the basis of plot (narrative thread) and style that 2 Sam. 2–4 may be connected to the narrative as its beginning. On the precarious nature of the consensus generally, see Harold O. Forshey, "Court Narrative (2 Samuel 9–1 Kings 2)," *ABD*, 1:1172–79.

It may be more helpful to view the materials in the book of 2 Samuel as revolving around David's adulterous relationship with Bathsheba: chapters 1–9 illustrate "David under the Blessing" and chapters 10–24 "David under the Curse."[3] In its current location in the book, our text is a concluding statement on David's rapid seizure of power, his construction of the new capital and palace, and his firm consolidation of power. At the height of his influence, David turns his attention to the house of Saul (or more to the point, the house of Jonathan) in order to show kindness. Again, David serves in this role as an ideal king of Israel, illustrating who may serve suitably in the role.

David Searches for a Descendant of Saul (9:1–5)

IN THE ANCIENT Near East, the family of a king replaced by a usurper did not generally expect to receive kindness. In fact, new dynasties were routinely accompanied by bloodletting among the family of the old order.[4] This is the way the new king solidified his power.[5] This background is precisely what makes David's treatment of Mephibosheth so surprising, because it comes immediately after the section most focused on consolidation of power in David's hands. David draws a line at Saul's family, beyond which he will not cross.

The connections between this chapter and chapter 8 are often overlooked. The opening phrase "David asked" means we have immediately returned to the historian's preferred means of narration (dialogue) after a long set of speeches (ch. 7) and a chronicle summary (ch. 8).[6] This compounds the problem created by the tendency among most interpreters to overemphasize the importance of chapter 9 as the beginning of an original "Court History" and thus with little relationship to the preceding chapters.

As we have seen often in this commentary, the historian responsible for 1–2 Samuel is skilled at relating a text thematically to the immediately

---

3. R. A. Carlson, *David, the Chosen King: A Traditio-Historical Approach to the Second Book of Samuel* (Stockholm: Almqvist & Wiksell, 1964). More specifically than I have proposed here, Carlson argues for a Deuteronomic redaction that sees 2 Sam. 2–5 and 9–24 as the units illustrating first blessing and then curse. Though not convinced by the details of his argument, I believe there is considerable value in analyzing the materials in this book in contrasting parts revolving around the Bathsheba incident, as we will see.

4. On the extirpation of royal lines as attainder in the Old Testament (i.e., confiscation of property and elimination of direct descendants), see Baruch Halpern, "Sybil, or the Two Nations? Archaism, Kinship, Alienation, and the Elite Redefinition of Traditional Culture in Judah in the 8th–7th Centuries B.C.E.," in *The Study of the Ancient Near East in the Twenty-First Century: The William Foxwell Albright Centennial Conference*, ed. J. S. Cooper and G. M. Schwartz (Winona Lake, Ind.: Eisenbrauns, 1996), 293–95.

5. Walton, Matthews, and Chavalas, *IVP Bible Background Commentary*, 336.

6. Alter, *David Story*, 240.

preceding text. So here the military summary provided in chapter 8 fulfills the words of Jonathan in 1 Samuel 20:15: "Do not ever cut off your kindness from my family—not even when the LORD has cut off every one of David's enemies from the face of the earth." Chapter 8 makes it clear that Yahweh has indeed cut David's enemies off, giving him victory wherever he went and providing the promised "rest" for the land. So now is the time for David to keep the covenant he and Jonathan established.

This opening paragraph contains numerous semantic links to Jonathan's covenant with David (1 Sam. 20:8, 14–17, 42). Primary among them is the importance of showing (lit., doing) "kindness" (*ḥesed*). This term has theological significance throughout the Old Testament, denoting the life-sustaining grace of God bestowed on humans and making it possible to have a loving relationship with him. More generally, "kindness" characterizes covenant relationships, whether between God and humans or simply among humans; therefore it can be translated in many ways: grace, loyalty, faithfulness, love, mercy, goodness.[7] What makes *ḥesed* an act of "kindness" is often the fact that one member in the relationship is in a position to render help or aid to the other, who is for one reason or another in need and unable to help or aid the other.[8] Such help is performed simply because of the deep and enduring relationship between the two covenant partners, which in the case of David and Jonathan was sealed in a formal covenant in 1 Samuel 20 (see v. 42). The need for *ḥesed* is particularly emphasized in situations where its performance is in question, where it seems unnatural, or where circumstances in the future may render it unlikely.

So Jonathan spoke prophetically when he charged David to show kindness faithfully to his family in that future day when Yahweh would give him rest from all his enemies (1 Sam. 20:15). Our text is further linked to Jonathan's earlier speech by the reference to "the *ḥesed* of God" in 9:3 (NIV "God's kindness"). Jonathan had asked for the "kindness of Yahweh" (NIV "unfailing kindness like that of the LORD") in 1 Samuel 20:14, which is probably an expression of the superlative: the greatest possible kindness.[9] So now David seeks to show the kindness of God to Saul's house.

The significance of these semantic links is to signify beyond doubt that David is now fulfilling his covenant obligation to Jonathan. Jonathan's

---

7. BDB, 338–39; *HALOT*, 1:336–37; *DCH*, 3:277–81. The concept has been defined generally as "a responsible keeping of faith with another with whom one is in a relationship" (Sakenfeld, *Meaning of Ḥesed*, 233). On the use of the term in the Old Testament in general, see the Bridging Contexts section for 1 Sam. 20:1–42.

8. Clark, *The Word Ḥesed*, 267.

9. It may also denote an oath to covenant kindness with Yahweh or God as witness. See BDB, 338, I.1; *DCH*, 3:279.

prophetic-like words have become a reality. Saul is dead; Jonathan is dead. God has silenced all David's and Israel's enemies in the neighboring territories. Now is the time for David to remember his old friend and to act benevolently toward Jonathan's family. This requires *ḥesed* because all expectations—indeed, the cultural momentum—is toward proper revenge.

We may question David's sincerity and his motives for showing kindness to Mephibosheth.[10] There can be no question that it is safe to elevate and bless him, because as a cripple Mephibosheth poses no threat to David personally or to David's rule, even though he is the only remaining descendant of King Saul.[11] Perhaps David is attempting to solidify the otherwise tenuous unity between northern Israel and southern Judah by incorporating into his royal household the vestiges of the Saulide dynasty, so popular among the northern tribes. Or perhaps this act of kindness is simply a desperate attempt to ease David's guilt-ridden conscience, assuming he somehow has felt responsible for the end of Saul's line.

But all such hypothetical and psychological speculation takes us beyond the message of 1–2 Samuel, which are clear in explaining David's motives at critical junctures. He was resolutely loyal to Saul himself, even after Saul set himself squarely as a bitter enemy who wanted David dead (1 Sam. 24:5–6). His friendship with Jonathan was unalloyed, pure companionship, and David refused to take advantage of or abuse Jonathan. As far as the text is concerned, David's motives are singularly focused on Jonathan; his reasons for showing kindness now are simply "for Jonathan's sake" (9:1, 7).[12]

David Shows Kindness to Mephibosheth (9:6–13)

AS WE HAVE seen, the name "Ish-Bosheth" was most probably a euphemistic substitution for Ish-Baal, "Man-of-Baal," referring to the Canaanite fertility god Baal.[13] Likewise, Mephibosheth's name is probably a substitution for Merib-Baal, though the substitution is far from obvious because of an additional phonemic change, raising questions about the reasons for such a

---

10. On the potential "calculated" motives of David, see Mauchline, *1 and 2 Samuel*, 241; Anderson, *2 Samuel*, 143.

11. Impressive physical features confirmed the right of a new king to rule (1 Sam. 9:2; 10:23; 16:12). Thus, Mephibosheth's debilitating condition make it unlikely he can mount a serious claim to the throne during a time of political instability and uncertainty.

12. The statement that "David can afford to be magnanimous" now that he is firmly established as the undisputed king misses the point (Youngblood, "1, 2 Samuel," 916). The location of this text immediately after ch. 8 makes it clear that Jonathan's words have come true only now that God has provided victory over all David's enemies; this is therefore the time to show kindness.

13. See comments in the Original Meaning section of 2 Sam. 2:8–11.

change.[14] The original name may have meant "Baal contends," and most scholars assume the current form Mephibosheth meant "One who scatters shame."[15]

Regardless of what Mephibosheth may have hoped, it can hardly be good news for him to be summoned to the royal palace. David brings him from obscurity in Lo Debar and identifies him as the son of Jonathan and grandson of Saul (9:6). In the central and pivotal section of our text (9:7),[16] David begins by alleviating his visitor's fears. Where Mephibosheth may have expected execution, he receives grace. The king will not only permit Mephibosheth to live, but he will show kindness to him for Jonathan's sake.

That kindness takes the form of two blessings. (1) David will give him the property of Saul's estate, making Mephibosheth a wealthy man instantly. He has apparently been dependent on the generosity of others, but now he becomes the holder of wealth-producing property.[17] Ziba's entire family will be needed to maintain and care for Mephibosheth's estate (9:9–10). (2) David grants the privilege that was lost to Mephibosheth when Saul and Jonathan were killed, that is, the right to eat at the king's table. The fact that this provision is granted for "always" (*tamid*) probably indicates that this is a permanent "pension" for Mephibosheth—one that grants honor and respect.[18]

THE MEANING OF KINDNESS. One potential obstacle to interpreting this passage for today is the word "kindness," which the NIV uses consistently for the three occurrences of *ḥesed* (all on the lips of David, 9:1, 3, 7). As we have seen, this is a perfectly adequate translation, but the English connotations are much weaker than the Hebrew (see above). For example, in English "kindness" carries no such covenantal connotations as is clear from the connections of our text with 1 Samuel 18,

---

14. See Youngblood, "1, 2 Samuel," 848; Anderson, 2 *Samuel*, 69–70; esp. McCarter, *II Samuel*, 124–25, 128.

15. Werner Weinberg, "Language Consciousness in the OT," *ZAW* 92 (1980): 201.

16. Youngblood, "1, 2 Samuel," 916–17; for a slightly different chiastic structure, see Kiyoshi K. Sacon, "A Study of the Literary Structure of 'The Succession Narrative,'" in *Studies in the Period of David and Solomon and Other Essays*, ed. Tomoo Ishida (Winona Lake, Ind.: Eisenbrauns, 1982), 48–49.

17. Baldwin, *1 and 2 Samuel*, 227. She notes that to restore the property of the previous regime to a member of its family was risky and held potential for future problems (see 2 Sam. 16:3).

18. Though this also made it possible for a reigning monarch to "keep an eye" on political prisoners. Walton, Matthews, and Chavalas, *IVP Bible Background Commentary*, 336.

20, and 23, in which David and Jonathan swore to remember each other in covenant faithfulness. To interpret the text for today, we will have to go beyond the implications of our English translations in order to make this point clearly.

David had accepted a covenant obligation regarding Jonathan. Once he is firmly established as king, he is obligated to be merciful to Jonathan's family. This passage shows that David wastes no time. Immediately after Yahweh has granted victory (ch. 8), David seeks out the remaining children of Saul in order to show them mercy. His benevolence to Mephibosheth surpasses his obligation to allow the unfortunate royal scion merely to stay alive. His "kindness" shows David to be a man of generosity, integrity and faithfulness, a "man of his word."

Looking at the literary context. Another potential obstacle occurs when we fail to consider the literary context sufficiently. I have emphasized the connections between this chapter and the rest of 1–2 Samuel. But these connections are subtle enough to miss in a casual reading, in which case we will miss the point of our unit. Most of the texts in this portion of 2 Samuel have been devoted to David's spectacular reign: his rise to the throne, his consolidation of power, the building of a new capital and palace, and the divine promises for an eternal dynasty. This chapter on Mephibosheth is transitional in that it leads us to reflect one final time on Saul and his failed rulership, but it also anticipates and provides important background for future events in 2 Samuel (16:1–4; 19:24–30). In the remainder of this section, I will seek to draw out more implications of this contextual reading.

From the outset Ziba emphasizes Mephibosheth's crippled condition, probably because he fears David might kill any remaining descendants of Saul (9:3, not an unfounded fear in light of 21:1–14). Ziba wants David to understand that it would be unlikely (or impossible?) for Mephibosheth to lay claim to the throne for the sake of his grandfather (thereby posing a threat to David). After all, Mephibosheth is dependent on Ziba entirely for his livelihood. The narrator returns to this point for added emphasis at the close of our text (9:13): "and he was crippled in both feet." This detail directs us back to 2 Samuel 4:4, where we first learn of Jonathan's son and the reason for his physical impairment. Mephibosheth's nurse dropped him when he was five years old in the panic following the deaths of his father and grandfather.

But all of this directs us further back to that fateful battle at Mount Gilboa and Saul's ignoble death (1 Sam. 31), and beyond that to his visit with the witch of Endor (1 Sam. 28). Mephibosheth himself is a casualty of Saul's failures. His very presence in our text recalls the failure of Israel's first king and highlights the pitiable end of his progeny. Saul does not even have a suitable heir for his estate, much less his kingdom.[19] Once the estate is given to Mephibosheth, it still requires caretakers because Mephibosheth himself is unable to maintain it.

In other words, Saul's grandson is not only incapable of posing a threat to David's new kingdom, he is even incapable of caring for himself (2 Sam. 9:10). Thus Samuel's prophecy against Saul has been fulfilled (1 Sam. 13:14): "Your kingdom will not endure; the LORD has sought out a man after his own heart and appointed him leader of his people, because you have not kept the LORD's command." In 2 Samuel, Saul's descendants gradually disappear until the only remaining trace is the pitiable Mephibosheth, who is graciously sustained at David's table.

By contrast, King David keeps moving from glory to glory. At this point in our story, he has fulfilled every promise and been granted every blessing. It is through David that Yahweh is making Israel the nation they have hoped to be all along and the nation that Yahweh can use in turn to bless the world. Thus, this passage contributes to the theme: What sort of man may serve suitably as king in Israel? Mephibosheth may not serve as king, for he is a continuation of Saul's line.[20] But David is ideal as king! His faithfulness to Jonathan moves him to be generous to Mephibosheth. His magnanimity goes far beyond any political benefits he may have received from having Mephibosheth in his court. He is lavish in his love for Jonathan, making his generosity appropriate. This is the character Israel wants and needs in its kings.

From this point forward in 2 Samuel, the book will continue to address the question about who may serve suitably as king. So far that question has been answered positively: David is the kind of person who may rule. But we will soon encounter negative answers: not Mephibosheth, not David when he acts like a typical ancient Near Eastern despot, not Amnon, not Absalom, and so on.

INTEGRITY. I once taught in a seminary that took a survey of the ecclesiastical administrators in all its constituent denominations. The school was hoping to do a better job preparing and training pastors for the denominations we were serving. We were planning to use the results of the survey to make curricular changes or to consider which topics needed more attention in ministerial education. At one point in the survey the

---

19. As we have seen, the events of David's reign are not presented chronologically in the books of Samuel. I assume here that the events of 2 Sam. 21:7–8 occurred prior to this episode, which is the only way to make sense of David's inquiry here in 9:1. For overview of the issues, see Gordon, *I & II Samuel*, 248.

20. His physical impairment may also have disqualified him (see comments at 4:4).

seminary asked what the church leaders thought was the single most important characteristic needed in its pastors.

The answer we received surprised us. An overwhelming majority of the church administrators said the most needed trait was integrity. But the answer was not only surprising; I think we were a little disappointed as well. We were hoping to add something to our curriculum or perhaps improve some neglected aspect in our courses to produce better pastors and serve our constituent denominations more effectively. But we had to face the fact: Integrity is not something you can teach in a classroom. We can attempt to model it more persuasively, but we cannot include "integrity" as an assessable course objective in our syllabi.

The church leaders struck a nerve. They had put their finger precisely on the pulse of their churches and identified the problem of the church today. Perhaps a long string of distasteful and unfortunate failures in the evangelical church have merely made us feel the need more acutely. But the fact remains, integrity is all too often missing in our leadership. We have an integrity crisis in the North American church today.

It is easy enough to give a formal dictionary definition of integrity: "the quality or state of being of sound moral principle; uprightness, honesty, and sincerity." However, this hardly exhausts the significance of David's actions in this unit. By integrity as illustrated here, I mean the determination to do what one believes is right even when there is no compelling reason to act rightly beyond the sheer "rightness" of the act. Scholars often debate about David's motives for his kindness to Mephibosheth. But as we have seen, this is not the concern of the text. Ziba and Mephibosheth himself expect anything but grace from the king, and they both appear to be surprised by the extent of David's generosity. Though there may have been modest benefits for David to allow Mephibosheth to live, he is motivated in this text solely by his commitments to Jonathan. Even though Jonathan is dead, the king faithfully keeps covenant.

(Ab)use of power. Another secondary theme that keeps recurring in the books of Samuel is the use and abuse of power. You and I are tempted to "show kindness" and to keep our covenant commitments only when it is convenient to do so or when it shows particular promise of return. In the workplace, in schools, dare I say even in the church, we tend to keep covenant with those who will repay us in some way. Such calculated covenant faithfulness manifests our falseness more than our integrity.

In this text, David serves as an example because he keeps covenant and shows mercy to someone who cannot advance his own causes.[21] Unlike

---

21. In fact, as we have seen, it was a risk to grant access to the royal palace and financial freedom to a grandson of Saul. It aroused the hopes that even Mephibosheth, crippled

Saul, who abused (or attempted to abuse) his royal power, David uses power *in this passage* in a way consistent with his calling as shepherd of God's flock. As such, he also anticipates his greater Son, who will never use power for self-aggrandizement but only for the advancement of his Father's kingdom. Unfortunately, David will not always represent such an example of the use of power, as we will soon see.

The following prayer from Africa is an appropriate way to tie these themes together.

> You asked for my hands
> that you might use them for Your purpose.
> I gave them for a moment,
> then withdrew them, for the work was hard.
>
> You asked for my mouth
> to speak out against injustice;
> I gave you a whisper that I might not be accused.
>
> You asked for my eyes
> to see the pain of poverty;
> I closed them, for I did not want to see.
>
> You asked for my life
> that you might work through me.
> I gave you a small part, that I might not get 'too involved'.
>
> Lord, forgive me for my calculated efforts to serve you
> only when it is convenient for me to do so,
> only in those places where it is safe to do so and
> only with those who make it easy to do so.
>
> Father, forgive me,
> renew me,
> send me out
> as a useable instrument
> that I might take seriously
> the meaning of your cross![22]

---

though he was, might someday take the throne from David for the sake of his grandfather (a possibility that comes into play later in the narrative, 2 Samuel 16:3).

22. Joe Seremane, "You Asked for My Hands," in *Celebrating One World: A Worship Resource on Social Justice*, ed. Linda Jones, A. Shilson-Thomas, and B. Farrell ([London]: Harper-Collins, [1998]), 136. Used by permission.

2 Samuel 10:1–12:31

I N THE COURSE of time, the king of the Ammonites died,
and his son Hanun succeeded him as king. ²David thought,
"I will show kindness to Hanun son of Nahash, just as his
father showed kindness to me." So David sent a delegation to
express his sympathy to Hanun concerning his father.

When David's men came to the land of the Ammonites,
³the Ammonite nobles said to Hanun their lord, "Do you
think David is honoring your father by sending men to you to
express sympathy? Hasn't David sent them to you to explore
the city and spy it out and overthrow it?" ⁴So Hanun seized
David's men, shaved off half of each man's beard, cut off their
garments in the middle at the buttocks, and sent them away.

⁵When David was told about this, he sent messengers to meet
the men, for they were greatly humiliated. The king said, "Stay at
Jericho till your beards have grown, and then come back."

⁶When the Ammonites realized that they had become a
stench in David's nostrils, they hired twenty thousand
Aramean foot soldiers from Beth Rehob and Zobah, as well
as the king of Maacah with a thousand men, and also twelve
thousand men from Tob.

⁷On hearing this, David sent Joab out with the entire army
of fighting men. ⁸The Ammonites came out and drew up in
battle formation at the entrance to their city gate, while the
Arameans of Zobah and Rehob and the men of Tob and
Maacah were by themselves in the open country.

⁹Joab saw that there were battle lines in front of him and
behind him; so he selected some of the best troops in Israel
and deployed them against the Arameans. ¹⁰He put the rest
of the men under the command of Abishai his brother and
deployed them against the Ammonites. ¹¹Joab said, "If the
Arameans are too strong for me, then you are to come to my
rescue; but if the Ammonites are too strong for you, then I
will come to rescue you. ¹²Be strong and let us fight bravely
for our people and the cities of our God. The LORD will do
what is good in his sight."

¹³Then Joab and the troops with him advanced to fight the
Arameans, and they fled before him. ¹⁴When the Ammonites

saw that the Arameans were fleeing, they fled before Abishai and went inside the city. So Joab returned from fighting the Ammonites and came to Jerusalem.

¹⁵After the Arameans saw that they had been routed by Israel, they regrouped. ¹⁶Hadadezer had Arameans brought from beyond the River; they went to Helam, with Shobach the commander of Hadadezer's army leading them.

¹⁷When David was told of this, he gathered all Israel, crossed the Jordan and went to Helam. The Arameans formed their battle lines to meet David and fought against him. ¹⁸But they fled before Israel, and David killed seven hundred of their charioteers and forty thousand of their foot soldiers. He also struck down Shobach the commander of their army, and he died there. ¹⁹When all the kings who were vassals of Hadadezer saw that they had been defeated by Israel, they made peace with the Israelites and became subject to them.

So the Arameans were afraid to help the Ammonites anymore.

^{11:1}In the spring, at the time when kings go off to war, David sent Joab out with the king's men and the whole Israelite army. They destroyed the Ammonites and besieged Rabbah. But David remained in Jerusalem.

²One evening David got up from his bed and walked around on the roof of the palace. From the roof he saw a woman bathing. The woman was very beautiful, ³and David sent someone to find out about her. The man said, "Isn't this Bathsheba, the daughter of Eliam and the wife of Uriah the Hittite?" ⁴Then David sent messengers to get her. She came to him, and he slept with her. (She had purified herself from her uncleanness.) Then she went back home. ⁵The woman conceived and sent word to David, saying, "I am pregnant."

⁶So David sent this word to Joab: "Send me Uriah the Hittite." And Joab sent him to David. ⁷When Uriah came to him, David asked him how Joab was, how the soldiers were and how the war was going. ⁸Then David said to Uriah, "Go down to your house and wash your feet." So Uriah left the palace, and a gift from the king was sent after him. ⁹But Uriah slept at the entrance to the palace with all his master's servants and did not go down to his house.

¹⁰When David was told, "Uriah did not go home," he asked him, "Haven't you just come from a distance? Why didn't you go home?"

¹¹Uriah said to David, "The ark and Israel and Judah are staying in tents, and my master Joab and my lord's men are camped in the open fields. How could I go to my house to eat and drink and lie with my wife? As surely as you live, I will not do such a thing!"

¹²Then David said to him, "Stay here one more day, and tomorrow I will send you back." So Uriah remained in Jerusalem that day and the next. ¹³At David's invitation, he ate and drank with him, and David made him drunk. But in the evening Uriah went out to sleep on his mat among his master's servants; he did not go home.

¹⁴In the morning David wrote a letter to Joab and sent it with Uriah. ¹⁵In it he wrote, "Put Uriah in the front line where the fighting is fiercest. Then withdraw from him so he will be struck down and die."

¹⁶So while Joab had the city under siege, he put Uriah at a place where he knew the strongest defenders were. ¹⁷When the men of the city came out and fought against Joab, some of the men in David's army fell; moreover, Uriah the Hittite died.

¹⁸Joab sent David a full account of the battle. ¹⁹He instructed the messenger: "When you have finished giving the king this account of the battle, ²⁰the king's anger may flare up, and he may ask you, 'Why did you get so close to the city to fight? Didn't you know they would shoot arrows from the wall? ²¹Who killed Abimelech son of Jerub-Besheth? Didn't a woman throw an upper millstone on him from the wall, so that he died in Thebez? Why did you get so close to the wall?' If he asks you this, then say to him, 'Also, your servant Uriah the Hittite is dead.'"

²²The messenger set out, and when he arrived he told David everything Joab had sent him to say. ²³The messenger said to David, "The men overpowered us and came out against us in the open, but we drove them back to the entrance to the city gate. ²⁴Then the archers shot arrows at your servants from the wall, and some of the king's men died. Moreover, your servant Uriah the Hittite is dead."

²⁵David told the messenger, "Say this to Joab: 'Don't let this upset you; the sword devours one as well as another. Press the attack against the city and destroy it.' Say this to encourage Joab."

²⁶When Uriah's wife heard that her husband was dead, she mourned for him. ²⁷After the time of mourning was over,

David had her brought to his house, and she became his wife and bore him a son. But the thing David had done displeased the LORD.

¹²:¹The LORD sent Nathan to David. When he came to him, he said, "There were two men in a certain town, one rich and the other poor. ²The rich man had a very large number of sheep and cattle, ³but the poor man had nothing except one little ewe lamb he had bought. He raised it, and it grew up with him and his children. It shared his food, drank from his cup and even slept in his arms. It was like a daughter to him.

⁴"Now a traveler came to the rich man, but the rich man refrained from taking one of his own sheep or cattle to prepare a meal for the traveler who had come to him. Instead, he took the ewe lamb that belonged to the poor man and prepared it for the one who had come to him."

⁵David burned with anger against the man and said to Nathan, "As surely as the LORD lives, the man who did this deserves to die! ⁶He must pay for that lamb four times over, because he did such a thing and had no pity."

⁷Then Nathan said to David, "You are the man! This is what the LORD, the God of Israel, says: 'I anointed you king over Israel, and I delivered you from the hand of Saul. ⁸I gave your master's house to you, and your master's wives into your arms. I gave you the house of Israel and Judah. And if all this had been too little, I would have given you even more. ⁹Why did you despise the word of the LORD by doing what is evil in his eyes? You struck down Uriah the Hittite with the sword and took his wife to be your own. You killed him with the sword of the Ammonites. ¹⁰Now, therefore, the sword will never depart from your house, because you despised me and took the wife of Uriah the Hittite to be your own.'

¹¹"This is what the LORD says: 'Out of your own household I am going to bring calamity upon you. Before your very eyes I will take your wives and give them to one who is close to you, and he will lie with your wives in broad daylight. ¹²You did it in secret, but I will do this thing in broad daylight before all Israel.'"

¹³Then David said to Nathan, "I have sinned against the LORD."

Nathan replied, "The LORD has taken away your sin. You are not going to die. ¹⁴But because by doing this you have made the enemies of the LORD show utter contempt, the son born to you will die."

¹⁵After Nathan had gone home, the LORD struck the child that Uriah's wife had borne to David, and he became ill. ¹⁶David pleaded with God for the child. He fasted and went into his house and spent the nights lying on the ground. ¹⁷The elders of his household stood beside him to get him up from the ground, but he refused, and he would not eat any food with them.

¹⁸On the seventh day the child died. David's servants were afraid to tell him that the child was dead, for they thought, "While the child was still living, we spoke to David but he would not listen to us. How can we tell him the child is dead? He may do something desperate."

¹⁹David noticed that his servants were whispering among themselves and he realized the child was dead. "Is the child dead?" he asked.

"Yes," they replied, "he is dead."

²⁰Then David got up from the ground. After he had washed, put on lotions and changed his clothes, he went into the house of the LORD and worshiped. Then he went to his own house, and at his request they served him food, and he ate.

²¹His servants asked him, "Why are you acting this way? While the child was alive, you fasted and wept, but now that the child is dead, you get up and eat!"

²²He answered, "While the child was still alive, I fasted and wept. I thought, 'Who knows? The LORD may be gracious to me and let the child live.' ²³But now that he is dead, why should I fast? Can I bring him back again? I will go to him, but he will not return to me."

²⁴Then David comforted his wife Bathsheba, and he went to her and lay with her. She gave birth to a son, and they named him Solomon. The LORD loved him; ²⁵and because the LORD loved him, he sent word through Nathan the prophet to name him Jedidiah.

²⁶Meanwhile Joab fought against Rabbah of the Ammonites and captured the royal citadel. ²⁷Joab then sent messengers to David, saying, "I have fought against Rabbah and taken its water supply. ²⁸Now muster the rest of the troops and besiege the city and capture it. Otherwise I will take the city, and it will be named after me."

²⁹So David mustered the entire army and went to Rabbah, and attacked and captured it. ³⁰He took the crown from the head of their king—its weight was a talent of gold, and it was set with precious stones—and it was placed on David's head. He took a great quantity of plunder from the city ³¹and brought out the people who were there, consigning them to labor with saws and with iron picks and axes, and he made them work at brickmaking. He did this to all the Ammonite towns. Then David and his entire army returned to Jerusalem.

WE HAVE SEEN THAT YAHWEH'S COVENANT with David in chapter 7 is the ideological mountain-top of 2 Samuel. Now with these chapters we come to the point at which the book begins its gradual descent into the valley. This is an all-time classic tale of betrayal, deception, adultery, and murder—and our leading hero is the culprit! We turn a corner with the Bathsheba episode that changes everything in the book.

Thus far 2 Samuel has narrated events surrounding the ideal king, and in the process the book answers the question: Who may serve suitably as Israel's king? The answer has come resoundingly: David may serve because he is perfect in every respect. But beginning with these chapters, we learn that David—to use a metaphor from a different Old Testament book—has "feet of clay" (Dan. 2:31–35). Though to all appearances David is the ideal king and looks invincible, he nonetheless has serious flaws and proves vulnerable at a number of points. Yet this narrative will demonstrate that even in his sins, David is ideal. How so? Because unlike Saul, David repents genuinely and quickly when confronted with the awful truth.

The books of Samuel were composed using certain earlier sources (see introduction). However, our historian has not simply strung them together like beads on a string. Rather, the book has been arranged thematically and is carefully structured around the event narrated here in order to make a theological point.[1] Collectively the narrative presents contrasting pictures of David revolving around the Bathsheba incident, so that this becomes the

---

1. For example, some scholars theorize that the Bathsheba episode recorded here took place prior to Absalom's revolt (chs. 15–19) or even that this war with the Ammonites occurred after David brought the ark into Jerusalem (6:1–19). J. W. Flanagan, "Court History or Succession Document? A Study of 2 Samuel 9–20 and 1 Kings 1–2," *JBL* 91 (1972): 172–81. For a different sequence, see Merrill, "The 'Accession Year' and Davidic Chronology," 107–12.

central pivotal text of 2 Samuel.[2] The king was blessed and protected by God in the first portion of the book. From this point forward, however, David will be a flawed character, who seems helpless to reverse the tide of sin and destruction he has unleashed on his own royal court.[3] Implicitly, the historian has traced all David's troubles in 2 Samuel 13–20 to his sin with Bathsheba recorded here.[4]

I will treat each part of these chapters separately below, though they actually have a chiastic structure; that is, the materials are arranged in concentric circles. The materials narrating the Ammonite war serve as a literary frame for the whole (10:1–11:1 and 12:26–31); within this, the sections on David and Bathsheba have their own concentric pattern (see below at 11:2–27).

Diplomacy with the Ammonites Breaks Down (10:1–5)

THE OPENING EXPRESSION ("in the course of time") is an idiomatic transition marker for the book, which seems to mark thematic arrangement of materials rather than strict chronology (see 2:1; 8:1; 13:1; 15:1; 21:18).[5] Since it is used both here and in 13:1, this expression complements the literary frame created by the narration of the Ammonite wars at the beginning and end of the narrative to tie off chapters 10–12 as a distinct literary unit.[6]

The Lord blessed David with good success against all Israel's near neighbors (see "The LORD gave David victory wherever he went" in ch. 8). The children of Ammon inhabited the territory just across the Jordan River from Jerusalem (their capital Rabbah, mentioned in 12:26, is modern Amman, capital of Jordan). This account of continued armed conflict between the

---

2. Alter muses that the narrator has "pulled out all the stops of his remarkable narrative art in order to achieve a brilliant realization of this crucially pivotal episode." He especially notes the orchestration of a variety of literary features, including thematic key words, shifting play of dialogue, and the intricate relation between instructions and their execution. The narrative has cultivated ambiguities of motive "with a richness that scarcely has an equal in ancient narrative" (Alter, *David Story*, 249).

3. For similar assessment though different in several details, see Carlson, *David, the Chosen King*. Carlson views 2 Sam. 2–5 as "David under the Blessing" and 2 Sam. 9–24 as "David under the Curse."

4. McCarter theorizes that Absalom's revolt in chs. 15–20 may have actually occurred prior to the Bathsheba episode, in which case chs. 10–12 have been affixed to chs. 13–20 as "a kind of theological preface," making the turmoil in the royal court recorded in 13–20 a result of David's sin with Bathsheba (McCarter, *II Samuel*, 276).

5. It may have the function of marking a sequence of events internal to a particular individual's reign. See Bailey, *David in Love and War*, 56–57; Conroy, *Absalom Absalom!* 41–42.

6. See Youngblood, "1, 2 Samuel," 920 for full treatment of why chs. 10–12 should be taken together as a single unit.

Israelites and Ammonites is interesting for the light it sheds on how David conducted warfare. But the narration of these events is no doubt included simply as background for the historian's main point of interest, that is, the story of David and Bathsheba.[7]

David apparently does not expect war with the Ammonites. Most likely Nahash, the Ammonite king who has died here (10:1) and an old adversary of Saul (1 Sam. 11), was David's ally during the difficult days of Saul's reign. It had been in Nahash's best interest to neutralize Saul by supporting a rival.[8] David logically seeks to maintain friendly relations with the Ammonites after Nahash's death. The specific terminology used to reveal David's intentions (2 Sam. 10:2, "I will show kindness," i.e., ḥesed) is reminiscent of David's kindness to Mephibosheth in the immediately preceding chapter (9:1, 3, 7) and may mean David has an actual covenant or treaty with Nahash. Just as David was faithful to his covenant with Jonathan by showing kindness to Mephibosheth, now he seeks to be faithful in his relationship with Nahash. The delegation David sends is clearly not military in nature, but was sent "to express sympathy" (lᵉnaḥᵃmo; lit., "comfort, console").

Details on why the shaved beard and cut garments represented the ultimate insult are not entirely clear (10:4).[9] The beard was apparently the pride and joy of an Israelite male, which was cut only for periods of mourning or as an act of humiliation (see Isa. 15:2; Jer. 41:5; 48:37). Since garments in the biblical world often reflected status, power, or identity, the added insult of cutting their garments at their hips exposes David's men to further humiliation.

It is important to note that verse 2 introduces an important theme word (or *Leitwort*) for our unit. The verb "send" (šlḥ) is used twenty-three times in these three chapters, an amount striking even for a word as common as this.[10] Its use in this chapter prepares for what follows in chapters 11−12 by illustrating the premeditated and deliberate maneuvering for power. After David *sends* the delegation to comfort Hanun, the Ammonite king humiliates them and *sends* them back. David then *sends* messengers to meet the beleaguered

---

7. Evans, *1 and 2 Samuel*, 178.

8. McCarter, *II Samuel*, 270, 273−74.

9. Anderson, *2 Samuel*, 146−47.

10. The verb occurs 844 times in the Old Testament (BDB, 1018; for breakdown by derived stems, see *HALOT*, 4:1512−16). The references in these three chapters are 10:2, 3 (2x), 4, 5, 6, 7, 16; 11:1, 3, 4, 5, 6 (3x), 12, 14, 18, 22, 27; 12:1, 25, 27. Three of these occurrences are not observable in the NIV: In 10:6 of the NIV, the Ammonites "hired twenty thousand Aramean foot soldiers" whereas the Heb. says they "sent and hired" them; in 10:16, Hadadezer "sent and brought forth" Arameans (NIV, "Hadadezer had Arameans brought"); in 11:27, David "sent and brought" Bathsheba to his house (NIV, "David had her brought").

men in order to minimize their humiliation. To prepare for war, the Ammonites *send* and hire mercenaries, whereupon David *sends* Joab and the Israelite army to prepare for war.

These two kings are busy "sending" to and against each other in the strategic play for power. Their "sending" is all about human power structures and about who has access to the most strength in order to dominate the other. David's decisive victory over the Arameans brings the power motif into focus and characterizes him as the legitimate king of Israel, who has the God-given power and authority to "send." David does indeed have royal power, and as we will see, this motif returns in frightening ways in chapters 11 and 12.[11]

Ammonite Wars (10:6–19)

HANUN'S HUMILIATION OF DAVID'S MEN is in effect a declaration of war. His next step is to form alliances that will enable him to limit David's power in Syria-Palestine, just as his father Nahash formed an alliance with David in order to limit Saul's power. The battle accounts recorded here (and at 12:26–31) have an official and authentic ring to them, and many scholars assume they have been taken directly from contemporary royal archives or annals.[12]

It seems clear from these battle accounts that the real power is not the Ammonites but their allies to the north, the Arameans.[13] Especially powerful is the kingdom of Zobah (also known as Aram-Zobah), which is the dominant political power of southern Syria during this time. Located to the extreme north of the Promised Land, Zobah probably extended from the northern Beqa Valley in what is modern Lebanon east of the Anti-Lebanon range to the north of Damascus.[14] During the eleventh century B.C., Zobah was the center of a small empire that encompassed most of the Aramean states surrounding it. The power of this empire under its king Hadadezer was growing as quickly as David's power in the south. Armed conflict between the two seems unavoidable, with political supremacy of Syria-Palestine at stake.[15]

The first battle described here takes place near the city of Rabbah itself (10:6–14). Once the Arameans arrived in the Transjordan, they successfully

---

11. Alter, *David Story*, 257; Brueggemann, *First and Second Samuel*, 279; Youngblood, "1, 2 Samuel," 920, 922, 941.

12. Hertzberg, *I and II Samuel*, 303.

13. For the locations of Beth Rehob, Maacah, and Tob, see Anderson, *2 Samuel*, 147; McCarter, *II Samuel*, 271–72, and esp. McCarter's map 6 on page 526.

14. Wayne T. Pitard, "Zobah," *ABD*, 6:1108; see Yohanan Aharoni and Michael Avi-Yonah, *Macmillan Bible Atlas*, 67.

15. Abraham Malamat, "Aspects of the Foreign Policies of David and Solomon," *JNES* 22 (1963): 1–6; Wayne T. Pitard, *Ancient Damascus* (Winona Lake, Ind.: Eisenbrauns, 1987), 89–95.

out-maneuver Joab so that he is forced to fight on two separate fronts (10:9–12). Joab divides his troops and encourages them to be strong and fight bravely, adding that Yahweh will do whatever seems best in his sight (10:12). The irascible general is seldom a paragon of virtue, but here Joab's quote illustrates the healthy balance between effort and faith. Effective servants in God's kingdom will exhaust their resources and energies doing whatever they can, while acknowledging that the fruit of their labors is ultimately in God's hands. Or, as someone has said, saints pray as though the outcome depends solely on God and work as though it depends on them.

To the disappointment of the Ammonites, their Aramean allies flee before Joab. The Israelite victory is probably tempered by losses, so that Joab is unable to continue his siege on the city itself and has no alternative but to return to Jerusalem (10:14).

The next battle is between Israel and the Arameans themselves and will determine the fate of all of Syria-Palestine (10:15–19). After acquiring reinforcements from beyond the Euphrates, Hadadezer moves into Helam. The exact location of Helam is uncertain, though presumably it is a city or region in northern Gilead, an area frequently contested by the Arameans of Damascus in subsequent centuries.[16] David leads the troops himself this time in what becomes a decisive victory.[17] From this time forward, Aram-Zobah loses its political influence and is replaced in the tenth century by Damascus as the most powerful Aramean state.

Our account concludes with the concise, "So the Arameans were afraid to help the Ammonites anymore." With the Aramean allies effectively neutralized, all that remains for David to control the Transjordan area is conquest of Ammon itself (which is recorded in 12:26–31). In the meantime, the account of these Ammonite wars is suspended in order to narrate the sad events in the royal palace back in Jerusalem, which are of paramount interest to our historian.

David Remains in Jerusalem (11:1)

DAVID SENDS JOAB and the Israelite army to capture the city of the Ammonites and finish what was begun in chapter 10. But instead of moving straight to the battle's culmination, the narrator uses subtle irony to include two further details that are strictly unnecessary in a simple military report: the precise time of year and the king's decision to stay in Jerusalem.

---

16. Henry O. Thompson, "Helam," *ABD*, 3:116–17.

17. David's march to the Euphrates in 8:3 must have been part of this victory, making the final victories over the Arameans recorded in 8:3–8 the decisive battle. See McCarter, *II Samuel*, 274–75.

This verse has three parts. The first is a temporal clause, translated literally "And at the return of the year, at the time of the marching forth of the kings," though most translations have something similar to the NIV's, "In the spring, at the time when kings go off to war."[18] We know from numerous citations in Assyrian annals concerning military campaigns that spring was in fact considered the propitious time for war.[19] A date around the spring equinox typically brought the end of the rainy season in the Middle East, resulting in favorable roads for armies to travel and food for troops and horses.[20]

That the events recorded in this chapter take place in the spring (a time for love, as well as war!) is probable, and therefore the NIV and most other translations are not entirely wrong, though somewhat misleading. Instead, the "return of the year" refers most likely to the coming around of the one-year anniversary of the time when the Aramean kings marched against Israel (10:6–19). This is further suggested by the fact that the phrase refers to specific kings in the context (lit., "*the* kings") rather than to kings generally.[21] In fact the preceding context makes mention of "the kings who were vassals of Hadadezer," making this interpretation likely (10:19).

Thus, although it probably is spring, the text is less concerned with this detail than it is to show that David's adultery with Bathsheba occurs approximately one year after the Ammonite-Aramean wars began. Regardless of the specifics, this temporal clause clearly places the events of chapter 11 in the historical context of David's Ammonite wars given in chapter 10, so that the military action of 11:1 is intended to finish what was begun by Hanun and his Aramean allies. In striking irony, David is thus described as performing his rightful (and righteous) role as king of Israel; that is, he is defending the nation against those who want to destroy her (1 Sam. 9:16). The irony, of course, is that David stays home, and rather than defend his subjects, he abuses them (i.e., Bathsheba and her family).

---

18. Contrast NJPS: "At the turn of the year, the season when kings go out [to battle]. . ."

19. "The month of March, named after Mars the Roman god of war, affords a parallel nearer home" (Gordon, *I and II Samuel*, 252).

20. De Vaux, *Ancient Israel*, 190, 251; see also Meir Sternberg, *The Poetics of Biblical Narrative: Ideological Literature and the Drama of Reading* (Bloomington, Ind.: Indiana Univ. Press, 1985), 194.

21. McCarter, *II Samuel*, 284–85; Sternberg, *Poetics*, 194; note Sternberg's two-part analysis of this verse instead of my three parts, 193–96. A fascinating alternative is to take seriously a textual variant ignored by most translations, which reads "the messengers" (or envoys) for "the kings," referring to David's original delegation sent to Hanun (10:1–2). If this is correct, David's deployment of Joab against the Ammonites described in 11:1 comes approximately one year later, aptly timed as revenge for the envoys' humiliation. See Fokkelman, *Narrative Art and Poetry in the Books of Samuel*, 1:50–51.

The second portion of verse 1 contains the central assertion in a series of three verbs: sent, destroyed, besieged.[22] In a way that is obscured by most translations, the original language uses "and" in an almost monotonous, and certainly innocent-sounding, chronicle of the war. The effect is to lure the reader in with facts, baiting us with yet another familiar report of great King David's victories on the battlefield.

But an unfamiliar uneasiness is created by the use of our unit's theme word highlighted as the central thesis: "David *sent* Joab..." (on "send" as *Leitwort*, see comments on 10:1–5). As in the previous chapter, David is in control. He has the royal power; as he sent and defeated the Arameans and Ammonites before, surely, we think, he will send and defeat again. The consecutive verbs confirm our belief: Joab and his men destroy and besiege.

But in reality, the series of "and" clauses prepares the reader for the third and final part of verse 1, which uses yet another coordinating "and" (Heb. *waw*) to tack on a final piece of information: "And [NIV "but"] David remained in Jerusalem."[23] Chapter 8's "the LORD gave David victory wherever he went" has now been turned into "David sent Joab" and "David remained in Jerusalem."

The narrator has baited us with a factual chronicle account of the war in the first two portions of the verse, only to switch our attention at the end of the verse to Jerusalem rather than the battlefield. The second portion of the verse seems emphatic that all able-bodied men are in the field: Joab, the king's servants, and *all* Israel. The last clause directs our attention to David *sitting*[24] alone at home, in contrast to all the others who are *destroying* and *besieging*, so that its "and" is turned quickly into "but" by the ironic association.[25]

However, in a fascinating way, this verse contrasts David not only with the Israelites on the battlefield but also with other kings who have gone forth for battle (i.e., the opening clause of the verse). "David remained in

---

22. The Hebrew *waw*-consecutive with prefix verbs most often associates actions sequentially in time or consequentially in logic (Bill T. Arnold and John H. Choi, *A Guide to Biblical Hebrew Syntax* [Cambridge: Cambridge Univ. Press, forthcoming], par. 3.5.2 a and b; Bruce K. Waltke and M. O'Connor, *An Introduction to Biblical Hebrew Syntax* [Winona Lake, Ind.: Eisenbrauns, 1990], 547–51; Paul Joüon, *A Grammar of Biblical Hebrew*, trans. T. Muraoka; 2 vols. [Rome: Pontifical Biblical Institute, 1991–1993], 389–92). The verb "destroyed" is consequential in this verse; "besieged" is sequential. Hence: "David sent Joab and his servants with him and all Israel, *and so* they destroyed the Ammonites, *and then* they besieged Rabbah."

23. Sternberg, *Poetics*, 195.

24. The literal meaning of the verb "remained" (*yšb*).

25. Word order also signals contrast here (Waltke and O'Connor, *Biblical Hebrew Syntax*, 650–51). For the most sensitive translation, taking into account these specific features of 11:1, see Alter, *David Story*, 249–50.

Jerusalem" is emphasized in a way that builds a "thematic bridge of irony between the beginning and the end of the verse."[26] By placing in the foreground the picture of Israel's adversary kings marching off to war, the narrator has put the spotlight on David sitting at home. The contrast would have been too transparent had the first and last phrases of verse 1 been placed together: "At the time of the marching forth of the kings, David stayed in." The narrator has chosen the much subtler method of separating them with the matter-of-fact report of the war.

So what is David doing in Jerusalem? Approximately one year after the Ammonites start the conflict, while Joab and the army are risking their lives for the good of the nation, David is at home "killing time."[27] The text does not explicitly condemn David for staying at home. In fact, a case can be made that David is acquiescing to the wishes of his men by staying out of harm's way (21:17).[28] But all narratives require a certain amount of "gap-filling" by the reader, and the contrasts of verse 1 are carefully and deliberately constructed to help us fill the gap.[29]

> As the narrative viewpoint moves into a close-up on David, we are reminded ... that while the king of Israel is home enjoying his siesta and then represented peeping at a bathing beauty on a neighboring roof, the fighting men of Israel—who in the past, including the last campaign just reported in Chapter 10, were commanded personally by their monarch—are out on the dusty plains of Ammon, risking their lives to protect the national interest.[30]

Thus, the three parts of verse 1 present a central assertion, modified by two additional pieces of information. The additional information, as it turns out, holds as much significance for our understanding of the rest of chapter 11 as the central assertion, only more subtly stated. David has sent Joab and the army against the Ammonites. His timing is good because it coincides with the first anniversary of the beginning of the war. But the final clause changes subjects. Instead of Joab and the army "destroying" and "besieging," David is

---

26. For this quote and more on what follows here, see Sternberg, *Poetics*, 195. By means of this "thematic bridge of irony," Sternberg says the narrator devises "an oblique and subtle exposure."

27. Baldwin, *1 and 2 Samuel*, 231.

28. For this line, see Bergen, *1, 2 Samuel*, 363–64. For the possibility that detail about David's staying at home is part of an original source that is not incriminating but is seen by the compiler/editor of the court history to have ironic potential and is used to introduce the subsequent narrative, see McCarter, *II Samuel*, 285.

29. Sternberg, *Poetics*, 186.

30. Alter, *The Art of Biblical Narrative*, 76.

"staying" at home. "All the terror of war and the confusion of battle are brack-eted out, making way for another kind of terror and confusion."[31]

David, Bathsheba, and Uriah (11:2–27)

THE BOOKS OF SAMUEL have so far illustrated by means of both negative and positive examples the nature of genuine Israelite kingship. Saul was a nega-tive example of how the monarch should appear; David in every case has been exemplary as the ideal king. But the shocking events narrated here reveal that David is capable of shameful actions that threaten his kingdom, his family, and his life. We would rather not read further. Yet the inspired text invites us to consider that we are all capable of such dark behavior, and taken together with chapter 12, we can learn even through these difficult narratives how to deal with sin and death.

The sad events narrated here may be divided into four episodes.[32] (1) The first is David's affair with Bathsheba reported in 12:2–5. After the care-fully crafted introduction in verse 1, verse 2 portrays the king loitering about on the roof of the palace after first lounging on his couch. Again we are reminded of the contrast with Joab and the Israelite soldiers, who are destroy-ing and besieging. While so occupied (or unoccupied!), David sees a beau-tiful woman bathing on a nearby rooftop.[33] The narrator emphasizes Bathsheba's beauty (she "was very beautiful," 11:2[34]) and immediately alarms the reader that danger lurks around the corner.

The narration is further characterized by three occurrences of our theme word, "send" (11:3, 4, 5; see comments on 10:1–5). David *sends* someone to

---

31. Brueggemann, *First and Second Samuel*, 273.

32. Anderson, *2 Samuel*, 152.

33. Occasionally someone suggests that Bathsheba is not entirely innocent for bathing publicly within plain view of the royal palace, and that she must bear a portion of the guilt. A. Schulz, *Das zweite Buch Samuel* (EHAT 8/2; Münster: Aschendorff, 1920), 114; Hertzberg, *I and II Samuel*, 309. But such an approach raises a *historical* question of an intensely *literary* presentation, in which the blame is carefully and deliberately placed only on David. The narrator is uninterested in the possibility and simply defers the question, making it impos-sible for us to speculate about her motives. Even Hertzberg admits that our narrator "lays the blame squarely on the king's shoulders" (Hertzberg, *I and II Samuel*, 310), which should make dubious all such speculation about Bathsheba's motives. Rather, the narrative gives us "no real reason to assume that Bathsheba actually intended to be seen by the king" (Ander-son, *2 Samuel*, 153). If we insist on looking for historical explanations for Bathsheba's actions, it is better to assume the heat of an unusually warm spring day in the late afternoon (the meaning of "evening" in v. 2) forces the woman to escape "the suffocatingly hot atmosphere of her house" (Youngblood, "1, 2 Samuel," 929).

34. A phrase reserved in the Old Testament for people of striking physical appearance (Youngblood, "1, 2 Samuel," 929).

find out more about Bathsheba. He is able to do so because he is, after all, the king. Just as his royal position qualified him to send messengers and generals and armies in the previous chapter (and in 11:1), so now he dispatches someone seeking information. The reported facts apparently do not deter David: The woman is the daughter of a prominent individual (Eliam) and the wife of Uriah the Hittite, whom we learn later is one of David's faithful fighting heroes (23:39; 1 Chron. 11:41).[35] Such details might arouse relief in the reader at first, but they eventually serve only to highlight the premeditated intent of David's next action.

David then *sends* again, this time with the intention of fetching Bathsheba to the palace (of course, David knows that Uriah, along with all the other mighty warriors, are conveniently occupied in Ammon). The specific verbs used in 11:4 to describe David's actions are painfully clear: He sends, he takes her ("take" is slightly obscured by the NIV's "David sent messengers *to get* her"), and he lies with her. Mercifully brief, with no account of conversation or mitigating circumstances, the verse coldly recounts David's crime.

The use of "take" here is probably also intended to recall what the wise prophet Samuel warned long ago: Kings are "takers" (1 Sam. 8:11–18): They will take your sons and your daughters (as David here takes Eliam's daughter), the best of your fields and vineyards, a tenth of your grain, your menservants and maidservants, and a tenth of your flocks, and they will make them all their own.[36] The Israelites requested a king like the other nations of Canaan. Samuel warned that such kings take and take, and when everything is gone, they force you into slavery. Now it appears that David is giving them what they requested.

---

35. Assuming the Eliam in 2 Sam. 23:34 is the same as Bathsheba's father mentioned here, he was also one of David's mighty warriors and the son of Ahithophel, one of David's key advisers (16:23). It seems likely that Eliam had been with David since the dark days of his exile, or at least since the beginning of David's Hebron kingship (R. C. Bailey, "Eliam," *ABD*, 2:459–60). This is another example of David marrying into a politically influential family, and at the same time another example of taking a wife who had been married previously (Levenson and Halpern, "The Political Import of David's Marriages," 507–18). Uriah's gentilic "the Hittite" does not necessarily imply he was either a foreigner or a mercenary, especially in light of his apparently Israelite name (ending as it does in the theophoric "-iah," that is "-yah" for Yahweh). It seems more likely that his ancestors had migrated to Israel from one of the predominantly Aramean Neo-Hittite states of northern Syria, and perhaps converted to Israelite Yahwism (see McCarter, *II Samuel*, 285–86).

36. The irony is that David is the king who was content to be *given* the kingdom (2 Sam. 2–4), whereas now he seizes a wife by force. See David M. Gunn, "David and the Gift of the Kingdom," *Semeia* 3 (1975): 14–45; Brueggemann, *First and Second Samuel*, 273. See also the Original Meaning section for 1 Sam. 8:10–18.

The little phrase near the end of 11:4 (in parentheses in the NIV) sounds an ominous note: "She had purified herself from her uncleanness." The point of the clause is that Bathsheba is cleansing herself ritually because of menstruation (as prescribed by the law of Lev. 15:19–24).[37] Such a detail clarifies a few further facts about the episode. (a) She has not been pregnant prior to intercourse with David. (b) Intercourse with David takes place precisely at the most opportune time for conception. (c) Since Uriah is off in the battlefield, he cannot possibly be the father. A small phrase with big implications!

David is not the only character who "sends" in this episode, for Bathsheba *sends* a succinct message (only two words in Hebrew) that changes everything: "I am pregnant." David exercised power in chapter 10 and thus far in chapter 11 by "sending." But when Bathsheba "sends," David must deal with a different kind of power. The power of wronged Bathsheba, the power of David's own sin—these are powers that David will now attempt to answer with more "sending" (11:6). But ultimately, Yahweh will "send," and David will relent (12:1).

(2) The second episode of chapter 11 narrates David's first attempts to cover up the unfortunate consequences of his affair with Bathsheba (11:6–13). His machinations reveal a pitiful dependence on human power structures reminiscent of King Saul. Has David learned nothing from Saul's failures? Will Israel ever understand the nature of an Israelite monarchy and how it must be different from Canaanite monarchies?

Our unit's theme word ("send") occurs three times in verse 6. David has the royal authority and power to *send* a decree to Joab, who has the military power to *send* Uriah back to Jerusalem from the battlefield. David believes he has a plan to hide the truth, and he does not hesitate to take action to enact the plan. In order to cover his guilt, David tries subterfuge and deceit, old and familiar friends of all who have walked this path (Gen. 3:12–13). He has faith in his plan, and he believes his royal power is sufficient for the task. So, as elsewhere, David *sends* in order to control and dominate, and also this time to conceal.

When Uriah arrives in Jerusalem, David appears to be greatly concerned about Joab, the army, and the progress of the war. His hypocritical questions in 11:7 are likely intended to give Uriah the impression that David has summoned him from the battlefield in order to get an accurate military report. But the reader knows better! In light of what David has just done, his feigned concern leaves the reader unsettled. How can our hero, the anointed of Yahweh, be so hypocritical? How can he maintain appearances of anxiety

---

37. For more on what follows in this paragraph, see McCarter, *II Samuel*, 286.

about the welfare of his troops after what he has done? Can such hypocrisy be allowed to stand? Will Israel's king be able to cover up this royal mess, all while appearing to have Joab's (and Uriah's) best interests at heart?

David's pathetic attempts to manipulate and control Uriah bring the king's hypocrisy to the foreground (11:8–13). His suggestion that Uriah go home and "wash his feet" may be a euphemism for sexual intercourse, which is evidently how Uriah understands these words. At the very least, the expression "wash your feet" connotes a return home from a journey, so that David is inviting Uriah to refresh himself in his own home.[38] Obviously, David wants Uriah to spend a night at home with his wife, creating the possibility later that Uriah is the father of Bathsheba's child. David may also be attempting to trap Uriah in a legal technicality, since soldiers on active duty were required to abstain from sexual activity (Deut. 23:9–11).[39] Whatever the cultural and legal implications, David was desperate. All would be well if Uriah would only spend a night relaxing at home with Bathsheba.

David has grossly underestimated Uriah's character. He refuses to go home despite the king's persistence and cajoling. He disregards the king's invitations for two reasons: religious convictions and loyalty to his fellow soldiers (note his reference to "the ark," "my master Joab," and "my lord's men," 11:11).[40] The great irony of our text is that this convert of foreign ancestry is more righteous than the Israelite king. Uriah, "the Hittite" (as he is labeled seven times in our text[41]), is a man of such character that he shuns any minor infraction of his duty as an Israelite soldier. He adamantly refuses to compromise his commitments to Yahweh's war against Ammon or to his fellow soldiers. Yet King David, the anointed one of Yahweh, has abused his God-given power and attempts to manipulate a faithful and righteous servant in a desperate scam to save himself. Repetition creates a striking irony: "Uriah drunk is more pious than David sober."[42]

(3) The third episode is the shocking account of murder (11:14–25). When David's attempts to cover his sins with subterfuge and deception fail to work, he does something more sinister. He is not finished *sending* yet; he

---

38. Keil and Delitzsch, *Samuel*, 384; Anderson, 2 *Samuel*, 154.

39. Evans, *1 and 2 Samuel*, 188; Anderson, 2 *Samuel*, 154.

40. Some have speculated that Uriah has heard rumors among the court officials and is suspicious of David's kindness (Hertzberg, *I and II Samuel*, 310). His refusal to see Bathsheba would be his only means of protection against a king who has wronged him. However, as with speculation about Bathsheba's ulterior motives, the text has no interest in explaining Uriah's actions as anything other than innocent loyalty. Uriah is a trusting servant of the king and is loyal to Yahweh's causes, which throws David's guilt into greater relief by contrast.

41. "Uriah the Hittite" occurs in 11:3, 6, 17, 21, 24; 12:9, 10 (and see also 23:39).

42. Ackroyd, *Second Book of Samuel*, 102.

has still other powerful means at his disposal. His next step is to write Uriah's own death warrant and "send" it to Joab by Uriah's own hand (11:14). As David had sent and taken Bathsheba (11:4), as he had sent and retrieved Uriah from the battlefield (11:6), now he sends and kills Uriah. His powerful royal prerogative has been turned to evil purposes. The nine-month gestation period does not allow David much time to act in order to create the appearance that Bathsheba's pregnancy resulted from her marriage. He becomes so intent on destroying Uriah in order to save himself that he jeopardizes his army's actions against Rabbah and trivializes the deaths of Israelite soldiers that he himself has caused.

David had shown the capacity to grieve deeply over the deaths of men who were his adversaries (Saul and Abner in 1:11–27 and 3:31–39 respectively). In this case, Uriah is no adversary but a faithful warrior who has apparently been with David many years. Yet David does not mourn. His flippant response to the news of Uriah's death (11:25) is shocking illustration of how far David has gone. His drive to cover up his sin leads him to sin again. Each new step of deceit and subterfuge seems easier than the last.

David carries out his deceit without even the remotest hint of remorse or sorrow recorded in the text. His words for Joab ("the sword devours one as well as another") is roughly equivalent to, "Oh well, such is a soldier's sad fate," or "Oh well, we all have to die sometime."[43] It seems justifiable in David's eyes that this good man should die in order to conceal the king's sin, which illustrates how hardened David has become about his own guilt. Everything in the text reminds us of the tragic consequences of sin in our lives. Sin, once it has been committed, if suppressed and concealed, will only lead to more sinning and, if left uncontested, will result in hardened, uncaring sinners. The escalation of sinful actions—illustrated also by Genesis 3–11—is known to all of us as ubiquitous and universal in human experience.

(4) The fourth part of our chapter is the (apparent!) conclusion of the story (11:26–27): David takes Bathsheba as his wife, and she bears him a son. After the official time of mourning is over, David "sent and brought her" (lit., 11:27; NIV "had her brought") to the royal palace. This is the last time in our text David is the subject of *sending* (the theme word *šlḥ*). From now on, God or Joab will do the *sending* (12:1, 25, 27). David has exercised his royal power for the last time; he has succeeded in manipulating everyone around him and has managed to cover his sin with Bathsheba. Thus far, everything seems normal, if not reflecting even a certain royal magnanimity in taking in a combat hero's widow. From David's perspective, that is the end of the matter; if the text ended with 11:26–27a, we would agree.

---

43. The phrase may have been a familiar soldier's cliché, on the order of "every bullet has its billet" (Alter, *David Story*, 255).

But this is why I called these verses the "apparent" conclusion. In reality, what ends the story in human eyes is really only the beginning of the struggle from God's perspective. The fact is that 11:27a does not end the matter. Sin has been concealed from human view, but there is much more to reality than only the human view. The little clause that ends the chapter injects a different element, a divine element, that reverberates throughout chapter 12: "But the thing David had done displeased the LORD" (lit., "was evil in the eyes of the LORD"). In David's eyes, sin has been concealed and the matter is over. But in Yahweh's eyes, evil must be confronted.[44]

A number of scholars have proposed a concentric structure for chapters 11 and 12. In such a structure, David's sending of Joab to besiege Rabbah in 11:1 corresponds with Joab's sending for David to besiege Rabbah in 12:26–31. These matching paragraphs constitute an outer frame for the whole, as we have seen. Within them are more matching paragraphs forming an inner concentric arrangement as follows:[45]

A. David sends Joab to besiege Rabbah (11:1)
  B. David sleeps with Bathsheba, who becomes pregnant (11:2−5)
    C. David has Uriah killed (11:6−17)
      D. Joab sends David a message (11:18−27a)
        E. The Lord is displeased with David (11:27b)
      D'. The Lord sends David a messenger (12:1−14)
    C'. The Lord strikes David's infant son, who dies (12:15−23)
  B'. David sleeps with Bathsheba, who becomes pregnant (12:24−25)
A'. Joab sends for David to besiege and capture Rabbah (12:26−31)

Though there are features of this arrangement that seem somewhat forced, I am intrigued by the literary fulcrum of the arrangement at 11:27b. This type of chiastic or concentric literary structure often emphasizes the central core, suggesting in this case that the Lord's displeasure with David's actions is the focus of chapters 11−12. As one of the few places in the court history where the inner thoughts of God are stated explicitly, this little phrase is determinative for the rest of chapters 12−20.[46]

---

44. The phrase appears also to be intentionally juxtaposed with 11:25, where the literal translation of David's message to Joab is "let not this deed be evil in your eyes" (NIV, "Don't let this upset you"). Verses 25 and 27 together show that "royal perceptions of reality are not congruent with Yahweh's perception" (Brueggemann, *First and Second Samuel,* 279).

45. Youngblood, "1, 2 Samuel," 927, and for a slightly more complex chiastic structure, see Sacon, "Literary Structure," 42−44.

46. Others are 12:24 and 17:14. See Gerhard von Rad, *The Problem of the Hexateuch and Other Essays,* trans. E. W. Trueman Dicken (New York: McGraw-Hill, 1966), 198−201; Gordon, *I and II Samuel,* 256; McCarter, *II Samuel,* 298.

Beginning with the death of Bathsheba's newborn, David's life is plagued by manifold problems. The contrast with the historian's account of David prior to the Bathsheba episode is striking. Though he previously had problems of a different nature (Saul's attempts to kill him, etc.), David has lived an almost enchanted life. He has always seemed to come out on top. But chapters 12–20 portray a different picture in which David is plagued with problems stemming mostly from his own family. The role of 11:27b is to connect the dots, to draw a line from David's sin and its consequences to the problems in his family. The ultimate reason is David's own sin, which he futilely attempts to conceal and which leaves him with unresolved problems.

Nathan the Prophet: You Are the Man! (12:1–12)

OUR TEXT HAS PRESENTED A DILEMMA: How does one challenge nearly absolute power? The books of Samuel slowly define the nature and limitations of the new Israelite monarchy, and the question now becomes: How does one correct this king who has assumed so much power? Will Yahweh permit this abuse of power to stand? Will Israel's king behave just like other Near Eastern kings? Will David be another Saul? The answer comes quickly and with prophetic certainty. Samuel had revived the role of prophecy in ancient Israel and had stood beside Saul to challenge and rebuke.[47] Now Nathan assumes the prophetic stance; he speaks on Yahweh's behalf in order to correct David.

This is the second time Nathan has appeared with little or no introduction (see 7:2). As we have seen, the books of Samuel recognize and value the preserving and rejuvenating power of God's word (see comments on 1 Sam. 3).[48] The arrival of a true prophet needs no other introduction. His authoritative speech demands attention, so that it seems unimportant where he has come from or who his family was (cf. Elijah's sudden appearance in 1 Kings 17:1, though at least his birthplace is given).

The return of our theme word "send" (*šlḥ*) in 12:1 is ironic: "The LORD *sent* Nathan to David."[49] David had sent, first in order to commit adultery, and then in order to cover up his crime. Now just when it appears David has gotten away with it and the story is over, Yahweh does some sending of his own.

---

47. When Samuel began his ministry, the "word of the LORD" and prophetic visions had been rare (1 Sam. 3:1). But God established Samuel as a prophet and revealed himself to Samuel through his word at Shiloh (3:20–21).

48. This led early Jewish scholars to attribute these books to prophets, much of it to Samuel himself (*b. B. Bat.* 14b).

49. On the use of this word in our text, see comments on 10:1–5.

How *does* a prophet correct a king who has assumed absolute power? The best way to expose David's hypocrisy is to have him condemn himself. Nathan's parable about the rich man and the poor man arouses David's indignation, and he quickly condemns himself by condemning the rich man (12:1–6). The parable's image of the rich man cruelly slaughtering the poor man's "one little ewe lamb" speaks directly to the heart of this former shepherd. With decisiveness and passion (he "burned with anger"), the king quickly declares that the rich man is guilty and deserving of death, though as king he will allow severe reparations as punishment (12:5–6).

David has announced his official royal judgment on any man who would behave in such a way.[50] Nathan comes immediately to the point of his parable (12:7): "You are the man!" David's sin is that he has "despised the word of the LORD" by committing evil in God's sight (cf. 1 Sam. 15:23, 26). The Lord has given him everything, but he wants more; especially he wants what is not rightfully his to have. As David chose the way of violence to cover his sin, using "the sword of the Ammonites," so the sword will never depart from his royal dynasty. God's punishment matches the crime. Furthermore, calamity (lit., "evil") will arise against David from within his own household (12:11–12).[51]

This judgment raises several questions for the reader and creates suspense in the narrative. David has been promised an eternal dynasty—his house will endure forever (ch. 7). But this punishment sounds similar to that pronounced against Saul and raises the possibility that David will be rejected as Saul had been (1 Sam. 15:10–31). This prophetic pronouncement also creates tension with the great covenant promises in 2 Samuel 7. Will David survive as king? Will his dynasty endure forever? Everything that follows in chapters 13–20 flows from this initial judgment. Amnon's rape of Tamar, his murder at the hands of Absalom, and Absalom's rebellion all represent threats to the great prophetic vision of 2 Samuel 7.[52] For the present, the historian leaves us in suspense about David's future.

---

50. Remember that one of the roles of the king was to adjudicate legal cases and ensure justice in the land (2 Sam. 8:15; 1 Kings 3:16–28).

51. In the Old Testament, divine punishment normally mirrors precisely the sin being punished. So, for example, here David is guilty of committing "evil" (*raʿ*, v. 9) and God responds by raising "evil" (*raʿah*, v. 11) from David's own house (NIV "calamity"). Similarly notice the words "evil" and "disaster" in 1 Kings 21:20–21 and Jer. 18:7–12 (all the same root in Heb.). So judgment and punishment in the Old Testament follow a sort of "poetic justice," meaning the penalty inflicted on the sinner matches repayment in kind for the harm done in the offense. Like the *lex talionis* principle in the ancient Near East ("eye for eye," "tooth for tooth"), the Old Testament uses a commensurate form of poetic justice through such wordplays. See Patrick D. Miller Jr., *Sin and Judgment in the Prophets: A Stylistic and Theological Analysis* (SBLMS 27; Chico, Calif.: Scholars Press, 1982).

52. Satterthwaite, "David in the Books of Samuel," 57–59.

Death of Newborn; Birth of Solomon (12:13−25)

HERE WE LEARN DAVID'S REAL CHARACTER. Certainly he is remembered for the heinous sins of chapter 11. But his response to the prophetic word in 12:13 is why David became known as Israel's ideal king. Unlike Saul's repentance in 1 Samuel 15, David's words "I have sinned" are full of genuine remorse and sorrow.[53] Saul, too, confessed using similar language (1 Sam. 15:24, 30). But before confession, Saul first tried deflection and argumentation. When those strategies failed, he confessed wrongdoing but exhibited no signs of contrition or repentance. Saul's "I have sinned" was followed by equivocation, with words roughly equivalent to "but we can fix it, right?" By contrast, David's simple phrase "I have sinned against the LORD" (only two words in Hebrew) is spoken alone.[54] There is no attempt to blame or dodge. In fact, it is possible that David has been miserable with guilt and actually welcomes Nathan's reproach.[55]

In order to appreciate fully David's terse confession in verse 13, we should remember the roles of kings and prophets in other cultures of the ancient world. Simply put, David does not *have* to confess! Other kings did as much as or more than David has done, and prophets in their courts had no right to deny them the royal privileges (see 1 Kings 21, esp. v. 7). In fact, a king in David's position could easily have simply killed Nathan and asked for another prophet, one who would say only nice things (of course!).

But the books of Samuel are teaching us that Israel's kings are different—indeed, they have to be different, because in reality it is Yahweh who rules. On a more personal level, this passage also shows that David is someone who wants to be what he is called to be. He quickly confesses and repents, not because he is trapped but because he recognizes it as the best way. Ultimately, this is the difference between believers and unbelievers, the difference between Saul and David, between David and lesser kings.

The biblical understanding of sin is defined elsewhere but is illustrated in chapter 11. Likewise, biblical understandings of repentance and forgiveness are defined elsewhere but are illustrated here.[56] True repentance (12:13a) is

---

53. Many Hebrew manuscripts have a space in the text after the words, "I have sinned," which some have suggested was intended to invite a cross reference to Ps. 51, considering it a commentary on this passage. Such correlating of poetry and narrative provides an early commentary on both. See Ackroyd, *Second Book of Samuel*, 111; Anderson, *2 Samuel*, 163.

54. Brueggemann has observed the way the entire narrative may be summarized in three phrases spoken by the leading characters, each phrase of only two words in Heb.: "I am pregnant" (11:5), "You are the man" (12:7), and "I have sinned against the LORD" (12:13) (*First and Second Samuel*, 282–83).

55. Evans, *1 and 2 Samuel*, 185. Compare also David's "I have sinned greatly" in 24:10.

56. As we have seen throughout this commentary, historical narratives such as we have in the books of Samuel often illustrate implicitly truths taught explicitly elsewhere in Scripture. See the Bridging Contexts section.

met instantly with genuine forgiveness (12:13b). Israel's law at times in their history prescribed death for the one guilty of David's sin (see, e.g., Lev. 20:10). But God is merciful. Nathan's reassuring words contain one of several metaphors for forgiveness in the Old Testament: "The LORD has taken away your sin." Its implication is essentially spatial: Sin is removed, carried off to a great distance (see Bridging Contexts).[57]

As wonderful as this lesson is, the big question is "why?" Why would Yahweh suspend his judgment as prescribed by the Sinai covenant, and why does he not make an example of David for his sin? The response demanded by a holistic reading of our text is twofold. (1) David's repentance is genuine, especially when compared to Saul's in 1 Samuel 15. The ideal quality of the anointed one is found here: He sincerely regrets his misdoing and longs for atonement. He immediately submits to Yahweh's messenger with a contrite heart.

(2) More importantly, the text illustrates the truth expressed in one of Israel's ancient creeds: Yahweh is a "compassionate and gracious God, slow to anger, abounding in love and faithfulness, maintaining love to thousands, and forgiving wickedness, rebellion and sin" (Ex. 34:6–7; cf. texts dependent on it, e.g., Num. 14:18–19; Neh. 9:17; Ps. 86:15; 103:8; 145:8; Joel 2:13; Jonah 4:2).[58] In contrast to Aristotle's "unmoved Mover," Israel's God is characterized by love and compassion, moved into gracious action by the penitent servant. He therefore overrides his plan for judgment (see esp. Jer. 18:7–12).

At the same time as 12:13 illustrates God's merciful forgiveness, 12:14 illustrates the unmitigated consequences of sin, even though forgiven by God. The punishment of death has been turned aside from David because of his repentance, but the aftermath of sin remains; the child will die. Sin that has been forgiven and forgotten by God may still leave human scars.

It is possible that 12:13 and 14, taken together, convey the concept that the guilt has been removed from David and placed instead on the newborn son. That is, the guilt of sin cannot simply be forgiven but must be transferred

---

57. The most common verb to express forgiveness in the Old Testament is *slḥ* ("forgive, pardon") (*HALOT*, 2:757; BDB, 699). But biblical Hebrew also uses several powerful metaphors to connote various aspects of forgiveness, such as healing of disease (2 Chron. 7:14; Ps. 103:3), God's not remembering (Jer. 31:34), God's treading sin underfoot and casting sins into the depths of the sea (Mic. 7:19), cleansing from impurity (Jer. 33:8), and God's wiping away or erasing sin (Ps. 51:2; Isa. 43:25). In Nathan's phrase, he uses the Hiphil of a verb meaning (lit.) "to make pass by/over" (*heᶜ ʾbir*), so that David's sin has been put away, removed at a distance. Some scholars have thought the verb also implies David's sin has been removed by being transferred to the newborn. But the metaphor may be spatial without requiring this interpretation.

58. Bergen, *1, 2 Samuel*, 373.

from one person (i.e., David) to another (the newborn).[59] Thus, the death of the son atones for David's sin, who is allowed to live. The child has died vicariously for David. However, it is equally possible (perhaps more likely) that David's sin has been removed while the consequences of that sin are allowed to continue, resulting in the death of the son. Similar terminology ("You are not going to die," 12:13, compared to "the son born to you will die," 12:14) does not necessarily require a causal correspondence between them, as if to say: "You may live *because* he will die."

Moreover, as we have suggested, 2 Samuel in general invites us to see the ensuing troubles in David's family as the *sum total* of David's punishment. If the death of the newborn was the punishment for David's crime, the book-level reading would be redundant.[60] The problems with Amnon and Absalom cannot be consequences of David's crime if the son's death has already paid the penalty of that crime. The death of the newborn was one consequence of David's sin, but it is not David's punishment.

Nonetheless, the death of Bathsheba's new son leaves today's readers with one of the most difficult aspects of Old Testament faith. Why is David forgiven while the innocent newborn has to die? The answer lies in the Bible's distinction between punishment and consequence.[61] The child's death is a result of David's sin, but this is not the same as punishment. It is a fundamental principle of life that God may forgive and cleanse us of all wrongdoing, but the consequences of our sin may, and in fact often, remain. The innocent suffer for crimes committed by someone else, but such suffering is not punishment for those crimes. A crack baby may die soon after birth because the mother used crack during pregnancy. The child dies; the mother lives. The child's death is not the punishment but the consequences of the mother's sin. Her punishment will take a different form.

A second part of the ancient creed just quoted from Exodus 34:7 acknowledges the fact that Yahweh visits "the iniquity of the parents upon the children and the children's children, to the third and the fourth generation."[62] A variant of this creed in the Ten Commandments (Ex. 20:5–6) emphasizes that God may allow sin's consequences to endure for three, perhaps four gener-

---

59. McCarter, *II Samuel*, 301. Compare NEB, "The LORD has laid on another the consequences of your sin." But this is tempered somewhat by Ackroyd (*Second Book of Samuel*, 111).

60. As hinted by Anderson, 2 *Samuel*, 163.

61. Evans, *1 and 2 Samuel*, 190.

62. So NRSV. The NIV's "he punishes" the children for the collocation *paqad ʿal*, "visit [iniquities] upon [someone]," may miss the gracious aspect of this visitation. The expression presupposes the children are treated in accord with their own participation in the crimes of the parents. For an attempt to understand this credal expression in light of contradictory statements in Deut. 24:16 and Ezek. 18:4, see Peter Enns, *Exodus* (NIVAC; Grand Rapids: Zondervan, 2000), 415–17.

ations, but his love extends for "a thousand generations of those who love me." In other words, Yahweh graciously limits the duration of sin's consequences that would otherwise continue on their own indefinitely, but his love is extended to a thousand generations of one's descendants. Because of Yahweh's nature, sin has a limited life span, but love lasts forever.

The episode of the child's death and David's reversal of conventional mourning customs leaves many interpreters perplexed (12:15–23). The normal period of mourning lasted seven days (1 Sam. 31:13; cf. Gen. 50:10), and the child died on the seventh day (12:18). Since David assumes an attitude of mourning while he prays for the sick boy, he has already fulfilled the customary period of mourning proleptically, and there was no need to continue his futile prayers for the boy's life (12:21–23).[63] Though modern scholars (like his ancient courtiers) are confused by David's disregard for social customs, there may be nothing more intended here than the depth of David's passion and hope in God. "He was counting on the open door of the divine 'perhaps': 'Who knows?' (cf. similarly Joel 2:13–14; Jonah 3:9)."[64]

The mention of David's worshiping in the "house of the LORD" (12:20) requires brief comment since it normally refers to Solomon's temple built years after David. Interpreters have suggested one of two possibilities: (1) Solomon's temple was in fact only a renovation of an old Jebusite cult center captured by David and used here as a place for Yahwistic worship; (2) this is an anachronistic reference to Solomon's temple mistakenly left in the text by later editors.[65]

But let us note again that the Mosaic tabernacle seems to have been used for years at Shiloh, and the traditions coming from that period use both "Tent of Meeting" and "house" to describe a semipermanent structure built around the ancient tabernacle (see comments at 1 Sam. 1:9–18; 3:1–4:1a). Subsequently, David brought the ark of the covenant into his new capital city and placed it in "the tent that David had pitched for it" (2 Sam. 6:17).[66] The

---

63. Gordon, I and II Samuel, 259; on the difficulties some interpreters see here, see McCarter, II Samuel, 301–2. Theodore J. Lewis suggests this text contains a vestige of ancient death-cult practices. It is possible that David's vigil in 12:15–24 intentionally imitated a person mourning the dead, and the narrator has used specific terminology reminiscent of "ritual descents" known elsewhere in Scripture and in Ugaritic literature. Thus David "was ritually acting out a descent into the underworld to try to bring his son back from the clutches of death" (Lewis, Cults of the Dead, 43–44).

64. Youngblood, "1, 2 Samuel," 948. Joyce Baldwin says this shows David is not fatalistic; rather, he responded as "a child hears the statement of a parent, who sometimes changes his mind about a punishment if the child behaves acceptably" (Baldwin, 1 and 2 Samuel, 240).

65. McCarter, II Samuel, 302; Anderson, 2 Samuel, 162.

66. Thus, David is unsatisfied with his new royal palace, while "the ark of God remains in a tent" (7:2).

Hebrew word for "house" (*bet*, like its cognate in Akkadian, *bītu*) was common for a divine temple, and it eventually came to be used for the semipermanent structure at Shiloh (1 Sam. 1:7, 24; 3:15) and likely continued to be used for the tent-shrine temporarily set up by David in Jerusalem.

The birth of another son between David and Bathsheba holds great symbolic significance (12:24–25). Bathsheba is called David's "wife" rather than the "wife of Uriah the Hittite" (cf. 11:3; 12:10). More importantly, Yahweh loves the new son, who bears two names, Solomon and Jedidiah.[67] Though other children are born to this union (Solomon, in fact, is the fourth, 1 Chron. 3:5), he will have special significance in fulfilling the covenant promises of 2 Samuel 7.

Nathan the prophet returns to declare, not another oracle of judgment against David, but Yahweh's love for the new son. Such a blessing confirms that David has been restored in his relationship with Yahweh; he has put his sin behind him. Fittingly, the historian uses one of the last occurrences of the unit's theme word to narrate Nathan's return (see comments on 10:1–5 for "send"). Yahweh holds the power now, and he *sends* (*šlḥ*) a message through the prophet to name the lad Jedidiah (12:25). Yahweh holds no grudges; David's dynasty is not in danger.

David Captures Rabbah (12:26–31)

THE HISTORIAN NOW returns to an annalistic style military report of David's Ammonite wars, narrating the capture of the royal city. This paragraph is a historical flashback used as a literary frame. It serves together with 10:1–11:1 to create a literary envelope for the whole.[68]

---

67. Not uncommon in the Old Testament, especially for kings, who occasionally have a personal name and a throne name (Anderson, *2 Samuel*, 165). The name "Solomon" probably means "his replacement," which means his parents see him as a replacement for his lost sibling. Symbolically, this comes to have powerful significance, since Solomon is also to become David's replacement. See G. Gerleman, "Die Wurzel *šlm*," *ZAW* 85 (1973): 1–14; J. J. Stamm, "Der Name des Königs Salomo," *TZ* 16 (1960): 285–97.

68. Since the beginning of the siege (11:1), Bathsheba has given birth, conceived again, and given birth to Solomon (who, as we have seen, is actually the fourth son born to David and Bathsheba, 1 Chron. 3:5). It is unlikely that the siege of Rabbah lasted so long, which illustrates again the nonchronological nature of these narratives. The narrator has concluded the personal drama prior to recording the national victory over Rabbah, revealing the organizing principle of using the war materials as a framing device. "The tale's principle of montage sacrifices chronology to structural-thematic considerations, and the narrator so manipulates the sequence as to introduce the victory only *after* bringing the personal story to an end" (Sternberg, *Poetics*, 196); see also Jan P. Fokkelman, *Narrative Art and Poetry in the Books of Samuel*, 1:94–96.

Joab and the army (formerly including Uriah the Hittite) capture Rabbah's water supply, and it will only be a matter of time before the city falls into Israelite hands. In the last occurrence of our passage's theme word, Joab uses his power to "send" (12:27, šlḥ) a message to David. Just as the war was precipitated by the sending of messengers (10:2, 4), so now it is concluded. In a book that routinely gives few military details, this paragraph is striking. But the details themselves merely highlight the irony of David stealing the credit for Joab's work while he has also stolen Uriah's wife.

THIS UNIT'S LITERARY POWER and classic themes give it a universal appeal, which explains why it has inspired artists and authors for centuries. One of my personal favorites is the way in which Sir Arthur Conan Doyle used the story of David, Bathsheba, and Uriah as a clue for solving one of his wonderful Sherlock Holmes mysteries.[69] However, as Christian readers we recognize this text has more to offer than remarkable literary qualities. With captivating poignancy, the text traces through the actions and responses of one of Israel's great heroes of the faith three of the most salient components of that faith: sin, repentance, and forgiveness.

Sin and its consequences. This is one of Israel's classic passages on the nature of sin and its consequences. It powerfully and subtly strips David of his luster and turns the focus on us as readers. It is "more than we want to know about David and more than we can bear to understand about ourselves."[70] The text painfully recounts David's premeditated and methodical disobedience of three of the Ten Commandments: "You shall not covet your neighbor's wife," "You shall not commit adultery," and "You shall not murder."[71]

It may be useful when building a bridge from this text to current readers to associate it with other important Old Testament texts that deal with sin and then to connect these to pertinent New Testament texts. Thus, David's actions in 11:2–5 illustrate and complement the origin and progression of temptation and sin (from perception and deception to covetousness, transgression, and death) as we learn them from Genesis 3:1–7 and James 1:14–15.[72] This alone is enough to give this unit immediate pertinence for today's

---

69. Sir Arthur Conan Doyle, "The Crooked Man," in *The Works of Sir Arthur Conan Doyle* (London: Longmeadow, 1981), 279–90.

70. Brueggemann, *First and Second Samuel*, 272.

71. Ex. 20:17, 14, and 13 respectively. See Youngblood, "1, 2 Samuel," 928.

72. Other passages helpful to correlate with our text are the entire unit Gen. 3–11 as well as Ps. 32 and 51 (the first commentaries on 2 Sam. 11–12); Hos. 2:2–13; and Rom. 1:18–3:20.

readers. It teems with forceful lessons on sin and death; as we all know, our day needs to hear these lessons again and again. It would be tempting to stop here, because this is an easy way to apply this text to our times.

However, it would be a mistake to interpret the passage as a single-dimensional example of what happens when we break the commandments. There are at least two indications in the text that the unit has more in view. (1) This passage plays an important role in the overall structure of 1–2 Samuel. As we have seen, the books are answering questions urgent for that ancient day: What is the acceptable nature of the new Israelite monarchy? Who may serve suitably as Yahweh's anointed one? The monarchy has been carefully circumscribed by Samuel as a vassalage of Yahweh; that is, the Israelite king is not really king but only a coregent for Yahweh.

Furthermore, Saul is presented as a negative example of who may serve in the new institution. In 2 Samuel, David has been established thus far as a positive example, as God-ordained and God-blessed in his role as king of Israel. This text takes us to the next level by demonstrating that no Israelite king, *not even David*, is permitted to behave like other ancient Near Eastern kings. If and when Israel's kings do so behave, they will not be free of guilt and responsibility. A prophet of Yahweh will hold them accountable.

(2) In addition, the unit's theme word (*šlḥ*) makes it clear that David has a problem with power. In fact, his abuse of power lies at the root of his sin. He has overstepped his boundaries as the vassal of Yahweh, chosen and anointed to represent Yahweh before Israel and the world. David exercises his royal power by sending and taking, and such abuse of power lies at the foundation of his sin. He *sends* instead of going in battle, and he abuses instead of serving.

In other words, this text is more than a moral lesson against breaking the Ten Commandments. It *is* that, but to stop there is to miss its grandest themes. It contributes to the books' overall concerns by teaching that manipulative abuses of power will destroy us or those around us. Whenever we are seduced by the misappropriation of human power structures, we incur guilt and deserve to die (12:5). Regardless of whether our attitudes come to fruition in external transgressions against the Ten Commandments, as with David, we cannot escape the implications: The way we use power reflects either our faithfulness to God or our treason.

The account of David's adultery with Bathsheba and his subsequent murder of Uriah confronts us as readers with our own manipulative and abusive ways. We may rigidly obey the Ten Commandments, but if we abuse the people around us, our hypocrisy will eventually be exposed, as Nathan's parable exposed David's hypocrisy. The way we impose our will on people around us, the way we "send" in order to "take," certainly displeases the Lord, just as David's displeased the Lord (11:27). Our actions are tantamount to despising "the word of the LORD" (12:9). Moreover, the book structure reveals that there are no exceptions. No matter how much power we wield, or how little, we are still responsible for the way we use it.

One further point might be necessary on the Old Testament's understanding of sin. In certain respects, today's readers find it easy to bridge the cultural contexts on this issue. Wherever we share similar ethical or legal assumptions with ancient Israel, we transfer the concepts into today's context without difficulty, as for example happens when the Bible refers to disobedience, rebellion, or crime.

The Old Testament, however, has one important aspect relating to its understanding of sin that is foreign to today's Western reader, one that may cause problems when interpreting texts like this one when it says that "the LORD has taken away your sin" (12:13). I refer here to the Pentateuch's priestly understanding of ritual impurity from unatoned guilt as an aerial contaminant, mystically settling down over the community and attaching itself to the tabernacle (and later to the temple), resulting in pollution.[73] The book of Leviticus, where this concept is established, does not always express its theology explicitly. But through prescriptions for ritual and sacrifice, it becomes clear that human sin resulted in impurity that polluted the sanctuary (Lev. 15:31; 20:3; cf. Num. 19:13, 20). Such pollution was perceived as a physical substance, an airborne contaminant magnetically attracted to and attached to the realm of the sacred, or in this case, the sanctuary.

This background is only vaguely apparent in our current text, though it has several important implications that affect our interpretation. (1) Personal sin in the Old Testament resulted in *corporate* guilt. When an individual Israelite sinned, the guilt contributed to the contamination of the sanctuary, for which the entire community was responsible. Because of our extreme

---

73. Tikva Frymer-Kensky, "Pollution, Purification, and Purgation in Biblical Israel," in *The Word of the Lord Shall Go Forth: Essays in Honor of David Noel Freedman in Celebration of His Sixtieth Birthday*, ed. C. L. Meyers and M. O'Connor (Winona Lake, Ind.: Eisenbrauns, 1983), 399–414, esp. 406. Thus the Day of Atonement, on which blood was sprinkled in the Most Holy Place and on the outer shrine (or "Tent of Meeting") and was rubbed on the altar of burnt offering, was a "day of purgation" (Lev. 16). The blood purged the cultic space and furniture and reconsecrated the altar, so that in effect, the entire sanctuary was purged of accumulated pollution (Lev. 16:16, 17b, 19b). After the day of purgation, the tabernacle was clean of all pollution, making it possible for the people to continue in the land. See Jacob Milgrom, *Cult and Conscience: The Asham and the Priestly Doctrine of Repentance* (SJLA 18; Leiden: Brill, 1976), 392; idem, "The Graduated ḤAṬṬAʾT of Leviticus 5:1–13," *JAOS* 103 (1983): 250–51; John H. Hayes, "Atonement in the Book of Leviticus," *Int* 52 (1998): 5–15; Gary A. Anderson, "Sacrifice and Sacrificial Offerings (OT)," *ABD*, 5:870–86, esp. 879–80; Robin C. Cover, "Sin, Sinners (OT)," *ABD*, 6:34–36.

individualism in North America, you and I may think we alone bear the guilt and punishment for our own sins. But we are wrong. The Old Testament has a healthy understanding of the suffering caused to the whole community when one of its members sinned.

(2) When left unatoned, sin was *cumulative*. The need for an annual decontamination of the sanctuary (the Day of Atonement, Lev. 16) illustrates that the guilt of sin accumulated whenever it was not expiated. Wherever it was ignored or suppressed, guilt eventually returned to the sinner (national or individual) later in life to exact punishment. Sin set a series of consequences in motion, and if unchecked it led inevitably to death.

(3) God provided an effective *cure* for sin. I will discuss this further below when we consider God's forgiveness of David's sin, but it is important to note at this point that the Old Testament devotes a great deal of attention to atonement (Ex. 25–31; 35–40; the book of Leviticus; Num. 1–10). Decontamination was possible, thanks to God's sacrificial system. Many of the Old Testament's images for the act of decontamination have to do with separating or removing the presence of the accumulated pollutant (Lev. 16:22). Sin may be cumulative and result in corporate guilt—but the good news is, there is a cure.

Repentance. The second component of Israel's faith illustrated in this text is repentance. David's words alone, "I have sinned against the LORD," might be construed to denote mere confession.[74] But in the context of the whole unit, David exemplifies the repentance Nathan required. As a result, Yahweh takes away David's sin and suspends the death penalty (12:13).

Furthermore, David's immediate and genuine penitence stands in stark contrast with that of Saul, who serves as the stubborn and recalcitrant counterpoint to repentance (1 Sam. 15:24, 30). The historian seems to be inviting us to make these contrasts ourselves. Saul's confession (1 Sam. 15:24, 30) and David's (2 Sam. 12:13) appear to be facing each other, stretching across the pages of the books of Samuel to present contrasting lessons on repentance. In David, we have an example of the correct attitude of repentance; in Saul, we have an example of equivocal and self-serving repentance (see comments on 12:13–25, above).

As we have seen many times, historical narratives such as these often illustrate implicitly the truths taught explicitly elsewhere in Scripture. The books of Samuel have been characterized from the beginning by prophetic interests, and primary among these is the definition and nature of repen-

---

74. That is, the words taken alone might indicate only an acknowledgement that he has committed sin, without displaying repentance fully. Repentance involves confession, but also a turning away from sin and a returning unto God.

tance. The opening chapters of 1 Samuel condemned the Elide priesthood at Shiloh as perverse (1 Sam. 1–3). In addition, the nation Israel tried to manipulate God for personal gain and was generally plagued with sin and failure (chs. 4–6). At a critical juncture in Israel's history, the prophet Samuel seized a moment of tragedy and suffering in order to call the nation to repentance. Using terminology characteristic of later prophetic preaching, Samuel called for a "return" (šwb) to Yahweh.[75] To restore a right relationship with Yahweh implies at once both a turning away from the sins that have caused the separation and a returning unto God.

This return to God must be "wholehearted," implying there can be no divided loyalties or opinions when one returns to Yahweh. In the specific case of Israel in 1 Samuel 7, repentance involved a repudiation of their allegiance to Canaanite gods and a renewed commitment to serve Yahweh exclusively. Samuel's message synopsizes the Old Testament prophetic concern for repentance and stands like a watchtower over the rest of 1–2 Samuel. Though the specific terminology for repentance is not used in 2 Samuel 12, David's "I have sinned" in response to Nathan's "You are the man" is a powerful lesson in Samuel's message of repentance. This text serves as a historical illustration for the sermon Samuel preached so many years before.

Forgiveness. The third prominent feature of Old Testament faith illustrated by our text is forgiveness. As we noted above on 12:14, Nathan's words of forgiveness raise questions. Why did Yahweh suspend the just penalty for David's sin? Why did Yahweh choose not to deal with David as prescribed by the Sinai covenant? If David were in charge of the universe, we know what he would have done! His verdict on the rich man in Nathan's parable makes it clear (12:5): "The man who did this deserves to die!" Yet Nathan is quick to reassure: "You are not going to die." Why not? We have seen that forgiveness in this text proves David's repentance was genuine, and so it does. But more importantly, forgiveness in this text proves Yahweh is a compassionate and gracious God.[76] God loves and forgives because that is his nature.

Two dramatic statements are held closely together in our text (12:13): "I have sinned," and "The LORD has taken away your sin." They are separated only by the barest minimum narration ("Nathan replied"). Their very proximity begs us to understand this forgiving nature of God. Yet we, like the prophet Jonah, sometimes cannot quite get over the fact that God forgives, and sometimes we, again like Jonah, do not like it when he does! But this text

---

75. See comments on 1 Sam. 7:2–4 for details. The importance of the terminology is clear from its widespread use elsewhere in Old Testament prophetic literature (Hos. 14:1–2; Joel 2:12–13, frequently in Jer.).

76. This very fact is what upset the irascible Jonah, who got it all wrong (Jonah 4:1–3).

is a powerful example of God's forgiving nature. As such it takes its place among many in the Old Testament that emphasize the separation and removal of guilt from the confessing and penitent sinner.

In fact, the Old Testament is awash with metaphors for forgiveness, and this rich assortment often emphasizes the separation or removal of guilt. Sin may be healed like a disease, forgotten like a fleeting thought, stomped underfoot, thrown behind the back or thrown into the depths of the sea, cleansed, washed, wiped away, blotted out, or erased. Sin can be separated as far as east is from the west, borne away, or covered over. Several verbs are associated with forgiving, but the authors of the Old Testament found them inadequate to express fully the joy and celebration associated with forgiveness.[77]

There are few other obstacles to interpretation of this text because its themes are so powerfully and memorably narrated and, more importantly, because they are so universal. All of us know the truth of David's failure because we have all lived it to one degree or another. All of us know David's hypocrisy because we have all been hypocritical. Those of us who have faced our own sin and have cried in the night, "I have sinned," need to hear afresh the profound truth contained in Nathan's beautiful words, "The LORD has taken away your sin."

Finally, we all need to understand again the message of 1–2 Samuel, that the anointed one who is worthy of God's anointing must be willing to confess and repent of sin quickly in order to maintain the unique relationship he has with God. In this manner, the books of Samuel prepare us in a way we could never have anticipated for David's greater Son, who needed no confession or repentance but who carried forgiveness in his blood (2 Cor. 5:21; Eph. 1:7; 1 John 3:5).

SATURATION WITH SEX. The contemporary application of this passage is multifaceted. On a basic level, it speaks to the need in our society to address sexual sin and the guilt and alienation caused by its infatuation with sexual pleasure. Over the decades, American culture has fallen prey to the lie that our highest human fulfillment is partially

---

77. John S. Kselman, "Forgiveness (OT)," *ABD*, 2:831–33; J. P. J. Olivier, "סלח," *NIDOTTE*, 3:259–64. One is reminded of the New Testament's rich variety of atonement images, suggesting that modern theologians do violence to the significance of Jesus' death by limiting it to one interpretation. See Joel B. Green and Mark D. Baker, *Recovering the Scandal of the Cross: Atonement in New Testament and Contemporary Contexts* (Downers Grove, Ill.: InterVarsity Press, 2000), 35–86.

attainable through self-indulgent, unrestrained erotic expression rather than through faithful, enduring, monogamous love.

But this falsehood is as old as human civilization itself, and this text reveals the ancient lie for what it is. David surrenders impulsively to his most basic instincts, which lead him down a path that grows darker with each step. Rather than reaching his highest level of personal fulfillment, David discovers the darkness of his own soul. Likewise, instead of enabling us to reach our highest human fulfillment, reckless and illicit eroticism ensnares us in animalistic self-destruction. It is a hopeless cycle that ends only and always in death (Prov. 7:21–23, 27).

Yet our culture becomes more and more enamored with each passing decade. As the pornography industry grows with each new advance in technology and as the homosexual subculture expands, our culture falls deeper into the clutches of the ancient lie. All the while, the Bible's emphasis on the surpassing value of a loving and lasting monogamous relationship is pushed farther back into the recesses of our national memory. The message of 2 Samuel 10–12 is as pertinent and necessary today as ever.

Abuse of power. However, the truths revealed in this text far transcend this basic understanding of human sexuality and fulfillment. On a larger scale, the passage addresses the tendency in all of us to abuse power in our interpersonal relationships. Whether considering one's relationship with God or with mortals, our greedy attempts to control and manipulate lead only to pain and loss. One should always remember to read this unit in the larger literary context of the books of Samuel, which will add depth perception to an already vivid portrayal of lust, deception, betrayal, and murder. Such a holistic reading prevents an application limited to warnings about lust and sexual sin.

The full characterization of King David in the books of Samuel to this point makes his actions here more disturbing. He has towered over the literary landscape, looming ever larger in our sight and growing ever more central to our hopes for godly leadership in Israel. Because we gloried in his rise, we recoil at his fall. And we learn that no matter how close we live to God, no matter how much responsibility we are given in God's kingdom, no matter how much power we hold, we too can fall. We must learn from David to guard our relationships carefully and to use power in ways that are never tyrannical and despotic.[78]

So these multifaceted applications make our text important when considering the use and abuse of power, sexual sins in our society, or the nature

---

78. For further illustration of the destructive consequences of our sin, see the illustration at the conclusion of the Contemporary Significance section for 2 Sam. 13–14.

and consequence of sin in general. As we have seen in the Bridging Contexts section, this text has much to say also about repentance and forgiveness. Today's audience is undoubtedly in need of the truth about sin, but we should also consider what this text teaches by way of illustration on the nature of repentance and forgiveness as well. In what follows, I offer a few reflections on the application of these themes.

Sin. To begin, I think it fair to say that the topic of sin has all but disappeared from the mainline denominations and even in many of our evangelical contexts. Well I remember a book I was required to read during my college days. Its title summarized the author's thesis beautifully: *Whatever Became of Sin?*[79] Its author, Karl Menninger, was a renowned psychiatrist who described the malaise of Western society and noted that one misses any mention of "sin."

> It was a word once in everyone's mind, but now rarely if ever heard. Does that mean that no sin is involved in all our troubles... ? Is no one any longer guilty of anything? Guilty perhaps of a sin that could be repented and repaired or atoned for? Is it only that someone may be stupid or sick or criminal—or asleep? Wrong things are being done, we know.... But is no one responsible, no one answerable for these acts? Anxiety and depression we all acknowledge, and even vague guilt feelings, but has no one committed any sin? Where, indeed, did sin go? What became of it?[80]

Exploring the causes of sin's disappearance, Menninger concluded that many former sins have become crimes, so that responsibility for dealing with them has passed from church to state, from priest to policeman. Others have dissipated into illness, or at least into symptoms of illness, so that in their case punishment has been replaced with treatment.[81] But these are changes of definition and societal mores, and sin, as Menninger argues, has not really gone away no matter how much we humans attempt to suppress it or redefine it. He proposes reviving public discourse on sin and enlisting the physician, the psychiatrist, the lawyer, the teacher—and above all, the clergy—to recognize the reality of sin in an effort to offer a needy world more than the hope of belated treatment, but of prevention.

Though we might bicker today over the details of Menninger's argument, there is no question that he put his finger on a societal change that is profound and has continued during the last decades of the twentieth century. In

---

79. Karl Menninger, *Whatever Became of Sin?* (New York: Hawthorn Books, 1973).
80. Ibid., 13.
81. Ibid., 50, 74–93.

fact, the collapse of modernism and the emergence of a more pluralistic society has left us in a situation far more severe than Menninger predicted. The church has not only lost its voice on issues related to sin and its consequences, but the church itself is guilty of raising a new voice in order to justify sin in different garb. Not only has sin taken up residence in our hearts; we have redefined it and given expression to it as a justifiable good!

For example, in 1988, a prominent bishop of a mainline denomination advocated reviving an old concept—betrothal.[82] He argued that the church today should confirm those young people who feel led to determine their own standards of morality. Since they believe sex before marriage is acceptable as long as it is confined to a meaningful relationship, the church should support and bless betrothal as a legalized period before marriage when couples can live together. The bishop argued that such a relationship would carry the possibility of life-giving "holiness." It would help to order and make holy the world of sexual testing that marks the lives of so many single young adults.

Of course for decades mainline denominations have struggled with questions of human sexuality, including the appropriate Christian response to homosexuals who feel called to ministry or who simply want to find acceptance in a local church. These are legitimate questions, which should always be approached in humility and respect. Unfortunately, some Christians would rather beat the questioners over the head with an oversized Bible than actually discuss the questions sanely and reasonably. Just as unfortunately, others in the church would address the questions without ever once raising the issue of biblical authority and the possibility of God's preventing and life-changing grace. Once "sin" is no longer in the church's theological vocabulary, there is no longer a need for words such as "forgiveness" or "grace." Sin really has taken up residence in our hearts and found expression in less offensive ways.

I discovered through an article published in *U.S. News & World Report* in 1997 the logical extremes to which such reasoning may take us.[83] The author spoke of a problem in today's American universities, which he defined as "absolutophobia," or an unwillingness to say anything is wrong. The point of the article is that our pop culture has pushed nonjudgmentalism to the limit so that now some students have difficulty condemning large moral horrors, such as human sacrifice, ethnic cleansing, and slavery. We have raised a generation of children so "dogmatically committed to moral relativism" that some of them are reluctant to say anything negative

---

82. John Shelby Spong, *Living in Sin? A Bishop Rethinks Human Sexuality* (San Francisco: Harper & Row, 1988), 177–87.

83. For what follows, see John Leo, "A No-Fault Holocaust," *U. S. News & World Report* (July 21, 1997), 14.

about mass slaughter! They argue that no one has the right to criticize the moral views of another group or culture.

The article told of classes studying human sacrifice in which many of the students had trouble expressing any moral reservations or objections to it. In another example, one professor asserted that in twenty years of teaching, he had never met a student who denied that the Holocaust happened. What he has encountered, however, may be worse. Approximately 10 to 20 percent of his students acknowledge the fact of the Holocaust but cannot bring themselves to say that killing millions of people is wrong! Students may deplore what the Nazis did, but their disapproval is expressed as a matter of taste or personal preference, not moral judgment. The professor quoted one student as saying, "Of course I dislike the Nazis, but who is to say they are morally wrong?"

The application of this passage's assumptions about sin and its consequences are complicated by such fuzzy thinking in our day. One can no longer simply call a congregation to repentance. It will not do to merely exhort one's hearers to lay aside all sinful impulses, sexual tendencies, and abuses of power. Instead, the ideological foundation needs to be carefully established and the moral compass explained. People now need to hear not only what sin is but why it is wrong. In this text we might emphasize the point that David understood his actions as sin "against the LORD" (12:13). In other words, David's relationship with Yahweh provided a moral standard for his actions, a standard external to himself and superior in every respect. Yahweh's character and self-revelation determined for David what was right and wrong for David's behavior (see Contemporary Significance section for 1 Sam. 13:23–14:52). Such basic teaching, even remedial theology, is now necessary for the life of the church.

In exposing the falsehood of David's sin, Nathan used logic and reason to persuade David of his guilt. I have also mentioned at various points the hypocrisy inherent in David's actions. Hypocrisy is implied in his "killing time" at home while his army was away (11:1), but it becomes explicit in his sanctimonious concern for Uriah (11:7) and his indifference to Uriah's death (11:25). Irony in biblical literature (as in history) is often used to expose the hypocrite. So here Uriah is ironically more devout and faithful than David (11:9, 11), putting David in a bad light. Further, David unwittingly condemns himself when he condemns the rich man in Nathan's parable (12:5), providing Nathan with the ironic punch line for his sermon (12:7): "You are the man!" More generally, it is ironic that the king as Israel's "covenant administrator" has become the covenant breaker.[84]

---

84. Gerbrandt, *Kingship According to the Deuteronomistic History*, 99.

I was reminded of the role of irony and hypocrisy recently when I read what one leading historian of American history had to say about the combatants of World War II in the European Theater of Operations: "The world's greatest democracy fought the world's greatest racist with a segregated army."[85] He was referring, of course, to the incongruity of the U.S. Army's struggle against the racist forces of Adolf Hitler and Nazism, all while segregating African American soldiers into isolated units.

He relates one ironic incident from the home front during the war that highlights the hypocrisy of the situation. In April, 1944, Corporal Rupert Timmingham, an African American soldier, was traveling with eight other African American soldiers through the South on their way to a new assignment. Timmingham reported having difficulty finding places to eat or buying a cup of coffee. Finally, the lunchroom manager at a Texas railroad depot said the GIs could go around back to the kitchen for a sandwich and coffee. As they were making their way around to the back of the depot, approximately two dozen German prisoners of war from a nearby prisoner camp, along with two American guards came to the station. Timmingham later wrote in *Yank* magazine, "They entered the lunchroom, sat at the tables, had their meals served, talked, smoked, in fact had quite a swell time. I stood on the outside looking on, and I could not help but ask myself why are they treated better than we are?"[86]

The magazine that published Timmingham's letter received thousands of letters outraged by his treatment, mostly from GIs. The hypocrisy of the army's segregation policy was further exposed by the efficiency of the African American soldiers during the war. Within a decade of the war's end, the army had changed from one of the most segregated organizations in the United States to the most successfully integrated.[87] Unfortunately, it would take our nation as a whole much longer to see the hypocrisy of it all.

The point of Nathan's parable (12:1–6) is something akin to Jesus' warning not to look for a speck in our neighbor's eye at the same time we miss the log in our own (Matt. 7:3–5). David was quick to see the cruelty and inconsiderate nature of the rich man's actions but missed the fact that his own cruel and inconsiderate actions came to fruition in adultery and murder. It is certainly appropriate when applying this text to warn our society against the dangers of unrestrained sexual promiscuity. But today's Christian church also needs to hear this passage's teaching on the use and abuse of power.

---

85. Stephen E. Ambrose, *Citizen Soldiers: The U. S. Army from the Normandy Beaches to the Bulge to the Surrender of Germany, June 7, 1944–May 7, 1945* (New York: Simon & Schuster, 1997), 345.
86. As quoted in ibid., 346.
87. Ibid., 346–50.

My own experience has taught me that many believers today fall into one of two extreme categories. They are either uncomfortable with authority and hesitant to take the reins of power because they are unsure of how to deal with it, or they are greedy when it comes to power. Believers I have met in the first category tend to shrink from responsibility in the church, while those of the latter category tend to squash those who disagree with them as "enemies" in the church's political power structure. These believers presumably consider David's adultery and murder deplorable, but they miss the significance of his abuse of power as a negative object lesson for their own lives. We need to be reminded of the dictum of Immanuel Kant: "Out of timber so crooked as that from which man is made nothing entirely straight can be carved."[88]

Repentance. On the issue of repentance, we have seen how this text illustrates a larger theme in the books of Samuel (cf., e.g., comments on 1 Sam. 7:2–4). It is entirely appropriate to follow the long-standing tradition of reading Psalm 51 as an early Israelite commentary on David's words, "I have sinned against the LORD":

> For I know my transgressions,
>> and my sin is always before me.
> Against you, you only, have I sinned
>> and done what is evil in your sight,
> so that you are proved right when you speak
>> and justified when you judge. (Ps. 51:3–4)

Our society's loss of any sensibilities about the nature of sin has equally impacted our understanding of biblical repentance. How can we repent adequately if we fail to understand the depths to which sin has affected our lives? A full appreciation of the self-destructive nature of our own actions should lead us emphatically, even drive us relentlessly, to genuine repentance:

> Surely I was sinful at birth,
>> sinful from the time my mother conceived me.
> Surely you desire truth in the inner parts;
>> you teach me wisdom in the inmost place. (Ps. 51:5–6)

In the following quote from perhaps the greatest theologian of the early church, Augustine of Hippo (354–430) describes the self-realization that occurs when he was being convicted and convinced of his sin:

---

88. "Idee zu einer allgemeinen Gesichte in weltburgerlicher Absicht" (1784), quoted in Isaiah Berlin, *The Crooked Timber of Humanity: Chapters in The History of Ideas*, ed. H. Hardy (London: J. Murray, 1990; repr., Princeton, N.J.: Princeton Univ. Press, 1997), v.

But you, Lord . . . were turning me around so that I could see myself; you took me from behind my own back, which was where I had put myself during the time when I did not want to be observed by myself, and you set me in front of my own face so that I could see how foul a sight I was. . . . If I tried to look away from myself . . . you were setting me in front of myself, forcing me to look into my own face, so that I might see myself and hate it. I did know it, but I pretended that I did not. I had been pushing the whole idea away from me and forgetting it.[89]

Forgiveness. Finally this text teaches that such genuine penitence results in forgiveness. But this may be the hardest part for today's readers to accept. Indeed, retribution and vengeance seem to rule in our day. *The Sunflower*, a book written by Simon Wiesenthal, makes the point forcefully.[90] By 1944, eighty-nine of his Jewish relatives had been killed by the Nazis. He had witnessed the execution of his grandmother in her home and his mother being forced into a freight car crammed with elderly Jewish women.

One day, while himself a prisoner of the Nazis, he was taken by a nurse into the room where a young soldier lay dying. The young man, whose name was Karl, summarized for Wiesenthal his Catholic upbringing and his childhood faith, which he had abandoned in the Hitler Youth Corps. Karl had volunteered for the SS and became an officer. But now, having been badly wounded on the Russian front, he had summoned a Jew to hear his deathbed confession. "I must tell you of this horrible deed—tell you because you are a Jew." As the soldier began to describe horrible atrocities against the Jews in the Ukraine, Wiesenthal pulled away three times in order to leave the room. But the soldier grabbed his arm and desperately pleaded for him to stay and hear him out. Karl had participated in the ruthless execution of three hundred Jewish men, women, and children, in the town of Dnyepropetrovsk. The memory haunted him. He complained of suffering from miserable grief and despair, and he longed for forgiveness.

In the last hours of my life you are with me. I do not know who you are, I know only that you are a Jew and that is enough. I know that what I have told you is terrible. In the long nights while I have been

---

89. Augustine, *Confessions* 8.7 (Warner translation). Quoted in Merold Westphal, "Taking Suspicion Seriously: The Religious Uses of Modern Atheism," *Faith and Philosophy* 4 (1987): 33.

90. Simon Wiesenthal, *The Sunflower* (New York: Schocken, 1976). For the summary that follows, see Philip Yancey, *What's So Amazing About Grace?* (Grand Rapids: Zondervan, 1997), 109–13.

waiting for death, time and time again I have longed to talk about it to a Jew and beg forgiveness from him. Only I didn't know whether there were any Jews left.... I know what I am asking is almost too much for you, but without your answer I cannot die in peace.[91]

After a long period of reflection, Wiesenthal eventually decided what to do. Without a word, he turned from the room and walked away.

Decades later, still haunted by his decision that fateful day, Wiesenthal wrote down the story and mailed it to thirty-two of the brightest ethical minds he knew and asked this question: What would you have done in my place? Only six said that Wiesenthal erred in not forgiving the dying SS officer. Several concluded the enormity of Nazi atrocities precluded the possibility of forgiveness. Most of the non-Jewish respondents were reticent to speak to the heirs of the Holocaust about forgiveness at all, and justifiably so. But as Philip Yancey explains in his summary of this ethical dilemma, "Forgiveness may be unfair—it is, by definition—but at least it provides a way to halt the juggernaut of retribution."[92] His main point is that unforgiveness is an unending cycle that creates a monstrous past, awaking in unexpected places and times from hibernation to devour the present. The only thing that breaks the cycle is the blessed word from the cross (Luke 23:34): "Father, forgive them...."

Though human forgiveness is always wise, it is often fickle and at times nearly impossible to grant. The immense burden placed on the shoulders of the young Simon Wiesenthal that day in 1944 was too much for any mere human to bear. Who among us could claim they would have done differently? But that is just the beauty of the biblical message, especially as illustrated by David's forgiveness in 2 Samuel 12:13: Forgiveness is not based on human sentiment, it is not placed on the shoulders of mortals.

It was unfair of the SS officer to place such a burden on Wiesenthal, who could not bear to represent his race at that terrible moment in history. But note the words of Nathan, "*The LORD* has taken away your sin." Our hope is not in the hands of fragile humans, who are incapable of fathoming the depths of our sin and granting us restoration and peace. But David's forgiveness was authentic because it was granted by Yahweh.

That experience of forgiveness, shared by all who name the name, is graphically captured in the immortal words of John Bunyan:

Now I saw in my dream that the highway which Christian was to go, was fenced on either side with a wall, and that wall was called Salva-

---

91. Yancey, *What's So Amazing About Grace?*, 110–11.
92. Ibid., 115.

tion, Isa. 26:1. Up this road therefore did burdened Christian run, but not without great difficulty, because of the load on his back. He ran thus till he came to a place somewhat ascending; and upon that place stood a cross, and a little below, in the bottom, a sepulcher. So I saw in my dream that just as Christian came up with the cross, his burden loosed from off his shoulders, and fell from off his back, and began to tumble, and so continued to do till it came to the mouth of the sepulcher, where it fell in, and I saw it no more.[93]

---

93. John Bunyan, *Pilgrim's Progress* (Chicago: Moody, [n.d.]), 28.

2 Samuel 13:1–14:33

𝕝

I N THE COURSE OF TIME, Amnon son of David fell in
love with Tamar, the beautiful sister of Absalom son
of David.

²Amnon became frustrated to the point of illness on
account of his sister Tamar, for she was a virgin, and it seemed
impossible for him to do anything to her.

³Now Amnon had a friend named Jonadab son of Shimeah,
David's brother. Jonadab was a very shrewd man. ⁴He asked
Amnon, "Why do you, the king's son, look so haggard morn-
ing after morning? Won't you tell me?"

Amnon said to him, "I'm in love with Tamar, my brother
Absalom's sister."

⁵"Go to bed and pretend to be ill," Jonadab said. "When
your father comes to see you, say to him, 'I would like my sister Tamar to come and give me something to eat. Let her prepare the food in my sight so I may watch her and then eat it
from her hand.'"

⁶So Amnon lay down and pretended to be ill. When the
king came to see him, Amnon said to him, "I would like my
sister Tamar to come and make some special bread in my
sight, so I may eat from her hand."

⁷David sent word to Tamar at the palace: "Go to the house
of your brother Amnon and prepare some food for him." ⁸So
Tamar went to the house of her brother Amnon, who was
lying down. She took some dough, kneaded it, made the
bread in his sight and baked it. ⁹Then she took the pan and
served him the bread, but he refused to eat.

"Send everyone out of here," Amnon said. So everyone left
him. ¹⁰Then Amnon said to Tamar, "Bring the food here into
my bedroom so I may eat from your hand." And Tamar took
the bread she had prepared and brought it to her brother
Amnon in his bedroom. ¹¹But when she took it to him to eat,
he grabbed her and said, "Come to bed with me, my sister."

¹²"Don't, my brother!" she said to him. "Don't force me.
Such a thing should not be done in Israel! Don't do this
wicked thing. ¹³What about me? Where could I get rid of my
disgrace? And what about you? You would be like one of the

wicked fools in Israel. Please speak to the king; he will not keep me from being married to you." ¹⁴But he refused to listen to her, and since he was stronger than she, he raped her.

¹⁵Then Amnon hated her with intense hatred. In fact, he hated her more than he had loved her. Amnon said to her, "Get up and get out!"

¹⁶"No!" she said to him. "Sending me away would be a greater wrong than what you have already done to me."

But he refused to listen to her. ¹⁷He called his personal servant and said, "Get this woman out of here and bolt the door after her." ¹⁸So his servant put her out and bolted the door after her. She was wearing a richly ornamented robe, for this was the kind of garment the virgin daughters of the king wore. ¹⁹Tamar put ashes on her head and tore the ornamented robe she was wearing. She put her hand on her head and went away, weeping aloud as she went.

²⁰Her brother Absalom said to her, "Has that Amnon, your brother, been with you? Be quiet now, my sister; he is your brother. Don't take this thing to heart." And Tamar lived in her brother Absalom's house, a desolate woman.

²¹When King David heard all this, he was furious. ²²Absalom never said a word to Amnon, either good or bad; he hated Amnon because he had disgraced his sister Tamar.

²³Two years later, when Absalom's sheepshearers were at Baal Hazor near the border of Ephraim, he invited all the king's sons to come there. ²⁴Absalom went to the king and said, "Your servant has had shearers come. Will the king and his officials please join me?"

²⁵"No, my son," the king replied. "All of us should not go; we would only be a burden to you." Although Absalom urged him, he still refused to go, but gave him his blessing.

²⁶Then Absalom said, "If not, please let my brother Amnon come with us."

The king asked him, "Why should he go with you?" ²⁷But Absalom urged him, so he sent with him Amnon and the rest of the king's sons.

²⁸Absalom ordered his men, "Listen! When Amnon is in high spirits from drinking wine and I say to you, 'Strike Amnon down,' then kill him. Don't be afraid. Have not I given you this order? Be strong and brave." ²⁹So Absalom's men did to Amnon what Absalom had ordered. Then all the king's sons got up, mounted their mules and fled.

³⁰While they were on their way, the report came to David: "Absalom has struck down all the king's sons; not one of them is left." ³¹The king stood up, tore his clothes and lay down on the ground; and all his servants stood by with their clothes torn.

³²But Jonadab son of Shimeah, David's brother, said, "My lord should not think that they killed all the princes; only Amnon is dead. This has been Absalom's expressed intention ever since the day Amnon raped his sister Tamar. ³³My lord the king should not be concerned about the report that all the king's sons are dead. Only Amnon is dead."

³⁴Meanwhile, Absalom had fled.

Now the man standing watch looked up and saw many people on the road west of him, coming down the side of the hill. The watchman went and told the king, "I see men in the direction of Horonaim, on the side of the hill."

³⁵Jonadab said to the king, "See, the king's sons are here; it has happened just as your servant said."

³⁶As he finished speaking, the king's sons came in, wailing loudly. The king, too, and all his servants wept very bitterly.

³⁷Absalom fled and went to Talmai son of Ammihud, the king of Geshur. But King David mourned for his son every day.

³⁸After Absalom fled and went to Geshur, he stayed there three years. ³⁹And the spirit of the king longed to go to Absalom, for he was consoled concerning Amnon's death.

¹⁴:¹Joab son of Zeruiah knew that the king's heart longed for Absalom. ²So Joab sent someone to Tekoa and had a wise woman brought from there. He said to her, "Pretend you are in mourning. Dress in mourning clothes, and don't use any cosmetic lotions. Act like a woman who has spent many days grieving for the dead. ³Then go to the king and speak these words to him." And Joab put the words in her mouth.

⁴When the woman from Tekoa went to the king, she fell with her face to the ground to pay him honor, and she said, "Help me, O king!"

⁵The king asked her, "What is troubling you?"

She said, "I am indeed a widow; my husband is dead. ⁶I your servant had two sons. They got into a fight with each other in the field, and no one was there to separate them. One struck the other and killed him. ⁷Now the whole clan has risen up against your servant; they say, 'Hand over the one who struck his brother down, so that we may put him to death for the life of his brother whom he killed; then we will get rid of the heir as well.' They would put out the only burning coal I have left, leaving my husband neither name nor descendant on the face of the earth."

⁸The king said to the woman, "Go home, and I will issue an order in your behalf."

⁹But the woman from Tekoa said to him, "My lord the king, let the blame rest on me and on my father's family, and let the king and his throne be without guilt."

¹⁰The king replied, "If anyone says anything to you, bring him to me, and he will not bother you again."

¹¹She said, "Then let the king invoke the LORD his God to prevent the avenger of blood from adding to the destruction, so that my son will not be destroyed."

"As surely as the LORD lives," he said, "not one hair of your son's head will fall to the ground."

¹²Then the woman said, "Let your servant speak a word to my lord the king."

"Speak," he replied.

¹³The woman said, "Why then have you devised a thing like this against the people of God? When the king says this, does he not convict himself, for the king has not brought back his banished son? ¹⁴Like water spilled on the ground, which cannot be recovered, so we must die. But God does not take away life; instead, he devises ways so that a banished person may not remain estranged from him.

¹⁵"And now I have come to say this to my lord the king because the people have made me afraid. Your servant thought, 'I will speak to the king; perhaps he will do what his servant asks. ¹⁶Perhaps the king will agree to deliver his servant from the hand of the man who is trying to cut off both me and my son from the inheritance God gave us.'

¹⁷"And now your servant says, 'May the word of my lord the king bring me rest, for my lord the king is like an angel of God in discerning good and evil. May the LORD your God be with you.'"

¹⁸Then the king said to the woman, "Do not keep from me the answer to what I am going to ask you."

"Let my lord the king speak," the woman said.

¹⁹The king asked, "Isn't the hand of Joab with you in all this?"

The woman answered, "As surely as you live, my lord the king, no one can turn to the right or to the left from anything my lord the king says. Yes, it was your servant Joab who instructed me to do this and who put all these words into the mouth of your servant. 20Your servant Joab did this to change the present situation. My lord has wisdom like that of an angel of God—he knows everything that happens in the land."

21The king said to Joab, "Very well, I will do it. Go, bring back the young man Absalom."

22Joab fell with his face to the ground to pay him honor, and he blessed the king. Joab said, "Today your servant knows that he has found favor in your eyes, my lord the king, because the king has granted his servant's request."

23Then Joab went to Geshur and brought Absalom back to Jerusalem. 24But the king said, "He must go to his own house; he must not see my face." So Absalom went to his own house and did not see the face of the king.

25In all Israel there was not a man so highly praised for his handsome appearance as Absalom. From the top of his head to the sole of his foot there was no blemish in him. 26Whenever he cut the hair of his head—he used to cut his hair from time to time when it became too heavy for him—he would weigh it, and its weight was two hundred shekels by the royal standard.

27Three sons and a daughter were born to Absalom. The daughter's name was Tamar, and she became a beautiful woman.

28Absalom lived two years in Jerusalem without seeing the king's face. 29Then Absalom sent for Joab in order to send him to the king, but Joab refused to come to him. So he sent a second time, but he refused to come. 30Then he said to his servants, "Look, Joab's field is next to mine, and he has barley there. Go and set it on fire." So Absalom's servants set the field on fire.

31Then Joab did go to Absalom's house and he said to him, "Why have your servants set my field on fire?"

32Absalom said to Joab, "Look, I sent word to you and said, 'Come here so I can send you to the king to ask, "Why have I come from Geshur? It would be better for me if I were still there!" ' Now then, I want to see the king's face, and if I am guilty of anything, let him put me to death."

³³So Joab went to the king and told him this. Then the king summoned Absalom, and he came in and bowed down with his face to the ground before the king. And the king kissed Absalom.

WE HAVE SEEN THAT THE DAVIDIC COVENANT in 2 Samuel 7 is the ideological summit of 2 Samuel. Building on the powerful images of Jerusalem and Zion established in chapters 5–6, the extended narrative took a long pause to consider the magnitude of David, his new capital city, and the importance of his dynasty in the overarching salvation history. Then, David's abuse of power resulted in adultery and murder and threatened the promises of that royal covenant. The narration of David's sins in the preceding unit (chs. 10–12) began the gradual descent from the heights of chapter 7. The descent culminates here at the behavioral nadir of 2 Samuel.

Nothing in 2 Samuel will be the same after David's sin with Bathsheba and his murder of Uriah.[1] Amnon's rape of Tamar and its consequences drive us forward to the account of Absalom's rebellion, since this text provides information required for our reading of those events (chs. 15–20). These intensely personal events provide the necessary backdrop for the public events recorded there.[2] But this unit also forces us to look back constantly at David's own sexual indulgence and, by subtle implication, draws a causal connection between his own sins (chs. 10–12) and the sins of his family. "In short, because of his behavior in the matter of Bathsheba and Uriah, the David of 2 Samuel 12–20 is a man under judgement, reaping publicly, through his family, the fruit of his cloistered sin."[3]

Amnon's Love for His Half-Sister, Tamar (13:1–2)

THE OPENING PHRASE (NIV "In the course of time") is a Hebrew idiom used as a transition marker (see comments on 2:1; cf. also 8:1; 10:1; 15:1; 21:18).[4] Its repeated use in 15:1 (with slight modification) serves to mark chs. 13–14 as

---

1. The extended narrative of chs. 13–20 flows from the initial judgment of David at 12:10, and the events described there represent threats to, or even reversals of, the vision of ch. 7. See Satterthwaite, "David in the Books of Samuel," 57–59.

2. McCarter, *II Samuel*, 350.

3. Gordon, *I and II Samuel*, 252.

4. It does not mark a completely new beginning but a new episode sharing something with the preceding. See Conroy, *Absalom Absalom!* 41; Bailey, *David in Love and War*, 56–57.

a distinct literary unit within the extended narrative of Absalom's rebellion (chs. 13–20).[5]

Verse 1 sets the stage for the new episode by introducing the principal actors, Amnon and Tamar.[6] However, the Hebrew syntax (obscured by NIV; cf. NRSV, NJPS) highlights Absalom's role: "And it happened thereafter—Absalom, David's son, had a beautiful sister named Tamar, and Amnon, David's son, loved her."[7] Thus the narrator lifts Absalom into the foreground and makes us aware that this is not simply a story about Amnon and Tamar, for it participates in the larger narrative of Absalom.

Since chapter 14 ends with the word "Absalom" (both in Heb. and the NIV), these two chapters begin and end with Absalom.[8] Furthermore, the narrator identifies both Amnon and Absalom as sons "of David," which reminds the reader that these actions are rooted in David's sin. Amnon's offense is sexual in nature, which ensures that the specter of David's own crimes is never far beneath the surface of this episode. As we say in English, "the apple doesn't fall far from the tree" or "like father like son."[9] David's sin is returning to haunt him, and since the main players are his own sons and daughter, the drama to be played out will be intensely personal.

Another important feature about the way the characters are introduced is the way the sons of David frame (and trap!) the daughter of David. The names of Absalom and Amnon surround and silence that of Tamar, an effect created by the Hebrew syntax: Absalom had a sister . . . Tamar . . . Amnon loved her. Tamar is viewed from the outset as a secondary (i.e., passive) character—the sister of Absalom and the object of Amnon's desire.[10] Her dilemma is palpable. As a woman with no recognized power of her own, she becomes the victim of the power struggle in which one brother is hungry for political advancement, the other for passionate pleasure.

---

5. See Youngblood, "1, 2 Samuel," 955, for other indications of the literary isolation of chapters 13–14.

6. For the meaning of the names, including Absalom's, see Anderson, 2 *Samuel*, 173.

7. Conroy, *Absalom Absalom!* 41–42. The translation here is from Alter, *David Story*, 265. Cf. also Cotterell and Turner, who use 13:1–22 in order to illustrate the salient elements of discourse analysis (Peter Cotterell and Max Turner, *Linguistics and Biblical Interpretation* [Downers Grove, Ill.: InterVarsity Press, 1989], 248–53).

8. Except for the temporal phrase ("In the course of time"), the first and last word of chs. 13–14 is *lᵉʾabšalom* (lit., "to Absalom"). Such a literary inclusio is another reason to read these two chapters together.

9. Or as Fokkelman has it, Amnon and Absalom prove to be "chips off the old block" (Fokkelman, *Narrative Art and Poetry in the Books of Samuel*, 1:99).

10. Phyllis Trible, *Texts of Terror: Literary-Feminist Readings of Biblical Narratives* (Philadelphia: Fortress, 1984), 38.

The reference to Tamar's virginity (13:2) may be "a cynical commentary on the morals of the royal court: had she been married she would have been available."[11] David had taken the married Bathsheba, but Amnon feels prevented from taking Tamar.[12] Amnon's crude but honest explanation for his love-sickness (13:2) shows that his "love" for Tamar is not love in any meaningful sense, but only lust.

Amnon Rapes Tamar (13:3–22)

THE PREVIOUS TWO verses presented Amnon's problem: that he cannot have the woman he desires. Here we meet his solution: the nefarious advice of a friend. By way of introducing Amnon's friend, Jonadab, the Hebrew syntax uses a grammatical parallel missed in most all translations: "There was to Absalom a beautiful sister, whose name was Tamar.... But there was to Amnon a friend, whose name was Jonadab" (13:1 and 3). Tamar may be beautiful, but Jonadab is shrewd.[13] More than a "friend," Jonadab is the "son of Shimeah, David's brother." Now we get a picture of the strife pervading David's extended family, which seems divided into opposing camps. Tamar and Absalom are allies on the one hand, while Amnon and his cousin Jonadab are on the other.[14] The battle lines for future combat seem established.[15]

Amnon's speech explaining his illness to Jonadab (13:4) uses an impressive literary device to stress the aroused nature of his passion. The result is that the explanation ("I'm in love with Tamar, my brother Absalom's sister") gives the impression of a succession of faltering, gasping sighs, in which alliteration intensifies the grip that his passion has over him.[16] Amnon's speech proclaims love for Tamar, but his actions are about to unveil a more sinister passion.

Amnon follows Jonadab's advice by feigning illness in order to draw Tamar into the trap (13:6–14). The Hebrew of this text uses a wide array of literary devices to emphasize the irony and injustice of the shameful act.[17] The

---

11. Cotterell and Turner, *Linguistics*, 250.

12. However, it is also possible her virgin status simply means she was carefully guarded and Amnon had no opportune moment to abuse her. See Ackroyd, *Second Book of Samuel*, 121.

13. Youngblood, "1, 2 Samuel," 957.

14. Conroy, *Absalom Absalom!* 27.

15. As we will see, Amnon is heir to the throne, which means the politically ambitious Absalom has much to gain by killing him. It is possible that Jonadab is a coconspirator with Absalom, who is willing to sacrifice his sister Tamar in order to remove Amnon. See Andrew E. Hill, "A Jonadab Connection in the Absalom Conspiracy?" *JETS* 30 (1987): 389.

16. Conroy, *Absalom Absalom!* 29; McCarter, *II Samuel*, 321–22. Each word in Amnon's speech in v. 4 begins with an *ʾalep* followed by -o and -a sounds.

17. See Cotterell and Turner, *Linguistics*, 251–53; Youngblood, "1, 2 Samuel," 959–63.

interchanging use of "sister" and "brother" in the dialogue focuses on the familial relationship between Amnon and Tamar and heightens the tragedy about to occur. After driving everyone out of the room so they can be alone, Amnon reveals his true intent to Tamar (13:11): "Come to bed with me, my sister." The NIV here has obscured two separate imperative verbs, the second of which is "lie down" (*škb*) further modified by "with me." This locution ("lie down with") normally denotes sexual relations that are illicit.[18]

Tamar's impressive speech desperately raises numerous objections and shows her to be a woman of integrity (12:12–13).[19] She begins with a firm and resolute refusal, with another subtle use of "my brother." Amnon may have hoped for consensual relations with Tamar in the privacy of his bed chamber. But her prohibition, "Don't force me!" uses a specific verb decrying the act for what it would be: rape.[20] Her objections involve several elements. (1) Israel is not Canaan, and such abusive force is not acceptable here. His proposal is a "wicked thing" (*nᵉbalah*, folly, an outrageously disgraceful act) and will only make a fool of him. (2) In a more practical vein, Tamar uses great foresight in warning that if he rapes her, he will ruin both their lives. She will be forced to live in shame, and he will become "one of the wicked fools in Israel." (3) Finally, Tamar asserts that marriage is not out of the question and that following the proper procedures may work in Amnon's favor.[21] Taken together, these objections are an unmistakable indictment of Amnon's proposal.

Secondarily, Tamar's stirring appeal in the current arrangement of the narrative (i.e., coming in this unit immediately after chs. 10–12) serves also as another indictment of David. This narrator is fond of thematic analogies between episodes. So here it seems likely that Amnon's lying on his feigned sickbed is similar to David's rising from his siesta bed. One summons his forbidden sister in order to abuse her; the other summons another man's wife to abuse her.[22] Thus, Amnon's actions are subtly drawn together with David's

---

18. Hebrew normally describes sexual relations that are approved by the community by other expressions ("know," "go into," etc.). See Williams, "שכב," *NIDOTTE*, 4:101–2.

19. Trible, *Texts of Terror*, 37–63. Tamar's panicked list of reasons for refusal appears to be a "structural allusion to Joseph and Potiphar's wife," which further characterizes Tamar as a woman of the highest moral rectitude. Alter, *David Story*, 268; idem, *The Art of Biblical Narrative*, 73.

20. The Piel of *ᶜnh* is widely used in the Old Testament for rape or forced intercourse. See *HALOT*, 2:853; *BDB*, 776; Paul Wegner, "ענה," *NIDOTTE*, 3:450.

21. It is not at all clear whether in fact marriage would have been possible, or whether Tamar was desperately "grasping at straws" in an attempt to thwart Amnon's advances. On the difficulties of her concluding statement, see McCarter, *II Samuel*, 323–24; Anderson, *2 Samuel*, 175.

22. Alter, *David Story*, xxii–xxiii.

in a cause-and-effect relationship: David's sin has come to rest now in his immediate family.

Amnon is not to be deterred. With staccato-like precision and brevity, details of the deplorable act are recorded (13:14–15). Verse 14 begins with his refusal to hear any more pleas from Tamar. This is followed quickly by three action verbs used only with their objects: "he overpowered her and abused her and bedded her."[23] Having earlier seized Tamar (13:11), Amnon has not released her to this point. He now "overpowers" her, which emphasizes the raw physical violence with which he forces himself on her, removing any trace of doubt about Tamar's innocence.[24]

Next the narrator uses the same word chosen by Tamar in 13:12 in her attempt to dissuade him ("Don't *force* me"), denoting rape or forced intercourse ("raped her"). The final verb in 13:14 (*škb*, omitted in the NIV) contains subtle connotations that are difficult to convey in translation. When used in an intransitive construction with a preposition phrase, it often means "lie with," in the sense of seduction and consensual sexual relations (cf. v. 11, where Amnon hopes for Tamar's cooperation).[25] But here in verse 14, the verb is in fact a transitive, using the direct object marker to identify Tamar, reducing her as the victim to a mere object: "bedded her."[26] The repetition integrates three verbs in an escalating sequence of violence.[27] Amnon dehumanizes Tamar and then ravages her, leaving her "a desolate woman" (13:20).

Recent literary studies of 13:1–22 have focused on its chiastic structure with a center at verses 14–15.[28] Here Amnon's violence against Tamar turns love into hatred. The movement from passion to self-gratification to revulsion is difficult to explain and has evoked interesting psychological

---

23. The translation is that of Alter, *David Story*, 269. The NIV coalesces three verbs into two and misses the pulsating intensity of the verbal succession, in which the object (Tamar!) is represented all three times as a pronominal suffix, first with a preposition, then directly on the verb, and finally with the direct object marker.

24. For more on the three verbs used to describe the rape, see Fokkelman, *Narrative Art and Poetry in the Books of Samuel*, 1:107.

25. The NIV's "Come to bed with me" is lit., "Come, lie with me" (v. 11).

26. Or perhaps, more lit., "laid her." See Trible, *Texts of Terror*, 46. This verb is used in the same way in Shechem's rape of Dinah (Gen. 34:2). On that passage and the comparisons to ours, see Sternberg, *Poetics*, 446, 536–37.

27. "The nadir is thus characterized by an immense acceleration, suggesting how Amnon is conditioned merely to reach orgasm" (Fokkelman, *Narrative Art and Poetry in the Books of Samuel*, 1:107).

28. Specifically, vv. 14b–15a. See Fokkelman, ibid., 1:99–102; Shimon Bar-Efrat, "Some Observations on the Analysis of Structure in Biblical Narrative," *VT* 30 (1980): 154–73, esp. 162–63. Fokkelman comments further that there are three links where the narrator explicitly mentions emotions: vv. 1–2, 14b–15a, and 21–22, connecting the key words, love and hatred (1:101–2).

speculation.[29] But the point of the narrator is that Amnon's repugnance for Tamar becomes central and must be addressed in the rest of the passage. Just as his unrelenting love (lust) for Tamar drove the first portion of the narrative forward, now his hatred drives the next.

The next sequence of events is clarified when we keep the Pentateuchal law in view, regardless of how much or little it was enforced in the royal court of David. In his hatred, Amnon wants to drive Tamar away (13:15). But Israelite law (and presumably earlier Hebrew mores) required that a man who had sexual intercourse with a virgin must marry her (Ex. 22:16–17; Deut. 22:28–29).[30] Tamar objects that "sending" her away now will be worse than Amnon's first offense (2 Sam. 13:16)—a reference to the Old Testament provision for divorcing a wife (notice "sends" in Deut. 24:1).[31] Amnon and Tamar are not married, of course, but Tamar's use of the technical term for divorce is a plea, a reminder that two wrongs do not make a right. By treating her now as a divorced and shamed woman, Amnon will only compound a difficult situation. She is again acting morally and wisely in order to divert tragedy for both of them.

The mention of Tamar's "richly ornamented robe" is interesting because this is the only other example of the expression used to describe Joseph's famous "coat of many colors" (NIV "richly ornamented robe," Gen. 37:3). As in the Joseph narrative, we have no clear indication of the precise nature of the robe that makes it so distinctive.[32] Whatever the term's etymological significance, the narrator has thankfully left us a note explaining the symbolism of Tamar's robe: It signified her status as an unmarried princess (2 Sam. 13:18). Once she tears it, the robe symbolizes the ruin of her life.[33]

The laconic verse 21 states that when David learns what has happened, he is furious. The abrupt ending of the verse is an indictment of his inactivity. Commentators often speculate about his failure to defend Tamar and punish Amnon, perhaps insisting on marriage as prescribed by law. It seems likely that David's consciousness of his own guilt paralyzes him.[34] How can he chastise Amnon in light of his own sin? Perhaps David could have pre-

---

29. McCarter, *II Samuel*, 324; Hertzberg, *I and II Samuel*, 324.

30. McCarter, *II Samuel*, 324; Bergen, *1, 2 Samuel*, 382.

31. Perhaps this is also a literary echo of the use of this verb (*šlḥ*) in chs. 10–12, see Original Meaning section of that section.

32. Though McCarter offers an impressive argument that the phrase *kᵉtonet passim* denotes "a long-sleeved gown" (McCarter, *II Samuel*, 325–26).

33. Conroy, *Absalom Absalom!* 34. There may have been more involved, though Baldwin assumes that tearing the robe after the bolting of the door to Amnon's bedroom means "the door to marriage was bolted against her for life" (Baldwin, *1 and 2 Samuel*, 249).

34. Keil and Delitzsch, *Samuel*, 401; Gordon, *I and II Samuel*, 264.

vented what will soon take place. Instead, he appears the overindulgent father, who becomes a passive, silent sufferer throughout the rest of the extended narrative (i.e., through ch. 20). Absalom refuses to speak to Amnon, but he treasures the hatred in his heart (13:21). The narrative that began with love (13:1–2) now ends with hatred (13:21–22). At its center stands the act of violence that has turned love into hatred (13:14–15).[35]

Absalom Kills Amnon (13:23–39)

THE FINAL NOTE OF HATRED in the previous paragraph warns us that this episode is not over. Absalom is disciplined and patient when it comes to revenge! He waits two years before setting a trap for Amnon (13:23). David's reluctance may imply also suspicion of Absalom's game, which once again indicts him as an overindulgent father (13:26). Once again, David is manipulated by the people around him, unable to resist Absalom's urging (13:27; cf. 13:6–7).

Absalom's two-year wait, during which he likely nurtures his hatred and plots his revenge, comes to fruition in the murder of Amnon. Though rape is roundly condemned in the Old Testament, the punishment was not murder, and Absalom's actions are totally unjustified.[36] Not unlike David's murder of Uriah, Absalom's execution of Amnon involves cold-blooded intrigue and secrecy. The motive in this case, however, is unadulterated hatred and perhaps greed for political gain, whereas David struck Uriah for the sake of self-preservation.

The expression "all the king's sons" (13:23, 29, 30, 33; without "all" in 13:35, 36) is probably a technical term designating those sons of David besides the crown prince, who is himself in line to inherit the throne.[37] Thus, Amnon is the crown prince and the object of Absalom's plot, while the other princes are only a decoy (13:27). The question of succession to David's kingdom is a theme just below the surface of this text. Amnon's murder serves both to avenge his shameful rape of Tamar and to clear the way for Absalom to claim the royal throne. The motive for violence in the previous paragraphs was pure lust. The violent mistreatment of Tamar has now resulted in further violence, the fratricidal revenge of Absalom, who is motivated by hate and greed. Sadly, the prophecy of Nathan against David is already coming to fruition (12:10): "The sword will never depart from your house."

In 13:37–39, the narrator gives a brief report of the ensuing three years. Absalom is forced into exile in Geshur, where he receives the hospitality

---

35. Youngblood, "1, 2 Samuel," 955.
36. Raymond Westbrook, "Punishments and Crimes," ABD, 5:546–56, esp. 552.
37. Hertzberg, I and II Samuel, 327.

and protection of his grandfather on his mother's side.[38] The narrative seems to have reached an impasse: David is incapable of administering justice in his own family, and Absalom is unable to return home. The narrator tells us Absalom stayed in Geshur for only "three years," which promises a resolution to the impasse and also creates a transition to the next chapter. In addition, David is now able to deal with the loss of Amnon and is ready for reconciliation with Absalom (13:39).[39]

The Wise Woman of Tekoa (14:1–20)

THIS PARAGRAPH RELIES on the role of the king as the one responsible for establishing divine justice in the land. In ancient Israel, the king was the possessor of the divine law (Deut. 17:18–20), the "supreme justice" in the land.[40] Just as Nathan's parable in 12:1–4 was given to elicit a judgment from the king, so the wise Tekoite woman's ruse evokes David's judgment. In both cases, the king's pronouncement turns out to be a self-indictment.

Joab takes action presumably because Absalom remains the crown prince, and his absence from Jerusalem could complicate a smooth transition of royal power to a new leader when the time is right.[41] But David is inactive (as he was when he heard of Amnon's rape of Tamar). David seems incapable of disciplining his children. Being fully aware of David's desire ("the king's heart longed for Absalom," 14:1), Joab makes arrangements to persuade David it is acceptable to bring Absalom home. Some scholars have assumed Tekoa must have been a village particularly noted for its wisdom, based on this passage and the fact that Amos, the eighth-century prophet, was from Tekoa. But more likely, Joab simply needs to be sure that the king will not recognize the woman, as might happen in the case of a local woman. Tekoa is in the hills of Judah, approximately ten miles south of Jerusalem.[42]

Wisdom in the Old Testament is a skill or tool for accomplishing one's purposes. It finds fruition in a number of skills and crafts, but it is particularly evident in sages who have an ability to use words or speech artfully. Indeed, there

---

38. King Talmai's daughter Maacah gave birth to Absalom during David's rule in Hebron (2 Sam. 3:3; 1 Chron. 3:2). Amnon was firstborn, and Chileab (Kileab in NIV) plays no further role in the succession question. It is often assumed that Chileab died young. Geshur was a small kingdom left unconquered west of the half-tribe of Manasseh and north of Gilead (Josh. 12:5, 13:11; see Aharoni and Avi-Yonah, *The Macmillan Bible Atlas*, 61).

39. A difficult verse, but one that has been clarified by evidence from Qumran (see McCarter, *II Samuel*, 338, 344).

40. Gösta W. Ahlström, "Administration of the State in Canaan and Ancient Israel," *CANE*, 1:598.

41. Gordon, *I and II Samuel*, 266.

42. Lars Axelsson, "Tekoa," *ABD*, 6:343–44; Anderson, *2 Samuel*, 187.

may have been an Israelite tradition in which rhetoricians were trained to use language artfully in order to achieve desired results.[43] Joab is in need of a gifted and eloquent actress in order to persuade David to take action. In Tekoa, he finds a remarkable woman, noted for her articulate, persuasive speech. Joab supplies the words, the Tekoite woman the rhetorical and thespian skills.

As supreme judge of the nation, David must have felt an obligation to avenge Amnon's death as required by law, even though Absalom is the crown prince (see Ex. 21:12; Lev. 24:17). Keeping Absalom safely tucked away in Geshur saves David from any unpleasantness and makes it possible for him to avoid taking action. Joab has apparently made other attempts to gain Absalom's freedom (implied by 14:19, 22), but David has continued to do nothing, perhaps afraid of further fratricidal retaliation. David needs to think in wholly different categories. Once he declares that the Tekoite woman's son will be spared, it suddenly becomes admissible to consider an exception in the case of Absalom.

> [As in Nathan's parable in chapter 12] the case is the shadow of a real situation in David's own life, a situation he had been unable to resolve. Blind to the pertinence of the case to himself, he is now able to pass judgment with a sense of justice befitting a king.[44]

Joab's strategy forces the king to perceive the dilemma differently, which Joab has apparently been unable to do directly. The Tekoite woman is a remarkable character, who uses persuasive speech mixed with flattery to move David beyond the impasse.[45]

David and Absalom Reconciled (14:21–33)

THE RESULT OF THE IMPRESSIVE TEKOITE WOMAN'S AUDIENCE with David is a changed situation. Once David places the woman's only remaining son under

---

43. The origins for Israelite wisdom have been sought in a court "school" in Jerusalem, but also in the family and tribe. See Roland E. Murphy, "Wisdom in the OT," *ABD*, 6:920–31, esp. 921; Gerald H. Wilson, "Wisdom," *NIDOTTE*, 4:1276–85; idem, "חכם," *NIDOTTE*, 2:130–34. McCarter makes the interesting observation that there are three wise women in the books of Samuel, all of whom make eloquent speeches to achieve certain desired results: Abigail (1 Sam. 25:24–31), the wise woman of Abel Beth Maacah (2 Sam. 20:16–19), and the Tekoite woman here. See McCarter, *II Samuel*, 345. Mary Evans comments further: "There seems to have been no problem, theologically or otherwise, with accepting advice or teaching from a woman (cf. 2 Kgs. 22:14–20)" (*1 and 2 Samuel*, 200).

44. McCarter, *II Samuel*, 350.

45. When she twice refers to David as "an angel of God" (14:17, 20), she is probably using flattery to soften the blow of her other words (see 1 Sam. 29:9; 2 Sam. 19:27; Sternberg, *Poetics*, 90).

royal protection, David is forced to reconsider his own position on Absalom. His situation is considerably different: Her two sons fought outdoors and one killed the other because there was no one to intervene, whereas Absalom's murder of Amnon was cold-blooded and premeditated. But the wise woman is able to press on David the parallels between her case and his. David relents, and Absalom is allowed to return to Jerusalem. The sad events recorded in the next several chapters prove Joab's strategy leading to this decision is a big mistake. Absalom not only goes unpunished, but he nearly brings down David's kingdom. Ironically, because David is reluctant to take up arms against his son, that very son will soon take up arms against him.[46]

The rest of this chapter characterizes Absalom further and prepares us as readers for the tragic events to follow. Absalom's impressive appearance is prelude to his claim to be king. Just as Saul's height and David's manly appearance served them well (1 Sam. 9:2; 10:23–24; 16:12; 17:42), so Absalom's striking good looks will serve him well. The physical characteristic of full, thick hair is an important detail that the narrator hopes we will remember (see 18:9). His manipulative and violent treatment of Joab further warns us of an avaricious side to Absalom that does not bode well for the future. The reconciliation between father and son is described briefly and formally (2 Sam. 14:33). But our reading of the next unit indicates the long "delay in restoration has left its mark on Absalom."[47]

VIOLENCE AND HATRED. In a word, this text is about violence. The Bible has much to say about violence in general. One of the reasons God sent a flood in Noah's day was because "the earth was corrupt in God's sight and was full of violence (ḥamas)" (Gen. 6:11). The Old Testament prophets were vigilant in their condemnation of violence as a ruthless abuse of power, especially wherever it resulted in loss or injury to the unprotected.[48] Seizure and abuse of power for personal gain (or gratification of selfish lusts) are uniformly condemned throughout the Bible.

As we have seen many times, these historical narratives illustrate truths taught explicitly elsewhere in Scripture. The violence David unleashed in the previous unit has now taken up residence in his family. Literarily, this unit mirrors the sins of David in chapters 10–12. The king was guilty of sexual transgression and murder, both of which come back to haunt him here among his own children. Amnon's act of sexual violence leads to an act of deadly revenge.

46. Baldwin, 1 and 2 Samuel, 253.
47. Hertzberg, I and II Samuel, 335.
48. Cf. Isa. 53:9; 60:18; Ezek. 7:23; 45:9; Amos 3:10; Mic. 2:2; 6:12; Hab. 1:3; 2:8.

But it would be a mistake to interpret the text as only and simply about violence, as though this were a one-dimensional portrait. The narrator has linked the two acts of violence—the rape of Tamar and the murder of Amnon—with the common thread of hatred, which gives the account depth and perspective. Amnon's "intense hatred" of Tamar after he has ravaged her (13:15) leads to Absalom's hatred of Amnon (13:22). One act of unbridled passion leads to vicious retribution, which unleashes monstrous hatred and fury. With Absalom's sojourn in Geshur, the reader fully expects the violence to continue.

One of the dangers of interpretating this passage is to read it in isolation, missing its contribution to the message of 2 Samuel as a whole. Indeed, many scholars have devoted considerable time to 2 Samuel 1–10 in order to learn as much as possible about the history of David's reign but neglect the prominence given in the narrative to the personal and societal consequences of the king's sins detailed in chapters 11–20. While our historian is interested in the grandeur of David's reign (he seems to rejoice in what God did through David), the focus in this last half of the book is to draw the reader into his prophetic evaluation of David and of all kings generally. As readers, we are invited to consider the full weight of sin, to see the social and public consequences of David's personal adultery and murder.

Thus, what we learn here about violence and hatred should be read together with the lessons on sin, repentance, and forgiveness in the previous unit. Chapters 13–20 are also the gradual unfolding of that which Yahweh promised, the fulfillment of his judgment through Nathan the prophet (2 Sam. 12:10–12). Baldwin has said it well:

> To concentrate on the historical aspect of David's reign, therefore, and to stop there, is to miss the point of the book. What we are meant to find is guidance to live by, a clue to the deceptions that distort our understanding of what is beneficial and what ought to be done. In other words, these chapters, like many more, are meant to be "a lamp to my feet and a light to my path" (Ps. 119:105).[49]

VIOLENCE AND HUMAN NATURE. The vicious cycle of apparently unending hatred and violence is characteristic of human nature and is what one recent author has called "ungrace."[50] Our world is filled with examples of ungrace, each with its own lengthy

---

49. Baldwin, *1 and 2 Samuel*, 282.
50. Philip Yancey, *What's So Amazing About Grace?* 75–93; see esp. p. 83 for some of what follows.

string of unforgiving acts of violence. The teenage bomb-thrower in Northern Ireland, the rock-throwing youth in Palestine, or the gun-toting Israeli soldier often has no knowledge, or at least no recollection, of the long history of violent hatred behind his actions. Ireland is still burdened with atrocities committed by Oliver Cromwell in the seventeenth century, Palestinians are avenging memories from five decades of injustices, and the Jews of modern Israel live with the haunting memories of centuries of anti-Semitism and pogroms in Europe.

This feature of human nature (why not call it human sin?) is spinning out of control. The twentieth century proved to be the most violent century of world history, dispelling the myth of humanism that things are improving and that the human spirit is gradually evolving into greater and better things. The statistics tell the story. Though scholars who study such things are not agreed about the specifics—admittedly, it is impossible to be confident of such computations—most estimates range between 160 million and 200 million deaths in the twentieth century related to war and genocide.[51] About half of these are war related, while the remainder are credited to politically motivated carnage, typically communist oppression.

As the twentieth century ended, this trend has not been slowing. According to news reports, our world in the post–Cold War era is not getting less violent. There are now more and more "hotspots" around the world, often enflamed by racial and religious hatred and each threatening to erupt into ethnic cleansing at any moment. In the former USSR, Abkhazia and south Ossentia both seek secession from Georgia, while Kurds want to carve a state out of Turkey. Deaths in Kashmir's Muslim insurgency against Hindu-dominated India passed the six thousand mark. Ethnic Kazakhs in Kazakhstan hate the Russian Cossacks, while Scots in Britain, Tutsis in Rwanda, Basques and Catalans in Spain, and Tauregas in Mali and Niger all seek varying degrees of self-rule or statehood. Even in North America, French Quebec edges toward separation from Canada.

Indeed, this period of post–Cold War world history seems destined to be characterized as the time of reemerging ancient tribal hatreds that have divided humankind for centuries by race, faith, and nationality. One leading authority has concluded: "The explosion of communal violence is the paramount issue facing the human rights movement today. And containing the abuses committed in the name of ethnic or religious groups will be our foremost challenge for the years to come."[52]

---

51. See most notably Zbigniew Brzezinski, *Out of Control: Global Turmoil on the Eve of the Twenty-First Century* (New York: Charles Scribner's Sons, 1993), 7–18.

52. Kenneth Ross, quoted in Miroslav Volf, *Exclusion and Embrace: A Theological Exploration of Identity, Otherness, and Reconciliation* (Nashville: Abingdon, 1996), 15.

"Like a spiritual defect encoded in the family DNA, ungrace gets passed on in an unbroken chain."[53] The sad fact is that our individual sins—our private hatreds and vitriolic passions—contribute to "ungrace" in our own tribes (families, churches, working environments, etc.). In one way or another, each of us repeats the failures of Adam and Eve in the primeval garden, eating the goodly fruit of the tree of the knowledge of good and evil to learn for ourselves whether what has been "told" us is the real "right" and "wrong" of things.[54] Thus, each of us contributes to the communal hatred that plagues humankind and constantly threatens to erupt at any moment in self-destructive violence. For this is the additional lesson of the story of David's family: All hate-driven violence inflicts as much harm on the avenger as the victim. Amnon and Absalom both come to an ignoble and violent death, which contributes further to our full-orbed understanding of the nature of sin.

This consuming, self-destructive nature of sin is graphically illustrated by the following story of how an Eskimo kills a wolf, related by radio personality Paul Harvey.

First, the Eskimo coats his knife blade with animal blood and allows it to freeze. Then he adds another layer of blood, and another, until the blade is completely concealed by frozen blood. Next, the hunter fixes his knife in the ground with the blade up. When a wolf follows his sensitive nose to the source of the scent and discovers the bait, he licks it, tasting the fresh frozen blood. He begins to lick faster, more and more vigorously, lapping the blade until the keen edge is bare. Feverishly now, harder and harder the wolf licks the blade in the arctic night. So great becomes his craving for blood that the wolf does not notice the razor-sharp sting of the naked blade on his own tongue, nor does he recognize the instant at which his insatiable thirst is being satisfied by his "own" warm blood. His carnivorous appetite just craves more—until the dawn finds him dead in the snow![55]

---

53. Yancey, What's So Amazing About Grace? 79.

54. Karl Menninger, Whatever Became of Sin? 20.

55. Chris T. Zwingelberg, quoted in Illustrations for Preaching and Teaching from Leadership Journal, ed. C. B. Larson (Grand Rapids: Baker, 1993), 146.

2 Samuel 15:1–20:26

Introduction: Absalom's Conspiracy and Its Outcome

THIS EXTENDED NARRATIVE leads us through court intrigue, seditious insurrection, the death of another crown prince, and eventually civil war. By the overall structure of the book, we are to understand all of this as the result of David's sin in the matter of Bathsheba and Uriah. The large amount of material devoted to Absalom's rebellion and its aftermath reveals just how serious the threat was: David nearly lost his throne.[1] Here he reaps what he has sown in chapters 10–12, made worse by his inability to deal with his children's crimes in chapters 13–14. My primary objective in this chapter is to emphasize the message of the book as discerned through analysis of its current arrangement and structure, not to speculate about what literary traditions might underlie the text (for which the reader may consult the technical commentaries).

We have ample reason to take these several chapters together as a single unit. Scholars have long recognized the intentional arrangement, especially in the transition from a "desire/fulfillment of desire" pattern (chs. 13–14) to a "departure/return" pattern (chs. 15–20).[2] Moreover, the rape of Tamar and its consequences (chs. 13–14) serve as a prologue for Absalom's rebellion (chs. 15–20), which explains the prominence of Absalom even there (see comments on 13:1). Thus the preceding unit provides a knowledge of private matters required for our reading of the public events narrated in chapters 15–20.[3]

THE "DEPARTURE/RETURN" MOTIF has contributed an internal coherence and structure to these chapters, but the details of that structure have been analyzed in a variety of ways.[4] In perhaps its simplest form, this structure entails a concentric arrangement in which the beginning of the rebellion (15:1–12) corresponds to the conclusion and its aftermath (20:1–22). The next internal layer of the chiastic structure

---

1. Ackroyd, *Second Book of Samuel*, 119.

2. Youngblood, "1, 2 Samuel," 987; Anderson, *2 Samuel*, 202.

3. McCarter, *II Samuel*, 327.

4. Most prominent among them is that of Charles Conroy, *Absalom Absalom!* 89. For variations of this chiastic structure for chs. 15–20, see Fokkelman, *Narrative Art and Poetry in the Books of Samuel*, 1:338–41; Sacon, "Literary Structure," 31–38.

---

begins with David's flight from Jerusalem and a series of "meeting scenes" (15:13–16:14). This in turn corresponds to David's return to the city and the matching "meeting scenes" (19:8b–43). At the center of the structure stands the confrontation of counselors (16:15–17:23) and the confrontation of armies (17:24–19:8a). Thus the following symmetry is discernible:[5]

A. Rebellion breaks out (15:1–12)
    B. David's flight: meeting scenes (15:13–16:14)
        C. Clash of counselors (16:15–17:23)
        C'. Clash of armies (17:24–19:8a)
    B'. David's return: meeting scene (19:8b–43)
A'. Rebellion finally crushed (20:1–22)

Geography also plays an essential role in this structure. In the opening section, the action takes place in Jerusalem, where the rebellion is planned, and in Hebron, where the rebellion begins. The next unit describes David's departure from Jerusalem. The "clash of counselors" takes place in Jerusalem and its environs, while the next unit describes the battle itself in the forest of Ephraim and events in and around Mahanaim. David's journey back to Jerusalem with its corresponding meeting scenes gives shape to 19:8b–43, while the final episode narrates the northern rebellion.

As a result of the literary unity of these chapters, I will treat sections of the narrative individually under Original Meaning. Then under the Bridging Contexts and Contemporary Significance sections, I will discuss the issues arising from the extended narrative as a whole.

Absalom Steals the Hearts of the People of Israel (15:1–12)

[1]In the course of time, Absalom provided himself with a chariot and horses and with fifty men to run ahead of him. [2]He would get up early and stand by the side of the road leading to the city gate. Whenever anyone came with a complaint to be placed before the king for a decision, Absalom would call out to him, "What town are you from?" He would answer, "Your servant is from one of the tribes of Israel." [3]Then Absalom would say to him, "Look, your claims are valid and proper, but there is no representative of the king to hear you." [4]And Absalom would add, "If only I were appointed judge in the land! Then everyone who has a complaint or case could come to me and I would see that he gets justice."

---

5. Again, following mostly Conroy, *Absalom Absalom!* 89.

⁵Also, whenever anyone approached him to bow down before him, Absalom would reach out his hand, take hold of him and kiss him. ⁶Absalom behaved in this way toward all the Israelites who came to the king asking for justice, and so he stole the hearts of the men of Israel.

⁷At the end of four years, Absalom said to the king, "Let me go to Hebron and fulfill a vow I made to the LORD. ⁸While your servant was living at Geshur in Aram, I made this vow: 'If the LORD takes me back to Jerusalem, I will worship the LORD in Hebron.'"

⁹The king said to him, "Go in peace." So he went to Hebron.

¹⁰Then Absalom sent secret messengers throughout the tribes of Israel to say, "As soon as you hear the sound of the trumpets, then say, 'Absalom is king in Hebron.'" ¹¹Two hundred men from Jerusalem had accompanied Absalom. They had been invited as guests and went quite innocently, knowing nothing about the matter. ¹²While Absalom was offering sacrifices, he also sent for Ahithophel the Gilonite, David's counselor, to come from Giloh, his hometown. And so the conspiracy gained strength, and Absalom's following kept on increasing.

The opening phrase ("In the course of time") has become familiar by now. We have frequently seen this idiom used as a transition marker in 2 Samuel, flagging a temporal introduction that at one and the same time separates and links this unit with what has gone before (see comments on 2:1; 8:1; 10:1; 13:1; 21:18).[6] By means of this phrase, the insurrection recorded here is linked to Amnon's rape of Tamar and David's seizure of Bathsheba.

The theme of this paragraph is the summarizing statement that Absalom "stole the hearts" of the Israelites (15:6).[7] Our English uses of "heart" may mistakenly lead us to read this phrase as connoting warm fondness, implying that Absalom had the ability to attract the affections of the people of Israel. But in this context and in at least one similar expression elsewhere in the Old Tes-

---

6. Randall Bailey, *David in Love and War*, 56–57; Conroy, *Absalom Absalom!* 41–42.

7. In this literature, the name "Israel" may refer to the whole people or to the northern tribes. Many have speculated whether Absalom was aiming in these actions to raise support for his subversive actions particularly among the northern tribes and whether Judah was involved in the rebellion at all (Ackroyd, *Second Book of Samuel*, 137). Most today believe Judah was involved from the beginning, making this a rebellion of national proportions. For the issues, see McCarter, *II Samuel*, 357–58.

tament,[8] this is not a positive or even a neutral idiom. The "heart" in Old Testament Hebrew is often the seat of one's intellect as well as one's emotions.[9] Thus, rather than win the affections of the Israelites, Absalom stole their minds—that is, he deceived or duped them.[10] This paragraph, then, is the account of the precise strategies Absalom uses in his seditious efforts to deceive and distort in order to overthrow David.

Absalom begins building support for his rebellion against David by means of three strategies.[11] (1) He acquires a chariot and horses, with a personal escort of fifty men (15:1). This constitutes no less than a claim to royal status, since such accessories were normally the privilege of the king.[12] (2) Absalom assumes the position and role of judge for the people, which ordinarily was the function of the king (15:2–4). His accusatory tones assume that David, in Absalom's opinion, no longer fulfills his responsibility to provide justice for the people. (3) Absalom begins to receive anyone coming to him—not as a crown prince but as the king himself (15:5). By fawning over his petitioners, Absalom displays more than simple courtly form. He receives homage from Israelites with warmth as though he were king instead of David. Indeed, "in his own mind he is already king."[13]

After four years of building his base, Absalom is now ready to instigate open rebellion against his father (15:7). He appears as patient and calculated

---

8. In Gen. 31:20, Jacob "stole the heart" of Laban, which is translated by many modern translations as "deceived." See NIV, NRSV, and NASB. The NJPS has "Jacob kept Laban the Aramean in the dark."

9. "Heart" (lebab and leb) is the locus of a variety of emotions as well as of thought (HALOT, 2:513–16, esp. 514; DCH, 4:497–509, esp. 498; BDB, 523–25, esp. 524, # 9). The term often translated "soul" or "living being" (nepeš) can also serve as the seat of emotions (HALOT, 2:711–13, esp. 713, # 8; BDB, 660, # 6). The plural form "kidneys" and other words for innards may also serve as the seat of emotion and affection (kᵉlayot, see HALOT, 2:479; DCH, 4:424–25; BDB, 480, # 2). Generally speaking, the Israelites associated emotions physiologically as follows: Anger was located in the head (esp. the nose and mouth), a range of emotions in the heart, and distress in the innards or liver. See Mark S. Smith, "The Heart and Innards in Israelite Emotional Expressions: Notes from Anthropology and Psychobiology," JBL 117 (1998): 427–36, esp. 434.

10. Smith, Samuel, 340.

11. There are undoubtedly complex reasons that Absalom's rebellion is so effective initially. One of the possible historical causes is the suggestion that David simply mismanages domestic affairs, and Absalom capitalizes on the king's weaknesses (Gordon, I & II Samuel, 270; see further McCarter, II Samuel, 358–59).

12. McCarter, II Samuel, 356; see 1 Sam. 8:11; 1 Kings 1:5.

13. Baldwin, 1 and 2 Samuel, 258. Ugaritic literature yields a remarkable parallel in Prince Yassib's challenge to King Kirta. See Victor H. Matthews and Don C. Benjamin, Old Testament Parallels: Laws and Stories from the Ancient Near East (New York/Mahwah, N.J.: Paulist, 1991), 205; for more bibliography, see Bill T. Arnold and Bryan E. Beyer, eds., Readings from the Ancient Near East (Grand Rapids: Baker, 2002), text #2 (esp. pp. 94–95).

---

in rebellion as he was in revenge. His request to go to Hebron to fulfill a vow to the Lord sounds suspiciously like his earlier request to allow Amnon his brother to join his sheepshearers at Baal Hazor (13:23–27). We suggested there that David was suspicious of Absalom's earlier request, though he remained inactive. There is no hint here that David suspects Absalom's ulterior motives, so his "go in peace" is an ironic blessing of Absalom's initiatives. Once again, David appears as exceedingly vulnerable when it comes to his family.

Absalom must have felt that four years of building his popular support is sufficient to overturn his father's authority.[14] The narrator is clear that the two hundred men accompanying Absalom are duped into being present; they do not know about "the matter" (15:11). Once there, they will automatically be associated with the sedition, and any attempts to extract themselves will be nearly impossible. These two hundred men from Jerusalem will galvanize Judah to Absalom's side, while his "secret messengers" sent throughout the tribes of Israel will garner his supporters from northern tribes that he has apparently been preparing since his sojourn in Geshur. The important figure, Ahithophel, is introduced into the narrative here for the first time (15:12).[15] He is a powerful ally because his counsel is valued so highly by both Absalom and David (16:23).

David's Retreat (15:13–16:14)

¹³A messenger came and told David, "The hearts of the men of Israel are with Absalom."

¹⁴Then David said to all his officials who were with him in Jerusalem, "Come! We must flee, or none of us will escape from Absalom. We must leave immediately, or he will move quickly to overtake us and bring ruin upon us and put the city to the sword."

¹⁵The king's officials answered him, "Your servants are ready to do whatever our lord the king chooses."

¹⁶The king set out, with his entire household following him; but he left ten concubines to take care of the palace. ¹⁷So the king set out, with all the people following him, and they

---

14. Does he naively envisage a bloodless revolution? Evans, 1 and 2 Samuel, 202.

15. We may assume that Ahithophel is Bathsheba's grandfather and therefore needs no further motivation for joining the conspiracy. This association, however, must remain tentative since it assumes the identification of Eliam in 11:3 and the Eliam in 23:34 (Gordon, I and II Samuel, 272). On the name "Ahithophel," see Anderson, 2 Samuel, 196; McCarter, II Samuel, 357.

halted at a place some distance away. [18]All his men marched past him, along with all the Kerethites and Pelethites; and all the six hundred Gittites who had accompanied him from Gath marched before the king.

[19]The king said to Ittai the Gittite, "Why should you come along with us? Go back and stay with King Absalom. You are a foreigner, an exile from your homeland. [20]You came only yesterday. And today shall I make you wander about with us, when I do not know where I am going? Go back, and take your countrymen. May kindness and faithfulness be with you."

[21]But Ittai replied to the king, "As surely as the LORD lives, and as my lord the king lives, wherever my lord the king may be, whether it means life or death, there will your servant be."

[22]David said to Ittai, "Go ahead, march on." So Ittai the Gittite marched on with all his men and the families that were with him.

[23]The whole countryside wept aloud as all the people passed by. The king also crossed the Kidron Valley, and all the people moved on toward the desert.

[24]Zadok was there, too, and all the Levites who were with him were carrying the ark of the covenant of God. They set down the ark of God, and Abiathar offered sacrifices until all the people had finished leaving the city.

[25]Then the king said to Zadok, "Take the ark of God back into the city. If I find favor in the LORD's eyes, he will bring me back and let me see it and his dwelling place again. [26]But if he says, 'I am not pleased with you,' then I am ready; let him do to me whatever seems good to him."

[27]The king also said to Zadok the priest, "Aren't you a seer? Go back to the city in peace, with your son Ahimaaz and Jonathan son of Abiathar. You and Abiathar take your two sons with you. [28]I will wait at the fords in the desert until word comes from you to inform me." [29]So Zadok and Abiathar took the ark of God back to Jerusalem and stayed there.

[30]But David continued up the Mount of Olives, weeping as he went; his head was covered and he was barefoot. All the people with him covered their heads too and were weeping as they went up. [31]Now David had been told, "Ahithophel is among the conspirators with Absalom." So David prayed, "O LORD, turn Ahithophel's counsel into foolishness."

³²When David arrived at the summit, where people used to worship God, Hushai the Arkite was there to meet him, his robe torn and dust on his head. ³³David said to him, "If you go with me, you will be a burden to me. ³⁴But if you return to the city and say to Absalom, 'I will be your servant, O king; I was your father's servant in the past, but now I will be your servant,' then you can help me by frustrating Ahithophel's advice. ³⁵Won't the priests Zadok and Abiathar be there with you? Tell them anything you hear in the king's palace. ³⁶Their two sons, Ahimaaz son of Zadok and Jonathan son of Abiathar, are there with them. Send them to me with anything you hear."

³⁷So David's friend Hushai arrived at Jerusalem as Absalom was entering the city.

¹⁶:¹When David had gone a short distance beyond the summit, there was Ziba, the steward of Mephibosheth, waiting to meet him. He had a string of donkeys saddled and loaded with two hundred loaves of bread, a hundred cakes of raisins, a hundred cakes of figs and a skin of wine.

²The king asked Ziba, "Why have you brought these?"

Ziba answered, "The donkeys are for the king's household to ride on, the bread and fruit are for the men to eat, and the wine is to refresh those who become exhausted in the desert."

³The king then asked, "Where is your master's grandson?"

Ziba said to him, "He is staying in Jerusalem, because he thinks, 'Today the house of Israel will give me back my grandfather's kingdom.'"

⁴Then the king said to Ziba, "All that belonged to Mephibosheth is now yours."

"I humbly bow," Ziba said. "May I find favor in your eyes, my lord the king."

⁵As King David approached Bahurim, a man from the same clan as Saul's family came out from there. His name was Shimei son of Gera, and he cursed as he came out. ⁶He pelted David and all the king's officials with stones, though all the troops and the special guard were on David's right and left. ⁷As he cursed, Shimei said, "Get out, get out, you man of blood, you scoundrel! ⁸The LORD has repaid you for all the blood you shed in the household of Saul, in whose place you have reigned. The LORD has handed the kingdom over to your son Absalom. You have come to ruin because you are a man of blood!"

> [9]Then Abishai son of Zeruiah said to the king, "Why should this dead dog curse my lord the king? Let me go over and cut off his head."
>
> [10]But the king said, "What do you and I have in common, you sons of Zeruiah? If he is cursing because the LORD said to him, 'Curse David,' who can ask, 'Why do you do this?'"
>
> [11]David then said to Abishai and all his officials, "My son, who is of my own flesh, is trying to take my life. How much more, then, this Benjamite! Leave him alone; let him curse, for the LORD has told him to. [12]It may be that the LORD will see my distress and repay me with good for the cursing I am receiving today."
>
> [13]So David and his men continued along the road while Shimei was going along the hillside opposite him, cursing as he went and throwing stones at him and showering him with dirt. [14]The king and all the people with him arrived at their destination exhausted. And there he refreshed himself.

As we have noted, the narrative of Absalom's rebellion is partially structured by geography. This present unit is dominated by David's quick departure from Jerusalem and the meeting scenes that occur on the way to the Transjordan. The opening paragraphs begin David's flight and exile from Jerusalem (15:13–23). He wisely discerns that he will need time to organize his forces and prepare for a defense against Absalom (15:14). Otherwise all will be lost, and lost quickly. His route takes him from the royal palace out of the city, down into the Kidron Valley and "toward the desert," which implies across the Mount of Olives (15:23, 30). Though fleeing for his life, David's popularity among the country citizens is apparent by the loud weeping as he and his entire entourage cross the valley. "Prefiguring the passion of another anointed King centuries later," this narrative is full of sadness and anguish.[16]

While this long and sad processional is taking place, David pauses to consider the loyalty of those risking their lives to go with him and perhaps to evaluate the combat readiness of his troops. The reference to "a place some distance away" from the city is likely the last building on the eastern outskirts of Jerusalem, which may have been a well-known landmark.[17] The text emphasizes especially the foreign troops who have remained loyal to

---

16. Youngblood, "1, 2 Samuel," 995; see the J. A. Wharton quote on page 993 (from "A Plausible Tale: Story and Theology in II Samuel 9–20, I Kings 1–2," *Int* 35 [1981]: 353).

17. Anderson, *2 Samuel*, 203; McCarter, *II Samuel*, 360. Alter speculates that it was the "last house in the settled area beyond the walls of the city" (Alter, *David Story*, 286).

David over the years. The phrase "Kerethites and Pelethites" connotes a royal bodyguard he assembled while living in exile at Ziklag (15:18).[18] These men were professional troops distinct from Israel's regular army and were often instrumental in initial offensives against an enemy, while Israel's regular army was usually held in reserve for the final assault.[19] These crack troops were attached directly to the king and were loyal only to him.

David's magnanimous spirit and the fierce loyalty of his men are illustrated in the exchange with Ittai the Gittite (15:19–22). Having only just joined David's royal bodyguard, it seems unfair for Ittai to risk his life and family by getting involved in this dispute. David grants him a full pardon and releases him from his commitments. Ittai's moving statement of devotion to David, whether in life or death, is reminiscent of Ruth's classic expression of loyalty to Naomi (15:21; cf. Ruth 1:16–17).

The next portion of the narrative (15:24–16:14) continues David's flight from the city. Now begins the series of so-called "meeting scenes." David first encounters Zadok the priest, then Hushai, Ziba, and Shimei. The action is delayed while important speeches carry forward the salient ideas in this unit.

These scenes portray David's reactions under fire. He has several decisions to make. What role will the ark of the covenant play in this drama? Should he concede defeat as the just punishment of God and live in exile in the desert, as he had done in his youth when Saul was king? How should he respond to the news that his most valued counselor has defected to the conspiracy? David calmly works through his grief with resolve and wisdom, always with a righteous deference to Yahweh's will. Here David becomes exemplary once again, this time in his blend of devout resignation with sagacious action.[20] He is a man of great faith, but also of great planning and strategy. He is being humbled by the course of political events, but he need not be naïve.

(1) As to the meeting with Zadok, David's resignation expressed in 15:25–26 is not simple fatalism. Rather, he seems to acknowledge the events as the just punishment for his sins, and he submits to the will of God, whatever the

---

18. See 1 Sam. 30:14; 2 Sam. 8:18; 20:7, 23; 1 Kings 1:38, 44. They were likely of Aegean origin and settled in the southwest coasts of Palestine about the same time as the Philistines, though their precise relationship with the Philistines is unclear. See Carl S. Ehrlich, "Cherethites," *ABD*, 1:898–99; idem, "Pelethites," *ABD*, 5:219; de Vaux, *Ancient Israel*, 219–22; McCarter, *II Samuel*, 256.

19. Note that Joab was commander of the army, while Benaiah was the commanding officer of the Kerethites and Pelethites (8:16, 18; 20:23).

20. Or, as Robert Gordon has eloquently put it, the portrait of David here is a "combination of the pious and the prudential," which Gordon says further is typified in Neh. 4:9: "We prayed to our God and posted a guard day and night" (see Gordon, *I and II Samuel*, 274).

outcome. But the outcome remains in doubt, as the double conditional clauses make clear. If, on the one hand, his punishment proves to be a temporary humiliation, then Yahweh will graciously restore David, and he will once again worship God before the ark of the covenant in Jerusalem. Therefore, he sends the ark back into the city. If, on the other hand, his punishment should prove fatal, David is prepared to accept whatever seems right in God's judgment. The NIV's "then I am ready" (15:26) is literally "here I am" (hin'ni). Often a common greeting, this utterance is sometimes a more subtle indication that a servant hears and obeys, and it takes on special theological significance when someone hears and obeys the divine call (Gen. 22:1, 11; Ex. 3:4; Isa. 6:8). At this sad moment in his life, David is not the least bit grasping or manipulative. He appears utterly submissive to Yahweh's will.

We should not move too quickly past David's decision to send the ark of the covenant back into Jerusalem. As we have seen in 1–2 Samuel, the ark is the most important symbol of God's approval among the unified tribes of Israel. In the past, Israelites tried to turn possession of the ark into political or military advantage in attempts essentially to manipulate God (1 Sam. 4:1b–11; 2 Sam. 6:1–19). But David illustrates here that he has learned to see beyond personal ambition and accomplishment. He would rather be right in his relationship with Yahweh than be the winner of this conflict. He refuses to turn possession of the ark to political advantage, but he humbly trusts God to do what is best in his life.

At the same time, David will also do whatever he can to answer Absalom's challenge. His most pressing need is information: What is Absalom doing and when is he doing it? When he turns Zadok and Abiathar back into Jerusalem, David sees the opportunity to establish a system of priestly spies to inform him of Absalom's activities (15:27–28). The venerated priests will themselves learn the most up-to-date information available, and they will use their sons, Ahimaaz and Jonathan, as runners to carry the news to David, who sets "the fords in the desert" as the rendezvous point.[21] This ring of espionage agents will eventually serve David well.

(2) As if David needs more bad news, he learns that his trusted counselor, Ahithophel, is among the conspirators (15:31). In a text revolving around the question of loyalty, this news of a disloyal adviser is devastating. But again, we see a combination of faith and strategy. David's prayer is that Yahweh will turn Ahithophel's counsel—otherwise always dependable—into foolishness. But this is followed immediately by David's arrangement with

---

21. The "fords in the desert" are most likely well-known places along the west bank for crossing the Jordan Valley, and they serve here as specific locales for the exchange of information (see Anderson, 2 Samuel, 201).

Hushai the Arkite (15:32–37).[22] Hushai returns to Jerusalem prepared to serve as a double agent. He will offer his services to Absalom, but his mission will be to counter the advice of Ahithophel. David also informs Hushai of the ring of priestly spies prepared to carry the information to the king in the desert. The suspense and intrigue begin to build.

(3) The remainder of this section narrates two episodes linked to David's relationship to the house of Saul: the encounters with Ziba and Shimei. Just beyond the summit of the Mount of Olives, David meets Ziba (16:1–4). The background information in chapter 9 has prepared us for this encounter. Ziba was the steward of Saul's house and the person responsible for Mephibosheth's welfare (9:9–11). The motives for his support of David during the crisis are unclear, but he may have seen the insurrection as an opportunity to ingratiate himself to David at Mephibosheth's expense.[23] Mephibosheth himself will deny the charges in 19:24–28, and it seems likely that Ziba is the scoundrel of the two.

Regardless of who is duplicitous, the picture of a representative of Saul's house meeting and supporting David at this moment is somehow ironic. David is, after all, running from his own son, just as he once ran from Saul. This image contributes to the theme of loyalty in this extended narrative. Who is loyal to whom? Absalom is certainly not loyal, nor is Ahithophel. Mephibosheth is rumored not to be loyal, while Ziba appears to go the second mile because of his loyalty to David. Through it all, we wonder whether David will be loyal to Yahweh.

(4) The last episode, also related to the house of Saul, is the cursing by Shimei (16:5–14). As the king and his retinue pass his town, Shimei takes the opportunity to pour down on them insults and stones. He is a member of Saul's "family" (*mišpaḥah*), which is the clan section or next smallest unit in a tribe and emphasizes his blood relationship with Saul.[24] Like the narrator, Shimei believes David deserves the current crisis, but for different reasons. The narrator is clear in connecting Absalom's rebellion with David's adultery with Bathsheba and his murder of Uriah; Shimei assumes David is harvesting what he has sown by replacing the house of Saul (16:8).

It seems likely that Shimei is expressing the resentment of others who felt David's rise to power (and the ascendancy of Judah over Benjamin)

---

22. In v. 37, Hushai is the "friend" of the king, which probably indicates he is a high-ranking royal official, perhaps a private counselor. See Roland de Vaux, *Ancient Israel*, 122–23; McCarter, *II Samuel*, 372; Anderson, *2 Samuel*, 205.

23. Gordon, *I and II Samuel*, 276.

24. That is, within the tribe of Benjamin, Shimei is from the same clan section or "family" as Saul's house. On average, there appear to have been four or five such "families" per tribe during this period. See Halpern, "Sybil, or the Two Nations?" 295–96.

was illegitimate and not condoned by Yahweh.[25] But 1–2 Samuel have been partially devoted to refuting such a claim and to defending the legitimacy of David by emphasizing his innocence in the process of becoming king. Shimei is right that David is accursed, but not in his assessment of the reasons. Nor is Shimei justified in pronouncing the curse himself, which he subsequently regrets (19:19–20; for his eventual punishment, see 1 Kings 2:8–9, 36–46).

When Abishai offers to bring an end to such blasphemy, David demurs. Now is not the time for further violence, especially against the family of Saul, the former anointed of Yahweh. Moreover, David wants to be submissive to the Lord's will in every respect. Perhaps this curse is itself from God, even if wrongly motivated by its human agent, Shimei (16:10–11). David's response, therefore, displays a decisive image of loyalty in a context crying out for loyalty. Even these many years after Saul's death and in such extreme circumstances in which his own son and close advisers have proven disloyal, David by contrast remains loyal to Saul, the anointed of the Lord (cf. 1 Sam. 26:9–11), and to Yahweh's will, whatever his own fate.

Ahithophel's Advice Defeated (16:15–17:23)

[15]Meanwhile, Absalom and all the men of Israel came to Jerusalem, and Ahithophel was with him. [16]Then Hushai the Arkite, David's friend, went to Absalom and said to him, "Long live the king! Long live the king!"

[17]Absalom asked Hushai, "Is this the love you show your friend? Why didn't you go with your friend?"

[18]Hushai said to Absalom, "No, the one chosen by the LORD, by these people, and by all the men of Israel—his I will be, and I will remain with him. [19]Furthermore, whom should I serve? Should I not serve the son? Just as I served your father, so I will serve you."

[20]Absalom said to Ahithophel, "Give us your advice. What should we do?"

[21]Ahithophel answered, "Lie with your father's concubines whom he left to take care of the palace. Then all Israel will hear that you have made yourself a stench in your father's nostrils, and the hands of everyone with you will be strengthened." [22]So they pitched a tent for Absalom on the roof, and he lay with his father's concubines in the sight of all Israel.

---

25. Gordon, *I and II Samuel*, 277.

²³Now in those days the advice Ahithophel gave was like that of one who inquires of God. That was how both David and Absalom regarded all of Ahithophel's advice.

¹⁷·¹Ahithophel said to Absalom, "I would choose twelve thousand men and set out tonight in pursuit of David. ²I would attack him while he is weary and weak. I would strike him with terror, and then all the people with him will flee. I would strike down only the king ³and bring all the people back to you. The death of the man you seek will mean the return of all; all the people will be unharmed." ⁴This plan seemed good to Absalom and to all the elders of Israel.

⁵But Absalom said, "Summon also Hushai the Arkite, so we can hear what he has to say." ⁶When Hushai came to him, Absalom said, "Ahithophel has given this advice. Should we do what he says? If not, give us your opinion."

⁷Hushai replied to Absalom, "The advice Ahithophel has given is not good this time. ⁸You know your father and his men; they are fighters, and as fierce as a wild bear robbed of her cubs. Besides, your father is an experienced fighter; he will not spend the night with the troops. ⁹Even now, he is hidden in a cave or some other place. If he should attack your troops first, whoever hears about it will say, 'There has been a slaughter among the troops who follow Absalom.' ¹⁰Then even the bravest soldier, whose heart is like the heart of a lion, will melt with fear, for all Israel knows that your father is a fighter and that those with him are brave.

¹¹"So I advise you: Let all Israel, from Dan to Beersheba—as numerous as the sand on the seashore—be gathered to you, with you yourself leading them into battle. ¹²Then we will attack him wherever he may be found, and we will fall on him as dew settles on the ground. Neither he nor any of his men will be left alive. ¹³If he withdraws into a city, then all Israel will bring ropes to that city, and we will drag it down to the valley until not even a piece of it can be found."

¹⁴Absalom and all the men of Israel said, "The advice of Hushai the Arkite is better than that of Ahithophel." For the LORD had determined to frustrate the good advice of Ahithophel in order to bring disaster on Absalom.

¹⁵Hushai told Zadok and Abiathar, the priests, "Ahithophel has advised Absalom and the elders of Israel to do such and

such, but I have advised them to do so and so. ¹⁶Now send a message immediately and tell David, 'Do not spend the night at the fords in the desert; cross over without fail, or the king and all the people with him will be swallowed up.'"

¹⁷Jonathan and Ahimaaz were staying at En Rogel. A servant girl was to go and inform them, and they were to go and tell King David, for they could not risk being seen entering the city. ¹⁸But a young man saw them and told Absalom. So the two of them left quickly and went to the house of a man in Bahurim. He had a well in his courtyard, and they climbed down into it. ¹⁹His wife took a covering and spread it out over the opening of the well and scattered grain over it. No one knew anything about it.

²⁰When Absalom's men came to the woman at the house, they asked, "Where are Ahimaaz and Jonathan?"

The woman answered them, "They crossed over the brook." The men searched but found no one, so they returned to Jerusalem.

²¹After the men had gone, the two climbed out of the well and went to inform King David. They said to him, "Set out and cross the river at once; Ahithophel has advised such and such against you." ²²So David and all the people with him set out and crossed the Jordan. By daybreak, no one was left who had not crossed the Jordan.

²³When Ahithophel saw that his advice had not been followed, he saddled his donkey and set out for his house in his hometown. He put his house in order and then hanged himself. So he died and was buried in his father's tomb.

At this point in the book, the geographical arrangement of the extended narrative comes to the foreground. Now the text shifts scenes from David's departure from Jerusalem and the so-called "meeting scenes" to events in Jerusalem and its environs. The focus of this section is the conflicting advice of Ahithophel and Hushai, which essentially prepares the reader for the military conflict to follow.

The opening paragraph (16:15–19) reminds us of the narrative's central theme, that is, loyalty. When Absalom and his supporters come to Jerusalem, he seems assured of success, not only because David is on the run but because Ahithophel is "with him" (16:15). Ahithophel always seemed right, and his counsel was respected and valued by everyone as though he inquired directly from God (16:23).[26] His support of Absalom's rebellion gives it respectability and strength (15:12). Upon learning that his trusted counselor failed to remain loyal, David prayed that the Lord would turn Ahithophel's counsel into foolishness, and he enlisted Hushai to make it possible (15:31–37). Now the question becomes: Will Hushai be loyal, or will he too join the conspiracy?

When Hushai meets Absalom, he repeats the standard loyalty oath (16:16): "Long live the king!" This phrase (only two words in Heb.) is used frequently in the historical books to denote the popular acclamation of a king (1 Sam. 10:24; 1 Kings 1:25, 34, 39; 2 Kings 11:12). It implies more than warm good wishes for a new king; rather, it formally accepts the royal authority of the king and may actually serve as a sort of pledge of allegiance.[27] In this context, the expression raises further the question: Does Hushai intend to support Absalom or David? By pledging loyalty to "the king," does he mean the young usurper king or the banished King David? In some examples of this expression, the name of the king is included, thereby removing all doubt about one's loyalty (1 Kings 1:25): "Long live King Adonijah!" By contrast, Hushai's use of the phrase is ambiguous, though Absalom certainly assumes he is the intended object of his loyalty (see 2 Sam. 17).[28] The reader hopes (and will soon learn) that Hushai has David in mind.

Absalom may have become suspicious, so he pushes Hushai further about his loyalty to David. Is this the way Hushai expresses love for his friends (16:17)? The implication is that Absalom can do without Hushai's support if, in fact, he is so fickle. The term translated "love" in NIV is ḥesed, which as we have seen several times in this commentary has to do with covenant loyalty and faithfulness (translated "loyalty" by NRSV and NJPS). In the Old Testament, ḥesed is needed in situations in which one member of a covenant partnership is in a position to render help or aid to the other, who is in need and unable to help the other. Here David is in need of Hushai's assistance, though whether Hushai is willing and capable is still in doubt. The motivation for aid is simply the enduring relationship between the two covenant partners. This loyalty is particularly necessary in situations where its performance is in question.[29]

---

26. The expression describing Ahithophel's advice ("like that of one who inquires of God") denotes the practice of priests who used the Urim and Thummim to discern Yahweh's will. See comments at 1 Sam. 23:1–14; 30:7–25; 2 Sam. 2:1–4a; 5:17–25. David has consistently been the one in 1–2 Samuel to seek God's will through proper channels. His enemies typically make up their minds prior to seeking God's counsel or neglect to ask altogether. Absalom seems genuinely undecided and therefore particularly vulnerable to conflicting advice. Moreover, his need is related to military strategies, which implies his mind is set on rebellion against his father.

27. Mettinger, *King and Messiah*, 131–37.

28. Anderson, *2 Samuel*, 213; McCarter, *II Samuel*, 384.

29. See the Bridging Contexts section for 1 Sam. 20:1–42; also comments at 2 Sam. 9:1–5.

Absalom's question puts Hushai in a tight spot. He must justify his decision to abandon David and defend his right to advise Absalom, all while convincing Absalom that he is a counselor to be trusted. This is a delicate balancing act, but Hushai can only hope to deceive Absalom later by winning his confidence now. His response is the picture of diplomacy, and it admirably convinces Absalom that Hushai is great in wisdom and can be trusted (16:18–19).

Nonetheless, Hushai's task is a difficult one. Ahithophel's counsel is nearly always right, as though God himself has spoken from Mount Sinai (16:23). His first piece of advice is rather strange: Absalom should appear publicly sleeping with David's royal harem (16:21). As we have seen elsewhere in this commentary, royal women played a significant political role in these ancient societies (see comments on 2 Sam. 3:6–7). Sexual relations with a king's wife or concubine was tantamount to a claim to that king's throne and appears to have been common in the ancient Near East when a king was replaced with a new dynasty.[30] Absalom quickly obeys Ahithophel's advice, which must have given the impression to the inhabitants of Jerusalem that the insurrection is in fact successful and Absalom is king (16:22). It also constitutes a definite and irreversible break between Absalom and David. There is no turning back now; the insurrection will run its course.[31]

Of course, Absalom's appearance with David's concubines is also the fulfillment of Nathan's pronouncement to David in 2 Samuel 12:11–12:

> This is what the LORD says: "Out of your own household I am going to bring calamity upon you. Before your very eyes I will take your wives and give them to one who is close to you, and he will lie with your wives in broad daylight. You did it in secret, but I will do this thing in broad daylight before all Israel."

This explicit intertextuality ties together the events of chapters 13–20 (i.e., the sexual and violent acts of David's family) with the king's own violent and sexual sins in chapter 11. The unfolding of Nathan's curse "forms a dominant force in the succeeding chapters" and draws a cause-and-effect connection between Bathsheba and Tamar, between Uriah and Absalom.[32] David continues to reap what he has sown.

---

30. Matitiahu Tsevat, "Marriage and Monarchical Legitimacy in Ugarit and Israel," *JSS* 3 (1958): 237–43; Levenson and Halpern, "The Political Import of David's Marriages," 508. See also 1 Kings 2:13–25.

31. This first bit of advice also illustrates Ahithophel's ruthless nature, since it advocates the breaking of the taboo against intercourse provided in the Torah (Lev. 18:7–8). Ancient Near Eastern custom has taken precedence over Torah stipulations (see Baldwin, *1 and 2 Samuel*, 264).

32. Childs, *Introduction to the Old Testament*, 276.

The conflict between Ahithophel's counsel (16:20–17:4) and Hushai's (17:5–14) is not unlike our own English wisdom proverbs: "Strike while the iron is hot" and "Look before you leap." Ahithophel advocates striking while David's position is weakened, while Hushai argues that only a carefully planned and well-staffed attack will be successful against so experienced an opponent as David. Of course, as readers we are privy to information unavailable to Absalom. David is especially vulnerable just now, and Ahithophel's advice is right. But Absalom has no such information, and Hushai's speech is once again impressive, especially the subtle reminders of David's abilities in guerrilla warfare and his use of propaganda (17:8–10). Absalom and all the men of Israel are persuaded, and Ahithophel's advice is disregarded (17:14a).

This was indeed a remarkable achievement for Hushai, whose oratory skills must have been stellar. However, lest the reader place too much credit on Hushai's rhetorical flare, the narrator intrudes with a rare, explicitly stated theological assessment (17:14b): "For the LORD had determined to frustrate the good advice of Ahithophel in order to bring disaster on Absalom."[33] This pronouncement is the turning point—the moment at which the reader learns how the story will end. Yahweh has determined that Ahithophel's advice becomes null and void,[34] advice that is admittedly "good" advice. This being true, the suspense is over. God has acted, and we have only to follow the course of events as Absalom's otherwise successful rebellion comes to ruin and David is restored to the throne.

The next portion of this unit shows David's espionage ring in action (17:15–22). The sons of Zadok and Abiathar (Jonathan and Ahimaaz) are well positioned to take reports of Ahithophel's advice to David, who is waiting at the Jordan River (as previously arranged; see 15:27–29, 35–36). The two younger priests narrowly escape capture. En Rogel (17:17) is a spring located approximately six hundred feet south of the confluence of the Hinnom and Kidron Valleys, only a short distance south of the Spring Gihon.[35] Bahurim was a Benjamite village on the road from Jerusalem as one moves east into the Jordan Valley en route to the Transjordan.[36]

---

33. For Gerhard von Rad, this is one of three theologically explicit passages illuminating the succession narrative (G. von Rad, *The Problem of the Hexateuch and Other Essays*, 199–200). Youngblood has offered a fascinating theory on the use of the Heb. root "counsel, advise" in 16:23; 17:14; and 17:23 to show how the fortunes of Ahithophel rise to their zenith in 16:23 and then sink to their nadir in 17:23, with 17:14 as the turning point ("1, 2 Samuel," 1011).

34. Lit., Yahweh "commanded" Ahithophel's advice to become ineffectual. Compare NJPS, "The LORD had decreed that Ahithophel's sound advice be nullified" (see also NRSV).

35. W. Harold Mare, "En-Rogel," *ABD*, 2:503–4; see Aharoni and Avi-Yonah, *The Macmillan Bible Atlas*, 74, map #114.

36. D. G. Schley, "Bahurim," *ABD*, 1:568; see map number 3 in McCarter, *II Samuel*, 523.

The informants manage to avert attention thanks to the benevolent aid of an unnamed couple in Bahurim, and they successfully reach David with the vital information. The text reads like a suspenseful spy novel at this point, with everything resting on the shoulders of two individuals. But the reader knows the secret agents will succeed at this high-stakes game. Yahweh has decreed that Ahithophel's advice will become null and void, and now he turns the news of events in Jerusalem to David's advantage. David and everyone with him cross the river and head to Mahanaim in order to prepare for the coming battle (17:22).

The brief note on Ahithophel's ignoble death is surprising (17:23). We can only assume this seasoned politician realizes his cause is irreversibly lost once Absalom rejects his advice. David's prayer has been answered (15:31). The miraculous acceptance of Hushai's advice over Ahithophel's gives David time to prepare for battle. As a result Absalom has lost the strategic advantage, and the rebellion can only fail. Once David is restored to power, Ahithophel is sure to face a torturous death, probably not unlike Absalom's (18:14–15). Ahithophel, the veteran politician and counselor, is wise enough to see he can have no future in a restored Davidic kingdom. He does what he can to avoid falling into the hands of David's men.

Most scholars admit the remarkable parallels with Matthew's report of Judas's death (Matt. 27:5): suicide by hanging, betrayal of the Son of David, the ascent of the Mount of Olives, and so on. It is even likely that Gethsemane, where Jesus' betrayal was enacted, is near the place where David learns of Ahithophel's betrayal (15:30–31).[37] Thus, the author of the first Gospel has fashioned his report of Judas with his eye on this account of David's traitor, just as he shaped his good news about Jesus as the promised Messiah from the line of David (Matt. 1:1–17).

Absalom's Forces Defeated (17:24–19:8a)

24David went to Mahanaim, and Absalom crossed the Jordan with all the men of Israel. 25Absalom had appointed Amasa over the army in place of Joab. Amasa was the son of a man named Jether, an Israelite who had married Abigail, the daughter of Nahash and sister of Zeruiah the mother of Joab. 26The Israelites and Absalom camped in the land of Gilead.

27When David came to Mahanaim, Shobi son of Nahash from Rabbah of the Ammonites, and Makir son of Ammiel from Lo Debar, and Barzillai the Gileadite from Rogelim

---

37. McCarter, II Samuel, 389.

²⁸brought bedding and bowls and articles of pottery. They also brought wheat and barley, flour and roasted grain, beans and lentils, ²⁹honey and curds, sheep, and cheese from cows' milk for David and his people to eat. For they said, "The people have become hungry and tired and thirsty in the desert."

¹⁸:¹David mustered the men who were with him and appointed over them commanders of thousands and commanders of hundreds. ²David sent the troops out—a third under the command of Joab, a third under Joab's brother Abishai son of Zeruiah, and a third under Ittai the Gittite. The king told the troops, "I myself will surely march out with you."

³But the men said, "You must not go out; if we are forced to flee, they won't care about us. Even if half of us die, they won't care; but you are worth ten thousand of us. It would be better now for you to give us support from the city."

⁴The king answered, "I will do whatever seems best to you."

So the king stood beside the gate while all the men marched out in units of hundreds and of thousands. ⁵The king commanded Joab, Abishai and Ittai, "Be gentle with the young man Absalom for my sake." And all the troops heard the king giving orders concerning Absalom to each of the commanders.

⁶The army marched into the field to fight Israel, and the battle took place in the forest of Ephraim. ⁷There the army of Israel was defeated by David's men, and the casualties that day were great—twenty thousand men. ⁸The battle spread out over the whole countryside, and the forest claimed more lives that day than the sword.

⁹Now Absalom happened to meet David's men. He was riding his mule, and as the mule went under the thick branches of a large oak, Absalom's head got caught in the tree. He was left hanging in midair, while the mule he was riding kept on going.

¹⁰When one of the men saw this, he told Joab, "I just saw Absalom hanging in an oak tree."

¹¹Joab said to the man who had told him this, "What! You saw him? Why didn't you strike him to the ground right there? Then I would have had to give you ten shekels of silver and a warrior's belt."

¹²But the man replied, "Even if a thousand shekels were weighed out into my hands, I would not lift my hand against

the king's son. In our hearing the king commanded you and Abishai and Ittai, 'Protect the young man Absalom for my sake.' ¹³And if I had put my life in jeopardy—and nothing is hidden from the king—you would have kept your distance from me."

¹⁴Joab said, "I'm not going to wait like this for you." So he took three javelins in his hand and plunged them into Absalom's heart while Absalom was still alive in the oak tree. ¹⁵And ten of Joab's armor-bearers surrounded Absalom, struck him and killed him.

¹⁶Then Joab sounded the trumpet, and the troops stopped pursuing Israel, for Joab halted them. ¹⁷They took Absalom, threw him into a big pit in the forest and piled up a large heap of rocks over him. Meanwhile, all the Israelites fled to their homes.

¹⁸During his lifetime Absalom had taken a pillar and erected it in the King's Valley as a monument to himself, for he thought, "I have no son to carry on the memory of my name." He named the pillar after himself, and it is called Absalom's Monument to this day.

¹⁹Now Ahimaaz son of Zadok said, "Let me run and take the news to the king that the LORD has delivered him from the hand of his enemies."

²⁰"You are not the one to take the news today," Joab told him. "You may take the news another time, but you must not do so today, because the king's son is dead."

²¹Then Joab said to a Cushite, "Go, tell the king what you have seen." The Cushite bowed down before Joab and ran off.

²²Ahimaaz son of Zadok again said to Joab, "Come what may, please let me run behind the Cushite."

But Joab replied, "My son, why do you want to go? You don't have any news that will bring you a reward."

²³He said, "Come what may, I want to run."

So Joab said, "Run!" Then Ahimaaz ran by way of the plain and outran the Cushite.

²⁴While David was sitting between the inner and outer gates, the watchman went up to the roof of the gateway by the wall. As he looked out, he saw a man running alone. ²⁵The watchman called out to the king and reported it.

The king said, "If he is alone, he must have good news." And the man came closer and closer.

²⁶Then the watchman saw another man running, and he called down to the gatekeeper, "Look, another man running alone!"

The king said, "He must be bringing good news, too."

²⁷The watchman said, "It seems to me that the first one runs like Ahimaaz son of Zadok."

"He's a good man," the king said. "He comes with good news."

²⁸Then Ahimaaz called out to the king, "All is well!" He bowed down before the king with his face to the ground and said, "Praise be to the LORD your God! He has delivered up the men who lifted their hands against my lord the king."

²⁹The king asked, "Is the young man Absalom safe?"

Ahimaaz answered, "I saw great confusion just as Joab was about to send the king's servant and me, your servant, but I don't know what it was."

³⁰The king said, "Stand aside and wait here." So he stepped aside and stood there.

³¹Then the Cushite arrived and said, "My lord the king, hear the good news! The LORD has delivered you today from all who rose up against you."

³²The king asked the Cushite, "Is the young man Absalom safe?"

The Cushite replied, "May the enemies of my lord the king and all who rise up to harm you be like that young man."

³³The king was shaken. He went up to the room over the gateway and wept. As he went, he said: "O my son Absalom! My son, my son Absalom! If only I had died instead of you— O Absalom, my son, my son!"

¹⁹:¹Joab was told, "The king is weeping and mourning for Absalom." ²And for the whole army the victory that day was turned into mourning, because on that day the troops heard it said, "The king is grieving for his son." ³The men stole into the city that day as men steal in who are ashamed when they flee from battle. ⁴The king covered his face and cried aloud, "O my son Absalom! O Absalom, my son, my son!"

⁵Then Joab went into the house to the king and said, "Today you have humiliated all your men, who have just saved your life and the lives of your sons and daughters and the lives of your wives and concubines. ⁶You love those who hate you and hate those who love you. You have made it clear today

that the commanders and their men mean nothing to you. I
see that you would be pleased if Absalom were alive today
and all of us were dead. [7]Now go out and encourage your
men. I swear by the LORD that if you don't go out, not a man
will be left with you by nightfall. This will be worse for you
than all the calamities that have come upon you from your
youth till now."

[8]So the king got up and took his seat in the gateway. When
the men were told, "The king is sitting in the gateway," they
all came before him.

The war to determine who will be king in Jerusalem takes only one battle on a single day (18:6–8). This unit describes preparations for that battle
and the quick end of hostilities. But our narrator is more interested in the personal aspects than in the military details, so the passage is dominated by the
specifics of Absalom's death and the emotional impact it has on David.

The action takes place in the Transjordan, having moved now from the
halls of power in Jerusalem. Heading east, David and his entourage crossed
the Jordan Valley at the close of the previous section (17:22). In the opening verse here, Absalom and "all the men of Israel" enter the Transjordan and
set up camp in Gilead (17:24–26). Interestingly, Mahanaim was the center
of Ish-Bosheth's power (2:8–9), and the northern Transjordan area was important for Saul's reign.[38] The irony of David escaping from Absalom and finding shelter here is heightened when he is met by friendly local authorities who
support him and his troops with much needed provisions (17:27–29). It is
possible to speculate about Ammonite and Gileadite strategies to support a
weakened central government in Jerusalem.[39] However, in this extended narrative, in which the central theme is the need for loyalty in a time of rebellion, it is also possible the narrator wants to contrast these erstwhile enemies
of Israel in territories that once belonged to King Saul with the traitorous
Absalom and Ahithophel. When David's own son and closest adviser forsake
him, he finds loyal friends in interesting places.

Apparently Hushai's delay tactics have given David enough time to reach
Mahanaim, which is presumably well fortified, and has provided time to
organize his supporters into three companies (18:1–2).[40] He originally

---

38. Partly because Jabesh Gilead had been the location of Saul's one shining victory
(1 Sam. 11) and remained loyal to Saul ever since (1 Sam. 31:11–13).

39. McCarter, *II Samuel*, 395.

40. Our knowledge of ancient combat tactics is limited, but it appears that when a
mobile force was needed, the strategy was to use three assault corps. See Roland de Vaux,
Ancient Israel, 252.

planned to join the troops in the field but is dissuaded by their pleas that he will be worth more in the city than in the field of battle (18:3). Thus, the conflicting pieces of advice from Hushai and Ahithophel continue to set the pattern for the outcome of the war. Ahithophel's strategy centered on the hopes of striking only David, so that Absalom could acquire all of David's supporters for his own cause and unite all Israel in a renewed national force (17:2–3). But this strategy was dependent on moving quickly to kill David before he could escape into the Transjordan. By contrast, Hushai specifically encouraged Absalom to muster a large contingent of troops from all Israel and to lead them himself in the battle (17:11). When the Lord turned Ahithophel's good advice into folly, it indeed doomed Absalom to disaster (17:14).

The account of the actual battle is brief (18:6–8). The rebellion has a superior force, "the army of Israel," and it appears to command an impressive advantage. Implicit in the words of David's men ("you are worth ten thousand of us," 18:3) is the realization that they are grossly outnumbered. The location of the "forest of Ephraim" is uncertain, though with most commentators, we should assume it was east of the Jordan River, probably south or southwest of Mahanaim.[41] The significance of the forest, however, is clear: It is difficult terrain for fighting and gives the advantage to David's men.[42] It is even possible to imagine that David and Joab intentionally draw Absalom into a trap. By choosing Mahanaim as David's headquarters, they effectively choose a battle site amenable to David's private warriors, who specialize in guerrilla warfare.[43] Thus, the forest of Ephraim is part of a larger military stratagem intended to counter the superior numbers of Absalom's army. The historian is content to make passing reference to the outcome (18:8): "The forest claimed more lives that day than the sword."

In fact, the biblical historian seems little interested in the details of David's victory. As we have said, this narrative is more interested in the specifics of Absalom's gruesome death and its impact on David. The tone of this portion of the narrative leaves the reader in doubt about whether this is indeed a victory at all, or rather a defeat for David. "The battle is no doubt a victory; the coup is defeated and David returns in power. Yet David returns in grief, and the grief nearly overrides the victorious power."[44] The sorrow of the king

---

41. Henry O. Thompson, "Ephraim, Forest of," ABD, 2:557; McCarter, II Samuel, 405; see McCarter's map #7 on page 527.

42. The term "forest" in this context probably refers to "rough country with trees and scrub and uneven ground, dangerous terrain for both battle and flight" (Ackroyd, Second Book of Samuel, 167). See also I. Cornelius, "יַעַר," NIDOTTE, 2:492.

43. McCarter, II Samuel, 405.

44. Brueggemann, First and Second Samuel, 318.

seems to permeate the remainder of the text as it relates the death of Absalom (18:9–18) and the report of his death to David (18:19–19:7).

The historian tells us that Absalom's head is caught in a tree and the mule rides on, leaving him dangling between heaven and earth (18:9). The symbolism of Absalom's predicament is related to the use of the mule during the early monarchy as the usual mount for princes and kings (rather than the horse or jackass, see 2 Sam. 13:29; 1 Kings 1:33, 38, 44; 10:25; 18:5). As Absalom has lost his mule from under him, so he has also lost his royal seat.[45]

There may be further symbolism intended in Absalom's suspension "between heaven and earth" (lit. trans. of NIV "in midair"; cf. NRSV and NJPS). He has become "a nowhere man."[46] His rebellion has left him without the ground beneath his feet, unable to fulfill his life as prince or king and incapable of serving in the kingdom of God. He is "suspended between life and death, between the sentence of a rebel and the value of a son, between the severity of the king and the yearning of the father."[47] David's troops do not have to hunt him down in order to kill him. Absalom's own sedition has left him helplessly suspended, powerless to defend himself, much less to lead a rebellion against David.

How did Absalom get his head caught in a tree? Beginning with the Jewish historian Josephus (A.D. 37–100), most interpreters have assumed Absalom became entangled by his luxuriant hair, taking this as an implicit reference to 14:26.[48] If in fact this text has in view the previous mention of Absalom's proud head of hair, this "hanging" emphasizes the tragedy of Absalom's death. He is the paradigmatic promising young man brought to ignoble death by his own pride.[49]

The description of Absalom's death occupies the center of this section.[50] David's prebattle instructions are preoccupied with Absalom's safekeeping (18:5): "Be gentle with the young man Absalom for my sake." Once Absalom is captured, one of Joab's men reminds him (and us!) of David's concerns (18:12). After his death is reported to David, the king's severe and prolonged mourning threatens to drive the entire Israelite army into desertion

---

45. Alter, *David Story*, 265; or, as Conroy aptly says, "losing his mule Absalom has lost his kingdom" (*Absalom Absalom!* 60).

46. Fokkelman, *Narrative Art and Poetry in the Books of Samuel*, 1:242.

47. Brueggemann, *First and Second Samuel*, 319.

48. Josephus, *Antiquities* 7.239. See McCarter, *II Samuel*, 406, for further references and discussion.

49. There are other explanations, however, less graphic. See G. R. Driver, "Plurima Mortis Imago," in *Studies and Essays in Honor of Abraham A. Neuman*, eds. M. Ben-Horin, B. D. Weinryb, and S. Zeitlin (Leiden: Brill, 1962), 128–43, esp. 131.

50. For details of what follows, see McCarter, *II Samuel*, 410–11.

(19:7). The narrative may be partly intended to defend David's innocence in the death of Absalom, laying the blame entirely at the feet of Joab. Beyond the historical explanations and justifications, the text also seems to mourn with David the loss of an excellent son.

We have seen foreigners deliver to David what they thought would be received as good news before. When Joab sends a "Cushite" to David with the news of Absalom's death, one recalls the Amalekite who reported Saul's death (1:1–16; see also 4:9–11). Instead of good news, David saw the report as evidence the Amalekite was blasphemous and had him executed. However, in that case, the Amalekite actually claimed to have killed Saul himself, which was David's stated reason for the harsh response (1:14–16). Joab takes no chances here. This will not be unmitigated good news for David, and he refuses to send Ahimaaz son of Zadok.[51]

The account of the two messengers running to David slowly builds suspense as we are forced to wait for David's reactions (18:19–19:7).[52] Ahimaaz appears to have been genuinely ignorant about the specifics of Absalom's death ("I saw great confusion ... but I don't know what it was," 18:29).[53] When he is forced to "stand aside" and wait for the Cushite to deliver the vital piece of missing information, we as readers are also left waiting for the moment when David learns of Absalom's death. We may have anticipated at least an ambivalent response: David rejoicing because of the military victory but melancholy because of the death of the prince. But there is no joy here—only grief.

David's powerful sense of loss ("If only I had died instead of you," 18:33) towers over the landscape of this narrative, turning the army's spectacular military achievement into defeat (19:2). His anguished "my son" is repeated five times in 18:33 (and another three times in 19:4) and reflects David's inconsolable attempt to fathom the loss. He seems to gather the past, with all his own sins and those of his family, into this one defining moment of sorrow. When all is said and done, David cannot begin to resolve the incompleteness of his loss.[54]

---

51. It is also possible that Joab simply wants someone he can rely on to report the outcome of the battle *and* the death of Absalom both as good news. Ahimaaz is too intimate with the details to be objective and would not report the death of Absalom as good news, as Joab wants. See McCarter, *II Samuel*, 408, for this possibility.

52. Second Sam. 18:33 is actually 19:1 in the Heb. text, leaving a one-verse difference between English translations and the Heb. throughout the chapter.

53. McCarter, *II Samuel*, 408, though it is possible that Ahimaaz suddenly loses his nerve when standing before David and chooses to let the Cushite break the news (Brueggemann, *First and Second Samuel*, 322).

54. See Brueggemann, *First and Second Samuel*, 323.

Life must go on, even if David cannot bear to imagine it without Absalom. If we see David here as "more father than king,"[55] it is Joab who makes the kingship possible. He takes the role of the realist, who forces David to continue with life without trying to talk him out of his grief (19:5–7). Joab is a man who understands power, so that this passage makes a contribution to the book's subtheme of the uses and abuses of power. With David's inconsolable grief, we learn that the lust for power often brings only sorrow and suffering to the powerful. Power often corrupts, and those who grasp for it (Absalom) as well as those who retain it (David) often find that power is incapable, in and of itself, of providing either joy or fulfillment.[56]

David's Return (19:8b–43)

[8b]Meanwhile, the Israelites had fled to their homes. [9]Throughout the tribes of Israel, the people were all arguing with each other, saying, "The king delivered us from the hand of our enemies; he is the one who rescued us from the hand of the Philistines. But now he has fled the country because of Absalom; [10]and Absalom, whom we anointed to rule over us, has died in battle. So why do you say nothing about bringing the king back?"

[11]King David sent this message to Zadok and Abiathar, the priests: "Ask the elders of Judah, 'Why should you be the last to bring the king back to his palace, since what is being said throughout Israel has reached the king at his quarters? [12]You are my brothers, my own flesh and blood. So why should you be the last to bring back the king?' [13]And say to Amasa, 'Are you not my own flesh and blood? May God deal with me, be it ever so severely, if from now on you are not the commander of my army in place of Joab.'"

[14]He won over the hearts of all the men of Judah as though they were one man. They sent word to the king, "Return, you and all your men." [15]Then the king returned and went as far as the Jordan.

Now the men of Judah had come to Gilgal to go out and meet the king and bring him across the Jordan. [16]Shimei son of Gera, the Benjamite from Bahurim, hurried down with the men of Judah to meet King David. [17]With him were a

55. Gordon, *I and II Samuel*, 283.
56. Evans, *1 and 2 Samuel*, 216.

thousand Benjamites, along with Ziba, the steward of Saul's household, and his fifteen sons and twenty servants. They rushed to the Jordan, where the king was. ¹⁸They crossed at the ford to take the king's household over and to do whatever he wished.

When Shimei son of Gera crossed the Jordan, he fell prostrate before the king ¹⁹and said to him, "May my lord not hold me guilty. Do not remember how your servant did wrong on the day my lord the king left Jerusalem. May the king put it out of his mind. ²⁰For I your servant know that I have sinned, but today I have come here as the first of the whole house of Joseph to come down and meet my lord the king."

²¹Then Abishai son of Zeruiah said, "Shouldn't Shimei be put to death for this? He cursed the LORD's anointed."

²²David replied, "What do you and I have in common, you sons of Zeruiah? This day you have become my adversaries! Should anyone be put to death in Israel today? Do I not know that today I am king over Israel?" ²³So the king said to Shimei, "You shall not die." And the king promised him on oath.

²⁴Mephibosheth, Saul's grandson, also went down to meet the king. He had not taken care of his feet or trimmed his mustache or washed his clothes from the day the king left until the day he returned safely. ²⁵When he came from Jerusalem to meet the king, the king asked him, "Why didn't you go with me, Mephibosheth?"

²⁶He said, "My lord the king, since I your servant am lame, I said, 'I will have my donkey saddled and will ride on it, so I can go with the king.' But Ziba my servant betrayed me. ²⁷And he has slandered your servant to my lord the king. My lord the king is like an angel of God; so do whatever pleases you. ²⁸All my grandfather's descendants deserved nothing but death from my lord the king, but you gave your servant a place among those who sat at your table. So what right do I have to make any more appeals to the king?"

²⁹The king said to him, "Why say more? I order you and Ziba to divide the fields."

³⁰Mephibosheth said to the king, "Let him take everything, now that my lord the king has arrived home safely."

³¹Barzillai the Gileadite also came down from Rogelim to cross the Jordan with the king and to send him on his way

from there. ³²Now Barzillai was a very old man, eighty years of age. He had provided for the king during his stay in Mahanaim, for he was a very wealthy man. ³³The king said to Barzillai, "Cross over with me and stay with me in Jerusalem, and I will provide for you."

³⁴But Barzillai answered the king, "How many more years will I live, that I should go up to Jerusalem with the king? ³⁵I am now eighty years old. Can I tell the difference between what is good and what is not? Can your servant taste what he eats and drinks? Can I still hear the voices of men and women singers? Why should your servant be an added burden to my lord the king? ³⁶Your servant will cross over the Jordan with the king for a short distance, but why should the king reward me in this way? ³⁷Let your servant return, that I may die in my own town near the tomb of my father and mother. But here is your servant Kimham. Let him cross over with my lord the king. Do for him whatever pleases you."

³⁸The king said, "Kimham shall cross over with me, and I will do for him whatever pleases you. And anything you desire from me I will do for you."

³⁹So all the people crossed the Jordan, and then the king crossed over. The king kissed Barzillai and gave him his blessing, and Barzillai returned to his home.

⁴⁰When the king crossed over to Gilgal, Kimham crossed with him. All the troops of Judah and half the troops of Israel had taken the king over.

⁴¹Soon all the men of Israel were coming to the king and saying to him, "Why did our brothers, the men of Judah, steal the king away and bring him and his household across the Jordan, together with all his men?"

⁴²All the men of Judah answered the men of Israel, "We did this because the king is closely related to us. Why are you angry about it? Have we eaten any of the king's provisions? Have we taken anything for ourselves?"

⁴³Then the men of Israel answered the men of Judah, "We have ten shares in the king; and besides, we have a greater claim on David than you have. So why do you treat us with contempt? Were we not the first to speak of bringing back our king?"

But the men of Judah responded even more harshly than the men of Israel.

According to the concentric structure we have seen in this portion of the book devoted to Absalom's conspiracy, we are now ready for David's return to Jerusalem. This unit corresponds to David's departure narrated in 15:13–16:14. As geography has played an important role in the structure to this point, so here we begin with a debate about how David will be brought back into the royal capital city. Furthermore, the so-called "meeting scenes" of 15:13–16:14 raised concerns that are resolved here with a corresponding set of meeting scenes as David returns to Jerusalem. However, even as these concerns are being resolved, a new conflict emerges in this passage that has potential to be more devastating than Absalom's rebellion, namely, hostilities between the northern and southern tribes.[57]

Though David's men have won the battle and Absalom is dead, the conflict is far from settled. Absalom's demagoguery tapped into legitimate complaints against David, especially in Judah where the rebellion started (15:10). Now that Absalom is dead, the pro-David voices return. He is, after all, the one who defeated the Philistines, and it is not likely that the nation will find a better ruler. These pro-David voices among the northern tribes argue that they should move quickly to bring David back into power in Jerusalem (19:9–10).

However, Judah is apparently slower to act, and David realizes he can never rule effectively in Jerusalem without Judah's support. He sends messengers to the "elders of Judah" (cf. 1 Sam. 30:26; 2 Sam. 2:1–4), stressing his kinship with them and offering to make Amasa the general of the Israelite army (19:11–13; see 17:25). This is a bold offer, which presumably addresses complaints about Joab's leadership as well. David's strategy works. All Judah acts to bring David back across the Jordan River. They meet him at Gilgal to escort him back into the city (which itself causes resentment among those tribes omitted from this reception, see 19:41).

(1) At this point in the narrative, we read of three encounters corresponding to the meetings David had on his way out of Jerusalem across the river into the Transjordan (15:13–16:14).[58] First comes Shimei, who, of course, is anxious to make amends for his severe cursing of David (19:16–23). As a relative of King Saul, it might have been expected that David would simply execute Shimei for his treason, which is the recommendation of David's trusted troops (esp. Abishai, 19:21). Shimei hopes to dissuade David by

---

57. The fact that Sheba's rebellion held such potential is not missed by David (see 20:6) (see McCarter, *II Samuel*, 423).

58. The sequence of Shimei, Mephibosheth, and Barzillai roughly reverses the sequence of Zadok, Hushai, Ziba, and Shimei in 15:24–16:14. The pattern is symmetrical if Ziba stands for Mephibosheth and the supporter Barzillai stands for two supporters, Zadok and Hushai. For a different analysis, see Youngblood, "1, 2 Samuel," 1032; cf. Alter, *David Story*, 315.

offering the support of a thousand Benjamite soldiers and displaying genuine repentance ("I have sinned," 19:20). David's magnanimity is a picture of a true anointed one, who is confident enough of his reign to forgive a man like Shimei.[59]

(2) David meets Mephibosheth, who argues fervently for his innocence against the slander of Ziba (19:24–30; see 16:3).[60] He has lived as though in mourning since David's departure from Jerusalem, which would be an easy check against Ziba's accusation, especially since neither man could possibly have foreseen the outcome of the conflict between David and Absalom. But this is a case of conflicting testimonies and counterclaims, and David sees immediately that he will never be able to sort it all out (just as we as readers are left in the dark, though most assume Mephibosheth's innocence). David's compromise leaves Mephibosheth with something and still rewards Ziba for his support during the crisis. In the end, we have to consider Mephibosheth the loser since a portion of his estate goes to Ziba. The point of the narrative, however, is likely that both men are less than unblemished, and the house of Saul is finally discredited.[61]

(3) David meets the aged Barzillai the Gileadite (19:31–39). Barzillai had been part of the delegation from the Transjordan that supported David during the crisis (17:27–29). David always appears ready to reward loyalty, and he wants particularly to reward the powerful Barzillai. The Transjordan was often a place of unrest for kings in Jerusalem, and having such a strong ally ensconced permanently in the palace and indebted to the royal treasury would be desirable for David. But Barzillai is beyond caring for palace attractions (19:35) and prefers instead to live out the rest of his life at home. In his place he offers Kimham, assumed by most interpreters to be one of his younger sons.[62]

Unfortunately, the end of Absalom's conspiracy is not the end of difficulties for David (as Nathan predicted, 12:10). The final paragraph of this unit illustrates the divide between Judah and the northern tribes (19:40–43).

---

59. We may speculate further about the prudence of forgiveness in this case. David is in need of the support of a local tribe such as Benjamin, and amnesty in that unstable situation will help him build more confidence and political leverage than punitive actions (see Evans, *1 and 2 Samuel*, 220).

60. The evidence that this meeting most likely takes place subsequent to David's return to Jerusalem (McCarter, *II Samuel*, 421; Gordon, *I and II Samuel*, 291) only highlights this narrator's practice of arranging materials thematically instead of chronologically.

61. Anderson, *2 Samuel*, 238.

62. Following some of the Greek manuscripts and Josephus's interpretation. See Stephen G. Dempster, "Chimham," *ABD*, 1:909. A dying David instructed Solomon to continue the favor he has shown to the sons of Barzillai at the palace (1 Kings 2:7).

The tenuous union in national Israel is achieved only through the strong personal leadership of David. But even during his reign the union threatens to dissolve into intertribal conflict at the slightest provocation. The problem may be intimated in the reference to "all the troops of Judah and half the troops of Israel" accompanying David across the Jordan River (19:40). Tensions escalate when the Israelites (here meaning *northern* Israelites) complain that Judah has been given pride of place in the celebratory parade across the river (19:41). The people of Judah respond with an appeal to their closer kinship to David (19:42), to which the Israelites counter that they have more tribes represented in David's leadership (19:43).

The narrator leaves us with the alarming note that the debate continues without detailing specifically what the Judahites say in response to this last Israelite complaint: "The men of Judah responded even more harshly than the men of Israel." Such acrimony sets the stage for the open conflict described in chapter 20. Thus, the aftermath of the Absalom rebellion provides an instigation for another, thus again illustrating the truth of Nathan's prophecy (12:10).[63]

Rebellion Finally Crushed (20:1–22)

¹Now a troublemaker named Sheba son of Bicri, a Benjamite, happened to be there. He sounded the trumpet and shouted,

> "We have no share in David,
>   no part in Jesse's son!
> Every man to his tent, O Israel!"

²So all the men of Israel deserted David to follow Sheba son of Bicri. But the men of Judah stayed by their king all the way from the Jordan to Jerusalem.

³When David returned to his palace in Jerusalem, he took the ten concubines he had left to take care of the palace and put them in a house under guard. He provided for them, but did not lie with them. They were kept in confinement till the day of their death, living as widows.

⁴Then the king said to Amasa, "Summon the men of Judah to come to me within three days, and be here yourself." ⁵But when Amasa went to summon Judah, he took longer than the time the king had set for him.

---

63. Gordon, *I and II Samuel*, 287.

⁶David said to Abishai, "Now Sheba son of Bicri will do us more harm than Absalom did. Take your master's men and pursue him, or he will find fortified cities and escape from us." ⁷So Joab's men and the Kerethites and Pelethites and all the mighty warriors went out under the command of Abishai. They marched out from Jerusalem to pursue Sheba son of Bicri.

⁸While they were at the great rock in Gibeon, Amasa came to meet them. Joab was wearing his military tunic, and strapped over it at his waist was a belt with a dagger in its sheath. As he stepped forward, it dropped out of its sheath.

⁹Joab said to Amasa, "How are you, my brother?" Then Joab took Amasa by the beard with his right hand to kiss him. ¹⁰Amasa was not on his guard against the dagger in Joab's hand, and Joab plunged it into his belly, and his intestines spilled out on the ground. Without being stabbed again, Amasa died. Then Joab and his brother Abishai pursued Sheba son of Bicri.

¹¹One of Joab's men stood beside Amasa and said, "Whoever favors Joab, and whoever is for David, let him follow Joab!" ¹²Amasa lay wallowing in his blood in the middle of the road, and the man saw that all the troops came to a halt there. When he realized that everyone who came up to Amasa stopped, he dragged him from the road into a field and threw a garment over him. ¹³After Amasa had been removed from the road, all the men went on with Joab to pursue Sheba son of Bicri.

¹⁴Sheba passed through all the tribes of Israel to Abel Beth Maacah and through the entire region of the Berites, who gathered together and followed him. ¹⁵All the troops with Joab came and besieged Sheba in Abel Beth Maacah. They built a siege ramp up to the city, and it stood against the outer fortifications. While they were battering the wall to bring it down, ¹⁶a wise woman called from the city, "Listen! Listen! Tell Joab to come here so I can speak to him." ¹⁷He went toward her, and she asked, "Are you Joab?"

"I am," he answered.

She said, "Listen to what your servant has to say."

"I'm listening," he said.

¹⁸She continued, "Long ago they used to say, 'Get your answer at Abel,' and that settled it. ¹⁹We are the peaceful and

faithful in Israel. You are trying to destroy a city that is a mother in Israel. Why do you want to swallow up the LORD's inheritance?"

²⁰"Far be it from me!" Joab replied, "Far be it from me to swallow up or destroy! ²¹That is not the case. A man named Sheba son of Bicri, from the hill country of Ephraim, has lifted up his hand against the king, against David. Hand over this one man, and I'll withdraw from the city."

The woman said to Joab, "His head will be thrown to you from the wall."

²²Then the woman went to all the people with her wise advice, and they cut off the head of Sheba son of Bicri and threw it to Joab. So he sounded the trumpet, and his men dispersed from the city, each returning to his home. And Joab went back to the king in Jerusalem.

The concentric literary arrangement of Absalom's conspiracy comes to closure with this unit. Chapter 20 corresponds to the beginning of the rebellion narrated in 15:1–12. Here David reenters Jerusalem but still must contend with the conspiracy's aftermath, which consists mostly of Sheba's revolt among the northern tribes. Though the revolt is easily quelled, it exposes a dangerous fragility in the union of the kingdom.[64] David rightly understands the seriousness of the northern revolt, even if the danger it poses is more for the future than the immediate present (20:6): "Now Sheba son of Bicri will do us more harm than Absalom did."

Sectional rivalry among the tribes of Israel emerges during David's return to Jerusalem, indicating that Absalom's revolt itself is symptomatic of a larger problem (19:41–43). Absalom seems to have simply played on regional jealousies in order to arouse support for his personal ambitions. Apparently, David has held north and south together in a unified kingdom through the sheer force of his personality. It is a personal union, effected through his skills and charisma.[65] But after Absalom's rebellion, David returns to Jerusalem a weakened monarch. In the wake of one disaster, a greater disaster looms because the tribes threaten to break into open civil war.

---

64. The connections between Absalom's conspiracy and Sheba's revolt may be more literary than historical. The extended narrative clearly associates the two thematically, though in time they may have been more separated from each other than the text indicates. See Gordon, *I and II Samuel*, 293; Evans, *1 and 2 Samuel*, 223.

65. John Bright, *A History of Israel*, 205; Miller and Hayes, *A History of Ancient Israel and Judah*, 168–88; Meyers, "Kinship and Kingship," 192–203.

An unscrupulous individual named Sheba capitalizes on the instability in the north and takes the opportunity to incite a rebellion (20:1–2).[66] The description of him as "a troublemaker" uses the expression "man of Belial," which is the Old Testament way of describing someone who is at least a worthless scoundrel (here, *beliyyaʿal*).[67] However, some have argued on the basis of etymology that the expression more specifically denotes "man of hell, hellfiend, damnable fellow," assuming a compound word meaning something like "[the place of] not-coming-up," or better, "of no return."[68] His cry of revolution in 20:1 is similar to that of secessionists after Solomon's death (1 Kings 12:16) and may be a conventional rallying cry for traditionalists in the north.[69] Consistent with the extended narrative, it portrays rebellion and raises questions of loyalty. The phrase "all the men of Israel" (20:2) denotes the geography of the secessionists, not the extent of their rebellion.

The information about the ten concubines seems bizarre for contemporary readers (20:3; cf. 15:16; 16:21). Their presence in the royal court may indicate how much the Israelite monarchy embraced the royal ideology of the ancient Near East.[70] David's action in confining them to house arrest for the remainder of their lifetimes may be an act of repentance. On the other hand, royal women have played an important political role in Israel's early monarchy, as illustrated elsewhere in 1–2 Samuel (see comments on 2 Sam. 3:6–7). Sexual relations with a king's wife or concubine was tantamount to a claim to that king's throne and appears to have been common in the ancient Near East when a king was replaced with a new dynasty.[71] Beyond these historical realities, the narrator's inclusion of this reference to the fate of the innocent victims of Absalom's conspiracy illustrates "the human tragedy so often found among the women in David's life."[72]

---

66. The expression "happened to be there" emphasizes the opportunistic nature of Sheba's actions. Alter creatively translates "And there chanced to be there. . ." (*David Story*, 321).

67. So NRSV and NJPS have "scoundrel."

68. Frank Moore Cross and David N. Freedman, "A Royal Song of Thanksgiving: 2 Samuel 22 = Psalm 18," *JBL* 72 (1953): 22 note 6. Others believe it means "swallower," based on an entirely different root, see D. Winton Thomas, "*Beliyaʿal* in the Old Testament," in *Biblical and Patristic Studies in Memory of Robert Pierce Casey*, ed. J. N. Birdsall and R. W. Thomson (Freiburg/New York: Herder, 1963), 11–19. For other biblical references and summary, see Paul D. Wegner, "בלה," *NIDOTTE*, 1:661–62.

69. Brueggemann, *First and Second Samuel*, 330.

70. Ibid.

71. Tsevat, "Marriage and Monarchical Legitimacy," 237–43; Levenson and Halpern, "The Political Import of David's Marriages," 508. See 2 Sam. 3:6–7; 16:21–22; 1 Kings 2:13–25.

72. Evans, *1 and 2 Samuel*, 223.

Joab is a ruthless general.[73] The citizenry must have resented him for his cruel treatment of any potential rivals in the military (3:26–27). When David returned to the throne after Absalom's conspiracy, he promised to replace Joab with Amasa as the commander of the army (19:13). Since Amasa himself commanded Absalom's army during the revolt, this is a certain compromise meant to appease those who objected to Joab's leadership (17:25). However, in Amasa's first assignment as the commander of the army for David, he fails (20:5). When he is unable to assemble the army of Judah to confront Sheba, David decides to take action. After all, delay tactics served David well in his own defense of the throne against Absalom. Timing is everything; allowing Sheba to fortify his defenses might result in defeat for the army of Judah.

David understands that Absalom's rebellion posed a threat to the king, whereas Sheba's revolt threatens the kingdom itself.[74] He can ill afford to delay in responding to the threat, and perhaps he is having doubts about Amasa's loyalty. His solution is to send out his crack troops (the Kerethites and Pelethites, see comments on 15:18) as an advance party under the leadership of Joab's brother, Abishai (1 Sam. 26:6). When Amasa meets the group near Gibeon, Joab shows himself again to be merciless in his treatment of any rival, even one related by birth.[75] Amasa greets Joab as an ally, but Joab strikes him down in a single blow. As Amasa draws his last breath, no one cares beyond removing him as a mere inconvenience from the path so the troops can get on with their business (20:12–13). As elsewhere, our historian defends David's innocence in the whole affair and does not hesitate to blame Joab.[76]

As it turns out, Sheba's revolt is not serious. After going through "all the tribes of Israel," he is apparently able to garner only a limited force. Joab (who appears fully in control again) is able to corner easily this rebel force in the northern town of Abel Beth Maacah.[77] But ironically, in the midst of all this military power and strategy, it is a "wise woman" who intervenes and delivers the town from destruction.[78] Her persuasive use of words and skillful rhetoric save the town and the kingdom.

---

73. He killed Abner (2 Sam. 3) and contributed to the deaths of Uriah and Absalom (2 Sam. 11; 18). His murder of Amasa here seems motivated by unmitigated selfish opportunism (Evans, *1 and 2 Samuel*, 226).

74. McCarter, *II Samuel*, 431.

75. Amasa appears to have been David's nephew and Joab's cousin (see 2 Sam. 17:25; 1 Chron. 2:10–17); for discussion, see Richard D. Nelson, "Amasa," *ABD*, 1:182.

76. McCarter, *II Samuel*, 431–32.

77. The site was just west of the city of Dan and was probably known simply as Abel, the rest of the name being descriptive. See Volkmar Fritz, "Abel-Beth-Maacah," *ABD*, 1:10. See map in McCarter, *II Samuel*, map 8 on p. 528.

78. A subplot in the books of Samuel is the role played by women in David's career. Mary J. Evans observes that this is consistent with the rest of the Old Testament. "Few women

This passage has verbal parallels with 14:1–20, which narrates David's interview with the wise woman of Tekoa.[79] Thus, these "wise woman" passages serve as bookends on either side of Absalom's conspiracy (chs. 15–19). In both cases, a wise woman defended Israel's integrity and David's self-respect. But she does so through the use of wisdom rooted in the most ancient religious traditions of Israel. This is the contrast created by her presence: Her power is not generated by political machinations like that of David or Joab. "She stands as an alternative to the relentlessness of David and the ruthlessness of Joab."[80] In the face of such peaceful and persuasive power, even Joab must relent and end the violence.

David's Officials (20:23–26)

[23]Joab was over Israel's entire army; Benaiah son of Jehoiada was over the Kerethites and Pelethites; [24]Adoniram was in charge of forced labor; Jehoshaphat son of Ahilud was recorder; [25]Sheva was secretary; Zadok and Abiathar were priests; [26]and Ira the Jairite was David's priest.

The literary unit beginning in chapter 15 is now concluded with a little paragraph corresponding to a similar list at 8:15–18 (cf. also 1 Kings 4:1–6). These were probably lists of officials from, respectively, early and late in David's reign.[81] They serve literarily to conclude extended narratives in 2 Samuel and to summarize the organization of David's government. Thus, the entire narrative in chapters 9–20 finds conclusion in these words, which signal the end of the action of Absalom's rebellion and Sheba's revolt. Things are getting back to normal in Jerusalem.

Ironically, Joab is back in power (20:23): "Joab was over Israel's entire army." David attempted to replace him, but Joab is not a man easily persuaded to give up power. The lessons of the wise woman of Abel seem to have been lost on Joab.

---

had leadership roles within Israel, but those who did (e.g., Deborah, Judg. 4–5; and Huldah, 2 Kgs. 22:14) were accepted without question. This woman had no problem in speaking on behalf of the town or in persuading the townspeople to act on her advice" (*1 and 2 Samuel*, 226).

79. McCarter, *II Samuel*, 345, 350–51.

80. Brueggemann, *First and Second Samuel*, 331–33 (quote on p. 333).

81. McCarter, *II Samuel*, 435; Gordon, *I and II Samuel*, 297. Differences in this list compared to the one in 8:16–18 seem to suggest that a controlling authority was introduced after Absalom's failed secession (note esp. the new position of minister of "forced labor"). The new authority is probably independent of the earlier kinship system. See Schäfer-Lichtenberger, "Sociological and Biblical Views," 102–3.

Bridging Contexts

THIS UNIT'S LITERARY power and classic themes have inspired modern authors. Especially moving is the image of David's profound grief over the loss of Absalom (18:33–19:4). While David at other times is capable of eloquent laments (e.g., over Saul; see 1:19–27), the tragic death of Absalom leaves him using unique language, which seems to throb with his inconsolable sobs and weeping. This portrait of the passionate king has inspired literary giants such as George Gordon Lord Byron and William Faulkner.[82]

However, as Christian readers we recognize a deeper, more meaningful power in these texts beyond their sheer literary greatness. The theological import of this passage is complex in its presentation but clear in its powerful central themes. In a word, this unit is about rebellion.

That rebellion is connected by means of an unbroken chain of cause-and-effect links to David's own personal sin; in this narrative his personal failure becomes familial and national. Moreover, this rebellion raises questions of loyalty, loyalty to one's commitments to God and fellow humans. It also raises troubling questions about power and the proper uses of power, confronting us again with an important subtheme of 1–2 Samuel. Finally, Absalom's conspiracy gives us further insight into one of the overarching questions of the books of Samuel: Who may serve suitably as messiah, the anointed king of Israel?

Consequences of sin. In order to build a bridge effectively from this narrative to contemporary readers, we must first consider the relationship between the narrative and its preceding context. Several literary features reveal the intended connections between it and the immediately preceding units, specifically chapters 10–12 and 13–14. For example, Absalom's abuse of David's concubines is an obvious fulfillment of Nathan's curse against David, which is pronounced because of David's sin (cf. 16:22 with 12:11–12). Again, the presence of Absalom as a character in the unit devoted to Amnon's rape of Tamar (chs. 13–14) prepares us for Absalom's conspiracy narrated here. Such literary features also communicate the intended theological connection between sin and unmitigated consequences.

Thus, the book's very structure invites us to see the troubles in David's family and kingdom as the natural consequences of David's sin committed in chapters 10–12. David's private and personal sins are linked in a cause-and-effect continuum with subsequent sins within his own family, which eventually explode into public rebellion and national tragedy.

---

82. William Faulkner wrote a novel entitled *Absalom, Absalom!* (New York: Random House, 1936), and Lord Byron produced "Hebrew Melodies" in 1815.

One potential problem for the present-day reader is this causal connection itself, because it means several other people suffer as a result of David's sin with Bathsheba and his murder of Uriah. David reaps in this narrative what he has sown in chapters 10–12. That much is clear. But what of Tamar and David's ten concubines? Why must they also suffer the punishment? As we have noted elsewhere, we should avoid confusing what are natural consequences of sin with actual punishment for sin (see comments on 12:13–25). The Old Testament honestly faces the sad fact that others suffer when we sin.

The great confession of faith in the Old Testament asserts boldly that Yahweh is a "compassionate and gracious God, slow to anger, abounding in love and faithfulness, maintaining love to thousands, and forgiving wickedness, rebellion, and sin." This much we love to celebrate. But the confession continues: "Yet he does not leave the guilty unpunished; he punishes the children and their children for the sin of the fathers to the third and fourth generation."[83] We should also learn to celebrate this portion of the confession, because it teaches that God does not allow sin to continue unpunished indefinitely. Furthermore, the love and compassion of God are proven by the fact that he allows the consequences of sin to filter through to the fourth generation while maintaining his love to thousands of generations (cf. Ex. 20:5–6). God limits the life span of sin, while his love lasts forever.

Rebellion. As a text narrating rebellion, we learn much about rebellion. Though biblical Hebrew is rich in words for the semantic field "rebellion," we have few such specifics in this text.[84] Absalom's conspiracy is termed a *qešer* (15:12), and those who participated in it are "conspirators" (*qošᵉrim*, 15:31). This term frequently refers to rebellious conniving that is political as here, though rebellion against Yahweh may also be involved.[85]

However, specific terminology is not determinative here because biblical narrative frequently teaches by illustration rather than explication. So here the narration itself teaches much about the nature of rebellion without labeling it as such. Absalom comes to power by duping the men of Israel (15:6). He intentionally keeps them in the dark (15:11[86]) until it is too late

---

83. For this confession see Ex. 34:6–7 and the several related texts: Num. 14:18–19; Neh. 9:17; Ps. 86:15; 103:8; 145:8; Joel 2:13; Jonah 4:2. As we have seen, "punishes" is an unfortunate translation in the NIV, for the idea is more that God "visits" the iniquity upon the children. They suffer consequences, which is not the same as suffering punishment.

84. Henri A. G. Blocher, "Sin," *New Dictionary of Biblical Theology*, ed. T. Desmond Alexander and Brian S. Rosner (Downers Grove, Ill.: InterVarsity Press, 2000), 781–88, esp. 782; Robin C. Cover, "Sin, Sinners (OT)," *ABD*, 6:32.

85. Eugene Carpenter and Michael A. Grisanti, "קשר," *NIDOTTE*, 3:1000–1003.

86. Compare the NJPS translation of Gen. 31:20 for a similar idiom, "to keep [someone] in the dark."

for them to express reservations. This is no legitimate claim to the throne but a duplicitous and insidious power play using strictly human power structures for legitimacy.

Likewise, Sheba is an unscrupulous rapscallion who maliciously takes advantage of the political weakness after Absalom's conspiracy (20:1). Such rebellion is accomplished in the dark among conniving miscreants, who rely on secrecy and trickery to acquire power. But the anointed one—Yahweh's anointed—patiently waits for the Lord's time and place to become king. The location of Absalom's conspiracy and Sheba's revolt in the books of Samuel alongside the narratives of David create a striking contrast. Even though these rebellions are the consequence of David's sin, David himself is still the example of the messiah. Samuel anointed him, but he refuses to demand the throne in his timing. Yahweh's anointed (our historian's way of designating "the legitimate holder of royal authority") is not a power-hungry rebel. There are proper and holy ways to become king of Israel, and Absalom and Sheba represent the opposite. Rebellion itself is antithetical to righteous patience, respect, and reverence for God's will.

Loyalty. Furthermore, such rebellion raises questions of loyalty. Absalom's rebellion is itself an expression of a son's disloyalty, and it forces everyone else in Israel's young monarchy to choose sides between the king and his son. Who will be loyal to David? When the king is compelled to flee Jerusalem, he learns who his loyal friends are. On the eastern outskirts of the city, he pauses to consider the loyalty of those risking their lives by going with him (15:17–18). Ironically, it is foreign troops attached to David personally who prove the most loyal (esp. the Kerethites and Pelethites) and foreigners in the Transjordan who support him in his most desperate hour (17:27–29).

The disloyalty of someone who was a trusted friend, such as Ahithophel, is devastating news; the fidelity of Hushai a source of hope. Zadok and Abiathar (and their sons Ahimaaz and Jonathan) prove their loyalty to David beyond doubt. Then there are those whose loyalties are unknown (Ziba and Mephibosheth) and those who take the opportunity to make public their hatred for David (Shimei and Sheba). Through it all the reader is forced to ask: Will David remain loyal to Yahweh? At every turn, David passes the test.

Power. As we have seen throughout the books of Samuel, the use of power has been a subtheme for this historian. It should not surprise us that Israel's first historians, who carefully narrate the rise and establishment of Israel's monarchy, are interested in this topic. Obviously, Absalom and Sheba are examples of individuals who abuse their power. David represents a man who has learned (finally!) how to use power judiciously. Joab presents perhaps the most complex example. He appears loyal to David, though the reader is forced to wonder if Joab is motivated simply by his need to preserve his access to power. At times he appears unconcerned about divine mandate or royal decree while he uses his military might ruthlessly.

One of the great ironies of the narrative occurs near the end when Joab encounters the wise woman of Abel (20:15–22). While the famous general brings all his awesome military power to bear against the city of Abel in order to defeat the rebel Sheba, the unnamed woman used only her words of wisdom. Her power was of a different sort, with different origins. Joab's power was observable and awe-inspiring; hers unassuming and rational. The narrative seems to lift the two as examples of power conceived differently and used differently. In the end, we may conclude that the wise woman of Abel is more powerful than the general.

Messiah. Finally, Absalom's conspiracy contributes generally to one of the overarching questions of the books of Samuel: Who may serve suitably as messiah, the anointed king of Israel? David's devout resignation while fleeing Jerusalem is expressed most vividly in the conditional clauses of his speech to Zadok concerning the ark of the covenant (15:25–26):

> "Take the ark of God back into the city. If I find favor in the LORD's eyes, he will bring me back and let me see it and his dwelling place again. But if he says, 'I am not pleased with you,' then I am ready; let him do to me whatever seems good to him."

As we argued in the Original Meaning section, this is no blind fatalism, as though David sees his future as some predetermined and inevitable destiny reflecting either God's punishment or pleasure. In such a state, the king of Israel would have nothing to do but wait it out, tarrying long enough to see how God would settle the dispute with Absalom. Instead, David appears here as one who has finally learned not to grasp at every means available to manipulate, to maneuver in order to control the final outcome. He certainly takes action to meet the challenge of Absalom's rebellion, but not by seizing the ark of the covenant and turning it to his advantage. In *this* portrait at least, David is an anointed one content to submit to God's will, even when that will is so far unknowable.

Thus, the hints of parallels in the New Testament's passion narratives between Jesus and David as anointed one are appropriate.[87] David's procession through the Kidron Valley and up the Mount of Olives anticipates Jesus' Maundy Thursday walk to the Mount of Olives and has been called David's

---

87. Suicide by hanging, betrayal of the Son of David, and the ascent of the Mount of Olives (see discussion of Matt. 27:5 at 2 Sam. 17:23). Possibly, the Gospel writers were intentional about these parallels, as suggested by Wharton, "A Plausible Tale," 353.

Via Dolorosa.[88] Just as David submitted to the will and authority of Yahweh, so Jesus chose submission rather than resistance (Matt. 26:39). In this and many other ways, the books of Samuel deliberately emphasize the Davidic ideal while at the same time portraying the disappointing shortcomings of David himself. By addressing these questions about the nature of Israel's monarchy and the one who may suitably serve as king, 1–2 Samuel move Israel forward along the messianic continuum that finds its fulfillment in the Gospels.[89]

REBELLION AND ABUSE OF POWER. Rebellion is a topic we all know well. Most of us have plenty of experience at it! Our world is in need of hearing this narrative's message on the nature and consequences of human rebellion. However, it may be helpful first to make another brief comment on the role of this extended narrative in 2 Samuel as a whole.

The Absalom story, as we have seen, is intentional about relating this conspiracy and its aftermath to David's own sins; there is a clear cause-and-effect pattern here. We also recognize a well-known pattern from the Bible's classic text on sin (Gen. 3–11); that is, when unchecked, sinful actions tend to grow until they become both more extensive and more intensive. So here, David's personal sin (chs. 11–12) evolves into a family trait that plagues his family for years (chs. 13–14) and eventually becomes a national characteristic that plagues the rest of his reign (chs. 15–20). Just as David "sent" and "took" Bathsheba (review the significance of those terms at 11:4), so Amnon *took* Tamar, and Absalom *took* the kingdom.

The warnings of the wise prophet Samuel have become a reality. Kings are takers, and they will take your children, the best of your fields and vineyards, a tenth of your grain, your servants, and a tenth of your flocks, and they will make them all their own (1 Sam. 8:11–18). What began as a personal sin of passion in David's heart quickly becomes a plague threatening the entire people of God. This portion of the book illustrates the principle we all know too well to be true: "After the first blush of sin comes its indifference," and subsequently more sin.[90]

We have seen that vocabulary alone is inadequate to illustrate the Old Testament's understanding of rebellion (see Bridging Contexts section). Rather

---

88. Gordon, *I and II Samuel*, 272.

89. For more on this deliberate "antinomy" in 1–2 Samuel, see Philip Satterthwaite, "David in the Books of Samuel," 41–65.

90. Henry David Thoreau, *On the Duty of Civil Disobedience* (1849).

than specific terminology, this narrative illustrates rebellion as disloyalty expressed through an abuse of power, which further illustrates a broad definition of sin itself. Indeed, it may be safely assumed that sin includes a willful, disloyal quality, in that someone else (God or human) is defied or hurt. "The willful disregard or sacrifice of the welfare of others for the welfare or satisfaction of the self is an essential quality of the concept of *sin*."[91] St. Augustine understood sin to contain this element of rebellion, since it involves a turning "away from the universal whole to the individual part."[92] So rebellion is a rejection of the greater and more desirable whole in order to satisfy the desires or longings of the individual.

The greatest danger in all of this, and the point at which many Christians get into trouble, is that rebellion can often look like vocation. In other words, we easily justify our rebellion because it appears to be a way to accomplish something we are genuinely called to accomplish. Taking Absalom as our departure point, it is clear that he, as crown prince, had at his disposal large amounts of legitimate power. He could probably assume that he would one day become David's successor and rule all Israel. Over time, he began to believe he had no reason to wait for David's (and God's!) timing. As David sent and took Bathsheba simply because he *could*, so Absalom took the kingdom because he believed it was eventually to be his anyway, and *he had the ability* to take it. It was one way of fulfilling his calling.

This is often the nature of temptation. In fact, temptations are hard to recognize because they regularly offer us ways to take control and use our own power (God-given power!) to falsely realize a true vocation.[93] Rebellion is often a distortion of our calling, an evil means to accomplish a righteous aim. Thus, Matthew's third recorded temptation of Jesus was a temptation to abuse his power (Matt. 4:8–10; second in Luke's sequence, Luke 4:5–8). God intended for Jesus to reign supreme over all the kingdoms of the earth. Alone in the desert, the devil offered him precisely a quick way to obtain "all the kingdoms of the world and their splendor." Could any vice have been more tempting to Jesus?

The abuse of God-given power to accomplish a God-given mission is a great temptation for contemporary believers today. Absalom serves precisely in this way as a warning for all of us who fail to resist this temptation. Henri Nouwen has argued that rebellion, or the abuse of God-given power, is one of the great weaknesses of the modern church:

---

91. Karl Menninger, *Whatever Became of Sin?* 19.

92. *De Trinitate* 12.14, as quoted in Menninger, *Whatever Became of Sin?* 19.

93. Tom Wright, *The Way of the Lord: Christian Pilgrimage Today* (Grand Rapids: Eerdmans, 1999), 39.

When I ask myself the main reason for so many people having left the Church during the past decades in France, Germany, Holland, and also in Canada and America, the word "power" easily comes to mind. One of the greatest ironies of the history of Christianity is that its leaders constantly gave into the temptation of power—political power, military power, economic power, or moral and spiritual power—even though they continued to speak in the name of Jesus, who did not cling to his divine power but emptied himself and became as we are.... Every time we see a major crisis in the history of the Church, such as the Great Schism of the eleventh century, the Reformation of the six-teenth century, or the immense secularization of the twentieth century, we always see that a major cause of rupture is the power exercised by those who claim to be followers of the poor and powerless Jesus.[94]

When Nouwen attempts to explain why the temptation of power seems so irresistible, he concludes, "It seems easier to be God than to love God, eas-ier to control people than to love people, easier to own life than to love life."[95]

There may also be lessons here about human relationships in general and the need to forge better families within the church. David's inability to relate to and influence his children certainly contributes to his problems. Nouwen emphasizes the connection between how we relate to those around us and the temptation to abuse our power:

One thing is clear to me: the temptation of power is greatest when inti-macy is a threat. Much Christian leadership is exercised by people who do not know how to develop healthy, intimate relationships and have opted for power and control instead. Many Christian empire-builders have been people unable to give and receive love.[96]

Who of us can deny the church has suffered great misdeeds by those more committed to personal empire-building than character-building? In this and many other ways, David and Absalom serve as warnings to today's believers about rebellion and the abuse of power.

---

94. Henri J. M. Nouwen, *In the Name of Jesus: Reflections on Christian Leadership* (New York: Crossroad, 1989), 58–59.
95. Ibid., 59.
96. Ibid., 60.

2 Samuel 21–24

❦

Epilogue: Yahweh, David, and the Ideal King of Israel

THIS COLLECTION OF disparate materials traces a number of different incidents from David's reign, which have little or no chronological or sequential connection. Having followed the consequences of David's sin in the matter of Bathsheba and Uriah throughout the court history (chs. 10–20), our narrator now brings the treatment of David to a close with these final chapters. The overarching concern throughout most of 2 Samuel has been with the question: Who may serve suitably as king of Israel? In order for 1–2 Samuel to arrive at a satisfactory answer, these remaining materials had to be included. Here we encounter poetry, annalistic lists, and historical narratives, all of which are necessary in order to form adequately an authentic, well-rounded portrait of David, the king of Israel. The variety of literary types here produces a sort of mosaic of David's reign, a tapestry of diverse materials rather than a picture cut from whole cloth.

The various materials collected here are often said to be of independent origin from the Deuteronomistic History.[1] It seems likely that our historian has supplemented his primary sources ("The Court History") with this collection of other materials that seem pertinent to the portrait of David. As elsewhere in this commentary, my primary objective will be to emphasize the message of the book as discerned through analysis of its current narratological structure rather than to speculate about the sources and history of the traditions used here.

 *Original Meaning*

SCHOLARS ARE VIRTUALLY UNITED about the intentional arrangement of 2 Samuel 21–24, and we are therefore justified in treating them here as a single unit. On the surface, these four chapters appear to have little in the way of a common theme or motif to hold them together. But after closer examination, they display a symmetry of structure that beautifully complements the historian's desire to round off the portrait of the ideal anointed one.

As with chapters 15–20 (see above), this unit displays a concentric arrangement, this time with two poems framed by layers of similar types of materials

---

1. See our introduction; for summary of the issues, see Nelson, *Historical Books*, 67–70, and esp. note 2 on p. 179.

before and after them. On the inner frame around the poems stand two lists of David's heroes and their mighty deeds (21:15—22 and 23:8—39). Serving as bookends on the outer frame are two narratives about public disasters (21:1—14 and 24:1—25). The poems themselves are attributed to David—one a song of praise (22:1—51) and the other labeled his "last words" (23:1—7).

A rather striking inclusio (or literary envelope) can be detected in the references to three years of famine at the beginning and the end of the unit (21:1 and 24:13).[2] Such inclusios often occur in this type of structure and neatly wrap up the unit as a self-contained whole. It is possible to name the six individual units in order to highlight this arrangement as follows:[3]

A. Yahweh's wrath against Israel (21:1—14)
    B. David's heroes (21:15—22)
        C. David's song of praise (22:1—51)
        C'. David's last words (23:1—7)
    B'. David's mighty men (23:8—39)
A'. Yahweh's wrath against Israel (24:1—25)

This "ring composition" is hardly accidental.[4] Scholars over a century ago observed this phenomenon, though they hardly knew what to make of it.[5] Even those less enamored with such literary observations admit the intentional chiastic structure in 2 Samuel 21—24.[6]

In such literary arrangements, it is normally the center of the pattern that the narrative emphasizes. So here the narrative highlights the Lord's

---

2. Note also the reference to God's answering of prayer on behalf of the land as another inclusio for the unit (21:14 and 24:25). On this "double inclusio" see Youngblood, "1, 2 Samuel," 1051.

3. Youngblood, "1, 2 Samuel," 1051. Or more succinctly, the outline of Richard Nelson: (A) famine story, (B) warriors, (C) psalm, (C') poem, (B') warriors, (A') plague story (*Historical Books*, 58). See also Gordon, *I and II Samuel*, 45.

4. I use the terms "ring composition," "chiasm," and "concentric" synonymously, though to be precise, these are all separate patterns of structure characterized by symmetry but having slightly different connotations. See Shimon Bar-Efrat, "Analysis of Structure in Biblical Narrative," *VT* 30 (1980): 154—73. For 2 Sam. 21—24, Fokkelman further observes the "quantitative alternation," by which he means that each genre is represented in a short and a long form: short story, short list, long poem followed by short poem, long list, and long story. See Jan P. Fokkelman, *Narrative Art and Poetry in the Books of Samuel*, 3:12—13. On the symmetric structure in general, see further Ackroyd, *Second Book of Samuel*, 193; Alter, *David Story*, 329; Anderson, *2 Samuel*, 248; Baldwin, *1 and 2 Samuel*, 282—83; Bergen, *1, 2 Samuel*, 442; Brueggemann, *First and Second Samuel*, 335; David Damrosch, *The Narrative Covenant: Transformations of Genre in the Growth of Biblical Literature* (San Francisco: Harper & Row, 1987), 237; Hertzberg, *I and II Samuel*, 415—16; McCarter, *II Samuel*, 18—19; and Sternberg, *Poetics*, 40.

5. Smith, *Samuel*, 373.

6. Gordon, *I and II Samuel*, 45.

deliverance of David (22:1–51) and the covenant relationship between God and king (23:1–7). It would be easy to emphasize the role of these poetic sections as theological summaries of David's reign. But it is more likely that the entire four-chapter unit offers, as suggested by Brevard Childs, "a highly reflective, theological interpretation of David's whole career adumbrating the messianic hope, which provides a clear hermeneutical guide for its use as sacred scripture."[7]

On a broader scale, the units of poetry also serve together with Hannah's prayer (1 Sam. 2:1–11) and David's lament for Saul and Jonathan (2 Sam. 1:17–27) as organizing features for all of 1–2 Samuel. The location of David's lament makes a fitting bookmark near the center, while Hannah's prayer and David's psalms play particularly important roles as bookends.[8] As we have noted periodically in this commentary, historical narrative normally teaches by illustration rather than by direct exhortation. Now we can see more clearly how the poetic sections are being used not only to form literary benchmarks but to emphasize explicitly what is implicit in the narratives. These are the theological promontories, providing vistas overlooking the narrative landscape. They elevate the image of Israel's king to the ideal, to the anointed one longed for by Israel.[9] This is, in effect, the full-orbed portrait of the one well-suited for Israel's kingship.

As a result of the literary structure of these closing chapters, I will treat each section individually under Original Meaning. Then under the Bridging Contexts and Contemporary Significance sections, I will discuss the issues arising from all four chapters together.

Famine As a Result of the Gibeonite massacre (21:1–14)

[1]During the reign of David, there was a famine for three successive years; so David sought the face of the LORD. The LORD said, "It is on account of Saul and his blood-stained house; it is because he put the Gibeonites to death."

[2]The king summoned the Gibeonites and spoke to them. (Now the Gibeonites were not a part of Israel but were survivors of the Amorites; the Israelites had sworn to spare them,

---

7. Childs, *Introduction to the Old Testament*, 275.

8. In Fokkelman's terminology, they establish a beginning, middle, and end of the books of Samuel (Jan P. Fokkelman, *Narrative Art and Poetry in the Books of Samuel*, 3:11). See also Childs, *Introduction*, 272–73; J. W. Watts, *Psalm and Story: Inset Hymns in Hebrew Narrative* (JSOTSup 139; Sheffield: JSOT Press, 1992), 19–40, 99–117; Robert Polzin, *Samuel and the Deuteronomist* (San Francisco: Harper & Row, 1989), 31–36.

9. Satterthwaite, "David in the Books of Samuel," 43–47.

but Saul in his zeal for Israel and Judah had tried to annihilate them.) ³David asked the Gibeonites, "What shall I do for you? How shall I make amends so that you will bless the LORD's inheritance?"

⁴The Gibeonites answered him, "We have no right to demand silver or gold from Saul or his family, nor do we have the right to put anyone in Israel to death."

"What do you want me to do for you?" David asked.

⁵They answered the king, "As for the man who destroyed us and plotted against us so that we have been decimated and have no place anywhere in Israel, ⁶let seven of his male descendants be given to us to be killed and exposed before the LORD at Gibeah of Saul—the Lord's chosen one."

So the king said, "I will give them to you."

⁷The king spared Mephibosheth son of Jonathan, the son of Saul, because of the oath before the LORD between David and Jonathan son of Saul. ⁸But the king took Armoni and Mephibosheth, the two sons of Aiah's daughter Rizpah, whom she had borne to Saul, together with the five sons of Saul's daughter Merab, whom she had borne to Adriel son of Barzillai the Meholathite. ⁹He handed them over to the Gibeonites, who killed and exposed them on a hill before the LORD. All seven of them fell together; they were put to death during the first days of the harvest, just as the barley harvest was beginning.

¹⁰Rizpah daughter of Aiah took sackcloth and spread it out for herself on a rock. From the beginning of the harvest till the rain poured down from the heavens on the bodies, she did not let the birds of the air touch them by day or the wild animals by night. ¹¹When David was told what Aiah's daughter Rizpah, Saul's concubine, had done, ¹²he went and took the bones of Saul and his son Jonathan from the citizens of Jabesh Gilead. (They had taken them secretly from the public square at Beth Shan, where the Philistines had hung them after they struck Saul down on Gilboa.) ¹³David brought the bones of Saul and his son Jonathan from there, and the bones of those who had been killed and exposed were gathered up.

¹⁴They buried the bones of Saul and his son Jonathan in the tomb of Saul's father Kish, at Zela in Benjamin, and did everything the king commanded. After that, God answered prayer in behalf of the land.

After three years of famine, David fervently prays in order to discern the cause of the plague. The Lord reveals to David that the famine is the result of Saul's treason against the Gibeonites. The text assumes Joshua 9:3–27, in which the Gibeonites, non-Israelite residents of cities north of Jerusalem, tricked Joshua into a peace treaty. Though we do not know the circumstances of Saul's subsequent hostilities against the Gibeonites, their presence in his own tribe of Benjamin so near his capital city (Gibeah) must have been troubling to Saul. David seeks restitution as a means of assuaging the guilt of Saul's actions. When the Gibeonites request that seven of Saul's male descendants be executed, David complies, saving only Mephibosheth because of his loyalty to Jonathan.[10]

We have no way of knowing precisely when this three-year famine occurred. The slaughter of the sons of Saul may be implied in the words of Shimei (2 Sam. 16:8), which would mean the famine and the execution of Saul's descendants occurred prior to Absalom's revolt. As we have seen, the historian is less concerned with precise chronology than with the need to narrate the end of Saul's line because of the consequences of blood-guilt and the innocence of David in the whole affair.

One leading scholar has suggested that this text is intended as a deliberate protest to the preceding "official" portrait of David, proposing instead a more suspicious reading.[11] David in this alternative interpretation is an opportunist, who takes advantage of a famine in order to brutally kill Saul's descendants, who may have otherwise posed a threat to the throne. David himself benefits from the slaughter and does not need to be concerned about preserving the life of the unfortunate Mephibosheth, who as a cripple could never challenge David's authority as king. All of this, it is suggested, is performed in a cold-blooded attempt to solidify David's royal power and is justified in the name of "responsible religion and justifiable politics."[12]

In response, it must be argued that this alternative interpretation depends too much on suppressing verse 1, in which divine speech specifically blames the famine on the blood-guilt of Saul's house. Furthermore, the text itself is clear that David is sincere in his reliance on Yahweh for answers in a time of crisis, which is certainly in agreement with other such cases in the David narratives. Moreover, the narrative is careful to portray David as a king concerned with justice for the Gibeonites and as loyal to Jonathan. When we read the text as it stands without suppressing verse 1, we conclude there is no reason to suspect that David has masterminded the plot as a means of removing

---

10. Review 1 Sam. 20; 2 Sam. 9:1–13.
11. For what follows, see Brueggemann, *First and Second Samuel*, 336–38.
12. Ibid., 337.

potential rivals. "That he could have benefited from the Gibeonites' revenge is no proof of machiavellian plotting on his part."[13]

In addition, we now have a rather remarkable parallel to this episode in the fourteenth-century prayer of a Hittite king.[14] In this prayer, the Hittite king seeks to discern the causes of a catastrophic plague destroying his kingdom. He appeals to the Hattian storm god and other deities in order to discern by omen, dream, or prophecy the causes of the plague. By means of an oracle, he learns that a peace treaty between the Hittites and the Egyptians had been violated by his father, who repeatedly attacked Egyptian troops. The plague first broke out among prisoners of war taken during these conflicts, who carried the plague back to Hatti. But beyond these facts of how the plague began, the Hittite king understands the broken treaty as the cause for the wrath of the storm god.

> In both sources, the Hittite and the biblical, the guilt is laid to a king, who, as the representative of the entire people, seems to have been held responsible for a disaster of national proportions.... But the most notable parallel between the two sources lies in the phenomenological structure of cause and effect, as revealed in the sequence: conclusion of treaty, violation of treaty and consequent national catastrophe.[15]

Evidently, the Israelites were not alone in their belief that "covenant breaches of the fathers could be visited upon the children."[16] The parallel confirms not only the historical likelihood of the event narrated here but also the text's interpretation as consistent with ancient Near Eastern historiography and, to some degree, worldview.

Rizpah loses two sons in the carnage (21:8). Her extreme actions are perhaps motivated by a desire to prevent the most shameful burial possible for an ancient Israelite, that of exposure to the birds and wild animals (21:10). However, it is also possible she is protecting her sons and the others from the curse reserved for covenant violators (as in Jer. 34:20).[17] Her loyalty to these descendants of Saul reminds David of Saul's and Jonathan's own igno-

---

13. Gordon, *I and II Samuel*, 300–301.

14. For the text of the Hittite prayer, see the second prayer in Arnold and Beyer, *Readings from The Ancient Near East*, text #77; Gary Beckman, "Plague Prayers of Muršili II," *COS*, 1.60:157–59. The significance of the parallel was first recognized by Abraham Malamat ("Doctrines of Causality in Hittite and Biblical Historiography: A Parallel," *VT* 5 [1955]: 1–12), who also suggested the Hittites introduced historiography as a literary genre into the ancient Near East, which was brought to artistic perfection by the Israelites.

15. Malamat, "Doctrines of Causality," 12.

16. Gordon, *I and II Samuel*, 299; see also McCarter, *II Samuel*, 444–45.

17. Youngblood, "1, 2 Samuel," 1055.

minious deaths and moves him into action. He does what Rizpah cannot do; he gives the fallen from the house of Saul a proper burial in their own family tomb. All these many years later, and near the conclusion of 1–2 Samuel, the house of Saul is finally laid to rest.

Apparently these actions meet the needs of justice and honor, and God answers prayer "in behalf of the land" (21:14). Israel is delivered from the famine. This formula for answered prayer is repeated in the last verse of the book (24:25), which illustrates the chiastic structure of chapters 21–24 (see above) and emphasizes the effectiveness of King David's prayer. The portrait of Israel's king, established by these parallel accounts, fixes the ideal anointed one for Israel's future: David's repentant leadership provides a context in which Yahweh can answer prayer.

Notes on Wars Against Philistine Giants (21:15–22)

¹⁵Once again there was a battle between the Philistines and Israel. David went down with his men to fight against the Philistines, and he became exhausted. ¹⁶And Ishbi-Benob, one of the descendants of Rapha, whose bronze spearhead weighed three hundred shekels and who was armed with a new sword, said he would kill David. ¹⁷But Abishai son of Zeruiah came to David's rescue; he struck the Philistine down and killed him. Then David's men swore to him, saying, "Never again will you go out with us to battle, so that the lamp of Israel will not be extinguished."

¹⁸In the course of time, there was another battle with the Philistines, at Gob. At that time Sibbecai the Hushathite killed Saph, one of the descendants of Rapha.

¹⁹In another battle with the Philistines at Gob, Elhanan son of Jaare-Oregim the Bethlehemite killed Goliath the Gittite, who had a spear with a shaft like a weaver's rod.

²⁰In still another battle, which took place at Gath, there was a huge man with six fingers on each hand and six toes on each foot—twenty-four in all. He also was descended from Rapha. ²¹When he taunted Israel, Jonathan son of Shimeah, David's brother, killed him.

²²These four were descendants of Rapha in Gath, and they fell at the hands of David and his men.

These four episodes presumably occur at various times in David's early wars with the Philistines and are held together literarily by two common threads (summarized in the concluding v. 22). (1) Each relates the victory of one of David's warriors in crucial battles against the Philistines. (2) In each episode, one of David's impressive soldiers is credited with the execution of one of the "descendants of Rapha" (21:22).

The list reads in formulaic fashion and may in fact have been taken from an official military archive. It contributes to the symmetry of the overall structure in chapters 21–24 by balancing the list in 23:8–39. Its location immediately before David's psalm of thanksgiving is fitting since it illustrates the great victories David celebrates over his traditional enemy, the Philistines. Moreover, we do well to remember that victory over the Philistines is perhaps the single most important raison d'être for Israel's institutional monarchy (1 Sam. 9:16): "He will deliver my people from the hand of the Philistines."

The "descendants of Rapha" are a frightening lot. They were probably a distinct group of the Rephaim in the Old Testament and may have been the Transjordanian equivalent of the Anakites west of the Jordan.[18] In light of references to the weight and size of their spears (21:16, 19), we can probably assume they are giants like Goliath in 1 Samuel 17, making this a list of David's "giant-killers." The unnamed "huge man" with six digits on each hand and foot (21:20) is especially compelling. More importantly, this list illustrates that giants in the Bible generally portray a negative image, usually representing pagans who deserve God's displeasure and are worthy of his wrath.[19] They appear as grotesque freaks, which is probably the point of narrating the unique fingers and toes of the "huge man" of verse 20. When he taunts Israel, David's nephew Jonathan justifiably cut him down (21:21).

Abishai's deliverance of David from Ishbi-Benob may signal for us other episodes when David is not leading the troops in battle personally. In the conflict against Absalom, the king's troops pled with him not to accompany them in battle, arguing that he was much more valuable lending support from Mahanaim (18:3). Some interpreters find here an explanation for David's presence in Jerusalem while his army was besieging Rabbah (11:1).[20]

The verse about Elhanan of Bethlehem is difficult for a number of reasons (21:19). The patronymic ("son of Jaare-Oregim") is almost certainly a corrupted text, and the footnote in the NIV should be followed instead: "son of Jair."[21]

---

18. Ronald F. Youngblood, "Giants, Heroes, Mighty Men," *NIDOTTE*, 4:676–78; on the possibility of pituitary abnormalities as a cause of the Old Testament's giantism and acromegaly, see Max Sussman, "Sickness and Disease," *ABD*, 6:6–15, esp. 13.

19. "Giant," *DBI*, 328.

20. But see our comments in the Original Meaning section for 11:1.

21. As supported by the parallel in 1 Chron. 20:5, without, however, "the weaver." The second element of the patronymic ("Oregim") is probably dittography, repeating a word from the end of the verse denoting "weaver." For details on these problems, see McCarter,

The larger problem, however, is the statement that this Elhanan (who is probably distinct from the Elhanan "son of Dodo from Bethlehem," 23:24) kills
"Goliath the Gittite." In light of the importance of the David and Goliath
account of 1 Samuel 17, one must ask: Who then killed Goliath, Elhanan or
David? Our summary will briefly consider three standard approaches.[22]

(1) Many scholars simply accept the two narratives as a contradiction. The
most popular approach is to assume Elhanan's victory over Goliath has been
transferred to the traditions about David in order to add to the splendor of
the king. Since the name "Goliath" itself is not a dominant feature in 1 Samuel
17, it has been suggested that the Philistine warrior killed by David was originally anonymous. Because deeds of obscure heroes tended to become coa-
lesced with those of more famous heroes, the name of Elhanan's victim,
"Goliath," has simply been inserted into the narrative of 1 Samuel 17.[23]
Among the problems with this interpretation, the most obvious is that
Goliath's name *does* in fact occur in 1 Samuel 17, and that chapter's use of "the
Philistine" in the place of his personal name may have been for literary
effect.[24] The idea that the anonymous Philistine killed by David has been
given a name imported from 2 Samuel 21:19 has little in the way of objec-
tive evidence and remains unconvincing.

(2) Others have suggested that there were perhaps two Philistine giants
by the same name. In favor of this view is the possibility that the name had
come to designate a "type," or a Philistine title, rather than a personal name.[25]
Thus "Goliath" is used in both places as a common term for a particular
group of large Gittites. Again, this suggestion has no evidence to support
it, and as a matter of fact, "Goliath" is specifically designated a "name" in
1 Samuel 17.[26]

(3) The most preferred attempts at harmonization originated in early
Jewish interpretation and removes the difficulty by claiming "Elhanan" is an

---

II Samuel, 449, who also takes "Jair" as "Jearite," assuming it refers to Kiriath-jearim, which
was closely associated with Bethlehem. See also Smith, Samuel, 378.

22. For details on this complicated issue, the reader should consult the technical commentaries.

23. For the most persuasive version of this argument, see McCarter, I Samuel, 291; II
Samuel, 450; and Alter, David Story, 334. This interpretation has been taken up in a rather
fascinating recent biography of David (Steven L. McKenzie, King David: A Biography [Oxford:
Oxford Univ. Press, 2000], 76).

24. The personal name occurs in 1 Sam. 17:4, 23. The NIV's inclusion of the name
"Goliath" in 17:8 is interpretive and not reflected in the Hebrew.

25. Hertzberg, I and II Samuel, 387.

26. Verses 4 and 23, though both are obscured by NIV (note NRSV's "by name" in 17:23;
see also NJPS at 17:4, 23).

alternative name for "David."[27] Thus 1 Samuel 17 and 2 Samuel 21:19 are referring to the same event. But this suggestion requires the further step of asserting that "son of Jaare" is a textual error for "son of Jesse," while at the same time requiring this exceptional use of "Elhanan" in a passage where "David" is common (2 Sam. 21:15, 17, 21, 22).[28] More compellingly, the inclusion of Elhanan/David in a list of his own mighty men is problematic. Is it really possible that his own victory over Goliath was nonchalantly included as third in a list of four such battles attributed to his mighty warriors?[29] Ultimately, this explanation is wholly unsatisfying.

It must be admitted that we currently have no easy answer to this question. Most scholars dismiss the parallel in 1 Chronicles 20:5 as an obvious harmonization: "Elhanan son of Jair killed Lahmi the brother of Goliath the Gittite."[30] In light of the textual corruption of 2 Samuel 21:19, it is best to leave open the possibility that this verse originally referred to a brother of Goliath, who was the more famous of the two, as in the Chronicles parallel.[31] Another way around the impasse is to admit that contradictions of this sort were not necessarily as disconcerting to ancient Israelite authors and editors as they are to modern readers.

---

27. In modern scholarship, this has become popular since the article of A. M. Honeyman, who argued that "David" was a throne name for an individual whose personal name was "Elhanan" ("The Evidence for Regnal Names Among the Hebrews," *JBL* 67 [1948]: 13–25, esp. 23–24). See also Baldwin, *1 and 2 Samuel*, 286; Gordon, *I and II Samuel*, 303.

28. The geography may also be problematic, since the conflict occurred near Socoh and Azekah, in the Valley of Elah, in 1 Sam. 17 and at Gob here, though the location of Gob is unknown.

29. The summary verse's "they fell at the hands of David and his men" (21:22b) does not remove the awkwardness of the proposal.

30. "The Chronicler's solution to the contradiction, therefore, was to invent a brother for Goliath. He then made up a name for him out of the word 'Bethlehemite' from 2 Sam. 21:19" (McKenzie, *King David*, 76).

31. Keil and Delitzsch, *Samuel*, 466; Youngblood, "1, 2 Samuel," 1060–61; Bergen, *1, 2 Samuel*, 449.

David's Song of Thanksgiving (22:1–51)

¹David sang to the L ORD the words of this song when the
L ORD delivered him from the hand of all his enemies and from
the hand of Saul. ²He said:

"The LORD is my rock, my fortress and my deliverer;
3   my God is my rock, in whom I take refuge,
     my shield and the horn of my salvation.
He is my stronghold, my refuge and my savior—
     from violent men you save me.
⁴I call to the LORD, who is worthy of praise,
     and I am saved from my enemies.

⁵"The waves of death swirled about me;
     the torrents of destruction overwhelmed me.
⁶The cords of the grave coiled around me;
     the snares of death confronted me.
⁷In my distress I called to the LORD;
     I called out to my God.
From his temple he heard my voice;
     my cry came to his ears.

⁸"The earth trembled and quaked,
     the foundations of the heavens shook;
     they trembled because he was angry.
⁹Smoke rose from his nostrils;
     consuming fire came from his mouth,
     burning coals blazed out of it.
¹⁰He parted the heavens and came down;
     dark clouds were under his feet.
¹¹He mounted the cherubim and flew;
     he soared on the wings of the wind.
¹²He made darkness his canopy around him—
     the dark rain clouds of the sky.
¹³Out of the brightness of his presence
     bolts of lightning blazed forth.
¹⁴The LORD thundered from heaven;
     the voice of the Most High resounded.
¹⁵He shot arrows and scattered the enemies,
     bolts of lightning and routed them.
¹⁶The valleys of the sea were exposed
     and the foundations of the earth laid bare

at the rebuke of the LORD,
    at the blast of breath from his nostrils.

17 "He reached down from on high and took hold of me;
    he drew me out of deep waters.
18 He rescued me from my powerful enemy,
    from my foes, who were too strong for me.
19 They confronted me in the day of my disaster,
    but the LORD was my support.
20 He brought me out into a spacious place;
    he rescued me because he delighted in me.

21 "The LORD has dealt with me according to my righteousness;
    according to the cleanness of my hands he has rewarded me.
22 For I have kept the ways of the LORD;
    I have not done evil by turning from my God.
23 All his laws are before me;
    I have not turned away from his decrees.
24 I have been blameless before him
    and have kept myself from sin.
25 The LORD has rewarded me according to my righteous-
    ness,
    according to my cleanness in his sight.

26 "To the faithful you show yourself faithful,
    to the blameless you show yourself blameless,
27 to the pure you show yourself pure,
    but to the crooked you show yourself shrewd.
28 You save the humble,
    but your eyes are on the haughty to bring them low.
29 You are my lamp, O LORD;
    the LORD turns my darkness into light.
30 With your help I can advance against a troop;
    with my God I can scale a wall.

31 "As for God, his way is perfect;
    the word of the LORD is flawless.
He is a shield
    for all who take refuge in him.
32 For who is God besides the LORD?
    And who is the Rock except our God?
33 It is God who arms me with strength
    and makes my way perfect.

³⁴ He makes my feet like the feet of a deer;
    he enables me to stand on the heights.
³⁵ He trains my hands for battle;
    my arms can bend a bow of bronze.
³⁶ You give me your shield of victory;
    you stoop down to make me great.
³⁷ You broaden the path beneath me,
    so that my ankles do not turn.

³⁸ "I pursued my enemies and crushed them;
    I did not turn back till they were destroyed.
³⁹ I crushed them completely, and they could not rise;
    they fell beneath my feet.
⁴⁰ You armed me with strength for battle;
    you made my adversaries bow at my feet.
⁴¹ You made my enemies turn their backs in flight,
    and I destroyed my foes.
⁴² They cried for help, but there was no one to save them—
    to the LORD, but he did not answer.
⁴³ I beat them as fine as the dust of the earth;
    I pounded and trampled them like mud in the streets.

⁴⁴ "You have delivered me from the attacks of my people;
    you have preserved me as the head of nations.
  People I did not know are subject to me,
⁴⁵   and foreigners come cringing to me;
    as soon as they hear me, they obey me.
⁴⁶ They all lose heart;
    they come trembling from their strongholds.

⁴⁷ "The LORD lives! Praise be to my Rock!
    Exalted be God, the Rock, my Savior!
⁴⁸ He is the God who avenges me,
    who puts the nations under me,
⁴⁹   who sets me free from my enemies.
  You exalted me above my foes;
    from violent men you rescued me.
⁵⁰ Therefore I will praise you, O LORD, among the nations;
    I will sing praises to your name.
⁵¹ He gives his king great victories;
    he shows unfailing kindness to his anointed,
    to David and his descendants forever."

As we have suggested, the poems at the beginning and end of the books of Samuel serve an important function as literary frames for the whole (Hannah's prayer in 1 Sam. 2:1–11 and David's psalm and last words in 2 Sam. 22:1–23:7). As is often the case in the Old Testament, poetry also has an important theological role, complementing the prose narrative.[32] The extended narratives in 1–2 Samuel have instructed us about the nature and purpose of Israel's monarchy, though the instruction itself is illustrative and the lessons are often stated implicitly. The poetic frame articulates more directly and explicitly the books' core theological assertions. "The songs of Hannah and David offer the definitive opinion on kingship, which embraces and interprets whatever else the book of Samuel says on the topic."[33] Fittingly, then, in these concluding sections of 1–2 Samuel, the historian has included this praise song, which should be taken as a theological commentary on the entire history of David.[34]

The scholarly literature on David's song is enormous for a number of reasons, not the least of which is its repetition in Psalm 18. There are few structural or compositional differences between them, making it certain that they "stem from an original poem."[35] The differences that are present are mostly minor textual or scribal variations, making the parallel editions a textbook example of the way ancient writings were preserved and transmitted.[36] Moreover, our poem contains grammatical and orthographic indications of genuine archaic poetry,[37] which makes its double retention in the Bible all the more remarkable. It seems likely that other minor changes were intended to make one rendition suitable for use in a liturgical collection (Ps. 18) and the other for a theological summation of narrative related to David (2 Sam. 22).[38]

The Old Testament psalmic literature has been categorized into various literary types or forms since the days of Hermann Gunkel (1862–1932).[39]

---

32. S. P. Weitzman, *Song and Story in Biblical Narrative: The History of a Literary Convention in Ancient Israel* (Bloomington, Ind.: Indiana Univ. Press, 1997); J. W. Watts, *Psalm and Story*.

33. Nelson, *Historical Books*, 127.

34. Hertzberg, *I and II Samuel*, 393; Childs, *Introduction to the Old Testament*, 275.

35. McCarter, *II Samuel*, 473; see also Hertzberg, *I and II Samuel*, 391–93.

36. Cross and Freedman, "A Royal Song," 15.

37. Probably from the tenth century itself. See Cross and Freedman, "A Royal Song," 20, 23; William F. Albright, *Yahweh and the Gods of Canaan: A Historical Analysis of Two Contrasting Faiths* (Garden City, N.Y.: Doubleday, 1968; repr., Winona Lake, Ind.: Eisenbrauns, 1990), 25. Most agree that Davidic authorship is not improbable (with few exceptions, e.g., Anderson, *2 Samuel*, 261).

38. Keil and Delitzsch, *Samuel*, 469.

39. For introduction, see David M. Howard Jr., "Recent Trends in Psalms Study," in *The Face of Old Testament Studies: A Survey of Contemporary Approaches*, ed. David W. Baker and Bill T. Arnold (Grand Rapids: Baker, 1999), 329–68, esp. 360–65.

This particular psalm is of a type most often called a "song of thanksgiving," though it is also a "royal psalm."[40] At the heart of thanksgiving psalms is typically a story of deliverance or salvation, which may be summarized succinctly at the beginning, as it is in the introduction to our psalm (22:4): "I call to the LORD, who is worthy of praise, and I am saved from my enemies."

In general the psalm in 2 Samuel 22 can be summarized by the keywords that recur in its stanzas and give the overall hymn a unified theme: "rock" and "save, deliver."[41] (1) "Rock" (sur) is a common epithet for God in the Old Testament, as it was among other nations of the ancient world to describe their own deities.[42] Referring to God in this way is similar to our "solid as a rock" or to the metaphorical ways we use "mountain" to connote stability and strength. The four occurrences of "rock" in our psalm are concentrated at the beginning and end and emphasize Yahweh as David's protector and savior (vv. 3, 47 [2x]), as well as the uniqueness of Yahweh's goodness (v. 32).[43]

(2) The other key word is the verb "save, deliver" ($yš^c$, vv. 3, 4, 28, 42) and its related noun "salvation" ($yeša^c$, vv. 3, 36, 47; also 23:5). David celebrates the assurance that Yahweh is a God who can be trusted, who rescues him and delivers him from certain death.

The brief historical introduction in verse 1 is almost identical to the superscription of Psalm 18. Its formulaic nature is similar to other songs inserted into narrative contexts: "David sang to the LORD the words of this song."[44] This is followed by the introduction to the poetry proper, which launches

---

40. A thanksgiving psalm may be called a *todah* (Heb. for "thanksgiving"), and these psalms frequently use the related verb (ydh), which may more accurately be translated "praise" than "give thanks." See Claus Westermann, *Praise and Lament in the Psalms*, trans. K. R. Crim and R. N. Soulen (Atlanta: John Knox, 1981), 25–30. See comments below on verse 50.

41. Robert Alter, *Art of Biblical Poetry*, 32; Youngblood, "1, 2 Samuel," 1065. On the impressive verbal and thematic links between this poem and Hannah's prayer (1 Sam. 2:1–10), see J. W. Watts, *Psalm and Story*, 23–24.

42. Though Israel used the name without polytheistic ramifications. Albright, *Yahweh and the Gods*, 188–89; David Noel Freedman, "Divine Names and Titles in Early Hebrew Poetry," in *Magnalia Dei, The Mighty Acts of God: Essays on the Bible and Archaeology in Memory of G. Ernest Wright*, ed. F. M. Cross, W. E. Lemke, and P. D. Miller Jr. (Garden City, N.Y.: Doubleday, 1976), 55–107; repr. in *Pottery, Poetry, and Prophecy: Studies in Early Hebrew Poetry* (Winona Lake, Ind.: Eisenbrauns, 1980), 131–66, esp. 155–56.

43. Our word sur is also used in 23:3. The NIV's "rock" in 22:2 translates a Hebrew synonym, $sela^c$ ("crag, cliff"). Interestingly, the use of "rock"(sur) is one of a handful of features used also in Hannah's song, tying these two poetic sections together (1 Sam. 2:2): "There is no Rock like our God."

44. See, e.g., Ex. 15:1; Num. 21:17; Deut. 31:30; Judg. 5:1, etc. See Peter Enns, *Exodus* (NIVAC; Grand Rapids: Zondervan, 2000), 307–8.

us immediately into a celebration of Yahweh's deliverance (22:2–4).[45] The "horn" of salvation (v. 3) should remind the reader of the way this term is used as a literary device in Hannah's song (1 Sam. 2:1, 10).[46] The deliverance theme so central to the psalm is stated generally in 2 Samuel 22:4 in the call-answer motif, which is particularized in the next paragraph.

As is typical for Hebrew thanksgiving psalms, the general statement of deliverance in 22:4 is expanded significantly in 22:5–20. David defines his situation as that of certain and imminent death (note the theme "death," "destruction," and "grave/Sheol," vv. 5–6). This is followed again by the assertion that he called out to God in the midst of his distress, and God heard his cry from his heavenly abode. David claims that earnest and righteous prayer is effective.

There follows in 22:8–20 a theophany (or divine appearance) phrased in language similar to other such appearances in the Old Testament. These descriptions of Yahweh's appearance show evidence of early Hebrew poetry and may even belong "to the earliest literary remains of Israelite history."[47] The general theme is that Yahweh delivers the king in his time of trouble and equips him for warfare. The primary image associated with Yahweh throughout the theophany is that of the divine warrior.[48] As in other such appearances of God, his arrival is accompanied by the quaking of the earth and mountains (v. 8). He comes as the warrior storm god, breathing smoke and consuming fire (v. 9). His thunderous arrival is meant to strike terror in the hearts of his enemies, a terror justified because of the arrows and bolts of lightning he uses against them (vv. 13–15).[49] Such imagery is well known from ancient Ugaritic mythology, in which the storm god, Baal, thunders from his heavenly abode against his enemies. The Israelite version of the theophany describes Yahweh's victory not over mythological forces but over David's flesh-and-blood enemies in order to rescue the king (v. 18).[50]

---

45. One of the most noticeable differences between 2 Sam. 22 and Ps. 18 is the insertion of an additional sentence before this introduction in Ps. 18: "I love you, O LORD, my strength."

46. See Original Meaning section for 1 Sam. 2:1–11.

47. Miller, *The Divine Warrior*, 74. See esp. Ex. 15; Deut. 33:2–5, 26–29; Josh. 10:12–13; Judg. 5; Ps. 68; Hab. 3:3–15, which like our psalm are early Israelite theophanies containing imagery and religious phenomena reflecting the early conceptions of Israelite faith, esp. the warrior character of Yahweh.

48. Ibid., 121–23.

49. A feature in the theory of holy war, which is also indicated by his riding upon the ark of the covenant as a war chariot in verse 11 (ibid., 122).

50. Ibid., 122, and for more on Yahweh in holy war generally, see Longman and Reid, *God Is a Warrior*, 31–47.

Unlike most other thanksgiving psalms, this one is not limited to a specific act of deliverance. The introduction can be applied to a number of times that God saved David, and the poem is used fittingly here to summarize the life of the king (v. 1): "when the LORD delivered [David] from the hand of all his enemies and from the hand of Saul." The conclusion of the spectacular theophany is that Yahweh has brought David out "into a spacious place" (v. 20). He has reached into David's tight spot, depicted as hemmed in by the cords of the grave, covered with the waves of death, and plunged into deep waters (vv. 5, 6, and 17), and God has set him down safely in the open.

Thus far the poem is a beautiful assertion that the honest and earnest prayer uttered in distress is effective. The warrior God of Israel appears on the scene with all the forces and power of nature specifically in order to rescue his servant from a tight spot.[51] "The concept of God and nature moving in concert to answer prayer for one man is bold almost beyond belief, if it were not affirmed in Scripture."[52]

David's hymn of praise now takes a turn that seems unusual for modern readers. In the next section, the king maintains his innocence and righteousness and asserts that Yahweh was only being faithful in saving David (22:21–30). Yahweh has dealt with David in wonderful ways in accordance with the king's righteousness and clean hands (v. 21). In general, David claims to have maintained his relationship with God by keeping the law and spurning evil (vv. 22–25).

David is not claiming here to have never sinned, a claim that can hardly be read seriously in light of the previous narration about Bathsheba and Uriah. Rather, he is taking the standard Old Testament view that deliverance is also vindication of one's relationship with God. It is precisely *because* he has been delivered that David can assume his actions concerning Saul were in the right and therefore pleasing to God. Another of the psalms claims similarly:

> If I had cherished sin in my heart,
> the LORD would not have listened;
> but God has surely listened
> and heard my voice in prayer. (Ps. 66:18–19)

Since God responds to human behavior in like kind (2 Sam. 22:26–28), so David can rejoice in his own standing before God. His deliverance verifies it.

---

51. The language and imagery is reminiscent of the song of Moses after Yahweh's deliverance at the Red Sea in Ex. 15 (see Gordon, *I and II Samuel*, 305; Enns, *Exodus*, 309).

52. Baldwin, *1 and 2 Samuel*, 288.

The psalmist is not talking about justification by works, much less about sinless perfection, but about "a conscience void of offence toward God and men" (Acts 24:16).... Within the shortened perspective of a largely this-world theodicy the absence of vindication could prove almost unbearable, yet it was by this route that a deeper faith was won—as may be seen, for example, in the "Psalm of Habakkuk", whose indebtedness to our psalm is evident at one point, but whose author goes on to declare himself for Yahweh even if the signs of his approval are withheld (Hab. 3:17f).[53]

The next section of the poem celebrates David's military victories, all of which have been won in the strength of Yahweh (22:31–46). David begins with a sort of confession of faith, declaring God's way is perfect and his word flawless (v. 31). This leads him to extol the incomparability of Yahweh in the form of two rhetorical questions (v. 32):

> For who is God besides the Lord?
> And who is the Rock except our God?

These questions call for an emphatic negative answer ("No one!"), and they contain an implicit monotheism.[54] God is incomparable, and it is God alone who provided David's strength and military skill, making it possible for the king to be victorious. It is Yahweh who made David swift in flight (which he often needed against Saul) and strong in battle (vv. 33–35). David's indebtedness to God is clear from the fact that God is the subject of all the verbs in verses 32–36.[55] David then lists his great military victories, in which he has subdued all his enemies (vv. 38–46). As a hymn of praise, the poem offers these victories as evidence of God's strength and power, not of David's own military prowess. It celebrates the king as a great warrior—but only penultimately, because it knows that Yahweh, not David, is the one who wins the battles.[56]

At the close of the hymn, the psalmist bursts forth in exultant praise (22:47–51). The NIV's "therefore I will praise you, O LORD" (v. 50) translates

---

53. Gordon, *I and II Samuel*, 306–7.

54. Ibid., 307. Some have argued, in fact, that such monotheism was not present in Israel until the seventh century B.C., and therefore this is a later insertion into the psalm (see McCarter, *II Samuel*, 469). But such a conclusion is not necessary, since a "theology of exaltation" developed during the second millennium in the ancient Near East and moved in the direction of monotheism in certain contexts (see K. van der Toorn, "Theology, Priests, and Worship in Canaan and Ancient Israel," *CANE*, 3:2056–57).

55. Baldwin, *1 and 2 Samuel*, 289.

56. Brueggemann, *First and Second Samuel*, 344.

a verb characteristic of Old Testament thanksgiving psalms (*ydh*) and jubilantly celebrates what God has done for David.[57] In this closing stanza, we encounter again themes used elsewhere in the psalm: God as rock and salvation (our two key words discussed above),[58] and victory over enemies.

There is, however, something new here. For the first time in the poem (and only the second time in 1–2 Samuel[59]), the term "anointed" (*mᵉšiaḥ*) is used specifically to refer to David (2 Sam. 21:51): "[The LORD] shows unfailing kindness [*ḥesed*, steadfast love] to his anointed." This is yet another way in which our psalm is similar to Hannah's prayer because it likewise concludes with a reference to the anointed one of God (1 Sam. 2:10).

But the way in which blessing and favor are specifically tied to David in 2 Samuel 22:51 is noteworthy. As we near the conclusion of this book, in which we learned about the Lord's promise of an eternal dynasty for David (ch. 7), the final phrase of the poem becomes even more significant, especially for Christian readers.[60] God's blessing and favor will be poured out on his anointed one, David, and on his "descendants forever."[61] This king whom God has blessed with such favor is no singular individual but David *and* his offspring forever, which refers then to the royal family of David and ultimately to Christ (Matt. 1:6–16).[62]

---

57. See discussion above on thanksgiving psalms. Westermann prefers to call this category of psalm-type a "narrative praise of the individual" (Westermann, *Praise and Lament*, 25–30).

58. The NIV translates *yišᶜi* as "my Savior" in v. 47, but "my salvation" is better, leaving a translation "the rock of my salvation" (see NRSV, NKJV, ASV, NASB).

59. The other being Abishai's speech in 2 Sam. 19:21.

60. The specific terminology of the last verse is that used of Nathan's oracle in 2 Sam. 7 and is probably an intentional intertextual reference (see McCarter, *II Samuel*, 472–73).

61. The term "descendants" is a singular collective noun (*zarᶜo*) and is perhaps better translated "offspring" (NJPS) or "seed" (KJV, ASV).

62. Keil and Delitzsch, *Samuel*, 484.

David's Last Words (23:1–7)

[1]These are the last words of David:

"The oracle of David son of Jesse,
the oracle of the man exalted by the Most High,
the man anointed by the God of Jacob,
Israel's singer of songs:

[2]"The Spirit of the LORD spoke through me;
his word was on my tongue.
[3]The God of Israel spoke,
the Rock of Israel said to me:
'When one rules over men in righteousness,
when he rules in the fear of God,
[4]he is like the light of morning at sunrise
on a cloudless morning,
like the brightness after rain
that brings the grass from the earth.'

[5]"Is not my house right with God?
Has he not made with me an everlasting covenant,
arranged and secured in every part?
Will he not bring to fruition my salvation
and grant me my every desire?
[6]But evil men are all to be cast aside like thorns,
which are not gathered with the hand.
[7]Whoever touches thorns
uses a tool of iron or the shaft of a spear;
they are burned up where they lie."

In the thanksgiving psalm of the previous section, David has looked back at the mercy and faithfulness of Yahweh during his life and reign. Here in his "last words" he looks forward, trusting in the promises he has received from God.[63] David extols the benefits and virtues of a righteous kingship. His must be just such a kingship, because God has made "an everlasting covenant" with him.

Most commentators believe this little poem is of genuine tenth-century origin, marked as it is by significant archaic features.[64] After the brief prose

---

63. Ibid., 458.

64. McCarter, *II Samuel*, 484–86; Hertzberg, *I and II Samuel*, 400; Cross, *Canaanite Myth and Hebrew Epic*, 234–37.

introduction (23:1a), there follows a stanza introducing the poem as "the oracle of David." Here David is characterized richly not only as the son of Jesse but as one exalted and anointed by God and as a beloved singer of Israel.[65] The designation of David as "the man anointed" (23:1) or "messiah" (*m^e šîaḥ*) links this poem with the preceding one because of its use of the same term in its concluding verse (22:51).[66] Together they form a poetic core at the center of the passage's chiastic structure (see above).

The prophet-like speech of David commends the beautiful benefits of righteous rulership for all who are so ruled (23:2–4).[67] The metaphors draw on our common human experience with nature. Such a righteous ruler may be compared to the grandeur of the early morning sunrise, to warm sunshine on a cloudless morning, and to fresh life-giving rain.

But David then turns to an even more meaningful concept. His own kingship is regarded by Yahweh as acceptable because his dynasty has been granted an "everlasting covenant" (23:5, *b^e rit ʿolam*). This is a technical term in the Old Testament, which has semantic parallels in the ancient Near East related to legal contracts with no anticipated terminus point; that is, they exist in perpetuity.[68] The expression is used in the Old Testament for all of the covenants (Noah, Abraham, Moses, and David).[69] Thus, David's kingship is both a blessing for all humankind and an enduring promise more specifically to Israel. David's rule is just and right and is a lasting blessing for all his subjects. Such concepts became foundational for Israel's messianic hopes, and it is just such a king that Israel longs for.

David's conviction that Yahweh has made such a perpetual covenant is no doubt dependent on Nathan's oracle in 2 Samuel 7:4–17. The terminology is particularly reminiscent of 7:12–16, which is reflected further in Psalm

---

65. This last phrase is uncertain Hebrew. Compare the NRSV's "the favorite of the Strong One of Israel," which follows Cross, *Canaanite Myth and Hebrew Epic*, 236.

66. And consequently with the concluding verse of Hannah's prayer (1 Sam. 2:10).

67. The now familiar "Rock" metaphor returns, again linking these two poems with Hannah's prayer (1 Sam. 2:2).

68. Moshe Weinfeld, "The Covenant of Grant in the Old Testament and in the Ancient Near East," *JAOS* 90 (1970): 184–203.

69. See the Bridging Contexts section on 2 Sam. 7:1–29 for a description of the covenants generally. For the Noah covenant, see Gen. 9:16; for the Abraham covenant, see Gen. 17:7, 13, 19. In the case of the Mosaic covenant, at least the Sabbath is called an eternal covenant (Ex. 31:16; Lev. 24:8). Other occurrences of *b^e rit ʿolam* are 1 Chron. 16:17; Ps. 105:10; Isa. 24:5; 55:3; 61:8; Jer. 32:40; 50:5; Ezek. 16:60; 37:26. Slight variations of the phrase occur as an everlasting covenant of salt (Num. 18:19) and an everlasting priesthood covenant (Num. 25:13). Such an "eternal" or "perpetual" covenant is not necessarily unconditional (see Matitiahu Tsevat, "Studies in the Book of Samuel, III," *HUCA* 34 [1963]: 71–82, esp. 76–77; Cross, *Canaanite Myth and Hebrew Epic*, 236).

89:28–37 as well as in prophetic expectations (Isa. 55:3; Jer. 32:40; 50:5; Ezek. 16:60; 37:26).[70] There can be no doubt that these "last words of David" contributed much to the intertestamental period's view of a messiah, along with the preceding poem in 2 Samuel 22.

More specifically, the three poetic sections that provide literary shape for 1–2 Samuel also give theological shape to the books' portrayal of David (1 Sam. 2:1–10; 2 Sam. 22:1–51; 23:1–7). In fact, the messianic themes of the narratives are clarified, perhaps even intensified, by the poetic frame. Certain claims central to the messianic expectations expressed in these books are reiterated in the three poems and may be summarized as follows:[71]

1. The messiah or anointed one is God's appointed ruler (1 Sam. 2:10; 2 Sam. 22:51; 23:1).
2. David trusts in God and is upheld and rescued by him (2 Sam. 22:2, 38–43, 49).
3. David leads God's people in battle, and God gives him power over the surrounding nations (2 Sam. 22:28, 45–46, 48).
4. The king is to rule God's people justly (2 Sam. 23:3–4).[72]

Thus Hannah's prayer, David's thanksgiving psalm, and his last words bring into sharp focus the most important themes in the narratives, especially those with messianic implications. In short, "the David of the narratives in Samuel has, in effect, been elevated in the poetic texts to an ideal."[73]

Soldiers' Hall of Fame (23:8–39)

⁸These are the names of David's mighty men:

Josheb-Basshebeth, a Tahkemonite, was chief of the Three; he raised his spear against eight hundred men, whom he killed in one encounter.

⁹Next to him was Eleazar son of Dodai the Ahohite. As one of the three mighty men, he was with David when they taunted the Philistines gathered at Pas Dammim for battle. Then the men of Israel retreated, ¹⁰but he stood his ground and struck

---

70. For discussion of Ps. 89, see Bridging Contexts section on 2 Sam. 7:1–29.

71. For what follows, see Satterthwaite, "David in the Books of Samuel," 41–65, esp. 43–47.

72. Satterthwaite (ibid., 45–46) has carefully demonstrated how each of these themes from the poetic sections also runs throughout the main narratives of 1–2 Samuel.

73. Ibid., 47.

down the Philistines till his hand grew tired and froze to the sword. The LORD brought about a great victory that day. The troops returned to Eleazar, but only to strip the dead.

¹¹Next to him was Shammah son of Agee the Hararite. When the Philistines banded together at a place where there was a field full of lentils, Israel's troops fled from them. ¹²But Shammah took his stand in the middle of the field. He defended it and struck the Philistines down, and the LORD brought about a great victory.

¹³During harvest time, three of the thirty chief men came down to David at the cave of Adullam, while a band of Philistines was encamped in the Valley of Rephaim. ¹⁴At that time David was in the stronghold, and the Philistine garrison was at Bethlehem. ¹⁵David longed for water and said, "Oh, that someone would get me a drink of water from the well near the gate of Bethlehem!" ¹⁶So the three mighty men broke through the Philistine lines, drew water from the well near the gate of Bethlehem and carried it back to David. But he refused to drink it; instead, he poured it out before the LORD. ¹⁷"Far be it from me, O LORD, to do this!" he said. "Is it not the blood of men who went at the risk of their lives?" And David would not drink it.

Such were the exploits of the three mighty men.

¹⁸Abishai the brother of Joab son of Zeruiah was chief of the Three. He raised his spear against three hundred men, whom he killed, and so he became as famous as the Three. ¹⁹Was he not held in greater honor than the Three? He became their commander, even though he was not included among them.

²⁰Benaiah son of Jehoiada was a valiant fighter from Kabzeel, who performed great exploits. He struck down two of Moab's best men. He also went down into a pit on a snowy day and killed a lion. ²¹And he struck down a huge Egyptian. Although the Egyptian had a spear in his hand, Benaiah went against him with a club. He snatched the spear from the Egyptian's hand and killed him with his own spear. ²²Such were the exploits of Benaiah son of Jehoiada; he too was as famous as the three mighty men. ²³He was held in greater honor than any of the Thirty, but he was not included among the Three. And David put him in charge of his bodyguard.

²⁴Among the Thirty were:

Asahel the brother of Joab,
Elhanan son of Dodo from Bethlehem,
²⁵Shammah the Harodite,
Elika the Harodite,
²⁶Helez the Paltite,
Ira son of Ikkesh from Tekoa,
²⁷Abiezer from Anathoth,
Mebunnai the Hushathite,
²⁸Zalmon the Ahohite,
Maharai the Netophathite,
²⁹Heled son of Baanah the Netophathite,
Ithai son of Ribai from Gibeah in Benjamin,
³⁰Benaiah the Pirathonite,
Hiddai from the ravines of Gaash,
³¹Abi-Albon the Arbathite,
Azmaveth the Barhumite,
³²Eliahba the Shaalbonite,
the sons of Jashen,
Jonathan ³³son of Shammah the Hararite,
Ahiam son of Sharar the Hararite,
³⁴Eliphelet son of Ahasbai the Maacathite,
Eliam son of Ahithophel the Gilonite,
³⁵Hezro the Carmelite,
Paarai the Arbite,
³⁶Igal son of Nathan from Zobah,
the son of Hagri,
³⁷Zelek the Ammonite,
Naharai the Beerothite, the armor-bearer of Joab son of Zeruiah,
³⁸Ira the Ithrite,
Gareb the Ithrite
³⁹and Uriah the Hittite.
There were thirty-seven in all.

We come now to a military honor roll, which matches the list at 21:15–22 and like it may have come from an official military archive. In succinct fashion, this passage lists the heroes who supported David, along with a few of their more spectacular exploits. From a human perspective, these are the valiant and loyal soldiers who made David's kingdom possible, and our historian honors them enthusiastically with this Soldiers' Hall of Fame. At the same time, the narrator reminds us that the human perspective is inadequate to explain their successes. After relating two of their amazing feats, the text adds "the LORD brought about a great victory" (23:10, 12). Even when celebrating the decorated war heroes, one must remember the source of their strength.

We read here of military institutions, the precise nature of which is lost to us. David, like Saul before him, recruited mercenaries from among both Israelites and foreigners. Early in his exile, David had four hundred men, later six hundred (1 Sam. 22:2; 25:13).[74] From foreign mercenaries, David recruited a special corps of "Kerethites and Pelethites," who became a royal bodyguard attached only to him (1 Sam. 30:14; 2 Sam. 8:18; 15:18; 20:7, 23; 1 Kings 1:38, 44).[75] The "Three" and the "Thirty" referred to in this text were presumably ranks of honor, whose precise relationship to the other, larger groups is unclear. Their members changed over time as some died and others were replaced, so at the time of this list there are actually thirty-seven in the "Thirty" (2 Sam. 23:39).[76] These two groups were special corps of David's elite troops.

The lists illustrate the way King David organized and administered his kingdom. When he became king, he was faced with territorial differences between north and south, with both regions having conflicting convictions about the nature of kingship itself.[77] He made Jerusalem his personal possession by right of conquest, and it became "the city of David." This provided him with a central power base, independent of both northern and southern authorities and controlled by him alone. This administrative philosophy is reflected also in David's organization of the military, which has concentric rings as revealed here: an inner circle of foreign mercenaries loyal only to him and serving as his personal Secret Service; a standing, professional army, which included the "Three" and the "Thirty"; and the militias of Judah and Israel.[78]

Our passage has a simple two-part structure. (1) The narrator has included stories about "The Three," who are honored above the rest (23:8–12). (2) The text describes "The Thirty," first by relating particularly striking examples of

---

74. See de Vaux, *Ancient Israel*, 219–20.

75. They were likely of Aegean origin and settled in the southwest coasts of Palestine about the same time as the Philistines, though their precise relationship with the Philistines is unclear. See Carl S. Ehrlich, "Cherethites," *ABD*, 1:898–99, idem, "Pelethites," *ABD*, 5:219.

76. How the historian arrived at the number thirty-seven remains a mystery (see McCarter, *II Samuel*, 499).

77. For what follows, see Cross, *Canaanite Myth and Hebrew Epic*, 230.

78. Ibid., 230; B. Mazar, "The Military Élite of King David," *VT* 13 (1963): 310–20.

their heroism and loyalty and then simply listing their names (23:13–39).[79] The notes on Abishai and Benaiah (23:18–23) are included to explain that both were honored above the Thirty but did not belong to the rank of the Three.[80]

The water retrieved by the three unnamed soldiers illustrates not only their love and loyalty to David but his own devout instincts, which, of course, made his men love him all the more (23:13–17). David longs for water not simply to quench his physical thirst. He longs specifically for water "from the well near the gate of Bethlehem," his hometown (v. 15). "He longingly remembers the draughts that quenched the harvest-time thirsts of his childhood."[81]

After his men risked their lives to bring him the very water to satisfy his nostalgia, his reaction may seem ungrateful to modern readers. But the particular verb for "poured it out" refers to the pouring out of libations, and when poured out "before the LORD," this is terminology specifically reminiscent of offerings to Yahweh as an act of devotion.[82] Instead of selfishly consuming water bought at such a great risk, David honors his men even more by offering it to Yahweh as a sacrifice. As Israelites were not allowed to drink the blood of a sacrificial animal, so David refuses to drink this water, turning it into sacred blood worthy of sacrifice to Yahweh (Lev. 17:10–13).

The names of the soldiers appear to have no particular order in the list of 23:24–39.[83] Surprisingly Joab is not mentioned, though his armor bearer is powerful enough to make the list (23:37). Perhaps Joab is so powerful it is not necessary to include him. His influence and power stand at the top of this list, just as his presence is felt throughout the narratives related to David.

If so much subtlety is involved in the list, then certainly the last item is intended to convey irony: "and Uriah the Hittite." The historian could have said much more about Uriah and his role in David's history. But "the mere mention of Uriah's name is enough to evoke the full memory."[84] As impressive as these war heroes were, it was enough to recall that even the greatest warrior of them all was flawed.

---

79. More extensive versions of these lists can be found in 1 Chron. 11 and 12. It seems logical to assume this list in 2 Samuel was current at the time of Uriah's death, and the Chronicles version updates the list during the whole reign of David (see Evans, *1 and 2 Samuel*, 241).

80. And possibly because they were well known within the main narratives of the books of Samuel.

81. McCarter, *II Samuel*, 496.

82. The Hiphil of *nsk*, as used in Gen. 35:14; Num. 28:7; and elsewhere. See Richard E. Averbeck, "נסך," *NIDOTTE*, 3:113–17, esp. 114.

83. The soldiers may have originally been listed in order of rank or geographical origins. But details are obscure to us in the present text (see McCarter, *II Samuel*, 500–501).

84. Brueggemann, *First and Second Samuel*, 350.

David Conducts a Census (24:1–25)

¹Again the anger of the LORD burned against Israel, and he incited David against them, saying, "Go and take a census of Israel and Judah."

²So the king said to Joab and the army commanders with him, "Go throughout the tribes of Israel from Dan to Beersheba and enroll the fighting men, so that I may know how many there are."

³But Joab replied to the king, "May the LORD your God multiply the troops a hundred times over, and may the eyes of my lord the king see it. But why does my lord the king want to do such a thing?"

⁴The king's word, however, overruled Joab and the army commanders; so they left the presence of the king to enroll the fighting men of Israel.

⁵After crossing the Jordan, they camped near Aroer, south of the town in the gorge, and then went through Gad and on to Jazer. ⁶They went to Gilead and the region of Tahtim Hodshi, and on to Dan Jaan and around toward Sidon. ⁷Then they went toward the fortress of Tyre and all the towns of the Hivites and Canaanites. Finally, they went on to Beersheba in the Negev of Judah.

⁸After they had gone through the entire land, they came back to Jerusalem at the end of nine months and twenty days.

⁹Joab reported the number of the fighting men to the king: In Israel there were eight hundred thousand able-bodied men who could handle a sword, and in Judah five hundred thousand.

¹⁰David was conscience-stricken after he had counted the fighting men, and he said to the LORD, "I have sinned greatly in what I have done. Now, O LORD, I beg you, take away the guilt of your servant. I have done a very foolish thing."

¹¹Before David got up the next morning, the word of the LORD had come to Gad the prophet, David's seer: ¹²"Go and tell David, 'This is what the LORD says: I am giving you three options. Choose one of them for me to carry out against you.'"

¹³So Gad went to David and said to him, "Shall there come upon you three years of famine in your land? Or three months of fleeing from your enemies while they pursue you? Or three

days of plague in your land? Now then, think it over and decide how I should answer the one who sent me."

¹⁴David said to Gad, "I am in deep distress. Let us fall into the hands of the LORD, for his mercy is great; but do not let me fall into the hands of men."

¹⁵So the LORD sent a plague on Israel from that morning until the end of the time designated, and seventy thousand of the people from Dan to Beersheba died. ¹⁶When the angel stretched out his hand to destroy Jerusalem, the LORD was grieved because of the calamity and said to the angel who was afflicting the people, "Enough! Withdraw your hand." The angel of the LORD was then at the threshing floor of Araunah the Jebusite.

¹⁷When David saw the angel who was striking down the people, he said to the LORD, "I am the one who has sinned and done wrong. These are but sheep. What have they done? Let your hand fall upon me and my family."

¹⁸On that day Gad went to David and said to him, "Go up and build an altar to the LORD on the threshing floor of Araunah the Jebusite." ¹⁹So David went up, as the LORD had commanded through Gad. ²⁰When Araunah looked and saw the king and his men coming toward him, he went out and bowed down before the king with his face to the ground.

²¹Araunah said, "Why has my lord the king come to his servant?"

"To buy your threshing floor," David answered, "so I can build an altar to the LORD, that the plague on the people may be stopped."

²²Araunah said to David, "Let my lord the king take whatever pleases him and offer it up. Here are oxen for the burnt offering, and here are threshing sledges and ox yokes for the wood. ²³O king, Araunah gives all this to the king." Araunah also said to him, "May the LORD your God accept you."

²⁴But the king replied to Araunah, "No, I insist on paying you for it. I will not sacrifice to the LORD my God burnt offerings that cost me nothing."

So David bought the threshing floor and the oxen and paid fifty shekels of silver for them. ²⁵David built an altar to the LORD there and sacrificed burnt offerings and fellowship offerings. Then the LORD answered prayer in behalf of the land, and the plague on Israel was stopped.

At first glance, our historian appears to have chosen a peculiar way in which to conclude 1–2 Samuel. David conducts a census against Joab's advice, and the nation suffers a bitter plague as a result. Under the direction of Gad the prophet, David acquires a new piece of land in Jerusalem, builds an altar, and offers a sacrifice to Yahweh. The books of Samuel conclude with a brief statement that Yahweh answers David's prayer and stops the plague. Technically, the story of David continues into the first two chapters of 1 Kings, making this chapter especially odd as a conclusion to 1–2 Samuel.

Upon further reflection, this narrative plays a role in the overall contribution of chapters 21–24 generally to the message of 1–2 Samuel. As the poetic sections (22:1–51; 23:1–7) confirm and strengthen the messianic themes of previous narratives (see above), so chapter 24 returns to one of the central characterizing features of David as the ideal king of Israel. David here is the repentant king, who puts the needs of his people before his own personal ambition. In short, this narrative reinforces the ideal portrait of David as someone willing to place aside his royal power in deference to Yahweh's will and authority. He becomes the willful and prayerful servant of God, who is the one really in control. Yahweh is king, David is only viceroy. Thus, one of the central questions of these books is addressed again: Who may serve suitably as king of Israel? David may, and only someone like him.

The opening verse of this text presents modern readers with a number of perplexing questions. Why is the Lord angry? Why does the Lord incite David to do something sinful? Why is taking a census sinful? We as readers must learn to be content with incomplete answers, or sometimes no answers at all. Here we are simply not told why Yahweh is angry with David, and to read emotions or motivations into the text is to be guilty of "psychologizing" the character of God.[85]

On the question of census-taking in Israel generally, we have the aid of other references in the Old Testament that assume a natural link between census-taking and plagues (Ex. 30:12). Moreover, this text assumes through the words of Joab that the census reflects a shift in David's object of faith— a shift from reliance on Yahweh to win battles to a reliance on access to

---

85. It is possible to answer the question by reasoning that David's census and a plague have occurred in sequence, and that David (and the author) simply assume a cause-and-effect relationship between the two. But such a historical explanation is not the same as interpreting a biblical text. The fact is that the narrative simply creates a gap it has no intention of filling (Nelson, *Historical Books*, 49; see 45–63 generally, where Nelson uses 2 Sam. 24 as a test case to introduce various critical methodologies).

military might (2 Sam. 24:3).[86] It is sinful because David is acting like a typical ancient Near Eastern king instead of an Israelite king.

The question on why the Lord would incite David to sin in the first place is more complicated. In the closely parallel passage in 1 Chronicles 21:1, the source of the problem has been redefined: "Satan rose up against Israel and incited David to take a census of Israel." Traditionally, Jewish and Christian interpreters have harmonized these two statements by asserting that God's permissive action is expressed in 2 Samuel 24:1 and Satan's instrumentality is the emphasis of the Chronicles parallel.[87] This sometimes gives the impression of exegetical sleight of hand and is often less than satisfying.

Without attempting to address this question thoroughly here, I suggest simply that we need to give more credence to ancient Israelite formulations of theology and the way that theology evolved over time during the Old Testament period. As we have seen elsewhere in this commentary, ancient Israelites were not initially concerned with secondary causes. Their emphasis on Yahweh as the creator and supreme God of the universe often found expression in the Bible in their crediting him with disaster or calamity (usually the Heb. word ra^c, "evil"). We modern readers are usually more interested in defending God's goodness than ancient Israelite authors, who were first and foremost interested in his power. Subsequently and late in their history, they saw a role for "Satan" in the power structures of world administration.

Ultimately, however, it must be admitted once again that we may need to learn to live without neat and tidy answers to questions raised by this text. As elsewhere in the biblical story of redemption (Job 1:12; 2:7, 10; 2 Cor. 12:7), our text is faced with "a complementarity of roles which is unresolvable" because it is "grappling with the mystery of evil."[88]

After nearly ten months of arduous work, Joab is able to give David a report of the census (24:8–9). But then David has a change of heart. Interestingly, 24:10 gives no hint of prophetic intervention or condemnatory oracle. The narrator simply states that the king is "stricken to the heart" because

---

86. Censuses were used for purposes of taxation and military conscription. This text seems concerned with military conscription, which is contrary to ancient Israel's reliance on voluntary militia (see Cross, *Canaanite Myth and Hebrew Epic*, 227).

87. Thus, "the Lord through Satan 'incited' David" (Youngblood, "1, 2 Samuel," 1096). John H. Sailhamer's attempt to explain the Chronicles passage as midrashic commentary on the Samuel text is fascinating and instructive ("1 Chronicles 21:1—A Study in Inter-Biblical Interpretation," in *Introduction to Old Testament Theology: A Canonical Approach* [Grand Rapids: Zondervan, 1995], 298–311; repr. from *TrinJ* 10 [1989]: 33–48). For critique, see Youngblood, "1, 2 Samuel," 1095–96.

88. Gordon, *I and II Samuel*, 317.

of what he has done (NRSV; NIV has "conscience-stricken"). The real point of the narrative seems to be David's important words, "I have sinned greatly." The confession is strategically placed to remind us of another time David used almost the identical words to admit his guilt before Nathan and Yahweh (12:13), only this time there is no prophetic "You are the man" to expose David's hypocrisy and call for repentance.

Gad the prophet comes to David the next day, *after* David has confessed and pleaded for forgiveness (24:11–13). This final narrative of 1–2 Samuel portrays David as a king who has learned how to confess and seek forgiveness and restoration. This time he does not need a prophetic intermediary to threaten him or parabolic sermons to persuade him of his guilt (12:1–12). David sees his own guilt, and he quickly and genuinely repents and seeks to reverse what he has done.

The narrator's invitation to read David's confession in light of 12:13 drives us further back into 1 Samuel as well. David's confession before Nathan was itself linked to another royal confession, Saul's before Samuel (see Original Meaning section for 2 Sam. 12:13–25 as well as 1 Sam. 15:24, 30). Saul's blustering and verbose confession became for our historian a prototype of the disingenuous and insincere ruler who repents only when caught in the act. Even then, Saul's repentance is exploitive, trying to recuperate his losses by using Samuel. Israel's first king *confesses*, but he does not *repent* (see Bridging Contexts section for 2 Sam. 10–12).

By contrast, David becomes a prototype of the sincere Israelite king who repents immediately and genuinely. He suffers the consequences of his sin, but he receives forgiveness and enjoys restored fellowship with Yahweh. Now, the final episode narrated in 2 Samuel further reinforces the picture of David, the repentant king. But it also takes the reader one step further and one step deeper in appreciating David's repentance: Here he repents without prophetic prodding. As he spoke prophetically in his last words (23:1–7), David now *lives* prophetically.

Yahweh makes David "pick his poison."[89] Required to choose between famine, military defeat, or plague (24:13), David surprises us again. He concludes that the judgment of mortals is unpredictable, whereas God's judgment is consistently moderated by his mercy (24:14): "Let us fall into the hands of the LORD, for his mercy is great." His repentance in verse 10 is genuine because he has become first and foremost a man of faith. He trusts God enough to fling himself on God's mercy rather than calculate the costs of suffering at the hands of mortals. In this again, David has become this narrative's portrait of the ideal king of Israel.

---

89. Brueggemann, *First and Second Samuel*, 352.

In the closing paragraphs of 2 Samuel, we encounter another rather bizarre episode. The tender-hearted King David is tortured by the realization that his people (his flock of "sheep," 24:17) suffer because of his actions. He intervenes on their behalf, pleading that the Lord lay his vengeful wrath on him and his own family rather than on the people of Jerusalem, which the angel of death is about to strike with the plague (24:16). At Gad's instruction, David acquires "the threshing floor of Araunah the Jebusite," builds an altar to Yahweh on it, and offers burnt offerings and fellowship offerings. The Lord responds, and the plague ends (24:18–25). At the end of the day, it is David's relationship with Yahweh that saves Jerusalem. All is well.

But why the details about Araunah the Jebusite? And who is he? His name has a variety of forms in different manuscript traditions and has been explained as having either Hurrian or Hittite origins.[90] Araunah is likely a title rather than a personal name, and many assume he was the last Jebusite king of Jerusalem. Still, this hardly explains why our historian includes these details as the final episode of 1–2 Samuel. The text clearly places great significance in the fact that the pestilence ceases in Araunah's threshing floor, which is then transferred to David's possessions.

Threshing floors were normally on a hill where the grain was collected for threshing and winnowing. They were also traditional sites for theophanies and receiving divine messages.[91] The context of this final paragraph implies that the threshing floor in question is north of David's city.[92] The Chronicler provides the missing detail that, in fact, this threshing floor becomes the site chosen for Solomon's temple, having been duly purchased with David's money and made sacred by his offerings (1 Chron. 22:1; 2 Chron. 3:1).[93] The final paragraph, therefore, establishes the sanctity of the future site of the temple.[94]

---

90. Note the Chronicler routinely uses "Ornan" for Araunah (see KJV, ASV, NAS, NRSV and NJPS, though obscured in NIV). For more on the name, see Richard D. Nelson, "Araunah," *ABD*, 1:353.

91. This suggests that Araunah's threshing floor already had sacred traditions associated with it. See Walton, Matthews, and Chavalas, *The IVP Bible Background Commentary*, 354; Mark D. Futato, "גֹּרֶן," *NIDOTTE*, 1:893–94; McCarter, *II Samuel*, 511–12.

92. The NRSV's "when Araunah looked down. . ." in v. 20 seems implied by the Hebrew. See Baldwin, *1 and 2 Samuel*, 297.

93. It seems likely that the narrator in 2 Samuel assumes knowledge of this connection to Solomon's temple (Gordon, *I and II Samuel*, 317).

94. It seems likely that David had selected the temple site, amassed significant material and human resources, and was well on his way to building the temple (as in the parallel Chronicles accounts). This census may have been preparatory to taxing the population in order to complete the project. But the plague coincided with the census and was naturally interpreted as God's punishment, thus forcing David to leave the last of his goals to Solomon. See Meyers, "David As Temple Builder," 357–76, esp. 370–72.

Moreover, the cost of Araunah's threshing floor is significant. David insists on paying a fair price, and his assertion about the nature of sacrifice in 24:24 has profound significance: "I will not sacrifice to the LORD my God burnt offerings that cost me nothing." David understands the need to sacrifice a portion of his personal wealth to honor Yahweh.[95] Otherwise, his worship will be cheap and his service meaningless.

The final verse of the books of Samuel therefore produces an interesting reminder (24:25): "David built an *altar* to the LORD there" instead of "David built the *temple* of the LORD there." David is the ideal anointed one—but not because he is invincible and accomplishes everything he wants. He is ideal because he is repentant and forgiven. He is ideal because while David is king, he is only viceroy of Israel; Yahweh is the true king. He is ideal because he banks on the mercy of God rather than trusting the fickle judgement of mortals (24:14) and because he pays the cost of true worship (24:24). David is someone well suited for kingship in Israel.

All others in Israel's future will be measured by David as the standard of Israelite kingship. But few measure up. Each royal failure only serves to drive the hope, the longing, for an ideal Son of David further into the future. So Jesus becomes the fulfillment of this longing for another David—not because David is perfect, but because he is submissive to God's rulership and is used by God to establish the kingdom. Jesus fulfills David's promise in an unexpected way and in a way no one else could (Matt. 4:17).

Bridging
Contexts

ONE LEADING SCHOLAR commenting on 2 Samuel 24 made the following observation:

As the concluding episode of the book of Samuel, this chapter serves as a canonical commentary on all that has been reported about David and a guide for how the various stories about David ought to be read. David is a model of repentant faith, and his accomplishments are the result of God's mercy and purpose.[96]

---

95. Coinage was invented three centuries after these events, in the seventh century B.C. However, for the purposes of trade and commerce, it is probable that there were fixed weights of silver and/or gold much earlier. This price of fifty silver shekels is modest compared to the Chronicler's version of the account, where David paid six hundred shekels of gold for "the site," referring perhaps to a much larger area (1 Chron. 21:25). Youngblood, "1, 2 Samuel," 1103; Marvin A. Powell, "Weights and Measures," OEANE, 5:339–42.
96. Nelson, *Historical Books*, 63.

In a sense, this may be said in general about the entire unit under consideration here. In order to build a bridge effectively to modern readers, the interpreter should focus on the internal concentric structure of chapters 21–24, especially the way this unit concludes and summarizes the message of 1–2 Samuel.

The unit's internal cohesiveness is impressive (see introduction to the Original Meaning section). The famine/plague narratives both begin with an offended Yahweh, who strikes Israel with disaster (21:1–14; 24:1–25).[97] Ultimately, King David is able to avert each disaster by assuaging the anger of the Lord. These two narratives create a literary frame for the whole. The two lists of military officers and their exploits form an inner literary frame for the whole (21:15–22 and 23:8–39). The sections of poetry at the center of the ring buttress the messianic themes of the Davidic narratives from the books of Samuel generally (22:1–51; 23:1–7).

Literary tapestry. However, this pleasing concentric symmetry is more than simple literary ingenuity. Rather, it shapes the way the unit contributes to the overall message of 1–2 Samuel. The internal structure picks up themes and motifs from elsewhere, weaving them together into an elaborate tapestry of review and offering a more complete portrait of the ideal King David. The structure within points the reader outside chapters 21–24 and substantiates the narratives of the whole.

Thus, for example, the famine/plague narratives of the outer frame look backward to Saul and forward to Solomon. The famine of 21:1–14 is a result of Saul's failure (21:1), and the plague of chapter 24 is a prelude to Solomon's temple. David stands between them. He becomes the king that Saul could never have been, and he makes possible Solomon's grandeur. The portrait of a repentant and restorative David confirms the contrast between Saul and David so prevalent in 1–2 Samuel (1 Sam. 15:24, 30; 2 Sam. 12:13–25). Likewise, the poems of the center clarify and intensify messianic themes implied elsewhere in Samuel.

It is not difficult to see why our narrator has concluded Samuel in such a way. The Absalom rebellion and its aftermath is logically continued in the opening chapters of 1 Kings, which narrate the succession of Solomon. But in those episodes, David appears impotent and helpless, at the mercy of people around him. Our narrator has woven 2 Samuel 21–24 together to portray David in his prime; here he is at the top of his game. They describe David in all his military greatness and full of reverential faith. This is indeed

---

97. The occurrence of "God/the LORD answered prayer in behalf of the land" in 21:14 and 24:25 is a clear editorial link between the two narratives, as is apparently the "again" in 24:1.

an admirable conclusion to the books intended to answer the question: Who may serve suitably as king of Israel?[98]

Having now reviewed the way chapters 21–24 relate to each other and to the books of Samuel as a whole, the next task for today's interpreter is to consider this elaborately woven tapestry in order to determine which of its themes to expound. As I have said, much of what has been addressed elsewhere in 1–2 Samuel is reiterated here, and any number of different themes can be explored. I have also suggested that certain central themes of these books are not only reiterated but clarified and intensified in these final chapters. Specifically, the poetic center of chapters 21–24 brings into sharper focus the messianic expectations stated only implicitly elsewhere in 1–2 Samuel. This could be said for the entire unit, which contributes substantially to Israel's expectation of an ideal Son of David.[99] In the rest of this section, I want to explore briefly a few of these themes.

Zion theology. In the most general way, it should be stated that David and his capital city, Jerusalem, play enormous roles in the Bible's story of redemption. David comes to symbolize the ideal vice-regent, while Yahweh alone is the real king of Israel. These closing chapters further characterize him as the righteous ruler who is miraculously delivered because of his intimate relationship with Yahweh (cf. esp. the thanksgiving hymn, 22:1–51). David is victorious over his foes (the military lists, 21:15–22 and 23:8–39) and saves his people from famine and plague (21:1–14; 24:1–25). Even when he falls, he is the humble, repentant servant (24:10). Together these materials present a focused portrait of David, which directs us to other Old Testament texts along the same messianic trajectory.

Moreover, Yahweh, the great king, has chosen the lovely Jerusalem as his dwelling place.[100] Yahweh's original mountain abode was Mount Sinai. But

---

98. There is, however, no agreement about the precise relationship between chs. 21–24 and the rest of Samuel. Brueggemann proposes a "suspicious reading" that sees chs. 21–24 as "deliberately intended as a protest against the preceding 'official' portrayal of David." These chapters, in his view, counter the royal ideology established elsewhere in the book and criticize especially David's abuses of power (Brueggemann, *First and Second Samuel*, 336–339; idem, "2 Samuel 21–24: An Appendix of Deconstruction?" *CBQ* 50 [1988], 383–97). By contrast, see J. W. Watts, *Psalm and Story*, 116–17, and the approach taken here.

99. See again the Original Meaning section for 23:1–7, where I summarize the four points of Philip Satterthwaite. These four chapters, and indeed all of 1–2 Samuel, express this messianic ideal with a certain tension between the promised ideal and the unsatisfactory present (David's shortcomings), which is everywhere acknowledged in the books of Samuel. This leads Satterthwaite to speak of a "deliberately emphasised antinomy" in the books (Satterthwaite, "David in the Books of Samuel," 65). David's history is less than ideal, but the promise of a dynasty remains in force.

100. Review the Bridging Contexts section for 2 Sam. 5–6 and the bibliography there.

once David captured Jebus and moved the ark of the covenant to the new capital, Mount Zion becomes Yahweh's chosen mountain (Ps. 9:11; 76:2; 78:68–69; Isa. 8:18, etc.). This "Zion theology" begins with David's coronation and his new capital at Jerusalem (2 Sam. 5–6). In the last chapter of 1– 2 Samuel, Jerusalem becomes Israel's last stand, her last hope of survival against a deadly plague. Even Yahweh is tormented by the thought of the destruction of Jerusalem (24:16): "When the angel stretched out his hand to destroy Jerusalem, the Lord was grieved. . . ."

The location of this event on the threshing floor of Araunah the Jebusite gives it special significance, as we have seen. The building of the temple of the Lord on this spot, as planned by David and executed by Solomon, will become another important component of this "Zion theology." Its features will be developed further in the Psalms and the Prophets, especially the picture of Zion as a life-giving stream or river flowing from the very presence of God on the mountain and Yahweh's subjugation of all Israel's enemies.

Everlasting covenant. The significance of David and the messianic themes of 1–2 Samuel are particularly central in the reference to the "everlasting covenant" of 2 Samuel 23:5. As we have seen, this text is dependent on 7:12– 16 and anticipates the expectations of many other Old Testament texts. Specifically, "David's last words" use the term "covenant" to describe the relationship established in chapter 7, which is itself an important contribution to the Bible's understanding of that relationship (*bᵉrit*).[101] So David's "covenant" with Yahweh incorporates the momentous promises of 2 Samuel 7, which assures for David all any ancient Near Eastern monarch could desire.

Thus, it is through this "everlasting covenant" that Yahweh has promised to make David's name great, to provide descendants to rule after him, to extend loving-kindness (*ḥesed*) to him forever, to establish a father-son relationship with his descendants, to build an enduring house (or royal dynasty) for David, to allow David's son to build a temple in Jerusalem, and finally, to provide peace and security ("rest") in the land.[102] Labeling these promises here an "everlasting covenant" is, in a sense, a commentary on chapter 7, explicating the real meaning of the promises stated there. This covenant relationship between David and God defined ideal kingship in Israel and provided hope for future glory (1 Kings 15:4–5).

Ideal king. Finally, this passage clarifies that David is the ideal king of Israel not because he is perfect but because he is repentant and redemptive. His repentance in chapter 24 recalls his earlier repentance (12:13–25) and, of

---

101. See the Bridging Contexts section for 2 Sam. 7.

102. For the promises of the Davidic covenant, see Original Meaning section for 2 Sam. 7:4–17.

course, Saul's failure in this area (1 Sam. 15:24, 30). Through David's repentance and submission to God's leadership, he brings redemption and salvation to his people. The ideal is intact. It is a fragile ideal, because God's promises are extended to human agents, who are prone to failure. But as long as David is vice-regent and submits to Yahweh's sovereign rulership, the ideal will endure and be projected into the future.

CHRISTOLOGY. AS WE move to contemporary application for today's Christian readers, it becomes apparent that the New Testament found this portrait of the ideal king of Israel useful for its Christological affirmations. Direct links between 2 Samuel 21–24 and the New Testament may be less than obvious. But in general, this unit brings the messianic themes and motifs of 1–2 Samuel into greater focus, and it is that greater clarity that marks out the contours of messianism in the Old Testament's psalms and prophetic literature and in Second Temple Judaism.[103] For contemporary Christian readers, we need only to trace briefly how the ideal King David and the Old Testament's Davidic messianism are worked out in New Testament Christology.

David appears in the New Testament predominantly as a mighty king, inspired psalmist, and ancestor of the Messiah. In the first Gospel, the prophecy-fulfillment motif leans heavily on the Davidic ancestry of the Messiah. This is especially apparent in Matthew's carefully constructed genealogy of Jesus, where Abraham and David are benchmarks (Matt. 1:1, 17). The title "Son of David" is common on the lips of those who need help from Jesus (9:27; 15:22; 20:30; see also 12:23; 21:9, 15). This title in Matthew is equivalent to "Messiah" and provides an explicit link to the Davidic roots of Israel's messianic expectation.[104]

In Luke-Acts, the promise-fulfillment pattern gives way to an emphasis on the flow of salvation history, which nonetheless continues to give a central role to Davidic messianism. In a paradigmatic text for Luke's Gospel, several features of the Nathan oracle appear together (Luke 1:32–33): Jesus will be made great, he will be considered Son of God, he will inherit the throne of

---

103. The imagery of "marking contours" comes from Satterthwaite, who asserts that the books of Samuel mark out the contours of a tension between the *ideal* King David and the *flawed* King David (his "deliberately emphasised antinomy"). See Satterthwaite, "David in the Books of Samuel," 64–65.

104. See Ben Witherington III, *Jesus the Sage: The Pilgrimage of Wisdom* (Minneapolis: Fortress, 1994), 349–68.

his ancestor David, and he will rule over God's people forever.[105] Jesus is the Lord's Anointed One, born in Bethlehem of David (Luke 1:27; 2:4, 11, 26). Jesus' resurrection is the fulfillment of the Davidic promise in Psalm 16 (Acts 2:24–32), and Jesus' ascension into heaven is the fulfillment of the Davidic promise in Psalm 110 (Acts 2:33–36).[106] Paul assumes Jesus' Davidic descent, but in general these messianic themes are not as central in Pauline formulations of Christology. However the expression "descendant of David" (lit., "seed of David") appears to be a proof of Jesus' messiahship based on the Davidic covenant (Rom. 1:3–5; 2 Tim. 2:8; cf. 2 Sam. 7:12, 14).[107]

Thus the books of Samuel have established David as the ideal king, the anointed one of the Lord. This theme has been refined and developed in royal psalms, prophetic literature, several texts of Second Temple Judaism, and the New Testament.[108] This commentary has attempted to demonstrate that several of the categories by which New Testament writers understood Jesus have been established in 1–2 Samuel, though in some cases we have to look to later biblical texts to explain their full significance.

Thus, Jesus comes to establish the kingdom of God, as David established and built the kingdom of God in old Israel. Jesus is upheld and vindicated by God's power and is victorious over God's enemies. Jesus is God's "Anointed One," the Messiah, who rules his people in justice and truth. As the one sent from God, Jesus prods us, as he did his first disciples, with the question (Mark 8:29): "But what about you . . . who do you say I am?" With Peter and Christians everywhere, we assert, "You are the Messiah." At least a portion of what we mean in our confession of Jesus as the Christ is to affirm the messianic expectations of 1–2 Samuel, their interpretation in Israel's Scriptures, and the Christological development of these expectations in the pages of the New Testament.

The nature of our faith. Finally, to assert that Jesus of Nazareth is the fulfillment of the Old Testament's messianic expectations has enormous

---

105. Following Isa. 9:7 and Dan. 7:14, Luke foresees a single ruler in an everlasting kingship rather than an enduring dynasty as promised in 2 Sam. 7. This is the result of an eschatological convergence of David's reign with the definitive, everlasting dominion of Yahweh. See Mark L. Strauss, *The Davidic Messiah in Luke-Acts: The Promise and Its Fulfillment in Lukan Christology* (JSNTSup 110; Sheffield: Sheffield Academic Press, 1995), 88–89.

106. See also Acts 7:46; 13:22–23.

107. Elsewhere in the New Testament, see also John 7:41–44; Rev. 5:5–6; 22:16. For more details, see Mark L. Strauss, "David," in *New Dictionary of Biblical Theology*, ed. T. Desmond Alexander and Brian S. Rosner (Downers Grove, Ill.: InterVarsity Press, 2000), 441–43.

108. See, e.g., Ps. 2; 18:50; 45:6, 16–17; 72; 89; 132:10–12, 17; Jer. 23:5–8; Ezek. 37:21–23; Hag. 2:21–22; Zech. 3:8–10; 12:10–13:1; 4 Ezra 12:31–32; *Psalms of Solomon* 17–18; 1QM 11:1–18; 4QFlor 1:11–14; 4QTest 9–13.

implications for the nature of our faith in general. It forces us to take our stand on one side or the other of what has been called "the great divide among the religions" of the world.[109] It forces us to confess that history really means something. Religion attempts to understand what directs and unifies all experience, even the multiplicity and incoherence of our present human experiences. But we are limited to two ways in which to explain reality. We can seek unity and coherence as "an existent reality" behind the multiplicity of our experiences, or we can seek unity and coherence as "an end yet to be obtained."[110]

The first option is to describe reality with the familiar imagery of a wheel: Life is inextricably enmeshed in the cycle of birth, growth, maturity, and death. We humans are part and parcel of the great cycles of nature, with their endless motion, constant turning, going nowhere, and meaning nothing. The second option is a road, inviting us to a journey or pilgrimage. Our same experiences of life (birth, growth, maturity, and death) are events in our movement toward a goal, one that we perceive only dimly. It is not a meaningless movement but results in the joy of unity and coherence at the end of the journey.

All of this is implied by the confession of faith that Jesus is the culmination of the Davidic messianic hopes. This confession forces us to affirm Jesus' role in salvation history and that, in fact, history is going somewhere to accomplish a specific purpose. It leads us to embrace Augustine's philosophy of history as a meaningful duration and to reject Aristotle's meaningless cycles of history glimmering endlessly—in short, to embrace Christ and to reject naturalism.[111] To say yes to Jesus as Messiah is to ally oneself with him and to become part of the momentous story of God's redemption of the world. "Yes" to Jesus is to own our responsibilities and to lay down our lives with him as his followers. "To claim finality for Jesus Christ . . . is to claim that commitment to him is the way in which [humans] can become truly aligned to the ultimate end for which all things were made."[112]

---

109. Nicol Macnicol, as quoted by Lesslie Newbigin, *The Finality of Christ* (Richmond, Va.: John Knox, 1969), 65.

110. Newbigin, *Finality of Christ*, 65.

111. For this discussion of Augustine and Aristotle, see Emile Cailliet, *Journey into Light* (Grand Rapids: Zondervan, 1968), 34–35.

112. Newbigin, *Finality of Christ*, 115.

Scripture Index

Subject Index

Author Index

Bring ancient truth to modern life with the
NIV Application Commentary *series*

Covering both the Old and New Testaments, the **NIV Application Commentary** series is a staple reference for pastors seeking to bring the Bible's timeless message into a modern context. It explains not only what the Bible means but also how that meaning impacts the lives of believers today.

Genesis
This commentary demonstrates how the text charts a course of theological affirmation that results in a simple but majestic account of an ordered, purposeful cosmos with God at the helm, masterfully guiding it, and what this means to us today.

John H. Walton
ISBN: 0-310-20617-0

Exodus
The truth of Christ's resurrection and its resulting impact on our lives mean that to Christians, the application of Exodus is less about how to act than it is about what God has done and what it means to be his children.

Peter Enns
ISBN: 0-310-20607-3

Judges, Ruth
This commentary helps readers learn how the messages of Judges and Ruth can have the same powerful impact today that they did when they were first written. Judges reveals a God who employs very human deliverers but refuses to gloss over their sins and the consequences of those sins. Ruth demonstrates the far-reaching impact of a righteous character.

K. Lawson Younger Jr.
ISBN: 0-310-20636-7

Esther
Karen H. Jobes shows what a biblical narrative that never mentions God tells Christians about him today.

Karen H. Jobes
ISBN: 0-310-20672-3

Psalms Volume 1

Gerald Wilson examines Books 1 and 2 of the Psalter. His seminal work on the shaping of the Hebrew Psalter has opened a new avenue of psalms research by shifting focus from exclusive attention to individual psalms to the arrangement of the psalms into groups.

Gerald H. Wilson
ISBN: 0-310-20635-9

Ecclesiastes, Song of Songs

Ecclesiastes and Songs of Songs have always presented particular challenges to their readers, especially if those readers are seeking to understand them as part of Christian Scripture. Revealing the links between the Scriptures and our own times, Iain Provan shows how these wisdom books speak to us today with relevance and conviction.

Iain Provan
ISBN: 0-310-21372-X

Jeremiah/Lamentations

These two books cannot be separated from the political conditions of ancient Judah. Beginning with the time of King Josiah, who introduced religious reform, Jeremiah reflects the close link between spiritual and political prosperity or disaster for the nation as a whole.

J. Andrew Dearman
ISBN: 0-310-20616-2

Ezekiel

Discover how, properly understood, this mysterious book with its obscure images offers profound comfort to us today.

Ian M. Duguid
ISBN: 0-310-20147-X

Daniel

Tremper Longman III reveals how the practical stories and spellbinding apocalyptic imagery of Daniel contain principles that are as relevant now as they were in the days of the Babylonian Captivity.

Tremper Longman III
ISBN: 0-310-20608-1

Hosea, Amos, Micah

Scratch beneath the surface of today's culture and you'll find we're not so different from ancient Israel. Revealing the links between Israel eight centuries B.C. and our own times, Gary V. Smith shows how the prophetic writings of Hosea, Amos, and Micah speak to us today with relevance and conviction.

Gary Smith
ISBN: 0-310-20614-6

Mark

Learn how the challenging Gospel of Mark can leave recipients with the same powerful questions and answers it did when it was written.

David E. Garland
ISBN: 0-310-49350-1

Luke

Focus on the most important application of all: "the person of Jesus and the nature of God's work through him to deliver humanity."

Darrell L. Bock
ISBN: 0-310-49330-7

John

Learn both halves of the interpretive task. Gary M. Burge shows readers how to bring the ancient message of John into a modern context. He also explains not only what the book of John meant to its original readers but also how it can speak powerfully today.

Gary M. Burge
ISBN: 0-310-49750-7

Acts

Study the first portraits of the church in action around the world with someone whose ministry mirrors many of the events in Acts. Biblical scholar and worldwide evangelist Ajith Fernando applies the story of the church's early development to the global mission of believers today.

Ajith Fernando
ISBN: 0-310-49410-9

Romans

Paul's letter to the Romans remains one of the most important expressions of Christian truth ever written. Douglas Moo comments on the text and then explores issues in Paul's culture and in ours that help us understand the ultimate meaning of each paragraph.

Douglas J. Moo
ISBN: 0-310-49400-1

1 Corinthians

Is your church struggling with the problem of divisiveness and fragmentation? See the solution Paul gave the Corinthian Christians over 2,000 years ago. It still works today!

Craig Blomberg
ISBN: 0-310-48490-1

2 Corinthians

Often recognized as the most difficult of Paul's letters to understand, 2 Corinthians can have the same powerful impact today that it did when it was first written.

Scott J. Hafemann
ISBN: 0-310-49420-6

Galatians

A pastor's message is true not because of his preaching or people-management skills, but because of Christ. Learn how to apply Paul's example of visionary church leadership to your own congregation.

Scot McKnight
ISBN: 0-310-48470-1

Ephesians

Explore what the author calls "a surprisingly comprehensive statement about God and his work, about Christ and the gospel, about life with God's Spirit, and about the right way to live."

Klyne Snodgrass
ISBN: 0-310-49340-4

Philippians

The best lesson Philippians provides is how to encourage people who actually are doing quite well. Learn why not all the New Testament letters are reactions to theological crises.

Frank Thielman
ISBN: 0-310-49340-4

Colossians/Philemon

The temptation to trust in the wrong things has always been strong. Use this commentary to learn the importance of trusting only in Jesus, God's Son, in whom all the fullness of God lives. No message is more important for our postmodern culture.

David E. Garland
ISBN: 0-310-48480-4

1&2 Thessalonians

Paul's letters to the Thessalonians say as much to us today about Christ's return and our resurrection as they did in the early church. This volume skillfully reveals Paul's answers to these questions and how they address the needs of contemporary Christians.

Michael W. Holmes
ISBN: 0-310-49380-3

1&2 Timothy, Titus

Reveals the context and meanings of Paul's letters to two leaders in the early Christian Church and explores their present-day implications to help you to accurately apply the principles they contain to contemporary issues.

Walter L. Liefeld
ISBN: 0-310-50110-5

Hebrews

The message of Hebrews can be summed up in a single phrase: "God speaks effectively to us through Jesus." Unpack the theological meaning of those seven words and learn why the gospel still demands a hearing today.

George H. Guthrie
ISBN: 0-310-49390-0

James
Give your church the best antidote for a culture of people who say they believe one thing but act in ways that either ignore or contradict their belief. More than just saying, "Practice what you preach," James gives solid reasons why faith and action must coexist.

David P. Nystrom
ISBN: 0-310-49360-9

1 Peter
The issue of the church's relationship to the state hits the news media in some form nearly every day. Learn how Peter answered the question for Christians surviving under Roman rule and how it applies similarly to believers living amid the secular institutions of the modern world.

Scot McKnight
ISBN: 0-310-49290-4

2 Peter, Jude
Introduce your modern audience to letters they may not be familiar with and show why they'll want to get to know them.

Douglas J. Moo
ISBN: 0-310-20104-7

Letters of John
Like the community in John's time, which faced disputes over erroneous "secret knowledge," today's church needs discernment in affirming new ideas supported by Scripture and weeding out harmful notions. This volume will help you show today's Christians how to use John's example.

Gary M. Burge
ISBN: 0-310-486420-3

Revelation
Craig Keener offers a "new" approach to the book of Revelation by focusing on the "old." He stresses the need for believers to prepare for the possibility of suffering for the sake of Jesus.

Craig S. Keener
ISBN: 0-310-23192-2

We want to hear from you. Please send your comments about this
book to us in care of the address below. Thank you.

GRAND RAPIDS, MICHIGAN 49530 USA

WWW.ZONDERVAN.COM